Billy,

Inside JavaScript

Contents at a Glance

Inside JavaScript

Steven Holzner

New Riders

www.newriders.com

201 West 103rd Street, Indianapolis, Indiana 46290

An Imprint of Pearson Education

Boston • Indianapolis • London • Munich • New York • San Francisco

Inside JavaScript

International Standard Book Number: 0-7357-1285-9

Library of Congress Catalog Card Number: 2002100321

06 05 04 03 02   7 6 5 4 3 2 1

Interpretation of the printing code: The rightmost double-digit number is the year of the book's printing; the rightmost single-digit number is the number of the book's printing. For example, the printing code 02-1 shows that the first printing of the book occurred in 2002.

Printed in the United States of America

Trademarks

Warning and Disclaimer

Publisher
David Dwyer

Associate Publisher
Stephanie Wall

Production Manager
Gina Kanouse

Managing Editor
Kristy Knoop

Senior Marketing Manager
Tammy Detrich

Publicity Manager
Susan Nixon

Project Editors
Stacia Mellinger
Beth Trudell

Copy Editor
Keith Cline

Indexer
Brad Herriman

Manufacturing Coordinator
Jim Conway

Book Designer
Louisa Klucznik

Cover Designer
Aren Howell

Proofreader
Debra Williams

Composition
Amy Parker
Ron Wise

❖

To Nancy. No one else even comes close.

❖

Table of Contents

About the Author

Steven Holzner has been writing about JavaScript for as long as it's been around. He's the author of 75 books on programming and is a former contributing editor to *PC Magazine*. A number of his books have been programming bestsellers, and he's had books translated into 16 languages around the world, selling more than 1.5 million copies total. He received his Ph.D. from Cornell University, and has been on the faculty of both Cornell and MIT. His hobbies include travel, chess, classical music, and writing books on philosophy.

About the Technical Reviewers

These reviewers contributed their considerable hands-on expertise to the entire development process for *Inside JavaScript*. As the book was being written, these dedicated professionals reviewed all the material for technical content, organization, and flow. Their feedback was critical to ensuring that *Inside JavaScript* fits our reader's need for the highest-quality technical information.

Rory Macdonald currently lives in Glasgow, Scotland, and teleworks as a Senior Systems Engineer for one of Europe's largest domain registrars and Internet service providers. After a few years developing high-speed video conferencing and real-time operating systems, Rory took off around the world for a year. On his return, he became a web developer for university-level distance education projects before joining Cisco Systems, Inc., developing web-based intranet applications. Over the years, he has gained considerable experience in cross-platform dynamic web development. In his spare time, Rory loves to travel, snowboard, and ride motorbikes.

Joel Lee is the Chief Operations Officer of JTL Networks, Inc. (www.jtlnet.com) in Columbus, Ohio. JTL Networks is an internet service provider, offering remote support staff augmentation, dedicated connectivity, enterprise software design, and managed shared and dedicated hosting solutions.

Bryan Gintz is the Senior Software Engineer for JTL Networks. He has worked with various aspects of JavaScript since 1996. He graduated from Wheaton College with a B.S. in Computer Science, and works with various Internet technologies specializing in some of the core scripting languages for Web Development, HTML, JavaScript, and PHP.

Acknowledgments

A book such as the one you're holding is the result of many people's hard work. I would particularly like to thank Stacia Mellinger and Beth Trudell, project editors extraordinaire; the two technical editors, Joel Lee and Rory Macdonald; Associate Publisher Stephanie Wall, copy editor Keith Cline, and indexer Brad Herriman. Thanks to you all; good job!

Tell Us What You Think

As the reader of this book, you are the most important critic and commentator. We value your opinion and want to know what we're doing right, what we could do better, what areas you would like to see us publish in, and any other words of wisdom you're willing to pass our way.

As the Associate Publisher for New Riders Publishing, I welcome your comments. You can fax, email, or write me directly to let me know what you did or didn't like about this book—and also what we can do to make our books stronger.

Please note that I cannot help you with technical problems related to the topic of this book, and that due to the high volume of mail I receive, I might not be able to reply to every message.

When you write, please be sure to include this book's title and author as well as your name and phone or fax number. I will carefully review your comments and share them with the author and editors who worked on the book.

Fax: 317-581-4663
Email: stephanie.wall@newriders.com
Mail: Stephanie Wall
          Associate Publisher
          New Riders Publishing
          201 West 103rd Street
          Indianapolis, IN 46290 USA

Introduction

Welcome to *Inside JavaScript*. This book is designed to be as comprehensive—and as accessible—as is possible for a single book on JavaScript. You'll find JavaScript just about everywhere you look on the Internet today, and even in many places behind the scenes. Thus, you've come to the right place; I believe this book provides the most complete coverage of what's going on in JavaScript as compared to any other JavaScript book today.

We're going to put JavaScript to work in depth, pushing the envelope as far as it can go. The best way to learn any topic such as JavaScript is by example, and this is an example-oriented book. You'll find hundreds of tested examples here, ready to be used.

Writing JavaScript is not some ordinary and monotonous task: It inspires artistry, devotion, passion, exaltation, and eccentricity—not to mention exasperation and frustration. I'll try to be true to that spirit and capture as much of the excitement and power of JavaScript in this book as I can.

Who Should Read This Book

Anyone who wants to learn as much as there is to learn about JavaScript should read this book. We're going to start with the basics. I do assume that you have some knowledge of HTML, but not necessarily very much. We'll see how to create JavaScript scripts from scratch in this book, starting at the very beginning.

Overview

Inside JavaScript is designed to give you as much of the whole JavaScript story as one book can hold. We'll not only see the full JavaScript syntax—from the most basic to the most advanced—but also dig into many of the ways in which JavaScript is used.

Unlike other JavaScript books, I'm also going to list which browser and which browser version supports every feature we're going to use. That information will enable you to develop JavaScript applications across multiple browsers with relative ease.

Here's a sample of some of the topics in this book—note that each of these topics themselves has many subtopics (too many to list here):

- The full JavaScript syntax
- Cross-browser issues: Which browser are you using?

- Dynamic HTML
- Handling errors
- Redirecting browsers
- Accessing HTML elements
- Accessing the status bar
- Creating dialog boxes
- Using the clipboard
- Alerts, confirmations, and prompts
- Creating popups
- Moving windows
- Opening and closing new windows
- Printing
- Scrolling a window
- Creating timed events
- Setting colors
- Creating cookies
- Handling file dates and sizes
- Tracking user navigation
- Creating new elements and nodes
- Finding elements by location
- Navigating to a new URL
- Using the `go`, `forward`, and `back` methods
- Finding and replacing text
- Selecting text
- Using forms
- Submitting forms
- Emailing forms
- Clicking a button from code
- Check boxes and radio buttons
- Working with HTML text and select controls
- Creating new options in a `select` control
- The file upload element

- Working with hyperlinks, lists, and tables
- Using JavaScript URLs
- Working with the mouse, keyboard, and images
- Mouse rollovers
- Precaching images and the image object
- Image maps
- Handling events
- Changing web pages on-the-fly
- Changing visual properties on-the-fly
- Rewriting documents with the `document.write` method
- Setting element visibility on-the-fly
- Adding visual effects with filters
- Using Internet Explorer visual transitions
- Changing pages with dynamic styles
- Drawing graphics with Vector Markup Language
- Using Internet Explorer Direct Animation
- Netscape Navigator layers
- Internet Explorer filters
- Internet Explorer visual transitions
- Dragging and dropping visual elements
- Dragging and dropping data
- Dragging and dropping using layers
- Data binding
- Using the Tabular Data Control
- Internet Explorer behaviors
- Working with regular expressions
- Cascading Style Sheets
- Using absolute positioning
- Using relative positioning
- Changing style classes on-the-fly
- Changing style sheets on-the-fly
- Changing mouse cursors

- Menus
- XML and XSLT
- Creating cookies and custom objects
- Mouse trails
- .NET and CGI programming

Here's something that's important to realize if you have an older browser: Note that not all examples will work in all browsers. Over time, browser manufacturers introduce new features, and of course, we have to cover those new features as well as the old—which means that not all examples are going to work in every browser version.

In fact, cross-browser issues are a serious consideration when programming in JavaScript, as we'll see throughout the book. As much as possible, I make it a point to indicate which examples will work in which browser; bear in mind that if you're trying to use an example with a newer feature in an older browser, however, it might not work. For that matter, many features that work in the Internet Explorer do not work in the Netscape Navigator, and vice versa.

As you can tell, this is an issue that raises its head over and over in JavaScript. To enable you to handle version and browser differences, this book lists the versions and browsers that support the features that we're going to see; so if an example doesn't work for you, that's the first thing to check. All the examples in the book were tested by three people—myself and two dedicated technical editors (working on different machines)—to make sure they work as advertised.

Conventions

I use one convention in this book that you should be aware of. When I add a new section of code, or want to emphasize something in code, I mark it like this for emphasis (this is from Chapter 4):

```
<HTML>
    <HEAD>
        <TITLE>Our first script!</TITLE>
    </HEAD>

    <BODY>
        <H1>Here we go!</H1>
        <SCRIPT LANGUAGE="JavaScript">
        <!--
        document.write("Hello from JavaScript!")
        // -->
        </SCRIPT>
    </BODY>
</HTML>
```

That's it. We're ready to go. If you have comments, I encourage you to write to me, in care of New Riders. This book is designed to be the new standard in JavaScript, more complete and more accessible than ever before. Please do keep in touch with me with ways to improve it and to keep it at the fore-front. If you think this book lacks anything, let me know—I'll add it, because I want to make sure this book stays on top. Thanks and happy programming!

1

Essential JavaScript

WELCOME TO THE WORLD OF JAVASCRIPT. This book is your guided tour to that world, so have no worries—you've come to the right place. That world is large and expanding in unpredictable ways every minute, but we're going to become familiar with the lay of the land in detail here. And there's a lot of territory to cover, because JavaScript is getting into the most amazing places, and in the most amazing ways, these days.

You'll see JavaScript just about everywhere you go on the Internet; it's the language of the web. JavaScript is a powerful, compact scripting language that gets embedded right in web pages, and brings them to life. In this book, we're going to see all of JavaScript at work, from the basics to the most advanced; from mouse rollovers to dynamic HTML; from status bar manipulations to opening new browser windows on command; from working with the mouse and keyboard to handling HTML controls such as buttons, check boxes, and drop-down menus; from working with XML and XSLT to working with .NET; from using style sheets to setting cookies. JavaScript supports a dazzling variety of options for your web pages, and it's all coming up in this book. We're going to see it all at work—and everything is going to be illustrated with at least one example.

This first chapter is our foundation chapter, where we'll get the necessary skills and techniques down to begin our guided tour of the language. To put things into perspective, a good place to start is with a history of JavaScript.

JavaScript Through the Ages

JavaScript is a unique language—despite its name, which has caused a great deal of confusion, it is not directly related to Java. When JavaScript was first introduced, Java was dominant, and it must have seemed like a good idea to tie JavaScript to Java.

Things have shifted dramatically, however; JavaScript has become far more popular than Java for web use. Whereas Java has gone on to become a relatively complex, involved language, JavaScript has remained remarkably the same over the years—a lightweight, fast, and *powerful* language that is, quite simply, the programmer's favorite—it's by far the favorite language of the web.

It all began in Netscape Communications Corporation in 1995, when a developer named Brendan Eich, who they had just lured away from MicroUnity Systems Engineering, was given a new project to work on. The original idea was to make programming more accessible than it was becoming in Java, and to somehow make the Netscape Navigator's new Java support more open to non-Java programmers. Eich took a look around and decided that what was needed was a scripting language that was fast and easy to use. Unlike Java, which first has to be compiled into "bytecodes," JavaScript was to be embedded right in the web page itself, and downloaded with that page. And as Java itself has become more and more inaccessible, JavaScript's star just continues to rise.

Brendan Eich called his creation *LiveScript*, but it was renamed JavaScript. (In fact, many people consider the name change a big mistake.) Although developed by Netscape, Sun had the trademarks on Java, and the name *JavaScript* is actually a trademark of Sun Microsystems, Inc. The new language was announced in a Netscape and Sun joint press conference on December 4, 1995. They originally positioned it as a "complement" to Java and HTML, rather than a simple support language for Java.

However, JavaScript rapidly slipped out of Java's shadow. Programmers took to it at once, and although there were problems with bugs and later with security, JavaScript was a success. It became clear that, as Eich had realized, programming a web page *in the browser* made all kinds of things possible that couldn't be done if you needed to reload the page from the server. (In fact, the most popular, original use for JavaScript was to swap images when the mouse rolled over them, and that continues to be a very popular thing to do.)

Web programmers found JavaScript programming *fun*. To some extent, that meant that many programmers didn't take it seriously. Java was a serious language, and as time has gone on, it has become much more serious— serious, unfortunately, to the point of inaccessibility for much of its intended audience. JavaScript, originally a guilty pleasure for many, started to be accepted by thousands of programmers. As browsers became more powerful and could run scripts faster (eliminating screen flicker and other problems), programmers discovered that JavaScript was indeed a viable development tool. And all it took was a few lines of code to get things working, making buttons work, and setting cookies.

As JavaScript started making waves, Netscape's chief competitor, Microsoft, could no longer ignore it. It's interesting to speculate how things would have gone if JavaScript had been a public standard in those days, developed, say, by a neutral third party. But JavaScript was a product of Microsoft's direct competitor in this area, Netscape, so Microsoft decided to create its own version of JavaScript, which it called *JScript*.

The first official version of JScript was released on July 16, 1996, in Internet Explorer 3.0. From then on, there was both JavaScript and JScript, and the resulting split personality for the language between Netscape and Microsoft has had repercussions that echo down to today. The original JScript was much like a reduced version of JavaScript 1.1, however, and the differences confused programmers. At that point, Microsoft had created its own scripting language, *VBScript*, based on its popular Visual Basic language, and was hoping to successfully rival JavaScript. JavaScript was triumphant, however, and VBScript is a very distant second these days.

To bring their JScript support up to full JavaScript 1.1, Microsoft later released a second version of Internet Explorer 3.0. So started the cross-browser and cross-browser version problems that have made life harder for the JavaScript programmer ever since. Programmers started to find that although JScript looked just like JavaScript, some scripts would run in Netscape and not in Internet Explorer, and vice versa.

Hoping to stave off chaos, Netscape and Sun looked for a third party to standardize JavaScript, and turned to the *European Computer Manufacturers Association* (ECMA, www.ecma.ch). Unfortunately for programmers, that standardization, which began in November 1996, has been a long time coming, and even longer to be adopted. You might expect the standardized language to be called JavaScript, or possibly JScript, but it's not called either—it's *ECMAScript*.

So now we actually have three standards: JavaScript, JScript, and ECMAScript. Although ECMAScript has brought some measure of coherence to the picture, both browsers also have gone their own ways. The result is that the Internet Explorer often has two ways of letting you do things (the JScript way and the ECMAScript way), and the Netscape Navigator has two ways of letting you do things (the JavaScript way and the ECMAScript way).

A big problem was that ECMAScript standardized the core JavaScript language itself, but not all the resources available in browsers that you work with—and those resources make up a much larger field than the JavaScript language does by itself.

These browser resources are made up of *browser objects* (discussed later in this chapter). Each browser had its own set of objects, such as the document object, which enables you to work with the web page, and the window object, which enables you to work with the browser itself. A great deal of JavaScript programming is all about working with these objects; and if they're entirely different in the two browsers, it's easy to see that the same JavaScript-enabled web pages are going to have problems in one or the other browser—so much so that people today are still coding different scripts in the same web page for the two browsers.

The chaos raised by different sets of browser objects threatened both JavaScript and JScript, so Microsoft, Netscape, and many other corporations went to the *World Wide Web Consortium* (W3C, www.w3.org) to bring some coherence to the objects browsers would make accessible to JavaScript. The original browser object set, before W3C started its work, became known as the *Document Object Model* (DOM) "level 0." The DOM level 1, which became an official W3C specification on October 1, 1998, standardized many aspects of the objects found in browsers, but left out many others. DOM level 2 was made a specification on November 13, 2000, and fills in many more details. However, both DOM models omit any discussion of many of the popular objects available in both browsers, which means that much of what we're going to do is try to reconcile programming issues between those browsers. Work on the DOM level 3, now in the working draft stage, has started.

The result of all this is that today, JavaScript is an amazingly powerful tool for web programmers, but it's still plagued by cross-browser issues. The current version of JavaScript in the Netscape Navigator is 1.5 (with 2.0 on the way), and the current JScript version is 5.6. With each new version, more power from other languages has been packed into JavaScript, borrowing from languages such as C++, Java, Perl, and even TCL.

Although the W3C DOM has brought some calm to the war between the browsers, it's also true that market share has dramatically shifted to Microsoft. It would be a shame if the only way JavaScript compatibility could finally be ensured were by the demise of one of the competitors, but it appears that might be happening. Nonetheless, we're going to work with both browsers in this book—in fact, if there's an incompatibility, I'll indicate not only which browser something applies to, but which versions of that browser. That's the only way to do it.

We'll take a look at cross-browser programming in more detail both in this chapter and in Chapter 4, "Handling the Browser Environment." The very fact that incompatibility issues exist indicates that both Netscape and Microsoft consider JavaScript very important. And despite the cross-browser problems, JavaScript continues to flourish. So, in just what kind of ways do people use JavaScript these days? I'll take an overview of the JavaScript world now.

What's JavaScript Good For?

There are many, many reasons for JavaScript's climbing popularity, and more are being invented all the time. Here are a few things that JavaScript can do for your web pages—this is just a starter list, of course:

- **Livening pages up.** The Internet already has too many static pages. Why add yours to the list? To get noticed, your page must be live, it must do something, or offer some service. What better way is there to liven pages up yourself than to use JavaScript, writing a short script that runs in the browser, right in front of the user? JavaScript puts all the elements in a web page—and the web page itself!—under your control.

- **Dynamic HTML.** *Dynamic HTML* (DHTML) has become a catch-all word for an entire world of techniques, from image manipulations to positioning a web page's elements as you like; from using special DHTML objects for optical effects (such as the filter and transition objects in the Internet Explorer) to rewriting web pages on-the-fly. How do you make these things happen? JavaScript.

- **Data entry validation.** Some web pages are designed to send data back to the web server, where that data is handled by *Common Gateway Interface* (CGI) programs such as Perl, *Active Server Pages* (ASP) programs, and *Java Server Pages* (JSP) programs. However, sending data back to the server takes time, and the server itself has limited resources. As a result, one popular use of JavaScript is to check the data a user has entered in a web page before that data is sent back to the server. Does the credit card number look like a valid number? Has the user entered his phone number? All that can be checked using JavaScript in the browser, after the user clicks the Submit button—we'll see how to use JavaScript to intercept the Submit button and check the data the user has entered before sending that data back to the server. (Note that to handle that data on the server, you have to have code on the server.)

- **Client-side "CGIs."** Server-side programming can be difficult—although JavaScript is starting to be supported on some servers, very few support it so far; and learning Perl, C++, ASP, and other programming languages is a more involved task than many people want to undertake. For that reason, their entire applications are written in JavaScript—no data has to be sent back to the server at all. They write entire mortgage calculators, news tickers, stock market trackers, all in JavaScript.

- **Unburdening busy servers.** If your server has become so busy that it's a problem, why not shift some of the load to the browsers? JavaScript lets you do that, handling many programming tasks in the browser. Wasting your time processing loans for people not qualified? Maybe you should have JavaScript check them out first.

- **Handling cookies.** A popular use of JavaScript is to work with cookies, storing information on the user's machine. Some people love cookies, some hate them, but there's no doubt that JavaScript can let you use them, all without any programming on the server at all. Want to record a user's special settings for your web page? A cookie will do that.

JavaScript can be used in millions of ways—and is used in millions of web pages. We'll see all the ways listed previously in this book, and many more. In fact, we'll get started right now, creating our first script.

Creating Our First Script

This isn't one of those books that takes you through chapters of dry theory before getting started. This book is written from the scripter's point of view, which means that we want to put JavaScript to work. It's time to do that now. Some books wait until Chapter 3 or 4 before even getting to their first script, but not here. Here, we'll let JavaScript itself do the talking as we start our first script.

Our first script will use JavaScript to write the text `Hello from JavaScript!` in a browser; you can see that text in Netscape Navigator 6.2 in Figure 1.1, and in Internet Explorer 6.0 in Figure 1.2.

So how do we get this result using JavaScript? The first step is to actually create the web page that will hold the JavaScript, and for that, we'll need a text editor.

Figure 1.1   Our first example script in Netscape Navigator.

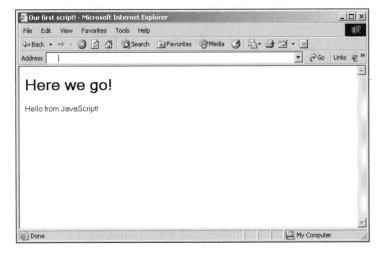

Figure 1.2   Our first example script in Internet Explorer.

Choosing a Text Editor

Any text editor you want to use to create web pages will be fine here—in fact, the less fancy the better. Your web pages have to be readable by web browsers as plain text, which means you must save them as plain text. Fancy word processors, such as Microsoft Word, do not save documents as plain text by default. You can still use them, but you must be sure to save your web pages as plain text documents. (In Microsoft Word, for example, save them using the .txt option in the Save As dialog box.)

A simpler text editor, such as WordPad in Windows or SimpleText in the Mac, is better. Make sure, however, that you're saving your documents in plain text format. (WordPad's default setting is rich text format, which won't work in browsers—select the Text Document format when you save your web pages using WordPad.) For example, you can see the first web page we'll create, first.html, in WordPad in Figure 1.3.

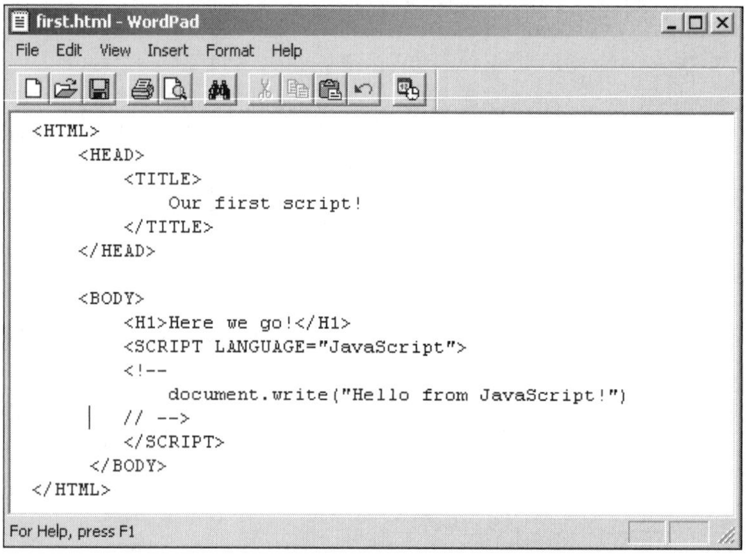

```
first.html - WordPad
File  Edit  View  Insert  Format  Help

<HTML>
    <HEAD>
        <TITLE>
            Our first script!
        </TITLE>
    </HEAD>

    <BODY>
        <H1>Here we go!</H1>
        <SCRIPT LANGUAGE="JavaScript">
        <!--
            document.write("Hello from JavaScript!")
        // -->
        </SCRIPT>
    </BODY>
</HTML>

For Help, press F1
```

Figure 1.3   Creating a web page in WordPad.

Selecting a Browser

The browser you use is up to you, of course. In this book, we'll cover the various versions available for both the Internet Explorer and the Netscape Navigator. Both are available for free online (Netscape Navigator at http://browsers.netscape.com/browsers/main.tmpl; Internet Explorer at www.microsoft.com/ie/default.asp). If you're programming for the general public, you should know that the Internet Explorer has the overwhelming market share at this point. However, the Netscape Navigator still has a lot to offer.

Creating Your Programming Environment

It's also worth giving a little thought to your programming environment. Although web pages generally available are stored on an Internet server, you can test your own web pages locally, on your own computer. There's no need to upload them to a server before looking at them in a browser. Knowing that can save you a great deal of time when you're developing your JavaScript-enabled pages and testing them.

To open a web page on your computer, just use the File | Open menu item in the Internet Explorer, or the File | Open File menu item in the Netscape Navigator, and browse to the HTML file you want to open. That's all it takes. (Note that the Netscape Navigator can have some problems opening files on your computer if you're already connected to the Internet; if that happens to you, the best thing is to open Netscape Navigator *before* connecting to the Internet, which will make local files available.) Now testing and debugging your web pages with JavaScript scripts in them becomes a matter of editing the page in your text editor, saving it, and clicking the Reload button in your web browser to reload the newly edited version of your page. That's all you need for a basic programming environment.

Note that if you're developing for a large audience, you also might want to have several versions of several browsers on your computer, loading your page into those browsers in turn to test for compatibility. This becomes more important the longer you program in JavaScript, and the longer your scripts become (unless you're programming for an audience that uses only one browser, of course, as on a corporate intranet).

That establishes our programming environment; now let's get to the web page itself.

Using HTML

We're going to be using a lot of HTML in this book. Our JavaScript will be embedded in these pages. That means you should have a knowledge of HTML to be able to work profitably with what's coming up. You don't need a profound or in-depth knowledge, but you should have some. For example, take a look at this element:

```
<A HREF="http://developer.netscape.com/docs/manuals/js/core/jsref15/contents.html">
    The JavaScript 1.5 Reference Manual
</A>
```

You should know that this is an `<A>` *element*, a hyperlink in this case. This hyperlink is to the JavaScript 1.5 Reference Manual at `developer.netscape.com`. This element starts with an `<A>` *opening tag* and ends with the `</A>` *closing tag*. This element has one HTML *attribute*, `HREF`. HTML attributes are used to specify something about an element; in this case, the `HREF` attribute specifies the target of the hyperlink.

If you are not comfortable with the level of HTML we'll be using here, take some time out and come up to speed on HTML. It won't take long, and will be well worth it for our work here.

Some of what you see in our first web page in Figures 1.1 and 1.2 come from the straight HTML in our web page, not from JavaScript. For example, for the title, Our first script!, you see in the browser's title bar comes from a <TITLE> element in the web page's head section, and the text Here we go! comes from an <H1> header element in the web page's body section.

Here, then, is how we start our first web page, first.html, making sure that the page's title and the heading text appear as it should:

```
<HTML>
    <HEAD>
        <TITLE>Our first script!</TITLE>
    </HEAD>

    <BODY>
        <H1>Here we go!</H1>
    </BODY>
</HTML>
```

Enter this HTML into your text editor now and save it as first.html. That's the HTML in our web page—but this book is all about JavaScript, and now it's time to embed JavaScript in this page.

Adding Some JavaScript

JavaScript scripts are downloaded with web pages; the scripts themselves don't actually have to be embedded in the page—they can be stored in separate script files as we'll see in this chapter—but they usually are. Here's the JavaScript we will embed in our first example, first.html:

(Listing 01-01.html on the web site)

```
<HTML>
    <HEAD>
        <TITLE>Our first script!</TITLE>
    </HEAD>

    <BODY>
        <H1>Here we go!</H1>
        <SCRIPT LANGUAGE="JavaScript">
        <!--
            document.write("Hello from JavaScript!")
        // -->
        </SCRIPT>
    </BODY>
</HTML>
```

Add this JavaScript to first.html now, save this document, and open it in a web browser. You should see the same kind of result that you see in Figures 1.1 and 1.2. The JavaScript part of the page writes the message `Hello from JavaScript!`, as you see in those figures. Congratulations, you're a JavaScript programmer! You've gotten your first JavaScript-enabled web page working.

Now let's take a look at what we've done.

Dissecting Our First Script

Our first JavaScript script wrote something in a web page—so how did it do that? We'll take it apart step by step here to see what's going on. First of all, like all scripts, we placed this script inside a `<SCRIPT>` HTML element so that the browser would know it's dealing with a script of some kind:

```
<HTML>
    <HEAD>
        <TITLE>Our first script!</TITLE>
    </HEAD>

    <BODY>
        <H1>Here we go!</H1>
        <SCRIPT LANGUAGE="JavaScript">
            .
            .
            .
        </SCRIPT>
    </BODY>
</HTML>
```

What is this `<SCRIPT>` element all about? Let's take a look.

The *<SCRIPT>* Element

The `<SCRIPT>` element will be an important one for us, so here are all its attributes, as set by W3C in the HTML 4.01 specification (www.w3.org/TR/html401):

- **CHARSET.** Specifies the character encoding of the script contents. Set to a language character set string. (The default is ISO-8859-1.)
- **CLASS.** Class of the element (used for rendering). Supported in IE4, IE5, and IE6.
- **DEFER.** Indicates to the browser that the script is not going to generate any document content (which means the browser can continue parsing and drawing the page). Standalone attribute. Supported in IE4, IE5, and IE6.

- **EVENT.** Gives the event the script is written for. Set to an event name (see "Using *<SCRIPT FOR>*" in this chapter for all the details). Supported in IE4, IE5, IE6, and NS6.

- **FOR.** Indicates which element is bound to the script. Set to an HTML element or element ID. Supported in IE4, IE5, and IE6.

- **ID.** Unique alphanumeric identifier for the tag, which you can use to refer to it. Supported in IE4, IE5, IE6, and NS6.

- **LANGUAGE.** Sets the scripting language. This attribute is required if the SRC attribute is not set and is optional otherwise. Set to the name of a scripting language, such as JavaScript or VBScript. Supported in IE3, IE4, IE5, IE6, NS3, NS4, and NS6.

- **SRC.** Gives an external source for the script code. Set to an URL. Supported in IE3, IE4, IE5, IE6, NS3, NS4, and NS6.

- **TITLE.** Holds additional information (which might be displayed in tool tips) for the element. Supported in IE4, IE5, and IE6.

- **TYPE.** Indicates the *Multipurpose Internet Mail Extension* (MIME) type of the scripting code. Set to an alphanumeric MIME type. Meant to replace the LANGUAGE attribute. Supported in IE4, IE5, IE6, and NS6.

We'll include the entire script in a <SCRIPT> element. Note that I'm using the LANGUAGE attribute of this element, and setting it to "JavaScript." I could set it to "JScript" if I wanted to target only the Internet Explorer, but that browser recognizes "JavaScript" as well as "JScript," and treats the two identically. There are other types of scripts out there, such as VBScript and PerlScript, so specifying the language you're using can be important. (In fact, the default if you omit the LANGUAGE attribute in both the Netscape Navigator and the Internet Explorer is "JavaScript.")

It's also worth noting that in the most recent version of HTML, version 4.01 as specified by W3C (you can see the specification at www.w3.org/TR/html1401), the LANGUAGE attribute has been replaced by the TYPE attribute. And, instead of setting TYPE to "JavaScript," you set it to "text/javascript." This new way of doing things is supported in both Netscape Navigator and Internet Explorer. However, the standard method of using the LANGUAGE attribute will be around for a long, long time yet in both the Netscape Navigator and Internet Explorer.

Hiding Scripts from Older Browsers

Note the next part of our script—it looks as though it's being hidden by an HTML comment (that is, <!-- -->):

```
<HTML>
    <HEAD>
        <TITLE>Our first script!</TITLE>
    </HEAD>

    <BODY>
        <H1>Here we go!</H1>
        <SCRIPT LANGUAGE="JavaScript">
        <!--
        document.write("Hello from JavaScript!")
        // -->
        </SCRIPT>
    </BODY>
</HTML>
```

What's going on here? In this case, I'm hiding our JavaScript from older browsers that don't support JavaScript. If a browser doesn't support JavaScript, it may display just our entire script in the web page without executing it, which looks less than professional. To avoid that, you can enclose the actual script statements in an HTML comment, as we've done here.

What really happens is that JavaScript-enabled browsers know enough to skip over an opening HTML comment tag, <!--, in <SCRIPT> elements. What about the closing comment tag, -->? To make sure the browser skips over that tag too, we're using a JavaScript single-line comment, which starts with two forward slashes (//). When JavaScript sees a comment marker, //, it ignores the rest of the line, which enables you to add comments to your code that programmers can read and JavaScript won't. Following the // marker here, I use the --> HTML closing comment tag so that older browsers will think the HTML comment is complete and will not show any of our script in the web page itself.

Most browsers you encounter will support JavaScript, but those that don't aren't necessarily old—they can be text-only browsers, or PDA browsers. Which means that you can't expect non-JavaScript browsers to fade away— which means it's good practice to surround your code with HTML comments. In fact, there's an entire HTML tag expressly for use with browsers that don't support JavaScript: <NOSCRIPT>.

Using *<NOSCRIPT>*

You might want to provide a non-JavaScript version of a web page for non-JavaScript browsers. You can do that in a <NOSCRIPT> element. Browsers that support JavaScript ignore this element and its contents. However, only the <NOSCRIPT> and </NOSCRIPT> *tags* are ignored by non-JavaScript browsers—all the HTML and text between these tags is still displayed.

That means you can put HTML for a non-JavaScript browser in a
<NOSCRIPT> element, including links or redirection directives to a non-
JavaScript page. Alternatively, you might just tell the user to get a browser
that supports JavaScript, like this:

(Listing 01-02.html on the web site)

```
<HTML>
    <HEAD>
        <TITLE>
            Our first script!
        </TITLE>
    </HEAD>

    <BODY>
        <H1>Here we go!</H1>
        <SCRIPT LANGUAGE="JavaScript">
        <!--
            document.write("Hello from JavaScript!")
        // -->
        </SCRIPT>
        <NOSCRIPT>
            Hey, get a browser that supports JavaScript!
        </NOSCRIPT>
    </BODY>
</HTML>
```

Here's an example: Microsoft Word is capable of opening HTML pages, but
it doesn't support JavaScript. You can see the preceding page opened in Word
in Figure 1.4, showing our prompt to the user about getting a new browser.

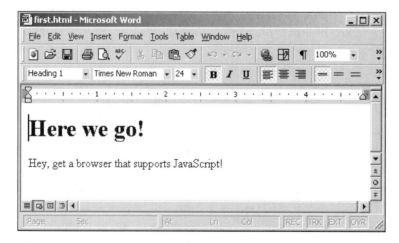

Figure 1.4   Using the <NOSCRIPT> element.

Here are the attributes for the <NOSCRIPT> element:

- **CLASS.** Class of the element (used for rendering).
- **DIR.** Gives the direction of directionally neutral text (text that doesn't have inherent direction in which you should read it). Possible values: LTR (left-to-right text or table) and RTL (right-to-left text or table).
- **ID.** Unique alphanumeric identifier for the tag, which you can use to refer to it. Supported in IE4, IE5, IE6, and NS6.
- **LANG.** Base language used for the tag.
- **STYLE.** Inline style indicating how to render the element. Supported in IE6 and NS6.
- **TITLE.** Holds additional information (which might be displayed in tool tips) for the element.

We have yet to dissect the part of our first script where we're actually using JavaScript itself. Let's do that now.

Writing JavaScript

Here's the actual JavaScript statement that does the work of displaying the text Hello from JavaScript!:

```
<HTML>
    <HEAD>
        <TITLE>Our first script!</TITLE>
    </HEAD>

    <BODY>
        <H1>Here we go!</H1>
        <SCRIPT LANGUAGE="JavaScript">
        <!--
        document.write("Hello from JavaScript!")
        // -->
        </SCRIPT>
    </BODY>
</HTML>
```

Here, we want to get something done in the browser—that is, display your message in a web page—and to do that, we have to interact with the browser. You interact with the browser through a set of objects, as we've discussed. In this case, we'll use the document object, which corresponds to the body of a web page (as well as several other parts).

Objects such as the document object have *properties*, which, like HTML attributes, enable you to configure a web page, setting its color and so on. They also have *methods*, which let you make something happen actively, such as writing in a web page. They also can handle *events*, which enable you to respond to user actions such as mouse clicks. Properties, methods, and events are all going to be very important to us, and we'll see more about them in this chapter; in this example, we're using the write method of the document object to write some text to our HTML page:

```
document.write("Hello from JavaScript!")
```

Note that we send the actual text to write to the web page, enclosed in quotation marks, to the write method by enclosing that text in parentheses. And that's all it takes; when this JavaScript statement is executed, our message is written to the web page. We've been able to make the document object do something for us by using one of its methods. We'll see all the methods of the various browser objects in this book laid out in detail.

Here's another thing to note—JavaScript is case-sensitive, which means that, *unlike HTML*, capitalization counts. If we had written this instead, JavaScript wouldn't have executed it:

```
Document.Write("Hello from JavaScript!")
```

That completes our first script; we've made considerable progress already. Let's take a look at a few more foundation issues now that will become important as we progress.

What About Semicolons?

JavaScript was written to follow the lead of Java in many ways, and one of those ways was to require a semicolon (;) at the end of each statement. Technically, we should have written our JavaScript statement followed by a semicolon, like this:

```
<HTML>
    <HEAD>
        <TITLE>Our first script!</TITLE>
    </HEAD>

    <BODY>
        <H1>Here we go!</H1>
        <SCRIPT LANGUAGE="JavaScript">
        <!--
        document.write("Hello from JavaScript!");
        // -->
        </SCRIPT>
    </BODY>
</HTML>
```

However, through popular usage, the semicolon is almost completely a thing of the past in JavaScript. Browsers don't require it, and programmers don't use it for the most part. Following common usage, we won't use it here either.

Tip

In at least one case, however, you must use semicolons. You can place two or more JavaScript statements on the same line if you want to; but if you do, you need to separate them with semicolons.

Commenting Your JavaScript

We've already seen that JavaScript supports a one-line comment with the // marker. JavaScript will stop reading anything on a line past //, so you can add comments for people to read to your code like this:

```
<HTML>
    <HEAD>
        <TITLE>
            Welcome To JavaScript
        </TITLE>

    </HEAD>

    <BODY>

        <SCRIPT LANGUAGE="JavaScript">
        <!--
            //Write "Welcome to JavaScript!" in the page.
            document.write("Welcome to JavaScript!")
        //-->
        </SCRIPT>

        <NOSCRIPT>
            Sorry, your browser doesn't support JavaScript!
        </NOSCRIPT>

        <H1>
                Welcome To JavaScript!
        </H1>
    </BODY>
</HTML>
```

In fact, JavaScript also supports a second type of comment, which you can use for multiple lines. This comment starts with /* and ends with */. When JavaScript sees /*, it ignores everything else until it sees */. Here's an example:

```
<SCRIPT LANGUAGE="JavaScript">
<!--
    /* This script
        writes "Welcome to JavaScript!"
        in the page.
    */
    document.write("Welcome to JavaScript!")
//-->
</SCRIPT>
```

Or you can create an entire comment block like this:

```
<SCRIPT LANGUAGE="JavaScript">
<!--
    /*.....................................
    |    This script                      |
    |    writes "Welcome to JavaScript!"  |
    |    in the page.                     |
    .....................................*/
    document.write("Welcome to JavaScript!")
//-->
</SCRIPT>
```

Where Does the *<SCRIPT>* Element Go?

One question to ask is where exactly is the <SCRIPT> element supposed to go
in a web page. When JavaScript first came out, many purists insisted that the
<SCRIPT> element could go only in a page's head section, because the head
contained meta information about the page that wasn't supposed to be
displayed:

```
<HTML>
    <HEAD>
        <TITLE>Our first script!</TITLE>
        <SCRIPT LANGUAGE="JavaScript">
        <!--
        .
        .
        .
        // -->
        </SCRIPT>
    </HEAD>

    <BODY>
        <H1>Here we go!</H1>
    </BODY>
</HTML>
```

However, JavaScript outgrew that and started to be able to create elements
that were indeed to be displayed, as in our first script, which displayed some
text in a web page. That can happen when the body of the page is loaded; so
when you're writing to the web page with document.write, you can place
your script in the body, not in the head:

```
<HTML>
    <HEAD>
        <TITLE>Our first script!</TITLE>
    </HEAD>

    <BODY>
        <H1>Here we go!</H1>
```

```
        <SCRIPT LANGUAGE="JavaScript">
        <!--
        document.write("Hello from JavaScript!")
        // -->
        </SCRIPT>
    </BODY>
</HTML>
```

The reason for this is that when the head is loaded and your script executes, the body section of the page, which it works with, may not have been loaded yet. In fact, you can have scripts in both the head and the body:

```
<HTML>
    <HEAD>
        <TITLE>Our first script!</TITLE>
        <SCRIPT LANGUAGE="JavaScript">
        .
        .
        .
        </SCRIPT>
    </HEAD>

    <BODY>
        <H1>Here we go!</H1>
        <SCRIPT LANGUAGE="JavaScript">
        .
        .
        .
        </SCRIPT>
    </BODY>
</HTML>
```

Alternatively, you can have multiple scripts in the head and/or the body:

```
<HTML>
    <HEAD>
        <SCRIPT LANGUAGE="JavaScript">
        .
        .
        .
        </SCRIPT>
        <TITLE>Our first script!</TITLE>
        <SCRIPT LANGUAGE="JavaScript">
        .
        .
        .
        </SCRIPT>
    </HEAD>

    <BODY>
        <H1>Here we go!</H1>
    </BODY>
</HTML>
```

So the answer to the question of where the <SCRIPT> element goes is this: Wherever it fits best. Usually, it's best to place <SCRIPT> elements in the head section of a web page. When you're writing to the web page directly, however, or may otherwise end up trying to access body elements before the body is loaded, it can be a good idea to place the <SCRIPT> element in the body of the web page.

Tip
In fact, there's another option: You can even place code that accesses the page's body in the head section of a page if you let the browser itself tell you when it's safe to run that code. See the discussion in "When Does a Script Run?" later in this chapter to learn how to run a script only after the whole page has loaded into the browser.

There are still more options to consider here; we've placed all our code in the web page itself—but you can store JavaScript outside the web page and still have it downloaded with that page.

Using Separate Script Files

If you want to store your JavaScript code in a file outside the web page you'll use it in, store it in a file with the extension .js. This can be a good idea when you're dealing with cross-browser issues, for example, because you can load one .js file for one browser and another .js file for another browser.

To associate a .js script file with a <SCRIPT> element, you use the <SCRIPT> element's SRC attribute, like this. (Note that the <SCRIPT> element is empty here, as it should be when you use the SRC attribute.)

```
<HTML>
    <HEAD>
        <TITLE>
            Here's my script!
        </TITLE>
        <SCRIPT LANGUAGE="JavaScript" SRC="script.js">
        </SCRIPT>
    </HEAD>

    <BODY>
        <H1>Like my script?</H1>
    </BODY>
</HTML>
```

You set the SRC attribute to a URL, so you can even get the .js file from another server, like this:

```
<HTML>
    <HEAD>
        <TITLE>
            Here's my script!
```

```
        </TITLE>
        <SCRIPT LANGUAGE="JavaScript" SRC="www.myjavascripts/steve/script.js">
        </SCRIPT>
    </HEAD>

    <BODY>
        <H1>Like my script?</H1>
    </BODY>
</HTML>
```

The .js file, script.js here, contains only the code you want to execute, like this:

```
document.write("Hello from JavaScript!")
```

> **Tip**
>
> Note, however, that when you're doing something like what this statement does—write to the body of a document—you can run into problems with external script files, because the browser may well load the external script file before the body is fully loaded, which means your JavaScript will not do anything.

Specifying the Language Version

You can use the LANGUAGE attribute in <SCRIPT> elements to specify the version of JavaScript you want to use. If your script is written for JavaScript 1.1, for example, you can specify that you want to use that version of the language like this:

```
<HTML>
    <HEAD>
        <TITLE>Our first script!</TITLE>
        <SCRIPT LANGUAGE="JavaScript 1.1">
        .
        .
        //JavaScript 1.1 Code
        .
        .
        </SCRIPT>
    </HEAD>

    <BODY>
        <H1>Here we go!</H1>
    </BODY>
</HTML>
```

Note that if the browser you're working with doesn't support JavaScript 1.1, your code won't be run. You can code for different levels of JavaScript like this, where I'm using multiple <SCRIPT> elements to handle browsers that support JavaScript 1.0, 1.1, and so on—note that these <SCRIPT> elements must be in ascending order:

```
<HTML>
    <HEAD>
        <TITLE>Our first script!</TITLE>
        <SCRIPT LANGUAGE="JavaScript">
        .
        //JavaScript 1.0 Browsers
        .
        </SCRIPT>
        <SCRIPT LANGUAGE="JavaScript 1.1">
        .
        //JavaScript 1.1 Browsers
        .
        </SCRIPT>
        <SCRIPT LANGUAGE="JavaScript 1.2">
        .
        //JavaScript 1.2 Browsers
        .
        </SCRIPT>
        <!--
        document.write("Hello from JavaScript!")
        // -->
        </SCRIPT>
    </HEAD>

    <BODY>
        <H1>Here we go!</H1>
    </BODY>
</HTML>
```

Tip

This is also a good way to determine what version of JavaScript a browser supports—<SCRIPT> elements specifying more recent versions will not be executed.

We've seen what <SCRIPT> elements are for, where they go, and what their attributes are for. But when does the code in them actually run? In our first example, the code ran automatically, as soon as the page loaded. However, that's not a good thing for every page, of course; for example, you might be writing a web page that calculates loan interest, and it wouldn't be a good idea to do anything until the user entered some data. So when do scripts run?

When Does a Script Run?

Code in a JavaScript script runs at three main times:

- While the document is loading
- Just after the document loads
- When the user performs some action

I'll take a look at these in overview, because knowing when a script will run is an important part of our JavaScript foundation. Note, however, that this is only an overview, because it deals with some topics, such as functions, that we won't see until Chapter 3, "The JavaScript Language: Loops, Functions, and Errors."

Our first script ran automatically as the document loaded, because we simply placed our JavaScript statements in a <SCRIPT> element:

```
<HTML>
    <HEAD>
        <TITLE>Our first script!</TITLE>
    </HEAD>

    <BODY>
        <H1>Here we go!</H1>
        <SCRIPT LANGUAGE="JavaScript">
        <!--
        document.write("Hello from JavaScript!")
        // -->
        </SCRIPT>
    </BODY>
</HTML>
```

In this case, the browser runs our code as that code is loaded from the HTML document the browser is opening.

However, JavaScript code does not have to run immediately as it is loaded into the browser—you can wait until after the entire document has been loaded before running your code. That's often a good idea because HTML documents load piece by piece, which means you might find yourself trying to work with an HTML element that hasn't been loaded into the browser yet, and that would cause an error.

You can let the browser inform you when a web page is fully loaded with an *event*. When an event occurs in a browser, you know that something happened—for example, the user pressed a mouse button or a key on the keyboard. You can handle events in JavaScript by specifying code to run when a particular event occurs, such as when a button is clicked in a web page.

We'll cover events in detail in Chapter 6, "Using Core HTML Methods and Events," but here's a preview (which you can skip and come back to later if you want). The event that occurs when a page is fully loaded is the onload event, and like other events, you can handle it using attributes of HTML elements—in this case, you use the ONLOAD attribute of the <BODY> element. (We'll see the onload event in depth in Chapter 8, "Using *window* and *frame* Methods and Events"—see the section "Window Loading and Unloading" in that chapter.)

We'll need some way of connecting the code we want to run to the <BODY> element's ONLOAD attribute, and we can do that with a JavaScript *function*. We'll see all the details about functions in Chapter 3; what's important to know here is that they will give us a way to collect our code into easily handled packages that are run *only* when you want them to be run (not automatically as the browser reads your code).

Suppose, for example, that I want to use the window object's alert method to display a message in a simple dialog box—called an *alert box*—indicating that the page has finished loading. To do that, I'll create a function named alerter and connect this function to the ONLOAD attribute of the <BODY> element. (Chapter 3 contains details about creating functions.) Doing so makes sure that the code in that function is run *only* when the page is fully loaded. Here's how this looks in JavaScript:

(Listing 10-03.html on the web site)

```
<HTML>
    <HEAD>
        <TITLE>
            Executing Scripts After a Document Loads
        </TITLE>
        <SCRIPT LANGUAGE="JavaScript">
            <!--
            function alerter()
            {
                window.alert("All loaded.")
            }
            // -->
        </SCRIPT>
    </HEAD>

    <BODY ONLOAD="alerter()">
        <H1>Executing Scripts After a Document Loads</H1>
    </BODY>
</HTML>
```

That's all it takes—now that we've packaged our code in a function, that code is run *only* when we want it to run, not automatically when the page loaded, as would happen if the code were not enclosed in a function. You can see the result of this code in Figure 1.5 in the Internet Explorer, and Figure 1.6 in the Netscape Navigator, where those browsers are being made to display an alert box to indicate that the current web page has finished loading.

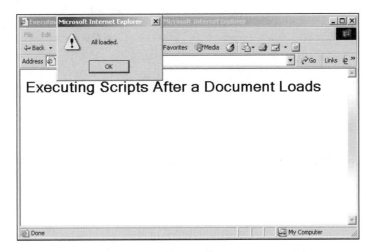

Figure 1.5   Using ONLOAD in the Internet Explorer.

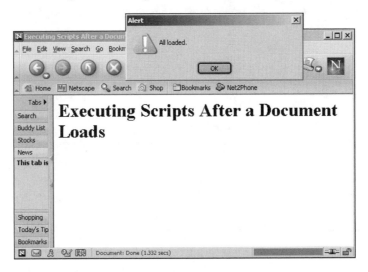

Figure 1.6   Using ONLOAD in the Netscape Navigator.

We've seen how loading a page can trigger an event—the onload event—but user actions, such as button clicks, can trigger events as well. We'll see how this works starting in Chapters 6, "Using Core HTML Methods and Events," and and 12, "Working with Forms, Buttons, Checkboxes, and Radio Buttons," but here's a preview. For example, just as we used the ONLOAD attribute of the <BODY> element to handle onload events, we can also handle button onclick events, which occur when you click a button, with the ONCLICK attribute of HTML button elements. Here's how I can display an alert box when the user clicks a button:

(Listing 01-04.html on the web site)

```
<HTML>
    <HEAD>
        <TITLE>
            Executing Scripts in Response to User Action
        </TITLE>
        <SCRIPT LANGUAGE="JavaScript">
            <!--
            function alerter()
            {
                window.alert("You clicked the button!")
            }
            // -->
        </SCRIPT>
    </HEAD>

    <BODY>
        <H1>Executing Scripts in Response to User Action</H1>
        <FORM>
            <INPUT TYPE="BUTTON" ONCLICK="alerter()" VALUE="Click Me!">
        </FORM>
    </BODY>
</HTML>
```

When the user clicks the button, the function named alerter is run, which displays the alert box. We'll see more on functions in Chapter 3, but what's important to know now is that they'll give us a way to decide when our code should be run, as opposed to letting the browser run that code automatically as the code is loaded from the HTML document.

Inline Scripts

Here's another option that you should be aware of: *inline scripts*. So far, we've placed all our code in <SCRIPT> elements or .js files, but there actually is another way, for very short code. Instead of connecting a JavaScript function to an event such as the onload event with the ONLOAD attribute, you can actually assign the JavaScript code you want to execute directly to the ONLOAD attribute. For example, here's how I display an alert box with the message All loaded. when a page loads:

```
<HTML>
    <HEAD>
        <TITLE>
            Executing Scripts After a Document Loads
        </TITLE>
    </HEAD>

    <BODY ONLOAD="alert('All loaded.')">
        <H1>Executing Scripts After a Document Loads</H1>
    </BODY>
</HTML>
```

This is a good technique to know for short scripts, but only for short scripts. For anything longer, place your script in a <SCRIPT> element.

Tip
If you want to place multiple statements in an inline script, you must separate them with semicolons.

Using *<SCRIPT FOR>*

And here's something else—in the Internet Explorer since version 4.0, you can use the <SCRIPT> element's FOR attribute to connect a script to a particular HTML element. For example, here's how I connect a script to the onclick event of the HTML button I've named button1 (I've named the button by setting the NAME attribute in the <INPUT> element that defines the button):

(Listing 01-05.html on the web site)

```
<HTML>
    <HEAD>
        <TITLE>
            Using the SCRIPT FOR Element
        </TITLE>
        <SCRIPT FOR="button1" EVENT="onclick" LANGUAGE="JavaScript">
            <!--
            alert("You clicked the button!")
            // -->
        </SCRIPT>
    </HEAD>

    <BODY>
        <H1>Using the SCRIPT FOR Element</H1>
        <FORM NAME="form1">
            <INPUT TYPE="BUTTON" NAME="button1" VALUE="Click Me!">
        </FORM>
    </BODY>
</HTML>
```

Now when the user clicks the button, an alert box appears with the message You clicked the button! (see Figure 1.7). This won't work in the Netscape Navigator, which will just run the script as soon as the page loads.

This is a useful technique to know to handle events, although it's not much used because it conflicts with the Netscape Navigator. We'll see more on this when we start working with events in Chapter 6.

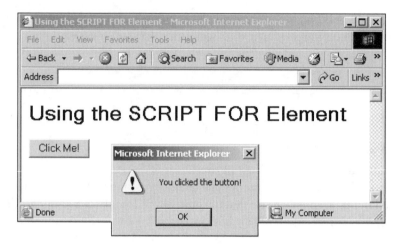

Figure 1.7   Using SCRIPT FOR in the Internet Explorer.

Viewing Script Errors

Sometimes, the JavaScript you and I write will have errors in it. (Well, maybe not you, but it sure happens to me.) The two browsers we're working with have the ability to tell us what the error is, and that's a useful thing to know in this chapter, where we're establishing our JavaScript foundation.

For example, what if we had misspelled document.write as documnt.write in our first script? Here's how that would look:

```
<HTML>
    <HEAD>
        <TITLE>
            Our first script!
        </TITLE>
    </HEAD>

    <BODY>
        <H1>Here we go!</H1>
        <SCRIPT LANGUAGE="JavaScript">
            <!--
            documnt.write("Hello from JavaScript!")
            // -->
        </SCRIPT>
    </BODY>
</HTML>
```

Both browsers would have trouble with this JavaScript. If there's a JavaScript error in the Internet Explorer, you'll see a small icon at right in the status bar at the bottom of the browser (see Figure 1.8). Double-clicking that icon opens an error dialog box, as you also see in Figure 1.8, telling you what the error is.

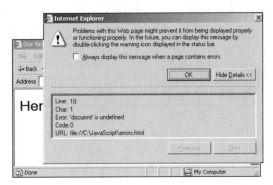

Figure 1.8   Locating an error in the Internet Explorer.

In fact, you can have a dialog box come up automatically for every error. In the Internet Explorer 6, you do that with the Tools | Internet Options | Advanced | Browsing item, and select the check box labeled Display a Notification About Every Script Error.

In the Netscape Navigator version 4 and later up to 6, you'll see a message in the status bar indicating that there is an error and directing you to navigate to the URL "javascript:". To do that, you can use the File | Open Page menu item, opening the Open Page dialog box. Type javascript: into that dialog box and click the Open button. This opens the JavaScript console, which is a separate window that displays errors.

In Netscape Navigator 6, you don't see an error icon in the taskbar if there's an error. If your script isn't running as it should, however, select the Tasks | Tools | JavaScript Console item to open the JavaScript console window. You can even leave this window open as you continue to work in the browser. You can see the JavaScript console for Netscape Navigator 6 in Figure 1.9.

Locating errors like this can be invaluable in helping you deal with them, and it's a good foundation item for our foundation chapter.

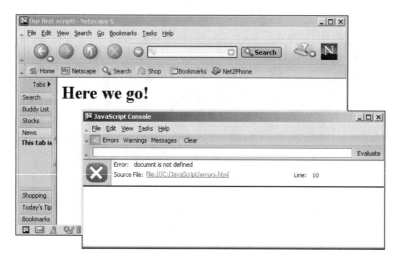

Figure 1.9   Locating an error in the Netscape Navigator.

Server-Side JavaScript

JavaScript is even becoming available on web servers these days, not just in web browsers. Only a few web servers support server-side JavaScript at the moment, but their number is growing. To embed JavaScript to be run on the web server in a web page, you use the <SERVER> element.

This element holds server-side JavaScript code, which is code that runs on the server. For example, here's how you would display a server's Internet address in a web page if server-side JavaScript is enabled:

```
<HTML>
    <HEAD>
        <TITLE>
            Server-Side JavaScript
        </TITLE>
        .
        .
        .
    </HEAD>

    <BODY>
        .
        .
        .
        Hello - your server's address is
```

```
<SERVER>
    write(request.ip)
</SERVER>
    .
    .
    .
    </BODY>
</HTML>
```

You can find Netscape's documentation for server-side JavaScript at `http://developer.netscape.com/docs/manuals/index.html?content=javascript.html`.

Working with Browser Objects in JavaScript

Many beginning JavaScript programmers have the idea that all they'll need is built in to the JavaScript language itself, but that's not so. The JavaScript language is actually very simple, and, more often than not, really serves just as a way to manipulate the objects already built in to a browser. In fact, the real richness is in those browser objects that JavaScript can work with, not so much in the language itself.

Through objects such as the `document` and `window` objects, you have access to the HTML in a web page, can open new browser windows, write to the web page, handle user events such as mouse clicks, make the browser navigate to a new location or to a page it's already been to, support drag and drop, and so on. For example, our first script used the `document` object's `write` method to write to a web page:

```
<HTML>
    <HEAD>
        <TITLE>Our first script!</TITLE>
    </HEAD>

    <BODY>
        <H1>Here we go!</H1>
        <SCRIPT LANGUAGE="JavaScript">
        <!--
        document.write("Hello from JavaScript!")
        // -->
        </SCRIPT>
    </BODY>
</HTML>
```

It's not just JavaScript that has access to these browser objects—any scripting language does. Programmers use JavaScript because they like the simplicity and power of the language itself, but a great deal of what people mean when they say "JavaScript programming" really is all about working with browser objects. We'll see that in this book, where there are whole chapters are devoted to the `document`, `window`, `location`, `history`, and other browser objects.

As you might gather from the name browser objects, however, there are going to be many compatibility issues here, because the Internet Explorer and the Netscape Navigator are different, and they've started off with very different sets of objects. The set of objects a browser uses is organized into an *object model.* An object model specifies the hierarchy of browser objects in a browser—for example, the `document` object (which corresponds to a web page's content) is contained inside the `window` object (which corresponds to the web browser window itself), and the browser's object model will show that.

Working with the different object models in the two browsers is the most difficult cross-browser issue we'll come up against. However, the story is no longer hopeless, as it once was, because of the W3C's work on the cross-browser DOM specification. Both Internet Explorer 6 and Netscape Navigator 6 do a good job of implementing the object model in the W3C DOM, as we'll see when we start discussing browser objects in depth in Chapter 4. (In fact, both browsers implement not only the W3C DOM, but also their own object models for backward compatibility.)

In this, our foundation chapter, it's essential to get an overview of the object model we'll be using in various browsers. To make things simpler and more coherent, in this chapter, I'm going to stick to the basic parts of the object models common to both browsers—we'll have time enough for browser differences in Chapter 4 and later. Here, let's take a look at what will work in any scriptable browser.

In Figure 1.10, you can see a version of the object model common to both browsers. (I'll call this basic object set the *common DOM model*, and you can count on it being available in any browser that supports scripting.) The figure shows which objects contain which other ones. You can see in the figure, for example, how the `window` object contains the `document` object, how the `document` object contains `form` objects, and so on.

Here's a basic list of browser objects and what they are good for; familiarity with these objects is an important part of the JavaScript foundation we're building in this chapter:

- **document.** Corresponds to the current web page's body and some parts of the head. Using this object, you have access to the HTML of the page itself, including all the links, images, and anchors in it.
- **form.** Holds information about HTML forms in the current page; forms can contain buttons, text fields, check boxes, and all kinds of other HTML *controls.* An HTML control is one the user can interact with by clicking, entering text, and so on.

- **frame.** Refers to a frame in the browser window.
- **history.** Holds the record of the sites the web browser has visited before reaching the current page. Gives you access to methods that enable you to move back to previous pages.
- **location.** Holds information about the location of the current web page, such as its URL, the domain name, path, server port, and more.
- **navigator**. Refers to the browser itself, enabling you to determine what browser the user has.
- **window.** Refers to the current browser window.

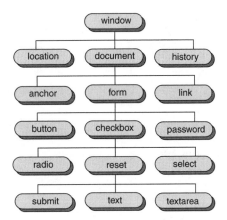

Figure 1.10   The common DOM model.

So how do you actually interact with these browser objects in JavaScript? You do that using three aspects of these objects, which we've already discussed: properties, methods, and events.

Browser Object Properties, Methods, and Events

We've seen that the document object refers to the current page, but how do you actually *use* this object? We've already seen one way, which is to use object methods, such as the write method, to write text to the web page. You use a method of an object by giving the object's name a dot (.) followed by the method name, such as document.write. Here are a few examples of methods:

- **document.write.** Writes text to the current web page.
- **document.writeln.** Writes a single line to the current web page and skips to the next line.

- **history.go.** Navigates the web browser to a location in the browser's history.

- **window.alert.** Displays an alert dialog box.

- **window.open.** Opens a new browser window.

As you can see, these methods provide a lot of ready-made power for you to work with the browser interactively. Besides performing actions with objects using methods, you can read and change settings in those objects using properties. A property holds some setting of an object. For example, the document.linkcolor property holds the color of hyperlinks in the current web page, and by changing the document.linkcolor property, you can change that color. Here are some example properties and the objects to which they belong:

- **document.bgcolor.** Background color of the current page.

- **document.fgcolor.** Foreground color of the current page.

- **document.lastmodified.** Date the page was last modified.

- **document.title.** Title of the current page.

- **location.hostname.** Name of the *Internet service provider* (ISP) host.

- **navigator.appName.** Name of the browser, which you can use to determine what browser the user has.

Object properties and methods give you access to what's going on in the browser, enabling you to change just about everything under programmatic control. Besides properties and methods, there is one more very important concept in working with browser objects: events.

How do you know when such an action has occurred? For example, what if you want to change the color of a web page when the user clicks that page? To inform you when something's happened, JavaScript uses events, such as mouse clicks, as we've already seen when we used the onload event to display an alert box like this:

```
<HTML>
    <HEAD>
        <TITLE>
            Executing Scripts After a Document Loads
        </TITLE>
        <SCRIPT LANGUAGE="JavaScript">
            <!--
            function alerter()
            {
                window.alert("All loaded.")
```

```
        }
        // -->
    </SCRIPT>
</HEAD>

<BODY ONLOAD="alerter()">
    <H1>Executing Scripts After a Document Loads</H1>
</BODY>
</HTML>
```

When the user clicks the page, an `onmousedown` event occurs. To handle that event, you can use the `ONMOUSEDOWN` event attribute. Here's an example showing one way of responding to such events. In this case, I'll change the document's background color to red when the mouse is clicked using an inline script:

(Listing 01-06.html on the web site)

```
<HTML>
    <HEAD>
        <TITLE>
            JavaScript Event Example
        </TITLE>
    </HEAD>

    <BODY ONMOUSEDOWN="document.bgColor='red'">
        <H1>
            Click this page to turn it red!
        </H1>
    </BODY>
</HTML>
```

In this case, I've indicated that I want to assign the browser-predefined color "red" to `document.bgcolor` when the user clicks the mouse (both Netscape Navigator and Internet Explorer understand basic color names like "red," "blue," "green," and so on), and I do that with the JavaScript assignment `document.bgColor='red'`. (As we'll see in Chapter 2, "The JavaScript Language: Data, Operators, and Branching," the equals sign here means that I want to set the `document.bgColor` property to `'red'`, much like the way we've assigned values to HTML attributes already.) The results of this example, in glorious black and white, appear in Figure 1.11 in the Netscape Navigator.

Tip

While we're on this example, here's something to note about inline scripts: The entire script is enclosed in quotation marks, because it's assigned to an HTML event attribute, such as ONMOUSEDOWN. If the script itself uses quotes, however, such as `document.bgColor="red"`, you should make sure you use different quotation marks from those that enclose the script so that the browser doesn't get confused. If you use double quotation marks around the script, for example, use single quotation marks in the script, and vice versa. Both of these will work: `<BODY ONMOUSEDOWN="document.bgColor='red'">` and `<BODY ONMOUSEDOWN='document.bgColor="red"'>`.

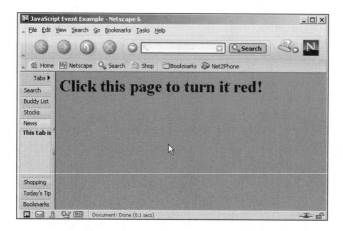

Figure 1.11 Turning a web page red.

So what HTML event attributes are available? Here are some common ones that we'll run into (discussed in more detail in Chapter 6):

- **ONABORT.** Occurs when an action is aborted.
- **ONBLUR.** Occurs when an element loses the input focus.
- **ONCHANGE.** Occurs when data in a control, such as a text field, changes.
- **ONCLICK.** Occurs when an element is clicked.
- **ONDBLCLICK.** Occurs when an element is double-clicked.
- **ONDRAGDROP.** Occurs when a drag-and-drop operation is undertaken.
- **ONERROR.** Occurs when there's been a JavaScript error.
- **ONFOCUS.** Occurs when an element gets the focus.
- **ONKEYDOWN.** Occurs when a key goes down.
- **ONKEYPRESS.** Occurs when a key is pressed and the key code is available.
- **ONKEYUP.** Occurs when a key goes up.
- **ONLOAD.** Occurs when the page loads.
- **ONMOUSEDOWN.** Occurs when a mouse button goes down.
- **ONMOUSEMOVE.** Occurs when the mouse moves.
- **ONMOUSEOUT.** Occurs when the mouse leaves an element.
- **ONMOUSEOVER.** Occurs when the mouse moves over an element.
- **ONMOUSEUP.** Occurs when a mouse button goes up.
- **ONRESET.** Occurs when the user clicks a Reset button.

- **ONRESIZE.** Occurs when an element or page is resized.
- **ONSUBMIT.** Occurs when the user clicks a Submit button.
- **ONUNLOAD.** Occurs when a page is unloaded.

I've presented the common DOM model here, but beyond these basics, the object models between the two browsers diverge. As mentioned, one of the biggest issues JavaScript programmers have to deal with is cross-browser compatibility; a web page with a script that works in one browser may not work in another. We'll be looking at this issue throughout the book—it's one of the most important topics we'll cover. I'll take a look at it in overview here in our foundation chapter.

Handling Cross-Browser Programming Issues

Nothing's more annoying than working hard on a script that performs beautifully when you test it, only to get email from users telling you that your script doesn't work at all—and that you should test your JavaScript before embedding it in web pages. With so many browser types, and so many browser versions, it's very hard to get any but the most rudimentary scripts to run for all users unless you pay attention to cross-browser compatibility issues.

The biggest such issue is what properties, methods, and events are supported by what browser objects, and I'll start by taking a look at that issue here.

Cross-Browser Issues: Differing Object Models

Unlike other books, this book is designed to make dealing with cross-browser object models easy—or at least easier. When there's an incompatibility, I'll point it out. For each property, method, and event of the various browser objects, I'm going to list which browser, and which version of which browser, supports them.

That information will give you what you need to deal with nearly all cross-browser issues. You don't have to worry about what will work in what browser—you'll be able to look it up directly in the reference material for the properties, methods, and events of the various objects. For example, you can quickly see all the browser versions that support the reset method in the sample entry in Table 1.1—here, NS2 stands for Netscape Navigator 2.0, IE5 stands for Internet Explorer 5.0, and so on. (I'll present all objects' properties, methods, and events this way—as well as all the syntax of the JavaScript language itself—enabling you to deal with cross-browser issues easily.)

Table 1.1 **Sample Object Method Entry**

Method	NS2	NS3	NS4	NS6	IE3a	IE3b	IE4	IE5	IE5.5	IE6
reset		x	x	x			x	x	x	x
Returns: Nothing										

This method simulates clicking the Reset button in a form, which resets the data in the form's controls back to their default values (which you can set with most controls' VALUE attribute). This method causes the onreset event to occur. Syntax: *form*.reset().

Note in particular the two entries for Internet Explorer versions 3a and 3b in Table 1.1; two different Internet Explorer versions 3.0 were released, and I'll label them 3a and 3b. You can tell the difference between these browsers with *object detection*—detecting the existence of objects on-the-fly—as discussed in Chapter 4.

Cross–Browser Issues: Built-in JavaScript Objects

Besides the browser objects that you work with in most JavaScript scripts, JavaScript itself has some built-in objects that deserve mention, and a few chapters in this book are devoted to them. The available objects differ to some degree between JavaScript and JScript. In particular, here are the built-in objects in JavaScript 1.5 and what they do:

- **Array.** Supports creation of arrays.
- **Boolean.** Supports Boolean values (which can hold only values of True or False).
- **Date.** Supports working with dates and times.
- **Function.** Specifies a string of JavaScript code to be compiled as a function.
- **Math.** Support for many math routines, such as square root.
- **Number.** Supports numeric data types.
- **Object.** Provides functionality common to all JavaScript objects.
- **RegExp.** Supports regular expression string matching.
- **String.** Supports manipulation of text strings.

And here are the built-in language objects in JScript 5.6:

- **ActiveXObject.** Supports Internet Explorer ActiveX objects.
- **Array.** Supports creation of arrays.
- **Boolean.** Supports Boolean values (which can hold only values of True or False).

- **Date.** Supports working with dates and times.

- **Dictionary.** Supports storing key/value data item pairs.

- **Enumerator.** Supports working with collections of objects.

- **Error.** Contains information about the errors that have occurred in a script.

- **FileSystemObject.** Gives you some access to the computer's file system.

- **Function.** Specifies a string of JavaScript code to be compiled as a function.

- **Global.** Collects various methods available anywhere in a script together into one object.

- **Math.** Support for many math routines, such as square root.

- **Number.** Supports numeric data types.

- **Object.** Provides functionality common to all JavaScript objects.

- **RegExp.** Supports regular expression string matching.

- **String.** Supports manipulation of text strings.

- **VBArray.** Gives you access to Microsoft Visual Basic safe arrays in the Internet Explorer.

When covering the properties, methods, and events of these objects, I'll indicate which browsers, and what versions of those browsers (just as with the browser objects).

Cross-Browser Issues: Core Language and Language Version

One area where some compatibility has finally appeared is in the core JavaScript language itself. Both the JavaScript language in the Netscape Navigator and the JScript language in the Internet Explorer are now compliant with the ECMA standard ECMAScript version 3. That means when it comes to the core language itself, which we'll be learning in the next two chapters, you usually don't have to worry about incompatibilities if you're dealing with recent browsers.

The JavaScript language itself is made up of various keywords, and we'll become familiar with these keywords in the next two chapters, which are on the syntax of JavaScript. These keywords are called *reserved words* in JavaScript, because they are already part of the JavaScript language and may not be used for any other purpose. For reference, you'll find the reserved words in JavaScript 1.5 in Table 1.2, and the reserved words in JScript 5.6 in Table 1.3. JScript 5.6 also reserves some words for possible future use, and you'll find them in Table 1.4.

Table 1.2   **Netscape's JavaScript 1.5 Reserved Words**

abstract	boolean	break	byte
case	catch	char	class
const	continue	debugger	default
delete	do	double	else
enum	export	extends	false
final	finally	float	for
function	goto	if	implements
import	in	instanceof	int
interface	long	native	new
null	package	private	protected
public	return	short	static
super	switch	synchronized	this
throw	throws	transient	true
try	typeof	var	void
volatile	while	with	

Table 1.3   **Microsoft's JScript 5.6 Reserved Words**

break	delete	function	return	typeof
case	do	if	switch	var
catch	else	in	this	void
continue	false	instanceof	throw	while
debugger	finally	new	true	with
default	for	null	try	

Table 1.4   **Microsoft's JScript 5.6 Future Reserved Words**

abstract	double	goto	native	static
boolean	enum	implements	package	super
byte	export	import	private	synchronized
char	extends	int	protected	throws
class	final	interface	public	transient
const	float	long	short	volatile

Despite the recent compliance with the ECMA version 3 standard, however, earlier versions of the browsers support different versions of JavaScript, and that introduces incompatibilities.

That means it's often important to know what version of JavaScript you're working with; so I'll put that information into a set of tables here. You'll find the JavaScript version listed by Netscape Navigator version in Table 1.5, and the JScript version (as well as which JavaScript version each JScript version matched) listed by Internet Explorer version in Table 1.6. Note that Internet Explorer 3.0 actually had two releases, which I'll call 3a and 3b throughout the book, which supported JavaScript 1.0 and 1.1 respectively.

Table 1.5   **Netscape Navigator JavaScript Version by Browser Version**

JavaScript Version	Netscape Navigator Version
1.0	2.0
1.1	3.0
1.2	4.0 to 4.05
1.3	4.06 to 4.7
1.4	Not implemented
1.5	6.0 (ECMA 3 compliant)

Table 1.6   **Internet Explorer JScript Version by Browser Version**

JScript Version	JavaScript Version	Internet Explorer Version
1.0	1.0	3a
2.0	1.1	3b
3.0	1.2	4.0
4.0	Not implemented	Not implemented
5.0	1.3	5.0
5.5	1.5	5.5 (partly ECMA 3 compliant)
5.6	1.5	6.0 (ECMA 3 compliant)

In fact, to further complicate the version issue, Netscape is already hard at work on JavaScript 2.0, now in the planning stages. You can find information about this version of JavaScript as it's being designed at http://www.mozilla.org/js/language/js20/introduction/index.html.

How will JavaScript 2.0 differ from JavaScript 1.5? Here's the current list of additions in JavaScript 2.0 as it appears on the JavaScript 2.0 site—these items are quoted from that site. (Note that these items will make sense only if you've already programmed in JavaScript and have some object-oriented programming experience.)

- Class definition syntax, both static and dynamic
- Packages, including a versioning mechanism
- Types for program and interface documentation
- Invariant declarations such as const and final
- Private, internal, public, and user-defined access controls
- Introspection facilities
- Overridable basic operators, such as + and [ ]
- Machine types, such as int32, for more faithful communication with other programming languages

With all these compatibility issues going on, it is often important to know which browser and version you're using. So how do you know? I'll take a look at that now.

Cross-Browser Issues: Which Browser Are You Using?

We'll deal in depth with cross-browser programming throughout the book, especially in Chapter 4, and an important part of that is knowing what browser version your script is executing in. That's where the navigator browser object comes in; this object is another of the browser objects you work with in JavaScript. Here are the relevant properties of this object:

- **navigator.AppName.** The name of the browser application.
- **navigator.AppVersion.** The version of the browser.
- **navigator.UserAgent.** More details about the browser.

The following script displays these properties in a web page:

(Listing 01-07.html on the web site)

```
<HTML>
    <HEAD>
        <TITLE>
            Checking Your Browser Type
        </TITLE>
    </HEAD>
```

```
<BODY>
    <SCRIPT LANGUAGE="JavaScript">
        document.write("navigator.appName: " + navigator.appName)
        document.write("<BR><BR>")
        document.write("navigator.appVersion: " + navigator.appVersion)
        document.write("<BR><BR>")
        document.write("navigator.userAgent: " + navigator.userAgent)
    </SCRIPT>

    <H1>Checking Your Browser Type</H1>
</BODY>
</HTML>
```

The + *operators* in this code are used to join text strings together, as we'll see in the next chapter. (Here, I'm joining the text "navigator.appName:" to the actual value of navigator.appName, and so on for navigator.appVersion and navigator.userAgent.) You can see the results of this script in the Internet Explorer in Figure 1.12, and in the Netscape Navigator in Figure 1.13. Note the appVersion property does not give you what you might expect—I'm using Internet Explorer 6.02, but appVersion is reported as 4.0, and I'm also using Netscape Navigator 6.2, but appVersion is reported as 5.0. To find the true browser version, you must search the userAgent text—you can see the text "MSIE 6.0" for Internet Explorer and "Netscape6/6.2" for Netscape Navigator in these two figures, which give the correct version.

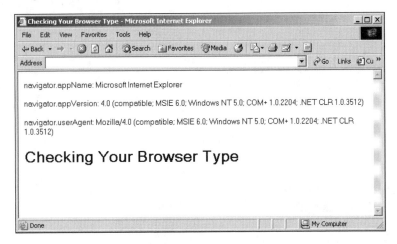

Figure 1.12   Getting browser information in the Internet Explorer.

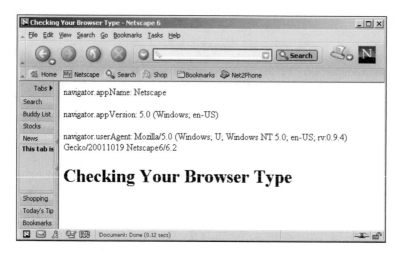

Figure 1.13 Getting browser information in the Netscape Navigator.

Why do both `userAgent` property values begin with "Mozilla" (as seen in these figures)? Mozilla is Netscape's free development browser that is a developer community effort to test new innovations in web browsing. In the early days of JavaScript, many scripts would search the `userAgent` property for the word *Mozilla* to determine whether the browser supported JavaScript, and that's why that property still begins with `"Mozilla"`.

Tip

The Mozilla browser is available at www.mozilla.org for free; it's a cutting edge browser that implements the various ECMA and W3C standards for JavaScript, but it's not in widespread use compared to the two main browsers available.

Checking the properties of the `navigator` object is one way to see what type of browser you're working with, and we'll work with this technique in Chapter 4. However, even the same version of a browser can have different capabilities on different platforms (such as Windows or the Mac). A better technique, as we'll see in Chapter 4, is to use direct object detection, which enables you to check for the existence of a browser object before you try to use it in your script. More on this in Chapter 4.

JavaScript Resources You Should Know About

Before finishing our foundation chapter, we should point out that tons of JavaScript resources are available on the Internet. (A casual search for "JavaScript" on the Internet turns up a mere 15,265,065 pages that discuss the topic). I'll put together a starter list here. As with all the Internet resources listed in this book, however, bear in mind that URLs can change in time.

To start, you can find the documentation for Netscape's JavaScript 1.5 online here:

- The JavaScript 1.5 user's guide is at `http://developer.netscape.com/docs/manuals/js/core/jsguide15/contents.html`.

- The JavaScript 1.5 reference manual is at `http://developer.netscape.com/docs/manuals/js/core/jsref15/contents.html`.

- You can download the JavaScript 1.5 user's guide and reference manual from `http://developer.netscape.com/docs/manuals/index.html?content=javascript.html`.

You can find the documentation for JScript 5.6 online as well:

- The JScript 5.6 user's guide and reference manual is available at `http://msdn.microsoft.com/library/default.asp?url=/library/en-us/script56/html/js56jsconjscriptfundamentals.asp`. Click the links in the navigation bar to find these items.

- You also can download the JScript 5.6 user's guide and reference manual. The URL for that currently is `http://msdn.microsoft.com/downloads/default.asp?URL=/downloads/sample.asp?url=/msdn-files/027/001/733/msdncompositedoc.xml`.

The ECMAScript specifications are also online:

- The ECMAScript Language Specification, 3rd edition is at `www.ecma.ch/ecma1/STAND/ECMA-262.HTM`.

- The ECMAScript Components Specification is at `www.ecma.ch/ecma1/STAND/ECMA-290.HTM`.

- The ECMAScript 3rd Edition Compact Profile specification is at `www.ecma.ch/ecma1/STAND/ecma-327.htm`.

Here's where to find the W3C DOM specifications that give the object models for the browser objects to which browsers are now conforming:

- W3C DOM level 1: `www.w3.org/TR/REC-DOM-Level-1/`
- W3C DOM level 2: `www.w3.org/TR/DOM-Level-2-Core/`
- W3C DOM level 3: `www.w3.org/TR/DOM-Level-3-Core/`

Many general sites also have some good JavaScript resources—here's a starter list:

- Netscape's JavaScript resources page is at `http://developer.netscape.com/docs/manuals/jsresource.html`.

- You can find some useful JavaScript resources at `http://javascript.com/ Good JavaScript resource`.

- A good source of JavaScript information is at `http://javascript.about.com/`.

- You can find additional JavaScript resources at `http://www.javascriptgate.com/`.

Here are a few free JavaScript tutorials on the web:

- `www.scriptsearch.com/javascript/tips_and_tutorials/`

- `www.scriptsearch.com/javascript/web_sites/`

- `http://javascript.about.com/cs/beginner/index.htm`

- `www.w3schools.com/js/default.asp` (JavaScript school)

- `www.echoecho.com/javascript.htm`

- `www.iboost.com/build/programming/js/tutorial/876.htm`

- `www.bitafterbit.com/english/jscript/basic/index.html`

- `www.javascriptmall.com/learn/index.htm`

And here are some sites that offer free, prewritten JavaScript scripts:

- `www.scriptsearch.com/javascript/scripts/`

- `www.scriptsearch.com/javascript/web_sites/`

- `http://scriptsearch.internet.com/javascript/`

- `http://webdeveloper.earthweb.com/webjs`

- `www.webcoder.com/scriptorium/index.html`

- `http://javascript.internet.com/` (930 scripts at last count)

- `www.crays.com/jsc/` (The JavaScript Corral)

- `www.j-scripts.com/`

- `www.hotscripts.com/javascript/scripts_and_programs/`

- `www.javascriptmall.com/`

- `www.tek-tips.com/gfaq.cfm/lev2/4/lev3/32/spid/216`

- `www.a1javascripts.com/`

In addition, some groups on Usenet are devoted to discussing JavaScript (note that not all newsgroups will be supported on all news servers):

- `comp.lang.javascript`

- `microsoft.public.scripting.jscript`

- `microsoft.public.dotnet.languages.jscript`

- `microsoft.public.inetsdk.programming.scripting.jscript`

As you can see, you can access many JavaScript resources on the Internet. This book is designed to provide all you need, but if you can't find it here, you might check the Internet—and be sure to let me know what you've missed so I can add it to the next edition!

That's it for our foundation chapter. We've gotten a solid JavaScript start here, and a good foundation on which to build. We've created our first scripts, played around with the <SCRIPT> element, and even determined what browser a script is running in. Now we're going to start really digging into JavaScript, beginning in Chapter 2, where we start seeing how to handle data, including numbers and text.

2

The JavaScript Language: Data, Operators, and Branching

THIS AND THE NEXT CHAPTER COVER THE JAVASCRIPT language itself. To be able to tackle the built-in browser objects, the built-in JavaScript objects, Dynamic HTML, and more, we need to have a solid understanding of how to use JavaScript itself. The language is the glue that will bind our scripts together and put the various objects we'll work with come under our control.

In this chapter, we'll get started by seeing how JavaScript handles and stores data, how to work on that data, and how to test data values so we can take different actions in our code depending on what those values are. There's a lot coming up here, and I'll start by taking a look at how JavaScript handles data.

Working with Data

The data in your JavaScript programs can be of many different types. For example, you might have some text—called a text *string*—that you want to display, like this:

```
document.write("Hello, welcome to my Web page!")
```

Or you might be writing a compound interest calculator for users and need to keep in mind the interest rate, the amount the user has invested, and the length of time the user wants to collect interest for to be able to calculate what he wants to know. Or you might even have a database of items to sell and need to search that database for matches to what the user is looking for. To make your programs actually *do* something, you won't get very far without being able to handle some data and work on it.

Internally, JavaScript has several *data types* it uses. For example, the string data type lets JavaScript handle strings of text, the number data type lets JavaScript handle numeric values, and so on. Here are the different data types that JavaScript supports internally:

- **String.** A string of text, such as "Welcome to my web page!" or "I think that's an error."

- **Number.** These are numeric values, such as integers like 1, −1, 0, and 5014, or floating-point values such as 1.000, 3.1415, and 0.07.

- **Boolean.** Boolean values are "truth" values, and can hold only two values: true or false. These will be more important when we start testing our data—for example, checking whether a temperature is greater than 72 will give us a value of true or false.

- **Null.** Null values indicate a null result in JavaScript. If you try to access data past the end of a data list, for example, you may get a null value. The idea here is that there's nothing to report.

- **Object.** We've already seen a great deal about the objects built in to browsers and built in to JavaScript itself. Instead of simple data such as strings or numbers, these objects are handled using the object data type internally. Later on in this book, we'll see how to create our own custom objects.

- **Function.** Even function definitions, which we'll see in the next chapter, can be treated as data in JavaScript.

You can use data of these various types in two ways in your code. First, you can embed it directly in JavaScript statements, like this:

```
document.write("Hello")
document.write(3.1415926)
```

These directly embedded data items are called *literals*, they're values that appear in your code statements. Here, I'm writing the string "Hello" and the number 3.1415926 to a web page and storing those values as literals in the code.

The second way to store data is to use *variables*, and I'll take a look at working with variables now.

Variables

When you store data in a variable, you're setting aside space for it in your program and giving it a name that you can refer to it with in your code. Unlike literals, you can manipulate and *change* the value stored in a variable, such as the current temperature, the value in a bank account, the current amount the user owes, and so on.

In JavaScript, you should first *declare* a variable before you use it, and you use the var statement to do that. This statement has been around since the beginning, as you see in Table 2.1.

Table 2.1 **The *var* Statement**

Statement	NS2	NS3	NS4	NS6	IE3a	IE3b	IE4	IE5	IE5.5	IE6
var	x	x	x	x	x	x	x	x	x	x

Here's the formal syntax of the var statement, which we'll decipher fully over the next few pages:

```
var varname [= value] [, varname [= value] ...]
```

In its simplest form, you just use the var statement to declare a variable so that you can use that variable in your code. Here's an example; in this case, I want to store the number of days left until summer vacation in a variable named numberOfDaysLeft, so I declare that variable with var:

```
<SCRIPT LANGUAGE="JavaScript">
<!--
    var numberOfDaysLeft
    .
    .
    .
// -->
</SCRIPT>
```

Now I'm free to *assign* data to this new variable, and that data will be stored in the variable. Here, I'm using the = *assignment operator* to store the number 262 in numberOfDaysLeft:

```
<SCRIPT LANGUAGE="JavaScript">
<!--
    var numberOfDaysLeft
    numberOfDaysLeft = 262
    .
    .
    .
// -->
</SCRIPT>
```

Now that I've stored a value in this variable, all I have to do is to use the variable's name in code, and JavaScript will replace that name with the variable's value. For example, here's how I display the value in `numberOfDaysLeft` using `document.write` (as we saw in the preceding chapter, the + operator joins strings together):

(Listing 02-01.html on the web site)

```html
<HTML>
    <HEAD>
        <TITLE>
            Working With Variables
        </TITLE>
    </HEAD>

    <BODY>
        <H1>Working With Variables</H1>
        <FORM NAME="Form1">
        </FORM>
        <SCRIPT LANGUAGE="JavaScript">
        <!--
            var numberOfDaysLeft
            numberOfDaysLeft = 262
            document.write("Number of days until summer: " + numberOfDaysLeft + ".")
        // -->
        </SCRIPT>
    </BODY>
</HTML>
```

You can see the result in Figure 2.1, where the value in `numberOfDaysLeft` is displayed.

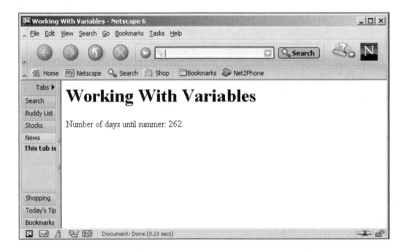

Figure 2.1   Using a variable in Netscape Navigator.

In this way, when you store data in a variable in your code, that data becomes accessible to your code. You can set the value in a variable, change the value if you want to, and access it from your code. Now we're able to start handling data in our code.

Note that we just used the `var` statement to declare `numberOfDaysLeft`; we didn't have to say what *type* of data would be stored in this variable (which you must do in many programming languages). JavaScript knows what type the data is in a variable depending on the data you assign to a variable; for example, assigning 262 to `numberOfDaysLeft` tells JavaScript that this variable will be storing numeric data:

```
numberOfDaysLeft = 262
```

If I had stored a string, JavaScript would know that the variable is storing string data:

```
numberOfDaysLeft = "Two hundred sixty two days left"
```

You can change the type of data stored in a variable at any time—just assign new data to it. Here, I'm changing the type of data stored in `numberOfDaysLeft` from a number to a string:

```
numberOfDaysLeft = 262
numberOfDaysLeft = "Two hundred sixty two days left"
```

Tip

Actually, JavaScript is a pretty forgiving language. It's not strictly necessary to use var, although you're supposed to, to declare variables before using those variables—just using the variables can declare them by default. I could just have used the statements numberOfDaysLeft = 262 and document.write("Number of days until summer: " + numberOfDaysLeft + ".") here. The only time JavaScript will actually insist that you declare variables before using them is when they might conflict with other variables of the same name, which we'll see more about in the next chapter.

Naming Variables

Note also the name of our first variable: `numberOfDaysLeft`. Here, I've put this name together using several words, and I'm using the Java variable-naming convention, which is the standard in JavaScript. That means the variable name starts with a small letter, and the first letter of each word that goes into the name is capitalized. The other standard option is to use underscores to assemble the variable name, like this: `number_of_days_left`. However, it's usually better to stick to the Java naming convention; JavaScript itself uses that convention to name its built-in functions, such as `toUpperCase`, which changes the case of a text string to upper case, as we'll see in this chapter.

You can't give a variable the same name as a JavaScript reserved word
(refer back to Tables 1.2, 1.3, and 1.4). Nor can JavaScript variables start with
a number, contain spaces, or any punctuation characters except underscores.
(In general, the rules for legal names for JavaScript variables are the same for
HTML identifiers.)

Initializing the Variable's Data

Here's what the syntax of the var statement is, as we've already seen:

```
var varname [= value] [, varname [= value] ...]
```

What does this mean? We'll see syntax statements such as this in this and the
next chapter. The terms *not* in italic are JavaScript keywords; the terms that
are in italic are *placeholders* where you can fill in your own items. For example, *varname* here is a placeholder for the name of the variable you're declaring. The square brackets, [and], are the standard way to indicate that
something is optional in syntax statements. (You'll see this in all JavaScript
documentation, so I'll use the same technique here.) Therefore, you can,
optionally, write a var statement like this:

```
var numberOfDaysLeft = 262
```

This declares a variable and assigns it a value, all in one step. It's the same as if
you had used these two statements:

```
var numberOfDaysLeft
numberOfDaysLeft = 262
```

Note also that, as you see in the preceding syntax statement, you can declare
multiple variables in the same var statement—and even initialize them, as in
this example:

```
var numberOfDaysLeft = 262, numberOfNightsLeft = 261, numberOfCustomersLeft = 2
document.write("Number of days until summer: " + numberOfDaysLeft + ".")
    .
    .
    .
```

This declares and initializes three variables with data—all in one var statement. This gives the same result as these three var statements:

```
var numberOfDaysLeft = 262
var numberOfNightsLeft = 261
var numberOfCustomersLeft = 2
document.write("Number of days until summer: " + numberOfDaysLeft + ".")
    .
    .
    .
```

Where Do You Use the *var* Statement?

Here's another thing to realize: So far, I've used the var statement as the first statement in our scripts, and in fact, variable declarations must be done first thing in many languages. In JavaScript, however, you can use the var statement wherever you need it; it doesn't have to be the first statement in a script at all:

```
<HTML>
    <HEAD>
        <TITLE>
            Working With Variables
        </TITLE>
    </HEAD>

    <BODY>
        <H1>Working With Variables</H1>
        <FORM NAME="Form1">
        </FORM>
        <SCRIPT LANGUAGE="JavaScript">
        <!--
            document.write("Welcome to my Web page!<BR>")
            var numberOfDaysLeft
            numberOfDaysLeft = 262
            document.write("Number of days until summer: " + numberOfDaysLeft + ".")
        // -->
        </SCRIPT>
    </BODY>
</HTML>
```

We'll see more on this in the next chapter when we cover the for loop.

Constants

As you can tell from the name "variable," the value in variables can change. However, you might *not* want the value in a variable to change—for example, you might want to store the value of pi, 3.1415926, for easy access throughout your script. Pi's not going to change; if you store it in a variable, however, you run the risk that its value might be inadvertently changed somewhere in your script. The Netscape Navigator version 6 enables you to declare *constants* instead, using the const statement, which you see in Table 2.2. Once declared, a constant can't change its value.

Table 2.2   **The *const* Statement**

Statement	NS2	NS3	NS4	NS6	IE3a	IE3b	IE4	IE5	IE5.5	IE6
const				x						

Here's the syntax for this statement, much like the syntax for the `var` statement:

```
const constname [= value] [..., constname [= value] ]
```

Constants are just like variables except that once initialized, they can't change their values. Here's an example where I'm using a constant named `pi` to hold the value of pi:

(Listing 02-02.html on the web site)

```
<HTML>
    <HEAD>
        <TITLE>
            Working With Arrays
        </TITLE>
    </HEAD>

    <BODY>
        <H1>Working With Arrays</H1>
        <FORM NAME="Form1">
        </FORM>
        <SCRIPT LANGUAGE="JavaScript">
        <!--
            const pi = 3.1415926
            document.write("Pi is " + pi + ".")
        // -->
        </SCRIPT>
    </BODY>
</HTML>
```

Working with Strings

We've been introduced to the various data types in JavaScript now, and one of them bears more investigation here: strings. There's more to this data type than meets the eye in JavaScript, and it's a good idea to understand this data type now, because we'll be seeing it throughout the book.

When you assign a string value to a variable, that string is just treated as a literal value, and stored as a *string literal*, which means that just the actual characters making up the text are stored in the variable:

```
var myText = "How do you like my text? Pretty good, huh?"
```

Tip

JavaScript itself has no limit on how long string literals can be. Note, however, that some older browsers have a maximum string length of 255 characters.

It's a very common thing to want to work with the actual characters in a string, such as converting them all to lower case, or searching for a certain substring, or replacing some characters with others. To enable you to do these kinds of things easily, JavaScript supports the string object, which has built-in methods for all these actions.

Tip

As mentioned in Chapter 1, "Essential JavaScript," you can enclose strings in either single or double quotation marks. If a string itself encloses a quote, it's best to alternate the types of quotation marks like this: `"'Hello,'` `he said."` or `'"Hello," he said.'` so that the browser isn't confused. Keep in mind that an apostrophe is treated as a single quotation mark, which can make things difficult. To avoid problems here, you can use the term `\'` rather than just `'` to tell the browser that it should just insert a `'` character in a string, but *not* treat it as the beginning or end of a string, like this: `'Welcome to Frank\'s web page!<BR>'`. You also can use `\"` in the same way, like this: `"\"Hello,\" he said."`.

The string object is supported in all scriptable browsers (in other words, since Netscape Navigator 2 and Internet Explorer 3). As we'll see in Chapter 18, "The *Date, Time*, and *String* Objects," where we deal with the string object in detail, to create a string object (not just a string literal), you use the new operator and specify the string's text, as here where I'm creating a string object named myString:

```
var myText = "How do you like my text? Pretty good, huh?"
var myString = new String("How do you like my text? Pretty good, huh?")
```

Now we can use all the built-in methods of the string object, such as toUpperCase—which converts the text in a string object to upper case—on myString, like this:

```
var myText = "How do you like my text? Pretty good, huh?"
var myString = new String("How do you like my text? Pretty good, huh?")
document.write(myString.toUpperCase())
```

So how does that help us with the simple string variable myText? Even though the text in myText is stored as simple characters, it turns out that JavaScript enables you to use all the string object's methods with myText; it converts myText to a string object temporarily for you in order to be able to do this. The upshot is that we can use all the string object's properties and methods on the simple variable myText, which is great to know when dealing with text:

```
var myText = "How do you like my text? Pretty good, huh?"
var myString = new String("How do you like my text? Pretty good, huh?")
document.write(myString.toUpperCase())
document.write(myText.toUpperCase())
```

Here's an example showing a few more `string` object properties and methods. In this case, I'm using the `length` property to find how many characters are in `myText`. It uses the `toUpperCase` method to see the text in upper case and the `toLowerCase` method to see the text in lower case. The example uses the `italics` method to see the text in italics, the `indexOf` method to find a single word in the text, and the `replace` method to replace one word with another, like this:

(Listing 02-03.html on the web site)

```
<HTML>
    <HEAD>
        <TITLE>
            Working With Strings
        </TITLE>
    </HEAD>

    <BODY>
        <H1>Working With Strings</H1>
        <SCRIPT LANGUAGE="JavaScript">
        <!--
            var text = "Here " + "is " + "the " + "text!"
            document.write("The text: " + text + "<BR>")
            document.write("The length of the text: " + text.length + "<BR>")
            document.write("In upper case: " + text.toUpperCase() + "<BR>")
            document.write("In lower case: " + text.toLowerCase() + "<BR>")
            document.write("In italics: " + text.italics() + "<BR>")
            document.write("Location of 'the': " + text.indexOf("the") + "<BR>")
            document.write("Replacing is with isn't: " + text.replace("is", "isn't")
            ➥+ "<BR>")
            if(navigator.appName == "Netscape") {
                document.write("The third letter is: " + text[2] + "<BR>")
            }
        // -->
        </SCRIPT>
    </BODY>
</HTML>
```

Figure 2.2 shows the results of this code. We'll see all these properties and methods of the `string` object in depth in Chapter 18, but it's good to know at this stage that they exist.

Note two more things here. First, as we've already mentioned in the preceding chapter, you can use the + *string operator* to join strings together, called *concatenating* them. In other words, these two statements do the same thing:

```
var text = "Here " + "is " + "the " + "text!"
var text = "Here is the text!"
```

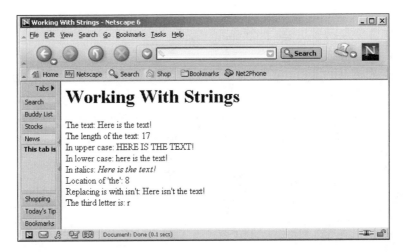

Figure 2.2   Using a string in Netscape Navigator.

Second, the Netscape Navigator—but not the Internet Explorer—lets you access the individual characters in a string in a simple way. For example, `text[0]` gives you the first character in `text`, `text[1]` gives you the second character, and so on:

```
if(navigator.appName == "Netscape") {
    document.write("The third letter is: " + text[2] + "<BR>")
}
```

This way of accessing characters, using a number inside square braces, [and], treats them as if they were in an *array*, and that's a perfect lead-in for our next topic: JavaScript arrays. Before moving on to arrays, however, it's essential to finish this topic by noting that strings and numbers are quite different in JavaScript—something that can be confusing if you're just starting out, as we'll see next.

Data Conversions

Strings are not the same as numbers in JavaScript. If you store the *number* 5 in a variable, that's not the same as storing the *string* "5" in a variable. The string "5" is a string, just like the string "Now is the time!"

This means that if you've stored the string "5" in a variable `myStringValue`, as follows, you should remember that it's stored as text:

```
var myStringValue = "5"
```

If you want a value stored as a number, store it as a number like this, where I'm creating a new variable named `myNumericValue`:

```
var myStringValue = "5"
var myNumericValue = 5
```

Now I can treat `myNumericValue` as a number. For example, if I wanted to add 1 to the value in `myNumericValue`, I could use the + addition operator (which we'll see in this chapter) like this:

```
var myStringValue = "5"
var myNumericValue = 5
document.write(myNumericValue + 1 + "<BR>")
```

This displays the number 6, as it should. If I tried to do the same thing, adding 1 to the value in `myStringValue` as follows, I would get an entirely different result:

```
var myStringValue = "5"
var myNumericValue = 5
document.write(myNumericValue + 1 + "<BR>")
document.write(myStringValue + 1 + "<BR>")
```

This time, JavaScript takes the string "5" and sees you're using the + operator on it, which, to JavaScript, means you're joining strings together, not adding numbers. The result is that JavaScript converts the number 1 you're adding here to a string, which means that `myStringValue` + 1 actually displays "51," not a value of 6!

So how do you convert the value in `myStringValue` to a number? JavaScript has two built-in functions that enable you to do that: `parseInt` and `parseFloat`. We were introduced to functions in the previous preceding chapter—when you place a function's name in your code, that function is called, and the code in it is executed. As we'll see in the next chapter, you can *pass* data values to a function for that function to work on, and that's how `parseInt` and `parseFloat` work.

You use `parseInt` to convert a quoted number (such as "5") into an integer and `parseFloat` to convert a quoted number (such as "2.7128") into a floating-point number. To pass a data value to a function like these, you place that value in parentheses after the function's name. That means I can convert the value in `myStringValue` to a number and add 1 to it (to get a result of 6) like this:

```
var myStringValue = "5"
var myNumericValue = 5
document.write(myNumericValue + 1 + "<BR>")
document.write(parseInt(myStringValue) + 1 + "<BR>")
```

That's all it takes; `parseInt` converted the string `myStringValue` into a number for us. For an example using `parseInt`, see the section, "The *onfocus* Event," in Chapter 6, "Using Core HTML Methods and Events."

Tip
You can also pass the `parseInt` function a base (called a *radix*) to convert numbers to. For example, `parseInt(myStringValue, 16)` converts `myStringValue` from a string into a hexadecimal (base 16) number.

More recently (since Netscape Navigator 4.0 and Internet Explorer 4.0), you can use the `Number` function, which converts strings to either integers or floating-point numbers, as appropriate:

```
var myStringValue = "5"
var myNumericValue = 5
document.write(myNumericValue + 1 + "<BR>")
document.write(parseInt(myStringValue) + 1 + "<BR>")
document.write(Number(myStringValue) + 1 + "<BR>")
```

Tip
To make sure the value returned by `parseInt`, `parseFloat`, or `Number` is a valid number, you can use the `isNaN` function (the name stands for "is not a number"), which we'll see in Chapter 3, "The JavaScript Language: Loops, Functions, and Errors," like this: `isNaN(myValue)`. If `myValue` is not a legal number, `isNaN(myValue)` will evaluate to true, which you can check with the `if` statement, coming up at the end of this chapter.

What about going the other way? What about converting numbers to strings? For example, what if you want to convert the number 5 into the string `"5"`? We've seen that when you add a number to a string where the string comes first, such as `"5"` + 1, the result is a string, `"51"`. So if you add an *empty* string, `""`, with no characters in it, to a number, the result is a string. That means to convert the number 5 to the string `"5"`, you can just add the number to the empty string like this: `""` + 5. Here's how it looks in code:

```
myStringValue = "" + 5
```

The fact that variables can hold both numeric and string data sometimes leads to problems, as when you add the wrong type of value to the data already in a variable, and it's something to watch out for if your scripts aren't performing as they should.

Arrays

The next step up from storing data in simple variables is to store data in arrays. Unlike a simple variable, an array stores multiple values, and each value is given an index number. To access a particular value, you specify not just the array name, but also the index number for the value you want. JavaScript arrays are supported by the array object, and you can see the support for this object in Table 2.3. Chapter 19, "The *Math, Number, Boolean,* and *Array* Objects," covers the array object in depth.

Table 2.3 **The *array* Object**

Statement	NS2	NS3	NS4	NS6	IE3a	IE3b	IE4	IE5	IE5.5	IE6
array		x	x	x		x	x	x	x	x

Let's take a look at an example to see how this works and what makes arrays useful. Here I'll start by creating an array called names, which I will use to store the names of friends. I'll set up that array and make it big enough to store four data items using the statement var names = new Array(4). Because Array is a type of object and not just a simple variable type, you need to use the new keyword to create an object of the Array type. In JavaScript, you must use the new keyword when explicitly creating objects, such as String or Array objects (but not when declaring plain variables)— that will be easy to keep track of, though, because we'll only create objects of a few types: String, Array, Date, and so on. Here's what the code looks like to create our new array:

```
<HTML>
    <HEAD>
        <TITLE>
            Working With Arrays
        </TITLE>
    </HEAD>

    <BODY>
        <H1>Working With Arrays</H1>
        <SCRIPT LANGUAGE="JavaScript">
        <!--
            var names = new Array(4)
            .
            .
            .
        // -->
        </SCRIPT>
    </BODY>
</HTML>
```

This creates a new array using the `Array` object's *constructor*. A constructor has the same name as the object type itself (like `String` or `Date`), and you use the constructor to create a new object of that type. You can send data to the object's constructor by enclosing that data in parentheses that follow the constructor's name (what data you can send depends on the type of object and what its constructor expects). For example, the code we're using here, `new Array(4)`, creates an array of four elements using the `Array` constructor. (We'll see more on constructors in Chapter 20, "The *RegExp* Object: Working with Regular Expressions.") So that sets up our array; but how do you actually store and retrieve data using this new array?

Accessing Array Data

To access the items in an array, you can use an index number. The first item in the `names` array is `names[0]`, the second is `names[1]`, and so on. (The first item in an array is always given the index number 0, which means the last item has the index number equal to the total number of items in the array minus one.) I can treat all these items as simple variables, assigning them values like this:

(Listing 02-04.html on the web site)

```
<HTML>
    <HEAD>
        <TITLE>
            Working With Arrays
        </TITLE>
    </HEAD>

    <BODY>
        <H1>Working With Arrays</H1>
        <SCRIPT LANGUAGE="JavaScript">
        <!--
            var names = new Array(4)
            names[0] = "Frank"
            names[1] = "Nancy"
            names[2] = "Dan"
            names[3] = "Claire"
            document.write(names[0])
        // -->
        </SCRIPT>
    </BODY>
</HTML>
```

Note also that I've displayed the value in `names[0]` with `document.write` at the end of the script. What's useful about arrays is that you have control over the index number in your code—for example, you can refer to items in an array using a variable for the index number, like this: `names[variable1]`. Your code can change `variable1`, and so access all the items in the `names` array easily.

This is especially useful when you have a long set of data—your script can access all the items in that set just by repeatedly adding 1 to `variable1`, accessing each data item and working with them all. Repetitive operations like that are what computers excel at (as we'll see in the next chapter where we deal with JavaScript *loops*, which are all about such repetitive action, executing the same code over and over on a whole set of data items).

In JavaScript, you don't have to use index numbers in arrays; you also can use index strings. That means you can store values in an array using strings, not just numbers. Here are some examples:

```
var names = new Array(4)
names["first"] = "Frank"
names["second"] = "Nancy"
names["third"] = "Dan"
names["fourth"] = "Claire"
document.write(names["first"])
```

This is useful if you want to store data using names such as "birthday," "address," "phoneNumber," and so on, and access that data using those names rather than index numbers. Arrays that use strings as indices for data like this are also called *associative arrays*.

Here's something else that's good to know: You can initialize the data in an array just by listing it when you create the array using the `Array` constructor, like this:

```
var values = new Array(1, 2, 3, 4)
```

To use this technique, you must specify more than one array element. You can even create and initialize a new array like this:

```
var values = [1, 2, 3, 4]
```

Determining the Array Length

We'll see the array object in depth in Chapter 19, but it's worth taking a look at one property of that object here: the `length` property, which tells you how many items are in an array. Here's an example showing how to use this property:

(Listing 02-05.html on the web site)

```
<HTML>
    <HEAD>
        <TITLE>
            Finding the Length of an Array
```

```
        </TITLE>
    </HEAD>

    <BODY>
        <H1>Finding the Length of an Array</H1>
        <SCRIPT LANGUAGE="JavaScript">
        <!--
            var names = new Array(4)
            names[0] = "Frank"
            names[1] = "Nancy"
            names[2] = "Dan"
            names[3] = "Claire"
            document.write("The names array has " + names.length + " items.")
        // -->
        </SCRIPT>
    </BODY>
</HTML>
```

Figure 2.3 shows the results.

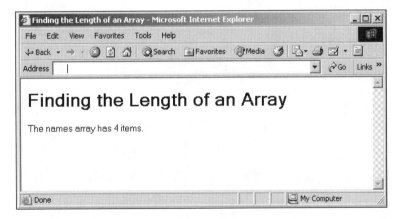

Figure 2.3   Finding an array's length.

We'll see more on arrays in Chapter 19.

Operators

At this point, we're ready to start taking the next step up from data storage and start really working with that data. To do that, we'll start working with JavaScript *operators*. We've already discussed operators briefly; they enable you to work on your data, as in this case, where I'm adding two numbers with the + addition operator:

```
result = 5 + 4
```

You also can use operators with the values in variables, as in this case, where I'm assigning the variable `numberOfDays` the value in the variable `numberOfWeeks` multiplied by seven, using the * multiplication operator:

```
numberOfDays = 7 * numberOfWeeks
```

Here's another example; this time, I'm using the JavaScript division operator, /, to convert pounds to kilograms:

(Listing 02-06.html on the web site)

```
<HTML>
    <HEAD>
        <TITLE>
            Working With Operators
        </TITLE>
    </HEAD>

    <BODY>
        <H1>Working With Operators</H1>
        <SCRIPT LANGUAGE="JavaScript">
        <!--
            var pounds = 5.0
            var kilograms = pounds / 2.2046
            document.write(pounds + " pounds = " + kilograms + " kilograms.")
        // -->
        </SCRIPT>
    </BODY>
</HTML>
```

You can see the results, to an excessive degree of accuracy, in Figure 2.4.

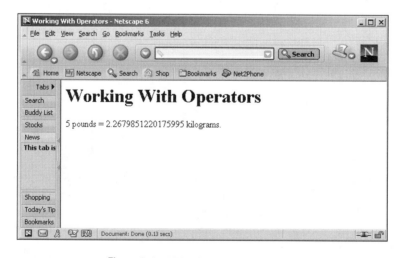

Figure 2.4   Using JavaScript operators.

JavaScript has all kinds of operators—assignment, comparison, arithmetic, bitwise, logical, string, and special operators. You can find them all listed in Table 2.4, along with what they do.

Table 2.4 **The JavaScript Operators**

Operator Category	Operator	Description
ARITHMETIC OPERATORS		
	+	(Addition) Adds two numbers together.
	++	(Increment) Adds one to a variable representing a number.
	-	(Unary negation, subtraction) As a unary operator, changes the sign of the value of its argument. As a binary operator, subtracts 2 numbers.
	- -	(Decrement) Subtracts one from a variable representing a number.
	*	(Multiplication) Multiplies two numbers together.
	/	(Division) Divides two numbers.
	%	(Modulus) Returns the integer remainder left after dividing two numbers.
STRING OPERATORS		
	+	(String addition) Joins two strings together.
	+=	Concatenates two strings and assigns the result to the first operand.
LOGICAL OPERATORS		
	&&	(Logical AND) When used with Boolean values, && returns true if both operands are true; otherwise, returns false.
	¦¦	(Logical OR) When used with Boolean values, ¦¦ returns true if either operand is true; if both are false, it returns false.
	!	(Logical NOT) Returns false if its single operand can be converted to true; otherwise, returns true.
BITWISE OPERATORS		
	&	(Bitwise AND) Returns a one in each bit position if bits of both operands are ones.
	^	(Bitwise XOR) Exclusive OR. Returns a one in a bit position if bits of one, but not both operands are one.

continues ▶

Table 2.4 **Continued**

Operator Category	Operator	Description
	¦	(Bitwise OR) Returns a one in a bit if bits of either operand are one.
	~	(Bitwise NOT) Flips the bits of its operand.
	<<	(Left shift) Shifts its first operand the number of bits to the left given in the second operand, shifting in zeros from the right.
	>>	(Sign-propagating right shift) Shifts the first operand the number of bits to the right given in the second operand, discarding bits shifted off.
	>>>	(Zero-fill right shift) Shifts the first operand the number of bits to the right given in the second operand, discarding bits shifted off, and shifting in zeros from the left.
ASSIGNMENT OPERATORS	=	Assigns the value of the second operand to the first operand.
	+=	Adds two numbers and assigns the result to the first.
	-=	Subtracts two numbers and assigns the result to the first.
	*=	Multiplies two numbers and assigns the result to the first.
	/=	Divides two numbers and assigns the result to the first.
	%=	Finds the modulus of two numbers and assigns the result to the first.
	&=	Performs a bitwise AND and assigns the result to the first operand.
	^=	Performs a bitwise XOR (exclusive OR) and assigns the result to the first operand.
	¦=	Performs a bitwise OR and assigns the result to the first operand.
	<<=	Performs a left shift and assigns the result to the first operand.
	>>=	Performs a sign-propagating right shift and assigns the result to the first operand.
	>>>=	Performs a zero-fill right shift and assigns the result to the first operand.

Operator Category	Operator	Description
COMPARISON OPERATORS		
	==	Equality operator. Returns true if the operands are equal.
	!=	Returns true if the operands are not equal.
	===	Strict equality operator. Returns true if the operands are equal and of the same type.
	!==	Returns true if the operands are not equal and/or not of the same type.
	>	Greater-than operator. Returns true if the left operand is greater than the right operand.
	>=	Greater-than-or-equal-to operator. Returns true if the left operand is greater than or equal to the right operand.
	<	Less-than operator. Returns true if the left operand is less than the right operand.
	<=	Less-than-or-equal-to operator. Returns true if the left operand is less than or equal to the right operand.
SPECIAL OPERATORS		
	?:	The conditional operator. Performs a simple "if...else" test.
	,	The comma operator. Evaluates two expressions. Returns the result of the second expression.
	delete	Deletes an object, an object's property, or an element at a given index in an array.
	function	Defines an anonymous function (discussed in Chapter 3).
	in	Returns true if the given property is in the given object.
	instanceof	Returns true if the given object is of the given object type.
	new	Creates an new object from a user-defined object type or a built-in object type.
	typeof	Returns a string indicating the type of its operand.
	void	Lets an expression be evaluated without returning a value.

Which operators are supported in which browsers? You'll find that information in Table 2.5.

Table 2.5 **JavaScript Operators by Browser**

Operator	NS2	NS3	NS4	NS6	IE3a	IE3b	IE4	IE5	IE5.5	IE6
Arithmetic	x	x	x	x	x	x	x	x	x	x
Assignment	x	x	x	x	x	x	x	x	x	x
Comparison	x	x	x	x	x	x	x	x	x	x
Bitwise	x	x	x	x	x	x	x	x	x	x
Logical	x	x	x	x	x	x	x	x	x	x
String	x	x	x	x	x	x	x	x	x	x
Conditional	x	x	x	x	x	x	x	x	x	x
Comma	x	x	x	x	x	x	x	x	x	x
delete		x	x	x			x	x	x	x
function				x					x	x
in				x					x	x
instanceof				x				x	x	x
new	x	x	x	x	x	x	x	x	x	x
typeof		x	x	x	x	x	x	x	x	x
void		x	x	x	x	x	x	x	x	x

Now that we're talking about operators, it's time to introduce a couple of terms, such as an *expression*. An expression is anything JavaScript can evaluate to get a single value. For example, 5 is a simple expression that evaluates, simply, to 5. The expression 5 + 4 evaluates to 9. If myValue holds 10, the expression myValue * 2 evaluates to 20. You'll see the term "expression" often in JavaScript documentation, and now you know what it means—a term or group of terms that JavaScript can evaluate to a single value.

In addition, in JavaScript, operators operate on *operands*. In the expression 5 + 4, for example, the operator is the + addition operator, 5 is the left operand, and 4 is the right operand. An operator that takes just one operand is a *unary* operator, one that takes two is a *binary* operator, and one that takes three is a *tertiary* operator. And that's it; now we're ready to start taking a look at the operators JavaScript offers us in detail, starting with the assignment operators.

Assignment Operators

An assignment operator assigns a value to its left operand based on the value of its right operand. The most common assignment operator is =, which just assigns the value of an expression to a variable, like this line of code we've already seen:

```
var kilograms = pounds / 2.2046
```

The other assignment operators are *shorthand assignment operators*. How do they work? If you want to add one to a value, you can do so as follows:

```
todaysDate = todaysDate + 1
```

However, using the += shorthand operator, you can do this a little easier, like this:

```
todaysDate += 1
```

In other words, the statement todaysDate = todaysDate + 1 does the same thing as the statement todaysDate += 1. You can use either in your code. Table 2.6 lists the JavaScript shorthand assignment operators.

Table 2.6 **JavaScript Shorthand Assignment Operators**

Shorthand Operator	Is the Same As
x += y	x = x + y
x -= y	x = x - y
x *= y	x = x * y
x /= y	x = x / y
x %= y	x = x % y
x <<= y	x = x << y
x >>= y	x = x >> y
x >>>= y	x = x >>> y
x &= y	x = x & y
x ^= y	x = x ^ y
x ¦= y	x = x ¦ y

Arithmetic Operators

As you can see in Table 2.6, the arithmetic operators enable you to work on numeric values, adding them (with the + operator), subtracting them (with the - operator), multiplying them (with the * operator), dividing them (with the / operator), and so on. We've already see these operators at work; here's an example we saw using the / operator to convert pounds to kilograms:

```
<HTML>
    <HEAD>
        <TITLE>
            Working With Operators
        </TITLE>
    </HEAD>

    <BODY>
        <H1>Working With Operators</H1>
        <SCRIPT LANGUAGE="JavaScript">
        <!--
            var pounds = 5.0
            var kilograms = pounds / 2.2046
            document.write(pounds + " pounds = " + kilograms + " kilograms.")
        // -->
        </SCRIPT>
    </BODY>
</HTML>
```

Another useful arithmetic operator is the modulus operator, %, which returns the modulus, or integer remainder, after dividing two numbers (for example, 18 % 5 = 3).

Besides the standard arithmetic operators +, -, *, /, and %, three more bear mention here: the increment, decrement, and unary negation operators.

The Increment Operator: ++

The increment operator, ++, adds one to its operand. For example, if myVariable holds 10, the expression myVariable++ will increment the value in myVariable to 11. This is a handy operator, but there's something you should know here: you can use ++ *before* or *after* a variable's name, like this: ++myVariable or myVariable++. When you use it before a variable's name, the value of the variable is incremented by one *before* the rest of the statement is executed; when you use it after a variable's name, the value of the variable is incremented by one *after* its value has been read and used in the statement. Here's an example:

(Listing 02–07.html on the web site)

```html
<HTML>
    <HEAD>
        <TITLE>
            Working With the Increment Operator
        </TITLE>
    </HEAD>

    <BODY>
        <H1>Working With the Increment Operator</H1>
        <SCRIPT LANGUAGE="JavaScript">
        <!--
            var votesDistrictOne = 5
            var votesDistrictTwo = 5
            document.write("The number of votes in district 1 is "
            ➥+ ++votesDistrictOne + ".")
            document.write("The number of votes in district 2 is "
            ➥+ votesDistrictTwo++ + ".")
        // -->
        </SCRIPT>
    </BODY>
</HTML>
```

You can see the difference between these two ways of incrementing values in Figure 2.5. After the increments are done, both votesDistrictOne and votesDistrictTwo end up with a value of 6, but note that votesDistrictTwo is incremented only after the rest of the statement is done executing, which means its value is still displayed as 5 in Figure 2.5.

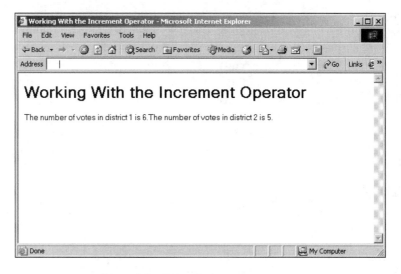

Figure 2.5 Using the increment operator.

The Decrement Operator: --

The decrement operator, `--`, is just decrements its operand by one. Like `++`, it can be used before and after a variable's name, like this: `--votesDistrictOne` and `votesDistrictOne--`; and for these cases, the operator works just as the increment operator `++` does, except that it decrements the variable's value.

The Unary Negation Operator: -

The unary negation operator just changes the sign of its operand. (It's called the unary negation operator because it's a unary operator that just takes one operand.) If the variable `temperature` holds a value of −30, and you execute the JavaScript statement `newTemperature = -temperature`, `newTemperature` will be left holding 30.

Comparison Operators

Comparison operators compare their two operands and return a *Boolean value of true or false*. As you recall from our discussion of data types, Boolean values can take only two values: true or false. This is very useful when you're testing your data to see whether various conditions are true or false, as when you test whether more people voted for pizza for dinner than for hamburgers, and so on.

To make this more clear, consider this example. The comparison operators are usually used with JavaScript statements, such as the `if` statement (discussed later in this chapter), and I'll use them in `if` statements here. An `if` statement enables you to execute code or not depending on whether a condition is true—and you can specify the condition with comparison operators. In this example, I'm comparing the number of votes for pizza to the number of votes for hamburgers. If there are more pizza votes than hamburger votes, the expression `votesForPizza > votesForHamburgers` that uses the `>` (greater-than) comparison operator will return a value of true, which means the code enclosed in curly braces, `{` and `}`, in the `if` statement will be executed and the message `Pizza wins!` will appear in the web page:

```
var votesForPizza = 5
var votesForHamburgers = 6
if(votesForPizza > votesForHamburgers) {
    document.write("Pizza wins!")
}
```

If the expression `votesForPizza > votesForHamburgers` is false, however, the code enclosed in curly braces in the `if` statement will not be executed. So I add additional `if` statements, using the `<` (less-than) and `==` (equal-to) comparison operators like this:

(Listing 02-08.html on the web site)

```
<HTML>
    <HEAD>
        <TITLE>
            Working With Comparison Operators
        </TITLE>
    </HEAD>

    <BODY>
        <H1>Working With Comparison Operators</H1>
        <SCRIPT LANGUAGE="JavaScript">
        <!--
            var votesForPizza = 5
            var votesForHamburgers = 6
            if(votesForPizza > votesForHamburgers) {
                document.write("Pizza wins!")
            }
            if(votesForPizza < votesForHamburgers) {
                document.write("Hamburgers win!")
            }
            if(votesForHamburgers == votesForPizza ) {
                document.write("Tie!")
            }
        // -->
        </SCRIPT>
    </BODY>
</HTML>
```

You can see the results in Figure 2.6, where hamburgers win. Getting to know the comparison operators is very important in JavaScript programming. Table 2.7 lists these operators.

Table 2.7 **JavaScript Comparison Operators**

Operator	Does This
==	Equality operator. Evaluates to true if both operands are equal. Be careful to use == when checking for equality, not =.
!=	Evaluates to true if the two operands are not equal.
===	Strict equality operator. Evaluates to true if the operands are equal—and they also must be of the same type.
!==	Evaluates to true if the operands are either not equal or not of the same type.
>	Greater-than operator. Evaluates to true if the left operand is greater than the right operand either numerically, lexicographically, or using object data conversion functions.
>=	Greater-than-or-equal-to operator. Evaluates to true if the left operand is greater than or equal to the right operand either numerically, lexicographically, or using object data conversion functions.

continues ▶

Table 2.7   **Continued**

Operator	Does This
<	Less-than operator. Evaluates to true if the left operand is less than the right operand either numerically, lexicographically, or using object data conversion functions.
<=	Less-than-or-equal-to operator. Evaluates to true if the left operand is less than or equal to the right operand either numerically, lexicographically, or using object data conversion functions.

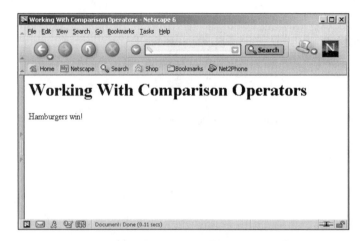

Figure 2.6   Using the comparison operators.

Note, in particular, the equality comparison operator, ==:

```
if(votesForHamburgers == votesForPizza ) {
    document.write("Tie!")
}
```

The first thing to note is that to check whether two values are equal, you must use the == *comparison operator*, not the = *assignment operator*. I'm stressing that in particular, because using = when you should use == is a common error. If I had said votesForHamburgers = votesForPizza here, that would just have assigned the value in votesForPizza to votesForHamburgers, without making a comparison.

So when are values considered equal? Two strings are considered equal when they have the same sequence of characters, and the same length. Two numbers are considered equal when they are numerically equal. Two objects are equal if they refer to the same object. And two Booleans are equal if they are both either true or false.

It's easy to see how JavaScript can compare numbers, but what about comparing strings? When is one string "greater" than another? This kind of comparison is done lexicographically, which means, for example, that when you compare apples to oranges, "oranges" is considered greater than "apples" because "oranges" comes after "apples" alphabetically.

When comparing two values, JavaScript automatically tries to convert them to be of the same type for the comparison. When you're comparing a string and a number, JavaScript tries to convert the string to a numeric value. If you're comparing a Boolean value to a number, true is converted to 1 and false to 0. If you compare an object to a string or number, JavaScript checks whether the object has a method named `toString` for string comparisons, and `valueOf` for numeric comparisons. If not, it creates an error.

You might also notice the two other equality operators in Table 2.6, first introduced in JavaScript 1.3: `===` (strict equals) and `!==` (strict not equals). If you want to make sure two values are the same *and* that they are of the same data type, you use the strict equals and strict not equals operators instead.

Logical Operators

Like the comparison operators we just took a look at, you use *logical operators* when creating test conditions that evaluate to a value of true or false. Using logical operators, you can create more powerful test conditions than just using comparison operators alone.

Suppose, for example, that you want to make sure the value in a variable named `temperature` is *between* 65 and 75. You can use the greater-than comparison operator, `>`, to make sure temperature is greater than 65, and the less-than comparison operator, `<`, to make sure that temperature is less than 75. But how can you make sure both conditions are true in the same `if` statement?

That's where the logical operators come in, because they enable you to tie test conditions together. For example, the `&&` logical operator is called the logical AND operator. If you use it like this: `expression1 && expression2`, both `expression1` *and* `expression2` must be true for the whole expression `expression1 && expression2` to be true; otherwise the whole expression's value is false. Here's how that looks in an example, where I'm checking the temperature:

(Listing 02-09.html on the web site)

```
<HTML>
    <HEAD>
        <TITLE>
            Working With Logical Operators
```

continues ▶

```
        </TITLE>
    </HEAD>

    <BODY>
        <H1>Working With Logical Operators</H1>
        <SCRIPT LANGUAGE="JavaScript">
        <!--
            var temperature = 68
            if(temperature > 65 && temperature < 75) {
                document.write("In the comfort zone!")
            }
        // -->
        </SCRIPT>
    </BODY>
</HTML>
```

Figure 2.7 shows the results of this code (which shows inside the comfort zone, temperature-wise).

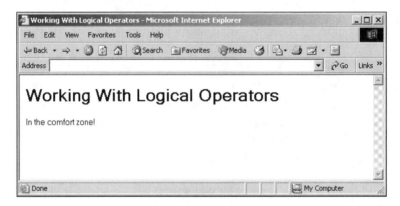

Figure 2.7   Using the logical operators.

Besides the && logical AND operator, you can also use the ¦¦ logical OR operator. The OR operator returns true if its first operand *or* its second operand is true (unlike AND, where you need both operands to be true to get a value of true), and false otherwise. In the following example, I use the <= less-than-or-equal-to and >= greater-than-or-equal-to operators to check whether we're *outside* a temperature comfort zone:

(Listing 02-10.html on the web site)

```
<HTML>
    <HEAD>
        <TITLE>
            Working With Logical Operators
        </TITLE>
```

```
    </HEAD>

<BODY>
    <H1>Working With Logical Operators</H1>
    <SCRIPT LANGUAGE="JavaScript">
    <!--
        var temperature = 62
        if(temperature <= 65 || temperature >= 75) {
            document.write("Outside the comfort zone!")
        }
    // -->
    </SCRIPT>
</BODY>
</HTML>
```

There's also another logical operator: the logical NOT operator, !. You use this operator to reverse the logical sense of an expression. For example if `expression1` evaluates as true, `!expression1` will return false; and if `expression1` evaluates as false, `!expression1` will return true.

> **Tip**
>
> The `&&` and `||` operators are also called *short-circuit operators* in JavaScript. In particular, because `false` `&&` *anyExpression* is *always* false, and `true` `||` *anyExpression* is *always* true, so in both cases, JavaScript does not even evaluate *anyExpression*. That means if evaluating *anyExpression* has side effects, such as calls to functions, those calls—and so their side effects—will *not* occur, which is why these operators are called short-circuit operators.

String Operators

Another category of operator is the string operators, which only contain two operators. We've already seen the string operator +, which we used to concatenate (join) strings together:

```
<HTML>
    <HEAD>
        <TITLE>
            Working With Strings
        </TITLE>
    </HEAD>

<BODY>
    <H1>Working With Strings</H1>
    <SCRIPT LANGUAGE="JavaScript">
    <!--
        var text = "Here " + "is " + "the " + "text!"
        document.write("The text: " + text + "<BR>")
```

continues ▶

```
        document.write("The length of the text: " + text.length + "<BR>")
        document.write("In upper case: " + text.toUpperCase() + "<BR>")
        document.write("In lower case: " + text.toLowerCase() + "<BR>")
        document.write("In italics: " + text.italics() + "<BR>")
        document.write("Location of 'the': " + text.indexOf("the") + "<BR>")
        document.write("Replacing is with isn't: " + text.replace("is", "isn't") +
        ➥"<BR>")
        if(navigator.appName == "Netscape") {
            document.write("The third letter is: " + text[2] + "<BR>")
        }
     // -->
     </SCRIPT>
  </BODY>
</HTML>
```

You also can use the shorthand assignment operator += to concatenate strings, and that's the other string operator. If the variable myText holds the value "Now is the ", the expression myText += "time." is evaluated to "Now is the time." and assigns this string to myText.

Bitwise Operators

Computers actually deal with data in terms of bits, that is, in terms of *binary values*, 0 and 1. For example, the number 9 is really stored in binary as 1001. JavaScript gives you access to the actual binary bits of the data it's working on with its bitwise operators. This probably won't concern you very much, and if not, feel free to skip on. For the sake of completeness, however, I'll include these details here.

You can see the JavaScript bitwise operators and what they do in Table 2.8.

Table 2.8 **JavaScript Bitwise Operators**

Operator	Usage	Does This
Bitwise AND	x & y	Places a one in each bit position of the result for which the corresponding bits of both operands are ones.
Bitwise OR	x ¦ y	Places a one in each bit position of the result for which the corresponding bits of either or both operands are ones.
Bitwise XOR	x ^ y	Places a one in each bit position of the result for which the corresponding bits of either, *but not both*, operands are ones.
Bitwise NOT	~ x	Flips the bits of its operand.

Operator	Usage	Does This
Left shift	x << y	Shifts x by y bits to the left (shifting in zeros from the right).
Sign-propagating right shift	x >> y	Shifts x by y bits to the right (not preserving bits shifted off).
Zero–fill right shift	x >>> y	Shifts x by y bits to the right, not preserving bits shifted off, and shifting in zeros from the left.

These operators treat numeric values as 32-bit values; each bit in one operand is paired with the corresponding bit in the other operand. Here's an example: 4 is 0100 in binary, and 1 is 0001, so using bitwise OR, ¦, on these two yields 4 ¦ 1 = 0100 | 0001 = 0101, or 5. Here's what that looks like in code:

(Listing 02-11.html on the web site)

```
<HTML>
    <HEAD>
        <TITLE>
            Working With Bitwise OR
        </TITLE>
    </HEAD>

    <BODY>
        <H1>Working With Bitwise OR</H1>
        <SCRIPT LANGUAGE="JavaScript">
        <!--
            var result = 4 ¦ 1
            document.write("4 ¦ 1 = " + result)
        // -->
        </SCRIPT>
    </BODY>
</HTML>
```

Figure 2.8 shows the results of the code (4 ¦ 1 = 5).

The bitwise shift operators take two operands: the first is a quantity to be shifted, and the second specifies the number of bit *positions* by which the first operand is to be *shifted* (shifting a bit means moving it left or right to the adjoining places in the binary number). The direction of the shift operation is controlled by the operator used. Shift operators shift the bits of their operands and convert those operands to 32–bit integers. For example, 9 << 1 gives a result of 18, because 1001 shifted one bit to the left becomes 10010, which is 18.

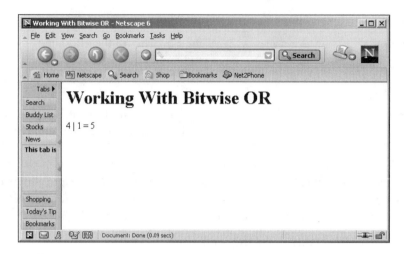

Figure 2.8   Using the bitwise OR operator.

Special Operators

JavaScript also contains a number of operators that don't fit into any other category, and it calls them *special operators*. I'll take a look at them here.

Two of these operators, new and this, are ones that most JavaScript programmers use a lot, but the others are not in such common use. Feel free to skim over these operators and come back to them when you actually need them in your code.

The Conditional Operator: *?:*

So far, the operators we've looked at have taken either one or two operands, but there is a JavaScript operator, the conditional operator, that takes *three* operands (making it JavaScript's only tertiary operator). Here's the syntax for this operator, which uses both a question mark (?) and a colon (:):

```
condition ? expression1 : expression2
```

If condition evaluates to true, the operator returns the value of expression1; otherwise, it returns the value of expression2. In other words, this operator provides you with a quick, each way to make a selection based on whether a certain condition is true. Here's an example: In this case, suppose a family is voting for pizza or hamburgers for dinner. I'll use the conditional operator to display the results:

(Listing 02–12.html on the web site)

```
<HTML>
    <HEAD>
        <TITLE>
            Working With the Conditional Operator
        </TITLE>
    </HEAD>

    <BODY>
        <H1>Working With the Conditional Operator</H1>
        <SCRIPT LANGUAGE="JavaScript">
        <!--
            var votesForPizza = 5
            var votesForHamburgers = 6
            var result = votesForPizza > votesForHamburgers ? "Pizza wins!" :
            ➥"Pizza didn't win."
            document.write(result)
        // -->
        </SCRIPT>
    </BODY>
</HTML>
```

Figure 2.9 shows the result.

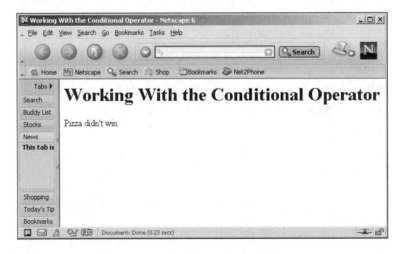

Figure 2.9   Using the conditional operator.

Tip

The conditional operator can be useful as a quick, one-line replacement for the `if` statement—see that statement later in this chapter.

The Comma Operator: ,

The comma operator enables you to specify two expressions to evaluate. This operator returns the value of the second operand. You use the comma operator when you want to include multiple expressions in a place that usually takes only one single expression.

It turns out that the most common place this operator is used is somewhere we won't cover until the next chapter: for loops. (If you've never seen for loops before, it's a good idea to wait until we do cover them, because I'll mention the comma operator there too.) The for loop enables you to repeat a series of statements a number of times; here's an example of the kind we'll decipher in the next chapter—the statements to be executed go between the curly braces, { and }:

```
for (loop_index = 0; loop_index < 100; loop_index++)
{
    .
    .
    .
}
```

The expressions separated by semicolons enable you to initialize the loop, terminate it, and perform some operation each time through the loop, as we'll see in the next chapter. Normally, only one expression can be used in each position here, unless you use the comma operator, as in this case, where I'm using that operator to initialize both a variable named loop_index *and* a variable named total to 0 in the initialization part of the loop:

```
for (loop_index = 0, total = 0; loop_index < 100; loop_index++)
{
    .
    .
    .
}
```

More on this example—and the comma operator—in the next chapter, when we cover the for loop.

The *delete* Operator

The delete operator deletes an object, a property of an object, or an element at a particular index in an array. Here's how you use this operator:

```
delete object
delete object.property
delete array[index]
```

When you delete an element in an array, the length of the array doesn't change. In fact, no element in the array is affected except the one you've deleted. Here's an example; in this case, I'll create an array named sandwiches with the elements "turkey", "cheddar", "ham", "tuna", and "egg". Next, I'll delete element 2, "ham" (remember that array indices start at 0, so element 2 is "ham" here) via the delete operator. Then I will check whether that element is really gone using the in operator, which is coming up next. In this case, if the expression 2 in sandwiches is false, element 2 was indeed deleted. I'll check that with an if statement of the kind we've already seen; in this case, the if statement will display the text Still here! if the element is still in the array; otherwise, the code in the else part of the if statement will be executed, displaying Sorry, that element is gone!:

(Listing 02-13.html on the web site)

```
<HTML>
    <HEAD>
        <TITLE>
            Working With the delete Operator
        </TITLE>
    </HEAD>

    <BODY>
        <H1>Working With the delete Operator</H1>
        <SCRIPT LANGUAGE="JavaScript">
        <!--
            sandwiches = new Array("turkey", "cheddar", "ham", "tuna", "egg")
            delete sandwiches[2]
            if (2 in sandwiches) {
                    document.write("Still here!")
            } else {
                    document.write("Sorry, that element is gone!")
            }
        // -->
        </SCRIPT>
    </BODY>
</HTML>
```

You can see the results of this code in Figure 2.10; element 2 was indeed deleted. We'll see more on the in operator in the next topic—and more on the if statement at the end of this chapter.

Figure 2.10   Using the delete operator.

The *in* Operator

The in operator returns true if a given element is in an array or a given property is in an object. We already saw the in operator in the preceding example using delete. In that example, we deleted an element from an array named sandwiches and checked to see whether it was really gone using in:

```
if (2 in sandwiches) {
    document.write("Still here!")
} else {
    document.write("Sorry, that element is gone!")
}
```

You also can check for properties in objects using in the in operator. For example, all arrays contain a length property, so the expression length in sandwiches would return true here.

The *instanceof* Operator

The instanceof operator returns true if a given object is of a particular object type. This operator is useful when you start working with different types of objects in JavaScript—a JavaScript variable can hold any type of object, so how do you know what kind of object you're dealing with? One way to check is with the instanceof operator.

To use this operator, you use this syntax: *object* instanceof *objectType*. This expression will return true if *object* is an object of type *objectType*. Here's an example; in this case, I'm creating a string object named actor using the new operator (the new operator is coming up next), and then checking whether actor is indeed a string object, using the instanceof operator:

```
<HTML>
    <HEAD>
        <TITLE>
            Working With the instanceof Operator
        </TITLE>
    </HEAD>

    <BODY>
        <H1>Working With the instanceof Operator</H1>
        <SCRIPT LANGUAGE="JavaScript">
        <!--
            var actor = new String("Cary Grant")
            if (actor instanceof String) {
                document.write("It's a string.")
            }
        // -->
        </SCRIPT>
    </BODY>
</HTML>
```

As you might expect, this example works as expected, displaying the text
`It's a string.`

The *new* Operator

The new operator is a useful one; you use this operator to create new objects
from a predefined object type such as string or array. Object types offer us a
great deal of functionality, as we'll see throughout this book. For example,
the string object type includes many built-in properties and methods—and
to use those properties and methods, you use the new operator to create
objects you can work with in your code from the various object types
available.

Here's how you use this operator:

```
object = new objectType(param1 [, param2] ...[, paramN])
```

In this case, you're creating a new object, *object*, of a particular type,
objectType. The values *param1*, *param2*, and so on are parameter values you
use when you create a new object, specifying, for example, the number of
items in an array or the text you want in a string.

Let's see an example. We've seen this operator at work already when we've
created new string and array objects; here's how we created a new string
object in the example in the preceding topic, using new:

```
var actor = new String("Cary Grant")
if (actor instanceof String) {
    document.write("It's a string.")
}
```

That's all it takes. When you create simple variables, you don't need to use new:

```
var taxes = 1000000        //Too much!!
```

But when you create an object from an *object type*, such as string or array, you do need to use new:

```
var myString = new String("Now is the time!")
```

Although we've only created objects of the built-in JavaScript object types array and string so far, the new operator works for any object type, whether that type is built in to JavaScript already, or whether it's an object type you've defined yourself (as we'll do in Chapter 23, "Cookies and Creating Your Own Objects").

The *typeof* Operator

Like instanceof, the typeof operator give you information about an operand's type. The instanceof operator enables you to compare an object's type to a known type, but the typeof operator tells you the object's type directly by returning a text string.

Here's an example; in this case, I'll declare a variable, store a number in it, and then check that variable's type:

(Listing 02-14.html on the web site)

```
<HTML>
    <HEAD>
        <TITLE>
            Working With the typeof Operator
        </TITLE>
    </HEAD>

    <BODY>
        <H1>Working With the typeof Operator</H1>
        <SCRIPT LANGUAGE="JavaScript">
        <!--
            var value = 5
            document.write("That item is a " + typeof value + ".")
        // -->
        </SCRIPT>
    </BODY>
</HTML>
```

As you can see in Figure 2.11, the typeof operator returned a string indicating that this variable holds a number.

The *void* Operator

The void operator is the last of the special operators, and its use is pretty specialized. All this operator does is to discard the value returned by an expression when that expression is evaluated. This proves useful when you want to evaluate an expression but don't want to do anything with the value the expression returns. Suppose, for example, that you have a function named checkData that performs some calculations you want performed, but it also returns a value that you want to discard. You can do that like this:

```
void(checkData)
```

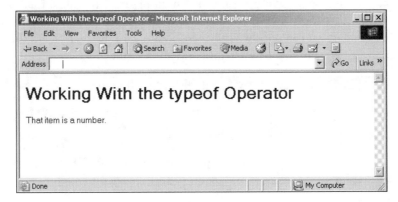

Figure 2.11   Using the typeof operator to check a variable's type.

> **Tip**
>
> We're not going to have a lot of use for the void operator, but I'm including it here for the sake of completeness; it does have occasional uses. One place it's sometimes used is in inline scripts that call functions that normally return values, because some browsers handle such values badly in inline scripts.

Understanding Operator Precedence

Now that we've covered the JavaScript operators, another issue becomes important: How does JavaScript handle multiple operators in the same statement? Take a look at this code, for example:

```
<HTML>
    <HEAD>
        <TITLE>
            Operator Precedence
        </TITLE>
    </HEAD>
```

continues ▶

```
<BODY>
    <H1>Working With the Conditional Operator</H1>
    <SCRIPT LANGUAGE="JavaScript">
    <!--
        var result = 5 + 3 * 2
        document.write("5 + 3 * 2 = " + result)
    // -->
    </SCRIPT>
</BODY>
</HTML>
```

The question here is, how does JavaScript evaluate the expression 5 + 3 * 2? Does it add 5 to 3 (giving 8) and then multiply by 2 (giving a total of 16)? Or does it multiply 3 by 2 (giving 6) and then add 5 to the result (giving a total of 11)? You can see the answer in Figure 2.12. JavaScript did the multiplication first, and then the addition, giving a result of 11.

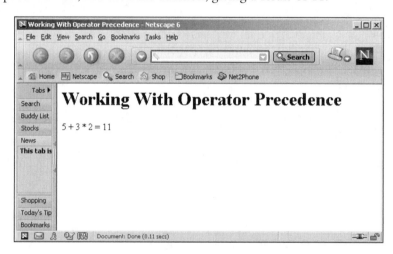

Figure 2.12   Checking operator precedence.

The reason for this is that the multiplication operator, *, has higher *precedence* than the addition operator, +, which means that multiplication operations are performed before addition operations. You can find the precedence of JavaScript operators in Table 2.9, from top (highest precedence) to bottom (lowest precedence). For example, you can see that * has higher precedence than +, so multiplication operations are performed before addition operations. If a number of operators appear on the same line, they all have the same precedence, and JavaScript evaluates expressions with such operators from left to right.

It's a bit much asking JavaScript programmers to memorize the operator precedence rules you see in Table 2.8, so it's good to know there's a shortcut: You can use *parentheses* to change the precedence of expressions to what you want. Expressions in parentheses are always evaluated before the rest of the expression.

If you really want to do the addition first in the example expression you just saw (5 + 3 ★ 2, for example), you could just write it this way: (5 + 3) ★ 2, which will evaluate to 16. That's all it takes. When in doubt, use parentheses to make it clear which part of an expression you want evaluated first.

Table 2.9   **Operator Precedence in JavaScript (top to bottom)**

Operator
. [] ()
++ -- - ~ ! delete new typeof void
* / %
+ - + (string concatenation)
<< >> >>>
< <= > >= instanceof
== != === !==
&
^
¦
&&
¦¦
?:
= *OP*= (shorthand assignments)
,

Tip

You also can *nest* parentheses, like this: ((2 + 3) + (3 * (8 + (1)))) * 2. This enables you to specify the order in which you want your expressions evaluated completely. Note that here, I'm even enclosing the number 1 in parentheses, which is legal—in JavaScript, numbers such as 1 are themselves expressions.

That completes our the look at operators for this chapter. Now it's time to take the next step up: *branching statements*.

Branching Statements

Branching statements enable you to make choices. JavaScript has two branching statements: `if` and `switch`. The `if` statement is so important that we've already seen it at work both in this and the previous chapter; we'll take a look at it in depth here.

This statement enables you to select which code to execute depending on whether a certain test condition (usually involving the comparison operators we've already seen, like this: `votesForPizza > votesForHamburgers`). In fact, the `if` statement is so important in JavaScript that the other branching statement, the `switch` statement, is really just a modified `if` statement that you use when you want to handle multiple test conditions. We'll see both of them here, starting with the `if` statement.

The *if* Statement

As we've already seen, the `if` statement enables you to execute a series of statements if a test condition is true. The `if` statement also includes an optional `else` clause that holds code to be executed if the test condition was false. Here's what the syntax of this statement looks like, formally speaking—note that the code to execute is between curly braces, { and }:

```
if (condition) {
    statements1
}
[else {
    statements2
}]
```

The `if` statement and `else` clause are so fundamental to JavaScript that they've been in it from the beginning, as you can see in Table 2.10.

Table 2.10   **The *if* Statement**

Statement	NS2	NS3	NS4	NS6	IE3a	IE3b	IE4	IE5	IE5.5	IE6
if	x	x	x	x	x	x	x	x	x	x

Here's an example using the > (greater-than), < (less-than), and == (equality) comparison operators. In this case, I'm checking to see what kind of dinner people have voted for:

(Listing 02-15.html on the web site)

```
<HTML>
    <HEAD>
        <TITLE>
            Working With the if Statement
        </TITLE>
```

```
    </HEAD>

    <BODY>
        <H1>Working With the if Statement</H1>
        <SCRIPT LANGUAGE="JavaScript">
        <!--
            var votesForPizza = 5
            var votesForHamburgers = 6
            if(votesForPizza > votesForHamburgers) {
                document.write("Pizza wins!")
            }
            if(votesForPizza < votesForHamburgers) {
                document.write("Hamburgers win!")
            }
            if(votesForHamburgers == votesForPizza ) {
                document.write("Tie!")
            }
        // -->
        </SCRIPT>
    </BODY>
</HTML>
```

Figure 2.13 shows the results. The `if` statement is at work finding out that hamburgers win.

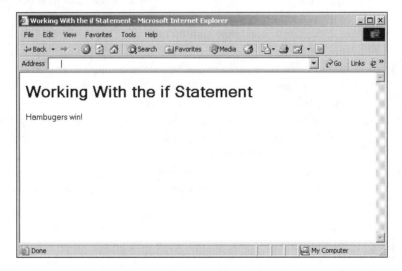

Figure 2.13   Using the `if` statement.

Omitting the Curly Braces

Interestingly, if the code to execute in an `if` statement is only one line, you can actually omit the curly braces (although it's good form to still use them, as I'll do throughout the book):

```
<HTML>
    <HEAD>
        <TITLE>
            Working With the if Statement
        </TITLE>
    </HEAD>

    <BODY>
        <H1>Working With the if Statement</H1>
        <SCRIPT LANGUAGE="JavaScript">
        <!--
            var votesForPizza = 5
            var votesForHamburgers = 6
            if(votesForPizza > votesForHamburgers)
                document.write("Pizza wins!")
            if(votesForPizza < votesForHamburgers)
                document.write("Hamburgers win!")
            if(votesForHamburgers == votesForPizza )
                document.write("Tie!")
        // -->
        </SCRIPT>
    </BODY>
</HTML>
```

In JavaScript, curly braces make a series of single statements into one *compound* statement, called a *block*. The way the if statement is defined technically is to execute only one code statement if the if statement's condition is true; by using curly braces, however, you can make that single statement a compound statement that includes multiple single statements.

Since the early days, however, using curly braces to enclose the code an if statement should execute—even if that's only a single statement—has become accepted usage. This is true of many statements in JavaScript. In the next chapter, for instance, we'll take a look at the for loop; if you place only a single statement in a for loop's body, you don't need to enclose it in curly braces. In this book, however, I'll always use the curly braces for consistency.

The if statement also includes an optional else clause, and I'll take a look at that next.

Using *else*

An if statement executes its code if its test condition is true. You also can handle the case where you want the code to execute when a certain statement is *false*—just use the ! logical NOT operator, which changes true to false and false to true:

```
if(!(votesForPizza > votesForHamburgers)) {
    document.write("Pizza loses.")
}
```

What if you want to execute some code if the test expression is true, and *other* code if it's false? In that case, you can use an else clause. The code in an if statement executes if the test condition is true, and the code in the if statement's else clause, if present, executes if the test condition is false, enabling you to execute code either way.

In fact, we've already seen the else clause at work when we deleted an element from an array. In that example, if the element was not deleted, we displayed the message Still here!; otherwise, because of the else clause, we displayed the message Sorry, that element is gone!:

```
<HTML>
    <HEAD>
        <TITLE>
            Working With the else Clause
        </TITLE>
    </HEAD>

    <BODY>
        <H1>Working With the else Clause</H1>
        <SCRIPT LANGUAGE="JavaScript">
        <!--
            sandwiches = new Array("turkey","cheddar","ham","tuna","egg")
            delete sandwiches[2]
            if (2 in sandwiches) {
                document.write("Still here!")
            } else {
                document.write("Sorry, that element is gone!")
            }
        // -->
        </SCRIPT>
    </BODY>
</HTML>
```

This enables you to respond correctly when a test statement is true—and also when it's false. What if it's not just a question whether a test condition is just true or false? What if, for example, you want to handle the case where an expression is equal to 1, as well as the case where it's equal to 2, and 3, and 4, and so on? In that case, you need a switch statement, coming right up.

Tip

When thinking about if statements, don't forget about the conditional operator, ?: (discussed earlier in this chapter). It can function as a one-line if statement, making your code shorter and cleaner.

You also can use if...else *ladders* of successive if and else statements, as in this example, as discussed more fully in Chapter 4, "Handling the Browser Environment":

```
var object1
if (document.all){
    object1 = document.all("IDobject1")
} else if (document.getElementByID) {
    object1 = document.getElementByID("IdObject1")
} else if (document.layers) {
    object1 = document.layers.document("NameObject1")
}
```

The *switch* Statement

The switch statement first appeared in the Netscape Navigator version 3.0, and then in the Internet Explorer 4.0, as you see in Table 2.11.

Table 2.11   **The *switch* Statement**

Statement	NS2	NS3	NS4	NS6	IE3a	IE3b	IE4	IE5	IE5.5	IE6
switch		x	x	x			x	x	x	x

This statement enables you to evaluate an expression and match the expression's value to a number of test values, executing code when you find a match. You place the expression to evaluate in parentheses after the switch keyword, and then give the test values you want to match in a set of case statements. If you match a test expression, the code in that case statement is executed up to a break statement (which ends the switch statement). Here's how it all looks formally:

```
switch (expression){
    case label1:
        statements
        break
    case label2:
        statements
        break
        .
        .
        .
    [default:
        statements]
}
```

Note the optional default statement at the end. If the value of the expression doesn't match any test value, the code in the default statement, if there is one, is executed. If you include a default statement, it should be the last statement, following all the case statements.

As with other programming constructs, this is all much more easily seen in an example. In this next example, I'll check the text in a variable named command, using a switch statement:

(Listing 02-16.html on the web site)

```
<HTML>
    <HEAD>
        <TITLE>
            Working With the switch Statement
        </TITLE>
    </HEAD>

    <BODY>
        <H1>Working With the switch Statement</H1>
        <SCRIPT LANGUAGE="JavaScript">
        <!--
            var command = "PANIC!"
            switch (command) {
                case "right":
                    document.write("Go right.")
                    break
                case "left":
                    document.write("Go left.")
                    break
                case "up" :
                    document.write("Go up.")
                    break
                case "down":
                    document.write("Go down.")
                    break
                case "PANIC!":
                    document.write("Head for the hills!")
                    break
                default:
                    document.write("Sorry, I did not understand.")
            }
        // -->
        </SCRIPT>
    </BODY>
</HTML>
```

As you can see in Figure 2.14, the test value "PANIC!" matched, and the code wrote out the corresponding message.

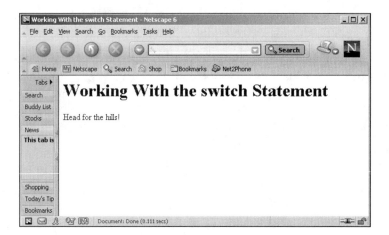

Figure 2.14 *Using the* switch *statement.*

Note that you can match more than strings in switch statements—for example, you can use numbers as test values. In fact, you can mix numbers and strings like this example, which displays the text Go left.:

```
var command = 5
switch (command) {
    case "right":
        document.write("Go right.")
        break
    case 5:
        document.write("Go left.")
        break
    case "up":
        document.write("Go up.")
        break
    case 12:
        document.write("Go down.")
        break
    case 9:
        document.write("Head for the hills!")
        break
    default:
        document.write("Sorry, I did not understand.")
}
```

Tip

If the break statement is omitted in a case statement, the program continues, executing the code in the next case statement. That can be useful to know in some cases, where you want to execute the following case statement(s) as well as the current one (sort of like singing "The Twelve Days of Christmas," where "five golden rings" falls through to "four calling birds" and so on). The usual way to write switch statements, however, is to end each case statement with a break statement. (The default statement, being the last statement, doesn't need a break statement, although you can include one if you prefer.)

That completes our chapter on data, operators, and branching. Now we can take the next step as we turn to loops, functions, and more in the next chapter.

3

The JavaScript Language: Loops, Functions, and Errors

IN THIS CHAPTER, WE'RE GOING TO BUILD on the work we started in the preceding chapter and continue building our JavaScript foundation. We've already taken a look at handling data, operators, and branching statements. Here, we're going to move up to working with loops, functions, and errors—all powerful parts of your JavaScript arsenal. I'll get started with loops immediately.

Loops

In JavaScript, loops enable you to execute a series of statements over and over on your data. At first, that might not seem very exciting—what's the good of executing the same code on your data more than once? However, each time through the loop, the data can be different—for example, imagine that you have 10,000 students at a university and you need to calculate their average final grade using the values in a JavaScript array. Adding those grades by hand to find the average grade would be a big and bothersome task—but using a loop, you can just loop over all members of the array with a few simple statements. No problem!

Several kinds of loops are available in JavaScript—the `for` loop, the `for...in` loop, the `while` loop, and the `do...while` loop. And we'll see them all here.

The *for* Loop

The most common loop is the for loop, which enables you to execute a series of statements a specific number of times. Here's the syntax of this loop:

```
for ([initial-expression]; [condition]; [increment-expression]) {
    statements
}
```

This loop enables you to use the three expression in parentheses to control the number of times the *statements* are executed. These statements make up the loop's body. Here's what the parts of this loop are all about:

- **initial-expression.** This part enables you to perform any initialization you'll need for the loop, and you can even declare new variables here using the var keyword.

- **condition.** This is an expression evaluated on each pass through the loop. If this condition evaluates to true, the statements are performed; otherwise the loop terminates. The condition in a for loop often involves checking the value in a loop index variable, which is incremented each time through the loop and so keeps track of the number of times the loop has executed.

- **increment-expression.** Performed after the body of the loop is executed. Usually used to increment a loop index, which counts the number of times the loop has executed.

- **statements.** This is the loop's *body*, a set of statements that are executed as long as condition evaluates to true. Although not required, it's usually good practice to indent these statements.

Tip

You can omit any of the *initial-expression*, *condition*, or *increment-expression* parts of a for loop, but you must not omit any of the semicolons separating these parts. If you omit the *condition* part, it always evaluates to true.

The for loop has always been a part of JavaScript, as you see in Table 3.1.

Table 3.1   **The *for* Loop**

Statement	NS2	NS3	NS4	NS6	IE3a	IE3b	IE4	IE5	IE5.5	IE6
for	x	x	x	x	x	x	x	x	x	x

The `for` loop is usually used with a *loop index* (also called a *loop counter*), which is just a variable that keeps track of the number of times the loop has executed. Here's an example. Suppose that I want to add the numbers from 1 to 5. To do that, I can use a loop index I'll call `loopIndex` to count the number of times the loop has executed, called *iterations*. I can start by declaring `loopIndex` and setting it to 1 in the initialization part of the for loop:

```
var loopIndex
for (loopIndex = 1;...) {
    .
    .
    .

}
```

This means that the first time through the loop, `loopIndex` will have a value of 1. In this example, we'll increment `loopIndex` by 1 each time through the loop, and to stop when we've added the numbers up to 5, we can set the termination condition to `loopIndex < 6`. While this condition is true, the loop will execute the statements in its body; and as soon as `loopIndex` equals or exceeds 6, the loop will stop. Here's how we put this condition into our `for` loop:

```
for (loopIndex = 1; loopIndex < 6; ...) {
    .
    .
    .

}
```

After the loop's body is executed, we have a chance to increment `loopIndex` in the `increment-expression` part of the `for` loop. This expression doesn't actually have to increment anything—it can be any expression you want— but because `for` loops are usually written to use a loop index/counter of some kind, this is where you usually increment that counter, as follows:

```
for (loopIndex = 1; loopIndex < 6; loopIndex++) {
    .
    .
    .

}
```

The way we've set up this loop, then, means that the first time through the loop, `loopIndex` will be 1, the next time 2, and so on up to 5, after which the loop terminates. Therefore, we can add the numbers 1 to 5 just by adding the current value of `loopIndex` to a running total in the loop's body, like this:

(Listing 03-01.html on the web site)

```html
<HTML>
    <HEAD>
        <TITLE>
            Using the for Loop
        </TITLE>
    </HEAD>

    <BODY>
        <H1>Using the for Loop</H1>
        <SCRIPT LANGUAGE="JavaScript">
            <!--
            var loopIndex, total
            total = 0
            for (loopIndex = 1; loopIndex < 6; loopIndex++) {
                total += loopIndex
                document.write("Loop iteration: "
                    + loopIndex + " Total: "  + total + "<BR>")
            }
            // -->
        </SCRIPT>
    </BODY>
</HTML>
```

Figure 3.1 shows the results of this code. The program displays the value of both `loopIndex` and the running total all the way through the loop. Our first `for` loop works as expected.

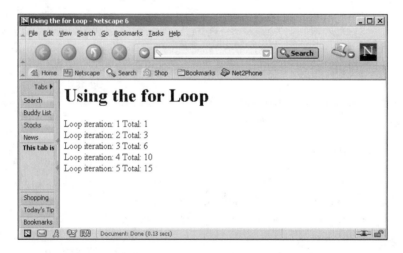

Figure 3.1 Using a for loop in the Netscape Navigator.

Using Local Variables in *for* Loops

You should be aware of a couple of shortcuts here—for example, we've used only the `loopIndex` variable in the `for` loop itself—and we can actually declare it in the `for` loop itself, using the `var` keyword. Here's how that looks:

```
<HTML>
    <HEAD>
        <TITLE>
            Using the for Loop
        </TITLE>
    </HEAD>

    <BODY>
        <H1>Using the for Loop</H1>
        <SCRIPT LANGUAGE="JavaScript">
            <!--
            var total
            total = 0
            for (var loopIndex = 0; loopIndex < 6; loopIndex++) {
                total += loopIndex
                document.write("Loop iteration: "
                    + loopIndex + " Total: "  + total + "<BR>")
            }
            // -->
        </SCRIPT>
    </BODY>
</HTML>
```

This loop works as before. In fact, using the comma operator we saw in the preceding chapter, we also can declare and initialize the running total variable, `total`, in the `for` loop, like this:

```
for (var loopIndex = 1, total = 0; loopIndex < 6; loopIndex++) {
    total += loopIndex
    document.write("Loop iteration: "
        + loopIndex + " Total: "  + total + "<BR>")
}
```

Using Arrays in *for* Loops

A primary use of `for` loops is to handle the data in an array. You can see how this would work well—you can access the data using a numeric index, and `for` loops can use a numeric loop index. This means you can iterate over all the data in an array just by using the array's length (which you can find with the array's length property) as the maximum possible value for the loop index. Here's an example showing how this works—just like the preceding example, we're adding the numbers from 1 to 5 here, but this time, those numbers are in an array named data:

(Listing 03-02.html on the web site)

```
<HTML>
    <HEAD>
        <TITLE>
            Using the for Loop With an Array
        </TITLE>
    </HEAD>

    <BODY>
        <H1>Using the for Loop With an Array</H1>
        <SCRIPT LANGUAGE="JavaScript">
            <!--
            var data = new Array(1, 2, 3, 4, 5)
            for (var loopIndex = 0, total = 0; loopIndex < data.length; loopIndex++) {
                total += data[loopIndex]
            }
            document.write("The total is " + total + ".<BR>")
            // -->
        </SCRIPT>
    </BODY>
</HTML>
```

Figure 3.2 shows the results.

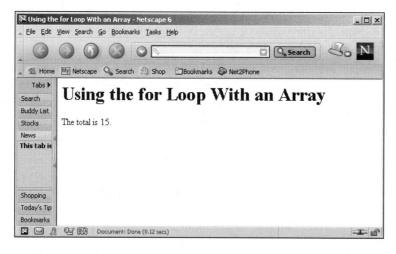

Figure 3.2   Using a for loop with an array in the Netscape Navigator.

The *for...in* Loop

Closely allied to the `for` loop is the `for...in` loop, which iterates a variable over all the properties of an object. For each property, JavaScript executes the statements in the loop's body. That might sound a little dry, but in fact, it's a great help when you want to find out which properties are available to you in a specific object, such as some unknown browser's `document` object. It's also handy because you can iterate over all the properties in an object without even knowing how many properties there are, because the loop handles that automatically. Here's the syntax of this loop:

```
for (variable in object) {
    statements
}
```

The following parts comprise this loop:

- **variable.** Variable to use when iterating over every property.
- **object.** Object you want the properties of.
- **statements.** The statements to execute for each property.

The `for...in` loop has been around for a long time, as you see in Table 3.2.

Table 3.2 **The *for...in* Loop**

Statement	NS2	NS3	NS4	NS6	IE3a	IE3b	IE4	IE5	IE5.5	IE6
for...in	x	x	x	x	x	x	x	x	x	x

Let's take a look at the `document` object in both the Netscape Navigator and Internet Explorer using a `for...in` loop. We'll take a look not only at the various properties, but also the current value of those properties; to find the current values of each property, we can treat the `document` object as an array of properties, giving the property name as the array index. Here's what the code looks like:

(Listing 03-03.html on the web site)

```
<HTML>
    <HEAD>
        <TITLE>
            Using the for...in Loop
        </TITLE>
    </HEAD>
```

continues ▶

```
<BODY>
    <H1>Using the for...in Loop</H1>
    <SCRIPT LANGUAGE="JavaScript">
        <!--
        for (var property in document) {
            document.write(property + ": " + document[property] + "<BR>")
        }
        // -->
    </SCRIPT>
</BODY>
</HTML>
```

That's all it takes. You can see the results of this code in Figure 3.3 for the
Netscape Navigator and in Figure 3.4 for the Internet Explorer. Try this
example yourself—it's instructive to see how differently these two browsers
report the properties of their document objects. For example, the Netscape
Navigator lists not only properties but also the document object's methods
(such as document.write), whereas the Internet Explorer lists properties and
event handlers (such as onclick), but not any methods of its document object.

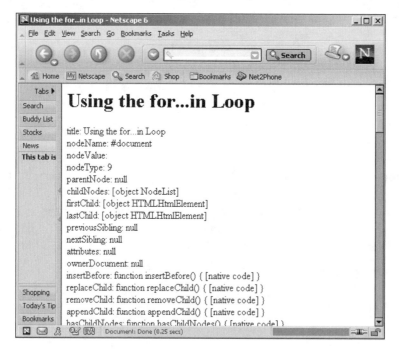

Figure 3.3   Displaying document object properties in the Netscape Navigator.

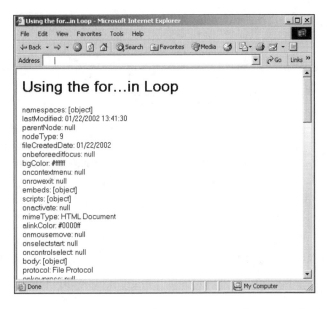

Figure 3.4 Displaying document object properties in the Internet Explorer.

The *while* Loop

Another powerful loop in JavaScript is the while loop. When you want a loop that uses a loop index, you naturally think of a for loop. However, you also might want a loop that doesn't use a loop index at all—you might want to loop only until a certain condition becomes false (such as when you haven't yet found the data item for which you're searching an array). That's where the while loop comes in. This loop evaluates an expression, and if it is true, executes a set of statements—no loop index needed. The loop keeps repeating as long as the specified condition is true.

```
while (condition) {
    statements
}
```

The following parts comprise this loop:

- **condition.** A condition that is evaluated before each time through the loop. If this condition evaluates to true, the statements in the loop's body are performed. When condition becomes false, the loop terminates.

- **statements.** The body of the loop. These are statements that are executed as long as *condition* evaluates to true. Although not required, it is good practice to indent these statements.

Like the `for` and `for...in` loops, the `while` loop has been around a long time, as you see in Table 3.3.

Table 3.3   **The *while* Loop**

Statement	NS2	NS3	NS4	NS6	IE3a	IE3b	IE4	IE5	IE5.5	IE6
while	x	x	x	x	x	x	x	x	x	x

Here's an example. In this case, I'll search an array for a person named Claire using a `while` loop; when I find Claire, I'll end the loop. Here's what the code looks like:

(Listing 03-04.html on the web site)

```html
<HTML>
  <HEAD>
    <TITLE>
      Using the while Loop
    </TITLE>
  </HEAD>

  <BODY>
    <H1>Using the while Loop</H1>
    <SCRIPT LANGUAGE="JavaScript">
      <!--
      var index = 0, data = new Array(5)
      data[0] = "Fank"
      data[1] = "Tom"
      data[2] = "Claire"
      data[3] = "Sara"
      data[4] = "Jane"

      while(data[index] != "Claire"){
          index++
      }
      alert("Found Claire at index " + index)
      // -->
    </SCRIPT>
  </BODY>
</HTML>
```

You can see the results in Figure 3.5, where we've found Claire. That's all it takes.

Here's one thing to note about the `while` loop: The condition is tested before the loop's body is executed even once. That's a problem where the code in the loop's body must be evaluated before the condition can be checked (as, for example, when you must perform some complex calculation to determine whether a result is over the maximum possible value). In cases like these, you can use the new `do...while` loop, which is just like a `while` loop, but where the loop's condition is checked *at the end* of each loop iteration, not before each iteration.

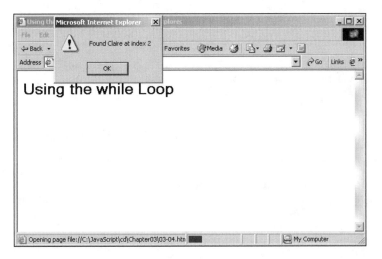

Figure 3.5 Using a while loop.

The *do...while* Loop

The do...while loop executes its statements until a test condition evaluates to false. Unlike a while loop, the statements in the body of the do...while loop are executed at least once. Here's the syntax of this loop:

```
do
    statements
while (condition)
```

The following parts comprise this loop:

- **statements.** The body of the loop, a set of statements that are executed at least once, and executed again each time the condition evaluates to true.

- **condition.** Evaluated after each pass through the loop. If *condition* evaluates to true, the statements in the loop's body are executed again. When *condition* evaluates to false, the loop terminates.

The do...while loop was new in version 4.0 of the Netscape Navigator and Internet Explorer, as you see in Table 3.4.

Table 3.4 **The *do...while* Loop**

Statement	NS2	NS3	NS4	NS6	IE3a	IE3b	IE4	IE5	IE5.5	IE6
do...while			x	x			x	x	x	x

Here's how we can search for "Claire" in an array, just as we did in the preceding example with a while loop—but this time, we're using a do...while loop:

(Listing 03-05.html on the web site)

```
<HTML>
    <HEAD>
        <TITLE>
            Using the do...while Loop
        </TITLE>
    </HEAD>

    <BODY>
        <H1>Using the do...while Loop</H1>
        <SCRIPT LANGUAGE="JavaScript">
            <!--
            var index = 0, data = new Array(5)
            data[0] = "Fank"
            data[1] = "Tom"
            data[2] = "Claire"
            data[3] = "Sara"
            data[4] = "Jane"

            do{
                index++
            }while(data[index] != "Claire")
            alert("Found Claire at index " + index)
            // -->
        </SCRIPT>
    </BODY>
</HTML>
```

The *with* Statement

You should know about another statement when working with loops: the with statement. This statement is not a loop by itself, but it's not all that different. It enables you to specify a default object with which the statements in the body of the with statement can work. If you make document the default object, for example, you can use write alone without having to specify document.write. Here is the syntax of this statement:

```
with (object){
    statements
}
```

The following parts comprise this statement:

- **object.** Specifies the default object to use for the statements. The parentheses around *object* are required.

- **statements.** Any set of statements.

The with statement has been around a long time, as you see in Table 3.5.

Table 3.5 **The *with* Statement**

Statement	NS2	NS3	NS4	NS6	IE3a	IE3b	IE4	IE5	IE5.5	IE6
with	x	x	x	x	x	x	x	x	x	x

Here's an example, using the JavaScript Math object, which we'll see more about in Chapter 19, "The *Math, Number, Boolean,* and *Array* Objects." This object has many useful built-in methods, such as cos and sqrt to take cosines and square roots respectively, and properties, such as PI, which holds the value of pi. If you're using the Math object a lot, it's easier to use a with statement than to always have to qualify every method and property name with the Math object (that is, Math.PI, Math.cos, and so on), like this:

(Listing 03-06.html on the web site)

```
<HTML>
    <HEAD>
        <TITLE>
            Using the with Statement
        </TITLE>
    </HEAD>

    <BODY>
        <H1>Using the with Statement</H1>
        <SCRIPT LANGUAGE="JavaScript">
            <!--
            with(Math){
                document.write("cos(pi) = " + cos(PI) + "<BR>")
                document.write("sqrt(4) = " + sqrt(4) + "<BR>")
            }
            // -->
        </SCRIPT>
    </BODY>
</HTML>
```

Getting More Control: Ending and Continuing Loops

You actually have more control over loops than is apparent in the for, while, and other statements we've already seen. JavaScript also enables you to end a loop partway through using the break statement, and skip on to the next iteration using the continue statement. Those statements are coming up next.

Ending a Loop Early

Sometimes, you might want to end a loop early—for instance, when you've found the data for which you were searching an array. To end loops early, you can use the break statement. Here's the syntax of this statement:

```
break [label]
```

This statement can take an optional label that indicates to JavaScript what loop you want to break out of, as we'll see. The break statement has been around in JavaScript as long as there have been loops, as you see in Table 3.6.

Table 3.6 **The *break* Statement**

Statement	NS2	NS3	NS4	NS6	IE3a	IE3b	IE4	IE5	IE5.5	IE6
break	x	x	x	x	x	x	x	x	x	x

Here's an example; in this case, I'll set up a while loop that'll loop forever by using the Boolean value true as the loop condition. How do you end such a loop? You can use the break statement, as I do here when we've found Claire in an array of people—when we've found Claire, the break statement will end the loop in this code:

(Listing 03-07.html on the web site)

```html
<HTML>
    <HEAD>
        <TITLE>
            Using the break Statement
        </TITLE>
    </HEAD>

    <BODY>
        <H1>Using the break Statement</H1>
        <SCRIPT LANGUAGE="JavaScript">
            <!--
            var index = 0, data = new Array(5)
            data[0] = "Fank"
            data[1] = "Tom"
            data[2] = "Claire"
            data[3] = "Sara"
            data[4] = "Jane"

            while(true){
                if(data[index] == "Claire") {
                    break
                }
                index++
```

```
        }
        alert("Found Claire at index " + index)
        // -->
    </SCRIPT>
  </BODY>
</HTML>
```

Tip

It's not usually good programming practice to write loops that would never terminate by themselves, called *endless loops*. If the break statements in such loops are never executed, those loops will just go on forever, wasting valuable computer time.

Continuing a Loop

Sometimes, you might not want to end a loop, as the break statement is designed to do, but you want to skip the processing of the current iteration and move on to the next iteration. You might have a loop where every iteration takes a great deal of time, for instance, and if you know you're in an iteration of the loop that won't yield anything useful, JavaScript enables you to use the continue statement to move on to the next iteration of the loop. Here's the syntax of the continue statement:

```
continue [label]
```

Like the break statement, this statement can take an optional label that indicates to JavaScript what loop you want to move on to the next iteration in. Like the break statement, the continue statement has been around in JavaScript as long as there have been loops, as you see in Table 3.7.

Table 3.7 **The *continue* Statement**

Statement	NS2	NS3	NS4	NS6	IE3a	IE3b	IE4	IE5	IE5.5	IE6
continue	X	X	X	X	X	X	X	X	X	X

Here's an example to make this clear. In this case, I'll search the array of names for "Claire" one last time—and each time through, if the current name isn't Claire, I'll continue on to the next iteration using the continue statement. Here's what the code looks like:

(Listing 03-08.html on the web site)

```html
<HTML>
    <HEAD>
        <TITLE>
            Using the continue Statement
        </TITLE>
    </HEAD>

    <BODY>
        <H1>Using the continue Statement</H1>
        <SCRIPT LANGUAGE="JavaScript">
            <!--
            var index = 0, claireIndex, data = new Array(5)
            data[0] = "Fank"
            data[1] = "Tom"
            data[2] = "Claire"
            data[3] = "Sara"
            data[4] = "Jane"

            while(true){
                if(data[index] != "Claire") {
                    index++
                    continue
                }
                claireIndex = index
                index++
            }
            alert("Found Claire at index " + claireIndex)
            // -->
        </SCRIPT>
    </BODY>
</HTML>
```

Using Labeled Statements

Both the break and continue statements can take labels that show what loop you want to break or continue, and that proves useful when you're inside a *nested* loop (that is, one loop nested inside another). If you have a for loop, for example, and a for loop *inside* that for loop, and try to use a break statement, which for loop are you breaking out of, the inner one or the outer one? Here's what that problem looks like in code:

```javascript
for(var outerLoopIndex = 1; outerLoopIndex < 3; outerLoopIndex++){
    for(var innerLoopIndex = 1; innerLoopIndex < 3; innerLoopIndex++){
        if(outerLoopIndex == 2 * innerLoopIndex) {
            break
        }
    }
}
```

To solve this problem, JavaScript now enables you to label loops. This is relatively recent, as you see in Table 3.8.

Table 3.8 **Labeled Statements**

Statement	NS2	NS3	NS4	NS6	IE3a	IE3b	IE4	IE5	IE5.5	IE6
Labeled			x	x			x	x	x	x

You label a statement with a text label of your choice, followed by a colon, just before the statement itself. And you can use the label in `break` and `continue` statements, as here, where I'm solving the problem we just saw by indicating that we want to break out of the outer loop (that is, end both loops):

```
<HTML>
    <HEAD>
        <TITLE>
            Using Labeled Statements
        </TITLE>
    </HEAD>

    <BODY>
        <H1>Using Labeled Statements</H1>
        <SCRIPT LANGUAGE="JavaScript">
            <!--
                outer:
                for(var outerLoopIndex = 1; outerLoopIndex < 3; outerLoopIndex++){
                    inner:
                    for(var innerLoopIndex = 1; innerLoopIndex < 3; innerLoopIndex++){
                        if(outerLoopIndex == 2 * innerLoopIndex) {
                        break outer
                        }
                    }
                }
                document.write("outerLoopIndex = " + outerLoopIndex +
                    " innerLoopIndex = " + innerLoopIndex)
            // -->
        </SCRIPT>
    </BODY>
</HTML>
```

That finishes our work with loops in this chapter—now we'll take the next step up in our JavaScript work, which is to start working with *functions*.

Functions

As we've already seen, a function is a set of statements that run when you *call* them, and not before, and you can call a function by treating its name as an expression to be evaluated. Here's the formal syntax for creating a function using the `function` statement:

```
function name([param1] [, param2] [..., paramN]) {
    statements
}
```

The following parts comprise this statement:

- **name.** The name of the function. (The same rules for naming variables apply.)
- **param1 to paramN.** The names of arguments to be passed to the function; using these arguments, you can pass data to the function for the function to work on. In JavaScript, a function can have up to 255 arguments.
- **statements.** The statements that make up the body of the function and which are executed when the function is called.

Functions are integral to JavaScript, and they've been around since the beginning, as you see in Table 3.9.

Table 3.9 **The *function* Statement**

Statement	NS2	NS3	NS4	NS6	IE3a	IE3b	IE4	IE5	IE5.5	IE6
function	x	x	x	x	x	x	x	x	x	x

Here's an example that we've already seen as far back as Chapter 1, "Essential JavaScript." In this example, we're connecting a function named alerter to an HTML button, using that button's ONCLICK event attribute. Here, the body of the function is just one statement, which displays an alert box with the message You clicked the button! when the function is called:

(Listing 03-09.html on the web site)

```
<HTML>
    <HEAD>
        <TITLE>Executing Scripts in Response to User Action</TITLE>
        <SCRIPT LANGUAGE="JavaScript">
            <!--
            function alerter()
            {
                alert("You clicked the button!")
            }
            // -->
        </SCRIPT>
    </HEAD>

    <BODY>
        <H1>Executing Scripts in Response to User Action</H1>
        <FORM>
```

```
            <INPUT TYPE="BUTTON" ONCLICK="alerter()" VALUE="Click Me!">
        </FORM>
    </BODY>
</HTML>
```

This shows us the basics of creating a function—you just use the `function` keyword, followed by the name you want to give to the function (you can use any valid JavaScript name—see the discussion of valid names at the beginning of the preceding chapter), followed by a parentheses-enclosed list of parameters used to pass data to the function—we won't use any parameters here, so the parentheses are empty—and the body of the function, enclosed in curly braces. The function in this example is called when the user clicks the button, and it displays an alert box, as you see in Figure 3.6.

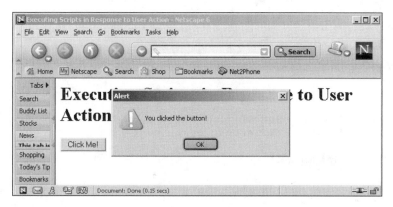

Figure 3.6   Using a function.

The value of placing the code in `alerter` in a function is that it isn't run until you call the function (if you just put code in a `<SCRIPT>` element, on the other hand, that code is run automatically when the page loads). However, functions can do a great deal more than just this.

Returning Values

Functions are often used to perform calculations, and they can *return* a value. If a function returns a value, you can use its name as an expression in your code, and JavaScript will replace that expression with the value returned by the function.

To return a value from a function, you use the `return` statement. Here's the syntax of that statement:

```
return expression
```

In this case, *expression* evaluates to the value you want to return from the function. The `return` statement has been around as long as JavaScript has, as you see in Table 3.10.

Table 3.10 **The *return* Statement**

Statement	NS2	NS3	NS4	NS6	IE3a	IE3b	IE4	IE5	IE5.5	IE6
return	x	x	x	x	x	x	x	x	x	x

For example, here's how I create a function, `getPi`, that returns the value of pi (using the JavaScript `Math.PI` property) when called:

(Listing 03-10.html on the web site)

```
<HTML>
    <HEAD>
        <TITLE>
            Using the return Statement
        </TITLE>
    </HEAD>

    <BODY>
        <H1>Using the return Statement</H1>
        <SCRIPT LANGUAGE="JavaScript">
            <!--
                function getPi()
                {
                    return Math.PI
                }
                document.write("pi = " + getPi())
            // -->
        </SCRIPT>
    </BODY>
</HTML>
```

Figure 3.7 shows the results of this code.

Tip

Although not a problem in current browsers, some older browsers may have trouble if you call a function before defining it. Note also that for the sake of organization, it's often a good idea to place your functions together in a `<SCRIPT>` element in the head section of you web page (unless the code in a function writes to the document body, in which case the code should go in the body section of the page).

You also can pass values to functions, as we've seen.

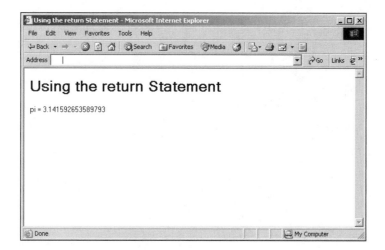

Figure 3.7 Returning a value from a function.

Passing Values

To pass data to a function so that it can work on that data, you can pass *arguments* (also called *parameters*) to the function. Here's an example; in this case, I'll write a function named `adder` that adds two arguments passed to it and returns their sum. When you set up the function, you indicate how many parameters it takes and what names you want to give to those parameters in the *argument list* inside parentheses:

```
function adder(operand1, operand2)
{
    .
    .
    .
}
```

Here, I've indicated that this function takes two parameters. I've named the first parameter `operand1` and the second parameter `operand2`. Now if I call adder like this: `adder(2, 5)`, then in the function's body, the variable `operand1` will hold 2, and the variable `operand2` will hold the value 5. That makes things easy—all I have to do to get the sum of these operands is to add `operand1` and `operand2` and return the result in the body of the function, as follows:

(Listing 03-11.html on the web site)

```
<HTML>
    <HEAD>
        <TITLE>
            Passing Data to Functions
        </TITLE>
    </HEAD>
```

continues ▶

```
<BODY>
    <H1>Passing Data to Functions</H1>
    <SCRIPT LANGUAGE="JavaScript">
        <!--
            function adder(operand1, operand2)
            {
                return operand1 + operand2
            }
            document.write("2 + 5 = " + adder(2, 5))
        // -->
    </SCRIPT>
</BODY>
</HTML>
```

Figure 3.8 shows the results; we learn that, surprisingly, 2 + 5 = 7.

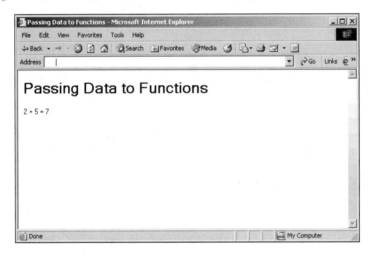

Figure 3.8 Passing values to a function.

Passing by Reference Versus Passing by Value

Now that we're discussing passing data to functions, you should know that you can pass data in two ways: by *reference* and by *value*. When you pass data by value, you pass only a copy of that data. When you pass data by reference, however, you're passing direct access to that data. In JavaScript, all data is passed to functions by value, except objects, which are passed by reference.

The upshot is that when you pass data, not objects, to a function, only a copy of that data is passed; so if you change that data, you're only changing the copy of the original data, which means the original data isn't affected. If you pass an object, such as a `String` object or an `Array` object, however, the function has direct access to the original object, which means that if you change the values in the object, the original object is affected.

Let's make this less theoretical with an example. In this case, I'll pass both a simple text string and an `Array` object to a function. Inside the function body, the function's code will change both the text in the string and an element in the array. When the function is done, we'll see that the element in the `Array` object was indeed changed, whereas the simple text variable was not:

(Listing 03–12.html on the web site)

```
<HTML>
    <HEAD>
        <TITLE>
            Passing by reference and by value
        </TITLE>
    </HEAD>

    <BODY>
        <H1>Passing by reference and by value</H1>
        <SCRIPT LANGUAGE="JavaScript">
            <!--
            function change(obj, text) {
                obj[2]=5
                text = "Changed text"
            }
            var array1 = new Array(1, 2, 3, 4), text = "Original text."
            change(array1)
            document.write("array1[2] = " + array1[2] + "<BR>text = " + text)
            // -->
        </SCRIPT>
    </BODY>
</HTML>
```

You can see the results of this code in Figure 3.9. As this figure shows, the text string variable's value was not changed by the function, but the data in the array *was*. The result is that you should be aware that when you pass an object to a function, that function has access to the actual object you've passed, not just a copy of it.

In JavaScript terms, what's really passed when you pass an object is an *object reference*. An object reference can be thought of as a special data item that stands for the object itself. When you store a reference to, say, a `document` object in a variable, you can use that variable from then on as you would the `document` object itself. (Behind the scenes, a reference holds the actual location of the object in memory, giving you direct access to that object.)

Tip

Why does JavaScript pass objects by reference? It does that to save time and resources—some objects can be very big, and if JavaScript had to create a copy of such objects when they were passed to a function, that could waste a lot of time and browser memory. Passing an object reference, which is a small data item that holds the location of the object in memory, not the object itself, is much more efficient.

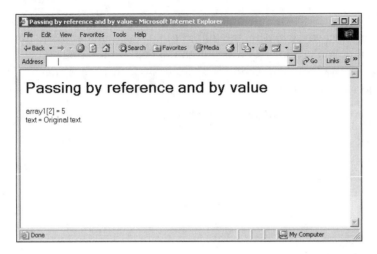

Figure 3.9   Passing by reference and by value.

Handling Recursion

Here's another aspect of functions that is good to know: Functions can actually *call themselves*. This process is called *recursion*, and it can be useful if you're clever and can divide a programming task into a number of identical levels.

Recursion is not something you'll probably use a lot, so feel free to skip this section. Because JavaScript supports it, however, we'll take a look at it here for completeness. The usual recursion example is to compute a factorial—the factorial of a positive integer is the product of that integer times the integer minus one times the integer minus two all the way down to one. Got that?

I'll create an example here to help. 6 factorial, which is written as 6!, is equal to 6 $\star$ 5 $\star$ 4 $\star$ 3 $\star$ 2 $\star$ 1 = 720. In programming terms, this can be broken up into identical stages, with the following rule for each stage, where I'm computing the factorial of *n*. First check whether *n* equals 1, in which case the factorial is done. Otherwise, just multiply *n* by the factorial of *n* −1 (which means calling the factorial function again—from the code inside that function). Here's how it looks in code, where I'm asking JavaScript to compute 6!:

(Listing 03-13.html on the web site)

```
<HTML>
    <HEAD>
        <TITLE>
            Using Recursion
        </TITLE>
    </HEAD>

    <BODY>
        <H1>Using Recursion</H1>
```

```
<SCRIPT LANGUAGE="JavaScript">
    <!--
    function fact(x)
    {
        if (x == 0) {
            return 1
        } else {
            return x * fact(x - 1)
        }
    }
    document.write("6! = " + fact(6))
    // -->
</SCRIPT>
    </BODY>
</HTML>
```

You can see the results of this code in Figure 3.10, where, using recursion, we learn that **6!** does indeed equal 720.

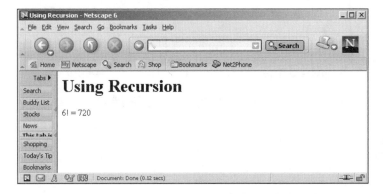

Figure 3.10   Using recursion.

All About Variable Scope

Now that we're achieving mastery over functions, another issue becomes important: *variable scope*. A variable's scope is made up of the part of the program in which is may be accessed—that is, where it's "visible" to your code. The scope of variables you declare in one function, for example, are limited to that function, and are not visible in other functions (unless those functions are nested inside the first function).

JavaScript has two types of scope: *local* and *global*. When you declare a variable in a function, it's *local* to that function, which means its scope is restricted to the body of the function. When you declare a variable in a `<SCRIPT>` element, outside any function, that variable is *global*. Any JavaScript code anywhere in the same page as a global variable—inside a function or not—has access to a global variable. If you declare a local variable with the same name as a global variable, however, that local variable overrides the global variable as long as the local variable is in scope. When you leave the local variable's scope, the global variable resumes its original value.

Here's an example to make all this clearer. In this case, I'll declare a variable named variable1 as a global variable in a web page's head section. Because it's a global variable, it's available to all JavaScript code *anywhere* in the page (unless overridden by a local variable of the same name), not just in the head section.

I'll also declare a global variable named variable2 in the body section and add a function, function1, to the body. In this function, we'll see that both global variables are visible. In another function, function2, however, I'll declare a new local variable, also named variable2. As we'll see, that local variable will override the global variable2 (but only in the function that declared a local version of variable2). Here's what it all looks like in code:

(Listing 03-14.html on the web site)

```
<HTML>
    <HEAD>
        <TITLE>Working With Variable Scope</TITLE>
        <SCRIPT LANGUAGE="JavaScript">
            <!--
                var variable1 = "Global, defined in the head."
            // -->
        </SCRIPT>
    </HEAD>

    <BODY onload="testValues()">
        <H1>Working With Variable Scope</H1>
        <SCRIPT LANGUAGE="JavaScript">
            var variable2 = "Global, defined in the body."
            function function1()
            {
                document.write("In function1: " + "<BR>")
                document.write("variable1 is: " + variable1 + "<BR>")
                document.write("variable2 is: " + variable2 + "<BR><BR>")
            }
            function function2()
            {
                document.write("In function2: " + "<BR>")
                var variable2 = "Local, defined in function2."
                document.write("variable1 is: " + variable1 + "<BR>")
                document.write("variable2 is: " + variable2 + "<BR>")
            }
            function1()
            function2()
        </SCRIPT>
    </BODY>
</HTML>
```

You can see the results of this code in Figure 3.11, where we get a picture of how scope works directly.

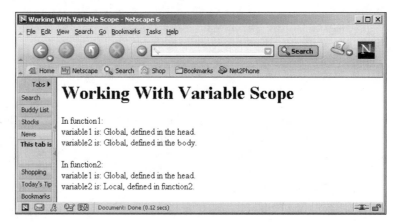

Figure 3.11 Handling variable scope.

Tip

Even though you can declare a variable throughout a function, as far as scope goes, after you have defined a local variable anywhere in a function, it overrides any global variables of the same name throughout the whole function. That means that the overridden global variable won't be visible in the function up to the point where you declare the local variable of the same name—the global variable will never be visible in the function at all.

The JavaScript *Function* Object

Believe it or not, JavaScript can treat functions as data types—with the result that you can declare a function as a variable. You can do this with the JavaScript `Function` object.

Here's an example showing how this works. In this case, I'll create a function named `adder` that will take two operands, which I'll name `operand1` and `operand2`, add them, and return their sum. You can do that with a new `Function` object as follows. (Recall that you have to use the `new` keyword when creating a new object.)

```
var adder = new Function("operand1", "operand2", "return operand1 + operand2")
```

Here, I pass the name of the first operand, then the second operand, and then the JavaScript code for the function. (You can specify as many function parameters as you want—up to 255 in JavaScript—not just the two I've used here.) Now you can use this new function as you would any other:

```
var adder = new Function("operand1", "operand2", "return operand1 + operand2")
document.write("2 + 3 = " + adder(2, 3))
```

The `Function` object has been available since Netscape Navigator version 3.0 and Internet Explorer version 3b, as you see in Table 3.11. (Earlier, unreliable versions of this object were available in Netscape Navigator version 2.0 and Internet Explorer version 3a.) You can find the properties of this object in Table 3.12 and the methods of this object in Table 3.13. (It has no events.)

Table 3.11 **The *Function* Object**

Object	NS2	NS3	NS4	NS6	IE3a	IE3b	IE4	IE5	IE5.5	IE6
Function		x	x	x		x	x	x	x	x

Table 3.12 **Properties of the *Function* Object**

Property	NS2	NS3	NS4	NS6	IE3a	IE3b	IE4	IE5	IE5.5	IE6
arguments		x	x	x		x	x	x	x	x
An array holding the arguments passed to a function.										
arguments.callee		x	x	x		x	x	x	x	x
Holds the function body of the executing function.										
arguments.caller		x	x	x		x	x	x	x	x
Holds the name of the function that called the currently executing function.										
arguments.length		x	x	x		x	x	x	x	x
Holds the number of arguments passed to the function.										
arity		x	x			x	x	x	x	x
Holds the number of arguments that were expected by the function.										
constructor		x	x	x		x	x	x	x	x
Gives the function that creates an object.										
length			x	x		x	x	x	x	x
Holds the number of arguments expected by a function.										

Table 3.13 **Methods of the *Function* Object**

Method	NS2	NS3	NS4	NS6	IE3a	IE3b	IE4	IE5	IE5.5	IE6
apply				x					x	x

Enables you to apply a method of another object while inside a
different object.
Syntax: `apply([obj[, argumentsArray]])`

Method	NS2	NS3	NS4	NS6	IE3a	IE3b	IE4	IE5	IE5.5	IE6
call				x					x	x

Enables you to call a method of another object while inside a
different object.
Syntax: `call(obj[, arg1[, arg2[...argN]]])`

Method	NS2	NS3	NS4	NS6	IE3a	IE3b	IE4	IE5	IE5.5	IE6
toSource		x	x			x	x	x	x	x

Returns a string representing the source code of the function.
Syntax: `Object.toSource()`

Method	NS2	NS3	NS4	NS6	IE3a	IE3b	IE4	IE5	IE5.5	IE6
toString		x	x			x	x	x	x	x

Returns a string representing the source code of the function.
Syntax: `Object.toString()`

Method	NS2	NS3	NS4	NS6	IE3a	IE3b	IE4	IE5	IE5.5	IE6
valueOf		x	x			x	x	x	x	x

Returns a string holding the actual source code of the function.
Syntax: `Object.valueOf()`

The *function* Operator

Besides the `Function` object, JavaScript also supports a `function` *operator*.
Following the lead of languages such as Perl and Java, the `function` operator
enables you to define a function without a name—that is, an *anonymous*
function. Here's the syntax of this statement—note how much this works
like just assigning a function definition to a variable:

```
var variableName = function([parameter1 [, parameter2...[, parameterN]]])
{functionBody}
```

As you see in Table 3.14, the `function` operator is fairly recent.

Table 3.14 **The *function* Operator**

Operator	NS2	NS3	NS4	NS6	IE3a	IE3b	IE4	IE5	IE5.5	IE6
function				x					x	x

The syntax for using this operator is much like that for using the `Function` object. Here's an example putting this operator to work, where I'm setting up a function to double the number you pass it, and assigning that function to a variable named `doubler`:

(Listing 03-15.html on the web site)

```
<HTML>
    <HEAD>
        <TITLE>
            Passing Data to Functions
        </TITLE>
    </HEAD>

    <BODY>
        <H1>Passing Data to Functions</H1>
        <SCRIPT LANGUAGE="JavaScript">
            <!--
                var doubler = function(operand1) {return 2 * operand1}
                document.write("2 * 10 = " + doubler(10))
            // -->
        </SCRIPT>
    </BODY>
</HTML>
```

Figure 3.12 shows the results of this code.

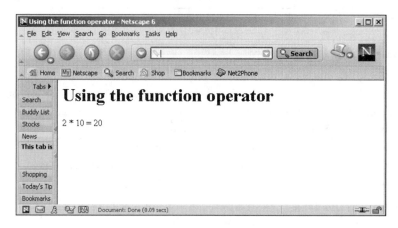

Figure 3.12   Using the `function` operator.

The *this* Keyword

Another important JavaScript resource, now that we're discussing functions, is the `this` keyword. This keyword refers to the object your code is in; and to pass that object to a function, you only have to pass the `this` keyword. We'll see more about the `this` object later, especially when dealing with HTML controls such as buttons and text fields, but we can get a preview here.

Suppose, for example, that I want to write a function to handle button clicks as we've already seen in Chapter 1. In this case, however, suppose that I want to display the *caption* of the clicked button in an alert box, so if the button's caption is Click Me!, I want to display `You clicked the Click Me! button`. I can do that if I pass this function the actual button object that was clicked, because I can use that object's `value` property to get the button's caption. Here's the JavaScript for the function, which I'll name `describer`, that will do this:

```
function describer(button)
{
    alert("You clicked the " + button.value + " button.")
}
```

Suppose, however, that I have *two* buttons in the web page—how can I pass the specific button object that was clicked to our function? I can do that with the `this` keyword—to pass the current button object to our function, all I have to do is to use `this` as you see here:

(Listing 03-16.html on the web site)

```
<HTML>
    <HEAD>
        <TITLE>Using the this keyword</TITLE>
    </HEAD>

    <BODY>
        <H1>Using the this keyword</H1>
        <SCRIPT LANGUAGE="JavaScript">
            <!--
            function describer(button)
            {
                document.write("You clicked the " + button.value + " button.")
                document.close()
            }
            // -->
        </SCRIPT>
        <FORM>
            <INPUT TYPE="BUTTON" ONCLICK="describer(this)" VALUE="Click Me!">
            <INPUT TYPE="BUTTON" ONCLICK="describer(this)" VALUE="Click Me Too!">
        </FORM>
    </BODY>
</HTML>
```

HTML controls such as buttons and text fields are treated as objects in JavaScript. When a button is clicked, the code in the clicked button executes, and in the button's code, you can refer to the button object itself with the `this` keyword. In the `onclick` event handler, then, all we have to do is to pass the current button object to the describer function, like this: `describer(this)`. You can see this web page in Figure 3.13. When the user clicks the Click Me! button, that button is passed to our function, and the caption of that button displays, as you see in Figure 3.14.

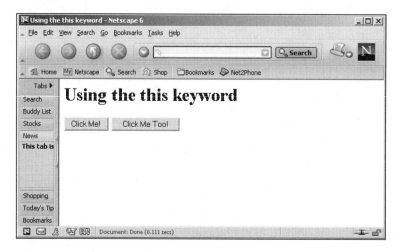

Figure 3.13   Using the `this` keyword, start page.

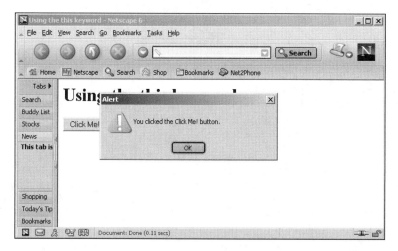

Figure 3.14   Using the `this` keyword, after clicking a button.

We'll see in more detail how to use the `this` keyword later in this book. Just keep in mind here that the `this` keyword always enables you to refer to the current object (whether that object has a formal name or not).

The JavaScript Built-in Functions

The last topic I'll take a look at in our coverage of JavaScript functions gives us a look at the functions that are already built in to JavaScript, and are available anywhere in your code. (In fact, these built-in functions are sometimes called global functions.) Table 3.15 lists these functions.

Table 3.15 **JavaScript's Global Functions**

Function	NS2	NS3	NS4	NS6	IE3a	IE3b	IE4	IE5	IE5.5	IE6
decodeURI				x					x	x

Decodes a *uniform resource identifier* (URI). URIs are encoded for use with browsers—for example, a space is encoded as a hex value, %20. This function decodes encoded URIs, substituting, for example, spaces for %20.
Syntax: decodeURI("URI")
Returns: String

Function	NS2	NS3	NS4	NS6	IE3a	IE3b	IE4	IE5	IE5.5	IE6
decodeURIComponent				x					x	x

Decodes a URI component. The same as decodeURI, except that this function works on components, which are parts of complete URIs.
Syntax: decodeURI("URIComponent")
Returns: String

Function	NS2	NS3	NS4	NS6	IE3a	IE3b	IE4	IE5	IE5.5	IE6
encodeURI				x					x	x

Encodes a URI for use in a browser, converting, for example, spaces into their hex equivalent, %20. More recent than the escape function, does not encode these characters—; / : @ & = + $, - _ . ! ~ * ' ( ) #—because these characters are now considered legal in URIs.
Syntax: encodeURI("Text")
Returns: String

Function	NS2	NS3	NS4	NS6	IE3a	IE3b	IE4	IE5	IE5.5	IE6
encodeURIComponent				x					x	x

Encodes a URI component for use in a browser. The same as encodeURI, except that this function works on URI components, which are parts of complete URIs.
Syntax: encodeURI("Text")
Returns: String

continues ▶

Table 3.15 **Continued**

Function	NS2	NS3	NS4	NS6	IE3a	IE3b	IE4	IE5	IE5.5	IE6
escape	X	X	X	X	X	X	X	X	X	X

"Escapes" a string into a URI that can be used in a browser. This function converts nearly all nonalphanumeric characters to their escaped version. (For example, spaces are converted to hex %20.) Performs more escaping than the more modern `encodeURI`.
Syntax: `escape("Text")`
Returns: String

Function	NS2	NS3	NS4	NS6	IE3a	IE3b	IE4	IE5	IE5.5	IE6
eval	X	X	X	X	X	X	X	X	X	X

Evaluates a JavaScript expression. See below for more information.
Syntax: `eval("string")`
Returns: Object reference

Function	NS2	NS3	NS4	NS6	IE3a	IE3b	IE4	IE5	IE5.5	IE6
isFinite	X	X	X	X	X	X	X	X	X	X

Checks whether an expression yields a number outside the maximum or minimum possible values JavaScript can store. Returns false if the expression's value is outside the maximum or minimum possible values.
Syntax: `isFinite(number)`
Returns: Boolean

Function	NS2	NS3	NS4	NS6	IE3a	IE3b	IE4	IE5	IE5.5	IE6
isNaN	X	X	X	X	X	X	X	X	X	X

Checks whether a value is a valid number (`isNaN` stands for *Is Not a Number*) and returns true if the value passed to it is not a number. Useful for checking the results of `parseInt` and `parseFloat`.
Syntax: `isNaN(value)`
Returns: Boolean

Function	NS2	NS3	NS4	NS6	IE3a	IE3b	IE4	IE5	IE5.5	IE6
Number			X	X			X	X	X	X

Converts a string to an integer or a floating-point number, as appropriate.
Syntax: `Number("string")`
Returns: Number

Function	NS2	NS3	NS4	NS6	IE3a	IE3b	IE4	IE5	IE5.5	IE6
parseFloat	X	X	X	X	X	X	X	X	X	X

Converts a string to a floating-point number. Syntax:
`parseFloat("string")`
Returns: Number

Function	NS2	NS3	NS4	NS6	IE3a	IE3b	IE4	IE5	IE5.5	IE6
parseInt	X	X	X	X	X	X	X	X	X	X

Converts a string to an integer. Can also take a base (also called a radix) to use when converting—for example, `parseInt(myString, 16)` creates a hexadecimal (base 16) value.
Syntax: `parseInt("string" [, radix])`
Returns: Number

Function	NS2	NS3	NS4	NS6	IE3a	IE3b	IE4	IE5	IE5.5	IE6
`toString`	x	x	x	x	x	x	x	x	x	x

This is a method of every JavaScript and DOM object, and is intended to convert the object into a string representation as meaningfully as it can. Can also take a radix if needed.
Syntax: `toString("string" [, radix])`
Returns: String

`unescape`	x	x	x	x	x	x	x	x	x	x

Converts an escaped URI into its unescaped version, the counterpart of the `escape` function.
Syntax: `unescape("URI")`
Returns: String

`unwatch`			x	x						

Directs an external debugger not to watch a particular property anymore.
Syntax: `unwatch(property)`
Returns: Nothing

`watch`			x	x						

Directs an external debugger to watch the value of a particular property.
Syntax: `watch(property, debugHandler)`
Returns: Nothing

One of the functions in Table 3.15 is particularly powerful—`eval`, which enables you to evaluate JavaScript code. I'll take a closer look at this function here, with an example that enables you to type in JavaScript expressions and evaluate them on-the-fly.

Tip

Also see the execScript method in Chapter 8, "Using *window* and *frame* Methods and Events."

Here's the code for that example—in this case, I'm reading the JavaScript expression the user has entered into a text field, evaluating it with `eval`, and displaying the result in another text field. We're anticipating our work with HTML text fields here—you might note in passing how this code refers to the text in a text field, which is stored in its HTML value property—as `document.forms[0].`*name*`.value`, where `forms` is a `document` object array that holds all the forms in the page, and *name* is the name given to the text field:

(Listing 03-17.html on the web site)

```
<HTML>
    <HEAD>
        <TITLE>
            Using the eval Function
        </TITLE>
        <SCRIPT LANGUAGE="JavaScript">
            <!--
            function evaluator()
            {
                document.forms[0].result.value
                    = eval(document.forms[0].expression.value)
            }
            // -->
        </SCRIPT>
    </HEAD>

    <BODY>
        <H1>Using the eval Function</H1>
        <FORM>
            <INPUT TYPE="TEXT" NAME="expression">
            <INPUT TYPE="BUTTON" ONCLICK="evaluator()" VALUE="  =  ">
            <INPUT TYPE="TEXT" NAME="result">
        </FORM>
    </BODY>
</HTML>
```

You can see the results in Figure 3.15, where I've typed in a JavaScript expression and clicked the = button, which makes the result appear in the second text field.

Tip

This example, which evaluates JavaScript expressions on-the-fly, can even be a useful tool as you develop your own code and want to check some JavaScript before putting it into your web page.

One use for the `eval` function is to get access to objects whose names you already know—for example, an `eval` statement can return a reference to the document object if you pass it the string `"document"`. What use is that? Well, the two major browsers have different object models, and if you try to execute a statement that uses an object that doesn't exist in the current browser, your script will crash. (Just having such statements in a script doesn't cause a problem—it's only if you try to *execute* those specific statements that your script will crash.) To avoid that, you can check which browser you're working with, and then use `eval` to get a set of objects legal for that browser by passing `eval` their names. Here's a simple example that gets a reference to the document object by passing the text `"document"` to `eval` (this is just an example—both browsers support a document object, of course):

(Listing 03-18.html on the web site)

```
<HTML>
    <HEAD>
        <TITLE>
            Using the eval Function
        </TITLE>
    </HEAD>

    <BODY>
        <H1>Using the eval Function</H1>
        <SCRIPT LANGUAGE="JavaScript">
            <!--
            var obj = "document"
            for (var property in eval(obj)) {
                document.write(property + ": " + document[property] + "<BR>")
            }
            // -->
        </SCRIPT>
    </BODY>
</HTML>
```

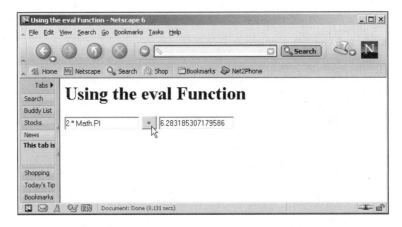

Figure 3.15   Using `eval` to evaluate a JavaScript expression.

Handling Errors

We'll turn now to the third topic in this chapter: handling errors. This topic isn't so much about syntax errors, which cause your script not to run in the first place, but handling errors that happen at runtime, such as when a numeric value is greater than can fit into a JavaScript variable.

You can handle runtime errors two ways in JavaScript: You can use the `onerror` event handler; and, more recently, you can use `try...catch` statements. I'll take a look at both techniques here.

Using the *onerror* Event Handler

The onerror event handler is built in to the window object. (As we saw in Chapter 1, the window object corresponds to the browser window itself, and it contains the document object.) Using the onerror event handler, you can specify a function the browser should call if there's been an error in your code. This event handler appeared in the Netscape Navigator 3.0 and the Internet Explorer 4.0, as you see in Table 3.16.

Table 3.16 **The *onerror* Event Handler**

Event	NS2	NS3	NS4	NS6	IE3a	IE3b	IE4	IE5	IE5.5	IE6
onerror		x	x	x			x	x	x	x

How do you connect a function to the onerror event handler? You just use the onerror property of the window object. For example, I can connect a function I'll name handleError to the onerror event as follows:

```
<HTML>
    <HEAD>
        <TITLE>Handling an Error</TITLE>
        <SCRIPT LANGUAGE="JavaScript">
            <!--
            window.onerror = handleError
            // -->
        </SCRIPT>
    </HEAD>
          .
          .
          .
</HTML>
```

When an error occurs, the browser will now try to call the handleError function, so we better write such a function. This function is automatically passed an error message, the URL of the web page that caused the error, and the line number in the script of the error itself, so here's how I set up the handleError function:

```
<HTML>
    <HEAD>
        <TITLE>Handling an Error</TITLE>
        <SCRIPT LANGUAGE="JavaScript">
            <!--
            function handleError(message, URL, lineNumber)
            {
              .
              .
              .
            }
```

```
        window.onerror = handleError
        // -->
    </SCRIPT>
</HEAD>
    .
    .
    .
</HTML>
```

We can display the error's information in an alert box using the `alert` method like this. Note the term `"\n"` here, which is a *newline* character that causes the text in the alert box to skip to the next line. (Using `"\n"` to skip to the next line is standard not just in JavaScript, but in languages such as C++ and Java as well. I use this term here because an alert box is designed to display text, not HTML; if we were displaying this text in a browser rather than an alert box, we would have to use the HTML `<BR>` tag to skip to the next line.) We can use the `alert` method to display the error's information in an alert box as follows:

```
<HTML>
    <HEAD>
        <TITLE>Handling an Error</TITLE>
        <SCRIPT LANGUAGE="JavaScript">
            <!--
            function handleError(message, URL, lineNumber)
            {
                alert("Error " + message + "\n" +
                "in file " + URL + "\n" +
                "at line " + lineNumber + ".\n")
                return true
            }
            window.onerror = handleError
            // -->
        </SCRIPT>
    </HEAD>
    .
    .
    .
</HTML>
```

Note that this error handler returns a value of true, which tells the browser we've handled the error. (This means the browser won't display an error icon or error dialog box.)

Tip

If you don't want to handle an error in an onerror event handling function, just return a value of false, and the browser will take over, as it would have as if there were no onerror event handling function.

Now when there's an error, an alert box will appear with all the details. So how do we cause an error? One way is to perform an illegal JavaScript operation, such as assigning a variable a value that you haven't yet defined. I'll do that here with a function named `causeError` that holds the statement `var myData = undefinedVariable`, where we haven't yet created the variable `undefinedVariable` (which means JavaScript won't know how to work with it). When the user clicks a button with the caption Create an Error, this statement will be executed, causing an error:

(Listing 03-19.html on the web site)

```
<HTML>
    <HEAD>
        <TITLE>Handling an Error</TITLE>
        <SCRIPT LANGUAGE="JavaScript">
            <!--
            function causeError()
            {
                var myData = undefinedVariable
            }

            function handleError(message, URL, lineNumber)
            {
                alert("Error " + message + "\n" +
                "in file " + URL + "\n" +
                "at line " + lineNumber + ".\n")
                return true
            }
            window.onerror = handleError
            // -->
        </SCRIPT>
    </HEAD>

    <BODY>
        <H1>Handling an Error</H1>
        <FORM>
            <INPUT TYPE="BUTTON" VALUE="Create an Error" onclick="causeError()">
        </FORM>
    </BODY>
</HTML>
```

You can see the results in Figure 3.16. When the user clicks the button, the script causes an error, and an alert box appears describing the error.

In this way, you can get information about the error, and even try to handle it in code if you like. However, the newer way of doing this is to use a `try...catch` statement, following the lead of languages such as C++ and Java. In fact, Netscape Navigator 6.0 no longer passes the error message, URL, and line number values to the `onerror` handler (so the preceding example doesn't display any values in the alert box)—perhaps in an attempt to switch to the `try...catch` way of doing things. I'll take a look at `try...catch` now.

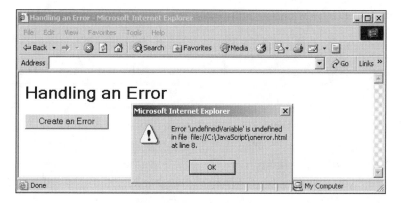

Figure 3.16   Working with errors.

Using the *try...catch* Statement

When you enclose a series of statements in a `try` statement, any error that happens when executing those statements will *throw* (that is, cause) an *exception*. When an exception is thrown, JavaScript will terminate the `try` statement and look for a `catch` statement, which "catches" the exception. If there is a `catch` statement, the code in that `catch` statement is executed, enabling you to deal with the error. There is also an optional `finally` statement, which is executed whether or not an exception occurs; here's the syntax:

```
try {
    tryStatements
}
[catch (exception)
    {catchStatements}]
[finally {finallyStatements}]
```

The following parts comprise these statements:

- **tryStatements**. A set of statements that executes once. If these statements throw an exception, execution transfers to a `catch` statement if there is one.

- *exception.* The name of the variable you want to use to hold the object (usually an `Error` object) passed to the catch statement.

- *catchStatements*. A set of statements that executes if an exception was thrown.

- *finallyStatements.* A set of statements that is executed before the try...catch statement completes. These statements execute whether or not an exception was thrown or caught.

The try...catch statement is relatively new, as you see in Table 3.17.

Table 3.17 **The *try...catch* Statement**

Statement	NS2	NS3	NS4	NS6	IE3a	IE3b	IE4	IE5	IE5.5	IE6
Try...catch				x				x	x	x

Let's put the try...catch statement to work now.

Unconditional *catch* Statements

When an exception occurs, execution transfers to the catch statement, if there is one. For example, we might cause the same error as in our onerror example—but this time, we'll use a try...catch statement. That means we place the error-causing code in a try statement and display the message There was an error. in the catch statement, as follows:

(Listing 03-20.html on the web site)

```html
<HTML>
    <HEAD>
        <TITLE>
            Reporting an Error
        </TITLE>
    </HEAD>

    <BODY>
        <H1>Reporting an Error</H1>
        <SCRIPT LANGUAGE="JavaScript">
        <!--
            try {
                var myData = undefinedVariable
            }
            catch(e) {
                document.write("There was an error.")
            }
        // -->
        </SCRIPT>
    </BODY>
</HTML>
```

Figure 3.17 shows this code at work.

The simple message There was an error. doesn't tell the user very much, however. The object that's passed to us in a catch statement is an Error object, and we can tell the user the name of the error by using this object's name property. The JavaScript error names are EvalError, RangeError, ReferenceError, SyntaxError, TypeError and URIError.

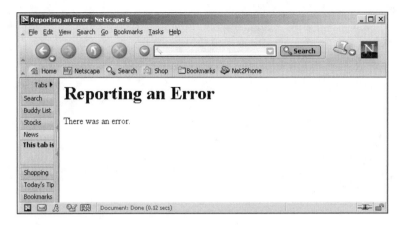

Figure 3.17   Using try...catch to catch an exception.

> **Tip**
>
> Other objects can throw their own error types in JavaScript. For example, W3C DOM objects can throw exceptions
> such as HIERARCHY_REQUEST_ERROR, WRONG_DOCUMENT_ERROR, NO_MODIFICATION_ALLOWED_ERROR, and
> so on.

In the parentheses following the catch keyword, you can assign a name to
the Error object passed to the catch statement; in this example, following
standard usage, I'll just call that object e:

```
try {
    var myData = undefinedVariable
}
catch(e) {
    document.write("There was an error.")
}
```

Now, in the catch statement, we can find the name of the error that
occurred with the e.name property, so here's how we let the user know what
error happened:

(Listing 03-21.html on the web site)

```
<HTML>
    <HEAD>
        <TITLE>
            Reporting an Error's Name
        </TITLE>
    </HEAD>
```

continues ▶

```
<BODY>
    <H1>Reporting an Error's Name</H1>
    <SCRIPT LANGUAGE="JavaScript">
    <!--
        try {
            var myData = undefinedVariable
        }
        catch(e) {
            document.write("An error of type " + e.name + " occurred.")
        }
    // -->
    </SCRIPT>
</BODY>
</HTML>
```

You can see this new, improved version of this example in Figure 3.18.

Figure 3.18   Reporting an exception's name.

Conditional *catch* Statements

Because you can determine the type of an error using the Error object's name property, you can add code to handle specific types of errors. Here's an example, where I'm using a switch statement to handle different types of exceptions:

(Listing 03-22.html on the web site)

```
<HTML>
    <HEAD>
        <TITLE>
            Handling Specific Errors
        </TITLE>
    </HEAD>
```

```
<BODY>
    <H1>Handling Specific Errors</H1>
    <SCRIPT LANGUAGE="JavaScript">
    <!--
        try {
            var myData = undefinedValue
        }
        catch (e){
            switch (e.name){
            case "EvalError":
                document.write("An EvalError error occurred.")
                break
            case "RangeError":
                document.write("A RangeError error occurred.")
                break
            case "ReferenceError":
                document.write("A ReferenceError error occurred.")
                break
            case "SyntaxError":
                document.write("A SyntaxError error occurred.")
                break
            case "TypeError":
                document.write("A TypeError error occurred.")
                break
            case "URIError":
                document.write("An URIError error occurred.")
                break
            default:
                document.write("An error occurred.")
            }
        }
    // -->
    </SCRIPT>
</BODY>
</HTML>
```

In this case, I'm just displaying the type of exception that occurred; in your own code, however, you could write code to actually handle and recover from the error. This example depends on using the name property of the Error object, which is a very useful property, but note that the Error object has other properties as well.

Using the *Error* Object

An Error object is usually passed to you in a catch statement (unless, for example, you throw the exception yourself and don't use an Error object). Table 3.18 lists the properties of this object.

Table 3.18   **Properties of the *Error* Object**

Property	NS2	NS3	NS4	NS6	IE3a	IE3b	IE4	IE5	IE5.5	IE6
description								x	x	x

Contains a description of the error; as of IE5.5 and NS6, however, the `message` property is preferred.

fileName				x						

Holds the name of the file that caused the error.

lineNumber				x						

Holds the line number of the statement that caused the error.

message				x					x	x

Contains a description of the error.

name				x					x	x

Contains the name of the error that was thrown. The JavaScript error names are `EvalError`, `RangeError`, `ReferenceError`, `SyntaxError`, `TypeError`, and `URIError`. General errors that you throw yourself are named `Error`.

number								x	x	x

Internet Explorer only. Holds the Internet Explorer number for each error.

Using these properties, you have access to a great deal of information about the error that occurred.

The *finally* Block

The `finally` statement contains statements to execute after the `try` and `catch` statements execute, but before the statements following the `try` and `catch` statements execute. The `finally` block executes whether or not an exception is thrown. (Note also that if an exception is thrown, the statements in the `finally` block execute even if no `catch` block handles the exception.)

If you're working with some crucial resource that you've locked in your code and an error occurs, for instance, that resource may never be unlocked if the error prevents the full code from running. To make sure that the resource is freed whether or not an error occurred, you can put code to unlock the resource in the `finally` statement, which executes regardless of whether an exception is thrown. Here's an example:

```
lockResource()
try {
    useResource()
}
catch(e){
    reportResourceError()
}
finally {
    unlockResource()
}
```

Throwing an Exception Yourself

You also can throw exceptions yourself, using the throw statement:

```
throw expression
```

Like the try and catch statements, the throw statement is relatively recent, as you see in Table 3.19.

Table 3.19 **The *throw* Statement**

Statement	NS2	NS3	NS4	NS6	IE3a	IE3b	IE4	IE5	IE5.5	IE6
throw				x				x	x	x

Here's an example. Suppose you bite into a pickle, but that you can't stand pickles. In that case, you could throw a bad taste exception like this:

```
<HTML>
    <HEAD>
        <TITLE>
            Throwing an Exception
        </TITLE>
    </HEAD>

    <BODY>
        <H1>Throwing an Exception</H1>
        <SCRIPT LANGUAGE="JavaScript">
        <!--
            try {
                throw "Bad Taste Exception"
            }
            catch (e){
                document.write("An error occurred: " + e)
            }
        // -->
        </SCRIPT>
    </BODY>
</HTML>
```

This throws the simple text string `"Bad Taste Exception"` as an exception, and that string is passed to the `catch` statement, where the code displays it. However, the more standard way to do this is to create an `Error` object, throw that object, and use the object's `message` property in a `catch` statement to find out what error occurred:

(Listing 03-23.html on the web site)

```
<HTML>
    <HEAD>
        <TITLE>
            Throwing an Exception
        </TITLE>
    </HEAD>

    <BODY>
        <H1>Throwing an Exception</H1>
        <SCRIPT LANGUAGE="JavaScript">
        <!--
            try {
                throw Error("Bad Taste Exception")
            }
            catch (e){
                document.write("An error occurred: " + e.message)
            }
        // -->
        </SCRIPT>
    </BODY>
</HTML>
```

Figure 3.19 shows the results of this code.

Figure 3.19 Throwing a custom exception.

Here's something else you should know about exceptions: You can *rethrow* an exception, using the `throw` statement. You can nest try...catch statements, for instance, and if you don't want to handle an exception in an inner try...catch pair of statements, you can throw it so that it'll be handled by the outer try...catch statements. Here's an example showing how this works; in this case, the inner `catch` statement will handle `EvalError` and `RangeError` errors—but will throw other exceptions. The thrown exception is then caught by the outer, more general `catch` statement:

(Listing 03-24.html on the web site)

```
<HTML>
    <HEAD>
        <TITLE>
            Handling Specific Errors
        </TITLE>
    </HEAD>

    <BODY>
        <H1>Handling Specific Errors</H1>
        <SCRIPT LANGUAGE="JavaScript">
        <!--
            try {
                try {
                    var myData = undefinedVariable
                }
                catch (e){
                    switch (e.name){
                    case "EvalError":
                        document.write("An EvalError error occurred.")
                        break
                    case "RangeError":
                        document.write("A RangeError error occurred.")
                        break
                    default:
                        throw e
                    }
                }
            }
            catch (e) {
                document.write("An error occurred: " + e.name)
            }
        // -->
        </SCRIPT>
    </BODY>
</HTML>
```

That completes our chapter on loops, functions, and handling errors. Now we have enough JavaScript under our belts to start working with what JavaScript was designed for in the first place: the browser environment.

4

Handling the Browser Environment

IN THIS CHAPTER, WE'RE GOING TO START PUTTING JAVASCRIPT to work where it was designed to be used: in browsers. That means we're going to start interacting with browsers using the various browser objects available to us in JavaScript, such as the `window`, `document`, and `navigator` objects. This chapter will provide us with an in-depth overview of not only those objects, but also the different object models available in various browsers and versions. We'll need that information in coming chapters.

Now that we're working with browsers, we'll also consider how to handle cross-browser programming issues, discussing how to determine what browser your script is executing in, and how to determine what objects are available to you.

Tip

In this book, it's not necessary to memorize which browser has which object model and try to guess whether your script will work as you plan. Instead, when you look up a language element or object property, method, or event here, you'll find a table showing directly which browser, and which browser version, supports that item. All you need to know is what browser and browser version you're working with, and you'll see how to determine that in this chapter.

We'll also take a look at how to access not only the big *Document Object Model* (DOM) objects, such as the `window` and `navigator` objects, but also all the HTML elements in a web page. In JavaScript, those HTML elements are represented as objects, and you'll see the many ways of accessing those elements in your scripts.

I'll start this chapter now by taking a look at the history of the various DOMs of various browsers.

The Document Object Models: A History

The primary power of JavaScript is that it's a straightforward language that enables you to script the objects available to you in browsers, and much of this book is an exploration of those objects. All browsers have had different object models, and as you know, that presents a programming challenge in JavaScript. You can see a basic overview of the browser objects available to you in JavaScript in Figure 4.1; you can count on these objects being available in all scriptable browsers.

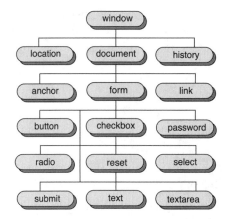

Figure 4.1   The common DOM model.

Beyond the basics you see in Figure 4.1, however, browsers diverge. You can see an overview of the various DOMs in various browsers in Table 4.1. I'll take a more in-depth look at each of these models next.

Table 4.1 **The DOM by Browser Version**

Model Name	Supported in These Browsers
DOM 0	NS2, NS3, IE3a, IE3b, NS4, IE4, IE5, IE5.5, NS6, IE6
DOM 0+Images	NS3, IE3a, IE3b, NS4, IE4, IE5, IE5.5, NS6, IE6
NS4 Extensions	NS4
IE4 Extensions	IE4, IE5, IE5.5, IE6
IE5 Extensions	IE5, IE5.5, IE6
Version 6 Extensions	NS6, IE6
W3C DOM 1 and 2	DOM level 1: NS6, IE6, Partial: IE5, IE5.5

The DOM 0

The original DOM, which you see more or less entirely in Figure 4.1, was supported by Netscape Navigator 2.0. This was the first DOM and provided the early support to JavaScript of the browser objects.

In fact, the DOM 0 introduced the browser objects that are familiar to us today: the `window`, `document`, `navigator`, and other objects. Using this DOM, you started to get access to the HTML elements in a web page. However, only the interactive elements of the web page—controls such as text fields, buttons, check boxes, links, and so on—became accessible. The rest of the page was still static.

DOM 0 was so successful that Internet Explorer 3.0 also implemented it virtually unchanged—a short, peaceful interlude before the browser wars really started.

Tip

Two versions of Internet Explorer 3.0 appeared that were slightly different, which we're calling versions 3a and 3b, as discussed in Chapter 1, "Essential JavaScript." So if you're scripting for version 3.0, you should think about using object detection, coming up in this chapter, to be sure of the browser's capabilities.

DOM 0+Images

Not long after Internet Explorer 3.0 appeared, Netscape Navigator 3.0 was released. Actually, not that much had changed from a scripting perspective in Netscape Navigator 3.0; more properties, methods, and events had been added to some browser objects. However, one change was to have far-reaching consequences for JavaScript: The `Image` object appeared.

The `Image` object itself was originally no great shakes—it just supported properties for the various attributes of `<IMG>` elements, and those properties were all read-only—with one exception: You could change the `SRC` attribute of the image at runtime. That meant you could swap the image displayed under script control, and that simple way of making web pages come alive has done a lot for JavaScript's reputation.

When the mouse rolled over an image, that image could suddenly change; when the mouse left the image, it could be restored, and the result was that web pages looked a lot more active. This wasn't something you could do with a roundtrip to the server—this had to be done in the browser itself, which meant using scripts.

Unfortunately, Internet Explorer 3.0 didn't support this property, and the cross-browser issues we face today got started then. Programmers had to start adding code to check which browser they were working in to avoid errors, and they didn't like it.

NS4 Extensions

In many ways, Netscape still had the upper hand in innovation in those days, and when Netscape Navigator 4.0 was released, that was truer than ever.

This browser gave you more control over creating and sizing new browser windows (something that users viewing pop-up ads may regret even to this day). It also gave programmers new power in two particular areas: event handling and layers.

Although event handling had existed before, Netscape Navigator 4.0 introduced more power and complexity by letting objects capture events. Keyboard and mouse events were added. In the Netscape Navigator, events started at the top of the object hierarchy and propagated downward to the actual cause of the event—for example, if a button was clicked, the event would move down through the `window`, `document`, and so on objects to eventually reach the button. You could now use the `window` or `document` (or `layer`, coming up next) `captureEvents` method to capture those events and so centralize event handling instead of having to handle such events in the objects that created them. To stop capturing events, you used the `releaseEvents` method.

Netscape Navigator 4.0 also introduced *layers*, a Netscape innovation that, although still supported, is no longer in widespread use. Layers let you "layer" your web page content, enabling you to move objects in different layers at runtime.

Layers were supported with the <LAYER> element, and the document object got a new array—now called a *collection*—the document.layers array, which held all the layers in the document. Layers had various properties and methods that let you move them. Each layer had its own document object, and you could access elements in a layer in any of one of these three ways:

```
document.layers[n].document.elementName
document.layersName.document.elementName
document.layers[layersName].document.elementName.
```

Layers introduced a major incompatibility between the Netscape Navigator and Internet Explorer—the Internet Explorer still does not support layers, and in fact, most of what you could do with layers is now commonly done with style sheets. At the time, however, layers were quite an innovation, and eagerly received by the JavaScript community. We'll see more on layers in Chapter 16, "Dynamic HTML: Changing Web Pages On-the-Fly." (Note that Netscape Navigator 6 no longer supports layers; their function has largely been taken over by style properties).

IE4 Extensions

Next came Internet Explorer 4.0, a major release for JavaScript programmers. The biggest change here was that all HTML elements could now be scripted, and all HTML elements now supported properties and methods available to JavaScript. This gave JavaScript programmers the most control over their web pages yet.

To access the elements in a web page without having to specify all the intervening objects (for example, document.forms[0].textField1), Microsoft introduced the all collection, which is a collection of all contained HTML elements. For example, if an element had the ID or name (as set with its ID or NAME attribute) textField1, you could then access that element as document.all.textField1. All you needed to know was an element's ID or name, and you had direct access to it. (See "Accessing HTML Elements" later in this chapter for the various ways to access elements using the all collection.)

The all collection was one way to make your page entirely scriptable; another was to give all elements their own properties (such as tagName, parentElement, offsetLeft, and offsetTop) and methods (such as scrollIntoView, setAttribute, and getAttribute). We'll see which elements and methods are supported by which HTML element in detail in the next two chapters.

Dynamic HTML also got a boost here, because Internet Explorer 4.0 introduced the innerText, outerText, innerHTML, outerHTML, `insertAdjacentHTML`, and `insertAdjacentText` properties and methods we'll see in Chapter 16; these enable you to change the content of individual HTML elements on-the-fly.

Cascading Style Sheets also got their start here with the `style` property. Now you could access individual style properties like this: `document.all.ID.style.styleProperty`, as discussed in Chapter 21, "Cascading Style Sheets and CGI Programming."

The Internet Explorer 4.0 also introduced a new event capture model: *event bubbling*. The Netscape Navigator event capture model had events moving downward from the topmost level, but the Internet Explorer has events moving upward, or "bubbling," from the object that caused the event up to the `window` object. And whereas Netscape event objects are passed to you in event handlers, Internet Explorer event objects are part of the `window` object. As we'll see in Chapter 6, "Using Core HTML Methods and Events," these conflicting event models are the cause of not a few headaches. (Note that these event models conflict when you start to capture events—they're still compatible at the basic level of adding a `click` event handler to a button using the `ONCLICK` event attribute.)

In addition, you could now bind scripts to specific elements using the new `FOR` and `EVENT` attributes of the `<SCRIPT>` element; we've already seen these attributes at work in Chapter 1.

Internet Explorer 4.0 also contained new features for Windows only, such as filters and transitions, which enable you to support impressive visual effects, as discussed in Chapter 16.

All in all, Internet Explorer 4.0 was a huge new release for scripting programmers. However, there was more to come.

IE5 Extensions

Microsoft introduced Internet Explorer 5 and then 5.5; from a scripting point of view, the big news was that these two browsers started to support the W3C DOM, although the support was only partial—see the next section to continue the W3C DOM story.

The other big news in Internet Explorer 5 and 5.5 was Internet Explorer *behaviors* and *HTML applications*, which we'll meet in Chapter 17, "Dynamic HTML: Drag and Drop, Data Binding, and Behaviors." A *behavior* is a customized script you can save as an external file that can be applied to any HTML element and that has access to some powerful techniques, such as blurring or highlighting elements. HTML applications are XML-based applications that you can download and initialize automatically.

The idea with behaviors and HTML applications was that Microsoft wanted to start separating data from code, and to some extent this has been successful. However, the adoption of behaviors has been hampered by the fact that they're not easy to script, and they're supported only in the Internet Explorer.

In fact, both browser corporations had for some time been realizing that the browser wars weren't doing much good for either browser, and they had already turned to W3C to standardize the DOM. Although the W3C DOM started to be implemented in Internet Explorer 5.0, it wasn't until version 6.0 of both browsers that we really made progress in this regard.

Version 6 Extensions

The current crop of browsers is the version 6 generation. The big story here is that finally, the two browsers are working toward some level of shared support using the W3C DOM. Both the Netscape Navigator and Internet Explorer support the W3C DOM level 1—as well as their own proprietary object models.

So what is the W3C DOM? It's the object model meant to bring the browsers together—and, of course, much of it is totally different from what we've already seen. For that reason, I'll take a look at it in some detail now.

The W3C DOM

The current version of the W3C DOM is level 2, although the DOM level 3 is in the working draft stage. Here are the various DOM documents online, and a brief history of each:

- **W3C DOM Level 1** (www.w3.org/TR/REC-DOM-Level-1/). Appeared during the reign of Netscape Navigator 4.0 and Internet Explorer 4.0. This is very similar to the object model of Netscape Navigator 3.0—but there is no event model here at all. Both the Internet Explorer 6.0 and Netscape Navigator 6.0 support the W3C DOM level 1 substantially.

- **W3C DOM Level 2** (www.w3.org/TR/DOM-Level-2-Core/). Added event handling, methods of inspecting the structure of a document, XML, methods of handling text *ranges*, style sheets, and various style properties.

- **W3C DOM Level 3** (www.w3.org/TR/DOM-Level-3-Core/). Currently in working draft form, this level is still up in the air.

There is also an *unofficial* W3C DOM level 0, which is the same as DOM 0, the original object model for browsers. This means that the basic object hierarchy you see in Figure 4.1 is supported in W3C DOM–compatible browsers.

It's important to realize that the W3C DOM does not attempt to codify all that's in the browser object models now—far from it. In fact, the first level W3C DOM didn't even have an event model. Layers are not part of the W3C DOM, and literally thousands of Internet Explorer objects, properties, methods, and events are left out. Also not supported: the `all` collection. Instead of using the `all` collection to address elements, you use a new method, `getElementById`. The Dynamic HTML properties `innerHTML`, `outerHTML`, `innerText`, and `outerText` are missing as well. Some properties that had been part of the `document` object (`alinkColor`, `bgColor`, `linkColor`, and `vlinkColor`) are part of the `body` object (which you access as `document.body`).

In fact, the W3C DOM is *literally* a document object model—it concerns itself only with the `document` object and the objects that are part of the document, such as the `body` object (although that may change in level 3). The `window`, `navigator`, and other such objects are not a significant part of the W3C DOM yet.

In addition, the W3C DOM adheres to HTML 4.01 (`www.w3.org/TR/html401`), which introduces some new HTML-authoring practices if you want to use W3C DOM capabilities. The biggest issue here is that, like XML, each HTML element must have both an opening and a closing tag. Earlier, you didn't have to use closing tags with many elements (such as `<P>`, `<IMG>`, `<LI>`, and so on), but to adhere to the HTML 4.01 specification, you should include a closing tag for each element. Also, HTML attribute values are all supposed to be enclosed in quotation marks now (like this: `<IMG SRC="image1.jpg">`).

In addition, several popular elements, such as `<CENTER>`, have been omitted from the HTML 4.01 specification. (In the case of `<CENTER>`, you can often use the style attributes of various elements instead, or use a `<DIV>` element and specify center justification in the `<DIV>` element's style properties—more on styles in Chapter 21.) Also, HTML 4.01, and the W3C DOM, emphasizes the `ID` attribute over the `NAME` attribute. (You can give an element both an ID and a name at the same time, because much server-side code still relies on names, not ID2s.)

Therefore, to identify your HTML elements, you use the `ID` attribute in the W3C DOM, not the `NAME` attribute. Instead of accessing such elements with the `all` collection, in the W3C DOM, you use the `getElementById` method. If you have a paragraph, created with a `<P>` element named paragraph1 (that is, `<P NAME="paragraph1"...>`), for example, you could reference it as `document.all.paragraph1` using the `all` collection. However, now you use `document.getElementById(paragraph1)`, where you've given the paragraph the ID paragraph1 (that is, `<P ID="paragraph1"...>`). The older way of accessing elements in a form, such as `document.forms[0].`*name* or `document.`*form1*`.name`, that we've already seen (and will see again in "Accessing HTML Elements" in this chapter) also still works.

TIP

Note that the `getElementById` method ends with a lower case *d*—many people type in `getElementByID` and can't understand why that doesn't work.

In fact, the whole way you think about an HTML document is different in the W3C DOM, and that bears some examination.

W3C DOM Nodes

The W3C DOM makes the elements available in both XML and HTML documents more accessible from scripts, but doing so introduces some more terminology for us. To define the structure of a web page, W3C introduces the concept of a *node*. For example, an HTML element is a node, the text content of an HTML element is a node, an element's attributes are all nodes, and so on. There are 12 node types defined for XML and HTML, but only 7 apply to HTML documents. You'll find them in Table 4.2. (All of these node types are supported in version 6.0 of the two browsers with which we're working.)

Table 4.2   **W3C DOM HTML Node Types**

Type	Number	*nodeName*	*nodeValue*	Means
Element	1	Tag's name	–	An HTML element
Attribute	2	name	attribute	An HTML attribute
Text	3	#text	text	Simple text
Comment	8	#comment	comment	An HTML comment
Document	9	#document	–	The document object
DocumentType	10	DOCTYPE	–	The Document Type Declaration (DTD)
Fragment	11	#document	–	One or more nodes making up a document fragment

Here's an example—take this short web page:

```
<HTML>
    <HEAD>
        <TITLE>
            Welcome to My Web Page
        </TITLE>
    </HEAD>

    <BODY ID="body1">
        <P ID="paragraph1">
            Welcome to my
            <I>
                terrific
            </I>
                Web page!
        </P>
    </BODY>
</HTML>
```

You can see this web page in Figure 4.2.

Figure 4.2   A short web page.

Rather than a haphazard collection of elements, the W3C DOM sees this page as a hierarchy of element, attribute, and text nodes. In particular, starting from the document node, first comes the <HTML> element node, then the <HEAD> element node, the <TITLE> element node, which itself encloses a text node that contains the text "Welcome to My Web Page", and so on. Here's the page's structure in node terms:

```
document
|___<HTML>
    |__<HEAD>
    |     |__<TITLE>
    |     |     |__"Welcome to My Web Page"
    |__<BODY ID="body1">
          |__<P ID="paragraph1">
                |__"Welcome to my"
                |__<I>
                |    |__"terrific"
                |__"Web page!"
```

In fact, the situation is even a little more complex than this, because in the W3C DOM, even the whitespace (spaces and/or tabs) used to indent this HTML document is counted as a text node. That means that all whitespace between element tags (not between an element tag and any text content of the element, because that whitespace is merged with the text content of the element) is technically considered a text node. Here's what this document looks like in node form if you include the whitespace text nodes:

```
document
|___<HTML>
    |__*whitespace text node*
    |__<HEAD>
    |     |__*whitespace text node*
    |     |__<TITLE>
    |     |     |__"Welcome to My Web Page"
    |     |__*whitespace text node*
    |__*whitespace text node*
    |__<BODY ID="body1">
          |__*whitespace text node*
          |__<P ID="paragraph1">
                |__"Welcome to my"
                |__<I>
                |    |__"terrific"
                |__"Web page!"
                |__*whitespace text node*
```

To make matters more confusing, the Internet Explorer currently ignores these whitespace nodes, whereas the Netscape Navigator treats them as bona-fide text nodes. We'll see more on this issue in the section "Accessing HTML Elements with the W3C DOM," later in this chapter.

W3C DOM Node Properties, Methods, and Events

To work with nodes, the W3C DOM includes new properties, methods, and event-handling techniques. You can see some of the properties shared by all nodes in W3C DOM level 2 in Table 4.3, and shared methods in Table 4.4.

(There are other properties and methods for specific nodes, as we'll see in the coming chapters.)

Table 4.3 **Common W3C DOM Level 2 Node Object Properties**

Property	Description
attributes	Array of attribute nodes
childNodes	Array of a node's child nodes
firstChild	Object reference to a node's first child node
lastChild	Object reference to a node's last child node
localName	Node name without the namespace part
nextSibling	Object reference to the next sibling node
nodeName	The name of the node
nodeType	The node number (see Table 4.2)
nodeValue	Content of the node
ownerDocument	Object reference to the node's containing document
parentNode	Object reference to node's parent node
previousSibling	Object reference to the previous sibling node

Table 4.4 **Common W3C DOM Level 2 Node Object Methods**

Method	Description
appendChild(node)	Adds a child node to the current node
cloneNode(deepClone)	Clones the current node, optionally including children
getAttributeNode(attrib)	Gets an attribute node
hasChildNodes()	Returns true if a node has child nodes
insertBefore(new ,refNode)	Inserts a child node before refNode
removeAttributeNode(attrib)	Removes an attribute node
removeChild(node)	Deletes a child node
replaceChild(newNode, oldNode)	Replaces an old node with a new node
setAttributeNode(attrib)	Sets an attribute node
swapNode(node)	Swaps a node with the current node

You can use the `nextSibling`, `lastChild`, `firstChild`, `parentNode`, and so on properties to navigate through an entire document, treated as a *node tree*. We'll see how to do this in "Accessing HTML Elements with the W3C DOM" in this chapter. Note that all this is added to the other ways that browsers enable you to access HTML elements—as of yet, no old way of accessing elements has been removed from the browsers in favor of doing things the W3C DOM way.

The W3C DOM also introduces a new way of handling events that we'll see in Chapter 6: using *event listeners*. Event listeners were introduced in Java earlier, and the W3C has followed that lead; a listener is an object that you can use to "listen" for particular types of events. For example, a `click` listener will listen for and handle `click` events.

To make a listener listen for an event, you use the `addEventListener` method of a node that can handle events. Because you specifically tailor how the event is handled and what nodes to add listeners to, you can configure your own event-handling model, whether you want to follow the traditional Netscape top-down or the Internet Explorer bubble-up model, or create your own custom model. More on handling events this way in Chapter 6.

By standardizing how you access elements in a web page, as well as the names of properties and method, the W3C DOM is intended to bring some sanity to the browser wars. However, it's an evolving standard, and currently, it covers only a relatively small part of the whole picture, focusing on the document object—and just a part of that object at that.

That provides us with an overview of what's going on in the W3C DOM; the primary innovation so far has been the introduction of the node model and event listeners. We'll see more on the W3C DOM throughout the book, as we cover the various HTML elements that support the W3C DOM properties and methods, as well as the standard properties and methods.

Now I'll turn back to the big picture, as we take a look at the various browser objects available to us in the browsers we're working with—the `navigator`, `window`, `document`, and other objects. I'll take a look at all of these objects in overview, because we'll be covering them all in depth in the upcoming chapters.

The *navigator* Object

The `navigator` object refers to the browser itself, enabling you to determine what browser the user has. In fact, we've already used the `navigator` object's `appName`, `appVersion`, and `userAgent` properties as far back as Chapter 1, with this script:

(Listing 04-01.html on the web site)

```
<HTML>
    <HEAD>
        <TITLE>
            Checking Your Browser Type
        </TITLE>
    </HEAD>

    <BODY>
        <SCRIPT LANGUAGE="JavaScript">
            document.write("navigator.appName: " + navigator.appName)
            document.write("<BR><BR>")
            document.write("navigator.appVersion: " + navigator.appVersion)
            document.write("<BR><BR>")
            document.write("navigator.userAgent: " + navigator.userAgent)
        </SCRIPT>

        <H1>Checking Your Browser Type</H1>
    </BODY>
</HTML>
```

You can see the results in Figure 4.3. The navigator object is often a very useful one in cross-browser programming, and we'll use it for that purpose in this chapter.

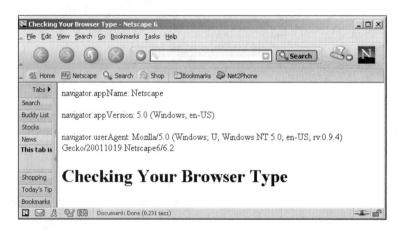

Figure 4.3 Determining browser type.

You'll find the properties and methods of the navigator object in Table 4.5; it has no events. Not all properties and methods will be supported in all browsers, of course. We'll get the full breakdown on browser version for each property and method in Chapter 10, "Using the *navigator*, *location*, and *history* Objects."

Table 4.5 **The Properties and Methods of the *navigator* Object**

Properties	Methods
appCodeName	javaEnabled
appMinorVersion	preference
appName	taintEnabled
appVersion	
browserLanguage	
cookieEnabled	
cpuClass	
language	
mimeTypes	
onLine	
oscpu	
platform	
plugins	
product	
productSub	
securityPolicy	
systemLanguage	
userAgent	
userLanguage	
userProfile	
vendor	
vendorSub	

The *window* Object

The window object is the big cheese object in the browser object model, and it contains other objects, such as the document object, the location object, and others. The window object refers to the current browser window, and it's got plenty of useful built-in methods, such as alert, which displays a new alert dialog box, and open, which opens a new browser window.

We've already seen the alert method in action, so here's an example putting the open method to work—when the user clicks a button here, a new browser window will open; when the user clicks the other button, the new window will close:

(Listing 04-02.html on the web site)

```
<HTML>
    <HEAD>
        <TITLE>Opening and Closing a Window</TITLE>
        <SCRIPT LANGUAGE="JavaScript">
            <!--
            var window1
            function openWindow()
            {
                window1 = window.open("", "", "HEIGHT=200,WIDTH=400")
            }

            function closeWindow()
            {
                window1.close()
            }
            // -->
        </SCRIPT>
    </HEAD>

    <BODY>
        <H1>Opening and Closing a Window</H1>
        <FORM>
            <INPUT TYPE="BUTTON" VALUE="Open a window"
                ONCLICK="openWindow()">
            <INPUT TYPE="BUTTON" VALUE="Close the window"
                ONCLICK="closeWindow()">
        </FORM>
    </BODY>
</HTML>
```

You can see the results of this code in Figure 4.4, where I've opened a new window. We'll see more on the open method in Chapter 8, "Using *window* and *frame* Methods and Events."

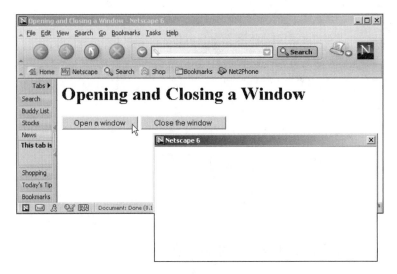

Figure 4.4   Opening a new browser window.

The `window.status` object also gives you access to the browser's status bar (which appears at the bottom of the browser), something that's very popular with JavaScript programmers. Here's an example—in this case, I'm displaying `Hello!` when the mouse rolls over a hyperlink, and `Good Bye!` when it leaves the hyperlink (the JavaScript functions called here must return a value of true, as we'll see when we cover the `window` object in Chapter 7, "Using *window* and *frame* Properties," and in Chapter 8, or the browser will just display the URL of the hyperlink—its default behavior, in this case):

(Listing 04-03.html on the web site)

```
<HTML>
    <HEAD>
        <TITLE>Using the Status Bar</TITLE>
        <SCRIPT LANGUAGE="JavaScript">
            <!--
            function sayHello() {
                window.status = "Hello!"
                return true
            }
            function sayGoodBye() {
                window.status = "Good Bye!"
                return true
            }
            // -->
        </SCRIPT>
    </HEAD>
```

continues ▶

```
<BODY>
    <H1>Using the Status Bar</H1>
    <A HREF="http://www.starpowder.com"
        onMouseOver="return sayHello()"
        onMouseOut="return sayGoodBye()">Here's my site!</A><P>
</BODY>
</HTML>
```

You can see the results of this code in Figure 4.5.

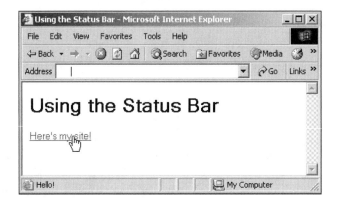

Figure 4.5   Using a browser's status bar.

You'll find the properties, methods, and events of the window object in Table 4.6. Not all properties, methods, and events will be supported in all browsers, of course. We'll get the full story on browser version for each property, method, and event of the window object in Chapters 7 and 8.

Table 4.6   **The Properties, Methods, and Events of the *window* Object**

Properties	Methods	Events
appCore	alert	onactivate
clientInformation	attachEvent	onafterprint
clipboardData	back	onbeforedeactivate
closed	blur	onbeforeprint
Components	captureEvents	onbeforeunload
controllers	clearInterval	onblur
crypto	clearTimeout	oncontrolselect
defaultStatus	close	ondeactivate
dialogArguments	confirm	onerror
dialogHeight	createPopup	onfocus
dialogLeft	detachEvent	onhelp

Properties	Methods	Events
dialogTop	disableExternalCapture	onload
dialogWidth	enableExternalCapture	onmove
directories	execScript	onmoveend
document	find	onmovestart
event	fireEvent	onresize
external	focus	onscroll
frameElement	forward	onunload
frames	getComputedStyle	
history	GetAttention	
innerHeight	handleEvent	
innerWidth	home	
length	moveBy	
loading	moveTo	
location	navigate	
locationbar	open	
menubar	print	
name	prompt	
navigator	releaseEvents	
offscreenBuffering	resizeBy	
opener	resizeTo	
outerHeight	routeEvent	
outerWidth	scroll	
pageXOffset	scrollBy	
pageYOffset	scrollByLines	
parent	scrollByPages	
personalbar	scrollTo	
pkcs11	setActive	
prompter	setCursor	
returnValue	setInterval	
screen	setTimeout	
screenLeft	showHelp	
screenTop	showModalDialog	
screenX	showModelessDialog	
screenY	sizeToContent	

continues ▶

Table 4.6   **Continued**

Properties	Methods	Events
scrollbars	stop	
scrollX		
scrollY		
self		
sidebar		
status		
statusbar		
toolbar		
top		
window		

The *document* Object

The document object is already a favorite of ours. This object corresponds to the current web page's body and some parts of the head. Using this object, you have access to the HTML of the page itself, including all the links, images, and anchors in it.

From a scripting point of view, the most popular document object method is document.write, which we've already seen, as in this example from Chapter 1, which wrote text to a web page:

```
<HTML>
    <HEAD>
        <TITLE>Our first script!</TITLE>
    </HEAD>

    <BODY>
        <H1>Here we go!</H1>
        <SCRIPT LANGUAGE="JavaScript">
        <!--
        document.write("Hello from JavaScript!")
        // -->
        </SCRIPT>
    </BODY>
</HTML>
```

You'll find the properties, methods, and events of the document object in Table 4.7. As before, not all properties, methods, and events will be supported in all browsers. We'll get all the details on browser version for each property, method, and event in Chapter 9, "Using the *document* and *body* Objects."

Table 4.7   **The Properties, Methods, and Events of the *document* Object**

Properties	Methods	Events
activeElement	attachEvent	onactivate
alinkColor	captureEvents	onbeforeactivate
all	clear	onbeforecut
anchors	clearAttributes	onbeforedeactivate
applets	close	onbeforeeditfocus
attributes	createAttribute	onbeforepaste
bgColor	createComment	onclick
body	createDocumentFragment	oncontextmenu
charset	createElement	oncontrolselect
characterSet	createEventObject	oncut
childNodes	createRange	ondblclick
cookie	createStyleSheet	ondeactivate
defaultCharset	createTextNode	ondrag
designMode	detachEvent	ondragend
doctype	elementFromPoint	ondragenter
documentElement	execCommand	ondragleave
domain	focus	ondragover
embeds	getElementById	ondragstart
expando	getElementsByName	ondrop
fgColor	getElementsByTagName	onfocusin
fileCreatedDate	getSelection	onfocusout
fileModifiedDate	handleEvent	onhelp
fileSize	hasFocus	onkeydown
firstChild	mergeAttributes	onkeypress
forms	open	onkeyup
frames	queryCommandEnabled	onmousedown
height	queryCommandIndeterm	onmousemove
ids	queryCommandState	onmouseout
images	queryCommandSupported	onmouseover
implementation	queryCommandValue	onmouseup
lastChild	recalc	onmousewheel
lastModified	releaseCapture	onpaste

continues ▶

Table 4.7 **Continued**

Properties	Methods	Events
layers	releaseEvents	onpropertychange
linkColor	routeEvent	onreadystatechange
links	setActive	onresizeend
location	write	onresizestart
mimeType	writeln	onselectionchange
namespaces		onstop
namespaceURI		
nextSibling		
nodeName		
nodeType		
ownerDocument		
parentNode		
parentWindow		
plugins		
previousSibling		
protocol		
readyState		
referrer		
scripts		
security		
selection		
styleSheets		
tags		
title		
uniqueID		
URL		
URLUnencoded		
vlinkColor		
width		

Tip

You might wonder about the documentElement property of the document object you see in Table 4.7; this property returns a reference to the <HTML> element at the very top of the document.

The *form* Object

You enclose HTML controls such as buttons, text fields, check boxes, and so on in *forms* in order to connect them to JavaScript functions. Form objects, supported by the <FORM> element, correspond to form objects in JavaScript.

We've already seen the form object at work; you use it to access the controls inside the form, as in this example that evaluated JavaScript expressions in the preceding chapter using the forms collection—an array of form objects—in the document object (you can see this code at work in Figure 3.15):

(Listing 04-04.html on the web site)

```
<HTML>
    <HEAD>
        <TITLE>
            Using the eval Function
        </TITLE>
        <SCRIPT LANGUAGE="JavaScript">
            <!--
            function evaluator()
            {
                document.forms[0].result.value
                    = eval(document.forms[0].expression.value)
            }
            // -->
        </SCRIPT>
    </HEAD>

    <BODY>
        <H1>Using the eval Function</H1>
        <FORM>
            <INPUT TYPE="TEXT" NAME="expression">
            <INPUT TYPE="BUTTON" ONCLICK="evaluator()" VALUE="  =  ">
            <INPUT TYPE="TEXT" NAME="result">
        </FORM>
    </BODY>
</HTML>
```

You'll find the properties, methods, and events of the form object in Table 4.8. We'll get all the details on browser version for each property, method, and event in Chapter 12, "Working with Forms, Buttons, Check Boxes, and Radio Buttons."

Table 4.8 **The Properties, Methods, and Events of the *form* Object**

Properties	Methods	Events
acceptCharset	addBehavior	onactivate
action	appendChild	onbeforeactivate
all	applyElement	onbeforecopy
attributes	attachEvent	onbeforecut
autocomplete	blur	onbeforedeactivate
begin	clearAttributes	onbeforeeditfocus
blockDirection	click	onbeforepaste
behaviorUrns	cloneNode	onblur
canHaveChildren	componentFromPoint	onclick
canHaveHTML	contains	oncontextmenu
childNodes	detachEvent	oncontrolselect
children	dragDrop	oncopy
className	fireEvent	oncut
clientHeight	focus	ondblclick
clientLeft	getAdjacentText	ondeactivate
clientTop	getAttribute	ondrag
clientWidth	getAttributeNode	ondragend
contentEditable	getBoundingClientRect	ondragenter
dir	getClientRects	ondragleave
disabled	getElementsByTagName	ondragover
disabled	getExpression	ondragstart
elements	hasChildNodes	ondrop
encoding	insertAdjacentElement	onfocus
enctype	insertAdjacentHTML	onfocusin
end	insertAdjacentText	onfocusout
firstChild	insertBefore	onhelp
hasMedia	item	onkeydown
hideFocus	mergeAttributes	onkeypress
id	namedItem	onkeyup
innerHTML	normalize	onlosecapture
innerText	releaseCapture	onmousedown
isContentEditable	removeAttribute	onmouseenter

Properties	Methods	Events
isDisabled	removeAttributeNode	onmouseleave
isMultiLine	removeBehavior	onmousemove
isTextEdit	removeChild	onmouseout
lang	removeExpression	onmouseover
language	removeNode	onmouseup
lastChild	replaceAdjacentText	onmousewheel
length	replaceChild	onmove
method	replaceNode	onmoveend
name	reset	onmovestart
nextSibling	scrollIntoView	onpaste
nodeName	setActive	onpropertychange
nodeType	setAttribute	onreadystatechange
nodeValue	setAttributeNode	onreset
offsetHeight	setCapture	onresize
offsetLeft	setExpression	onresizeend
offsetParent	submit	onresizestart
offsetTop	swapNode	onselectstart
offsetWidth	urns	onsubmit
onOffBehavior		ontimeerror
outerHTML		
outerText		
ownerDocument		
parentElement		
parentNode		
parentTextEdit		
previousSibling		
readyState		
scopeName		
scrollHeight		
scrollLeft		
scrollTop		
scrollWidth		
sourceIndex		

continues ▶

Table 4.8 **Continued**

Properties	Methods	Events
syncMaster		
tabIndex		
tagName		
tagUrn		
target		
timeContainer		
title		
uniqueID		

The *history* Object

The history object holds the record of the sites the web browser has visited before reaching the current page. It gives you access to methods that enable you to move back to previous pages.

Here's an example putting the history object to work. In this case, I'll use this object's back, forward, and go methods to navigate forward and backward in the browser's history, letting the user navigate one or two pages forward or backward (to navigate more than one page at a time, you use the go method):

(Listing 04-05.html on the web site)

```
<HTML>
    <HEAD>
        <TITLE>Using the history object</TITLE>
        <SCRIPT LANGUAGE="JavaScript">
            <!--
            function back()
            {
                window.history.back()
            }
            function forward()
            {
                window.history.forward()
            }
            function back2()
            {
                window.history.go(-2)
            }
            function forward2()
            {
                window.history.go(2)
            }
```

```
        // -->
    </SCRIPT>
    </HEAD>

    <BODY>
        <H1>Using the history object</H1>
        <FORM>
            <BR>
            Click a button to go forward or back one page:
            <BR>
            <INPUT TYPE = BUTTON VALUE = "< Go back" ONCLICK = "back()">
            <INPUT TYPE = BUTTON VALUE = "Go forward >" ONCLICK = "forward()">
            <BR>
            <BR>
            Click a button to go forward or back two pages:
            <BR>
            <INPUT TYPE = BUTTON VALUE = "<< Go back 2" ONCLICK = "back2()">
            <INPUT TYPE = BUTTON VALUE = "Go forward 2 >>" ONCLICK = "forward2()">
        </FORM>
    </BODY>
</HTML>
```

You can see this code at work in Figure 4.6—simply clicking the buttons is just like clicking the browser's forward and back buttons, except that we're offering the user the option of moving two pages in either direction as well.

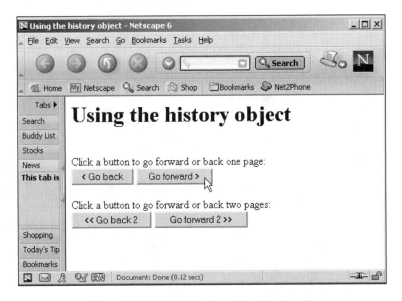

Figure 4.6 Navigating forward and backward.

You'll find the properties and methods (there are no events) of the `history` object in Table 4.9. We'll get all the details on browser version for each property, method, and event in Chapter 10.

Table 4.9   **The Properties and Methods of the *history* Object**

Properties	Methods
current	back
length	forward
next	go
previous	

The *location* Object

The `location` object holds information about the location of the current web page, such as its URL, the domain name, path, server port, and more. This object is part of the `window` object, and you can navigate to a new URL just by assigning that URL to the `location` object's `href` property (or, in most browsers, to the `location` object itself). Here's an example; in this case, we'll let the user enter a URL and make the browser navigate to that URL when the user clicks a button:

(Listing 04-06.html on the web site)

```
<HTML>
    <HEAD>
        <TITLE>
            Navigate to a URL
        </TITLE>
        <SCRIPT LANGUAGE = "JavaScript">
            <!--
            function Jump()
            {
                window.location.href = document.form1.text1.value
            }
            // -->
        </SCRIPT>
    </HEAD>

    <BODY>
        <H1>Navigate to a URL</H1>
        <FORM NAME = "form1">
            <BR>
            <INPUT TYPE = TEXT NAME="text1" SIZE = 80>
            <BR>
            <BR>
```

```
        <INPUT TYPE = BUTTON VALUE="Navigate to URL" ONCLICK="Jump()">
    </FORM>
  </BODY>
</HTML>
```

You can see this script at work in Figure 4.7.

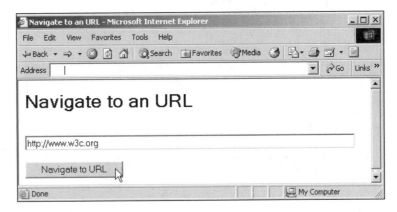

Figure 4.7   Navigating to an URL.

You'll find the properties and methods (there are no events) of the `location` object in Table 4.10. We'll get all the details on browser version for each property, method, and event in Chapter 10.

Table 4.10   **The Properties and Methods of the *location* Object**

Properties	Methods
hash	assign
host	reload
hostname	replace
href	
pathname	
port	
protocol	
search	

Tip

The `location` object is a great one to use when you want to redirect a browser to a new site. We'll see more on this object in this chapter when we want to redirect a browser to various documents tailored by browser version.

HTML Elements

Since Internet Explorer 4.0, all HTML elements in a web page are regarded as browser objects as well, just like the others we've been discussing in this chapter. For example, we've already seen this code in this and the preceding chapter, where I'm treating a text field named `result` as an object, and using its `value` property to assign text to that text field (see Figure 3.15):

```
<HTML>
    <HEAD>
        <TITLE>
            Using the eval Function
        </TITLE>
        <SCRIPT LANGUAGE="JavaScript">
            <!--
            function evaluator()
            {
                document.forms[0].result.value
                    = eval(document.forms[0].expression.value)
            }
            // -->
        </SCRIPT>
    </HEAD>

    <BODY>
        <H1>Using the eval Function</H1>
        <FORM>
            <INPUT TYPE="TEXT" NAME="expression">
            <INPUT TYPE="BUTTON" ONCLICK="evaluator()" VALUE="  =  ">
            <INPUT TYPE="TEXT" NAME="result">
        </FORM>
    </BODY>
</HTML>
```

Treating all HTML elements as objects makes for an immense number of new objects, all with their own properties, methods, and events. You can see all the elements supported in HTML 4.01, and what they do, in Table 4.11.

Table 4.11 **The HTML 4.10 Elements**

Element	Means
`<!-->`	Comments and server-side includes
`<!DOCTYPE>`	Starting an HTML page
`<A>`	Creating a hyperlink or anchor
`<ABBR>`	Displaying abbreviations
`<ACRONYM>`	Displaying acronyms
`<ADDRESS>`	Displaying an address

Element	Means
`<APPLET>`	Embedding applets in web pages
`<AREA>`	Creating clickable regions in image maps
`<B>`	Creating bold text
`<BASE>`	Setting the base for hyperlinks
`<BASEFONT>`	Setting the base font
`<BDO>`	Overriding the bidirectional character algorithm
`<BGSOUND>`	Adding background sounds
`<BIG>`	Creating big text
`<BLINK>`	Making text blink
`<BLOCKQUOTE>`	Indenting quotations
`<BODY>`	Creating a web page's body
` `	Inserting line breaks
`<BUTTON>`	Creating a customizable button
`<CAPTION>`	Creating a table caption
`<CENTER>`	Centering text
`<CITE>`	Creating a citation
`<CODE>`	Displaying program code
`<COL>`	Defining a column
`<COLGROUP>`	Grouping and formatting columns
`<DD>`	Creating definition list definitions
`<DEL>`	Displaying text as deleted
`<DFN>`	Defining new terms
`<DIR>`	Deprecated list
`<DIV>`	Formatting block text
`<DL>`	Creating definition lists
`<DT>`	Creating definition list terms
`<EM>`	Emphasizing text
`<EMBED>`	Embedding multimedia and plug-ins in a web page
`<FIELDSET>`	Grouping form elements
`<FONT>`	Specifying a font
`<FORM>`	Creating HTML forms
`<FRAME>`	Creating frames
`<FRAMESET>`	Containing frames
`<H1>` through `<H6>`	Creating web page headings

continues ▶

Table 4.11 **Continued**

Element	Means
<HEAD>	Creating a web page's head
<HR>	Creating horizontal rules
<HTML>	Starting an HTML page
<I>	Creating italic text
<IFRAME>	Creating inline or floating frames
<ILAYER>	Creating inline layers
<IMG>	Adding an image to a web page
<INPUT TYPE=BUTTON>	Creating buttons
<INPUT TYPE=CHECKBOX>	Creating check boxes
<INPUT TYPE=FILE>	Creating file input for a form
<INPUT TYPE=HIDDEN>	Creating hidden data
<INPUT TYPE=IMAGE>	Creating image submit buttons
<INPUT TYPE=PASSWORD>	Creating password controls
<INPUT TYPE=RADIO>	Creating radio buttons
<INPUT TYPE=RESET>	Creating reset buttons
<INPUT TYPE=SUBMIT>	Creating submit buttons
<INPUT TYPE=TEXT>	Creating text fields
<INS>	Displaying inserted text
<ISINDEX>	Using an index
<KBD>	Displaying text the user is to type
<KEYGEN>	Processing secure transactions
<LABEL>	Labeling form elements
<LAYER>	Arranging text in layers
<LEGEND>	Creating a legend for form elements
<LI>	Creating list items
<LINK>	Setting link information
<MAP>	Creating client-side image maps
<MARQUEE>	Displaying text in a scrolling marquee
<MENU>	Deprecated list
<META>	Giving more information about your web page
<MULTICOL>	Creating columns
<NOBR>	Avoiding line breaks

Element	Means
`<NOEMBED>`	Handling browsers that don't handle embedding
`<NOLAYER>`	Handling browsers that don't handle layers
`<NOSCRIPT>`	Handling browsers that don't handle JavaScript
`<OBJECT>`	Placing an object into a web page
`<OL>`	Creating ordered lists
`<OPTGROUP>`	Creating a select control item group
`<OPTION>`	Creating a select control item
`<P>`	Creating paragraphs
`<PARAM>`	Specifying a parameter
`<PRE>`	Displaying preformatted text
`<Q>`	Displaying short quotations
`<RT>`	Creating ruby text
`<RUBY>`	Creating rubies
`<S>` and `<STRIKE>`	Striking text out
`<SAMP>`	Displaying sample program output
`<SCRIPT>`	Creating a script
`<SELECT>`	Creating a select control
`<SERVER>`	Running server-side JavaScript scripts
`<SMALL>`	Creating small text
`<SPACER>`	Controlling horizontal and vertical spacing
`<SPAN>`	Formatting inline text
`<STRONG>`	Strongly emphasizing text
`<STYLE>`	Using embedded style sheets
`<SUB>`	Creating subscripts
`<SUP>`	Creating superscripts
`<TABLE>`	Creating a table
`<TBODY>`	Creating a table body when grouping rows
`<TD>`	Creating table data
`<TEXTAREA>`	Creating text areas
`<TFOOT>`	Creating a table foot when grouping rows
`<TH>`	Creating table headings
`<THEAD>`	Creating a table head when grouping rows
`<TITLE>`	Giving a web page a title

continues ▶

Table 4.11 **Continued**

Element	Means
<TR>	Creating a table row
<TT>	Creating "teletype" text
<U>	Underlining text
<UL>	Creating unordered lists
<VAR>	Displaying program variables and arguments
<WBR>	Allowing word breaks
<XML>	Accessing XML data with an XML data island

It would be very difficult to list and discuss all the properties, methods, and events for each of the many elements you see in Table 4.11 in this book, because we would be talking about well more than 10,000 different items. However, there's a great deal of overlap among these items, because all these HTML elements support what I'll call JavaScript's core set of HTML properties, methods, and events. You can find those core properties, methods, and events in Table 4.12. We'll be covering them in the next two chapters (in fact, there are some exceptions to the core properties, methods, and events in Table 4.12—some HTML elements don't support some of these properties, methods and events, and I'll note them on a case-by-case basis in the next two chapters).

Table 4.12 **Core HTML Properties, Methods, and Events**

Properties	Methods	Events
accessKey	addBehavior	onactivate
all	addEventListener	onbeforeactivate
attributes	appendChild	onbeforecopy
begin	applyElement	onbeforecut
behaviorUrns	attachEvent	onbeforedeactivate
canHaveChildren	blur	onbeforeeditfocus
canHaveHTML	clearAttributes	onbeforepaste
childNodes	click	onblur
children	cloneNode	onclick
className	componentFromPoint	oncontextmenu
clientHeight	contains	oncontrolselect
clientLeft	detachEvent	oncopy

Properties	Methods	Events
clientTop	dispatchEvent	oncut
clientWidth	dragDrop	ondblclick
contentEditable	fireEvent	ondeactivate
currentStyle	focus	ondrag
dataFld	getAdjacentText	ondragend
dataFormatAs	getAttribute	ondragenter
dataSrc	getAttributeNode	ondragleave
dir	getBoundingClientRect	ondragover
disabled	getClientRects	ondragstart
document	getElementsByTagName	ondrop
end	getExpression	onfilterchange
filters	hasChildNodes	onfocus
firstChild	insertAdjacentElement	onfocusin
hasMedia	insertAdjacentHTML	onfocusout
height	insertAdjacentText	onhelp
hideFocus	insertBefore	onkeydown
id	item	onkeypress
innerHTML	mergeAttributes	onkeyup
innerText	normalize	onlosecapture
isContentEditable	releaseCapture	onmousedown
isDisabled	removeAttribute	onmouseenter
isMultiLine	removeAttributeNode	onmouseleave
isTextEdit	removeBehavior	onmousemove
lang	removeChild	onmouseout
language	removeEventListener	onmouseover
lastChild	removeExpression	onmouseup
length	removeNode	onmousewheel
localName	replaceAdjacentText	onmove
namespaceURI	replaceChild	onmoveend
nextSibling	replaceNode	onmovestart
nodeName	scrollIntoView	onpaste
nodeType	setActive	onpropertychange
nodeValue	setAttribute	onreadystatechange

continues ▶

Table 4.12 **Continued**

Properties	Methods	Events
offsetHeight	setAttributeNode	onresize
offsetLeft	setCapture	onresizeend
offsetParent	setExpression	onresizestart
offsetTop	supports	onselectstart
offsetWidth	swapNode	ontimeerror
onOffBehavior	tags	
outerHTML	urns	
outerText		
ownerDocument		
parentElement		
parentNode		
parentTextEdit		
prefix		
previousSibling		
readyState		
recordNumber		
runtimeStyle		
scopeName		
scrollHeight		
scrollLeft		
scrollTop		
scrollWidth		
sourceIndex		
style		
syncMaster		
tabIndex		
tagName		

Cross-Browser Programming

As we've discussed, if you're programming for general users, the different levels of JavaScript and the various DOMs can make life difficult. In this chapter on the browser environment, therefore, I'll discuss the issue of cross-browser programming.

One solution to the problems of cross-browser programming is to use only those capabilities available in DOM level 0 (see Figure 4.1) and JavaScript 1.0. This means that, although you're restricted in what you can do (remember, for example, that even mouse rollover image-swapping wasn't supported in DOM 0), at least your script will run in all scriptable browsers (and you can use the <NOSCRIPT> element to handle nonscriptable browsers—see the discussion of <NOSCRIPT> in Chapter 1).

The next option is to detect the capabilities of the browser you're working with when your script executes; there are two main ways to do that: detecting version information and object detection. I'll take a look at detecting version information first.

Tip

You also can use the LANGUAGE attribute of the <SCRIPT> element; but of course, the version information varies between JavaScript and JScript, and that information still tells you nothing about the DOM for the browser.

Version Detection

In this book, I've listed the browser and version that each language element, each property, method, and event is supported in, which means that if you want to use a specific item, you know whether it'll work in a particular browser—if you know what the browser's version is. To determine the browser's version, you can use the appName and userAgent properties of the navigator object. This object also has a userVersion property, but that will not return correct version information—as we saw in Figures 1.12 and 1.13, this property returns 4.0 for Internet Explorer 6.0 and returns 5.0 for Netscape Navigator 6.0. You can use appName to determine the browser you're working in, and search the userAgent property for the correct version information.

Here's a script designed to do just that, filling a variable named version with the (floating-point) version number of the browser—it's designed to work with all scriptable versions of the two browsers, from version 3.0 to 6.0 of the Internet Explorer and from version 2.0 to 6.2 of the Netscape Navigator, but there are no guarantees—some interim or beta versions or versions for little-supported operating systems may use a different format for the userAgent property. Here's the code (this code uses some string methods we'll see in Chapter 18, "The *Date*, *Time*, and *String* Objects," such as the substring method):

(Listing 04-07.html on the web site)

```html
<HTML>
    <HEAD>
        <TITLE>
            Getting Browser Version
        </TITLE>
    </HEAD>

    <BODY>
        <H1>Getting Browser Version</H1>
        <SCRIPT LANGUAGE="JavaScript">
            <!--
            var start, end, version
            if(navigator.appName == "Netscape") {
                if(navigator.userAgent.indexOf("Netscape") < 0) {
                    start = "Mozilla/".length
                    end = navigator.userAgent.indexOf(" ", start)
                    version = parseFloat(navigator.userAgent.substring(start, end))
                    document.write("You are using Netscape Navigator " + version)
                } else {
                    start = navigator.userAgent.indexOf("Netscape") +
                    "Netscape".length + 2
                    end = navigator.userAgent.length
                    version = parseFloat(navigator.userAgent.substring(start, end))
                    document.write("You are using Netscape Navigator " + version)
                }
            }

            if (navigator.appName == "Microsoft Internet Explorer") {
                start = navigator.userAgent.indexOf("MSIE ") + "MSIE ".length
                if(navigator.userAgent.indexOf(";", start) > 0) {
                    end = navigator.userAgent.indexOf(";", start)
                } else {
                    end = navigator.userAgent.indexOf(")", start)
                }
                version = parseFloat(navigator.userAgent.substring(start, end))
                document.write("You are using Internet Explorer " + version)
            }
            // -->
        </SCRIPT>
    </BODY>
</HTML>
```

You can see the results for the Internet Explorer in Figure 4.8 and for the Netscape Navigator in Figure 4.9.

Figure 4.8   Determining the Internet Explorer's version.

Figure 4.9   Determining the Netscape Navigator's version.

Using the information in this book, you can determine whether a particular item is supported in a browser, now that you know the browser's version. On the other hand, it's sometimes easier not to have to work with browser version, but use *object detection* instead.

Object Detection

Sometimes the best thing to do is to determine whether a particular object—or property, or method—is available before using it. Doing so can be easier than tracking down the information about version support that you need if you use version detection. To determine whether you're dealing with a browser that enables you to swap images (that is, with the DOM 0+Images model), for example, you can check whether the document.images collection exists before trying to use it, using an if statement. If it does exist, you can proceed with your code, resetting the SRC attribute of an image, something like this:

```
if (document.images){
    document.images[0].src = imageURL
}
```

Here's another example; if you want to determine whether you can use Cascading Style Sheets, you can check whether a particular element supports the STYLE HTML attribute by looking for that element's JavaScript style property, like this:

```
if (element1.style){
    element1.style.color = "red"
}
```

Here's another example—in this case, I'm checking for the all collection, for support for layers, and for the getElementById method in order to read the text from a text field:

(Listing 04-08.html on the web site)

```
<HTML>
    <HEAD>
        <TITLE>
            Using Object Detection
        </TITLE>
    </HEAD>

    <BODY>
        <H1>Using Object Detection</H1>
        <FORM NAME="form1">
            <INPUT TYPE=TEXT VALUE="Hello!" NAME="nameObject1" ID="idObject1">
        </FORM>
        <SCRIPT LANGUAGE="JavaScript">
            <!--
                var object1
                if (document.all){
                    object1 = document.all("iDobject1")
                } else if (document.getElementById) {
                    object1 = document.getElementById("idObject1")
```

```
        } else if (document.layers) {
            object1 = document.form1.nameObject1
        }

        if(object1){
            document.write(object1.value)
        }
    // -->
    </SCRIPT>
  </BODY>
</HTML>
```

You also can check for W3C DOM support by checking for W3C DOM properties, such as `documentElement` (which returns a reference to the `<HTML>` element in a web page):

```
var W3CSupport = (document.documentElement) ? true : false
```

In fact, you can determine browser and browser version using object detection using a series of `if` statements in order, like this:

```
if (document.characterSet){
    window.location.href = "NS6.html"
}

if (document.docType){
    window.location.href = "IE6.html"
}

if (document.documentElement)
    window.location.href = "IE5.html"
}

if (document.all)
    window.location.href = "IE4.html"
}

if (document.layers)
    window.location.href = "NS4.html"
}

if (document.images)
    window.location.href = "NS3.html"
}
```

Redirecting Browsers

Although it's possible to embed scripts for different browsers in a web page, you also can redirect browsers to entirely new pages, one for each browser. Here's an example that does that, by setting the window.location.href property; note also that it redirects other browsers—and browsers that don't support scripting—using a <META> element:

(Listing 04-09.html on the web site)

```
<HTML>
    <HEAD>
        <TITLE>Redirecting Browsers</TITLE>
        <SCRIPT LANGUAGE="JavaScript">
            <!--
            if (navigator.appName == "Microsoft Internet Explorer") {
                window.location.href = "IE.html"
            }
            if(navigator.appName == "Netscape") {
                window.location.href = "NS.html"
            }
            //-->
        </SCRIPT>
        <META HTTP-EQUIV="refresh" CONTENT="0; URL=default.html">
    </HEAD>

    <BODY>
        <H1>Redirecting Browsers</H1>
    </BODY>
</HTML>
```

Creating Objects Based on Browser Type

Here's another alternative to providing multiple pages for different browsers—you can use the eval function to create objects appropriate to a particular browser on-the-fly, just passing their names. We saw how this works in the preceding chapter, where we created an object reference to the document object:

```
<HTML>
    <HEAD>
        <TITLE>
            Using the eval Function
        </TITLE>
    </HEAD>

    <BODY>
        <H1>Using the eval Function</H1>
        <SCRIPT LANGUAGE="JavaScript">
            <!--
```

```
var obj = "document"
for (var property in eval(obj)) {
    document.write(property + ": " + document[property] + "<BR>")
}
// -->
</SCRIPT>
</BODY>
</HTML>
```

Using Script Libraries

Here's another alternative for cross-browser programming—you can use different script files, .js files, for different browsers and browser versions:

```
<SCRIPT LANGUAGE="JavaScript">
    <!--
    if (navigator.appName == "Microsoft Internet Explorer") {
        document.write("<SCRIPT LANGUAGE='JavaScript' SRC=='ie.js'></SCRIPT>")
    }
    if(navigator.appName == "Netscape") {
        document.write("<SCRIPT LANGUAGE='JavaScript' SRC=='ns.js'></SCRIPT>")
    }
    //-->
</SCRIPT>
```

We'll see more on cross-browser issues throughout the book, such as cross-browser event handling.

Accessing HTML Elements

In the previous couple of chapters, we dealt with the built-in JavaScript syntax. In this chapter, we started working with the browser objects available to you in JavaScript. The built-in objects (such as the window, document, and navigator objects) are always available to you in your code—but what about the HTML elements in a web page? In modern JavaScript, all those elements are treated as objects—how do you get access to them?

Let's start with an example; suppose that I want to access the tagName property of the <P> element in this page (this property will return P in this case):

```
<HTML>
    <HEAD>
        <TITLE>
            Accessing HTML Elements
        </TITLE>
    </HEAD>

    <BODY>
        <H1>Accessing HTML Elements</H1>
```

```
<P NAME="text1" ID="text1">
    Here's the text.
</P>
<FORM NAME="form1">
    <INPUT TYPE="BUTTON" VALUE="Click Me!" ONCLICK="getText()">
</FORM>
    </BODY>
</HTML>
```

Using the Netscape Navigator, I could access the <P> element with the getElementsByName or getElementsByTagName methods, both of which return an array of elements. To use these methods, I can pick out the element we're interested using an array index of 0 (because this <P> element is the first element in these arrays):

- document.getElementsByName("text1")[0].tagName

- document.getElementsByTagName("P")[0].tagName

Note that neither of these methods are available in Netscape Navigator before version 6.0—there's no direct way to access elements that are not part of a form before that version.

In the Internet Explorer, you also can use the all collection. As we've discussed, there's an element in the all collection for each HTML element in the page. Here are some ways to access the text in the text field in the Internet Explorer—note also that the all collection includes a tags method that you can use to locate elements (as discussed in Chapter 6):

- document.all.text1.tagName

- document.all["text1"].nodeValue

- document.all.tags("P")[0].tagName

- document.getElementsByName("text1")[0].tagName

- document.getElementsByTagName("P")[0].tagName

TIP

In fact, you can drop the document.all and just use text1.tagName.

TIP

Here's an important thing to know: If you're having trouble accessing an HTML element, it may be because the browser hasn't loaded it yet. In that case, put your script after the point where the HTML element you're trying to access appears in the web page (which may mean moving your script from the head section to the body section of a page).

Here's a web page that puts all these techniques to work (note that you'll need version 6+ if you're using Netscape Navigator):

(Listing 04-10.html on the web site)

```
<HTML>
    <HEAD>
        <TITLE>
            Accessing HTML Elements
        </TITLE>
        <SCRIPT LANGUAGE="JavaScript">
            <!--
            function getText()
            {
                if(navigator.appName == "Netscape") {
                alert("document.getElementsByName(\"text1\")[0].tagName= "
                    + document.getElementsByName("text1")[0].tagName)
                alert("document.getElementsByTagName(\"P\")[0].tagName= "
                    + document.getElementsByTagName("P")[0].tagName)
                }

                if (navigator.appName == "Microsoft Internet Explorer") {
                alert("document.all.text1.tagName = "
                    + document.all.text1.tagName)
                alert("document.all[\"text1\"].tagName = "
                    + document.all["text1"].tagName)
                alert("document.all.tags(\"P\").tagName = "
                    + document.all.tags("P")[0].tagName)
                alert("document.getElementsByName(\"text1\")[0].tagName = "
                    + document.getElementsByName("text1")[0].tagName)
                alert("document.getElementsByTagName(\"P\")[0].tagName = "
                    + document.getElementsByTagName("P")[0].tagName)
                }
            }
            // -->
        </SCRIPT>
    </HEAD>

    <BODY>
        <H1>Accessing HTML Elements</H1>
        <P NAME="text1" ID="text1">
            Here's the text.
        </P>
        <FORM NAME="form1">
            <INPUT TYPE="BUTTON" VALUE="Click Me!" ONCLICK="getText()">
        </FORM>
    </BODY>
</HTML>
```

Let's take a look at another example—this time, let's access an HTML control in a form. In this case, I'll discuss how to access the text in a text field (ID and NAME attributes set to "text1") embedded in a form named form1 in this web page:

```
<HTML>
    <HEAD>
        <TITLE>
            Accessing HTML Elements
        </TITLE>
    </HEAD>

    <BODY>
        <H1>Accessing HTML Elements</H1>
        <FORM NAME="form1">
            <INPUT TYPE="TEXT" NAME="text1" ID="text1">
            <INPUT TYPE="BUTTON" VALUE="Click Me!" ONCLICK="getText()">
        </FORM>
    </BODY>
</HTML>
```

The text in this text field is accessible using the text field's value property in JavaScript (which matches its VALUE HTML attribute). There are several ways to access that property; here are some examples in the Netscape Navigator—note that only the first two are available before version 6.0 of that browser:

- document.form1.text1.value
- document.forms[0].text1.value
- document.getElementsByName("text1")[0].value
- document.getElementsByTagName("INPUT")[0].value

In the Internet Explorer, you also can use the all collection, like this:

- document.form1.text1.value
- document.forms[0].text1.value
- document.all.text1.value
- document.all["text1"].value
- document.all.tags("INPUT")[0].value
- document.getElementsByName("text1")[0].value
- document.getElementsByTagName("INPUT")[0].value

Here's a web page putting these various access techniques to work (again, note that you'll need version 6+ if you're using Netscape Navigator):

(Listing 04-11.html on the web site)

```html
<HTML>
    <HEAD>
        <TITLE>
            Accessing HTML Elements
        </TITLE>
        <SCRIPT LANGUAGE="JavaScript">
            <!--
            function getText()
            {
                if(navigator.appName == "Netscape") {
                alert("document.form1.text1.value = " + document.form1.text1.value)
                alert("document.forms[0].text1.value = " +
                document.forms[0].text1.value)
                alert("document.getElementsByName(\"text1\")[0].value = "
                    + document.getElementsByName("text1")[0].value)
                alert("document.getElementsByTagName(\"INPUT\")[0].value = "
                    + document.getElementsByTagName("INPUT")[0].value)
                }

                if (navigator.appName == "Microsoft Internet Explorer") {
                alert("document.form1.text1.value = " + document.form1.text1.value)
                alert("document.forms[0].text1.value = "
                    + document.forms[0].text1.value)
                alert("document.all.text1.value = "
                    + document.all.text1.value)
                alert("document.all[\"text1\"].value = "
                    + document.all["text1"].value)
                alert("document.all.tags(\"INPUT\")[0].value = "
                    + document.all.tags("INPUT")[0].value)
                alert("document.getElementsByName(\"text1\")[0].value = "
                    + document.getElementsByName("text1")[0].value)
                alert("document.getElementsByTagName(\"INPUT\")[0].value = "
                    + document.getElementsByTagName("INPUT")[0].value)
                }
            }
            // -->
        </SCRIPT>
    </HEAD>

    <BODY>
        <H1>Accessing HTML Elements</H1>
        <FORM NAME="form1">
            <INPUT TYPE="TEXT" NAME="text1" ID="text1">
            <INPUT TYPE="BUTTON" VALUE="Click Me!" ONCLICK="getText()">
        </FORM>
    </BODY>
</HTML>
```

TIP

When you use the `all` collection, you can use either square braces or parentheses, like this: `document.all["text1"].value` or this `document.all("text1").value`. If two elements have the same ID, you can specify the item you want if you use parentheses, like this: `document.all("text1", 1).value`.

Accessing HTML Elements with the W3C DOM

The W3C DOM adds the `getElementById` method. (Note that the W3C DOM doesn't support the `all` collection.) You can use that method to access elements that have an ID value in Netscape Navigator 6+ and Internet Explorer 5+:

```html
<HTML>
    <HEAD>
        <TITLE>
            Accessing HTML Elements
        </TITLE>
        <SCRIPT LANGUAGE="JavaScript">
            <!--
            function getText()
            {
                if(navigator.appName == "Netscape") {
                alert("document.form1.text1.value = " + document.form1.text1.value)
                alert("document.forms[0].text1.value = " +
                document.forms[0].text1.value)
                alert("document.getElementsByName(\"text1\")[0].value = "
                    + document.getElementsByName("text1")[0].value)
                alert("document.getElementsByTagName(\"INPUT\")[0].value = "
                    + document.getElementsByTagName("INPUT")[0].value)
                alert("document.getElementById(\"text1\").value = "
                    + document.getElementById("text1").value)
                }

                if (navigator.appName == "Microsoft Internet Explorer") {
                alert("document.form1.text1.value = " + document.form1.text1.value)
                alert("document.forms[0].text1.value = "
                    + document.forms[0].text1.value)
                alert("document.all.text1.value = "
                    + document.all.text1.value)
                alert("document.all[\"text1\"].value = "
                    + document.all["text1"].value)
                alert("document.getElementsByName(\"text1\")[0].value = "
                    + document.getElementsByName("text1")[0].value)
                alert("document.getElementsByTagName(\"INPUT\")[0].value = "
                    + document.getElementsByTagName("INPUT")[0].value)
                alert("document.all.tags(\"INPUT\")[0].value = "
                    + document.all.tags("INPUT")[0].value)
```

```
                alert("document.getElementById(\"text1\").value = "
                    + document.getElementById("text1").value)
            }
        }
        // -->
    </SCRIPT>
</HEAD>

<BODY>
    <H1>Accessing HTML Elements</H1>
    <FORM NAME="form1">
        <INPUT TYPE="TEXT" NAME="text1" ID="text1">
        <INPUT TYPE="BUTTON" VALUE="Click Me!" ONCLICK="getText()">
    </FORM>
</BODY>
</HTML>
```

The W3C DOM also supports properties and methods to enable you to navigate through a web page to the element you want; you can see some of these properties and methods in Tables 4.3 and 4.4. Here's an example that finds the text in the same text field as before; but this time, I'll use the W3C DOM properties and methods. Here's the web page we'll be using:

```
<HTML>
    <HEAD>
        <TITLE>
            Accessing HTML Elements
        </TITLE>
    </HEAD>

    <BODY>
        <H1>Accessing HTML Elements</H1>
        <FORM NAME="form1">
            <INPUT TYPE="TEXT" NAME="text1" ID="text1">
            <INPUT TYPE="BUTTON" VALUE="Click Me!" ONCLICK="getText()">
        </FORM>
    </BODY>
</HTML>
```

I start by getting a node object corresponding to the body element like this, using getElementById. (I could, of course, have accessed the text field directly this way; for the purposes of this example, however, I'll start from the <BODY> tag.)

```
var body1 = document.getElementById("body")
    .
    .
    .
```

Next, I get the first child node of the body node, which is the node corresponding to the `<H1>` element:

```
var body1 = document.getElementById("body")
var h1 = body1.childNodes[0]
    .
    .
    .
```

To get to the form, I can use the `nextSibling` property:

```
var body1 = document.getElementById("body")
var h1 = body1.childNodes[0]
var form1 = h1.nextSibling
    .
    .
    .
```

Finally, I reach the text field, which is the first child node of the form, and display the text field's value like this:

```
var body1 = document.getElementById("body")
var h1 = body1.childNodes[0]
var form1 = h1.nextSibling
var text1 = form1.childNodes[0]
alert(text1.value)
    .
    .
    .
```

That's how things work—in the Internet Explorer. The Netscape Navigator, on the other hand, treats the indentation whitespace in this HTML document as text nodes, as discussed in the beginning of this chapter, which means we have to get not the first child node of the `body` and `form` objects, but the second child node. That looks like this in a combined web page (you'll need Netscape Navigator 6+ or Internet Explorer 5+ here because this code uses the getElementById method, which isn't available before those browsers):

(Listing 04-12.html on the web site)

```
<HTML>
    <HEAD>
        <TITLE>
            Accessing HTML Elements
        </TITLE>
        <SCRIPT LANGUAGE="JavaScript">
            <!--
            function getText()
            {
```

```
            if(navigator.appName == "Netscape") {
            var body1 = document.getElementById("body")
            var h1 = body1.childNodes[1]
            var form1 = h1.nextSibling.nextSibling
            var text1 = form1.childNodes[1]
            alert(text1.value)
        }
            if (navigator.appName == "Microsoft Internet Explorer") {
            var body1 = document.getElementById("body")
            var h1 = body1.childNodes[0]
            var form1 = h1.nextSibling
            var text1 = form1.childNodes[0]
            alert(text1.value)
        }
    }
    // -->
    </SCRIPT>
</HEAD>

<BODY ID="body">
    <H1>Accessing HTML Elements</H1>
    <FORM NAME="form1">
        <INPUT TYPE="TEXT" NAME="text1" ID="text1">
        <INPUT TYPE="BUTTON" VALUE="Click Me!" ONCLICK="getText()">
    </FORM>
</BODY>
</HTML>
```

You can see the result of this code in Figure 4.10—now we're using W3C DOM navigation techniques to move around in web pages.

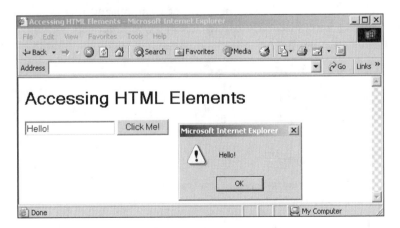

Figure 4.10   Using W3C DOM navigation techniques.

In general, the W3C DOM properties and methods are good for working with an HTML document as a tree of nodes—not only can you navigate through a document as we've just seen, you also can manipulate the nodes and node positions in a document. We'll see more on this in Chapter 16, but here's an example; in this case, I'll use the insertBefore method to change a list of items in an ordered HTML list from:

- Now
- is
- the
- time.

To this:

- Now
- is
- not
- the
- time.

Here's it works—I create the new <LI> element with the createElement method, and then use the innerHTML property to add text to this new element (more on innerHTML in Chapter 16). Then I use the insertBefore method to insert this new element into the list (note that once again, the node location is different in the Internet Explorer and Netscape Navigator because of whitespace, and note that you'll need Netscape Navigator 6+ or Internet Explorer 5+ here):

(Listing 04-13.html on the web site)

```
<HTML>
    <HEAD>
        <TITLE>Inserting New Nodes</TITLE>
        <SCRIPT LANGUAGE="JavaScript">
            <!--
            function addItem()
            {
                var listItem1 = document.createElement("LI")
                listItem1.innerHTML = "not"
                if(navigator.appName == "Netscape") {
                document.getElementById("List1").insertBefore(listItem1,
                    document.getElementById("List1").childNodes[3])
                }
```

```
                if(navigator.appName == "Microsoft Internet Explorer") {
                document.getElementById("List1").insertBefore(listItem1,
                    document.getElementById("List1").childNodes[2])
                }
            }
            // -->
        </SCRIPT>
    </HEAD>

    <BODY>
        <H1>Inserting New Nodes</H1>
            <FORM>
                <INPUT TYPE="button" VALUE="Insert Item" ONCLICK="addItem()">
            </FORM>

            <OL ID="List1">
                <LI>Now
                <LI>is
                <LI>the
                <LI>time.
            </OL>
    </BODY>
</HTML>
```

You can see the results of this code in Figure 4.11 before the new node is added, and in Figure 4.12 after the button was clicked and the new node was added.

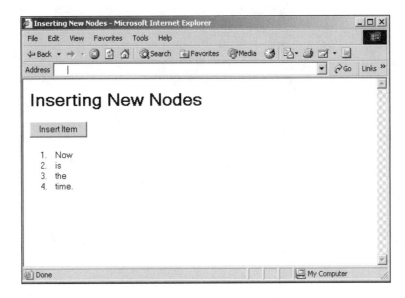

Figure 4.11   Inserting new nodes.

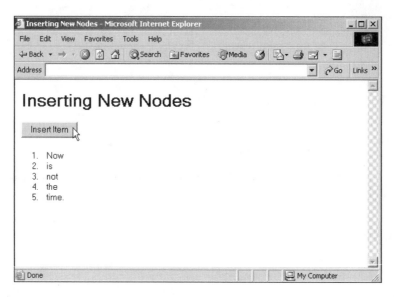

Figure 4.12   A new node.

We'll see more on using W3C DOM properties and methods for working with nodes in Chapter 16.

And that's it—that gives us the overview we'll need for the coming chapters. Here, we saw what's going on in the browser environment for us as JavaScript programmers, including an overview of the various DOM levels, the browser objects available, and cross-browser issues. Now it's time to start digging into all the details—in the next chapter, I'll start by taking a look at the core properties of HTML elements accessible in JavaScript and how to put them to work.

5

Using Core HTML Properties

IN THE COMING CHAPTERS, WE'RE GOING to see a great many HTML elements and browser objects. Each of these elements and objects has properties, methods, and events; and if we were to list them all for each item, we would need more space than there is in this book. However, a great many JavaScript properties, methods, and events are *common* to nearly all HTML elements and to many browser objects, so I'll collect them into this and the next chapter, calling them *JavaScript's core HTML properties, methods, and events*. This chapter covers JavaScript's core HTML properties, and the next chapter (Chapter 6, "Using Core HTML Methods and Events") covers JavaScript's core HTML methods and events.

So when you want to look up the properties, methods, and events of an object, such as the window object, or a text field, or a button, you turn to the chapter that covers the object you want—one of Chapters 7–15. Some of the properties, methods, and events you find in those chapters will be JavaScript core items, and those chapters will refer you back to Chapters 5 and 6 for those items.

Take a look at the Table 5.1, for example, which is a partial listing of the methods of the window object from Chapter 8, "Using *window* and *frame* Methods and Events;" it's the beginning of Table 8.3. The attachEvent method is marked "See Chapter 6," indicating that this method is covered in Chapter 6. The attachEvent method is also a method of the document object, covered in Chapter 9, "Using the *document* and *body* Objects."

And it's a method of the HTML text elements in Chapter 11, "Working with HTML Text Elements," as well as a method of the HTML form objects covered in Chapters 12, "Working with Forms, Buttons, Check Boxes, and Radio Buttons," 13, "Working with Text and Select Controls," 14, "Working with Links, Lists, and Tables," and so on. As you can see, collecting JavaScript's HTML core properties, methods, and events here in Chapters 5 and 6 will save us an immense amount of duplication in later chapters (in fact, more duplication than would fit into the book).

Table 5.1 **Partial List of the Methods of the *window* Object (from Table 8.3)**

Method	NS2	NS3	NS4	NS6	IE3a	IE3b	IE4	IE5	IE5.5	IE6
alert		x	x	x	x	x	x	x	x	x	x

Returns: Nothing
Displays an alert box.
Syntax: `window.alert([msg])`, where *msg* is a string holding the message to display in the alert box.

Method	NS2	NS3	NS4	NS6	IE3a	IE3b	IE4	IE5	IE5.5	IE6
attachEvent	See Chapter 6.									
back				x	x					

Returns: Nothing
Navigates the Netscape Navigator back one page in the browser's history. Not available in the Internet Explorer; so for cross-browser compatibility, it's probably best to stick with the `history` object (see Chapter 10, "Using the Navigator, Location, and History Objects").

...	...
...	...
...	...

In this chapter, therefore, we're going to take a look at JavaScript's core HTML properties; these properties apply to nearly all HTML elements (such as `<BODY>`, `<P>`, `<INPUT>`, and so on) and to many browser objects (such as `window`, `document`, and so on) as well, as we'll see in the coming chapters. For example, the `id` property holds an object's ID value, as set in its `ID` attribute. The `tagName` property holds an element's tag name (such as `"P"` for a `<P>` element). The `children` property holds any child elements enclosed in an element, and so on.

Note that to cover *all* JavaScript's core HTML properties, methods, and events, we'll occasionally need to cover some topics that we haven't discussed yet and which are coming up in later chapters, such as style sheets or Dynamic HTML. That won't be a problem for the most part, but feel free to skip that material until you need it when dealing with the programming in later chapters.

So from where do JavaScript's core HTML properties that we're going to cover come? Although more have developed over the years, they originally came from HTML attributes.

From HTML Attributes to JavaScript Properties

Take a look at this HTML element, a text field:

```
<INPUT TYPE="TEXT" NAME="text1" ID="text1" VALUE="Type here!">
```

Here, the VALUE attribute holds the original text in the text field. To give you access to items such as this text in scripts, HTML attributes became JavaScript properties. The case of these properties were changed to match the Java naming convention, which means the VALUE attribute of this text field is accessible as the value property of the text field's JavaScript object. Here's how I access that text, using the value property, in a web page when the user clicks a button:

```
<HTML>
    <HEAD>
        <TITLE>
            Accessing HTML Elements
        </TITLE>
        <SCRIPT LANGUAGE="JavaScript">
            <!--
            function getText()
            {
                alert("The text is " + document.form1.text1.value)
            }
            // -->
        </SCRIPT>
    </HEAD>

    <BODY>
        <H1>Accessing HTML Elements</H1>
        <FORM NAME="form1">
            <INPUT TYPE="TEXT" NAME="text1" ID="text1" VALUE="Type here!">
            <INPUT TYPE="BUTTON" VALUE="Click Me!" ONCLICK="getText()">
        </FORM>
    </BODY>
</HTML>
```

You can see the results of this code in Figure 5.1.

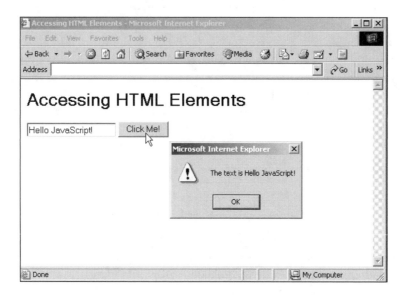

Figure 5.1 Using a JavaScript property.

That's how it worked—HTML attributes became JavaScript properties you could access in code; the STYLE attribute became the style property, and so on. Hyphenated attributes, such as the LIST-STYLE attribute, use the Java naming convention, so LIST-STYLE becomes the listStyle property in JavaScript. (You can't use hyphens in JavaScript names.)

You can find JavaScript's core HTML properties in Table 5.2. (Not all properties are supported by all browsers, of course.) These properties are shared by nearly all HTML elements, as well as many of the big browser objects, and we're going to cover them in this chapter.

Table 5.2 **JavaScript's Core HTML Properties**

Properties

accessKey	all	attributes
begin	behaviorUrns	canHaveChildren
canHaveHTML	childNodes	children
className	clientHeight	clientLeft
clientTop	clientWidth	contentEditable
currentStyle	dataFld	dataFormatAs
dataSrc	dir	disabled

Properties

document	end	filters
firstChild	hasMedia	height
hideFocus	id	innerHTML
innerText	isContentEditable	isDisabled
isMultiLine	isTextEdit	lang
language	lastChild	length
localName	namespaceURI	nextSibling
nodeName	nodeType	nodeValue
offsetHeight	offsetLeft	offsetParent
offsetTop	offsetWidth	onOffBehavior
outerHTML	outerText	ownerDocument
parentElement	parentNode	parentTextEdit
prefix	previousSibling	readyState
recordNumber	runtimeStyle	scopeName
scrollHeight	scrollLeft	scrollTop
scrollWidth	sourceIndex	style
syncMaster	tabIndex	tagName
tagUrn	timeContainer	title
uniqueID		

In fact, a number of HTML elements don't have any properties, methods, or events beyond the core set, and you'll find them in Table 5.3.

Table 5.3   **Core HTML Elements**

Properties

ACRONYM	ADDRESS	B	BIG
CENTER	CITE	CODE	DEL
DFN	DIV	EM	HR
HTML	I	INS	KBD
LISTING	NOBR	P	PLAINTEXT
PRE	RT	RUBY	S
SAMP	SMALL	SPAN	STRIKE
STRONG	SUB	SUP	TT
U	VAR	WBR	XMP

As you can see in Table 5.2, there are many core HTML properties, and their functionality is all over the map, covering many different aspects of programming. Because these properties are so scattered, it's best to just cover them one after the other, instead of trying to collect them into larger programming topics—no larger programming topics would work. So here it goes—the rest of this chapter is all about the core HTML properties you see in Table 5.2, one after the other, and I'll cram in as many examples as I can. Just skip any material you're not interested in now, and come back to it later when you need information on a specific core property.

The *accessKey* Property

The accessKey property enables you to specify a keyboard character that you can press with the Alt key to give an HTML element the focus (that is, make it the element that will receive keystrokes). You can see the support for this property in Table 5.4.

Table 5.4 **The *accessKey* Property**

Method	NS2	NS3	NS4	NS6	IE3a	IE3b	IE4	IE5	IE5.5	IE6
accessKey								x	x	x
		Read/Write								
		Type: String								

Here's an example that gives a button the access key "b" and a text field the access key "t":

(Listing 05-01.html on the web site)

```
<HTML>
    <HEAD>
        <TITLE>Using Access Keys</TITLE>
    </HEAD>

    <BODY>
        <H1>Using Access Keys</H1>
        <FORM>
            <INPUT TYPE="BUTTON" ID="button1" ONCLICK="alert('Hello!')" VALUE="Click
            ➥Me!">
            <INPUT TYPE="TEXT" ID="text1" VALUE="Click Me!">
        </FORM>

        <SCRIPT LANGUAGE="JavaScript">
            <!--
```

```
            document.all.button1.accessKey = "b"
            document.all.text1.accessKey = "t"
            // -->
        </SCRIPT>
    </BODY>
</HTML>
```

When you open this page in the Internet Explorer, you can give the focus to the button or text field simply by using Alt + the access key. (Note that giving the button the focus clicks the button.)

The *all* Property

In the Internet Explorer, the `all` collection for an HTML element is the same as the `all` collection for the `document` object—it holds the elements the HTML element contains. You can see the support for the `all` property in Table 5.5.

Table 5.5 **The *all* Property**

Property	NS2	NS3	NS4	NS6	IE3a	IE3b	IE4	IE5	IE5.5	IE6
all							x	x	x	x
		Read-only								
		Type: Object array								

As with the `document.all` collection, you can access any item by ID like this: `all("myID")` (`all["myID"]` also works). Here's an example; in this case, I'm displaying all the properties in the `all` collection of a form—not only are the two HTML elements, `button1` and `text1`, displayed when you load this page, but so is the `all` collection's `length` property, which gives the number of items in the collection:

(Listing 05-02.html on the web site)

```
<HTML>
    <HEAD>
        <TITLE>Using the all Property</TITLE>
    </HEAD>

    <BODY>
        <H1>Using the all Property</H1>
        <FORM NAME="form1">
            <INPUT TYPE="BUTTON" ID="button1" ONCLICK="alert('Hello!')" VALUE="Click
            ➥Me!">
            <INPUT TYPE="TEXT" ID="text1" VALUE="Click Me!">
        </FORM>
```

continues ▶

```
<SCRIPT LANGUAGE="JavaScript">
    <!--
        for(var obj in document.form1.all){
            alert(obj)
        }
    // -->
</SCRIPT>
</BODY>
</HTML>
```

The *attributes* Property

The attributes property is a very useful one; it returns a collection—that is, an array—of the attributes of an element. You can see the support for the attributes property in Table 5.6.

Table 5.6   **The *attributes* Property**

Property	NS2	NS3	NS4	NS6	IE3a	IE3b	IE4	IE5	IE5.5	IE6
attributes				x				x	x	x
Read-only										
Type: Object array										

This property returns an array of attribute objects; you can see the properties of attribute objects in Table 5.7.

Table 5.7   **The attribute Object Properties**

Property	IE6	NS6	Means
attributes		x	Contained (nested) attributes
childNodes		x	Array of child nodes
expando	x		Indicates whether variables can be created within the object
firstChild	x	x	First child node
lastChild	x	x	Last child node
localName		x	Local name (not qualified with the name-space, if there is one)
name	x	x	Name of the attribute
nameSpaceURI		x	XML namespace Uniform Resource Identifier (URI)

Property	IE6	NS6	Means
nextSibling	x	x	Next sibling node
NodeName	x	x	Name of the attribute
NodeType	x	x	Node type, set to 2
NodeValue	x	x	Value of the attribute
ownerDocument	x	x	Object reference to the current document
ownerElement		x	Object reference to the containing element
parentNode	x	x	Object reference to the attribute's parent
prefix		x	Prefix of the namespace, if there is one
previousSibling	x	x	Previous sibling node
specified	x	x	True if the attribute is explicitly listed, false if it's implicit
value	x	x	Value of the attribute

Here's an example; in this case, I'll take a look at the value of the `onclick` attribute's value in a button element:

(Listing 05-03.html on the web site)

```
<HTML>
    <HEAD>
        <TITLE>Using the attributes Property</TITLE>
    </HEAD>

    <BODY>
        <H1>Using the attributes Property</H1>
        <FORM NAME="form1">
            <INPUT TYPE="BUTTON" ID="button1" ONCLICK="alert('Hello!')" VALUE="Click
            ➥Me!">
            <INPUT TYPE="TEXT" ID="text1" VALUE="Click Me!">
        </FORM>

        <SCRIPT LANGUAGE="JavaScript">
            <!--
                document.write(document.form1.button1.attributes["onclick"].name +
                " = " +
                document.form1.button1.attributes["onclick"].value)
            // -->
        </SCRIPT>
    </BODY>
</HTML>
```

You can see the results in Figure 5.2.

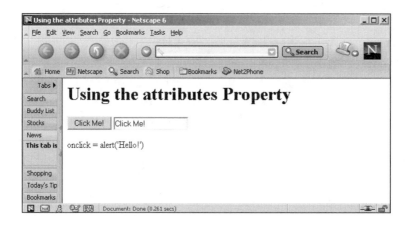

Figure 5.2   Looking at an attribute in the Netscape Navigator.

The *begin* Property

This property is for use with the `time` and `time2` behaviors built into the Internet Explorer, and first appeared in Internet Explorer 5.5. The `begin` property is a read/write property that sets or gets the delay time before a "timeline" begins playing in an element and enables you to coordinate multimedia actions. You can assign this property a string in clock format like `"h:min:s.f"`; or an event occurrence, given an element ID such as this: `id.event[+"h:min:s.f"]` (where the time in square brackets is optional); or a value of `"indefinite"`, which means the `begin` time is determined by a call to the `beginElement` method. See Chapter 15, "Working with the Mouse, Keyboard, and Images," for more on Internet behaviors, such as `time` and `time2`.

The *behaviorUrns* Property

The `behaviorUrns` property returns an array of *Uniform Resource Names* (URNs) of any Internet Explorer behaviors, which we'll see in Chapter 17, "Dynamic HTML: Drag and Drop, Data Binding, and Behaviors" (and which we discussed in the preceding chapter), that are attached to a specific object, such as an HTML element. You can see the support for this property in Table 5.8.

Table 5.8   **The *behaviorUrns* Property**

Property	NS2	NS3	NS4	NS6	IE3a	IE3b	IE4	IE5	IE5.5	IE6
behaviorUrns								x	x	x
Read-only										
Type: String array										

We'll see more about behaviors in Chapter 17.

The *canHaveChildren* Property

When you're constructing your own web pages in JavaScript (using Dynamic HTML or W3C DOM methods), it can be useful to see whether you're dealing with an element that can contain children or not (for example, `<BR>` elements cannot). You can see the support for this property in Table 5.9.

Table 5.9   **The *canHaveChildren* Property**

Property	NS2	NS3	NS4	NS6	IE3a	IE3b	IE4	IE5	IE5.5	IE6
canHaveChildren							x	x	x	
Read-only										
Type: Boolean										

Here's an example—this code loops over all elements in a web page and colors them green if they can have children:

(Listing 05-04.html on the web site)

```
<HTML>
    <HEAD>
        <TITLE>Using the canHaveChildren Property</TITLE>
        <SCRIPT LANGUAGE="JavaScript">
            <!--
            for (var loopIndex =0; loopIndex <document.all.length; loopIndex++){
                if (document.all[loopIndex].canHaveChildren){
                    document.all[loopIndex].style.color = "green"
                }
            }
            // -->
        </SCRIPT>
    </HEAD>

    <BODY>
        <H1 NAME="header">Using the canHaveChildren Property</H1>
        <P NAME="p1">Here's a paragraph.</P>
        <DIV NAME="div1">Here's a DIV.</DIV>
    </BODY>
</HTML>
```

You can see the results in Figure 5.3 in glorious black and white—although you can't tell, all the text in this figure is green. Give this one a try—load it into the Internet Explorer (this property isn't supported in the Netscape Navigator) yourself.

Figure 5.3 Using the `canHaveChildren` property.

The *canHaveHTML* Property

The `canHaveHTML` property is much like the `canHaveChildren` property, except that the `canHaveHTML` property indicates whether an element can contain HTML content (for example, a `<DIV>` element can, but a `<BR>` element can't) rather than children. You can see the support for this property in Table 5.10.

Table 5.10 **The *canHaveHTML* Property**

Property	NS2	NS3	NS4	NS6	IE3a	IE3b	IE4	IE5	IE5.5	IE6
canHaveHTML									x	x
Read-only										
Type: Boolean										

The *childNodes* **Property**

The `childNodes` property is one we've already seen in Chapter 4, "Handling the Browser Environment"—this property returns an array of the child nodes of the current node. You can see the support for this property in Table 5.11.

Table 5.11 **The *childNodes* Property**

Property	NS2	NS3	NS4	NS6	IE3a	IE3b	IE4	IE5	IE5.5	IE6
childNodes				x			x	x	x	x

Read-only

Type: Node array

In the following example, I'm using the `childNodes` property to read the text in a text field:

(Listing 04-12.html on the web site)

```
<HTML>
    <HEAD>
        <TITLE>
            Accessing HTML Elements
        </TITLE>
        <SCRIPT LANGUAGE="JavaScript">
            <!--
            function getText()
            {
                if(navigator.appName == "Netscape") {
                var body1 = document.getElementById("body")
                var h1 = body1.childNodes[1]
                var form1 = h1.nextSibling.nextSibling
                var text1 = form1.childNodes[1]
                alert(text1.value)
                }
                if (navigator.appName == "Microsoft Internet Explorer") {
                var body1 = document.getElementById("body")
                var h1 = body1.childNodes[0]
                var form1 = h1.nextSibling
                var text1 = form1.childNodes[0]
                alert(text1.value)
                }
            }
            // -->
        </SCRIPT>
    </HEAD>

    <BODY ID="body">
        <H1>Accessing HTML Elements</H1>
        <FORM NAME="form1">
            <INPUT TYPE="TEXT" NAME="text1" ID="text1">
```

continues ▶

```
            <INPUT TYPE="BUTTON" VALUE="Click Me!" ONCLICK="getText()">
        </FORM>
    </BODY>
</HTML>
```

You can see this code at work in Figure 4.10.

Tip
If there are no child nodes, the `length` property of the `childNodes` array will be 0.

The *children* Property

In the Internet Explorer, the `children` property holds the HTML elements that are children of the current element. This property is not the same as `childNodes`, which includes text nodes and so on—the `children` property contains only child HTML elements. You can see the support for this property in Table 5.12.

Table 5.12 **The *children* Property**

Property	NS2	NS3	NS4	NS6	IE3a	IE3b	IE4	IE5	IE5.5	IE6
children							x	x	x	x
		Read-only
		Type: Object Array

Here's an example that displays the names of the child HTML elements of a form (there are two, `button1` and `text1`):

(Listing 05-05.html on the web site)

```
<HTML>
    <HEAD>
        <TITLE>Using the children Property</TITLE>
    </HEAD>

    <BODY>
        <H1 NAME="header1">Using the children Property</H1>
        <FORM NAME="form1">
            <INPUT NAME="button1" TYPE="BUTTON" ONCLICK="alerter()" VALUE="Click Me!">
            <INPUT NAME="text1" TYPE="TEXT">
        </FORM>
        <SCRIPT LANGUAGE="JavaScript">
            <!--
```

```
for(var loopIndex=0; loopIndex < form1.children.length; loopIndex++){
    document.write(form1.children[loopIndex].name + "<BR>")
        }
    // -->
    </SCRIPT>
    </BODY>
</HTML>
```

You can see the results in Figure 5.4.

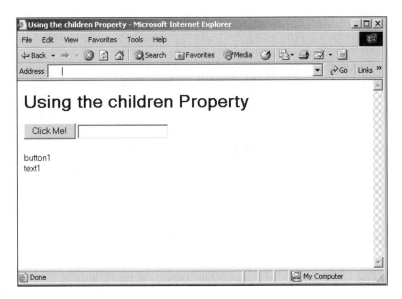

Figure 5.4 Using the `children` property.

The *className* Property

You use the `className` property with style sheets; this property holds the
Cascading Style Sheet (CSS) class name assigned to an object. You can see the
support for this property in Table 5.13.

Table 5.13 **The *className* Property**

Property	NS2	NS3	NS4	NS6	IE3a	IE3b	IE4	IE5	IE5.5	IE6
className				X			X	X	X	X
Read/Write										
Type: String										

Here's an example using CSS styles, which we'll see in Chapter 21, "Cascading Style Sheets and CGI Programming;" in this case, I'm creating two CSS classes, redText and blackText, and assigning them to the text in a <DIV> using the className property to turn text black or red when the user clicks a button:

(Listing 05-06.html on the web site)

```html
<HTML>
    <HEAD>
        <TITLE>Coloring Text with Dynamic CSS Classes</TITLE>
        <STYLE TYPE="text/css">
            .blackText {color:Black}
            .redText {color:Red}
        </STYLE>
        <SCRIPT LANGUAGE="JavaScript">
            <!--
            function turnBlack()
            {
                document.all.div1.className = "blackText"
            }
            function turnRed()
            {
                document.all.div1.className = "redText"
            }
            // -->
        </SCRIPT>
    </HEAD>

    <BODY>
        <DIV ID = "div1">
            <H1>Coloring Text With Dynamic CSS Classes</H1>
            <BR>
            <FORM>
                <INPUT TYPE = BUTTON Value = "Turn text black" onClick =
                ➥"turnBlack()">
                <INPUT TYPE = BUTTON Value = "Turn text red" onClick = "turnRed()">
            </FORM>
        </DIV>
    </BODY>
</HTML>
```

You can see the results in Figure 5.5, where I've turned the text red (although it's black and white here, of course).

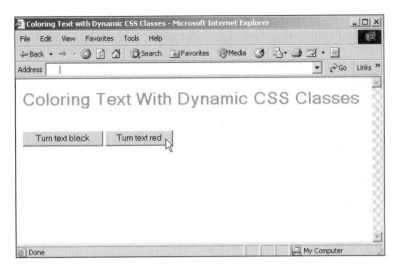

Figure 5.5   Using the `className` property.

The *clientHeight*, *clientLeft*, *clientTop*, and *clientWidth* Properties

These properties give you the dimensions, in pixels, of an object that you've set the height, width, left position, or top position for, using CSS styles. You can see the support for these properties in Table 5.14.

Table 5.14   **The *clientHeight*, *clientLeft*, *clientTop*, and *clientWidth* Properties**

Property	NS2	NS3	NS4	NS6	IE3a	IE3b	IE4	IE5	IE5.5	IE6
clientHeight							X	X	X	X
	Read-only									
	Type: Integer									
clientLeft							X	X	X	X
	Read-only									
	Type: Integer									
clientTop							X	X	X	X
	Read-only									
	Type: Integer									
clientWidth							X	X	X	X
	Read-only									
	Type: Integer									

Here's an example; in this case, the code reports the height you've set for a
<P> element using that element's width style:

(Listing 05-07.html on the web site)

```
<HTML>
    <HEAD>
        <TITLE>
            Using the clientHeight Property
        </TITLE>
        <SCRIPT LANGUAGE="JavaScript">
            <!--
            function getText()
            {
                alert("document.all.text1.clientHeight = "
                    + document.all.text1.clientHeight)
            }
            // -->
        </SCRIPT>
    </HEAD>

    <BODY>
        <H1>Using the clientHeight Property</H1>
        <P NAME="text1" ID="text1" STYLE="width:200">
            Here's the text.
        </P>
        <FORM NAME="form1">
            <INPUT TYPE="BUTTON" VALUE="Click Me!" ONCLICK="getText()">
        </FORM>
    </BODY>
</HTML>
```

The *contentEditable* Property

Internet Explorer 5.5 introduced a cool property, contentEditable, which
lets the user edit the content in a web page interactively. You can see the support for this property in Table 5.15.

Table 5.15   **The *contentEditable* Property**

Property	NS2	NS3	NS4	NS6	IE3a	IE3b	IE4	IE5	IE5.5	IE6
contentEditable									x	x
Read/Write										
Type: Boolean										

Here's an example. In this case, I'll make the text in a `<DIV>` element named `editableDIV` editable:

(Listing 05-08.html on the web site)

```
<HTML>
    <HEAD>
        <TITLE>Editing Content</TITLE>
    </HEAD>

    <BODY>
        <H1>Editing Content</H1>
        <DIV ID="editableDIV">Edit Me!</DIV>
        <SCRIPT LANGUAGE="JavaScript">
            <!--
            editableDIV.contentEditable = true
            // -->
        </SCRIPT>
    </BODY>
</HTML>
```

You can see the results in Figure 5.6; originally, the text there was just `Edit Me!`, but, just as you would in a word processor, I've changed that to `Edit Me Now!`.

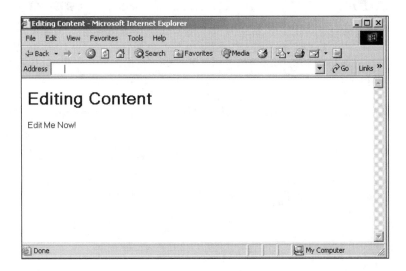

Figure 5.6   Using the `contentEditable` property.

The *currentStyle* Property

This property is for use with CSS styles, and gives you more information than the style property by returning style information that was not specifically set with CSS style statements. For example, the <I> element displays text in italics; unless you specifically set this element's CSS style to italics, however, the style property won't reflect that. The currentStyle property *will* reflect that, however. In this case, the currentStyle property holds a style object whose fontStyle is set to "italic". You can see the support for this property in Table 5.16.

Table 5.16   **The *currentStyle* Property**

Property	NS2	NS3	NS4	NS6	IE3a	IE3b	IE4	IE5	IE5.5	IE6
currentStyle								x	x	x
Read-only										
Type: Object										

The *dataFld*, *dataFormatAs*, and *dataSrc* Properties

You use the dataFld, dataFormatAs, and dataSrc properties with *Data Source Objects* (DSOs) in the Internet Explorer, which enable you to display data from a database in tabular and field-by-field format. These properties were introduced in Internet Explorer 4.0, as you see in Table 5.17.

Table 5.17   **The *dataFld*, *dataFormatAs*, and *dataSrc* Properties**

Property	NS2	NS3	NS4	NS6	IE3a	IE3b	IE4	IE5	IE5.5	IE6
dataFld							x	x	x	x
Read/Write										
Type: String										
dataFormatAs							x	x	x	x
Read/Write										
Type: String										
dataSrc							x	x	x	x
Read/Write										
Type: String										

The `dataSrc` property holds the source of the data, such as an HTML document. This HTML document can be divided into labeled data fields with `<SPAN>` elements; the `dataFld` property enables you to refer to specific data fields in that document. The `dataFormatAs` holds the data format, `"text"` (the default), `"html"`, or `"localized-text"` (which takes into account locale-specific data). These properties apply to these elements: `<APPLET>`, `<BUTTON>`, `<DIV>`, `<FRAME>`, `<IFRAME>`, `<IMG>`, `<INPUT>`, `<LABEL>`, `<MARQUEE>`, `<SELECT>`, `<SPAN>`, `<TABLE>`, and `<TEXTAREA>`.

Here's an example that displays data from an HTML document:

(Listing 05-09.html on the web site)

```
<HTML>
    <HEAD>
        <TITLE>
            Using the dataFld, dataFormatAs, and dataSrc Properties
        </TITLE>
    </HEAD>

    <BODY>
        <CENTER>
            <H1>
                Using the dataFld, dataFormatAs, and dataSrc Properties
            </H1>

            <OBJECT ID="dsoEmployees" DATA="05-10.html" HEIGHT=0 WIDTH=0>
            </OBJECT>

            Name: <INPUT TYPE="TEXT" DATASRC="#dsoEmployees"
                DATAFLD="NAME" SIZE=10>
            <P>
            ID: <INPUT TYPE="TEXT" DATASRC="#dsoEmployees"
                DATAFLD="ID" SIZE=5>
            <P>
            Hire date: <SPAN DATASRC="#dsoEmployees"
                DATAFLD="HIRE_DATE"></SPAN>
            <P>
            Title: <SPAN DATASRC="#dsoEmployees" DATAFLD="TITLE">
            </SPAN>
            <P>
            Department: <SELECT DATASRC="#dsoEmployees"
                DATAFLD="DEPARTMENT" SIZE=1>
                <OPTION VALUE="Shipping">Shipping
                <OPTION VALUE="Programming">Programming
                <OPTION VALUE="Editing">Editing
                <OPTION VALUE="Writing">Writing
            </SELECT>
            <P>
```

continues ▶

```
        <BUTTON ONCLICK=
            "dsoEmployees.recordset.MoveFirst()" >&lt;&lt;</BUTTON>
        <BUTTON ONCLICK="if (!dsoEmployees.recordset.BOF)
            dsoEmployees.recordset.MovePrevious()" >&lt;</BUTTON>
        <BUTTON ONCLICK="if (!dsoEmployees.recordset.EOF)
            dsoEmployees.recordset.MoveNext()" >&gt;</BUTTON>
        <BUTTON ONCLICK=
            "dsoEmployees.recordset.MoveLast()">&gt;&gt;</BUTTON>
    </CENTER>
  </BODY>
</HTML>
```

Here's the data HTML document that needs to be in the same directory for this code to read in:

(Listing 05-10.html on the web site)

```
<HTML>
    <HEAD>
        <TITLE>Data Page</TITLE>
    </HEAD>

    <BODY>
        <H1>This page holds data.</H1>
        Name: <SPAN ID="NAME">Frank</SPAN><BR>
        ID: <SPAN ID="ID">2345</SPAN><BR>
        Hire Date: <SPAN ID="HIRE_DATE">12-31-2003</SPAN><BR>
        Department: <SPAN ID="DEPARTMENT">Shipping</SPAN><BR>
        Title: <SPAN ID="TITLE">Packer</SPAN><BR>
        Name: <SPAN ID="NAME">Mike</SPAN><BR>
        ID: <SPAN ID="ID">2346</SPAN><BR>
        Hire Date: <SPAN ID="HIRE_DATE">12-31-2003</SPAN><BR>
        Department: <SPAN ID="DEPARTMENT">Programming</SPAN><BR>
        Title: <SPAN ID="TITLE">Programmer</SPAN><BR>
        Name: <SPAN ID="NAME">Sammy</SPAN><BR>
        ID: <SPAN ID="ID">2346</SPAN><BR>
        Hire Date: <SPAN ID="HIRE_DATE">12-31-2003</SPAN><BR>
        Department: <SPAN ID="DEPARTMENT">Shipping</SPAN><BR>
        Title: <SPAN ID="TITLE">Packer</SPAN><BR>
        Name: <SPAN ID="NAME">Tamsen</SPAN><BR>
        ID: <SPAN ID="ID">2347</SPAN><BR>
        Hire Date: <SPAN ID="HIRE_DATE">12-31-2003</SPAN><BR>
        Department: <SPAN ID="DEPARTMENT">Shipping</SPAN><BR>
        Title: <SPAN ID="TITLE">Packer</SPAN><BR>
        Name: <SPAN ID="NAME">Kim</SPAN><BR>
        ID: <SPAN ID="ID">2348</SPAN><BR>
        Hire Date: <SPAN ID="HIRE_DATE">12-31-2003</SPAN><BR>
        Department: <SPAN ID="DEPARTMENT">Shipping</SPAN><BR>
        Title: <SPAN ID="TITLE">Packer</SPAN><BR>
    </BODY>
</HTML>
```

You can see the results in Figure 5.7—here, the data from several records is displayed record by record. The user can move from record to record using the arrow navigation buttons at the bottom of the page.

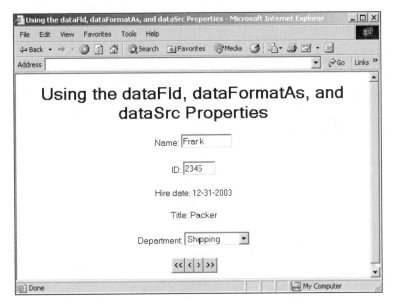

Figure 5.7   Using the `dataFld`, `dataFormatAs`, and `dataSrc` properties.

We'll see more on using these properties in Chapter 17.

The *dir* Property

The `dir` property gives the direction of text in text-oriented HTML components, and can be set to `"rtl"` (right to left) or `"ltr"` (left to right) for various languages. You can see the support for this property in Table 5.18.

Table 5.18   **The *dir* Property**

Property	NS2	NS3	NS4	NS6	IE3a	IE3b	IE4	IE5	IE5.5	IE6
dir				x				x	x	x
Read/Write										
Type: String										

> **Tip**
>
> If you want to use the `dir` property in the Internet Explorer, you may have to download an add-in component named Microsoft Uniscribe. You can find more information at www.microsoft.com/OpenType/developers/uniscribe/intro.htm.

The *disabled* Property

The `disabled` property lets you know—or enables you to set—whether an element is disabled. If a button is disabled, for example, its caption is grayed out, and you can't click it. You can find the support for this property in Table 5.19.

Table 5.19 **The *disabled* Property**

Property	NS2	NS3	NS4	NS6	IE3a	IE3b	IE4	IE5	IE5.5	IE6
disabled				X			X	X	X	X
Read/Write										
Type: Boolean										

Here's an example where I'm disabling a button:

(Listing 05-11.html on the web site)

```
<HTML>
    <HEAD>
        <TITLE>Using the disabled Property</TITLE>
    </HEAD>

    <BODY>
        <H1>Using the disabled Property</H1>
        <FORM>
            <INPUT ID="button1" TYPE="BUTTON" ONCLICK="alert('Hello!')" VALUE="Click
            ➥Me!">
        </FORM>
        <SCRIPT LANGUAGE="JavaScript">
            <!--
                document.all.button1.disabled = true
            // -->
        </SCRIPT>
    </BODY>
</HTML>
```

You can see the results in Figure 5.8.

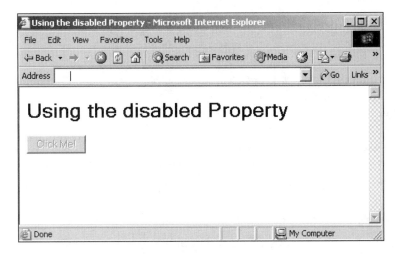

Figure 5.8   Using the `disabled` property.

The *document* Property

The `document` property holds the document object that contains the object. You can see the support for this property in Table 5.20.

Table 5.20   **The *document* Property**

Property	NS2	NS3	NS4	NS6	IE3a	IE3b	IE4	IE5	IE5.5	IE6
document							x	x	x	x
	Read-only Type: Object									

Here's an example; in this function, `warner`, I'll use an object's `document` property to write a warning message about the object to the object's document (the `isBad` method is fictitious):

```
function warner(object1)
{
    if(object1.isBad()){
        object1.document.write("WARNING: Bad Object Found!")
    }
}
```

The *end* Property

Like the `begin` property, this property is for use with the `time` and `time2` behaviors built in to the Internet Explorer, and first appeared in Internet Explorer 5.5. The end property is a read/write property that sets or gets a value indicating the end time for the element's timed actions, and enables you to coordinate multimedia actions. You can assign this property a string in clock format like `"h:min:s.f"`; or an event occurrence, given an element ID like this: `id.event[+"h:min:s.f"]` (where the time in square brackets is optional); or a value of `"indefinite"`, which means the end time is indeterminate. See Chapter 15 for more on Internet behaviors such as `time` and `time2`.

The *filters* Property

In the Internet Explorer, the `filters` property holds an array of *filters* defined for the current element. Filters support various visual effects, such as drop shadows and blurring. You can see the support for this property in Table 5.21.

Table 5.21   **The *filters* Property**

Property	NS2	NS3	NS4	NS6	IE3a	IE3b	IE4	IE5	IE5.5	IE6
filters							x	x	x	x
Read-only										
Type: Object array										

We'll see more on filters in Chapter 16, "Dynamic HTML: Changing Web Pages On-the-Fly," but here's a preview; this web page enables you to play with various filters, applying them to some text:

(Listing 05-12.html on the web site)

```
<HTML>
    <HEAD>
        <TITLE>
            Using Filters
        </TITLE>

        <SCRIPT LANGUAGE="JavaScript">
            <!--
            function applyFilter()
            {
                div1.style.filter=""

                if (document.form1.radio01.checked) {
                    div1.style.filter = "fliph(enabled=1)"
                }
```

```
            if (document.form1.radio02.checked) {
                div1.style.filter = "flipv(enabled=1)"
            }
            if (document.form1.radio03.checked) {
                div1.style.filter = "gray(enabled=1)"
            }
            if (document.form1.radio04.checked) {
                div1.style.filter = "invert(enabled=1)"
            }
            if (document.form1.radio05.checked) {
                div1.style.filter = "xray(enabled=1)"
            }
            if (document.form1.radio06.checked){
                var opacityValue = document.form1.opacity.value
                div1.style.filter = "alpha(opacity=" + opacityValue +
                    ", enabled=1)"
            }
            if (document.form1.radio07.checked) {
                div1.style.filter =
                    "blur(direction=45, strength=15, add=0, enabled=1)"
            }
            if (document.form1.radio08.checked) {
                div1.style.filter = "chroma(color=#FFFF00, enabled=1)"
            }
            if (document.form1.radio09.checked) {
                div1.style.filter = "dropshadow(offx=5, offy=9, " +
                    "color=#008fff, enabled=1)"
            }
             if (document.form1.radio10.checked) {
                div1.style.filter = "glow(strength=5, color=#ffff00, "
                + "enabled=1) "
            }
            if (document.form1.radio11.checked) {
                div1.style.filter = "mask(color=#FF0000 ,enabled=1)"
            }
            if (document.form1.radio12.checked) {
                div1.style.filter =
                    "shadow(color=#FF0088, direction=320, enabled=1)"
            }
            if (document.form1.radio13.checked) {
                div1.style.filter = "wave(freq=2, strength=6, phase=0, " +
                    "lightstrength=0, add=0, enabled=1)"
            }
        }
        // -->
    </SCRIPT>
</HEAD>

<BODY>
    <H1>Using Filters</H1>
    <FORM NAME="form1">
        <INPUT TYPE="RADIO" NAME="radiobuttons" ID="radio01">Flip Horizontal
```

continues ▶

```
            <INPUT TYPE="RADIO" NAME="radiobuttons" ID="radio02">Flip Vertical
            <INPUT TYPE="RADIO" NAME="radiobuttons" ID="radio03">Gray
            <INPUT TYPE="RADIO" NAME="radiobuttons" ID="radio04">Invert
            <INPUT TYPE="RADIO" NAME="radiobuttons" ID="radio05">XRay
            <BR>
            <BR>
            <INPUT TYPE="RADIO" NAME="radiobuttons" ID="radio07">Blur
            <INPUT TYPE="RADIO" NAME="radiobuttons" ID="radio08">Chroma
            <INPUT TYPE="RADIO" NAME="radiobuttons" ID="radio09">Drop Shadow
            <INPUT TYPE="RADIO" NAME="radiobuttons" ID="radio10">Glow
            <INPUT TYPE="RADIO" NAME="radiobuttons" ID="radio11">Mask
            <BR>
            <BR>
            <INPUT TYPE="RADIO" NAME="radiobuttons" ID="radio12">Shadow
            <INPUT TYPE="RADIO" NAME="radiobuttons" ID="radio13">Wave
            <INPUT TYPE="RADIO" NAME="radiobuttons" ID="radio06">
                Alpha   Opacity: 
            <INPUT TYPE="TEXT" ID="opacity" VALUE="60" SIZE="3" MAXLENGTH="3">
            <BR>
            <INPUT TYPE="BUTTON" NAME="startFilter" VALUE="Apply Filter"
                onclick="applyFilter()">
        </FORM>
        <DIV ID="div1" STYLE="POSITION:absolute; WIDTH:250; HEIGHT:100;
            TOP:220; LEFT:30; font-size:24pt;font-family:arial;
            font-style:bold; color:red;">
            Here is the text!
        </DIV>
    </BODY>
</HTML>
```

You can see the results in Figure 5.9, where I've applied a shadow filter to some text. More on filters in Chapter 16.

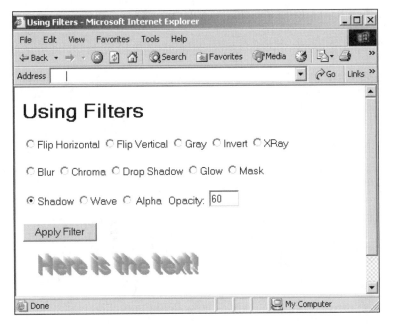

Figure 5.9   Using filters.

The *firstChild* and *lastChild* Properties

The firstChild and lastChild properties return the first and last child nodes of a specific node, or a value of null if there is no such child. You can see the support for these properties in Table 5.22.

Table 5.22   **The *firstChild* and *lastChild* Properties**

Property	NS2	NS3	NS4	NS6	IE3a	IE3b	IE4	IE5	IE5.5	IE6
firstChild				X				X	X	X
	Read-only									
	Type: Node object									
lastChild				X				X	X	X
	Read-only									
	Type: Node object									

Here's an example putting the firstChild and lastChild properties to work—in this case, the code will report the names of the two children of a form using these properties:

(Listing 05-13.html on the web site)

```
<HTML>
    <HEAD>
        <TITLE>
            Using the firstChild and lastChild Properties
        </TITLE>
    </HEAD>

    <BODY>
        <H1>Using the firstChild and lastChild Properties</H1>
        <FORM NAME="form1">
            <INPUT TYPE="BUTTON" NAME="button1" VALUE="Click Me!" ONCLICK="getText()">
            <INPUT TYPE="TEXT" NAME="text1"></FORM>
        <SCRIPT LANGUAGE="JavaScript">
            <!--
            document.write("document.all.form1.firstChild.name = "
                + document.all.form1.firstChild.name + "<BR>")
            document.write("document.all.form1.lastChild.name = "
                + document.all.form1.lastChild.name + "<BR>")
            // -->
        </SCRIPT>
    </BODY>
</HTML>
```

You can see the results in Figure 5.10.

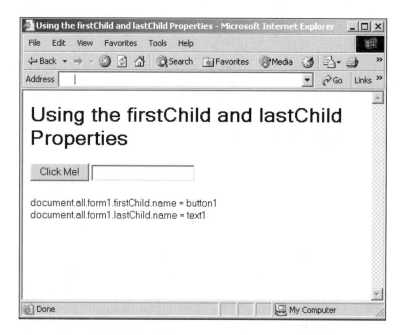

Figure 5.10   Using the `firstChild` and `lastChild` properties.

The *hasMedia* Property

Holds a Boolean value indicating whether the element is an Internet Explorer HTML+TIME media element. You can see the support for this property in Table 5.23.

Table 5.23 **The *hasMedia* Property**

Property	NS2	NS3	NS4	NS6	IE3a	IE3b	IE4	IE5	IE5.5	IE6
hasMedia									x	x
Read-only										
Type: Boolean										

The *height* and *width* Properties

The height and width properties correspond to the HEIGHT and WIDTH HTML attributes of elements that support these attributes. You can see the support for these properties in Table 5.24.

Table 5.24 **The *height* and *width* Properties**

Property	NS2	NS3	NS4	NS6	IE3a	IE3b	IE4	IE5	IE5.5	IE6
height			x	x			x	x	x	x
Read/Write										
Type: Integer or percentage										

These properties are measured in pixels or percentages, just as their corresponding HTML attributes. You can read them—or write them—in JavaScript.

> **Tip**
>
> Note that the height and width properties are *not* the same as the height and width properties set with an element's style property.

The *hideFocus* Property

The hideFocus property is an Internet Explorer-only property. When an HTML element in that browser gets the focus (that is, becomes the target for keystrokes), the element usually displays a dotted-line box (as surrounds the caption of clicked buttons). If you set an element's hideFocus property to true, that dotted-line box doesn't appear. You can see the support for this property in Table 5.25.

Table 5.25 **The *hideFocus* Property**

Property	NS2	NS3	NS4	NS6	IE3a	IE3b	IE4	IE5	IE5.5	IE6
hideFocus									x	x
Read/Write										
Type: Boolean										

The *id* Property

As you can guess, the id property corresponds to the ID HTML attribute, and holds an object's ID value. Working with ID values is relatively new for browsers, coming in largely because the W3C DOM emphasizes the ID attribute over the NAME attribute. You can see the support for these properties in Table 5.26.

Table 5.26 **The *id* Property**

Property	NS2	NS3	NS4	NS6	IE3a	IE3b	IE4	IE5	IE5.5	IE6
id				x			x	x	x	x
Read-only										
Type: String										

Here's an example extending the code in the document object topic earlier in this chapter; in this case, I'll report an object's ID when displaying a warning in the object's document:

```
function warner(object1)
{
    if(object1.isBad()){
        object1.document.write("WARNING: Bad Object Found! ID:" object1.id)
    }
}
```

The *innerHTML, innerText, outerHTML,* and *outerText* Properties

The innerHTML, innerText, outerHTML, and outerText properties are the basis of much Dynamic HTML, because they enable you to access an HTML element's HTML and text, and change them at runtime. We'll put these properties to work in Chapter 16. Here's an overview of these properties:

- **innerHTML.** Changes contents of element *between* start and end tags, can include HTML.

- **innerText.** Enables you to change the text *between* the start and end tags of an element.
- **outerHTML.** Contents of an element, *including* start and end tags, treats text as HTML.
- **outerText.** Enables you to change all the element's text, *including* the start and end tags.

You can see the support for these properties in Table 5.27 (note that only innerHTML is supported by the Netscape Navigator, and only in version 6 so far).

Table 5.27   **The *innerHTML, innerText, outerHTML,* and *outerText* Properties**

Property	NS2	NS3	NS4	NS6	IE3a	IE3b	IE4	IE5	IE5.5	IE6
innerHTML				x			x	x	x	x
		Read/Write								
		Type: String								
innerText							x	x	x	x
		Read/Write								
		Type: String								
outerHTML							x	x	x	x
		Read/Write								
		Type: String								
outerText							x	x	x	x
		Read/Write								
		Type: String								

Here's an Internet Explorer example using the innerHTML property that rewrites an <H1> header when you click that header, using the innerHTML property:

(Listing 05-14.html on the web site)

```
<HTML>
    <HEAD>
        <TITLE>Using the innerHTML Property</TITLE>
        <SCRIPT LANGUAGE = JavaScript>
            <!--
            function rewriteHeader()
            {
```

```
              document.all.Header.innerHTML = "Here's a New Header!"
          }
      </SCRIPT>
  </HEAD>

  <BODY>
      <H1 ID="Header" ONCLICK="rewriteHeader()">Click Me!</H1>
  </BODY>
</HTML>
```

You can see the results in Figure 5.11, where I've clicked the header to rewrite it.

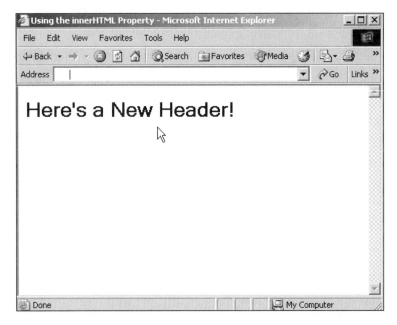

Figure 5.11   Using the `innerHTML`, `innerText`, `outerHTML`, and `outerText` properties.

We'll see more on these properties in Chapter 16.

The *isContentEditable* Property

The `isContentEditable` property returns true if the content of an element is editable (see the `contentEditable` property earlier in this chapter for all the details on making web page content editable). You can see the support for this property in Table 5.28.

Table 5.28   **The *isContentEditable* Property**

Property	NS2	NS3	NS4	NS6	IE3a	IE3b	IE4	IE5	IE5.5	IE6
isContentEditable									x	x
Read-only										
Type: Boolean										

The *isDisabled* Property

The isDisabled property lets you know whether an object is disabled—see the disabled property earlier in this chapter for more on disabling objects. You can see the support for the isDisabled property in Table 5.29.

Table 5.29   **The *isDisabled* Property**

Property	NS2	NS3	NS4	NS6	IE3a	IE3b	IE4	IE5	IE5.5	IE6
isDisabled									x	x
Read-only										
Type: Boolean										

The *isMultiLine* Property

The isMultiLine property indicates whether an element displayed its content (usually text) in multiple lines. For example, an HTML text field will return false, although an HTML text area can return true, as can a button (button captions can extend over several lines). You can see the support for this property in Table 5.30.

Table 5.30   **The *isMultiLine* Property**

Property	NS2	NS3	NS4	NS6	IE3a	IE3b	IE4	IE5	IE5.5	IE6
isMultiLine									x	x
Read-only										
Type: Boolean										

The *isTextEdit* Property

The isTextEdit property returns true if you can create an Internet Explorer TextRange object using its content. You can see the support for this property in Table 5.31.

Table 5.31 **The *isTextEdit* Property**

Property	NS2	NS3	NS4	NS6	IE3a	IE3b	IE4	IE5	IE5.5	IE6
isTextEdit							x	x	x	x

Read-only
Type: Boolean

We'll see more on text ranges in Chapter 11; they let you work with text grouped together into an object. Here's a preview, where I'm using a text range to rewrite the text in a <DIV> element, and using the isTextEdit:

(Listing 05-15.html on the web site)

```
<HTML>
    <HEAD>
        <TITLE>
            Using Text Ranges
        </TITLE>

        <SCRIPT LANGAUGE="JavaScript">
            <!--
            function replaceText()
            {
                if(document.body.isTextEdit){
                    var range = document.body.createTextRange()
                    range.moveToElementText(div1)
                    range.pasteHTML("Here is the replacement text!")
                }
            }
            // -->
        </SCRIPT>
    </HEAD>

    <BODY>
        <H1>Using Text Ranges</H1>
        <INPUT TYPE=BUTTON VALUE="Click Me!" onclick="replaceText()">
        <BR>
        <BR>
        <DIV ID="div1" STYLE="font-family:Arial, sans-serif; font-weight:bold">
            Click the button to replace all this text.
        </DIV>
    </BODY>
</HTML>
```

You can see the results in Figure 5.12, where I've clicked the button and replaced the original text with new text. More on text ranges in Chapter 11.

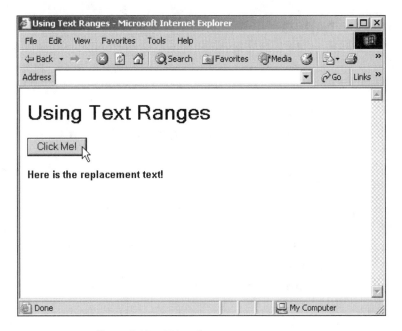

Figure 5.12   Using the `isTextEdit` property.

The *lang* and *language* Properties

The `lang` property holds an object's language (such as `"en"` for English), and the `language` property holds the scripting language for an element. You can see the support for these properties in Table 5.32.

Table 5.32   **The *lang* and *language* Properties**

Property	NS2	NS3	NS4	NS6	IE3a	IE3b	IE4	IE5	IE5.5	IE6
lang				x			x	x	x	x
		Read/Write Type: String								
language							x	x	x	x
		Read/Write Type: String								

Although these properties are primarily meant to be read, you *can* write them; here's an example:

```
document.all.germanLanguageDIV.lang ="de"
document.all.script1.language ="JavaScript"
```

The *length* Property

We've already used the `length` property, which just returns the number of items in an array or collection. You can see the support for this property in Table 5.33.

Table 5.33 **The *length* Property**

Property	NS2	NS3	NS4	NS6	IE3a	IE3b	IE4	IE5	IE5.5	IE6
length	x	x	x	x	x	x	x	x	x	x
	Read-only									
	Type: Integer									

Here's an example from earlier in this chapter where we're using the `length` property of the `children` collection to loop over all the child HTML elements in a form:

(Listing 05-05.html on the web site)

```
<HTML>
    <HEAD>
        <TITLE>Using the children Property</TITLE>
    </HEAD>

    <BODY>
        <H1 NAME="header1">Using the children Property</H1>
        <FORM NAME="form1">
            <INPUT NAME="button1" TYPE="BUTTON" ONCLICK="alerter()" VALUE="Click Me!">
            <INPUT NAME="text1" TYPE="TEXT">
        </FORM>
        <SCRIPT LANGUAGE="JavaScript">
            <!--
                for(var loopIndex=0; loopIndex < form1.children.length; loopIndex++){
                    document.write(form1.children[loopIndex].name + "<BR>")
                }
            // -->
        </SCRIPT>
    </BODY>
</HTML>
```

The *localName, namespaceURI,* and *prefix* Properties

You use the `localName`, `namespaceURI`, and `prefix` properties mostly with XML documents—or XML embedded in HTML documents—that uses namespaces. We won't have that much use for namespaces in this book, but, briefly, you can declare and use a namespace in XML like this:

```
<doc xmlns:ns="http://www.ns.com">
    <ns:myElement>Here is some data</ns:myElement>
</doc>
```

Here, "ns" is the namespace's prefix, "http://www.ns.com" is the namespace's URI, and the local name of an tag such as <ns:myElement> is just the part without the namespace prefix, "myElement". These items correspond to the localName, namespaceURI, and prefix properties, and you can find the support for these properties in Table 5.34.

Tip

For more on XML, see the W3C XML specification at www.w3.org/TR/REC-xml. See also the scopeName property in this chapter.

Table 5.34   **The *localName, namespaceURI,* and *prefix* Properties**

Property	NS2	NS3	NS4	NS6	IE3a	IE3b	IE4	IE5	IE5.5	IE6
localName				x						x
Read-only Type: String										
namespaceURI				x						x
Read-only Type: String										
prefix				x						x
Read-only Type: String										

The *nextSibling* and *previousSibling* Properties

The nextSibling and previousSibling properties are W3C DOM properties that are useful when navigating an HTML document as a node tree, enabling you to navigate between sibling nodes (that is, nodes at the same level in the document). You can see the support for these properties in Table 5.35.

Table 5.35   **The *nextSibling* and *previousSibling* Properties**

Property	NS2	NS3	NS4	NS6	IE3a	IE3b	IE4	IE5	IE5.5	IE6
nextSibling				x				x	x	x
Read-only Type: Object										
previousSibling			x				x	x	x	
Read-only Type: Object										

We've already seen the nextSibling property at work in the preceding chapter; this property returns the next node at the same level as the current node, letting us navigate through an HTML document like this:

(Listing 04-12.html on the web site)

```html
<HTML>
    <HEAD>
        <TITLE>
            Accessing HTML Elements
        </TITLE>
        <SCRIPT LANGUAGE="JavaScript">
            <!--
            function getText()
            {
                if(navigator.appName == "Netscape") {
                var body1 = document.getElementById("body")
                var h1 = body1.childNodes[1]
                var form1 = h1.nextSibling.nextSibling
                var text1 = form1.childNodes[1]
                alert(text1.value)
                }

                if (navigator.appName == "Microsoft Internet Explorer") {
                var body1 = document.getElementById("body")
                var h1 = body1.childNodes[0]
                var form1 = h1.nextSibling
                var text1 = form1.childNodes[0]
                alert(text1.value)
                }
            }
            // -->
        </SCRIPT>
    </HEAD>

    <BODY ID="body">
        <H1>Accessing HTML Elements</H1>
        <FORM NAME="form1">
            <INPUT TYPE="TEXT" NAME="text1" ID="text1">
            <INPUT TYPE="BUTTON" VALUE="Click Me!" ONCLICK="getText()">
        </FORM>
    </BODY>
</HTML>
```

Here's an example putting the previousSibling property to work; in this case, I'm navigating through the elements in a form, starting at the button and ending up with the text field, using previousSibling:

(Listing 05-16.html on the web site)

```
<HTML>
    <HEAD>
        <TITLE>
            Accessing HTML Elements
        </TITLE>
        <SCRIPT LANGUAGE="JavaScript">
            <!--
            function getText()
            {
                if(navigator.appName == "Netscape") {
                var button1 = document.getElementById("button1")
                var text1 = button1.previousSibling.previousSibling
                alert(text1.value)
                }

                if (navigator.appName == "Microsoft Internet Explorer") {
                var button1 = document.getElementById("button1")
                var text1 = button1.previousSibling.previousSibling
                alert(text1.value)
                }
            }
            // -->
        </SCRIPT>
    </HEAD>

    <BODY ID="body">
        <H1>Accessing HTML Elements</H1>
        <FORM NAME="form1">
            <INPUT TYPE="TEXT" NAME="text1" ID="text1">
            <INPUT TYPE="BUTTON" VALUE="Click Me!" ID="button1" ONCLICK="getText()">
        </FORM>
    </BODY>
</HTML>
```

The *nodeName* Property

The nodeName property gives you the name of a node, and it's a property you use when you're treating an HTML document as a W3C DOM node tree. You can see the support for this property in Table 5.36.

Table 5.36 **The *nodeName* Property**

Property	NS2	NS3	NS4	NS6	IE3a	IE3b	IE4	IE5	IE5.5	IE6
nodeName				x				x	x	x
	Read-only									
	Type: String									

The nodeName of an element is the element's name (just like the tagName property). The nodeName of an attribute is the name of the attribute. The nodeName for a text node is "#text", because text nodes don't have specific names.

Here's an example that puts the nodeName, nodeType, and nodeValue properties to work. In this case, I'll take a look at those properties for a text node:

(Listing 05-17.html on the web site)

```
<HTML>
    <HEAD>
        <TITLE>
            Using the nodeName, nodeType, and nodeValue Properties
        </TITLE>
    </HEAD>

    <BODY>
        <H1>Using the nodeName, nodeType, and nodeValue Properties</H1>
        <P NAME="text1" ID="text1">
            Here's the text.
        </P>
        <SCRIPT LANGUAGE="JavaScript">
            <!--
            var node = document.getElementById("text1").firstChild
            document.write("node.nodeName = "
                    + node.nodeName + "<BR>")
            document.write("node.nodeType = "
                    + node.nodeType + "<BR>")
            document.write("node.nodeValue = "
                    + node.nodeValue + "<BR>")
            // -->
        </SCRIPT>
    </BODY>
</HTML>
```

You can see the results in Figure 5.13, where the nodeName, nodeType, and nodeValue properties for the text node are displayed.

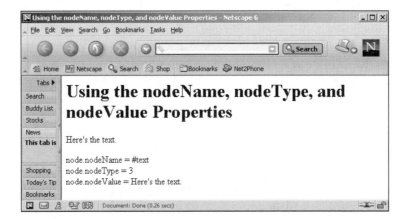

Figure 5.13　Using the `nodeName`, `nodeType`, and `nodeValue` properties.

The *nodeType* Property

The `nodeType` property returns a numeric value indicating the type of a node. You can see the support for this property in Table 5.37.

Table 5.37　**The *nodeType* Property**

Property	NS2	NS3	NS4	NS6	IE3a	IE3b	IE4	IE5	IE5.5	IE6
nodeType				x				x	x	x
Read/Write										
Type: Integer										

You can see the possible node type values in Table 5.38; here, I'm including all possible values for both XML and HTML documents, because you can mix HTML and XML documents in the Internet Explorer (more on this in Chapter 22, "XML and XSLT"). The only valid node types for HTML nodes are 1, 2, 3, 8, 9, 10, and 11.

Table 5.38　**W3C Node Types**

Number	Means
1	Element
2	Attribute
3	Text node

continues ▶

Table 5.38 **Continued**

Number	Means
4	CDATA (character data) section
5	Entity reference
6	Entity node
7	Processing instruction
8	Comment
9	Document node
10	Document Type Definition (DTD)
11	Document fragment
12	Notation

For an example using this property, see the nodeName topic earlier in this chapter.

The *nodeValue* Property

The nodeValue property returns a node's value—but note that this has meaning only for text nodes (where the node's value is the text itself) and attribute nodes (where the node's value is the value assigned to the attribute). For other nodes, such as element nodes, this property is null (which evaluates to false in Boolean conditions such as those you use in if statements). You can see the support for this property in Table 5.39.

Table 5.39 **The *nodeValue* Property**

Property	NS2	NS3	NS4	NS6	IE3a	IE3b	IE4	IE5	IE5.5	IE6
nodeValue				x				x	x	x
Read/Write										
Type: String, number, or null										

> **Tip**
> Technically, this property should always return a string, and it is a string in the Netscape Navigator; however, the Windows version of Internet Explorer (not the Mac version) returns a number if the attribute value is a number.

For an example using this property, see the nodeName topic earlier in this chapter.

The *offsetHeight*, *offsetWidth*, *offsetLeft*, *offsetRight*, and *offsetParent* Properties

The offsetHeight, offsetWidth, offsetLeft, and offsetRight properties give the offset, in pixels, of an object from its parent container (for both the object and the parent object, the origin, (0, 0), is at upper left). The offsetParent property holds the parent object that these properties are measured with respect to. You can see the support for this property in Table 5.40.

Table 5.40   **The *offsetHeight*, *offsetWidth*, *offsetLeft*, *offsetRight*, and *offsetParent* Properties**

Property	NS2	NS3	NS4	NS6	IE3a	IE3b	IE4	IE5	IE5.5	IE6
offsetHeight				X			X	X	X	X
Read-only Type: Integer										
offsetWidth				X			X	X	X	X
Read-only Type: Integer										
offsetLeft				X			X	X	X	X
Read-only Type: Integer										
offsetTop				X			X	X	X	X
Read-only Type: Integer										
offsetParent				X			X	X	X	X
Read-only Type: Object										

Here's an example putting these properties to work; in this example, I'm reporting the offset of an <H1> header from its parent, and reporting the parent's tag name (which is "BODY"):

(Listing 05-18.html on the web site)

```
<HTML>
    <HEAD>
        <TITLE>
            Using the Offset Properties
        </TITLE>
    </HEAD>

    <BODY>
        <H1 ID="Header">Using the Offset Properties</H1>
```

continues ▶

```
<SCRIPT LANGUAGE = "JavaScript">
    <!--
    alert("document.all.Header.offsetLeft = " + document.all.Header.offsetLeft)
    alert("document.all.Header.offsetTop = " + document.all.Header.offsetTop)
    alert("document.all.Header.offsetParent = " +
    ➥document.all.Header.offsetParent.tagName)
    // -->
</SCRIPT>
</BODY>
</HTML>
```

You can see the results in Figure 5.14.

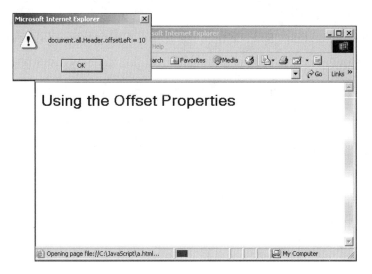

Figure 5.14 Using the offset properties.

The *onOffBehavior* Property

The onOffBehavior property holds a Boolean value indicating whether a particular Internet Explorer DirectAnimation behavior is running. This property was introduced in Internet Explorer 5.0, but is considered deprecated (in other words, obsolete, and probably won't be supported in the future). You can see the support for this property in Table 5.41.

Table 5.41 **The *onOffBehavior* Property**

Property	NS2	NS3	NS4	NS6	IE3a	IE3b	IE4	IE5	IE5.5	IE6
onOffBehavior								x	x	x
	Read-only									
	Type: Boolean									

The *ownerDocument* Property

Like the document property we saw earlier, ownerDocument holds a reference to a node or element's containing document object. You can see the support for this property in Table 5.42.

Table 5.42   **The *ownerDocument* Property**

Property	NS2	NS3	NS4	NS6	IE3a	IE3b	IE4	IE5	IE5.5	IE6
ownerDocument				x						x
Read-only Type: Object										

The *parentElement* Property

The parentElement property returns the parent element of the present element. Unlike the parentNode property, you only use this property with elements, not any kind of node. (Nodes can include text nodes, attribute nodes, and so on.) You can see the support for this property in Table 5.43.

Table 5.43   **The *parentElement* Property**

Property	NS2	NS3	NS4	NS6	IE3a	IE3b	IE4	IE5	IE5.5	IE6
parentElement							x	x	x	x
Read-only Type: Object										

Here's an example:

```
var parentElement = document.getElementById("element1").parentElement
```

The *parentNode* Property

The parentNode property returns the parent node of the present node. Unlike the parentElement property (see the previous topic), you can use this property with any W3C node, not just with elements. You can see the support for this property in Table 5.44.

Table 5.44 **The *parentNode* Property**

Property	NS2	NS3	NS4	NS6	IE3a	IE3b	IE4	IE5	IE5.5	IE6
parentNode				X				X	X	X
	Read-only									
	Type: Node object									

Here's an example:

```
var parentNode = document.getElementById("node1").parentNode
```

The *parentTextEdit* Property

You use this property with text ranges, which we'll see in Chapter 11. This property enables you to find the next outermost object containing the current object that can support text ranges. If there is such a containing object, parentTextEdit returns that object; otherwise it returns null to indicate a non-result. You can see the support for this property in Table 5.45.

Table 5.45 **The *parentTextEdit* Property**

Property	NS2	NS3	NS4	NS6	IE3a	IE3b	IE4	IE5	IE5.5	IE6
parentTextEdit							X	X	X	X
	Read-only									
	Type: Object									

See also the isTextEdit property, earlier in this chapter.

The *readyState* Property

The readyState property gives you some indication of the progress of an object loading its data. For example, an <IMG> element might take some time to load an image, and you can use this property to check when it's done. You can see the support for this property in Table 5.46.

Table 5.46 **The *readyState* Property**

Property	NS2	NS3	NS4	NS6	IE3a	IE3b	IE4	IE5	IE5.5	IE6
readyState							X	X	X	X
	Read-only									
	Type: String									

The possible strings returned, such as "complete" or "loaded" appear in Table 5.47. (The <OBJECT> element returns numbers rather than strings, and those numbers are also listed in Table 5.47.)

Table 5.47   **The *readyState* Property Values**

Value	Means
complete	All data is loaded (`<OBJECT>` value: 4).
interactive	Not all data is loaded, but the object can interact with the user (`<OBJECT>` value: 3).
loaded	All data is loaded—but object may be busy working on that data (`<OBJECT>` value: 2).
loading	Data is still being loaded (`<OBJECT>` value: 1).

For example, you can check the `readyState` property of an image named image1 like this: `document.all.image1.readyState`. Although Internet Explorer 4.0 supported this property for only a few elements (such as `<IMG>`, `<OBJECT>`, and `<EMBED>`), starting with Internet Explorer 5.0 you can use this property on nearly every element.

TIP

You can't use the `readyState` property to check whether an element itself is loaded, just whether its data is loaded—the element itself needs to be present before you can even use the `readyState` property.

The *recordNumber* Property

The `recordNumber` property is used with data binding in the Internet Explorer (see "The `dataFld`, `dataFormatAs`, and `dataSrc` Properties" in this chapter and Chapter 17 for more on data binding), and gives you the current record number when you're displaying multiple records. To display multiple records in a table, for example, the Internet Explorer will automatically add rows to a default table, and each row will have a different `recordNumber` property. You can see the support for this property in Table 5.48.

Table 5.48   **The *recordNumber* Property**

Property	NS2	NS3	NS4	NS6	IE3a	IE3b	IE4	IE5	IE5.5	IE6
recordNumber							x	x	x	x
	Read-only Type: Integer									

The *runtimeStyle* Property

The runtimeStyle property gives you the default style attributes of an object at the times a page loads, before they are changed. You can find the support for this property in Table 5.49.

Table 5.49 **The *runtimeStyle* Property**

Property	NS2	NS3	NS4	NS6	IE3a	IE3b	IE4	IE5	IE5.5	IE6
runtimeStyle								x	x	x
Read-only Type: Object										

The *scopeName* Property

You use the scopeName property with XML embedded in an HTML document in the Internet Explorer. Because you can create XML elements with your own tags, it's common to assign them to different *namespaces* to avoid overlap between XML elements with the same tag name. The scopeName property of an element gives its namespace. You can see the support for this property in Table 5.50.

Table 5.50 **The *scopeName* Property**

Property	NS2	NS3	NS4	NS6	IE3a	IE3b	IE4	IE5	IE5.5	IE6
scopeName								x	x	x
Read-only Type: String										

You also can set a namespace for HTML documents as an attribute of the <HTML> element. The default namespace is "HTML", but here I'm changing that by defining a namespace "NS", using that namespace in a <P> element, and then reporting the <P> element's namespace like this:

(Listing 05-19.html on the web site)

```
<HTML XMLNS:NS='http://www.starpowder.com'>
    <HEAD>
        <TITLE>Using the scopeName Property</TITLE>
    </HEAD>

    <BODY>
        <H1>Using the scopeName Property</H1>
```

```
<NS:P ID="data1">Here is a paragraph.</NS:P>
<SCRIPT LANGUAGE="JavaScript">
    <!--
        document.write("<BR>Scope name of the paragraph: "
            + document.getElementById("data1").scopeName)
    // -->
</SCRIPT>
    </BODY>
</HTML>
```

You can see the results in Figure 5.15.

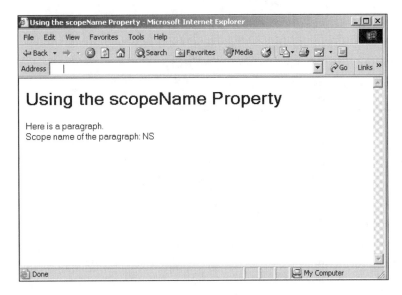

Figure 5.15   Using the scopeName property.

The *scrollHeight, scrollWidth, scrollLeft,* and *scrollTop* Properties

You use the scrollHeight, scrollWidth, scrollLeft, and scrollTop properties with elements that can be scrolled, such as <BODY> and <TEXTAREA> elements. The scrollHeight and scrollWidth properties give the actual height and width of an object (no matter how much of the object is visible currently). The scrollLeft and scrollTop properties give the distance in pixels from the upper left of the scrolling area to the upper left of the object you're scrolling. You can see the support for these properties in Table 5.51.

Table 5.51   **The *scrollHeight, scrollWidth, scrollLeft,* and *scrollTop* Properties**

Property	NS2	NS3	NS4	NS6	IE3a	IE3b	IE4	IE5	IE5.5	IE6
scrollHeight							x	x	x	x
Read-only Type: Integer										
scrollWidth							x	x	x	x
Read-only Type: Integer										
scrollLeft							x	x	x	x
Read-only Type: Integer										
scrollTop							x	x	x	x
Read-only Type: Integer										

Tip

In Internet Explorer, only a few objects supported this property; now almost all do. If the object doesn't actually support scrolling, however, these properties will always have a value of 0.

The *sourceIndex* Property

In the Internet Explorer, the sourceIndex property returns the numeric index of an object in the all collection. You can see the support for this property in Table 5.52.

Table 5.52   **The *sourceIndex* Property**

Property	NS2	NS3	NS4	NS6	IE3a	IE3b	IE4	IE5	IE5.5	IE6
sourceIndex							x	x	x	x
Read-only Type: Integer										

Here's an example where I find the numeric index of a text field, and then use that index in the document.all collection to get the text from the text field:

(Listing 05-20.html on the web site)

```
<HTML>
    <HEAD>
        <TITLE>Using the sourceIndex Property</TITLE>
    </HEAD>

<BODY>
        <H1>Using the sourceIndex Property</H1>
```

```
<INPUT ID="text1" TYPE="TEXT" VALUE="Hello!">
<SCRIPT LANGUAGE="JavaScript">
    <!--
    document.write("<BR>The text is: " +
    document.all[document.getElementById("text1").sourceIndex].value)
    // -->
</SCRIPT>
</BODY>
</HTML>
```

The *style* Property

You can use the `style` property to associate a CSS style with an element. You can see the support for this property in Table 5.53.

Table 5.53 **The *style* Property**

Property	NS2	NS3	NS4	NS6	IE3a	IE3b	IE4	IE5	IE5.5	IE6
style				X			X	X	X	X
Read/Write										
Type: Object										

The `style` property has many subproperties corresponding to the style attributes (such as `color`, `fontWeight`, and `fontStyle`) that we'll see in Chapter 21, but here's a preview. In this example, I'll change the style of an `<H1>` header to italic when the user clicks a button:

(Listing 05-21.html on the web site)

```
<HTML>
    <HEAD>
        <TITLE>Using the style Property</TITLE>
        <SCRIPT LANGUAGE="JavaScript">
            <!--
                function styler()
                {
                    document.body.style.fontStyle = "italic"
                }
            // -->
        </SCRIPT>
    </HEAD>

    <BODY>
        <H1 NAME="header1">Using the style Property</H1>
        <FORM>
            <INPUT TYPE="BUTTON" ONCLICK="styler()" VALUE="Click Me!">
        </FORM>
    </BODY>
</HTML>
```

You can see the results in Figure 5.16.

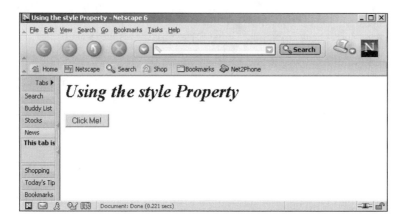

Figure 5.16   Using the style property.

The *syncMaster* Property

The syncMaster property sets or gets a Boolean value indicating whether an Internet Explorer time container has to synchronize playback to this element. You can see the support for this property in Table 5.54. See also the timeContainer property.

Table 5.54 **The *syncMaster* Property**

Property	NS2	NS3	NS4	NS6	IE3a	IE3b	IE4	IE5	IE5.5	IE6
syncMaster									x	x
		Read/Write								
		Type: Boolean								

The *tabIndex* Property

You can let the user move from element to element in your web page just by pressing the Tab key. When you do, the focus moves from element to element—and using the tabIndex property, you can specify the tab order of elements in a page. You can find the support for this property in Table 5.55.

Table 5.55 **The *tabIndex* Property**

Property	NS2	NS3	NS4	NS6	IE3a	IE3b	IE4	IE5	IE5.5	IE6
tabIndex				x			x	x	x	x
Read/Write										
Type: Integer										

Here's an example where I'm rearranging the tab order of three text fields in a web page:

(Listing 05-22.html on the web site)

```
<HTML>
    <HEAD>
        <TITLE>
            Using the tabIndex Property
        </TITLE>
    </HEAD>

    <BODY>
        <H1>
            Using the tabIndex Property
        </H1>
        <INPUT TYPE="TEXT" NAME="text1">
        <INPUT TYPE="TEXT" NAME="text2">
        <INPUT TYPE="TEXT" NAME="text3">
        <SCRIPT LANGAUGE="JavaScript">
            <!--
            document.all.text1.tabIndex = 2
            document.all.text2.tabIndex = 1
            document.all.text3.tabIndex = 0
            // -->
        </SCRIPT>
    </BODY>
</HTML>
```

When the user presses the Tab key repeatedly, the focus moves from the element with tab index 0 to the element with tab index 1, then tab index 2, and so on.

The *tagName* Property

As we know, the tagName property holds the tag name of an element—for example, a <P> element's tagName property will hold "P". You can find the support for this property in Table 5.56.

Table 5.56   **The *tagName* Property**

Property	NS2	NS3	NS4	NS6	IE3a	IE3b	IE4	IE5	IE5.5	IE6
tagName				x			x	x	x	x
	Read-only									
	Type: String									

We've already see the `tagName` property at work; this example from Chapter 4 shows several different ways of accessing HTML elements:

(Listing 04-10.html on the web site)

```
<HTML>
    <HEAD>
        <TITLE>
            Accessing HTML Elements
        </TITLE>
        <SCRIPT LANGUAGE="JavaScript">
            <!--
            function getText()
            {
                if(navigator.appName == "Netscape") {
                    alert("document.getElementsByName(\"text1\")[0].tagName= "
                        + document.getElementsByName("text1")[0].tagName)
                    alert("document.getElementsByTagName(\"P\")[0].tagName= "
                        + document.getElementsByTagName("P")[0].tagName)
                }

                if (navigator.appName == "Microsoft Internet Explorer") {
                    alert("document.all.text1.tagName = "
                        + document.all.text1.tagName)
                    alert("document.all[\"text1\"].tagName = "
                        + document.all["text1"].tagName)
                    alert("document.all.tags(\"P\").tagName = "
                        + document.all.tags("P")[0].tagName)
                    alert("document.getElementsByName(\"text1\")[0].tagName = "
                        + document.getElementsByName("text1")[0].tagName)
                    alert("document.getElementsByTagName(\"P\")[0].tagName = "
                        + document.getElementsByTagName("P")[0].tagName)
                }
            }
            // -->
        </SCRIPT>
    </HEAD>

    <BODY>
        <H1>Accessing HTML Elements</H1>
        <P NAME="text1" ID="text1">
            Here's the text.
        </P>
        <FORM NAME="form1">
            <INPUT TYPE="BUTTON" VALUE="Click Me!" ONCLICK="getText()">
```

```
        </FORM>
    </BODY>
</HTML>
```

The *tagUrn* Property

You can use the `tagUrn` property with XML you've embedded in an HTML page. (We'll see how to embed XML in Chapter 22.) This property returns an element's namespace Uniform Resource Name (URN). You can find the support for this property in Table 5.57.

Table 5.57 **The *tagUrn* Property**

Property	NS2	NS3	NS4	NS6	IE3a	IE3b	IE4	IE5	IE5.5	IE6
tagUrn								x	x	x
Read-only Type: String										

The *timeContainer* Property

The `timeContainer` property sets or gets the type of timeline associated with a timed element in the Internet Explorer. Here are the possible string values:

- **excl.** Indicates the exclusive timeline container element in a document. Only descendents of this element can play at one time.
- **none (the default).** The current element does not define a local timeline.
- **par.** All descendants of this element have independent (also called *parallel*) timing.
- **seq.** Indicates a sequence timeline container element. When the timeline of an element completes, the next element in the sequence starts playing.

You can find the support for this property in Table 5.58.

Table 5.58 **The *timeContainer* Property**

Property	NS2	NS3	NS4	NS6	IE3a	IE3b	IE4	IE5	IE5.5	IE6
timeContainer									x	x
Read/write Type: String										

The *title* Property

The title property is a W3C property that adds some explanatory data to HTML elements. Browsers use the title property as a tooltip (those small windows that pop up with descriptive text when the mouse rests on an object). You can find the support for this property in Table 5.59.

Table 5.59 **The *title* Property**

Property	NS2	NS3	NS4	NS6	IE3a	IE3b	IE4	IE5	IE5.5	IE6
title				x			x	x	x	x
		Read/Write								
		Type: String								

Here's an example that adds a tooltip to some text in a <P> element:

(Listing 05-23.html on the web site)

```
<HTML>
    <HEAD>
        <TITLE>
            Using the title Property
        </TITLE>
    </HEAD>

    <BODY>
        <H1>Using the title Property</H1>
        <P NAME="text1" ID="text1">
            Here's the text.
        </P>
        <SCRIPT LANGUAGE="JavaScript">
            <!--
            document.all.text1.title = "Here's a tooltip!"
            // -->
        </SCRIPT>
    </BODY>
</HTML>
```

You can see the results in Figure 5.17, where the tooltip is displaying its text.

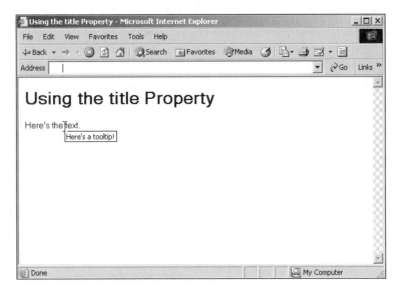

Figure 5.17   Using the `title` properties.

The *uniqueID* Property

In the Internet Explorer, you can create unique ID values to assign to elements using the `uniqueID` property, and that can be useful when you're creating new elements (as discussed in Chapter 16). You can find the support for this property in Table 5.60.

Table 5.60   **The *uniqueID* Property**

Property	NS2	NS3	NS4	NS6	IE3a	IE3b	IE4	IE5	IE5.5	IE6
uniqueID								x	x	x
	Read-only									
	Type: String									

Here's an example that creates a new ID for a header and displays that ID (typically, unique IDs are values, such as `"ms__id18"` and so forth):

```
<HTML>
    <HEAD>
        <TITLE>
            Using the uniqueID Property
        </TITLE>
    </HEAD>
```

continues ▶

```
    <BODY>
        <H1 ID="Header">Using the uniqueID Property</H1>

        <SCRIPT LANGUAGE = "JavaScript">
            <!--
            alert(Header.uniqueID)
            // -->
        </SCRIPT>
    </BODY>
</HTML>
```

And that's it—we've covered the core HTML properties. As you can see, there's a tremendous amount of JavaScript power here; and when working in future chapters, you'll be able to find the definition of any property marked as "core" in this chapter. Let's push ahead—in the next chapter, I'll take a look at the core HTML methods and events.

6

Using Core HTML Methods and Events

I N THE PRECEDING CHAPTER, WE SAW JAVASCRIPT'S core HTML properties; in this chapter, we'll take a look at JavaScript's core HTML methods and events. You can find JavaScript's core HTML methods and events in Table 6.1, and we'll cover them all in this chapter.

Tip

Note the capitalization in Table 6.1; methods use the Java capitalization scheme—for instance, removeChild—but events are all in lower case, such as onmousemove. Some books use the Java capitalization scheme for events too, such as onMouseMove, but that's incorrect; it's really onmousemove and because capitalization counts in JavaScript, using onMouseMove won't work.

Table 6.1 **Core Methods and Events of HTML Elements**

Methods	Events
addBehavior	onactivate
addEventListener	onbeforeactivate
appendChild	onbeforecopy
applyElement	onbeforecut
attachEvent	onbeforedeactivate
blur	onbeforeeditfocus
clearAttributes	onbeforepaste

continues ▶

Table 6.1   **Continued**

Methods	Events
click	onblur
cloneNode	onclick
componentFromPoint	oncontextmenu
contains	oncontrolselect
detachEvent	oncopy
dispatchEvent	oncut
dragDrop	ondblclick
fireEvent	ondeactivate
focus	ondrag
getAdjacentText	ondragend
getAttribute	ondragenter
getAttributeNode	ondragleave
getBoundingClientRect	ondragover
getClientRects	ondragstart
getElementsByTagName	ondrop
getExpression	onfilterchange
hasChildNodes	onfocus
insertAdjacentElement	onfocusin
insertAdjacentHTML	onfocusout
insertAdjacentText	onhelp
insertBefore	onkeydown
item	onkeypress
mergeAttributes	onkeyup
normalize	onlosecapture
releaseCapture	onmousedown
removeAttribute	onmouseenter
removeAttributeNode	onmouseleave
removeBehavior	onmousemove
removeChild	onmouseout
removeEventListener	onmouseover
removeExpression	onmouseup
removeNode	onmousewheel

Methods	Events
replaceAdjacentText	onmove
replaceChild	onmoveend
replaceNode	onmovestart
scrollIntoView	onpaste
setActive	onpropertychange
setAttribute	onreadystatechange
setAttributeNode	onresize
setCapture	onresizeend
setExpression	onresizestart
supports	onselectstart
swapNode	ontimeerror
tags	
urns	

Like the preceding chapter, this chapter is intended partly for reference; to cover all of JavaScript's core HTML methods and events, we'll occasionally need to cover some topics that we haven't discussed yet and which are coming up in later chapters, such as style sheets or Dynamic HTML. As in the preceding chapter, that won't be a problem for the most part, but feel free to skip that material until you need it when dealing with the programming in later chapters.

JavaScript's Core HTML Methods

We've already seen some of the core HTML methods at work, such as the getElementsByTagName method, which returns an array of elements based with the same tag name. Here's an example we saw in Chapter 4, "Handling the Browser Environment":

(Listing 04-11.html on the web site)

```
<HTML>
    <HEAD>
        <TITLE>
            Accessing HTML Elements
        </TITLE>
        <SCRIPT LANGUAGE="JavaScript">
            <!--
            function getText()
            {
                if(navigator.appName == "Netscape") {
                alert("document.form1.text1.value = " + document.form1.text1.value)
```

continues ▶

```
            alert("document.forms[0].text1.value = " +
            ➥document.forms[0].text1.value)
            alert("document.getElementsByName(\"text1\")[0].value = "
                + document.getElementsByName("text1")[0].value)
            alert("document.getElementsByTagName(\"INPUT\")[0].value = "
                + document.getElementsByTagName("INPUT")[0].value)
        }

        if (navigator.appName == "Microsoft Internet Explorer") {
            alert("document.form1.text1.value = " + document.form1.text1.value)
            alert("document.forms[0].text1.value = "
                + document.forms[0].text1.value)
            alert("document.all.text1.value = "
                + document.all.text1.value)
            alert("document.all[\"text1\"].value = "
                + document.all["text1"].value)
            alert("document.all.tags(\"INPUT\")[0].value = "
                + document.all.tags("INPUT")[0].value)
            alert("document.getElementsByName(\"text1\")[0].value = "
                + document.getElementsByName("text1")[0].value)
            alert("document.getElementsByTagName(\"INPUT\")[0].value = "
                + document.getElementsByTagName("INPUT")[0].value)
        }
    }
    // -->
    </SCRIPT>
</HEAD>

<BODY>
    <H1>Accessing HTML Elements</H1>
    <FORM NAME="form1">
        <INPUT TYPE="TEXT" NAME="text1" ID="text1">
        <INPUT TYPE="BUTTON" VALUE="Click Me!" ONCLICK="getText()">
    </FORM>
</BODY>
</HTML>
```

(As you can see in this code, we also saw the `getElementsByName` method, but
that method is a method of the `document` object only, and is not a core
HTML method that applies to all HTML elements and browser objects.)
Working with JavaScript's core HTML methods is straightforward—you just
pass any arguments to the method as you would with any method. Handling
events, on the other hand, is a different story.

Using JavaScript's Core HTML Events

Handling events in JavaScript has become complex in recent years because
you can now do things three ways: the Netscape Navigator way, the Internet
Explorer way, and the W3C way. We'll take a look at these various techniques

and event handling in depth in Chapter 15, "Working with the Mouse, Keyboard, and Images," but I'll introduce the topic here. Despite the complexities, we'll be able to cover at least 95 percent of the typical JavaScript event handling here in this chapter.

Connecting an Event Handler Using Event Attributes

We've already seen how to handle events in a general way—you can just use an HTML event attribute such as ONCLICK to connect an event to a JavaScript function, called an event handler. Here's an example from Chapter 1, "Essential JavaScript." In this case, I'm connecting a button's ONCLICK HTML attribute to a JavaScript function named alerter:

(Listing 01-04.html on the web site)

```
<HTML>
    <HEAD>
        <TITLE>
            Executing Scripts in Response to User Action
        </TITLE>
        <SCRIPT LANGUAGE="JavaScript">
            <!--
            function alerter()
            {
                window.alert("You clicked the button!")
            }
            // -->
        </SCRIPT>
    </HEAD>

    <BODY>
        <H1>Executing Scripts in Response to User Action</H1>
        <FORM>
            <INPUT TYPE="BUTTON" ONCLICK="alerter()" VALUE="Click Me!">
        </FORM>
    </BODY>
</HTML>
```

You can see the results in Figure 6.1, where I've clicked the button and the JavaScript code displays an alert box.

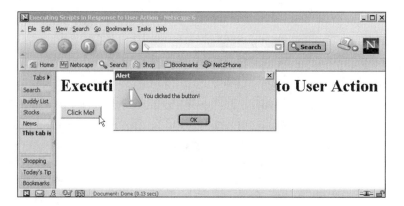

Figure 6.1   Using an event in the Netscape Navigator.

Connecting an Event Handler Using Object Properties

In the preceding example, I used the HTML event attribute ONCLICK to connect an event to an event handler. (Because this is an HTML attribute, it can
be any mix of capital and small letters; in this book, however, I'm capitalizing
HTML to distinguish it from JavaScript, so here it's ONCLICK.) In recent
browsers (NS3+ and IE4+), you also can connect an event handler in
JavaScript code, using JavaScript's events such as onclick (all small letters),
which enables you to change event handlers as you want. Here's an example
using the onclick event in JavaScript, where I'm connecting that event to
the button and the alerter function:

```
<HTML>
    <HEAD>
        <TITLE>
            Executing Scripts in Response to User Action
        </TITLE>
    </HEAD>

    <BODY>
        <H1>Executing Scripts in Response to User Action</H1>
        <FORM ID="form1" NAME="form1">
            <INPUT ID="button1" NAME="button1" TYPE="BUTTON" VALUE="Click Me!">
        </FORM>
        <SCRIPT LANGUAGE="JavaScript">
            <!--
            document.form1.button1.onclick = alerter
            function alerter()
            {
                window.alert("You clicked the button!")
            }
```

```
            // -->
        </SCRIPT>
    </BODY>
</HTML>
```

Connecting an Event Handler Using *<SCRIPT FOR>*

In the Internet Explorer 4+, you also can use the `<SCRIPT>` element's `FOR` attribute to connect a script to a particular event. We saw this as far back as Chapter 1; for example, here's how I connect a script to the `onclick` event of the HTML button `button1`:

(Listing 01-06.html on the web site)

```
<HTML>
    <HEAD>
        <TITLE>
            Using the SCRIPT FOR Element
        </TITLE>
        <SCRIPT FOR="button1" EVENT="onclick" LANGUAGE="JavaScript">
            <!--
            alert("You clicked the button!")
            // -->
        </SCRIPT>
    </HEAD>

    <BODY>
        <H1>Using the SCRIPT FOR Element</H1>
        <FORM NAME="FORM1">
            <INPUT TYPE="BUTTON" NAME="button1" VALUE="Click Me!">
        </FORM>
    </BODY>
</HTML>
```

Connecting an Event Handler Using the *attachEvent* Method

There's still another way to connect an event handler to an event—you can use the Internet Explorer `attachEvent` method (available in IE5+). You use this method on the HTML element you want to attach an event handler to, passing the name of the event to use (in quotes) and the event handler function (without quotes), like this:

```
<HTML>
    <HEAD>
        <TITLE>Using the attachEvent Method</TITLE>
    </HEAD>

    <BODY>
        <H1>Using the attachEvent Method</H1>
        <FORM NAME="form1">
```

continues ▸

```
        <INPUT TYPE="BUTTON" NAME="button1" VALUE="Click Me!">
    </FORM>
    <SCRIPT LANGUAGE="JavaScript">
        <!--
        document.form1.button1.attachEvent("onclick", alerter)
        function alerter()
        {
            alert("You clicked the button!")
        }
        // -->
    </SCRIPT>
  </BODY>
</HTML>
```

As you can see, you can connect events to event handlers in a number of ways. In fact, that's just the beginning. Here, we've used only the simple onclick event. However, events often have more data connected with them—for example, when an onmousedown event occurs, you know the user pressed the mouse button—but where did the mouse event actually occur? You can find that out by using an event object.

Using *event* Objects

Both the Netscape Navigator and the Internet Explorer have an event object, and you can retrieve event data from this object. As we'll see in Chapter 15, however, the properties of this object vary not only by browser, but also by version. You can see a summary of some common event object properties in Table 6.2 by browser and version.

Table 6.2 **Core *event* Object Properties**

NS4	NS6	IE4+	**Means**
–	clientX	clientX	X location in a window
–	clientY	clientY	Y location in a window
layerX	layerX	x	X location in a positioned item
layerY	layerY	y	Y location in a positioned item
modifiers	shiftKey	shiftKey	Keyboard modifier keys
	altKey	altKey	
	ctrlKey	ctrlKey	
–	–	offsetX	X location in a container
–	–	offsetY	Y location in a container
pageX	pageX	–	X location in the page
pageY	pageY	–	Y location in the page

NS4	NS6	IE4+	Means
screenX	screenX	screenX	X location in the screen
screenY	screenY	screenY	Y location in the screen
target	target	srcElement	Element the event was targeted to
type	type	type	Type of event that occurred
–	–	wheelDelta	The distance the wheel button rolled
which	keyCode	keyCode	Keyboard key that caused the event
which	button	button	Mouse button that caused the event

Tip

Here's another good property to know of the Internet Explorer's event object: `returnValue`. If you set `window.event.returnValue` to false in an event handler, the browser does not perform the default operation it usually performs for that event. See "The *oncopy* Event" in this chapter for an example, where we're overriding an attempt to copy text from a web page.

Cross-Browser Event Handling

There is another difference besides the differences you see in Table 6.2—in the Netscape Navigator, the `event` object is passed to your event handler; in the Internet Explorer before version 6.0, however, the `event` object is part of the `window` object, and you referenced it as `window.event` (in other words, as a global object, instead of being passed to event handlers). To account for this difference, you used to use code like this, where I'm placing the `event` object in a variable named e—if we're working in the Netscape Navigator, we'll use the event object passed to the event handler; otherwise I'll assign `window.event` to e, like this:

```
function handler(e)
{
    //For browsers before Internet Explorer 6.0
    if (!e){
        e = window.event
    }
    //event-handling code
}
```

Here's an example; in this case, I'll use the clientX and clientY properties common to the event object in both the Netscape Navigator and the Internet Explorer to discover where the mouse button was pressed. The origin for clientX and clientY is at upper left of the client area of the browser. (The client area is the display area, which doesn't include toolbars, status bars, menus, and so on.) Here's the code:

(Listing 06-01.html on the web site)

```html
<HTML>
    <HEAD>
        <TITLE>Handling Events</TITLE>
    </HEAD>

    <BODY ONMOUSEDOWN="display(event)">
        <H1>Handling Events: Click this Page!</H1>
        <FORM NAME="form1">
            <INPUT TYPE="TEXT" NAME="text1"></INPUT>
        </FORM>
        <SCRIPT LANGUAGE="JavaScript">
            <!--
            function display(e)
            {
                //For browsers before Internet Explorer 6.0
                if (!e){
                    e = window.event
                }
                document.form1.text1.value = "You clicked (" +
                    e.clientX + ", " + e.clientY + ")"
            }
            // -->
        </SCRIPT>
    </BODY>
</HTML>
```

Note how I've specified that the Netscape Navigator should pass an event object to the event handler here, by passing the keyword "event": <BODY ONMOUSEDOWN="display(event)">. This ensures that the Netscape Navigator will pass an event object to the event handler. Earlier versions of the Internet Explorer, on the other hand, will pass null here. You can see the results of this code in Figure 6.2.

Tip

The Netscape Navigator attaches special attention to the "event" argument. You can use multiple arguments like this: <BODY ONMOUSEDOWN="display(this, event)">, and the Netscape Navigator will pass the event object in the position given by the "event" argument.

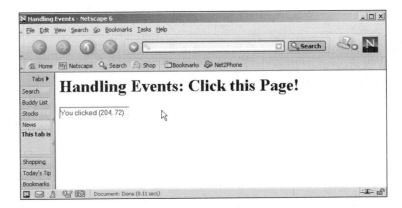

Figure 6.2   Using a mouse event in the Netscape Navigator.

The situation has changed in the Internet Explorer 6.0, however, making this kind of object detection less reliable. Perhaps because Microsoft realized that the trend is moving toward passing event objects to event handlers instead of using global event objects in the W3C DOM level 2 (which Microsoft has yet to implement), or to give programmers tackling both the Internet Explorer and Netscape Navigator a break, event handlers in Internet Explorer 6.0 now *are* passed to an event object (identical to window.event, which still exists and is still accessible) if you specify the "event" argument when connecting an event handler to an event, like this: `<BODY ONMOUSEDOWN="display(event)">`.

This makes things a little awkward for scripts that are used to checking for a passed event object in event handlers to distinguish between the two browsers. In some cases, those scripts will have to be updated to check the name of the browser directly (using the navigator.appName property), and I'll often use that technique in this chapter.

That introduces us to event handling in the Netscape Navigator and the Internet Explorer; we'll see more on event handling, and in more depth, in Chapter 15. Besides this type of event handling, there's also another type: the W3C DOM type.

Handling Events in the W3C DOM

The W3C technique of event handling, following the lead of Java, is that you must register for the events you want to catch using a *listener*, which is just an event handler.

There are several listener types, one for each type of event, as you see in Table 6.3. These listeners are implemented only in the Netscape Navigator 6.0 (and not all of them at that)—event handling was introduced only in the W3C DOM level 2, and the Internet Explorer supports only the W3C DOM level 1 fully. Note that there are far fewer W3C events than standard Internet Explorer and Netscape Navigator events (which you see in Table 6.1.)—and also note that there is no on prefixing these names: for example, here, you use the `click` event, not the `onclick` event.

Table 6.3   **W3C DOM Event Listener Types**

Listeners

abort	blur	change
click	DOMActivate	DOMAttrModified
DOMCharacterDataModified	DOMFocusIn	DOMFocusOut
DOMNodeInserted	DOMNodeInsertedIntoDocument	DOMNodeRemoved
DOMNodeRemovedFromDocument	DOMSubtreeModified	error
focus	load	mousedown
mousemove	mouseout	mouseover
mouseup	reset	resize
scroll	select	submit
unload		

The event object passed to a listener function in the Netscape Navigator is much like a standard NS6 event object. You can see some of the properties of W3C event objects in the Netscape Navigator in Table 6.4, which you can match up to those in Table 6.2, with the addition of the `currentTarget` property, which holds the current target element of an event that you've routed in ways we'll see in Chapter 15—the `originalTarget` property, which is holds original target element of the event, the `metaKey` property to handle meta key events, and the `timeStamp` property, which holds information about when the event occurred.

Table 6.4   **Some W3C DOM Event Object Properties**

Properties

currentTarget	type	target
originalTarget	timeStamp	altKey
ctrlKey	shiftKey	metaKey

Properties

charCode	keyCode	screenX
screenY	clientX	clientY
button	layerX	layerY
pageX	pageY	which

Tip

The W3C DOM event object has a method that corresponds to the Internet Explorer's returnValue property: cancelDefault. If you call an event object's cancelDefault method, the browser does not perform the default operation it usually performs for that event. For an example using the Internet Explorer's returnValue property, see "The *oncopy* Event" in this chapter for an example, where we're overriding an attempt to copy text from a web page.

Here's an example. In this case, I'll add an event listener to the click event of a <SPAN> element and display the ID of the <SPAN> element when the user clicks that element. To do that, I'll use the addEventListener method, passing that method the name of the event to listen for, the event handler function, and a value of true to indicate that I want to capture this event and not route it on to another event handler (this example, which uses the addEventListener method, is targeted at Netscape Navigator 6.0):

(Listing 06-02.html on the web site)

```
<HTML>
    <HEAD>
        <TITLE>Handling W3C Events</TITLE>
    </HEAD>

    <BODY>
        <H1>Handling W3C Events</H1>
        <P><SPAN ID="span1">Click Me.</SPAN></P>
        <FORM NAME="form1">
            <INPUT TYPE="TEXT" ID="text1"></INPUT>
        </FORM>
        <SCRIPT LANGUAGE="JavaScript">
            <!--
            document.getElementById("span1").addEventListener("click", display, true)
            function display(e)
            {
                document.form1.text1.value = "You clicked: " +
                    e.currentTarget.id
            }
            // -->
        </SCRIPT>
    </BODY>
</HTML>
```

You can see the results in Figure 6.3, where we're catching the <SPAN> element's W3C `click` event.

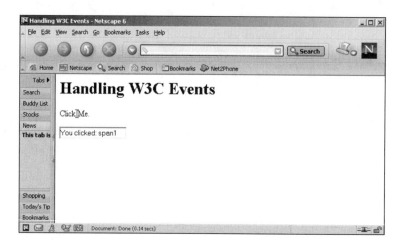

Figure 6.3 Using a W3C event in the Netscape Navigator.

JavaScript's Core HTML Methods

That gives us the overview we'll need of event handling in JavaScript; it's time now to turn to JavaScript's core HTML methods and events. I'll start with the core methods. As in the preceding chapter, the items here are all over the map, making it impossible to group them together into various programming topics. The best way of handling the core HTML methods and events is to just list them one after the other, explaining them all in turn. In the coming chapters, when we put these methods and events to work, you'll be able to come back to this chapter for all the details.

The *addBehavior* Method

You use the `addBehavior` method to add a new Internet Explorer behavior to an object, passing this method the URL of the behavior. You can see the support for this method in Table 6.5.

Table 6.5 **The *addBehavior* Method**

Method	NS2	NS3	NS4	NS6	IE3a	IE3b	IE4	IE5	IE5.5	IE6
addBehavior (*URL*)								x	x	x
Returns: Integer										

As discussed in Chapter 4, a behavior is a customized script you can save as an external file that can be applied to any HTML element and that has access to some powerful techniques. This method returns a behavior ID value that you can later pass to removeBehavior (covered later in this chapter) to remove the behavior. We'll see how to work with behaviors in Chapter 17, "Dynamic HTML: Drag and Drop, Data Binding, and Behaviors."

The *addEventListener* Method

You use the addEventListener method to add a W3C event listener to an object, as discussed earlier in this chapter (see "Handling Events in the W3C DOM"). You can see the support for this method in Table 6.6.

Table 6.6　The *addEventListener* Method

Method	NS2	NS3	NS4	NS6	IE3a	IE3b	IE4	IE5	IE5.5	IE6
addEventListener(*event*, *listenerFunction*, *capture*)				x						
No return value										

To use this method, you pass the W3C event you want to work with (see Table 6.3), the listener function you want to use to handle events, and a Boolean set to true if you want this event to "bubble" (that is, move upward to parent objects as we'll discuss in Chapter 15). Here's the example we saw earlier in this chapter that uses addEventListener to connect a listener function to a <SPAN> element's W3C click event:

```
<HTML>
    <HEAD>
        <TITLE>Handling W3C Events</TITLE>
    </HEAD>

    <BODY>
        <H1>Handling W3C Events</H1>
        <P><SPAN ID="span1">Click Me.</SPAN></P>
        <P><SPAN ID="span2">Click Me Too.</SPAN></P>
        <FORM NAME="form1">
            <INPUT TYPE="TEXT" ID="text1"></INPUT>
        </FORM>
        <SCRIPT LANGUAGE="JavaScript">
            <!--
            document.getElementById("span2").addEventListener("click", display, true)
            function display(e)
            {
                document.form1.text1.value = "You clicked: " +
                    e.currentTarget.id
            }
```

continues ▶

```
        // -->
    </SCRIPT>
  </BODY>
</HTML>
```

The *appendChild* Method

The `appendChild` method enables you to append a child HTML element (not a node) to another HTML element. You can see the support for this method in Table 6.7.

Table 6.7 **The *appendChild* Method**

Method	NS2	NS3	NS4	NS6	IE3a	IE3b	IE4	IE5	IE5.5	IE6
appendChild (node)				x				x	x	x
Returns: Node										

We'll see more about methods like this, which enable you to change the structure of a document on-the-fly, in Chapter 16, "Dynamic HTML: Changing Web Pages On-the-Fly." Here's an example that uses the `appendChild` method to add a new item to an unordered HTML list, and the `replaceChild` method (coming up later in this chapter) to replace the first item in the list. When the user clicks the Add New Item button, the `appendChild` method adds a new item to an unordered HTML list:

(Listing 06-03.html on the web site)

```
<HTML>
    <HEAD>
        <TITLE>
            Using the appendChild and replaceChild Methods
        </TITLE>

        <SCRIPT LANGUAGE="JavaScript">
            <!--
            function adder()
            {
                var item1 = document.createElement("LI")
                item1.innerHTML = "Next item"
                document.getElementById("list1").appendChild(item1)
            }

            function replacer(form)
            {
                var item1 = document.createElement("LI")
                item1.innerHTML = "Newer First Item"
```

```
                var lastItem = document.getElementById("list1").firstChild
                document.getElementById("list1").replaceChild(item1, lastItem)
            }
            -->
        </SCRIPT>
    </HEAD>
    <BODY>

        <H1>Using the appendChild and replaceChild Methods</H1>

        <FORM>
            <INPUT TYPE=BUTTON VALUE="Add New Item" onclick="adder()">
            <INPUT TYPE=BUTTON VALUE="Replace First Item" onclick="replacer()">
        </FORM>
        <UL ID="list1">
            <LI>First Item
            <LI>Second Item
        <UL>
    </BODY>
</HTML>
```

You can see the results in Figure 6.4. Originally, the list only had two items, First Item and Second Item; but when you click the Add New Item button, the code adds a new item, Next Item, to the list.

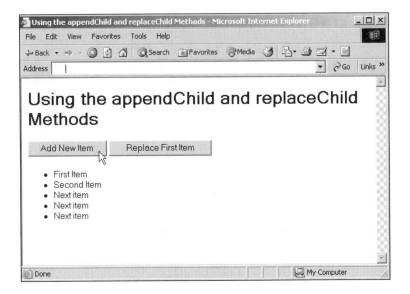

Figure 6.4   Using the `appendChild` and `replaceChild` Methods.

The *applyElement* Method

The `applyElement` method enables you to create parent or child elements in the Internet Explorer. You can see the support for this method in Table 6.8.

Table 6.8   **The *applyElement* Method**

Method	NS2	NS3	NS4	NS6	IE3a	IE3b	IE4	IE5	IE5.5	IE6
applyElement (*element* [, *type*]) No return value								x	x	x

You first create a new element with the `document` object `createElement` method and pass that element to this method, along with the *type* argument, which can be either of these strings:

- `"outside"` (the default). The indicated element becomes a parent of the current element.

- `"inside"`. The indicated element becomes a child of the current element—but contains all children of the current element.

The *attachEvent* Method

You can use the `attachEvent` method to attach an event handler to an event in the Internet Explorer. This method returns true if the event handler was connected successfully. You can see the support for this method in Table 6.9.

Table 6.9   **The *attachEvent* Method**

Method	NS2	NS3	NS4	NS6	IE3a	IE3b	IE4	IE5	IE5.5	IE6
attachEvent (*event*, *handlerFunction*) Returns: Boolean								x	x	x

You pass this method the event to handle (as a string) and the handler function. We've already seen an example using the `attachEvent` method in the beginning of this chapter; in that example, I attached an event handler to a button's `onclick` event:

```
<HTML>
    <HEAD>
        <TITLE>Using the attachEvent Method</TITLE>
    </HEAD>

    <BODY>
        <H1>Using the attachEvent Method</H1>
        <FORM NAME="form1">
            <INPUT TYPE="BUTTON" NAME="button1" VALUE="Click Me!">
        </FORM>
        <SCRIPT LANGUAGE="JavaScript">
            <!--
            document.form1.button1.attachEvent("onclick", alerter)
            function alerter()
            {
                alert("You clicked the button!")
            }
            // -->
        </SCRIPT>
    </BODY>
</HTML>
```

The *blur* Method

You use the `blur` method to remove the focus from an element. (After the focus is gone, the element will no longer be the target for keystrokes.) You can see the support for this method in Table 6.10.

Table 6.10 **The *blur* Method**

Method	NS2	NS3	NS4	NS6	IE3a	IE3b	IE4	IE5	IE5.5	IE6
blur()	x	x	x	x	x	x	x	x	x	x
No return value										

This method pairs with the `focus` method, which gives an element the focus. (The `focus` method is coming up in this chapter.)

The *clearAttributes* Method

The `clearAttributes` method deletes all attributes from an HTML element except the NAME and ID attributes. You can see the support for this method in Table 6.11.

Table 6.11 **The *clearAttributes* Method**

Method	NS2	NS3	NS4	NS6	IE3a	IE3b	IE4	IE5	IE5.5	IE6
clearAttributes()								x	x	x
No return value										

The *click* Method

Calling an object's click method is almost the same as triggering a click event for the object—before Netscape Navigator 4.0 and Internet Explorer 4.0; however, this method did not call the object's onclick event handler. You can see the support for this method in Table 6.12.

Table 6.12 **The *click* Method**

Method	NS2	NS3	NS4	NS6	IE3a	IE3b	IE4	IE5	IE5.5	IE6
click()	x	x	x	x	x	x	x	x	x	x
No return value										

Here's an example; in this case, when you click the second button in this page, the first button's onclick event is triggered:

(Listing 06-04.html on the web site)

```
<HTML>
    <HEAD>
        <TITLE>Using the click Method</TITLE>
        <SCRIPT LANGUAGE="JavaScript">
            <!--
            function alerter()
            {
                alert("You clicked the button!")
            }
            function clicker()
            {
                document.form1.button1.click()
            }
            // -->
        </SCRIPT>
    </HEAD>

    <BODY>
        <H1>Using the click Method</H1>
        <FORM NAME="form1">
```

```
            <INPUT TYPE="BUTTON" NAME="button1" ONCLICK="alerter()" VALUE="Click Me!">
            <INPUT TYPE="BUTTON" ONCLICK="clicker()" VALUE="Click the Other Button!">
        </FORM>
    </BODY>
</HTML>
```

The *cloneNode* Method

The `cloneNode` method copies the current node and returns a new object reference to the copy. You also can pass a Boolean, *deep*, that you set to true if you want all the node's child nodes to be copied as well; setting it false means only the node itself will be copied. You can see the support for this method in Table 6.13.

Table 6.13 **The *cloneNode* Method**

Method	NS2	NS3	NS4	NS6	IE3a	IE3b	IE4	IE5	IE5.5	IE6
cloneNode(*deep*)				x				x	x	x
Returns: Reference to a node										

The *componentFromPoint* Method

The `componentFromPoint` method returns the component of an object located at specified coordinates. This method, available as of Internet Explorer 5.0, can be used with any object that can be given scrollbars through *Cascading Style Sheets* (CSS), and it's used to determine where in an object a point is. You can see the support for this method in Table 6.14.

Table 6.14 **The *componentFromPoint* Method**

Method	NS2	NS3	NS4	NS6	IE3a	IE3b	IE4	IE5	IE5.5	IE6
componentFromPoint(*x, y*)								x	x	x
Returns: String										

You pass the client window X and Y coordinates of the point you want to check, and this method returns one of the following strings:

- **""**. Component is inside the client area of the object.
- **"handleBottom"**. Bottom sizing handle is at the indicated location.
- **"handleBottomLeft"**. Lower-left sizing handle is at the indicated location.

- `"handleBottomRight"`. Lower-right sizing handle is at the indicated location.
- `"handleLeft"`. Left sizing handle is at the indicated location.
- `"handleRight"`. Right sizing handle is at the indicated location.
- `"handleTop"`. Top sizing handle is at the indicated location.
- `"handleTopLeft"`. Upper-left sizing handle is at the indicated location.
- `"handleTopRight"`. Upper-right sizing handle is at the indicated location.
- `"outside"`. Component is outside the bounds of the object.
- `"scrollbarDown"`. Down scroll arrow is at the indicated location.
- `"scrollbarHThumb"`. Horizontal scroll thumb or box is at the indicated location.
- `"scrollbarLeft"`. Left scroll arrow is at the indicated location.
- `"scrollbarPageDown"`. Page-down scrollbar shaft is at the indicated location.
- `"scrollbarPageLeft"`. Page-left scrollbar shaft is at the indicated location.
- `"scrollbarPageRight"`. Page-right scrollbar shaft is at the indicated location.
- `"scrollbarPageUp"`. Page-up scrollbar shaft is at the indicated location.
- `"scrollbarRight"`. Right scroll arrow is at the indicated location.
- `"scrollbarUp"`. Up scroll arrow is at the indicated location.
- `"scrollbarVThumb"`. Vertical scroll thumb or box is at the indicated location.

The *contains* Method

The `contains` method indicates whether an object contains another object (in terms of nested HTML elements), returning a value of true if so, and false otherwise. You can see the support for this method in Table 6.15.

Table 6.15 **The *contains* Method**

Method	NS2	NS3	NS4	NS6	IE3a	IE3b	IE4	IE5	IE5.5	IE6
contains(*object*)							x	x	x	x
Returns: Boolean										

Here's an example where I'm checking whether `object1` contains `element1`:

```
var contained = object1.contains(element1)
```

The *detachEvent* Method

You use the detachEvent method to detach an event handler from an event; this method is the complement function to attacheEvent (see earlier in this chapter). You can see the support for this method in Table 6.16.

Table 6.16 **The *detachEvent* Method**

Method	NS2	NS3	NS4	NS6	IE3a	IE3b	IE4	IE5	IE5.5	IE6
detachEvent(*event, handlerFunction*)								x	x	x
Returns: Boolean										

Like the attacheEvent method, you pass the detachEvent method the event (in quotes) you want to detach and the handler function to detach (not in quotes). See the attacheEvent method for more information.

The *dispatchEvent* Method

The dispatchEvent method is a W3C method that enables you to send an event to an object. This is the W3C way of triggering events, as opposed to methods such as the click method. You can see the support for this method in Table 6.17.

Table 6.17 **The *dispatchEvent* Method**

Method	NS2	NS3	NS4	NS6	IE3a	IE3b	IE4	IE5	IE5.5	IE6
dispatchEvent(*eventObject*)				x						
Returns: Boolean										

To use this method, you use the document method createEvent to create an event object, and then pass the event object to the object in which you want to trigger the event. This method returns a value of true if the event was dispatched successfully, false otherwise.

The *dragDrop* Method

The dragDrop method creates a drag event. See Chapter 17 for more on dragging and dropping. You can see the support for this method in Table 6.18. This method returns true if the drag/drop operation was successful, false otherwise.

Table 6.18 **The *dragDrop* Method**

Method	NS2	NS3	NS4	NS6	IE3a	IE3b	IE4	IE5	IE5.5	IE6
dragDrop()									x	x
Returns: Boolean										

The *fireEvent* Method

The fireEvent method is much like the dispatchEvent method (see the previous topic), except fireEvent is an Internet Explorer-method only. You can see the support for this method in Table 6.19.

Table 6.19 **The *fireEvent* Method**

Method	NS2	NS3	NS4	NS6	IE3a	IE3b	IE4	IE5	IE5.5	IE6
fireEvent(*event* [, *eventObject*])									x	x
Returns: Boolean										

You pass this method the name of the event you want to "fire" (that is, trigger), and you can optionally pass an event object that you want to hold the data for this event. Here's an example where I'm causing an onclick event in a button:

(Listing 06-05.html on the web site)

```
<HTML>
    <HEAD>
        <TITLE>Using the click Method</TITLE>
        <SCRIPT LANGUAGE="JavaScript">
            <!--
            function alerter()
            {
                alert("You clicked the button!")
            }
            function clicker()
            {
                document.form1.button1.fireEvent("onclick")
            }
            // -->
        </SCRIPT>
    </HEAD>

    <BODY>
        <H1>Using the click Method</H1>
        <FORM NAME="form1">
            <INPUT TYPE="BUTTON" NAME="button1" ONCLICK="alerter()" VALUE="Click Me!">
```

```
                <INPUT TYPE="BUTTON" ONCLICK="clicker()" VALUE="Click the Other Button!">
            </FORM>
        </BODY>
</HTML>
```

This method returns a value of true if the event was triggered successfully, and false otherwise.

The *focus* Method

The focus method gives an object the focus. You can see the support for this method in Table 6.20.

Table 6.20 **The *focus* Method**

Method	NS2	NS3	NS4	NS6	IE3a	IE3b	IE4	IE5	IE5.5	IE6
focus()	x	x	x	x	x	x	x	x	x	x
	No return value									

Here's an example. When you click a button, the button gets the focus. However, suppose that button spell-checks the text in a text field—in that case, it would useful to transfer the focus back to the text field so that the user could just keep typing. Here's an example that does that:

(Listing 06-06.html on the web site)

```
<HTML>
    <HEAD>
        <TITLE>Using the focus Method</TITLE>
        <SCRIPT LANGUAGE="JavaScript">
            <!--
            function defocus()
            {
                document.form1.text1.focus()
            }
            // -->
        </SCRIPT>
    </HEAD>

    <BODY>
        <H1>Using the focus Method</H1>
        <FORM NAME="form1">
            <INPUT TYPE="TEXT" ID="text1"></INPUT>
            <INPUT TYPE="BUTTON" ONCLICK="defocus()" VALUE="Click Me"></INPUT>
        </FORM>
    </BODY>
</HTML>
```

The *getAdjacentText* Method

The getAdjacentText method enables you to get text directly from a web page. You can see the support for this method in Table 6.21.

Table 6.21 **The *getAdjacentText* Method**

Method	NS2	NS3	NS4	NS6	IE3a	IE3b	IE4	IE5	IE5.5	IE6
getAdjacentText(*position*)								x	x	x
Returns: String										

You can use this method to get the text part of an element (without any HTML tags). You pass this method a *position* argument that indicates where you want to get the text from in relation to the current object; this argument may be set to one of these values:

- **"beforeBegin"**. Text is returned from immediately before the element.
- **"afterBegin"**. Text is returned from after the start of the element (but before all other content in the element).
- **"beforeEnd"**. Text is returned from immediately before the end of the element (but after all other content in the element).
- **"afterEnd"**. Text is returned from immediately after the end of the element.

The *getAttribute* Method

As its name implies, the getAttribute returns the value of an attribute. You can see the support for this method in Table 6.22.

Table 6.22 **The *getAttribute* Method**

Method	NS2	NS3	NS4	NS6	IE3a	IE3b	IE4	IE5	IE5.5	IE6
getAttribute(*attribute*, [, *case*])	x						x	x	x	x
Returns: Attribute value										

You pass this method the name of the attribute to get, and, optionally, the *case* argument, which, if true, makes the browser search for attributes in a case-sensitive way. Here's an example where I'm getting the value of a <FORM> element:

(Listing 06-07.html on the web site)

```html
<HTML>
    <HEAD>
        <TITLE>Using the getAttribute Method</TITLE>
        <SCRIPT LANGUAGE="JavaScript">
            <!--
            function getAttr()
            {
                document.form1.text1.value = "The name of the form is " +
                    document.form1.getAttribute("NAME")
            }
            // -->
        </SCRIPT>
    </HEAD>

    <BODY>
        <H1>Using the getAttribute Method</H1>
        <FORM NAME="form1">
            <INPUT TYPE="TEXT" ID="text1" SIZE="50"></INPUT>
            <BR>
            <INPUT TYPE="BUTTON" ONCLICK="getAttr()" VALUE="Get Attribute"></INPUT>
        </FORM>
    </BODY>
</HTML>
```

You can see the results in Figure 6.5, where I'm retrieving the name of the form, form1.

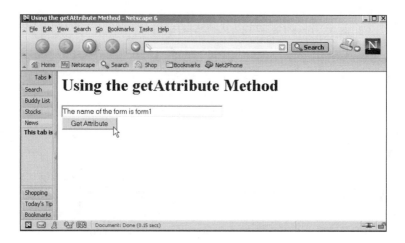

Figure 6.5   Getting an attribute's value.

The *getAttributeNode* Method

The getAttributeNode method returns an attribute object when you pass it the name of an attribute as a string. You can see the support for this method in Table 6.23.

Table 6.23 **The *getAttributeNode* Method**

Method	NS2	NS3	NS4	NS6	IE3a	IE3b	IE4	IE5	IE5.5	IE6
getAttributeNode(*attribute*)				x						x
Returns: Attribute object										

Tip

For a list of the properties of attribute objects, take a look at Table 5.7.

The *getBoundingClientRect* Method

The getBoundingClientRect method is an Internet Explorer method that returns a TextRectangle object that holds the rectangle that the object appears in, called its *bounding rectangle*. You can see the support for this method in Table 6.24.

Table 6.24 **The *getBoundingClientRect* Method**

Method	NS2	NS3	NS4	NS6	IE3a	IE3b	IE4	IE5	IE5.5	IE6
getBoundingClientRect()								x	x	x
Returns: TextRectangle object										

You can use the TextRectangle object's bottom, left, right, and top properties to get the actual bounding rectangle of an object.

The *getClientRects* Method

The getClientRects method returns a collection of TextRectangle objects (see the preceding topic) that describes the layout of the contents of an object or range within the client. Each rectangle describes a single line of content. You can see the support for this method in Table 6.25.

Table 6.25   **The *getClientRects* Method**

Method	NS2	NS3	NS4	NS6	IE3a	IE3b	IE4	IE5	IE5.5	IE6
getClientRects()								X	X	X
Returns: TextRectangle array

The *getElementsByTagName* Method

The getElementsByTagName method is a favorite method. This method
returns an array of elements in a page that have a particular tag name (such
as "P"). You can see the support for this method in Table 6.26.

Table 6.26   **The *getElementsByTagName* Method**

Method	NS2	NS3	NS4	NS6	IE3a	IE3b	IE4	IE5	IE5.5	IE6
getElementsByTagName(*tag*)				X				X	X	X
Returns: Element array

We've put this method to work back in Chapter 4 in this example (it's
Listing 04-11.html on the web site), where I'm searching for the text in an
<INPUT> element:

```
<HTML>
    <HEAD>
        <TITLE>
            Accessing HTML Elements
        </TITLE>
        <SCRIPT LANGUAGE="JavaScript">
            <!--
            function getText()
            {
                if(navigator.appName == "Netscape") {
                alert("document.form1.text1.value = " + document.form1.text1.value)
                alert("document.forms[0].text1.value = " +
                ➥document.forms[0].text1.value)
                alert("document.getElementsByName(\"text1\")[0].value = "
                    + document.getElementsByName("text1")[0].value)
                alert("document.getElementsByTagName(\"INPUT\")[0].value = "
                    + document.getElementsByTagName("INPUT")[0].value)
                }

                if (navigator.appName == "Microsoft Internet Explorer") {
                alert("document.form1.text1.value = " + document.form1.text1.value)
```

continues ▶

```
              alert("document.forms[0].text1.value = "
                  + document.forms[0].text1.value)
              alert("document.all.text1.value = "
                  + document.all.text1.value)
              alert("document.all[\"text1\"].value = "
                  + document.all["text1"].value)
              alert("document.all.tags(\"INPUT\")[0].value = "
                  + document.all.tags("INPUT")[0].value)
              alert("document.getElementsByName(\"text1\")[0].value = "
                  + document.getElementsByName("text1")[0].value)
              alert("document.getElementsByTagName(\"INPUT\")[0].value = "
                  + document.getElementsByTagName("INPUT")[0].value)
            }
          }
          // -->
        </SCRIPT>
      </HEAD>

      <BODY>
        <H1>Accessing HTML Elements</H1>
        <FORM NAME="form1">
            <INPUT TYPE="TEXT" NAME="text1" ID="text1">
            <INPUT TYPE="BUTTON" VALUE="Click Me!" ONCLICK="getText()">
        </FORM>
      </BODY>
</HTML>
```

The *getExpression* Method

The getExpression method is an Internet Explorer method that returns the
text of the expression that was assigned to an attribute using the setExpression
method (see the setExpression method later in this chapter). You can see the
support for this method in Table 6.27.

Table 6.27 **The *getExpression* Method**

Method	NS2	NS3	NS4	NS6	IE3a	IE3b	IE4	IE5	IE5.5	IE6
getExpression(*attribute*)								x	x	x
Returns: String										

The *hasChildNodes* Method

The hasChildNodes method returns true if a W3C node has child nodes, false
otherwise. You can see the support for this method in Table 6.28.

Table 6.28   **The *hasChildNodes* Method**

Method	NS2	NS3	NS4	NS6	IE3a	IE3b	IE4	IE5	IE5.5	IE6
hasChildNodes()				x				x	x	x
Returns: Boolean										

The hasChildNodes method is useful to check whether a node has any child nodes before you try to use a property such as childNodes, which holds all the child nodes. (If your code relies on childNodes not being empty, for instance, it can crash unless you check to make sure there are actually child nodes before using the childNodes collection.)

The *insertAdjacentElement* Method

The insertAdjacentElement method enables you to insert a new element into a web page. You can see the support for this method in Table 6.29.

Table 6.29   **The *insertAdjacentElement* Method**

Method	NS2	NS3	NS4	NS6	IE3a	IE3b	IE4	IE5	IE5.5	IE6
insertAdjacentElement(*position*, *element*)								x	x	x
Returns: Object										

We'll see more about methods such as this one in Chapter 16, where we change web pages on-the-fly. To use this method, you can use the document object's createElement method to create a new element, and then use the insertAdjacentElement to insert the new element next to an existing object. You specify where you want the new element with the *position* argument, which can take these values:

- **"beforeBegin".** Inserts the element immediately before the object.
- **"afterBegin".** Inserts the element after the start of the object (but before all other content in the object).
- **"beforeEnd".** Inserts the element immediately before the end of the object (but after all other content in the object).
- **"afterEnd".** Inserts the element immediately after the end of the object.

This method returns the element inserted.

The *insertAdjacentHTML* and *insertAdjacentText* Methods

The `insertAdjacentHTML` and `insertAdjacentText` methods are cornerstones of Dynamic HTML; these methods enable you to insert HTML and text into a web page. You can see the support for this method in Table 6.30.

Table 6.30 **The *insertAdjacentHTML* and *insertAdjacentText* Methods**

Method	NS2	NS3	NS4	NS6	IE3a	IE3b	IE4	IE5	IE5.5	IE6
`insertAdjacentHTML(position, HTML)`							x	x	x	x
No return value										
`insertAdjacentText(position, text)`							x	x	x	x
No return value										

We'll see more about methods like this one in Chapter 16, where we change web pages on-the-fly. Both arguments that both of these methods take are strings; the *position* argument indicates where the HTML or text should be inserted, and the second argument holds the HTML or the text to insert. Here are the possible values for the *position* argument:

- **"beforeBegin"**. Inserts text or HTML immediately before the object.
- **"afterBegin"**. Inserts text or HTML after the start of the object (but before all other content in the object).
- **"beforeEnd"**. Inserts text or HTML immediately before the end of the object (but after all other content in the object).
- **"afterEnd"**. Inserts text or HTML immediately after the end of the object.

If you are inserting HTML that you want the browser to treat as HTML, use `insertAdjacentHTML`; otherwise, use `insertAdjacentText`. (In `insertAdjacentText`, HTML tags are just treated as text.) Here's an example that inserts a new text field into a page when the user clicks a button:

(Listing 06-08.html on the web site)

```
<HTML>
    <HEAD>
        <TITLE>
            Using the insertAdjacentHTML Method
        </TITLE>
```

```
<SCRIPT LANGUAGE="JavaScript">
    <!--
    function addMore()
    {
        div1.insertAdjacentHTML("afterEnd",
        "<P>Here is a new text field: <input type=text VALUE='Hello!'>")
    }
    // -->
</SCRIPT>
</HEAD>

<BODY>
    <H1>Using the insertAdjacentHTML Method</H1>
    <DIV ID="div1">
        <INPUT TYPE=BUTTON VALUE="Click Me!" onclick="addMore()">
    </DIV>
</BODY>
</HTML>
```

You can see the results in Figure 6.6, where I've clicked the button a couple of times.

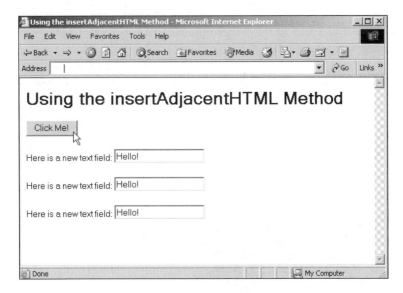

Figure 6.6   Using the `insertAdjacentHTML` Method.

The *insertBefore* Method

The insertBefore method enables you to insert a W3C node before another node. You can see the support for this method in Table 6.31.

Table 6.31 **The *insertBefore* Method**

Method	NS2	NS3	NS4	NS6	IE3a	IE3b	IE4	IE5	IE5.5	IE6
insertBefore(*node* [, *refNode*])				x				x	x	x
Returns: Node										

Here, you pass the node you want to insert, and a *reference node*. The reference is a child node of the current node, and the new node is inserted directly before the reference node. If the reference node is missing or null, the node is added as the last child node of the current node. This method returns the node that was inserted.

We'll see more on methods such as this one in Chapter 16, but here's an example where I'm creating a new <DIV> element using the document object's createElement method (which returns an element object that you also can treat as a node) and adding other objects—text and a text field—to that element using insertBefore:

(Listing 06-09.html on the web site)

```
<HTML>
    <HEAD>
        <TITLE>
            Creating New Elements
        </TITLE>

        <SCRIPT LANGUAGE="JavaScript">
            <!--
            function addMore()
            {
                var newDiv, newTextField, newText
                newDiv = document.createElement("DIV")
                newTextField = document.createElement("INPUT")
                newTextField.type = "TEXT"
                newTextField.value = "Hello!"
                newText = document.createTextNode("Here is a new text field: ")
                newDiv.insertBefore(newText, null)
                newDiv.insertBefore(newTextField, null)
                document.body.insertBefore(newDiv, null)
            }
            // -->
        </SCRIPT>
    </HEAD>
```

```
    <BODY>
        <H1>Creating New Elements</H1>
        <FORM>
            <INPUT TYPE=BUTTON VALUE="Click Me!" ONCLICK="addMore()">
        </FORM>
    </BODY>
</HTML>
```

This code gives you the same result you see in Figure 6.6.

The *item* Method

The item method gives you another way to access objects in a collection—you can use this method rather than an array index. You can see the support for this method in Table 6.32.

Table 6.32   **The *item* Method**

Method	NS2	NS3	NS4	NS6	IE3a	IE3b	IE4	IE5	IE5.5	IE6
item(number [, index])				X			X	X	X	X
Returns: Object										
item(text [, index])				X			X	X	X	X
Returns: Object										

Here are two ways to access the same node:

```
document.getElementById("span1").childNodes.item(5)
document.getElementById("span1").childNodes[5]
```

Tip

In the Internet Explorer, you also can use an item's ID value as the array index, or to access the item with the item method.

The *mergeAttributes* Method

The mergeAttributes method enables you to use an element as a sort of template when creating other elements—in this case, you pass an existing element whose attributes you want to duplicate in another element to this method. You can see the support for this method in Table 6.33.

Table 6.33   **The *mergeAttributes* Method**

Method	NS2	NS3	NS4	NS6	IE3a	IE3b	IE4	IE5	IE5.5	IE6
mergeAttributes(*Object*)								x	x	x
No return value										

The *normalize* Method

The `normalize` method enables you to merge adjacent text nodes in a document into a single node. Sometimes, when you're inserting text nodes into a document, you can end up with two or more side by side. That's not a problem for HTML browsers, but it can be for XML browsers. To fix this problem, you can merge adjacent text nodes with the `normalize` method. You can see the support for this method in Table 6.34.

Table 6.34   **The *normalize* Method**

Method	NS2	NS3	NS4	NS6	IE3a	IE3b	IE4	IE5	IE5.5	IE6
normalize()				x						x
No return value										

The *releaseCapture* Method

You can direct the Internet Explorer to capture all mouse events using the `setCapture` method. When you use `setCapture` on an object, all mouse events are channeled to that object; to stop capturing mouse events, you use `releaseCapture`. You can see the support for this method in Table 6.35.

Table 6.35   **The *releaseCapture* Method**

Method	NS2	NS3	NS4	NS6	IE3a	IE3b	IE4	IE5	IE5.5	IE6
releaseCapture()								x	x	x
No return value										

The *removeAttribute* Method

As you can guess from its name, the removeAttribute method enables you to remove an attribute from an element. You can see the support for this method in Table 6.36.

Table 6.36 **The *removeAttribute* Method**

Method	NS2	NS3	NS4	NS6	IE3a	IE3b	IE4	IE5	IE5.5	IE6
removeAttribute(*attribute*, [, *case*])				x			x	x	x	x
Returns: See text										

Here, *attribute* is the name of the attribute you want to remove when you invoke this method on an element object, and if the *case* argument is present and set to true, the browser will search for that attribute in a case-sensitive way. The Internet Explorer returns true if the attribute was removed, and false otherwise. The Netscape Navigator version of this method does not return any value.

The *removeAttributeNode* Method

The removeAttributeNode method is the W3C version of the removeAttribute method—if you've created an attribute with the setAttribute method, you can remove it with the removeAttribute method. You can see the support for this method in Table 6.37.

Table 6.37 **The *removeAttributeNode* Method**

Method	NS2	NS3	NS4	NS6	IE3a	IE3b	IE4	IE5	IE5.5	IE6
removeAttributeNode(*attributeNode*)	x								x	
Returns: attribute object										

The *removeBehavior* Method

You use the removeBehavior method to remove an Internet Explorer behavior. When you add a behavior to an object with the addBehavior method (discussed earlier in this chapter), addBehavior returns an ID value you can later pass to removeBehavior to remove the behavior. You can see the support for this method in Table 6.38.

Table 6.38 **The *removeBehavior* Method**

Method	NS2	NS3	NS4	NS6	IE3a	IE3b	IE4	IE5	IE5.5	IE6
removeBehavior(*behaviorID*)								x	x	x
Returns: Boolean										

The *removeChild* Method

You use the `removeChild` method to remove a child node from an object. Just pass the node you want to remove (which you can get from the `childNodes` collection); this method will remove the node and return it. You can see the support for this method in Table 6.39.

Table 6.39 **The *removeChild* Method**

Method	NS2	NS3	NS4	NS6	IE3a	IE3b	IE4	IE5	IE5.5	IE6
removeChild(*node*)				x				x	x	x
Returns: Node object										

The *removeEventListener* Method

You use the `removeEventListener` method to remove a W3C event listener. The arguments passed to this method are the same as you pass to the `addEventListener`, discussed earlier in this chapter. You can see the support for this method in Table 6.40.

Table 6.40 **The *removeEventListener* Method**

Method	NS2	NS3	NS4	NS6	IE3a	IE3b	IE4	IE5	IE5.5	IE6
removeEventListener(*event*, *listnerFunction*, *capture*)										
				x						
No return value										

The *removeExpression* Method

Using the Internet Explorer, you can assign expressions to object properties —see the `setExpression` method in this chapter. Using `removeExpression`, you can remove that expression. You can see the support for this method in Table 6.41.

Table 6.41 **The *removeExpression* Method**

Method	NS2	NS3	NS4	NS6	IE3a	IE3b	IE4	IE5	IE5.5	IE6
removeExpression(*property*)								x	x	x
Returns: Boolean										

To use this method, you pass the object property you want to remove the expression from; the method returns true if it was successful, and false otherwise.

The *removeNode* Method

You use the removeNode method to remove the current node. If you pass this method a value of false (the default), the node will remove itself; if you pass a value of true, the node will remove itself and any children. You can see the support for this method in Table 6.42.

Table 6.42 **The *removeNode* Method**

Method	NS2	NS3	NS4	NS6	IE3a	IE3b	IE4	IE5	IE5.5	IE6
removeNode([*children*])								x	x	x
Returns: Node object										

Unlike the removeChild method, removeNode is an Internet Explorer-only method.

The *replaceAdjacentText* Method

The replaceAdjacentText method is much like the insertAdjacentText method, discussed earlier in this chapter, except that this method enables you to replace text rather than insert it. You can see the support for this method in Table 6.43.

Table 6.43 **The *replaceAdjacentText* Method**

Method	NS2	NS3	NS4	NS6	IE3a	IE3b	IE4	IE5	IE5.5	IE6
replaceAdjacentText(*position*, *text*)								x	x	x
Returns: String										

You pass a *position* argument to this method, and the new text. Here's the values the *position* argument can take:

- **"beforeBegin"**. Replaces the text immediately before the element.
- **"afterBegin"**. Replaces the text after the start of the element (but before all other content in the element).
- **"beforeEnd"**. Replaces the text immediately before the end of the element (but after all other content in the element).
- **"afterEnd"**. Replaces the text immediately after the end of the element.

The *replaceChild* Method

The replaceChild method replaces an existing child node with a new child node. You can see the support for this method in Table 6.44.

Table 6.44 **The *replaceChild* Method**

Method	NS2	NS3	NS4	NS6	IE3a	IE3b	IE4	IE5	IE5.5	IE6
replaceChild(*newNode*, *oldNode*)				x				x	x	x
Returns: Node object										

To use this method, you pass the new node object and the old child node you want to replace. The replaced node is returned. For an example, take a look at the section "The *appendChild* Method" in this chapter.

The *replaceNode* Method

The replaceNode method replaces one node with another. You can see the support for this method in Table 6.45.

Table 6.45 **The *replaceNode* Method**

Method	NS2	NS3	NS4	NS6	IE3a	IE3b	IE4	IE5	IE5.5	IE6
replaceNode(*node*)								x	x	x
Returns: Node object										

To use this method on a node, you just pass the new node you want to replace that node with.

The *scrollIntoView* Method

The `scrollIntoView` method causes an object to scroll into view in the Internet Explorer, aligning it either at the top or bottom of the window as you specify. You can see the support for this method in Table 6.46.

Table 6.46 **The *scrollIntoView* Method**

Method	NS2	NS3	NS4	NS6	IE3a	IE3b	IE4	IE5	IE5.5	IE6
scrollIntoView([*top*])							x	x	x	x
No return value										

If the *top* argument is true, the top of the object is aligned to the top of the browser's client area; if it's false, the bottom of the object is aligned to the bottom of the browser's client area. Here's an example that uses `scrollIntoView` to scroll a text field into view:

(Listing 06-10.html on the web site)

```
<HTML>
    <HEAD>
        <TITLE>Using the scrollIntoView Method</TITLE>
        <SCRIPT LANGUAGE="JavaScript">
            <!--
            function scroller()
            {
                document.form1.text1.scrollIntoView(false)
            }
            // -->
        </SCRIPT>
    </HEAD>

    <BODY>
        <H1>Using the scrollIntoView Method</H1>
        <FORM NAME="form1">
            <INPUT TYPE="BUTTON" ONCLICK="scroller()" VALUE="Scroll Text
            ➥Field"></INPUT>
            <BR>
            <BR>
            <BR>
            <BR>
            <BR>
            <BR>
            <BR>
            <BR>
            <BR>
            <BR>
            <BR>
            <BR>
```

continues ▶

```
            <BR>
            <BR>
            <INPUT TYPE="TEXT" ID="text1" SIZE="50" VALUE="Hello"></INPUT>
        </FORM>
    </BODY>
</HTML>
```

The *setActive* Method

The setActive method makes an element into the current active HTML element. (The active element is the one that has the focus when the document enclosing it gets the focus, and may be found using the document object's activeElement property.) You can see the support for this method in Table 6.47.

Table 6.47   **The *setActive* Method**

Method	NS2	NS3	NS4	NS6	IE3a	IE3b	IE4	IE5	IE5.5	IE6
setActive()									x	x
No return value										

> **Tip**
> The element with the focus in a document is made into the active element by default.

The *setAttribute* Method

The setAttribute method sets the value of a specified attribute. You invoke this method on an element, passing it the name of an attribute, a new value for the attribute, and an optional *case* argument, which, if true, makes the browser search for the attribute in a case-sensitive way. You can see the support for this method in Table 6.48.

Table 6.48   **The *setAttribute* Method**

Method	NS2	NS3	NS4	NS6	IE3a	IE3b	IE4	IE5	IE5.5	IE6
setAttribute(*attribute*, *value* [, *case*])				x			x	x	x	x
No return value										

Here's an example that sets the VALUE attribute of a text field, which inserts text into that text field:

(Listing 06-11.html on the web site)

```
<HTML>
    <HEAD>
        <TITLE>Using the setAttribute Method</TITLE>
        <SCRIPT LANGUAGE="JavaScript">
            <!--
            function setAttr()
            {
                document.form1.text1.setAttribute("VALUE", "Hello there!")
            }
            // -->
        </SCRIPT>
    </HEAD>

    <BODY>
        <H1>Using the setAttribute Method</H1>
        <FORM NAME="form1">
            <INPUT TYPE="TEXT" ID="text1" SIZE="50"></INPUT>
            <BR>
            <INPUT TYPE="BUTTON" ONCLICK="setAttr()" VALUE="Set Attribute"></INPUT>
        </FORM>
    </BODY>
</HTML>
```

You can see the results in Figure 6.7, where we've inserted Hello there! into a text field.

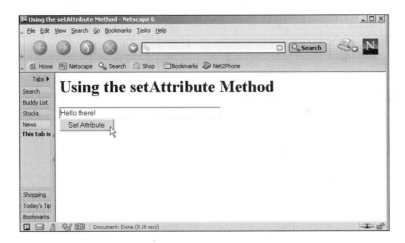

Figure 6.7   Using the setAttribute Method.

The *setAttributeNode* Method

The setAttributeNode method assigns an attribute node to a node. You can see the support for this method in Table 6.49.

Table 6.49   **The *setAttributeNode* Method**

Method	NS2	NS3	NS4	NS6	IE3a	IE3b	IE4	IE5	IE5.5	IE6
setAttributeNode(*attributeNode*)				x						x
Returns: Attribute object										

The setAttributeNode is the W3C analog to the setAttribute method discussed in the preceding section. To assign an attribute node to another node capable of supporting attributes, you just pass that attribute node to this method:

```
elementNode.setAttributeNode(attributeNode)
```

The *setCapture* Method

The setCapture method sets the mouse capture to the object belonging to the current document. You can see the support for this method in Table 6.50.

Table 6.50   **The *setCapture* Method**

Method	NS2	NS3	NS4	NS6	IE3a	IE3b	IE4	IE5	IE5.5	IE6
setCapture([*capture*])								x	x	x
No return value										

If you set the *capture* argument to true (the default), events originating within a container are captured by the container. Otherwise, events originating within a container are not captured by the container.

The *setExpression* Method

In the Internet Explorer, you can assign scripting expressions to object properties using setExpression. You can see the support for this method in Table 6.51.

Table 6.51   **The *setExpression* Method**

Method	NS2	NS3	NS4	NS6	IE3a	IE3b	IE4	IE5	IE5.5	IE6
setExpression(*property*, *expression*, *language*)								X	X	X
No return value										

Here, *property* is the property you're assigning an expression to, *expression* is the expression to assign, and *language* is the scripting language you're using. For example, here's how to assign the value in a text field to the width style property of another text field:

```
text2.style.setExpression("width", "eval(text1.value)", "JavaScript")
```

The *swapNode* Method

The swapNode method enables you to swap two nodes. You can see the support for this method in Table 6.52.

Table 6.52   **The *swapNode* Method**

Method	NS2	NS3	NS4	NS6	IE3a	IE3b	IE4	IE5	IE5.5	IE6
swapNode(*node*)								X	X	X
Returns: Node object										

Here's how you would swap two nodes, node1 and node2:

```
node1.swapNode(node2)
```

The *tags* Method

In the Internet Explorer, the tags method retrieves a collection of objects that have the specified HTML tag name. You can see the support for this method in Table 6.53.

Table 6.53   **The *tags* Method**

Method	NS2	NS3	NS4	NS6	IE3a	IE3b	IE4	IE5	IE5.5	IE6
tags(*tag*)							X	X	X	X
Returns: Element object array										

This method is part of collections like the `all` and `forms` collections. We've already put the `tags` method to work in Chapter 4:

(Listing 04-11.html on the web site)

```
<HTML>
    <HEAD>
        <TITLE>
            Accessing HTML Elements
        </TITLE>
        <SCRIPT LANGUAGE="JavaScript">
            <!--
            function getText()
            {
                if(navigator.appName == "Netscape") {
                alert("document.form1.text1.value = " + document.form1.text1.value)
                alert("document.forms[0].text1.value = " +
                ➥document.forms[0].text1.value)
                alert("document.getElementsByName(\"text1\")[0].value = "
                    + document.getElementsByName("text1")[0].value)
                alert("document.getElementsByTagName(\"INPUT\")[0].value = "
                    + document.getElementsByTagName("INPUT")[0].value)
                }

                if (navigator.appName == "Microsoft Internet Explorer") {
                alert("document.form1.text1.value = " + document.form1.text1.value)
                alert("document.forms[0].text1.value = "
                    + document.forms[0].text1.value)
                alert("document.all.text1.value = "
                    + document.all.text1.value)
                alert("document.all[\"text1\"].value = "
                    + document.all["text1"].value)
                alert("document.all.tags(\"INPUT\")[0].value = "
                    + document.all.tags("INPUT")[0].value)
                alert("document.getElementsByName(\"text1\")[0].value = "
                    + document.getElementsByName("text1")[0].value)
                alert("document.getElementsByTagName(\"INPUT\")[0].value = "
                    + document.getElementsByTagName("INPUT")[0].value)
                }
            }
            // -->
        </SCRIPT>
    </HEAD>

    <BODY>
        <H1>Accessing HTML Elements</H1>
        <FORM NAME="form1">
            <INPUT TYPE="TEXT" NAME="text1" ID="text1">
            <INPUT TYPE="BUTTON" VALUE="Click Me!" ONCLICK="getText()">
        </FORM>
    </BODY>
</HTML>
```

The *urns* Method

The urns method retrieves a collection of all objects to which a specified behavior is attached. You can see the support for this method in Table 6.54.

Table 6.54 **The *urns* Method**

Method	NS2	NS3	NS4	NS6	IE3a	IE3b	IE4	IE5	IE5.5	IE6
urns(*URN*)								x	x	x
Returns: Array of behaviors										

You pass this method the *Uniform Resource Name* (URN) of an Internet Explorer behavior, and it returns an array of objects that have that behavior associated with them. We'll see more on Internet Explorer behaviors in Chapter 17.

And that's it for JavaScript's core HTML methods. Next, I'll take a look at JavaScript's Core HTML Events.

JavaScript's Core HTML Events

In the beginning of this chapter, we took a look at event handling and how to implement it. There are many core HTML events in JavaScript, and we'll take a look at them next. To see how to handle these events, take a look at the event-handling information in the beginning of this chapter—especially Table 6.2, which holds the properties of event objects that hold data about the event, such as the keyCode property that holds the code of a struck key.

The *onactivate, onbeforedeactivate,* and *ondeactivate* Events

The onactivate event occurs in an object when that object becomes the active element in the document (as with the focus or setActive methods). The onbeforedeactivate event occurs when an object is the active element and is about to be deactivated (as when another object is going to become the active element), and the ondeactivate event occurs when an object is deactivated. You can find the support for these events in Table 6.55.

Table 6.55 **The *onactivate, onbeforedeactivate,* and *ondeactivate* Events**

Method	NS2	NS3	NS4	NS6	IE3a	IE3b	IE4	IE5	IE5.5	IE6
onactivate									X	X
onbeforedeactivate									X	X
ondeactivate										X

Only elements that can accept the focus can become the active element. Unless you're specifically handling the case when an element becomes the active element and gets the focus (a document can have only one active element, and that element is stored in the `activeElement` property), it's probably a good idea to stick to the `onfocus` and `onblur` events.

The *onbeforecopy* Event

The `onbeforecopy` event occurs before a selection is copied to the system clipboard (as with the browser's Edit | Copy menu item, or by pressing Ctrl+C in Windows). You can find the support for this event in Table 6.56.

Table 6.56 **The *onbeforecopy* Event**

Method	NS2	NS3	NS4	NS6	IE3a	IE3b	IE4	IE5	IE5.5	IE6
onbeforecopy								X	X	X

Unlike similar events such as `onbeforecut`, this event does *not* occur for form input elements.

Tip

For an example using the clipboard, see "The *oncopy* Event" in this chapter.

The *onbeforecut* Event

The `onbeforecut` event occurs before a selection is cut (as with the browser's Edit | Cut menu item, or by pressing Ctrl+X in Windows). You can find the support for this event in Table 6.57.

Table 6.57   **The *onbeforecut* Event**

Event	NS2	NS3	NS4	NS6	IE3a	IE3b	IE4	IE5	IE5.5	IE6
onbeforecut								x	x	x

For an example using the copying and pasting, see "The *oncopy* Event" in this chapter.

The *onbeforeeditfocus* Event

The onbeforeeditfocus event occurs just before content is edited in the Internet Explorer's DHTML ActiveX Editing control, or in editable text in the Internet Explorer 5.5+. You can find the support for this event in Table 6.58.

Table 6.58   **The *onbeforeeditfocus* Event**

Event	NS2	NS3	NS4	NS6	IE3a	IE3b	IE4	IE5	IE5.5	IE6
onbeforeeditfocus								x	x	x

For more information on editable text in the Internet Explorer 5.5+, see "The *contentEditable* Property" in Chapter 5, "Using Core HTML Properties."

The *onbeforepaste* Event

The onbeforepaste event occurs before a selection is pasted from the system clipboard (as when the user uses the browser's Edit | Paste menu item, or by pressing Ctrl+V in Windows). You can find the support for this event in Table 6.59.

Table 6.59   **The *onbeforepaste* Event**

Event	NS2	NS3	NS4	NS6	IE3a	IE3b	IE4	IE5	IE5.5	IE6
onbeforepaste								x	x	x

Tip

For an example using the clipboard, see "The *oncopy* Event" in this chapter.

The *onblur* Event

The `onblur` event occurs when an object loses the focus. (The idea is, if it's out of focus, it must be blurred). You can find the support for this event in Table 6.60.

Table 6.60 **The *onblur* Event**

Event	NS2	NS3	NS4	NS6	IE3a	IE3b	IE4	IE5	IE5.5	IE6
onblur	x	x	x	x	x	x	x	x	x	x

Here's an example that does a little data verification as the user enters numbers into a text field. If the user enters a value into the text field that is not a number (which we'll check with the `isNaN` function we saw in Chapter 2, "The JavaScript Language: Data, Operators, and Branching") and then clicks outside the text field, causing it to lose the focus, an alert box will appear with the message `Please enter a number!`:

(Listing 06-12.html on the web site)

```html
<HTML>
    <HEAD>
        <TITLE>Using the onblur Event</TITLE>
        <SCRIPT LANGUAGE="JavaScript">
            <!--
            function checker()
            {
                if(isNaN(document.form1.text1.value)){
                    alert("Please enter a number!")
                }
            }
            // -->
        </SCRIPT>
    </HEAD>

    <BODY>
        <H1>Using the onblur Event</H1>
        <FORM NAME="form1">
            <INPUT TYPE="TEXT" ID="text1" SIZE="50" ONBLUR="checker()"></INPUT>
        </FORM>
    </BODY>
</HTML>
```

The *onclick* Event

As we know, the `onclick` event occurs when an object is clicked. You can find the support for this event in Table 6.61.

Table 6.61 **The *onclick* Event**

Event	NS2	NS3	NS4	NS6	IE3a	IE3b	IE4	IE5	IE5.5	IE6
onclick	x	x	x	x	x	x	x	x	x	x

Starting in Internet Explorer 4.0, virtually every visible object can have an `onclick` handler, which was much more than was available in Netscape Navigator 4.0 (which supported `onclick` for only the `<INPUT>`, `<FORM>`, `<A>`, and `<SELECT>` elements). Support for `onclick` is still limited in Netscape Navigator 6.0 compared to Internet Explorer—for example, `<H1>`-`<H6>` headers don't have an `onclick` event in the Netscape Navigator 6.0.

We've worked with the `onclick` event for a long time already; here's an example from Chapter 1 that displays an alert box when the user clicks a button (it's Listing 01-04.html on the web site):

```
<HTML>
    <HEAD>
        <TITLE>
            Executing Scripts in Response to User Action
        </TITLE>
        <SCRIPT LANGUAGE="JavaScript">
            <!--
            function alerter()
            {
                window.alert("You clicked the button!")
            }
            // -->
        </SCRIPT>
    </HEAD>

    <BODY>
        <H1>Executing Scripts in Response to User Action</H1>
        <FORM>
            <INPUT TYPE="BUTTON" ONCLICK="alerter()" VALUE="Click Me!">
        </FORM>
    </BODY>
</HTML>
```

Tip
You can cancel the normal action connected to a click in the Internet Explorer by returning a value of false from the onclick event handler, or by setting window.event.returnValue to false in the event handler.

The *oncontextmenu* Event

The oncontextmenu event occurs when the user clicks the right mouse button in the client area, opening the context menu. You can find the support for this event in Table 6.62.

Table 6.62 **The *oncontextmenu* Event**

Event	NS2	NS3	NS4	NS6	IE3a	IE3b	IE4	IE5	IE5.5	IE6
oncontextmenu								x	x	x

This event occurs when the user clicks an object with the secondary mouse button (usually the right button), which causes the browser to display a context menu of commands.

> **Tip**
>
> You can cancel the normal action connected to a right-click in the Internet Explorer by returning a value of false from the oncontextmenu event handler, or by setting window.event.returnValue to false in the event handler. Doing so can stop the user from downloading images from your web page (assuming the user has not deactivated scripting in the browser).

The *oncontrolselect* Event

The oncontrolselect event occurs in the Internet Explorer when the user clicks a control once, selecting it. You can find the support for this event in Table 6.63.

Table 6.63 **The *oncontrolselect* Event**

Event	NS2	NS3	NS4	NS6	IE3a	IE3b	IE4	IE5	IE5.5	IE6
oncontrolselect									x	x

The *oncopy* Event

The oncopy event occurs when the user copies an object or a selection (as with the browser's Edit | Copy menu item or by pressing Ctrl+C in Windows), adding it to the system clipboard. You can find the support for this event in Table 6.64.

Table 6.64 **The *oncopy* Event**

Event	NS2	NS3	NS4	NS6	IE3a	IE3b	IE4	IE5	IE5.5	IE6
oncopy								x	x	x

In the Internet Explorer, the `window` object has a `clipboardData` object with `setData` and `getData` methods that enable you to handle clipboard data. You pass `setData` the data format (`"Text"` or `"URL"`) and the data to place in the clipboard. You pass `getData` the format of the data you want, and it returns the data.

Here's an example using `oncopy` and `onpaste`: When the user copies text from a `<SPAN>` element, we actually cancel the normal copy operation (by setting `event.returnValue` to false) and place our own text in the clipboard (which enables us to stop the user from copying sensitive data—assuming the user has not deactivated scripting in the browser). When the user pastes the text into a text field, we handle that operation ourselves as well:

(Listing 06-13.html on the web site)

```html
<HTML>
    <HEAD>
        <TITLE>Using the Clipboard</TITLE>
        <SCRIPT LANGUAGE="JavaScript">
            <!--
            function copy()
            {
                window.clipboardData.setData("Text", "Hello from JavaScript!")
                event.returnValue = false
            }

            function paste()
            {
                text1.value = window.clipboardData.getData("Text")
                event.returnValue = false
            }
            // -->
        </SCRIPT>
    </HEAD>

    <BODY>
        <H1>Using the Clipboard</H1>
        <SPAN oncopy="copy()">Here is some text to copy.</SPAN>
        <BR>
        <INPUT ID="text1" onpaste="paste()">
    </BODY>
</HTML>
```

You can see the results in Figure 6.8, where no matter what text you copy from the <SPAN> element, you'll see Hello from JavaScript! when you paste the text into the text field.

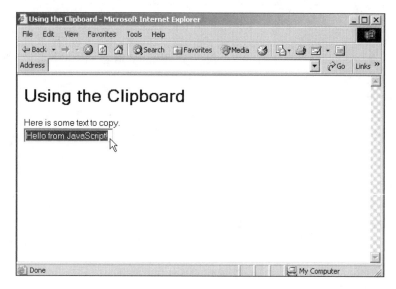

Figure 6.8 Using the clipboard.

The *oncut* Event

The oncut event occurs when the user cuts an object or selection from a web page (as with the browser's Edit | Cut menu item or by pressing Ctrl+X in Windows). You can find the support for this event in Table 6.65.

Table 6.65 **The *oncut* Event**

Event	NS2	NS3	NS4	NS6	IE3a	IE3b	IE4	IE5	IE5.5	IE6
oncut								x	x	x

In oncut events, your script is responsible for cutting the text or object from the page, if you want to do so. You can use properties such as innerHTML and innerText to do that.

The *ondblclick* Event

The `ondblclick` event occurs when the user double-clicks an object. You can find the support for this event in Table 6.66.

Table 6.66 **The *ondblclick* Event**

Event	NS2	NS3	NS4	NS6	IE3a	IE3b	IE4	IE5	IE5.5	IE6
ondblclick			x	x			x	x	x	x

When a user double-clicks an element, an `onclick` event occurs after the first click, and then an `ondblclick` event after the second click. Virtually all visible objects in the Internet Explorer from version 4.0 on support `ondblclick`, but support in the Netscape Navigator is much more limited—the Netscape Navigator 4.0 supported this event for `link` objects only, for example.

Here's an example that responds by displaying a message when you double-click a web page:

(Listing 06-14.html on the web site)

```
<HTML>
    <HEAD>
        <TITLE>Using the ondblclick Event</TITLE>
        <SCRIPT LANGUAGE="JavaScript">
            <!--
            function display()
            {
                document.form1.text1.value = "You double clicked this Web page!"
            }
            // -->
        </SCRIPT>
    </HEAD>

<BODY ONDBLCLICK="display()" ID="body1">
        <H1>Using the ondblclick Event</H1>
        <FORM NAME="form1">
            <INPUT TYPE="TEXT" ID="text1" SIZE="60"></INPUT>
        </FORM>
    </BODY>
</HTML>
```

You can see the results in Figure 6.9.

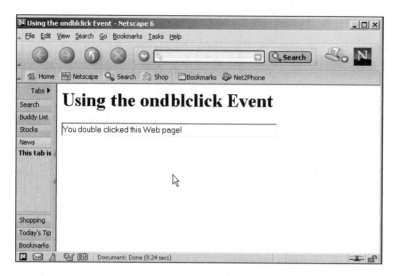

Figure 6.9 Using the ondblclick event.

The *ondrag, ondragend, ondragenter, ondragleave, ondragover, ondragstart,* and *ondrop* Events

These events are used in drag-and-drop operations, and we'll see them in more detail in Chapter 17. You can find the support for these events in Table 6.67.

Table 6.67 **The *ondrag, ondragend, ondragenter, ondragleave, ondragover, ondragstart,* and *ondrop* Events**

Event	NS2	NS3	NS4	NS6	IE3a	IE3b	IE4	IE5	IE5.5	IE6
ondrag								X	X	X
ondragend								X	X	X
ondragenter								X	X	X
ondragleave								X	X	X
ondragover								X	X	X
ondragstart							X	X	X	X
ondrop								X	X	X

We'll see more about dragging and dropping in Chapter 17, but here's a preview. In this example, I'll drag and drop not just a visual object, but *data*. Here, I'll connect some text data with an event object, and let the user drag that data to a target and drop it. We'll see more on how this works in Chapter 17:

(Listing 06-15.html on the web site)

```
<HTML>
    <HEAD>
        <TITLE>
            Dragging and Dropping Data
        </TITLE>

        <SCRIPT LANGUAGE="JavaScript">
            <!--
            function startDrag()
            {
                event.dataTransfer.setData("Text",
                    "The data was passed to the target!");
                event.dataTransfer.effectAllowed = "copy"
            }

            function endDrag()
            {
                event.returnValue = false
                event.dataTransfer.dropEffect = "copy"
                droptarget.innerHTML =
                    event.dataTransfer.getData("Text")
            }

            function dragOver()
            {
                event.returnValue = false
                event.dataTransfer.dropEffect = "copy"
            }
            // -->
        </SCRIPT>
    </HEAD>

    <BODY>
        <H1>Dragging and Dropping Data</H1>
        <IMG SRC="dragger.jpg" ondragstart="startDrag()">
        <DIV ID="droptarget"
            style="background:green; width:300; height:100;"
            ondragenter="dragOver()" ondrop="endDrag()"
            ondragover="dragOver()">
            Drop the data here...
        </DIV>
    </BODY>
</HTML>
```

You can see the results in Figure 6.10, where I'm dragging the data from the top image to the target, and Figure 6.11, where I've dropped the text data—and that text appears in the target. For the details, see Chapter 17.

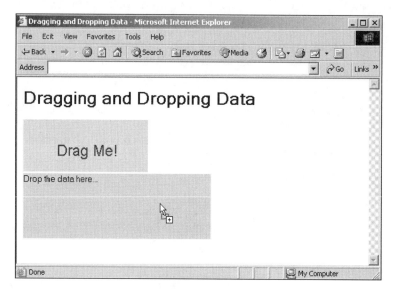

Figure 6.10   Dragging data.

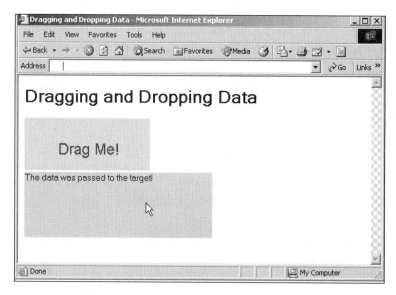

Figure 6.11   Dropping data.

The *onfilterchange* Event

The onfilterchange event occurs when an Internet Explorer visual filter changes state or completes its effect. You can find the support for this event in Table 6.68.

Table 6.68   **The *onfilterchange* Event**

Event	NS2	NS3	NS4	NS6	IE3a	IE3b	IE4	IE5	IE5.5	IE6
onfilterchange							x	x	x	x

For more on Internet Explorer visual filters, see "The *filters* Property" in Chapter 5, as well as Chapter 16.

The *onfocus* Event

The onfocus event occurs when an object gets the focus (that is, becomes the target of keystrokes). You can find the support for this event in Table 6.69.

Table 6.69   **The *onfocus* Event**

Event	NS2	NS3	NS4	NS6	IE3a	IE3b	IE4	IE5	IE5.5	IE6
onfocus	x	x	x	x	x	x	x	x	x	x

Here's an example that uses the onfocus event to display prompts to the user about what kind of data he should enter. This example is a web page–based calculator that adds numbers, and each time one of the two text fields the user is supposed to enter an integer into gets the focus, this code uses the window.status property to display the prompt Enter an integer. in the browser's status bar:

(Listing 06-16.html on the web site)

```
<HTML>
    <HEAD>
        <TITLE>An HTML Calculator</TITLE>
        <SCRIPT LANGUAGE="JavaScript">
            <!--
            function text1Prompt()
            {
                window.status = "Enter an integer."
            }
            function text2Prompt()
            {
```

continues ▶

```
            window.status = "Enter an integer."
        }
    function text3Prompt()
    {
            window.status = "The sum is displayed here."
        }
    function Add()
    {
            document.form1.text3.value =
            parseInt(document.form1.text1.value) +
            parseInt(document.form1.text2.value)
        }
        // -->
    </SCRIPT>
</HEAD>

<BODY>
    <H1>An HTML Calculator</H1>
    <FORM NAME="form1">
        <INPUT TYPE="TEXT" NAME="text1" ONFOCUS="text1Prompt()">
        +
        <INPUT TYPE="TEXT" NAME="text2" ONFOCUS="text2Prompt()">
        <INPUT TYPE="BUTTON" ONCLICK="Add()" VALUE = " = ">
        <INPUT TYPE="TEXT" NAME="text3" ONFOCUS="text3Prompt()">
    </FORM>
</BODY>
</HTML>
```

You can see the results in Figure 6.12—note the message `Enter an integer.` in the status bar.

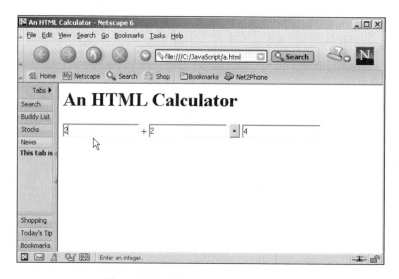

Figure 6.12   Using the onfocus event.

The *onfocusin* and *onfocusout* Events

The onfocusin event occurs for an object just before that object gets the focus. The onfocusin event occurs for the current object with the focus just after moving the focus to another object. You can find the support for these events in Table 6.70.

Table 6.70　**The *onfocusin* and *onfocusout* Events**

Event	NS2	NS3	NS4	NS6	IE3a	IE3b	IE4	IE5	IE5.5	IE6
onfocusin										x
onfocusout										x

The *onhelp* Event

The onhelp event occurs when an element has the focus and the user presses F1 in Windows or the Help key on the Mac. You can find the support for this event in Table 6.71.

Table 6.71　**The *onhelp* Event**

Event	NS2	NS3	NS4	NS6	IE3a	IE3b	IE4	IE5	IE5.5	IE6
onhelp							x	x	x	x

Tip

You can use this event to display your own help. (This event does not occur when the user clicks a help button in the browser or selects a help menu item.)

The *onkeydown, onkeypress,* and *onkeyup* Events

As you can guess, you use the onkeydown, onkeypress, and onkeyup events to handle keystrokes. You can find the support for these events in Table 6.72.

Table 6.72　**The *onkeydown, onkeypress,* and *onkeyup* Events**

Event	NS2	NS3	NS4	NS6	IE3a	IE3b	IE4	IE5	IE5.5	IE6
onkeydown			x	x			x	x	x	x
onkeypress			x	x			x	x	x	x
onkeyup			x	x			x	x	x	x

Form input controls such as text fields handle keystrokes by themselves; if you want to create your own key-handling routines, however, you can use these events. We'll cover this in more detail in Chapter 15, because it gets a little complex. For example, there are two types of codes: *key codes* and *character codes*. There is one key code for each key on the keyboard, and it'll be the same even if modifier keys, such as the Shift key, were also pressed. Character codes, on the other hand, correspond to the Unicode code for a character and include capital and small characters. Here are the three keystroke events, the order in which they occur, and what they do:

- **onkeydown.** Occurs when a key is struck or is held down and repeats (along with onkeyup) when you hold it down. Internet Explorer: event.keyCode holds the key's key code. Netscape Navigator: event.keyCode holds the key code, and event.charCode holds zero.

- **onkeypress.** Occurs after the onkeydown and before the onkeyup event when you press an alphanumeric key, as well as ! @ # $ % ^ & * ( ) _ - + = < [ ] { } , . / ? \ | ` ` " ~ Esc, Spacebar, and Enter. Internet Explorer: event.keyCode holds the key's character code. Netscape Navigator: event.charCode holds the character code, and event.keyCode holds zero.

- **onkeyup.** Occurs when a key is released or is held down and repeats (along with onkeydown) when you hold a key down. Internet Explorer: event.keyCode holds the key's key code. Netscape Navigator: event.keyCode holds the key code, and event.charCode holds zero.

When you're handling alphanumeric keys, use onkeypress; when you're handling nonalphanumeric keys (such as arrow keys), use onkeydown and/or onkeyup. In onkeydown and onkeyup, modifiers such as the Shift key haven't been applied to the key yet, and you have to check properties such as event.shiftKey yourself (see Table 6.2) to see whether a character should be capitalized.

Note that the character codes and key codes you get are just numbers—you still have to translate them into characters. Here's an example that reads keys in both browsers using the <BODY> element's ONKEYPRESS attribute and displays what you've typed—just load this page and type something (don't give the focus to the text field); the keys you type will be inserted into the text field automatically:

(Listing 06-17.html on the web site)

```html
<HTML>
    <HEAD>
        <TITLE>Reading Keys</TITLE>
        <SCRIPT LANGUAGE="JavaScript">
            <!--
            document.onkeypress = keyPress

            var instring = ""

            function keyPress(e)
            {
                if(navigator.appName == "Netscape") {
                    if(parseInt(navigator.appVersion) == 4) {
                        instring += unescape("%" + e.which.toString(16))
                        document.form1.text1.value = instring
                    }
                    if(parseInt(navigator.appVersion) > 4) {
                        instring += unescape("%" + e.charCode.toString(16))
                        document.form1.text1.value = instring
                    }
                }
                if (navigator.appName == "Microsoft Internet Explorer") {
                    instring += String.fromCharCode(window.event.keyCode)
                    document.form1.text1.value = instring
                }
            }
            // -->
        </SCRIPT>
    </HEAD>

    <BODY>
        <H1>Reading Keys Directly (Type some text!)</H1>
        <BR>
        <FORM NAME="form1">
            <INPUT NAME="text1" TYPE="TEXT" SIZE="20">
        </FORM>
    </BODY>
</HTML>
```

You can see the results in Figure 6.13—more on this code in Chapter 15.

Tip

If you want to cancel a keystroke in the Internet Explorer 4+, set the `event.returnValue` property to false in the keystroke event handlers.

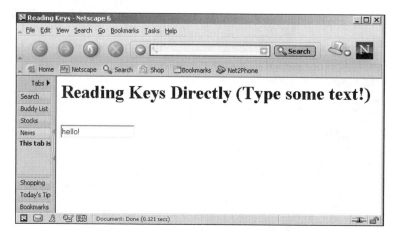

Figure 6.13   Using the onkeypress event.

The *onlosecapture* Event

The onlosecapture event occurs when the object loses the mouse capture the Internet Explorer. You can find the support for this event in Table 6.73.

Table 6.73   **The *onlosecapture* Event**

Event	NS2	NS3	NS4	NS6	IE3a	IE3b	IE4	IE5	IE5.5	IE6
onlosecapture								x	x	x

For more on mouse capture in the Internet Explorer, see the setCapture and releaseCapture methods in this chapter, and see Chapter 15.

The *onmousedown, onmouseenter, onmouseleave, onmousemove, onmouseout, onmouseover, onmouseup,* and *onmousewheel* Events

These are the mouse events, and we'll cover them in more detail in Chapter 15. You can find the support for these events in Table 6.74.

Table 6.74 **The *onmousedown, onmouseenter, onmouseleave, onmousemove,***
***onmouseout, onmouseover, onmouseup,* and *onmousewheel* Events**

Event	NS2	NS3	NS4	NS6	IE3a	IE3b	IE4	IE5	IE5.5	IE6
onmousedown			X	X			X	X	X	X
onmouseenter									X	X
onmouseleave									X	X
onmousemove			X	X			X	X	X	X
onmouseout	X	X	X	X	X	X	X	X	X	X
onmouseover	X	X	X	X	X	X	X	X	X	X
onmouseup			X	X			X	X	X	X
onmousewheel										X

Here's when these events occur:

- **onmousedown.** Occurs when the primary mouse button mouse is pressed.
- **onmouseenter.** Occurs when the mouse enters an object. This event was new in Internet Explorer 5.5 and is an alternative to onmouseover.
- **onmouseleave.** Occurs when the mouse leaves an object. This event was new in Internet Explorer 5.5 and is an alternative to onmouseout.
- **onmousemove.** Occurs when the mouse moves.
- **onmouseout.** Occurs when the mouse leaves an object (just like onmouseleave).
- **onmouseover.** Occurs when the mouse enters an object (just like onmouseenter).
- **onmouseup.** Occurs when the primary mouse button is released.
- **onmousewheel.** Occurs when the mouse wheel button is rotated.

We'll see more on mouse handling in Chapter 15, but here's a quick example. In this case, I'll just use the onmousedown event and display where on the page the mouse button was pressed:

(Listing 06-18.html on the web site)

```
<HTML>
    <HEAD>
        <TITLE>Using the onmousedown Event</TITLE>
        <SCRIPT LANGUAGE="JavaScript">
            <!--
            function display(e)
            {
```

continues ▶

```
                    if (!e){
                        e = window.event
                    }
                        document.form1.text1.value = "The mouse went down at (" +
                        e.clientX + ", " + e.clientY + ")"
                }
                // -->
            </SCRIPT>
        </HEAD>

    <BODY ONMOUSEDOWN="display(event)">
        <H1>Using the onmousedown Event: Click Anywhere!</H1>
        <FORM NAME="form1">
            <INPUT TYPE="TEXT" NAME="text1" SIZE="80"></INPUT>
        </FORM>
    </BODY>
</HTML>
```

You can see the results in Figure 6.14.

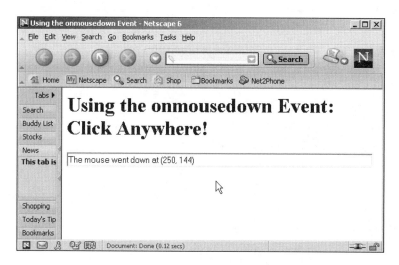

Figure 6.14   Using the onmousedown event.

The newest mouse event is the onmousewheel event, which occurs when the mouse wheel is turned. Here's an example that uses this event in the Internet Explorer 6.0. (It's not supported in the Netscape Navigator yet.) The change in the mouse wheel's position is recorded in the wheelDelta property, and if that value is greater than 120, the mouse wheel has been turned to a new position:

(Listing 06-19.html on the web site)

```
<HTML>
    <HEAD>
        <TITLE>Using the onmousewheel Event</TITLE>
        <SCRIPT LANGUAGE="JavaScript">
            <!--
            var count = 0

            function wheeler()
            {
                if (event.wheelDelta >= 120){
                    count++
                } else if (event.wheelDelta <= -120) {
                    count-- }
                document.form1.text1.value= "Wheel rotations: " + count
            }
            // -->
        </SCRIPT>
    </HEAD>

<BODY ONMOUSEWHEEL="wheeler()">
    <H1>Using the onmousewheel Event</H1>
    <BR>
    <FORM NAME="form1">
        <INPUT NAME="text1" TYPE="TEXT" SIZE="20">
    </FORM>
</BODY>
</HTML>
```

You can see the results in Figure 6.15.

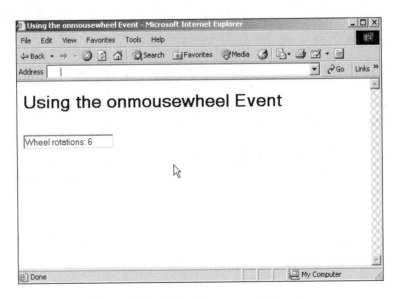

Figure 6.15 Using the onmousewheel event.

The *onmove, onmoveend,* and *onmovestart* Events

The onmove, onmoveend, and onmovestart events occur when you move an object, and when the move ends and starts, respectively. You can find the support for these events in Table 6.75.

Table 6.75 **The *onmove, onmoveend,* and *onmovestart* Events**

Event	NS2	NS3	NS4	NS6	IE3a	IE3b	IE4	IE5	IE5.5	IE6
onmove			x						x	x
onmoveend								x	x	x
onmovestart									x	x

Note that the onmove event in Netscape Navigator 4.0 is enabled for the window object only.

The *onpaste* Event

The onpaste event occurs when the user pastes data from the clipboard into an object (as with the Edit | Paste menu item, or by pressing Ctrl+V in Windows). You can find the support for this event in Table 6.76.

Table 6.76 **The *onpaste* Event**

Event	NS2	NS3	NS4	NS6	IE3a	IE3b	IE4	IE5	IE5.5	IE6
onpaste								x	x	x

For an example using this event, see "The *oncopy* Event" in this chapter.

The *onpropertychange* Event

The onpropertychange event occurs when an object's property value is changed. You can find the support for this event in Table 6.77.

Table 6.77 **The *onpropertychange* Event**

Event	NS2	NS3	NS4	NS6	IE3a	IE3b	IE4	IE5	IE5.5	IE6
onpropertychange								x	x	x

This is a cool event, because it enables you to monitor what's happening with various objects. Note that changing the `innerText` or `innerHTML` of child elements will not cause the `onpropertychange` event to occur in parent elements.

The *onreadystatechange* Event

The onreadystatechange event occurs when the ready state of an object changes. You can find the support for this event in Table 6.78.

Table 6.78 **The *onreadystatechange* Event**

Event	NS2	NS3	NS4	NS6	IE3a	IE3b	IE4	IE5	IE5.5	IE6
onreadystatechange							x	x	x	x

See "The *readyState* Property" in Chapter 5 for more information.

The *onresize, onresizeend,* and *onresizestart* Events

As you can guess from its name, the onresize event occurs when the size of an object is about to change. The onresizestart event occurs when the resizing operation starts, and the onresizeend event occurs when the resizing operation ends. You can find the support for these events in Table 6.79.

Table 6.79 **The *onresize* Event**

Event	NS2	NS3	NS4	NS6	IE3a	IE3b	IE4	IE5	IE5.5	IE6
onresize			x	x			x	x	x	x
onresizeend									x	x
onresizestart									x	x

The *onselectstart* Event

The `onselectstart` event occurs when an object is being selected. You can find the support for this event in Table 6.80.

Table 6.80 **The *onselectstart* Event**

Event	NS2	NS3	NS4	NS6	IE3a	IE3b	IE4	IE5	IE5.5	IE6
onselectstart							x	x	x	x

The *ontimeerror* Event

This event occurs when a time-specific error occurs in the Internet Explorer, usually as a result of setting a property to an invalid value. You can find the support for this event in Table 6.81.

Table 6.81 **The *ontimeerror* Event**

Event	NS2	NS3	NS4	NS6	IE3a	IE3b	IE4	IE5	IE5.5	IE6
ontimeerror									x	x

That's it for our coverage of JavaScript's core HTML methods and events—now we can start working with the objects that share these methods and events, as well as the core properties we saw in the preceding chapter. In the next chapter, we'll start taking an in-depth look at the window object.

7

Using *window* and *frame* Properties

I N THIS CHAPTER, WE'LL START WORKING WITH THE browser objects and HTML elements that we'll be seeing over the next several chapters. Working with JavaScript is all about working with these objects, such as the window browser object or button HTML objects. Literally thousands of properties, methods, and events are available to you in JavaScript, and we're going to cover them in depth in this book to give you the maximum possible programming advantage.

This chapter starts that coverage with the properties of the window object, which is the biggest browser object available, as well as the properties of windows in frames using the <FRAMESET>, <FRAME>, and <IFRAME> elements. In the next chapter, we'll take a look at methods and events of these objects.

Properties of the *window* Object

As we know, the window object is the big cheese of browser objects, corresponding to the browser window and containing, among other objects, the document, location, and history objects. Those objects are available through properties of the same name in the window object; for example, we've already seen how to navigate the browser to a URL the user types using the location object—which is part of the window object—like this (this is Listing 04-06.html on the web site—more on the location object in Chapter 10, "Using the *navigator, location,* and *history* Objects"):

```
<HTML>
    <HEAD>
        <TITLE>
            Navigate to an URL
        </TITLE>
        <SCRIPT LANGUAGE = "JavaScript">
            <!--
            function Jump()
            {
                window.location.href = document.form1.text1.value
            }
            // -->
        </SCRIPT>
    </HEAD>

    <BODY>
        <H1>Navigate to an URL</H1>
        <FORM NAME = "form1">
            <BR>
            <INPUT TYPE = TEXT NAME="text1" SIZE = 80>
            <BR>
            <BR>
            <INPUT TYPE = BUTTON Value="Navigate to URL" ONCLICK="Jump()">
        </FORM>
    </BODY>
</HTML>
```

Tip

Because the window object is the overall containing object in a browser, you can usually omit referring to it when using its properties, events, and methods if there's no possibility of confusion. For example, I could have written window.location.href = document.form1.text1.value above as location.href = document.form1.text1.value.

You can find an overview of the properties of the window object in Table 7.1 (note that not all properties apply to all browsers), and property-by-property coverage in Table 7.2. In this chapter, we'll discuss those properties.

Table 7.1 **Overview of the Properties of the *window* Object**

Properties

appCore	clientInformation	clipboardData	closed
Components	controllers	crypto	defaultStatus
dialogArguments	dialogHeight	dialogLeft	dialogTop
dialogWidth	directories	document	event
external	frameElement	frames	history

Properties

innerHeight	innerWidth	length	loading
location	locationbar	menubar	name
navigator	offscreenBuffering	opener	outerHeight
outerWidth	pageXOffset	pageYOffset	parent
personalbar	pkcs11	prompter	returnValue
screen	screenLeft	screenTop	screenX
screenY	scrollbars	scrollX	scrollY
self	sidebar	status	statusbar
toolbar	top	window	

Table 7.2 **The Properties of the *window* Object**

Property	NS2	NS3	NS4	NS6	IE3a	IE3b	IE4	IE5	IE5.5	IE6
appCore				x						

Read-only
This property is a Netscape 6.0 property that allows scripting access (called XPConnect) to COM objects and Netscape's XML-based XUL objects. See www.mozilla.org/scriptable/ for the details.

clientInformation							x	x	x	x

Read-only
Another name for the navigator object in the Internet Explorer.

clipboardData								x	x	x

Read/write
Allows access to the clipboard. See "Using the Clipboard" in this chapter for the details, as well as "The oncopy Event" in Chapter 6, "Using Core HTML Methods and Events."

closed	x	x	x					x	x	x

Read-only
Set to true if a window object has been closed, and false otherwise. Useful if you're handling multiple window objects at the same time. See "Working with New Windows" in this chapter for an example.

Components				x						

Read-only
This property is a Netscape 6.0 property that allows scripting access (Called XPConnect) to COM objects and Netscape's XML-based XUL objects. See www.mozilla.org/scriptable/ for the details.

continues ▶

Table 7.2 **Continued**

Property	NS2	NS3	NS4	NS6	IE3a	IE3b	IE4	IE5	IE5.5	IE6
controllers				X						

Read-only

This property is a Netscape 6.0 property that allows scripting access (Called XPConnect) to COM objects and Netscape's XML-based XUL objects. See www.mozilla.org/scriptable/ for the details.

| crypto | | | | X | | | | | | |

Read-only

This property is used in Netscape's public-key cryptography efforts; for more details, see www.mozilla.org/projects/security.

| defaultStatus | X | X | X | X | X | X | X | X | X | X |

Read/write

Holds the default text for the status bar (visible when the page first loads). If the mouse moves over a link, the default text will be replaced temporarily and restored when the mouse leaves the link. See "Accessing the Status Bar" in this chapter for an example.

| dialogArguments | | | | | | | X | X | X | X |

Read-only

Holds arguments passed to dialog boxes (used to initialize the dialog boxes), which are windows opened with the Internet Explorer methods showModalDialog and showModelessDialog. See "Creating Dialog Boxes" in this chapter for an example. More on the showModalDialog and showModelessDialog methods in Chapter 8, "Using *window* and *frame* Methods and Events."

| dialogHeight | | | | | | | X | X | X | X |

Read/write

Sets or gets the height of dialog boxes, which are windows opened with the Internet Explorer methods showModalDialog and showModelessDialog. See "Creating Dialog Boxes" in this chapter for an example. More on the showModalDialog and showModelessDialog methods in Chapter 8. Values include "px" to indicate pixel measurements, like this: "300px".

| dialogLeft | | | | | | | X | X | X | X |

Read/write

Sets the left position of dialog boxes, which are windows opened with the Internet Explorer methods showModalDialog and showModelessDialog. See "Creating Dialog Boxes" in this chapter for an example. More on the showModalDialog and showModelessDialog methods in Chapter 8. Values include "px" to indicate pixel measurements, like this: "300px".

Property	NS2	NS3	NS4	NS6	IE3a	IE3b	IE4	IE5	IE5.5	IE6
dialogTop							x	x	x	x

Read/write
Sets the top position of dialog boxes, which are windows opened with the Internet Explorer methods `showModalDialog` and `showModelessDialog`. See "Creating Dialog Boxes" in this chapter for an example. More on the `showModalDialog` and `showModelessDialog` methods in Chapter 8. Values include `"px"` to indicate pixel measurements, like this: `"300px"`.

Property	NS2	NS3	NS4	NS6	IE3a	IE3b	IE4	IE5	IE5.5	IE6
dialogWidth							x	x	x	x

Read/write
Sets the width of dialog boxes, which are windows opened with the Internet Explorer methods `showModalDialog` and `showModelessDialog`. See "Creating Dialog Boxes" in this chapter for an example. More on the `showModalDialog` and `showModelessDialog` methods in Chapter 8. Values include `"px"` to indicate pixel measurements, like this: `"300px"`.

Property	NS2	NS3	NS4	NS6	IE3a	IE3b	IE4	IE5	IE5.5	IE6
directories			x	x						

Read/write
One of the properties that enables you to customize the appearance of the Netscape Navigator by displaying or hiding menu bars, location bars, and so on. See "Displaying and Hiding Netscape Navigator Bars" in this chapter.

Property	NS2	NS3	NS4	NS6	IE3a	IE3b	IE4	IE5	IE5.5	IE6
document	x	x	x	x	x	x	x	x	x	x

Read-only
The `document` object. See Chapter 9, "Using the *document* and *body* Objects," for the details.

Property	NS2	NS3	NS4	NS6	IE3a	IE3b	IE4	IE5	IE5.5	IE6
event							x	x	x	x

Read/write
The global `event` object in the Internet Explorer, holding data about events that have occurred. See Chapter 6 for the details.

Property	NS2	NS3	NS4	NS6	IE3a	IE3b	IE4	IE5	IE5.5	IE6
external							x	x	x	x

Read-only
This property gives you access to a host application when the Internet Explorer is being run from such an application. This property corresponds to the `external` object, which includes methods such as `AddDesktopComponent(URL, Type [, Left] [, Top] [, Width] [, Height])` to add a desktop component (set `Type` to `"website"` or

continues ▶

Table 7.2 **Continued**

Property	NS2	NS3	NS4	NS6	IE3a	IE3b	IE4	IE5	IE5.5	IE6
	"image", and AddFavorite(URL [, Title]), which adds an URL to the Internet Explorer's favorites list; here's an example showing how to use AddFavorite: window.external.AddFavorite(location.href, document.title).									
frameElement								X		X
	Read-only If a window is being displayed in a frame, this property returns the parent <FRAME> or <IFRAME> element.									
frames	X	X	X	X	X	X	X	X	X	X
	Read-only Holds an array of frames contained by a window. See "Using Frame Properties" in this chapter for an example.									
history	X	X	X	X	X	X	X	X	X	X
	Read-only The history object, which holds the browser's past locations. See Chapter 10 for the details.									
innerHeight			X	X						
	Read/write Holds the height of the client area of the browser (where the document is displayed). The Netscape Navigator enables you to change this property on-the-fly. See "Setting the Netscape Navigator's Dimensions" in this chapter for an example.									
innerWidth			X	X						
	Read/write Holds the width of the client area of the browser (where the document is displayed). The Netscape Navigator enables you to change this property on-the-fly. See "Setting the Netscape Navigator's Dimensions" in this chapter for an example.									
length	A JavaScript HTML core property. See Chapter 5, "Using Core HTML Properties."									
loading			X							
	Read-only Returns true if a window is still being loaded, and false otherwise. Specific to Netscape Navigator 4.0 only!									

Property	NS2	NS3	NS4	NS6	IE3a	IE3b	IE4	IE5	IE5.5	IE6
location	x	x	x	x	x	x	x	x	x	x

Read/write
The location object. See Chapter 10 for the details.

Property	NS2	NS3	NS4	NS6	IE3a	IE3b	IE4	IE5	IE5.5	IE6
locationbar			x	x						

Read/write
One of the properties that enables you to customize the appearance of
the Netscape Navigator by displaying or hiding menu bars, location
bars, and so on. See "Displaying and Hiding Netscape Navigator Bars"
in this chapter for an example.

Property	NS2	NS3	NS4	NS6	IE3a	IE3b	IE4	IE5	IE5.5	IE6
menubar			x	x						

Read/write
One of the properties that enables you to customize the appearance of
the Netscape Navigator by displaying or hiding menu bars, location
bars, and so on. See "Displaying and Hiding Netscape Navigator Bars"
in this chapter for an example.

Property	NS2	NS3	NS4	NS6	IE3a	IE3b	IE4	IE5	IE5.5	IE6
name	x	x	x	x	x	x	x	x	x	x

Read/write
A window's name. By default, a top-level window has no name,
although you can supply one with the window.name property. Windows
are often given names in <FRAMESET> elements; see "Using Frame
Properties" in this chapter for an example.

Property	NS2	NS3	NS4	NS6	IE3a	IE3b	IE4	IE5	IE5.5	IE6
navigator				x			x	x	x	x

Read-only
The navigator object. See Chapter 10.

Property	NS2	NS3	NS4	NS6	IE3a	IE3b	IE4	IE5	IE5.5	IE6
offscreenBuffering							x	x	x	x

Read/write
Specifies whether the Internet Explorer draws a page in memory before
displaying it on the screen. A page saved in memory can be presented
immediately to the user (that is, the user won't have to watch the page
being constructed piece-by-piece on the screen). The default value here
is auto, which lets the Internet Explorer decide when to use offscreen
buffering. You can turn on offscreen buffering by setting this value to
true, or turn it off by setting it to false.

continues ▶

Table 7.2 **Continued**

Property	NS2	NS3	NS4	NS6	IE3a	IE3b	IE4	IE5	IE5.5	IE6
opener		x	x	x	x	x	x	x	x	x

Read-only
The window that opened the current window. This property gives you access to a parent window; see "Working with New Windows" in this chapter for an example.

Property	NS2	NS3	NS4	NS6	IE3a	IE3b	IE4	IE5	IE5.5	IE6
outerHeight			x	x						

Read/write
Holds the height of the browser itself. The Netscape Navigator enables you to change this property on-the-fly. See "Setting the Netscape Navigator's Dimensions" in this chapter for an example.

Property	NS2	NS3	NS4	NS6	IE3a	IE3b	IE4	IE5	IE5.5	IE6
outerWidth			x	x						

Read/write
Holds the width of the browser itself. The Netscape Navigator enables you to change this property on-the-fly. See "Setting the Netscape Navigator's Dimensions" in this chapter for an example.

Property	NS2	NS3	NS4	NS6	IE3a	IE3b	IE4	IE5	IE5.5	IE6
pageXOffset			x	x						

Read-only
The X coordinate (in document coordinates) of the top left of the client area (the area where the document is displayed) when the document has been scrolled.

Property	NS2	NS3	NS4	NS6	IE3a	IE3b	IE4	IE5	IE5.5	IE6
pageYOffset			x	x						

Read-only
The Y coordinate (in document coordinates) of the top left of the client area (the area where the document is displayed) when the document has been scrolled.

Property	NS2	NS3	NS4	NS6	IE3a	IE3b	IE4	IE5	IE5.5	IE6
parent	x	x	x	x	x	x	x	x	x	x

Read-only
Usually used when you're working with windows in frames. This property corresponds to the window's parent `window` object. See "Using Frame Properties" in this chapter for an example.

Property	NS2	NS3	NS4	NS6	IE3a	IE3b	IE4	IE5	IE5.5	IE6
personalbar			x	x						

Read/write
One of the properties that enables you to customize the appearance of the Netscape Navigator by displaying or hiding menu bars, location bars, and so on. See "Displaying and Hiding Netscape Navigator Bars" in this chapter for an example.

Property	NS2	NS3	NS4	NS6	IE3a	IE3b	IE4	IE5	IE5.5	IE6
pkcs11				x						

Read-only
This property is used in Netscape's public-key cryptography efforts; for more details, see www.mozilla.org/projects/security.

Property	NS2	NS3	NS4	NS6	IE3a	IE3b	IE4	IE5	IE5.5	IE6
prompter				x						

Read-only
This property is a Netscape 6.0 property that allows scripting access (called XPConnect) to COM objects and Netscape's XML-based XUL objects. See www.mozilla.org/scriptable/ for the details.

Property	NS2	NS3	NS4	NS6	IE3a	IE3b	IE4	IE5	IE5.5	IE6
returnValue							x	x	x	x

Read/write
Holds the return value from dialog boxes, which are windows opened with the Internet Explorer methods showModalDialog and showModelessDialog. This return value can be an array of values set by the user in the dialog box. See "Creating Dialog Boxes" in this chapter for an example.

Property	NS2	NS3	NS4	NS6	IE3a	IE3b	IE4	IE5	IE5.5	IE6
screen				x			x	x	x	x

Read-only
The screen object, which holds data about the screen, such as its dimensions. See "The screen Object" in this chapter for an example.

Property	NS2	NS3	NS4	NS6	IE3a	IE3b	IE4	IE5	IE5.5	IE6
screenLeft								x	x	x

Read-only
Holds the left position of the client area (the area where the document is displayed, excluding toolbars, menu bars, and so on) with respect to the top left of the screen (which is treated as (0, 0)). Measured in pixels.

Property	NS2	NS3	NS4	NS6	IE3a	IE3b	IE4	IE5	IE5.5	IE6
screenTop								x	x	x

Read-only
Holds the top of the client area (the area where the document is displayed, excluding toolbars, menu bars, and so on) with respect to the upper-left corner of the screen (which is treated as (0, 0)). Measured in pixels.

Property	NS2	NS3	NS4	NS6	IE3a	IE3b	IE4	IE5	IE5.5	IE6
screenX				x						

Read/write
Holds the X position of the left edge of the browser in screen coordinates (where the upper left corner of the screen is (0, 0)). Measured in pixels.

continues ▶

Table 7.2 **Continued**

Property	NS2	NS3	NS4	NS6	IE3a	IE3b	IE4	IE5	IE5.5	IE6
screenY				x						

Read/write
Holds the Y position of the top edge of the browser in screen coordinates (where the upper-left corner of the screen is (0, 0)). Measured in pixels.

| scrollbars | | | x | x | | | | | | |

Read/write
One of the properties that enables you to customize the appearance of the Netscape Navigator by displaying or hiding menu bars, location bars, and so on. See "Displaying and Hiding Netscape Navigator Bars" in this chapter for an example.

| scrollX | | | | x | | | | | | |

Read-only
Holds the horizontal position of a scrolled window. Measured in pixels.

| scrollY | | | | x | | | | | | |

Read-only
Holds the vertical position of a scrolled window. Measured in pixels.

| self | x | x | x | x | x | x | x | x | x | x |

Read-only
Refers to the current window (just like using the window object for the current window).

| sidebar | | | | x | | | | | | |

Read-only
This property is a Netscape 6.0 property that allows scripting access (called XPConnect) to COM objects and Netscape's XML-based XUL objects. See www.mozilla.org/scriptable/ for the details.

| status | x | x | x | x | x | x | x | x | x | x |

Read/write
Holds the text displayed in the browser's status bar. See "Accessing the Status Bar" in this chapter for an example.

| statusbar | | | x | x | | | | | | |

Read/write
One of the properties that enables you to customize the appearance of the Netscape Navigator by displaying or hiding menu bars, location bars, and so on. See "Displaying and Hiding Netscape Navigator Bars" in this chapter for an example.

Property	NS2	NS3	NS4	NS6	IE3a	IE3b	IE4	IE5	IE5.5	IE6
toolbar			x	x						

Read/write
One of the properties that enables you to customize the appearance of the Netscape Navigator by displaying or hiding menu bars, location bars, and so on. See "Displaying and Hiding Netscape Navigator Bars" in this chapter for an example.

top	x	x	x	x	x	x	x	x	x	x

Read-only
Refers to the top window in a window hierarchy. When you are using frames, for example, top refers to the topmost containing window. See "Using Frame Properties" in this chapter for an example.

window	x	x	x	x	x	x	x	x	x	x

Read-only
The same as the window object itself, even though this is a property of the window object. (There's no real reason to use this property.)

As you can see in Table 7.2, the window object has a great many properties. Let's put them to work.

Accessing the Status Bar

One of the most common uses for the properties of the window object is to display text in the browser's status bar, using the window.status object. You also can set default text in the status bar (which is displayed when the browser loads, and before and after the mouse moves over links) using the window.defaultStatus property.

In fact, we've already seen how this works as far back as Chapter 4, "Handling the Browser Environment." This example displays Hello! and Good Bye! in the status bar as the user moves the mouse over a link (note that both functions here return a value of true to make sure the browser does not perform its default action of displaying the link's URL; this is Listing 04-03.html on the web site—note also that some versions of Netscape Navigator 6 will not let you display anything but a hyperlink's URL when the mouse rolls over that hyperlink):

```
<HTML>
    <HEAD>
        <TITLE>Using the Status Bar</TITLE>
        <SCRIPT LANGUAGE="JavaScript">
            <!--
```

continues ▶

```
          function sayHello() {
              window.status = "Hello!"
              return true
          }
          function sayGoodBye() {
              window.status = "Good Bye!"
              return true
          }
          // -->
      </SCRIPT>
  </HEAD>

  <BODY>
      <H1>Using the Status Bar</H1>
      <A HREF="http://www.starpowder.com"
          ONMOUSEOVER="return sayHello()"
          ONMOUSEOUT="return sayGoodBye()">Here's my site!</A>
  </BODY>
</HTML>
```

You can see the results of this code in Chapter 4, Figure 4.5.

Here's another popular way of handling messages in the status bar—you can scroll such messages using the handy window object's setTimeout method (discussed in the next chapter). You pass setTimeout an expression to execute and a time, in milliseconds, to wait before evaluating that expression. In this case, I can use setTimeout to call a function recursively (that is, have the same function call itself—see "Handling Recursion" in Chapter 3, "The JavaScript Language: Loops, Functions, and Errors"), taking one character off the beginning of the status bar text and putting it on the end of the text with the String method substring (which we'll cover in depth in Chapter 18, "The *Date*, *Time*, and *String* Objects") like this:

(Listing 07-01.html on the web site)

```
<HTML>
    <HEAD>
        <TITLE>Scrolling Status Bar Text</TITLE>
        <SCRIPT LANGUAGE="JavaScript">
            <!--
            var text = "Hello from JavaScript! Hello from JavaScript! "
            function scroller()
            {
                window.status = text
                text = text.substring(1, text.length) + text.substring(0, 1)
                setTimeout("scroller()", 150)
            }
            // -->
        </SCRIPT>
    </HEAD>
```

```
<BODY ONLOAD="scroller()">
    <H1>Scrolling Status Bar Text</H1>
  </BODY>
</HTML>
```

Note that I start scrolling the text as soon as the document is loaded, using the `<BODY>` element's `ONLOAD` attribute (covered in Chapter 9). Working with the text in the status bar, this makes it appear to scroll, as you can see if you run this example; you can see a static snapshot in Figure 7.1.

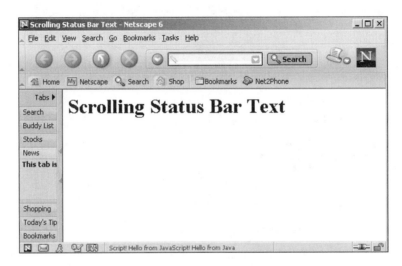

Figure 7.1   Scrolling text in the Netscape Navigator's status bar.

Working with New Windows

In the next chapter on `window` object methods and events, we'll cover one of the most popular ways of working with `window` objects—opening new browser windows with the `window.open` method. Two properties in this chapter are useful when working with new windows you've opened up—`closed` and `opener`. The `closed` property enables you to determine whether a window has been closed, and the `opener` property holds the window that opened the current window (the parent window).

Here's an example that puts these properties to work. In this case, I'll let the user open and close a new window using buttons. The open button will open a new window, and I'll use the `closed` property of the new window to check whether it's already been closed when the user clicks the close button in the main window—if the window is already closed, there's no reason to close it again.

I'll also give the new window access to the main window through the opener property. In this case, I'll display a button in the new window that lets the user close the main window by executing the window.opener.close method. Here's what the code looks like (we'll see the window object's open and close methods, used in this code, in the next chapter):

(Listing 07-02.html on the web site)

```
<HTML>
    <HEAD>
        <TITLE>Using the closed and opener Properties</TITLE>
        <SCRIPT LANGUAGE="JavaScript">
            <!--
            var window1

            function openWindow()
            {
                window1 = window.open("","window1", "HEIGHT=300,WIDTH=300")
                window1.document.write("<HTML><BODY><H1>A New Window</H1><BR>" +
                "<FORM><INPUT TYPE='button' VALUE='Close the original window'" +
                "ONCLICK='window.opener.close()'>" +
                "</FORM></BODY></HTML>")
                window1.document.close()
            }

            function closeWindow()
            {
                if (window1 && !window1.closed) {
                    window1.close()
                }
            }
            // -->
        </SCRIPT>
    </HEAD>

    <BODY>
        <H1>Using the closed and opener Properties</H1>
        <FORM>
            <INPUT TYPE="button" VALUE="Open New Window" ONCLICK="openWindow()">
            <INPUT TYPE="button" VALUE="Close New Window" ONCLICK="closeWindow()">
        </FORM>
    </BODY>
</HTML>
```

Tip

Why am I using the window1.document.close method after writing to the new window here? I do that to close the HTML stream to the new window (which the window1.document.write method opened)—otherwise, the mouse cursor will keep displaying a wait icon in both Netscape Navigator 6.0 and Internet Explorer 4.0, even after the new window is finished. See "Writing to a Document" in Chapter 9 for more details on why that happens.

You can see the results in Figure 7.2, where we're using the `closed` and `opener` properties to let the user work with parent and child windows—the `closed` property lets us determine whether a window we opened has already been closed, and the `opener` property gave us access to the window that is the parent of a newly opened window. We'll see a lot more on opening new windows and writing HTML to them in the next chapter.

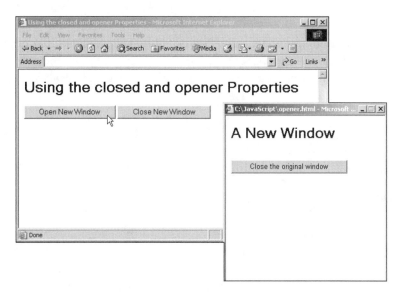

Figure 7.2 Working with parent and child windows.

Tip
When you're opening new windows and writing HTML to them, as we are here, it's sometimes wise to wait for a while after opening a new window to make sure it's ready to go before writing to it. You can do that with the window method `setTimeout`, discussed in the previous topic.

Creating Dialog Boxes

The Internet Explorer enables you to create dialog boxes with the `showModalDialog` and `showModelessDialog` methods that we'll see in the next chapter. (A modal dialog box won't let the user switch back to the main window while the dialog box is open—you have to deal with it before going back to what you were doing—but a modeless one will.) A dialog box is just an HTML document opened in a window that has a dialog box–like frame and which enables you to pass information back and forth between the opening window. When you create a new dialog box, you can use the `dialogHeight`, `dialogLeft`, `dialogTop`, and `dialogWidth` properties to set the dimensions of the box.

The most important properties here are the `dialogArguments` (which enables you to pass data to dialog boxes) and `returnValue` (which enables you to return data from dialog boxes) properties. Suppose, for example, that you want to let the user set some values using a dialog box. You can use the `dialogArguments` property to pass initial values to the dialog box's code that can be displayed when the dialog box opens, and the `returnValue` property enables you to pass data back to the opening window when the user clicks the OK button. Note that both the `dialogArguments` and `returnValue` properties can take arrays of values.

Tip

It's important to realize that you don't need dialog boxes to pass and return data between windows—the Internet Explorer just provides this dialog box functionality for convenience. For example, as we'll see in the next chapter, if you create a new child window object named window2, you can access, say, a text field in that child window from code in the parent window as window2.document.form1.text1.value.

Here's an example to show how this works. In this case, I'll display a window with two text fields originally holding the values 1 and 2. When the user clicks a button, a dialog box will open, displaying those original data values. If the user changes those values and clicks OK, the dialog box will close and the new values will appear in the main window.

Let's write some code to make this work. I'll store the original data values in an array named `values`, storing them as `"value1"` and `"value2"`. Next, I'll open the modal dialog box with the `showModalDialog` method (which we'll see in the next chapter), creating a new modal dialog box named `dialog1` and passing the `values` array to that dialog box:

```
<HTML>
    <HEAD>
        <TITLE>Using Modal Dialogs</TITLE>
        <SCRIPT LANGUAGE="JavaScript">
            <!--
            function openDialog()
            {
                var values = new Array()
                if(document.form1.text1.value){
                    values["value1"] = document.form1.text1.value
                }
                if(document.form1.text2.value){
                    values["value2"] = document.form1.text2.value
                }
```

```
                        var dialog1 = showModalDialog("07-04.html", values,
                            "dialogWidth:350px; dialogHeight:250px")
                            .
                            .
                            .
                }
                // -->
        </SCRIPT>
    </HEAD>

    <BODY>
        <H1>Using Modal Dialogs</H1>
        <FORM NAME="form1">
            <INPUT TYPE="BUTTON" ONCLICK="openDialog()" VALUE="Open the dialog box">
            <BR>
            Enter the first value:
            <BR>
            <INPUT TYPE="TEXT" ID="text1" VALUE="1">
            <BR>
            Enter the second value:
            <BR>
            <INPUT TYPE="TEXT" ID="text2" VALUE="2">
            <BR>
        </FORM>
    </BODY>
</HTML>
```

Now the dialog box we're opening (which is a separate HTML document, with its own code) has access to the values array using its dialogArguments property (this is a property of the dialog box's window object). For example, you can access the data I've stored using the name "value1" as window.dialogArguments["value1"] in the dialog box's code.

That means I can recover the two data items from the dialogArguments property and display them in text boxes in the dialog box when that dialog box opens. To do that, I'll use a JavaScript function I'll call initialize, which runs as soon as the dialog box is loaded. (This function is connected to the dialog's ONLOAD event attribute.) Here's what that looks like in the dialog box's code:

```
<HTML>
    <HEAD>
        <TITLE>Modal Dialog Box</TITLE>
        <SCRIPT LANGUAGE="JavaScript">
            <!--
            function initialize()
            {
                if (window.dialogArguments) {
                    if (window.dialogArguments["value1"]) {
                        document.form1.text1.value = window.dialogArguments["value1"]
                }
```

continues ▶

```
                   if (window.dialogArguments["value2"]) {
                       document.form1.text2.value = window.dialogArguments["value2"]
                   }
               }
           }
           // -->
       </SCRIPT>
   </HEAD>

<BODY ONLOAD="initialize()">
    <H1>Modal Dialog Box</H1>
    <FORM NAME="form1">
        Enter the new first value:
        <BR>
        <INPUT TYPE="TEXT" NAME="text1">
        <BR>
        Enter the new second value:
        <BR>
        <INPUT TYPE="TEXT" NAME="text2">
        <BR>
        <INPUT TYPE="BUTTON" ONCLICK="handleOK()"
        ➡VALUE="  OK  ">
        <INPUT TYPE="BUTTON" ONCLICK="handleCancel()" VALUE="Cancel">
    </FORM>
</BODY>
</HTML>
```

You can see the results so far in Figure 7.3, where I've clicked the "Open the dialog box" button to open the dialog box and display the initial data, as copied from the main window.

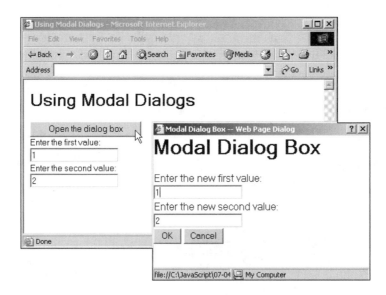

Figure 7.3 Displaying initial data in a dialog box.

When the user clicks the OK button in the dialog box, all I have to do is to load the data that the user entered into the dialog box's text fields into an array and assign that array to the `returnValue` property of the dialog box window—when I do, the code in the main window will get access to that data. Here's how that looks in the dialog box's code (note also that if the user clicks the Cancel button I've added to the dialog box, I don't assign any value to the `returnValue` property):

(Listing 07-04.html on the web site)

```html
<HTML>
    <HEAD>
        <TITLE>Modal Dialog Box</TITLE>
        <SCRIPT LANGUAGE="JavaScript">
            <!--
            function handleOK()
            {
                var returnValues = new Array()
                if (document.form1.text1.value) {
                    returnValues["value1"] = document.form1.text1.value
                }
                if (document.form1.text2.value) {
                    returnValues["value2"] = document.form1.text2.value
                }
                window.returnValue = returnValues
                window.close()
            }

            function handleCancel()
            {
                window.returnValue = ""
                window.close()
            }

            function initialize()
            {
                if (window.dialogArguments) {
                    if (window.dialogArguments["value1"]) {
                        document.form1.text1.value = window.dialogArguments["value1"]
                    }
                    if (window.dialogArguments["value2"]) {
                        document.form1.text2.value = window.dialogArguments["value2"]
                    }
                }
            }
            // -->
        </SCRIPT>
    </HEAD>

    <BODY ONLOAD="initialize()">
        <H1>Modal Dialog Box</H1>
```

continues ▶

```
        <FORM NAME="form1">
            Enter the new first value:
            <BR>
            <INPUT TYPE="TEXT" NAME="text1">
            <BR>
            Enter the new second value:
            <BR>
            <INPUT TYPE="TEXT" NAME="text2">
            <BR>
            <INPUT TYPE="BUTTON" ONCLICK="handleOK()"
            ➥VALUE="  OK  ">
            <INPUT TYPE="BUTTON" ONCLICK="handleCancel()" VALUE="Cancel">
        </FORM>
    </BODY>
</HTML>
```

Finally, in the main window's code, I can access the returned values I've named "value1" and "value2" simply as dialog1["value1"] and dialog1["value1"] (where dialog1 is the dialog box we created with showModalDialog). In this case, I'll display the new values the user entered in the dialog box in the main window's text fields like this in the main window's code:

(Listing 07-03.html on the web site)

```
<HTML>
    <HEAD>
        <TITLE>Using Modal Dialogs</TITLE>
        <SCRIPT LANGUAGE="JavaScript">
            <!--

            function openDialog()
            {
                var values = new Array()
                if(document.form1.text1.value){
                    values["value1"] = document.form1.text1.value
                }
                if(document.form1.text2.value){
                    values["value2"] = document.form1.text2.value
                }

                var dialog1 = showModalDialog("07-04.html", values,
                    "dialogWidth:350px; dialogHeight:250px")
                if (dialog1) {
                    if (dialog1["value1"]) {
                        document.form1.text1.value = dialog1["value1"]
                    }
                    if (dialog1["value2"]) {
                        document.form1.text2.value = dialog1["value2"]
                    }
                }
```

```
        }
        // -->
    </SCRIPT>
</HEAD>

<BODY>
    <H1>Using Modal Dialogs</H1>
    <FORM NAME="form1">
        <INPUT TYPE="BUTTON" ONCLICK="openDialog()" VALUE="Open the dialog box">
        <BR>
        Enter the first value:
        <BR>
        <INPUT TYPE="TEXT" ID="text1" VALUE="1">
        <BR>
        Enter the second value:
        <BR>
        <INPUT TYPE="TEXT" ID="text2" VALUE="2">
        <BR>
    </FORM>
</BODY>
</HTML>
```

Let's see this in action. After the dialog box opens (see Figure 7.3), I'll enter 3 and 4 in the dialog box's text fields and then close the dialog box. Those new values will then appear in the main window, as you see in Figure 7.4. And that's all it takes—now we're passing and returning data between windows and dialog boxes.

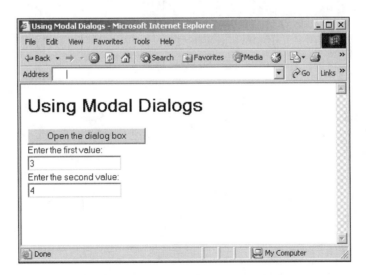

Figure 7.4   Retrieving values from a dialog box.

Using the Clipboard

One of the useful window properties in the Internet Explorer is the `clipboardData` property, which holds data copied to the clipboard. We saw how to use this property in "The `oncopy` Event" in Chapter 6. In that topic, we saw an example using `oncopy` and `onpaste`; when the user copies text from a `<SPAN>` element, we canceled the normal copy operation (by setting `event.returnValue` to false) and placed our own text in the clipboard using the `setData` method. When the user pasted data from the clipboard, we handled that operation ourselves using the `getData` method.

(Listing 06-13.html on the web site)

```
<HTML>
    <HEAD>
        <TITLE>Using the Clipboard</TITLE>
        <SCRIPT LANGUAGE="JavaScript">
            <!--
            function copy()
            {
                window.clipboardData.setData("Text", "Hello from JavaScript!")
                event.returnValue = false
            }

            function paste()
            {
                text1.value = window.clipboardData.getData("Text")
                event.returnValue = false
            }
            // -->
        </SCRIPT>
    </HEAD>

    <BODY>
        <H1>Using the Clipboard</H1>
        <SPAN oncopy="copy()">Here is some text to copy.</SPAN>
        <BR>
        <INPUT ID="text1" onpaste="paste()">
    </BODY>
</HTML>
```

You can see the results in Chapter 6, in Figure 6.8. For all the details, take a look at "The *oncopy* Event" in Chapter 6.

The *screen* Object

Another useful property of the `window` object is the `screen` property, which returns the `screen` object—which holds a great deal of information about the screen dimensions and color capabilities. You can see the various properties of the `screen` object in Table 7.3.

Table 7.3 **The Properties of the *screen* Object**

Property	NS2	NS3	NS4	NS6	IE3a	IE3b	IE4	IE5	IE5.5	IE6
availHeight, availWidth		X	X				X	X	X	X

Read-only
The available height and width of the screen (omitting items such as the Windows taskbar) in pixels.

| availLeft, availTop | | X | X | | | | X | X | X | X |

Read-only
The available left and top positions on the screen (omitting items such as the Windows taskbar if positioned along the left edge of the screen, and so on) in pixels.

| bufferDepth | | | | | | | X | X | X | X |

Read/write
If you set this property to –1 (the default is 0), the Internet Explorer will set its offscreen buffer to the same color depth as the screen.

| colorDepth | | X | X | | | | X | X | X | X |

Read-only
Holds the number of bits used to store a color in the screen. Same as `pixelDepth`.

| fontSmoothingEnabled | | | | | | | X | X | X | X |

Read/write
Set to true if font smoothing is enabled, false otherwise. The default is false.

| height, width | | X | X | | | | X | X | X | X |

Read-only
The height and width of the screen in pixels.

| pixelDepth | | X | X | | | | X | X | X | X |

Read/write
Holds the number of bits used to store a color in the screen. Same as `colorDepth`.

| updateInterval | | X | X | | | | X | X | X | X |

Read-only
Holds the number of milliseconds between screen updates.

> **Tip**
>
> The screen object is a great one if you want to determine whether you can display large graphics (for example, you can check the screen's height and width properties)—and if not, you can load smaller graphics (by changing <IMG> elements' SRC property on-the-fly, for example, or even navigating to a new page with the location.href property).

Setting the Netscape Navigator's Dimensions

In the Netscape Navigator, you can resize the browser on-the-fly with the innerWidth, innerHeight, outerWidth, and outerHeight properties (see Table 7.2). Here's an example that puts these properties to work, resizing the browser as you click buttons:

(Listing 07-05.html on the web site)

```
<HTML>
    <HEAD>
        <TITLE>Setting Window Size</TITLE>
        <SCRIPT LANGUAGE="JavaScript">
            <!--
            var beginWidth = window.outerWidth
            var beginHeight = window.outerHeight

            function inner()
            {
                window.innerWidth = 400
                window.innerHeight = 400
            }

            function outer()
            {
                window.outerWidth = 400
                window.outerHeight = 400
            }

            function available()
            {
                window.outerWidth = screen.availWidth
                window.outerHeight = screen.availHeight
            }

            function restore()
            {
                window.outerWidth = beginWidth
                window.outerHeight = beginHeight
            }
            // -->
        </SCRIPT>
    </HEAD>
```

```
<BODY>
    <H1>Setting Window Size</H1>
    <BR>
    <FORM>
        <INPUT TYPE="button" VALUE="Set inner dimensions" onClick="inner()"><BR>
        <INPUT TYPE="button" VALUE="Set outer dimensions" onClick="outer()"><BR>
        <INPUT TYPE="button" VALUE="Use available space"
        ➡onClick="available()"><BR>
        <INPUT TYPE="button" VALUE="Restore original" onClick="restore()"><BR>
    </FORM>
    </BODY>
</HTML>
```

You can see the results in Figure 7.5, where I'm resizing the Netscape Navigator just by clicking buttons. Note that you also can restore the browser to its original dimensions with the "Restore original" button.

Figure 7.5 Resizing the Netscape Navigator by clicking buttons.

Displaying and Hiding Netscape Navigator Bars

Here's another capability of the Netscape Navigator—you can customize the appearance of this browser using window properties. To do that, you can use the locationbar, menubar, personalbar, scrollbars, statusbar, and toolbar properties you see in Table 7.2. These properties control whether the corresponding bars display. If you set the menubar property to false, for example, the menu bar disappears.

Here's an example that will let you toggle the various bars of the Netscape Navigator on and off just by toggling check boxes (which we'll see in Chapter 12, "Working with Forms, Buttons, Check Boxes, and Radio Buttons"). To avoid letting malicious scripts configure the browser without your consent, scripts such as these need special security privileges before working with these bars, and I'll use the `netscape.security.PrivilegeManager.enablePrivilege` method to set the needed security privilege here, and then revert back later to normal privilege levels with the `netscape.security.PrivilegeManager` `.revertPrivilege` method. The Netscape Navigator will check with you before giving higher privileges to the script. Here's what the code looks like:

(Listing 07-06.html on the web site)

```html
<HTML>
    <HEAD>
        <TITLE>Toggling Navigator Bars</TITLE>
        <SCRIPT LANGUAGE="JavaScript">
            <!--
            function handleBar()
            {
netscape.security.PrivilegeManager.enablePrivilege("UniversalBrowserWrite")
                window.locationbar.visible = document.form1.check01.checked
                window.menubar.visible = document.form1.check02.checked
                window.personalbar.visible = document.form1.check03.checked
                window.scrollbars.visible = document.form1.check04.checked
                window.statusbar.visible = document.form1.check05.checked
                window.toolbar.visible = document.form1.check06.checked
netscape.security.PrivilegeManager.revertPrivilege("UniversalBrowserWrite")
            }
        // -->
        </SCRIPT>
    </HEAD>

    <BODY>
        <H1>Toggling Navigator Bars</H1>
        <FORM NAME="form1">
            <INPUT TYPE="CHECKBOX" ID="check01" ONCLICK="handleBar()"
            ➥CHECKED>Location Bar
            <BR>
            <INPUT TYPE="CHECKBOX" ID="check02" ONCLICK="handleBar()" CHECKED>Menu Bar
            <BR>
            <INPUT TYPE="CHECKBOX" ID="check03" ONCLICK="handleBar()"
            ➥CHECKED>Personal Bar
            <BR>
            <INPUT TYPE="CHECKBOX" ID="check04" ONCLICK="handleBar()"
            ➥CHECKED>Scrollbars
            <BR>
            <INPUT TYPE="CHECKBOX" ID="check05" ONCLICK="handleBar()"
            ➥CHECKED>Status Bar
            <BR>
            <INPUT TYPE="CHECKBOX" ID="check05" ONCLICK="handleBar()" CHECKED>Tool Bar
        </FORM>
    </BODY>
</HTML>
```

When you click a check box in this document, the browser checks with you to see whether you want to give the script higher privileges with an "Internet Security" dialog box, as you see in Figure 7.6, where I've clicked the menu bar check box.

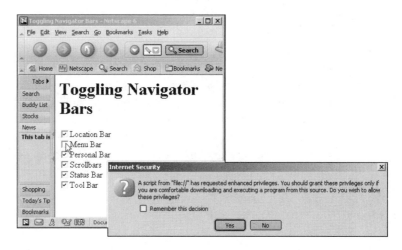

Figure 7.6   Requesting higher privileges in the Netscape Navigator.

If you click Yes in the Internet Security box, the menu bar will disappear, as shown in Figure 7.7. Now we're configuring the Netscape Navigator just by clicking check boxes.

Figure 7.7   Removing the menu bar in the Netscape Navigator.

Tip
You don't have to check with the user before turning bars on and off when you're displaying a *new* window, as we'll see in the next chapter.

Working with Frames

Windows can appear in *frames* in HTML. Some people love frames, some hate them, but there's little question that they're here to stay. You use the <FRAMESET> and <FRAME> HTML elements to create frames, and because the window object has many properties designed to be used with frames, I'll take a look at the <FRAMESET> and <FRAME> elements in this chapter.

Feeling rusty on frames? Here's an example to get us started; this example, Listing 07-07.html on the web site, displays three HTML documents (Listings 07-08.html, 07-09.html, and 07-10.html) in various frames using <FRAMESET> and <FRAME>:

(Listing 07-07.html on the web site)

```
<HTML>
    <HEAD>
        <TITLE>Working With Frames</TITLE>
    </HEAD>

    <FRAMESET COLS = "55%, 45%">
        <NOFRAMES>Sorry, your browser does not support frames!</NOFRAMES>

        <FRAMESET ROWS = "35%, 45%, 45%">
            <FRAME SRC="07-08.html">
            <FRAME SRC="07-09.html">
            <FRAME SRC="07-10.html">
        </FRAMESET>

        <FRAMESET ROWS = "25%, 25%, 50%">
            <FRAME SRC="07-08.html">
            <FRAME SRC="07-09.html">
            <FRAME SRC="07-10.html">
        </FRAMESET>
    </FRAMESET>
</HTML>
```

(Listing 07-08.html on the web site)

```
<HTML>
    <HEAD>
        <TITLE>
            Page 1
        </TITLE>
    </HEAD>
```

```
<BODY BGCOLOR="RED">
    <H1>
        Page 1
    </H1>
    Here is page 1.
</BODY>
</HTML>
```

(Listing 07-09.html on the web site)

```
<HTML>
    <HEAD>
        <TITLE>
            Page 2
        </TITLE>
    </HEAD>

    <BODY BGCOLOR="YELLOW">
        <H1>
            Page 2
        </H1>
        Here is page 2.
    </BODY>
</HTML>
```

(Listing 07-10.html on the web site)

```
<HTML>
    <HEAD>
        <TITLE>
            Page 3
        </TITLE>
    </HEAD>

    <BODY BGCOLOR="CYAN">
        <H1>
            Page 3
        </H1>
        Here is page 3.
    </BODY>
</HTML>
```

You can see the results in Figure 7.8, where we're displaying various documents in frames.

The main frame element is the <FRAMESET> element, and I'll take a look at working with this element in JavaScript now—including showing how to create new frames entirely in JavaScript.

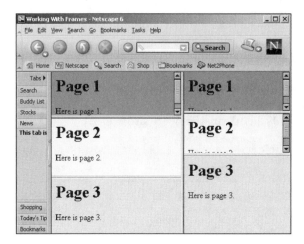

Figure 7.8 Working with frames.

The *<FRAMESET>* Element

I'll take a look at the <FRAMESET> element from the JavaScript point of view here. As with the other HTML elements we'll see, JavaScript's core HTML properties, methods, and events (covered throughout Chapters 5 and 6) apply to this element. Besides those core HTML properties, the <FRAMESET> element supports the JavaScript properties you see in overview in Table 7.4 and covered in depth in Table 7.5. We'll see methods and events for this element in the next chapter.

Table 7.4 **Overview of the Properties of the *<FRAMESET>* Element (See Chapter 5 and 6 for the JavaScript core HTML properties, methods, and events that also apply to this element.)**

Properties

border	borderColor	cols	frameBorder
frameSpacing	rows		

Table 7.5 **The Properties of the <*FRAMESET*> Element (See Chapter 5 and 6 for the JavaScript core HTML properties, methods, and events that also apply to this element.)**

Property	NS2	NS3	NS4	NS6	IE3a	IE3b	IE4	IE5	IE5.5	IE6
border							X	X	X	X

Read/write
Holds the thickness of the frames' borders, in pixels.

borderColor							X	X	X	X

Read/write
Holds the color of the frameset's border (the BORDERCOLOR attribute). Set to a color the browser can recognize (color triplet or predefined color). See the tip following this table for more information.

cols				X			X	X	X	X

Read/write
Using this value, you can actually change the COLS attribute of a <FRAMESET> element, changing the space distribution of columns in the element. Set this property to any valid COLS attribute value (including percent signs and asterisks).

frameBorder							X	X	X	X

Read/write
Specifies the value of the FRAMEBORDER attribute. May be set to "yes," "no," 1, or 0.

frameSpacing							X	X	X	X

Read/write
Holds the value of the FRAMESPACING attribute. Sets the spacing in pixels between frames.

rows				X			X	X	X	X

Using this value, you can actually change the ROWS attribute of a <FRAMESET> element, changing the space distribution of rows in the element. Set this property to any valid ROWS attribute value (including percent signs and asterisks).

Tip

Plenty of the JavaScript properties we'll see in this book, such as the <FRAMESET> object's borderColor property, correspond to HTML attributes used to set the colors displayed in a browser. You assign these properties colors that the browser can recognize (using the same values you would assign to HTML color attributes)—that is, a hexadecimal color triplet or a predefined color. Here are some examples—the hexadecimal color triplet "ff0000" is pure red, "ffffff" is bright white, "000000" is black, "00ff00" is bright green, and "808080" is gray. The red, green, and blue values here, *rr*, *gg*, and *bb* (each of which can go from 00 to ff in hexadecimal) are assembled into a color triplet: *rrggbb*. You also can use predefined colors (which differ by browser) such as "red," "yellow," "blue," or "pink".

Note the power you have in Table 7.5—using the cols and rows properties of <FRAMESET> objects in JavaScript, you can modify the COLS and ROWS attributes of <FRAMESET> elements, changing your frame layout on-the-fly.

The *<FRAME>* Element

Like the <FRAMESET> element, the <FRAME> element, which you use to create individual frames, shares JavaScript's core HTML properties, methods, and events that we covered in Chapters 5 and 6. And like the <FRAMESET> element, the <FRAME> element also has some additional properties beyond the core ones, and you can see them in overview in Table 7.6, and in detail in Table 7.7. We'll see methods and events for this element in the next chapter.

Table 7.6 **Overview of the Properties of the *<FRAME>* Element (See Chapter 5 and 6 for the JavaScript core HTML properties, methods, and events that also apply to this element.)**

Properties

allowTransparency	borderColor	contentDocument
contentWindow	frameBorder	height
longDesc	marginHeight	marginWidth
noResize	scrolling	src
width		

Table 7.7 **The Properties of the *<FRAME>* Element (See Chapter 5 and 6 for the JavaScript core HTML properties, methods, and events that also apply to this element.)**

Property	NS2	NS3	NS4	NS6	IE3a	IE3b	IE4	IE5	IE5.5	IE6
allowTransparency									X	X

Read/write
Specifies whether a frame can be transparent. When the property is set to false, the backgroundColor style property of the frame can only be that of the window. When the property is set to true, the backgroundColor property of the frame can be set to any value, including the default value of transparent.

borderColor							X	X	X	X

Read/write
Holds the color of the frame's border (the BORDERCOLOR attribute). Set to a color the browser can recognize (color triplet or predefined color).

contentDocument				X						

Read-only
Holds the document object that corresponds to the content of the frame.

contentWindow									X	X

Read-only
Retrieves the window object of the specified frame.

frameBorder							X	X	X	X

Read/write
Specifies the value of the FRAMEBORDER attribute. May be set to "yes," "no," 1 (means yes), or 0 (means no).

height							X	X	X	X

Read/write
Holds the height of the frame, in pixels.

longDesc				X						X

Read/write
The property corresponds to the LONGDESC attribute, and holds the URL of a document with a long description of the frame.

continues ▶

Table 7.7 **Continued**

Property	NS2	NS3	NS4	NS6	IE3a	IE3b	IE4	IE5	IE5.5	IE6
marginHeight				x			x	x	x	x

Read/write
Holds the height of the margin between a frame's content and its frame, in pixels.

marginWidth				x			x	x	x	x

Read/write
Holds the width of the margin between a frame's content and its frame, in pixels.

noResize				x			x	x	x	x

Read/write
Set to false to allow the user to resize frames, true otherwise.
Corresponds to the NORESIZE attribute.

scrolling				x			x	x	x	x

Read/write
Indicates whether the frame can be scrolled (and displays scrollbars if appropriate). May be set to "yes," "no," 1 (means yes), or 0 (means no).

src				x			x	x	x	x

Read/write
Enables you to set or read the SRC attribute of a frame, which sets the URL of the source document (as with images in the <IMG> element). Set to an URL.

width							x	x	x	x

Read/write
Holds the width of the frame, in pixels.

As you can see in Table 7.7, you have a lot of control over what happens in a frame using JavaScript. Here's one thing to note: You can use the src property to set the source URL for the frame's document, but this JavaScript property is still relatively new, and it's probably a better idea to use the location.href property for compatibility with old browsers.

Using Frame Properties

When you're working with frames, it's important to know your way around—when you're in a `<FRAMESET>` window, for example, how do you access the child frames using JavaScript? When you're in a frame, how do you access the parent `<FRAMESET>` window? Here are the `window` object properties that enable you to move from frame to parent and back again:

- **frames.** This property holds an array of the frames displayed in the window.

- **name.** This property holds a name for a window. (There is no default value for this property—it does not correspond to the `<TITLE>` element in `<HEAD>` sections.)

- **parent.** The parent window of the current window—this property is great for finding the `<FRAMESET>` that contains the current frame.

- **self.** Refers to the current window.

- **top.** This property holds the topmost window displayed. This is a good property if you have nested frames and don't want to work back through multiple parent properties—you can go right to the topmost window (which has the `<FRAMESET>` element that contains all the rest of the frames and their children) with this property.

If you're in one frame, for example, how do you refer to the document in another frame? You can use syntax like this: `parent.frames[2].document`. What about reading the name of the topmost window? You can use `top.name`. How about the value of a text field in a child frame? You can use syntax like `frames[1].document.form1.text1.value`. Here's an example that takes a look at the properties in the preceding list in a browser (note that I'm explicitly setting the `name` property of the top window here—otherwise, the `name` property of that window would be empty):

(Listing 07-11.html on the web site)

```
<HTML>
    <HEAD>
        <TITLE>Frame Properties</TITLE>
        <SCRIPT LANGUAGE="JavaScript">
            <!--
            self.name = "Top Dog"
            // -->
```

continues ▶

```
        </SCRIPT>
    </HEAD>
    <FRAMESET COLS="50%, 50%">
        <FRAME NAME="frame1" SRC="07-12.html">
        <FRAME NAME="frame2" SRC="07-12.html">
</FRAMESET>
</HTML>
```

(Listing 07-12.html on the web site)

```
<HTML>
    <HEAD>
        <TITLE>Frame</TITLE>
    </HEAD>

    <BODY>
        <H1>Frame Properties</H1>
        <SCRIPT LANGUAGE="JavaScript">
            <!--
            document.write(
                "window.name: " + window.name + "<BR>" +
                "parent.frames.length: " + parent.frames.length + "<BR>" +
                "parent.frames[0].name: " + parent.frames[0].name + "<BR>" +
                "parent.frames[1].name: " + parent.frames[1].name + "<BR>" +
                "window.name: " + window.name + "<BR>" +
                "self.name: " + self.name + "<BR>" +
                "self.document.title: " + self.document.title +
                "top.name: " + top.name + "<BR>" +
                "parent.name: " + parent.name + "<BR>" +
                "parent.document.title: " + parent.document.title + "<BR>"
            )
            // -->
        </SCRIPT>
    </BODY>
</HTML>
```

You can see the results in Figure 7.9, showing the properties that let you get from frame to frame.

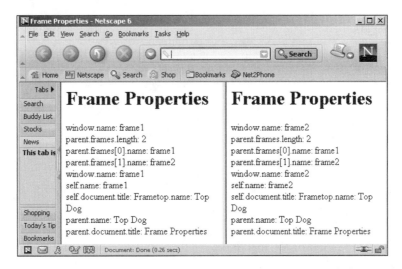

Figure 7.9 Looking at frame properties in the Netscape Navigator.

Insisting on Frames

Here's a useful thing to do with frames in JavaScript—if you've designed a window to be displayed only as a frame, you can make sure the user doesn't sneakily view it without frames, using code like this:

```
<HTML>
    <HEAD>
        <TITLE>Welcome to my frame!</TITLE>
        <SCRIPT LANGUAGE="JavaScript">
            <!--
            if(self == top){
                top.location.href = "frames.html"
            }
        // -->
        </SCRIPT>
    </HEAD>

    <BODY>
        <H1>Welcome to my frame!</H1>
    </BODY>
</HTML>
```

Avoiding Framing

Conversely, you can make sure a document is not viewed in a frame (as when someone jumps to your site from a site that uses frames)—here's how that might look in code:

```
<HTML>
    <HEAD>
        <TITLE>Welcome to my page!</TITLE>
        <SCRIPT LANGUAGE="JavaScript">
            <!--
            if(self != top){
                top.location.href = self.location.href
            }
            // -->
        </SCRIPT>
    </HEAD>

    <BODY>
        <H1>Welcome to my page!</H1>
    </BODY>
</HTML>
```

Creating Frames in JavaScript: JavaScript URLs

The document you load into the SRC attribute of a <FRAME> element doesn't have to be an actual HTML document. For example, you can use an URL built in to browsers—"about:blank"—to display a blank page:

```
<HTML>
    <HEAD>
        <TITLE>Frame Properties</TITLE>
    </HEAD>
    <FRAMESET COLS="50%, 50%">
        <FRAME NAME="frame1" SRC="frame1.html">
        <FRAME NAME="frame2" SRC="about:blank">
    </FRAMESET>
</HTML>
```

You also can create a document to display in a frame using a *JavaScript URL*. A JavaScript URL is actually a JavaScript function that the browser treats as a URL—you just preface the function name with "javascript:". When the browser jumps to that URL, it just runs the JavaScript function. If you want to create a frame document using a JavaScript function, you just return the HTML from the function you want in the document.

Tip

We'll see more on JavaScript URLs in Chapter 14, "Working with Links, Lists, and Tables."

Here's an example—in this case, I'm using a JavaScript function I'll name `filler` to create a new frame with an <H1> header in it that displays the text `A New Frame`:

(Listing 07-13.html on the web site)

```html
<HTML>
    <HEAD>
        <TITLE>Frame Properties</TITLE>
        <SCRIPT LANGUAGE="JavaScript">
            <!--
            self.name = "Top Dog"
            function filler()
            {
                return "<HTML><HEAD><TITLE>Frame</TITLE></HEAD>" +
                    "<BODY><H1>A New Frame</H1></BODY></HTML>"
            }
            // -->
        </SCRIPT>
    </HEAD>
    <FRAMESET COLS="50%, 50%">
        <FRAME NAME="frame1" SRC="07-12.html">
        <FRAME NAME="frame2" SRC="javascript:parent.filler()">
</FRAMESET>
</HTML>
```

You can see the results in Figure 7.10, where we're creating the frame on the right in JavaScript. Pretty cool.

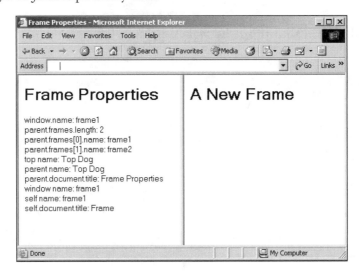

Figure 7.10 Creating a frame in JavaScript.

> **Tip**
>
> Note that you also can use the `document.write` method to rewrite a frame's contents on-the-fly.

The *<IFRAME>* Element

Iframes (inline floating frames) are supported in Internet Explorer 4+ and
Netscape Navigator 6 with the `<IFRAME>` element. These frames can "float,"
and need not just be aligned with the edges of a window. (In many ways,
they are much like Netscape Navigator layers.) Here's an example using
inline frames and the `<IFRAME>` element:

(Listing 07-14.html on the web site)

```
<HTML>
    <HEAD>
        <TITLE>
            Inline Frames!
        </TITLE>
    </HEAD>

    <BODY>
        <H1>Using the IFRAME Element</H1>
        <BR>
        <BR>
        <IFRAME WIDTH="50%" HEIGHT="25%" NAME="frame1"
            SRC="07-15.html" FRAMEBORDER="1" SCROLLING="NO" ALIGN="top">
        <BR>
        <BR>
    </BODY>
</HTML>
```

(Listing 07-15.html on the web site)

```
<HTML>
    <HEAD>
        <TITLE>
            Inline Frames!
        </TITLE>
    </HEAD>

    <BODY>
        <H1>An Inline Frame</H1>
    </BODY>
</HTML>
```

You can see the results in Figure 7.11, where we're creating an inline frame.

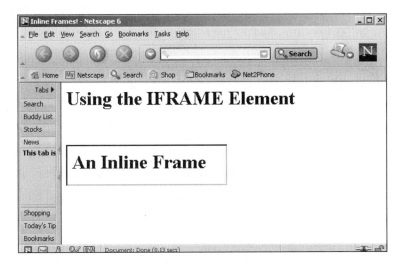

Figure 7.11   Creating an inline frame.

Like other HTML elements, `<IFRAME>` supports the JavaScript core HTML properties, methods, and events we saw in Chapters 5 and 6. You can see an overview of the additional properties of the `<IFRAME>` element in Table 7.8, and those properties in depth in Table 7.9. We'll see methods and events for this element in the next chapter.

Table 7.8   **Overview of the Properties of the *<IFRAME>* Element (See Chapter 5 and 6 for the JavaScript core HTML properties, methods, and events that also apply to this element.)**

Properties

align	allowTransparency	contentDocument
contentWindow	frameBorder	frameSpacing
hspace	longDesc	marginHeight
marginWidth	scrolling	src
vspace		

Table 7.9 **The Properties of the *<IFRAME>* Element (See Chapter 5 and 6 for the JavaScript core HTML properties, methods, and events that also apply to this element.)**

Statement	NS2	NS3	NS4	NS6	IE3a	IE3b	IE4	IE5	IE5.5	IE6
align				X			X	X	X	X

Read/write
Sets the alignment of the iframe. Can be set to `"left"` (aligns to the left edge of the available space), `"center"`, (aligns to the center of the available space), or `"right"` (aligns to the right edge of the available space).

allowTransparency									X	X

Read/write
Specifies whether a frame can be transparent. When the property is set to false, the `backgroundColor` style property of the frame can only be that of the window. When the property is set to true, the `backgroundColor` property of the frame can be set to any value, including the default value of `transparent`.

contentDocument				X						

Read-only
Holds the `document` object that corresponds to the content of the frame.

contentWindow									X	X

Read-only
Retrieves the `window` object of the specified frame.

frameBorder							X	X	X	X

Read/write
Specifies the value of the `FRAMEBORDER` attribute. May be set to "yes," "no," 1 (means yes), or 0 (means no).

frameSpacing							X	X	X	X

Although this property has been included since IE4, it has no meaning for iframes. (Some programmers believe it was included as a mistake originally and since then has been kept for backward compatibility.)

hspace							X	X	X	X

Read/write
Corresponds to the `HSPACE` attribute; sets the horizontal space between the `<IFRAME>` and the surrounding content.

Statement	NS2	NS3	NS4	NS6	IE3a	IE3b	IE4	IE5	IE5.5	IE6
longDesc				x						x

Read/write
The property corresponds to the `LONGDESC` attribute, and holds the URL of a document with a long description of the frame.

marginHeight				x			x	x	x	x

Read/write
Holds the height of the margin between a frame's content and its frame, in pixels.

marginWidth				x			x	x	x	x

Read/write
Holds the width of the margin between a frame's content and its frame, in pixels.

scrolling				x			x	x	x	x

Read/write
Indicates whether the frame can be scrolled (and displays scrollbars if appropriate). May be set to "yes," "no," 1 (means yes), or 0 (means no).

src				x			x	x	x	x

Read/write
Enables you to set or read the `SRC` attribute of a frame, which sets the URL of the source document (as with images in the `<IMG>` element). Set to an URL.

vspace							x	x	x	x

Read/write
Corresponds to the `VSPACE` attribute; sets the vertical space between the `<IFRAME>` and the surrounding content.

And that completes our look at the properties of the `window` object, as well as our look at the `<FRAMESET>`, `<FRAME>`, and `<IFRAME>` elements. In the next chapter, I'll turn to the methods and events of the `window` object.

8

Using *window* and *frame* Methods and Events

IN THE PRECEDING CHAPTER, WE TOOK a look at the properties of window object and frame elements. In this chapter, we'll take a look at their methods and events. To start us off, you can see the window object's methods and events in overview in Tables 8.1 and 8.2, and in depth in Tables 8.3 and 8.4. We'll discuss those methods and events in depth in this chapter.

Table 8.1 **Overview of the Methods of the *window* Object**

Methods		
alert	attachEvent	back
blur	captureEvents	clearInterval
clearTimeout	close	confirm
createPopup	detachEvent	disableExternalCapture
enableExternalCapture	execScript	find
fireEvent	focus	forward
getComputedStyle	GetAttention	getSelection
handleEvent	home	moveBy
moveTo	navigate	open
print	prompt	releaseEvents
resizeBy	resizeTo	routeEvent
scroll	scrollBy	scrollTo
scrollByLines	scrollByPages	setActive

continues ▶

Table 8.1 **Continued**

Methods		
setCursor	setInterval	setTimeout
showHelp	showModalDialog	showModelessDialog
sizeToContent	stop	

Table 8.2 **Overview of the Events of the *window* Object**

Events		
onactivate	onafterprint	onbeforedeactivate
onbeforeprint	onbeforeunload	onblur
oncontrolselect	ondeactivate	onerror
onfocus	onhelp	onload
onmove	onmoveend	onmovestart
onresize	onscroll	onunload

Table 8.3 **The Methods of the *window* Object**

Method	NS2	NS3	NS4	NS6	IE3a	IE3b	IE4	IE5	IE5.5	IE6
alert	x	x	x	x	x	x	x	x	x	x

Returns: Nothing
Displays an alert box. Syntax: `window.alert([msg])`, where *msg* is a string holding the message to display in the alert box. See "Alerts, Confirmations, and Prompts" in this chapter for an example.

attachEvent	See Chapter 6, "Using Core HTML Methods and Events."									
back			x	x						

Returns: Nothing
Navigates the Netscape Navigator back one page in the browser's history. Syntax: `back()`. Not available in the Internet Explorer, so for cross-browser compatibility, it's probably best to stick with the `history` object (see Chapter 10, "Using the *Navigator*, *Location*, and *History* Objects").

blur	See Chapter 6.									
captureEvents			x							

Returns: Nothing
Lets the `window` object capture events in Netscape navigator 4.0. Syntax: `captureEvents(eventTypeList)`. Here, *eventTypeList* holds a list of events to capture, OR'ed together like this: `Event.CLICK | Event.MOUSEUP`. See Chapter 15, "Working with the Mouse, Keyboard, and Images," for more details.

Method	NS2	NS3	NS4	NS6	IE3a	IE3b	IE4	IE5	IE5.5	IE6
clearInterval			x	x			x	x	x	x

Returns: Nothing
Clears an interval set with setInterval. (The interval sets the time between repeated automatic calls to the code you specify.) Syntax: clearInterval(*intervalID*), where *intervalID* is the ID returned by setInterval. See "Creating Timed Events" in this chapter for an example.

clearTimeout	x	x	x	x	x	x	x	x	x	x

Returns: Nothing
Clears a timer set with setTimeout and stops it from calling your code at some time in the future. Syntax: clearTimeout(*timerID*), where *timerID* is the ID returned by setTimer. See "Creating Timed Events" in this chapter for an example.

close	x	x	x	x	x	x	x	x	x	x

Returns: Nothing
Closes a window. Syntax: close(). See "Opening and Closing New Windows" for an example.

confirm	x	x	x	x	x	x	x	x	x	x

Returns: Boolean
Displays a confirmation dialog box that displays a message as well as OK and Cancel buttons. Syntax: window.confirm([*msg*]), where *msg* is the message to display. See "Alerts, Confirmations, and Prompts" in this chapter for an example.

createPopup									x	x

Returns: Popup object
Creates a popup window, which is typically used for dialog boxes, message boxes, tooltips, and other temporary windows. Syntax: createPopup(). (This method can actually take a parameter, but that parameter is not used in the current versions of the Internet Explorer). See "Creating Popups" in this chapter for an example.

detachEvent										

See Chapter 6.

disableExternal-			x							
Capture										

Returns: Nothing
Disables event capture in other frames in the Netscape Navigator 4.0. See Chapter 15 for more on this topic.

enableExternal			x							
Capture										

Returns: Nothing
Enables event capture in other frames in the Netscape Navigator 4.0. See Chapter 15 for more on this topic.

continues ▶

Table 8.3 **Continued**

Method	NS2	NS3	NS4	NS6	IE3a	IE3b	IE4	IE5	IE5.5	IE6
execScript							x	x	x	x

Returns: Nothing
Executes a script passed to the method as a string. Syntax:
`window.execScript(code, language)`, where *code* is the code to
execute and *language* is the scripting language to use (allowed values:
`"JScript"`—the default—`"JavaScript"` and `"VBScript"`). Unlike the
JavaScript `eval` function, this function does not return a result, although
it does have access to the global variables in your script. Good when
you want to execute some code in another scripting language, such as
VBScript.

find			x							

Returns: Boolean
This Netscape Navigator 4.0 method works like the Find dialog box in
this browser. Syntax: `find([text [, caseSensitive [, searchUp]]])`,
where *text* is the text to search for, *caseSensitive* is a Boolean value
indicating whether the search should be case-sensitive, and *searchUp*
is a Boolean value indicating whether the search should search upward.
Returns true if the text was found, false otherwise.

fireEvent	See Chapter 6.
focus	See Chapter 6.

forward				x	x					

Returns: Nothing
Navigates the Netscape Navigator forward one page in the browser's
history. Syntax: `forward()`. Not available in the Internet Explorer, so for
cross-browser compatibility, it's probably best to stick with the `history`
object (see Chapter 10).

getComputedStyle				x						

Returns: style object
Gets a computed style. Syntax: `getComputedStyle(style)`.

GetAttention				x						

Returns: Nothing
This Netscape Navigator 4.0 method gets the attention of the user if
the browser is already not the topmost window. In Windows, for exam-
ple, this method causes the browser's button in the taskbar to flash. The
MacOS beeps and displays a bullet next to the browser's entry in the
Application menu. Syntax: `GetAttention()`.

Method	NS2	NS3	NS4	NS6	IE3a	IE3b	IE4	IE5	IE5.5	IE6
getSelection				x						

Returns: String
Gets the text that is currently selected (highlighted) in a window.
Syntax: `window.getSelection()`. Replaces the deprecated
`document.getSelection()` (discussed in Chapter 9, "Using the
Document and *Body* Objects").

| handleEvent | | | x | | | | | | | |

Returns: Nothing
This Netscape Navigator 4.0 method handles events captured with
`setCapture`. Syntax: `handleEvent(event)`, where *event* is an event type
such as `Event.CLICK`. See Chapter 15 for more details.

| home | | | x | x | | | | | | |

Returns: Nothing
Navigates the Netscape Navigator to the web page that's been set as the
home page. Syntax: `home()`.

| moveBy | | | x | x | | | x | x | x | x |

Returns: Nothing
Moves a window. Syntax: `window.moveBy(iX, iY)`, where *iX* is the
horizontal change in pixels and *iY* is the vertical change in pixels.
See "Moving Windows" in this chapter for more details.

| moveTo | | | x | x | | | x | x | x | x |

Returns: Nothing
Moves a window. Syntax: `window.moveTo(iX, iY)`, where *iX* is the new
horizontal position in pixels and *iY* is the new vertical position in
pixels. See "Moving Windows" in this chapter for more details.

| navigate | | | | | x | x | x | x | x | x |

Returns: Nothing
Navigates to a new URL. Syntax: `navigate(URL)`, where *URL* is the
URL to navigate to. For cross-browser compatibility, it's better to use
`window.location.href`.

| open | x | x | x | x | x | x | x | x | x | x |

Returns: `window` object or null
Opens a new browser window. This is a big one—see "Opening and
Closing New Windows" in this chapter for the details and syntax.

continues ▶

Table 8.3 **Continued**

Method	NS2	NS3	NS4	NS6	IE3a	IE3b	IE4	IE5	IE5.5	IE6
print			x	x				x	x	x

Returns: Nothing
Prints a window. Syntax: `print()`. Note that Netscape Navigator 4.0 for Windows prints only the current frame. Netscape Navigator 6.0 enables you to print all frames. Internet Explorer gives you the option of printing all frames or a specific frame. See "Printing" in this chapter for an example.

prompt	x	x	x	x	x	x	x	x	x	x

Returns: Text or null
Displays a prompt box and returns user-entered text. Syntax: `window.prompt([msg] [, defaultValue])`, where *msg* is the prompt to display to the user and *defaultValue* is the text that originally appears in the prompt's text field. If the user enters text and clicks OK (not Cancel), this method returns the entered text. See "Alerts, Confirmations, and Prompts" for an example.

releaseEvents			x							

Returns: Nothing
This Netscape Navigator method releases event capture. Syntax: `releaseEvents(eventTypeList)`. Here, *eventTypeList* holds a list of events to release, OR'ed together like this: `Event.CLICK ¦ Event.MOUSEUP`. See Chapter 15 for more details.

resizeBy			x	x			x	x	x	x

Returns: Nothing
Resizes the browser window. Syntax: `window.resizeBy(iX, iY)`, where *iX* is the change in horizontal size in pixels and *iY* is the change in vertical size in pixels.

resizeTo			x	x			x	x	x	x

Returns: Nothing
Resizes the browser window. Syntax: `window.resizeTo(iX, iY)`, where *iX* is the new horizontal size in pixels and *iY* is the new vertical size in pixels.

routeEvent			x							

Returns: Nothing
If you've turned on event capture in Netscape Navigator 4.0, this method enables you to route an event after you have worked on the event and want to pass it along to the next event handler.
Syntax: `routeEvent(event)`. See Chapter 15 for more details.

Method	NS2	NS3	NS4	NS6	IE3a	IE3b	IE4	IE5	IE5.5	IE6
scroll		x	x	x			x	x	x	x

Returns: Nothing
Scrolls a window. Syntax: `window.scroll(`*hCoordinate,* *vCoordinate*`)`, where *hCoordinate* is the new horizontal position in pixels and *vCoordinate* is the new vertical position in pixels. This method has been gradually replaced by `scrollTo`, but is still available. See "Scrolling a Window" in this chapter for more details.

scrollBy			x	x	x			x	x	x

Returns: Nothing
Scrolls a window. Syntax: `window.scrollBy(`*hCoordinate,* *vCoordinate*`)`, where *hCoordinate* is the horizontal change in pixels and *vCoordinate* is the vertical change in pixels. See "Scrolling a Window" in this chapter.

scrollByLines				x						

Scrolls a window by a number of lines.
Syntax: `window.scrollBy(`*lines*`)`, where *lines* is the number of lines to scroll by. See "Scrolling a Window" in this chapter.

scrollByPages				x						

Scrolls a window by a number of pages.
Syntax: `window.scrollBy(`*pages*`)`, where *pages* is the number of pages to scroll by. See "Scrolling a Window" in this chapter.

scrollTo			x	x	x			x	x	x

Returns: Nothing
Scrolls a window. Syntax: `window.scrollTo(`*hCoordinate,* *vCoordinate*`)`, where *hCoordinate* is the new horizontal position in pixels and *vCoordinate* is the new vertical position in pixels. See "Scrolling a Window" in this chapter.

setActive	See Chapter 6									

setCursor				x						

Returns: Nothing
Sets the cursor in Netscape Navigator 4.0.
Syntax: `setCursor(`*type*`)`, where *type* can be one of: alias, auto, cell, context-menu, copy, count-down, count-up, count-up-down, crosshair, default, e-resize, grab, grabbing, help, move, n-resize, ne-resize, nw-resize, pointer, s-resize, se-resize, spinning, sw-resize, text, w-resize, or wait.

continues ▶

Table 8.3 **Continued**

Method	NS2	NS3	NS4	NS6	IE3a	IE3b	IE4	IE5	IE5.5	IE6
setInterval			x	x			x	x	x	x

Returns: Interval ID value (integer)
Sets an interval to use to call a function or execute code repeatedly.
Syntax: `window.setInterval(code, milliSeconds [, language])`. Here
are the arguments: *code* is code that specifies a function or text string of
code to be executed when the specified interval has elapsed, *milliSeconds*
is an integer that specifies the number of milliseconds between execu-
tions, and *language* is a string that specifies any one of the possible values
for the LANGUAGE attribute. (The Netscape Navigator does not support
the *language* argument.) Returns an ID value to use with `clearInterval`.
See "Creating Timed Events" in this chapter for an example.

Method	NS2	NS3	NS4	NS6	IE3a	IE3b	IE4	IE5	IE5.5	IE6
setTimeout	x	x	x	x	x	x	x	x	x	x

Returns: ID value
Sets an interval to use to call a function or execute code at some time
in the future. Syntax: `window.setTimeout(code, milliSeconds [,
language])`. Here are the arguments: *code* is the code that specifies a
function or text string of code to be executed when the specified time
has elapsed, *milliSeconds* is an integer that specifies the number of milliseconds to wait until execution, and *language* is a string that specifies
any one of the possible values for the LANGUAGE attribute. (The Netscape
Navigator does not support the *language* argument.) Returns an ID
value to use with `clearTimeout`. See "Creating Timed Events" in this
chapter for an example.

Method	NS2	NS3	NS4	NS6	IE3a	IE3b	IE4	IE5	IE5.5	IE6
showHelp							x	x	x	x

Returns: Nothing
This Internet Explorer method enables you to display a WinHelp
window for Windows .hlp files. Syntax: `window.showHelp(URL [,
ContextID])`, where *URL* specifies the URL of the file to be displayed
as help, and *ContextID* specifies a string or integer that indicates a context identifier in a Help file.

Method	NS2	NS3	NS4	NS6	IE3a	IE3b	IE4	IE5	IE5.5	IE6
showModalDialog							x	x	x	x

Returns: Nothing
Displays a modal dialog box. This is a big one—see "Dialog Boxes" in
this chapter for the syntax and details.

Method	NS2	NS3	NS4	NS6	IE3a	IE3b	IE4	IE5	IE5.5	IE6
showModelessDialog	x	x	x	x	x	x	x	x	x	x

Returns: Nothing
Displays a modeless dialog box. This is a big one—see "Dialog Boxes" in
this chapter for the syntax and details.

Method	NS2	NS3	NS4	NS6	IE3a	IE3b	IE4	IE5	IE5.5	IE6
sizeToContent				X						

Returns: Nothing
Resizes a window so that all the window's contents are visible.
Syntax: `sizeToContent()`.

Method	NS2	NS3	NS4	NS6	IE3a	IE3b	IE4	IE5	IE5.5	IE6
stop			X	X						

Returns: Nothing
Using this method is the same as clicking the Stop button in the
Netscape Navigator's toolbar. Syntax: `stop()`.

Table 8.4   **The Events of the *window* Object**

Event	NS2	NS3	NS4	NS6	IE3a	IE3b	IE4	IE5	IE5.5	IE6
onactivate	See Chapter 6.									
onafterprint								X	X	X

Occurs immediately after a document prints or previews for printing.
See "Printing" in this chapter.

Event	NS2	NS3	NS4	NS6	IE3a	IE3b	IE4	IE5	IE5.5	IE6
onbeforedeactivate	See Chapter 6.									
onbeforeprint								X	X	X

Occurs immediately before a document prints or previews for printing.
See "Printing" in this chapter.

Event	NS2	NS3	NS4	NS6	IE3a	IE3b	IE4	IE5	IE5.5	IE6
onbeforeunload							X	X	X	X

Occurs just before a page is unloaded. See "Window Loading and
Unloading" in this chapter.

Event	NS2	NS3	NS4	NS6	IE3a	IE3b	IE4	IE5	IE5.5	IE6
onblur	See Chapter 6.									
oncontrolselect	See Chapter 6.									
ondeactivate	See Chapter 6.									
onerror	See Chapter 3, "The JavaScript Language: Loops, Functions, and Errors."									
onfocus	See Chapter 6.									
onhelp	See Chapter 6.									
onload	X	X	X	X	X	X	X	X	X	X

Occurs when a document has been fully loaded and all parts of the
document are available for scripting. See "Window Loading and
Unloading" in this chapter for an example.

Event	NS2	NS3	NS4	NS6	IE3a	IE3b	IE4	IE5	IE5.5	IE6
onmove	See Chapter 6.									

continues ▶

Table 8.4 **Continued**

Event	NS2	NS3	NS4	NS6	IE3a	IE3b	IE4	IE5	IE5.5	IE6
onmoveend	See Chapter 6.									
onmovestart	See Chapter 6.									
onresize	See Chapter 6.									
onscroll							x	x	x	x
	Occurs when the window is scrolled.									
onunload	x	x	x	x	x	x	x	x	x	x
	Occurs when a document is unloaded. See "Window Loading and Unloading" in this chapter for an example.									

Alerts, Confirmations, and Prompts

Browsers have a few predefined window methods that enable you to display dialog boxes: `alert`, `confirm`, and `prompt`. The alert method just displays an alert dialog box with a message:

```
window.alert([msg])
```

Here, *msg* is a string that specifies the message to display in the dialog box. We've already seen how to use alert boxes as far back as Chapter 1, "Essential JavaScript;" here's Listing 01-03.html on the web site, which displays an alert box when a page loads:

```
<HTML>
    <HEAD>
        <TITLE>
            Executing Scripts After a Document Loads
        </TITLE>
        <SCRIPT LANGUAGE="JavaScript">
            <!--
            function alerter()
            {
                window.alert("All loaded.")
            }
            // -->
        </SCRIPT>
    </HEAD>

    <BODY ONLOAD="alerter()">
        <H1>Executing Scripts After a Document Loads</H1>
    </BODY>
</HTML>
```

You can see the results of this code in Figure 8.1, where you see that the alert displays only an OK button to let the user acknowledge the message.

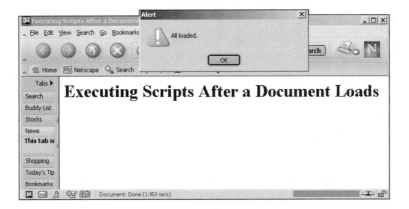

Figure 8.1 Displaying an alert box.

The `confirm` method enables the user to click an OK button to confirm a message or Cancel to deny it. Here's how you use this method:

answerBoolean = window.confirm([*msg*])

The *msg* argument is the text displayed in the confirm box. This method returns true if the user clicked the OK button, and false if the user clicked the Cancel button. Here's an example that displays a confirm box asking whether the user wants a greeting, and if so, writes `Hello!` to the page:

(Listing 08-01.html on the web site)

```
<HTML>
    <HEAD>
        <TITLE>Using the confirm Method</TITLE>
    </HEAD>

    <BODY>
        <H1>Using the confirm Method</H1>
        <SCRIPT LANGUAGE="JavaScript">
            <!--
            if(confirm("Do you want a greeting?")){
                document.write("Hello!")
            }
            // -->
        </SCRIPT>
    </BODY>
</HTML>
```

You can see the confirm box in Figure 8.2, and the results in Figure 8.3 if you click the OK button.

Figure 8.2   Displaying a confirm box.

Figure 8.3   Using data from a confirm box.

The prompt method displays a prompt to the user and accepts typed text, returning that text. Here's how you use this method:

```
text = window.prompt([msg [, defaultValue]])
```

Here, *msg* is a string that specifies the message to display in the dialog box (by default, this is set to ""), and *defaultValue* is a string that specifies the default value of the input text field (by default, this parameter is set to "undefined"). Here's an example using the prompt method, letting the user enter his own name (the default name here is Ralph):

(Listing 08-02.html on the web site)

```
<HTML>
    <HEAD>
        <TITLE>Using the prompt Method</TITLE>
    </HEAD>
```

```
<BODY>
    <H1>Using the prompt Method</H1>
    <SCRIPT LANGUAGE="JavaScript">
        <!--
        document.write("Hello " + prompt("What is your name?", "Ralph") + "!")
        // -->
    </SCRIPT>
</BODY>
</HTML>
```

You can see the prompt box in Figure 8.4, and the results in Figure 8.5 after I've entered Steve and clicked the OK button.

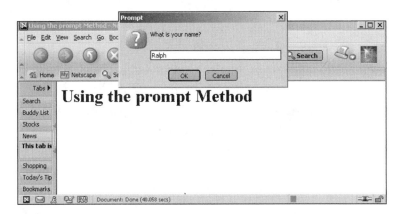

Figure 8.4   Displaying a prompt box.

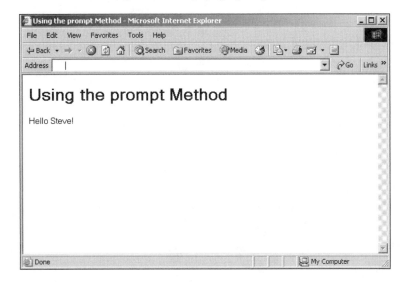

Figure 8.5   Using data from a prompt box.

Creating Popups

Popups are windows typically used for dialog boxes, message boxes, tooltips, and other temporary windows; and in the Internet Explorer, you can use the `createPopup` method to create a popup:

```
window.createPopup([arguments])
```

The optional *arguments* argument actually is ignored currently and is reserved for future use only. This method returns the popup window object itself. You can use two methods with popup windows, `show` and `hide`. The `show` method shows the popup:

```
popup.show(iX, iY, iWidth, iHeight [, element])
```

Here are the arguments for this method:

- **iX.** Integer that specifies the x coordinate of the popup window, in pixels.
- **iY.** Integer that specifies the y coordinate of the popup window, in pixels.
- **iWidth.** Integer that specifies the width of the popup window, in pixels.
- **iHeight.** Integer that specifies the height of the popup window, in pixels.
- **element.** Object that specifies the element to which the x,y coordinates are relative. If none is given, the x,y coordinates are relative to the screen, where (0,0) is the upper-left corner.

The `hide` method just hides the popup, and is called without arguments: `popup.hide()`.

Here's an example that displays a tooltip using a popup window when the user clicks a button:

(Listing 08-03.html on the web site)

```
<HTML>
    <HEAD>
        <TITLE>Popup Example</TITLE>
        <SCRIPT LANGUAGE="JavaScript">
            <!--
            var popup = window.createPopup()
            function ButtonClick()
            {
                popup.document.body.style.backgroundColor = "lightyellow"
                popup.document.body.style.border = "solid black 1px"
                popup.document.body.innerHTML = "This is a popup! Click outside the
                ➥popup to close it."
                popup.show(100, 100, 180, 40, document.body)
            }
            // -->
        </SCRIPT>
    </HEAD>
```

```
<BODY>
    <BUTTON ONCLICK="ButtonClick()">Click Me!</BUTTON>
</BODY>
</HTML>
```

You can see the results in Figure 8.6.

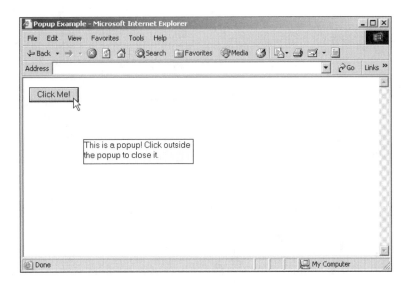

Figure 8.6   Displaying a popup.

Moving Windows

You can use the `moveBy` and `moveTo` methods to move windows. The `moveBy` method moves a window by a given (positive or negative) X and Y offset, and the `moveTo` method moves a window to a specific X and Y location. Both methods take two arguments—the X and Y offset (for `moveBy`) or new position (for `moveTo`), measured in pixels.

X and Y coordinates for the `moveBy` and `moveTo` methods are measured in screen coordinates, where (0, 0) is the upper-left corner of the screen; positive X is to the right, and positive Y is downward. To move 10 pixels down and 5 pixels to the left, for example, use `moveBy(-5, 10)`. Note that this is true for all JavaScript graphical methods: (0, 0) is at upper left (the upper left of the screen for the `moveBy` and `moveTo` methods, but possibly the upper left of other windows—such as the browser window—for certain other methods), positive X is to the right, and positive Y is downward.

Here's an example that moves the browser to the upper-left corner of the screen:

(Listing 08-04.html on the web site)

```
<HTML>
    <HEAD>
        <TITLE>Using the moveTo method</TITLE>
        <SCRIPT LANGUAGE="JavaScript">
            <!--
            function mover()
            {
                window.moveTo(0, 0)
            }
            // -->
        </SCRIPT>
    </HEAD>

    <BODY>
        <H1>Using the moveTo method</H1>
        <FORM>
            <INPUT TYPE="BUTTON" ONCLICK="mover()" VALUE="Click Me!">
        </FORM>
    </BODY>
</HTML>
```

Opening and Closing New Windows

The window.open method is a big one, because it enables you to open new browser windows. Here's how you use this method:

```
window.open( [URL] [, name] [, features] [, replace])
```

This method returns the new window object. The arguments for this method are *URL* and *name*.

The *URL* argument specifies the URL of the document to display. If no URL is specified and you pass an empty string (""), a new window with the title about:blank displays.

The *name* argument is a string that specifies the name of the window. (The name is a one-word name for the NAME attribute—not the title of the window—this name is used as the value for the TARGET attribute on a form or an element.) You also can use these values here:

- **replace.** Specifies that the new document is to replace the current entry in the history list.

- **_blank.** The document is loaded into a new, unnamed window.

- **_media.** The document is loaded into the HTML content area of the Internet Explorer Media Bar (available in Internet Explorer 6 or later).

- **_parent.** The document is loaded into the current frame's parent.

- **_search.** The document is opened in the browser's search pane (available in Internet Explorer 5 and later).

- **_self.** The current document is replaced with the specified document.

- **_top.** The document replaces any framesets that may be loaded. (As you would expect, if no framesets are defined, this value acts as the value _self.)

The *features* argument is a string list of items separated by commas. Each item consists of an option and a value, separated by an equals sign (for example, "fullscreen=yes,toolbar=yes", as we'll see in a page or two—note that you should not use spaces between these items, because NS4 can't handle such spaces). You can find the possible values in Table 8.5—all values are Boolean values you set to "yes," "no," 1 (same as yes), or 0 (same as no) unless otherwise noted.

Table 8.5 **The Features of Windows Opened with the *window.open* Method**

Feature	Means
alwaysLowered	New window appears behind other browser windows. (NS4+)
alwaysRaised	New window appears in front of other browser windows. (NS4+)
channelmode	Specifies whether to display the window in theater mode and show the channel band. The default is "no". (IE4+)
copyhistory	Copies the history for new window. (NS2+)
dependent	The new window should close if window that opened it closes. (NS4+)
directories	Specifies whether to add directory buttons. The default is "yes". (NS2+, IE3+)
fullscreen	Specifies whether to display the browser in full-screen mode. The default is "no". (IE4+)
height	Specifies the height of the window, in pixels. Set to an integer—the minimum value for the Internet Explorer is 100. (NS2+, IE3+)
hotkeys	This item disables menu shortcuts when the menu bar is not visible. (NS4+)
innerHeight	Height of the client area. Set to an integer. (NS4+)
innerWidth	Width of the client area. Set to an integer. (NS4+)
left	Horizontal position of upper-left corner of the window in screen coordinates. Set to an integer value, in pixels. (IE4+)

continues ▶

Table 8.5 **Continued**

Feature	Means
location	Specifies whether to display the input field for entering URLs directly into the browser. The default is "yes". (NS2+, IE3+)
menubar	Specifies whether to display the menu bar. The default is "yes". (NS2+, IE3+)
outerHeight	Outer height of the window. Set to an integer value, in pixels. (NS4+)
outerWidth	Outer width of the window. Set to an integer value, in pixels. (NS4+)
resizable	Specifies whether to display resize handles at the corners of the window. The default is "yes". (NS2+, IE3+)
screenX	Horizontal position of window's upper-left corner in screen coordinates. Set to an integer value, in pixels. (NS4+)
screenY	Vertical position of window's upper-left corner in screen coordinates. Set to an integer value, in pixels. (NS4+)
scrollbars	Specifies whether to display horizontal and vertical scrollbars if needed. The default is "yes". (NS2+, IE3+)
status	Specifies whether to display the status bar at the bottom of the new window. (NS2+, IE3+)
titlebar	Specifies whether to display a title bar for the window. The default is "yes". In the Internet Explorer, this parameter is ignored unless the calling application is an HTML application or a trusted dialog box. (NS4+, IE4+)
toolbar	Specifies whether to display the toolbar, displaying buttons such as Back, Forward, and Stop. The default is "yes". (NS2+, IE3+)
top	Vertical position of upper-left corner of the window in screen coordinates. Set to an integer value, in pixels. (IE4+)
width	Specifies the width of the window, in pixels. Set to an integer—the minimum value for the Internet Explorer is 100. (NS2+, IE3+)
z-lock	Locks the new window layer below other browser windows. (NS4+)

Tip

If you display a new window in full-screen mode, the browser's controls won't be visible, so you should provide a way for the user to close the browser, or at least let the users know they can close the window with Ctrl+W in both the Internet Explorer and the Netscape Navigator.

Finally, the *replace* argument is a Boolean value that holds *true* if the new document replaces the current document in the history list or *false* if the new document should create a new entry in the history list.

We've already seen the open method at work in Chapter 7, "Using *window and frame* Properties;" in this example (it's Listing 07-02.html on the web site), we opened a new blank window, creating the window object window1, and then wrote to the new window with the window1.docuent.write method like this (note that the only features we're setting here are the height and width: "height=300,width=300", but we could have done more like this "height=300,width=300,scrollbars=yes,toolbar =no" and so on):

```
<HTML>
    <HEAD>
        <TITLE>Using the closed and opener Properties</TITLE>
        <SCRIPT LANGUAGE="JavaScript">
            <!--
            var window1

            function openWindow()
            {
                window1 = window.open("","window1", "height=300,width=300")
                window1.document.write("<HTML><BODY><H1>A New Window</H1><BR>" +
                "<FORM><INPUT TYPE='button' VALUE='Close the original window'" +
                "ONCLICK='window.opener.close()'>" +
                "</FORM></BODY></HTML>")
                window1.document.close()
            }

            function closeWindow()
            {
                if (window1 && !window1.closed) {
                    window1.close()
                }
            }
            // -->
        </SCRIPT>
    </HEAD>

    <BODY>
        <H1>Using the closed and opener Properties</H1>
        <FORM>
            <INPUT TYPE="button" VALUE="Open New Window" ONCLICK="openWindow()">
            <INPUT TYPE="button" VALUE="Close New Window" ONCLICK="closeWindow()">
        </FORM>
    </BODY>
</HTML>
```

You can see the results in Chapter 7, in Figure 7.2.

Tip

When you're opening new windows and writing HTML to them, as we are here, it's sometimes wise to wait for a while after opening a new window to make sure it's ready to go (that is, fully loaded) before writing to it (especially with the Internet Explorer). You can do that with the `window` method `setTimeout`, discussed in the previous topic.

Working with Other Windows

When you open new windows, a `window` object is returned by the `open` method. When you have such a `window` object, you can access the `document` inside the new window with an expression such as `windowObject.document`. For example, here's how to access a text field in another window: `windowObject.document.form1.text1.value`. In this way, you can work with multiple windows in your code.

Here's an example where you can open a new window with a button, enter text in a text field in the new window, and click a button (labeled "Get text from new window") to read the text from the text field, displaying it in the main window:

(Listing 08-05.html on the web site)

```
<HTML>
    <HEAD>
        <TITLE>Working With Multiple Windows</TITLE>
        <SCRIPT LANGUAGE="JavaScript">
            <!--
            var window1

            function openWindow()
            {
                window1 = window.open("08-06.html","window1","HEIGHT=300, WIDTH=300")
            }

            function getText()
            {
                if (window1 && !window1.closed) {
                document.form1.text1.value = window1.document.form1.text1.value
                }
            }

            function closeWindow()
            {
                if (window1 && !window1.closed) {
                    window1.close()
                }
            }
            // -->
```

```
            </SCRIPT>
        </HEAD>

        <BODY>
            <H1>Working With Multiple Windows</H1>
            <FORM NAME="form1">
                <INPUT TYPE="BUTTON" VALUE="Open new window" ONCLICK="openWindow()">
                <INPUT TYPE="BUTTON" VALUE="Get text from new window" ONCLICK="getText()">
                <INPUT TYPE="BUTTON" VALUE="Close new window" ONCLICK="closeWindow()">
                <BR>
                <INPUT TYPE="TEXT" NAME="text1">
            </FORM>
        </BODY>
</HTML>
```

And here's the HTML for the new window:

(Listing 08-06.html on the web site)

```
<HTML>
    <HEAD>
        <TITLE>A New Window</TITLE>
    </HEAD>

    <BODY>
        <H1>A New Window</H1>
        <FORM NAME="form1">
            Enter some text:
            <INPUT TYPE="TEXT" NAME="text1">
        </FORM>
    </BODY>
</HTML>
```

You can see the results in Figure 8.7, where I've entered text in the new window, and read it from the main window.

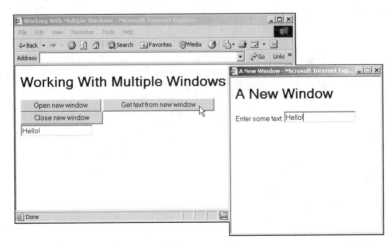

Figure 8.7   Working with multiple windows.

Printing

You also can print windows and frames using the print method like this:
`window.print()`.

The print method opens the Print dialog box, prompting the user to change print settings and click OK to print. The Netscape Navigator 4.0 for Windows prints only the current frame. Netscape Navigator 6.0 enables you to print all frames if you use the print method from the <FRAMESET> window. Internet Explorer gives you the option of printing all frames or a specific frame.

> **Tip**
>
> When the user clicks the OK button in the Internet Explorer's Print dialog box, the following sequence of events occurs: The onbeforeprint event occurs, the document prints, and then the onafterprint event occurs. These events are not supported in the Netscape Navigator.

Here's an example that prints the current window:

(Listing 08-07.html on the web site)

```
<HTML>
    <HEAD>
        <TITLE>
            Printing a Window
        </TITLE>
        <SCRIPT LANGUAGE="JavaScript">
            <!--
            function printer()
            {
                window.print()
            }
            // -->
        </SCRIPT>
    </HEAD>

    <BODY>
        <H1>Printing a Window</H1>
        <FORM>
            <INPUT TYPE="BUTTON" ONCLICK="printer()" VALUE="Click Me!">
        </FORM>
    </BODY>
</HTML>
```

Scrolling a Window

You can use the scroll, scrollBy, and scrollTo methods to scroll a window's content. Here's how you use these methods:

```
window.scroll(iX, iY)
window.scrollBy(iX, iY)
window.scrollTo(iX, iY)
```

Here are the arguments of these methods:

- *iX.* Integer that specifies the horizontal scroll offset (scrollBy) or new position (scroll and scrollTo), in pixels. Positive values scroll the window right, and negative values scroll it left.

- *iY.* Integer that specifies the vertical scroll offset (scrollBy) or new position (scroll and scrollTo), in pixels. Positive values scroll the window down, and negative values scroll it up.

Here's an example that uses the scroll method to scroll a window when the user clicks a button:

(Listing 08-08.html on the web site)

```
<HTML>
    <HEAD>
        <TITLE>
            Scrolling Windows
        </TITLE>
        <SCRIPT LANGUAGE="JavaScript">
            <!--
            function scroller()
            {
                window.scroll(0, 100)
            }
            // -->
        </SCRIPT>
    </HEAD>

    <BODY>
        <H1>Scrolling Windows</H1>
        <FORM>
            <INPUT TYPE="BUTTON" ONCLICK="scroller()" VALUE="Click Me!">
        </FORM>
        <BR>
        <BR>
        <BR>
        <BR>
        <BR>
        <BR>
        <BR>
        <BR>
        <BR>
        <BR>
        <BR>
        <BR>
        <BR>
        <BR>
        <BR>
        <BR>
        <BR>
    </BODY>
</HTML>
```

Actually, the `scroll` method has been more or less replaced by the `scrollTo` method these days—which does the same thing—although the `scroll` method is still available. The Netscape Navigator also supports two handy methods—`scrollByLines` and `scrollByPages` that enable you to scroll by a given number of lines and pages.

Creating Timed Events

On occasion, it can be useful to have the browser call your code at a later time, as when you want to display scrolling text in the status bar or display a clock. JavaScript gives you two ways to do this—using the `setInterval`/`clearInterval` methods and the `setTimeout`/`clearTimeout` methods.

You use `setInterval` to set the interval (measured in milliseconds, 1/1000ths of a second) between repeated calls to your code and `setTimeout` to set a length of time after which the browser will call your code. That is, `setInterval` is designed to be used for repeated calls, and `setTimeout` just for a single call sometime in the future. In practice, however, `setTimeout`, which was introduced before `setInterval`, is often used for repeated calls as well.

The `setInterval` method returns an interval ID (an integer), which you can pass to `clearInterval` to stop the repeated calls; and the `setTimer` method returns a timer ID (also an integer), which you can pass to `clearTimeout` to cancel the future call to your code. Here's how to use both methods:

```
window.setTimeout(code, milliSeconds [, language])
window.setInterval(code, milliSeconds [, language])
```

Here are the arguments for these methods:

- **code.** The function or string that holds the code to be executed when the specified time has elapsed.

- **milliSeconds.** Integer that specifies the number of milliseconds to wait.

- **language.** Internet Explorer only. String that specifies one of the following values: `"JScript"`, `"VBScript"`, `"JavaScript"`.

We've already seen the `setTimeout` method to display scrolling text in the browser's status bar in Chapter 7 like this (Listing 07-01.html on the web site):

```
<HTML>
    <HEAD>
        <TITLE>Scrolling Status Bar Text</TITLE>
        <SCRIPT LANGUAGE="JavaScript">
            <!--
```

```
                var text = "Hello from JavaScript! Hello from JavaScript! "
                function scroller()
                {
                    window.status = text
                    text = text.substring(1, text.length) + text.substring(0, 1)
                    setTimeout("scroller()", 150)
                }
                // -->
            </SCRIPT>
        </HEAD>

    <BODY onLoad="scroller()">
        <H1>Scrolling Status Bar Text</H1>
    </BODY>
</HTML>
```

Here's an example that uses setInterval and clearInterval to display a
clock, updated every second. To do that, this example uses the Date object's
toLocaleTimeString method (not available in NS4 or earlier) that we'll see in
Chapter 18, "The *Date*, *Time*, and *String* Objects"—this method returns a
string with the local time. If the user wants to stop the clock, she just has to
click the button to use the clearInterval method (to start the clock again,
you have to use setInterval to get a new interval ID):

(Listing 08-09.html on the web site)

```
<HTML>
    <HEAD>
        <TITLE>
            Using setInterval and clearInterval
        </TITLE>
        <SCRIPT LANGUAGE="JavaScript">
            <!--
            var intervalID = ""

            intervalID = window.setInterval("showTime()", 1000)
            function showTime()
            {
                var d = new Date()
                document.form1.text1.value = d.toLocaleTimeString()
            }
            function stopCounting()
            {
                window.clearInterval(intervalID)
            }
            // -->
        </SCRIPT>
    </HEAD>

    <BODY>
        <H1>Using setInterval and clearInterval</H1>
```

continues ▶

```
        <FORM NAME="form1">
            <INPUT TYPE="TEXT" NAME="text1">
            <INPUT TYPE="BUTTON" VALUE="Stop counting" ONCLICK="stopCounting()">
        </FORM>
    </BODY>
</HTML>
```

You can see the results in Figure 8.8.

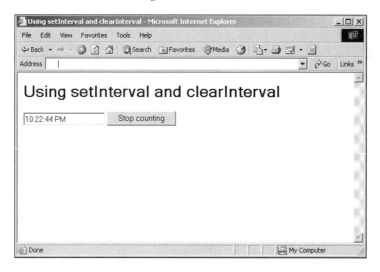

Figure 8.8   Displaying a clock.

You also can pass arguments to `setInterval` and `setTimeout` to be passed to a called function. The Netscape Navigator 4+ enables you to pass a list of comma-separated arguments to be passed to the function you're calling like this: `setInterval(dataCrunch, 1000, value1 , value2)`, where `value1` and `value2` will be passed to the `dataCrunch` function. (Note that the first argument is just the `dataCrunch` function name, without quotes and without parentheses.) For cross-browser compatibility, however, here's a better way:

```
interval = setInterval("dataCrunch(" + value1 + ", " + value2 + ")", 1000)
```

Dialog Boxes

In the Internet Explorer, you can use the `showModalDialog` to display modal dialog boxes (dialog boxes the user must dismiss before continuing with the browser) and `showModelessDialog` to display modeless dialog boxes (dialog boxes that enable the user to return to the browser before being dismissed) with `showModalDialog`. Here's how to use these two methods:

```
window.showModalDialog(URL [, arguments] [, features])
window.showModelessDialog(URL [, arguments] [, features])
```

The *URL* argument specifies the URL of the document to load and display.

The *arguments* argument specifies the arguments to use when displaying the dialog box. Use this parameter to pass a value of any type, including an array of values. The dialog box can extract the values passed by the caller from the `dialogArguments` property of the `window` object.

The *features* argument specifies how to configure the dialog box, using one or more of the following semicolon-delimited values—all these values can be set to Boolean values you can set to "yes," "no," 1 (same as yes), or 0 (same as no) unless otherwise noted:

- `dialogHeight`. Sets the height of the dialog window. Set to a value in pixels ending in `px`, such as `"250px"`.

- `dialogLeft`. Sets the left position of the dialog window relative to the upper-left corner of the desktop. Set to a value in pixels ending in `px`, such as `"250px"`.

- `dialogTop`. Sets the top position of the dialog window relative to the upper-left corner of the desktop. Set to a value in pixels ending in `px`, such as `"250px"`.

- `dialogWidth`. Sets the width of the dialog window. Set to a value in pixels ending in `px`, such as `"250px"`.

- `center`. Specifies whether to center the dialog window in the screen. The default is `"yes"`.

- `dialogHide`. Specifies whether the dialog window is hidden when printing or using print preview. The default is `"no"`.

- `edge`. Specifies the edge style of the dialog window. Set to `"sunken"` or `"raised"`. The default is `"raised"`.

- `help`. Specifies whether the dialog window displays a context-sensitive Help icon. The default is `"yes"`.

- `resizable`. Specifies whether the dialog window may be resized. The default is `"no"`.

- `scroll`. Specifies whether the dialog window displays scrollbars. The default is `"yes"`.

- `status`. Specifies whether the dialog window displays a status bar. The default is `"yes"` for untrusted dialog windows and `"no"` for Internet Explorer trusted dialog windows.

- `unadorned`. Specifies whether the dialog window displays the border elements. This feature is available only when a dialog box is opened from an Internet Explorer trusted application. The default is `"no"`.

You set these values with a colon and the value itself; for example, here's how we created a dialog box 350 pixels wide and 250 pixels high in Chapter 7:

```
var dialog1 = showModalDialog("07-04.html", values, "dialogWidth:350px;
dialogHeight:250px")
```

We've already seen how to use these methods in Chapter 7. In that chapter, we used showModalDialog to display a modal dialog box. In that example, the main window displayed two values in text fields; when the user opened the dialog box, those values were passed to and displayed in that dialog box. The user could enter new values, close the dialog box, and the new values would appear in the main window. Here is the code we used for the main window:

(Listing 07-03.html on the web site)

```
<HTML>
    <HEAD>
        <TITLE>Using Modal Dialogs</TITLE>
        <SCRIPT LANGUAGE="JavaScript">
            <!--
            function openDialog()
            {
                var values = new Array()
                if(document.form1.text1.value){
                    values["value1"] = document.form1.text1.value
                }
                if(document.form1.text2.value){
                    values["value2"] = document.form1.text2.value
                }

                var dialog1 = showModalDialog("07-04.html", values,
                    "dialogWidth:350px; dialogHeight:250px")
                if (dialog1) {
                    if (dialog1["value1"]) {
                        document.form1.text1.value = dialog1["value1"]
                    }
                    if (dialog1["value2"]) {
                        document.form1.text2.value = dialog1["value2"]
                    }
                }
            }
            // -->
        </SCRIPT>
    </HEAD>

    <BODY>
        <H1>Using Modal Dialogs</H1>
        <FORM NAME="form1">
            <INPUT TYPE="BUTTON" ONCLICK="openDialog()" VALUE="Open the dialog box">
            <BR>
            Enter the first value:
            <BR>
```

```
            <INPUT TYPE="TEXT" ID="text1" VALUE="1">
            <BR>
            Enter the second value:
            <BR>
            <INPUT TYPE="TEXT" ID="text2" VALUE="2">
            <BR>
        </FORM>
    </BODY>
</HTML>
```

And here's the code for the dialog box (Listing 07-04.html on the web site):

```
<HTML>
    <HEAD>
        <TITLE>Modal Dialog Box</TITLE>
        <SCRIPT LANGUAGE="JavaScript">
            <!--
            function handleOK()
            {
                var returnValues = new Array()
                if (document.form1.text1.value) {
                    returnValues["value1"] = document.form1.text1.value
                }
                if (document.form1.text2.value) {
                    returnValues["value2"] = document.form1.text2.value
                }
                window.returnValue = returnValues
                window.close()
            }

            function handleCancel()
            {
                window.returnValue = ""
                window.close()
            }

            function initialize()
            {
                if (window.dialogArguments) {
                    if (window.dialogArguments["value1"]) {
                        document.form1.text1.value = window.dialogArguments["value1"]
                    }
                    if (window.dialogArguments["value2"]) {
                        document.form1.text2.value = window.dialogArguments["value2"]
                    }
                }
            }
            // -->
        </SCRIPT>
    </HEAD>
```

continues ▶

```
<BODY ONLOAD="initialize()">
    <H1>Modal Dialog Box</H1>
    <FORM NAME="form1">
        Enter the new first value:
        <BR>
        <INPUT TYPE="TEXT" NAME="text1">
        <BR>
        Enter the new second value:
        <BR>
        <INPUT TYPE="TEXT" NAME="text2">
        <BR>
        <INPUT TYPE="BUTTON" ONCLICK="handleOK()"
    ➥VALUE="  OK  ">
        <INPUT TYPE="BUTTON" ONCLICK="handleCancel()" VALUE="Cancel">
    </FORM>
</BODY>
</HTML>
```

You can see the results of this code in Figures 7.3 and 7.4. For all the details, see Chapter 7.

Window Loading and Unloading

As you know, you have to be careful in JavaScript about accessing page elements that have not yet been loaded. For example, trying to write to the <BODY> of a page from the <HEAD> might cause problems, because the body might not be loaded yet:

```
<HTML>
    <HEAD>
        <TITLE>
            Writing to a Web page
        </TITLE>
        <SCRIPT LANGUAGE="JavaScript">
            <!--
            document.write("Hello!")
            // -->
        </SCRIPT>
    </HEAD>

    <BODY>
        <H1>Writing to a Web page</H1>
    </BODY>
</HTML>
```

One solution is to embed the script in the <BODY> of a page:

```
<HTML>
    <HEAD>
        <TITLE>
            Writing to a Web page
```

```
        </TITLE>
    </HEAD>

    <BODY ONLOAD="writer()">
        <H1>Writing to a Web page</H1>
        <SCRIPT LANGUAGE="JavaScript">
            <!--
            document.write("Hello!")
            // -->
        </SCRIPT>
    </BODY>
</HTML>
```

Another solution is to use the window object's onload and onunload events.
The onload event occurs when a window is fully loaded (after all elements
have been fully loaded and are running) and the onunload event occurs just
before a window is removed from the screen. You can assign an event handler
to those events using the <BODY> or <FRAMESET> elements, and the event handler will be attached to the corresponding window object's event. Here's how
that looks in code targeted to IE5+ and NS6+:

```
<HTML>
    <HEAD>
        <TITLE>
            Writing to a Web page
        </TITLE>
        <SCRIPT LANGUAGE="JavaScript">
            <!--
            function writer()
            {
                document.write("Hello!")
            }
            // -->
        </SCRIPT>
    </HEAD>

    <BODY ONLOAD="writer()">
        <H1>Writing to a Web page</H1>
    </BODY>
</HTML>
```

And there's another option in the Internet Explorer 4+ (only)—you can use
the <SCRIPT FOR> element, which we saw in Chapter 1:

```
<HTML>
    <HEAD>
        <TITLE>
            Writing to a Web page
        </TITLE>
```

continues ▶

```
<SCRIPT FOR="window" EVENT="ONLOAD" LANGUAGE="JavaScript">
    <!--
    document.write("Hello!")
    // -->
</SCRIPT>
</HEAD>

<BODY>
    <H1>Writing to a Web page</H1>
</BODY>
</HTML>
```

Tip

Internet Explorer 4+ also has another event that is of interest: onbeforeunload, which occurs before the
unloading process starts.

You also can use the onload and onunload events with the <FRAMESET>
element in the Internet Explorer, like this:

```
<HTML>
    <HEAD>
        <TITLE>Working With Frames</TITLE>
        <SCRIPT LANGUAGE="JavaScript">
            <!--
            function alerter()
            {
                window.alert("All loaded.")
            }
            // -->
        </SCRIPT>
    </HEAD>

<FRAMESET COLS = "55%, 45%" ONLOAD="alerter()">
    <NOFRAMES>Sorry, your browser does not support frames!</NOFRAMES>

    <FRAMESET ROWS = "35%, 45%, 45%">
        <FRAME SRC="frame1.html">
        <FRAME SRC="frame2.html">
        <FRAME SRC="frame3.html">
    </FRAMESET>

    <FRAMESET ROWS = "25%, 25%, 50%">
        <FRAME SRC="frame4.html">
        <FRAME SRC="frame5.html">
        <FRAME SRC="frame6.html">
    </FRAMESET>
</FRAMESET>
</HTML>
```

Methods and Events of the *<FRAMESET>* Element

JavaScript's core HTML methods and events we covered in Chapter 6 apply to the <FRAMESET> element as well. In addition, this element has a few more events, which you see in Table 8.6 in overview and in Table 8.7 in depth. (The <FRAMESET> element does not have any non-core methods.)

Table 8.6 **Overview of the Events of the *<FRAMESET>* Element (See Chapters 5 and 6 for the JavaScript core HTML properties, methods, and events that also apply to this element.)**

Events		
onafterprint	onbeforeprint	onload
onunload		

Table 8.7 **The Events of the *<FRAMESET>* Element (See Chapters 5 and 6 for the JavaScript core HTML properties, methods, and events that also apply to this element.)**

Method	NS2	NS3	NS4	NS6	IE3a	IE3b	IE4	IE5	IE5.5	IE6
onafterprint								x	x	x
Occurs immediately after a document prints or previews for printing. See "Printing" in this chapter.										
onbeforeprint								x	x	x
Occurs immediately before a document prints or previews for printing. See "Printing" in this chapter.										
onload							x	x	x	x
Occurs when frame contents are fully loaded and all parts of the document are available for scripting. See "Window Loading and Unloading" in this chapter.										
onunload							x	x	x	x
Occurs when frames are unloaded. See "Window Loading and Unloading" in this chapter.										

Methods and Events of the *<FRAME>* Element

Like the <FRAMESET> element, JavaScript's core HTML methods and events we covered in Chapter 6 apply to the <FRAME> element as well. This element has a few more events to add to the core set, which you see in Table 8.8 in overview and in Table 8.9 in depth. Note that although there is an onload event (ever since Internet Explorer 5.5), there is no onunload event. (The <FRAME> element does not have any non-core methods.)

Table 8.8   Overview of the Events of the *<FRAME>* Element (See Chapters 5 and 6 for the JavaScript core HTML properties, methods, and events that also apply to this element.)

Events		
onafterupdate	onbeforeupdate	onerrorupdate
onload		

Table 8.9   The Events of the *<FRAME>* Element (See Chapters 5 and 6 for the JavaScript core HTML properties, methods, and events that also apply to this element.)

Event	NS2	NS3	NS4	NS6	IE3a	IE3b	IE4	IE5	IE5.5	IE6
onafterupdate							x	x	x	x
Occurs in an Internet Explorer data-bound object after updating data in the data source object. For more on data binding, see Chapter 17, "Dynamic HTML: Drag and Drop, Data Binding, and Behaviors."										
onbeforeupdate							x	x	x	x
Occurs in an Internet Explorer data-bound object before updating data in the data source object. For more on data binding, see Chapter 17.										
onerrorupdate							x	x	x	x
Occurs in an Internet Explorer data-bound object when an error occurs while updating data in the data source object. For more on data binding, see Chapter 17.										
onload									x	x
Occurs when the contents of the frame are fully loaded.										

Methods and Events of the *<IFRAME>* Element

Like the <FRAMESET> and <FRAME> elements, JavaScript's core HTML methods and events we covered in Chapter 6 apply to the <IFRAME> element as well. As with the <FRAME> element, this element has a few more events to add to the core set, which you see in Table 8.10 in overview and in Table 8.11 in depth. Note that although there is an onload event (ever since Internet Explorer 5.5), there is no onunload event. (The <IFRAME> element does not have any non-core methods.)

Table 8.10 **Overview of the Events of the *<IFRAME>* Element (See Chapters 5 and 6 for the JavaScript core HTML properties, methods, and events that also apply to this element.)**

Events		
onafterupdate	onbeforeupdate	onerrorupdate
onload		

Table 8.11 **The Events of the *<IFRAME>* Element (See Chapters 5 and 6 for the JavaScript core HTML properties, methods, and events that also apply to this element.)**

Event	NS2	NS3	NS4	NS6	IE3a	IE3b	IE4	IE5	IE5.5	IE6
onafterupdate							X	X	X	X
Occurs in an Internet Explorer data-bound object after updating data in the data source object. For more on data binding, see Chapter 17.										
onbeforeupdate							X	X	X	X
Occurs in an Internet Explorer data-bound object before updating data in the data source object. For more on data binding, see Chapter 17.										
onerrorupdate							X	X	X	X
Occurs in an Internet Explorer data-bound object when an error occurs while updating data in the data source object. For more on data binding, see Chapter 17.										
onload									X	X
Occurs when the contents of the frame are fully loaded.										

And that's it. In this and the previous chapters, we've taken a look at the properties, methods, and events of window object and frame elements—in the next chapter, we'll do the same for the document object and the <BODY> element.

9

Using the *document* and *body* Objects

I N THIS CHAPTER, WE'LL TAKE A LOOK AT THE JAVASCRIPT properties, methods, and events of the document object and the `<BODY>` element. In the early days of JavaScript, before each element became a JavaScript object, the document object gave you access to many aspects of what's really the `<BODY>` element—for example, the colors used in the web page. And when you're writing to a web page, you're really writing to the `<BODY>` element. Because JavaScript programmers needed access to more than just the `<BODY>` element, the document object grew—for example, this object also has a `title` property that gives you access to the `<TITLE>` element in the `<HEAD>`, a `referrer` property that enables you to determine how the user got to the current page, and so on, even a `cookie` property that lets you set and retrieve cookie data.

That was how the document object developed before Internet Explorer 4.0—as a mix of the properties, methods, and events that belonged to various HTML elements. When Internet Explorer 4.0 appeared, the new DOM gave programmers access to every element in the web page directly—including the `<HEAD>` and `<BODY>` elements. By that time, however, JavaScript programmers had become used to the document object, which no longer corresponded to any one element.

And that brings us to today. The document object is still the huge object that JavaScript programmers have grown to know, but much of what it gives you access to is available in the `<BODY>` object as well—which is why I'm covering both objects in this chapter. For example, the document object's `alinkColor` property is the same as the `<BODY>` element's `alink` property. The document object's `linkColor` property is the same as the `<BODY>` element's `link` property, the `document` object's `fgColor` property is the `<BODY>` element's `text` property, and so on (although, interestingly, the `bgColor` property retains the same name in both objects). Although the `<BODY>` element doesn't have a `write` method to correspond to the popular `document.write`, you can perform much the same action with the `<BODY>` element's `innerHTML`, `innerText`, `outerHTML`, and `outerText` properties.

Although the `document` object overlaps with other objects in JavaScript, the `document` object isn't about to disappear, so there often will be two ways to get a particular task done. So how do you keep all this functionality straight between the `document` object and the `<BODY>` element? Easy—just refer to this chapter when you want to do something to find an appropriate property, method, or event. I'll list all that's going on with the `document` object and the `<BODY>` element here, and you can choose what you want from that data.

Tip

It's also worth keeping in mind that the document object has been around a lot longer than the `<BODY>` element has been accessible in JavaScript; so if you're going to be working with older browsers, stick with the document object's properties, methods, and events when possible.

In fact, this chapter starts us off working with real HTML web pages, element by element. For that reason, I'm going to take a quick look first at the other major HTML elements that appear in a page: the `<HTML>`, `<HEAD>`, and `<TITLE>` elements. They need only a short amount of discussion, and I'll start with them.

The *<HTML>*, *<HEAD>*, and *<TITLE>* Elements

As it turns out, the `<HTML>`, `<HEAD>`, and `<TITLE>` elements are all covered very well in the discussion about JavaScript's core HTML properties in Chapters 5, "Using Core HTML Properties," and 6, "Using Core HTML Methods and Events." (In JavaScript, these elements correspond to the `html`, `head`, and `title` objects.) Each of these elements has only one additional property not covered in those chapters (and no additional methods or events).

How do you get access to an element such as `<HTML>` in JavaScript? You do that just as you would get access to any element, such as giving this element an ID and then using methods like `getElementById` to get access to the element as an object in JavaScript. If you've given the `<HTML>` element the ID "html1" like this: <HTML ID="html1">, for example, you can access it like this: document.getElementById("html1"), and access properties like this: document.getElementById("html1").*property*, and methods like this: document.getElementById("html1").*method(...)*. As with other any other element, you can treat the <HTML> element as an object and assign it to a variable like this: var html1 = document.getElementById("html1"). In this way, any element in a web page becomes an object for you to work with in JavaScript.

Besides the core HTML properties, the <HTML> element also includes a read/write version property in JavaScript, as of Netscape Navigator 6 and Internet Explorer 6. This property sets or gets the HTML version for the current document. In fact, although this property is new in both browsers, it's been deprecated—rendered obsolete—by W3C, which says you should indicate the HTML version with the <!DOCTYPE> element. (If used, this element is the very first in an HTML document, before even the <HTML> element.) Here, for example, are three <!DOCTYPE> elements, which specify HTML 4.01 strict (strict adherence to the HTML 4.01 recommendation), HTML 4.01 transitional (includes support for deprecated features), and HTML 4.01 frameset (which is the same as the strict version, but includes support for frames):

```
<!DOCTYPE HTML PUBLIC "-//W3C//DTD HTML 4.0//EN"
        "http://www.w3.org/TR/REC-html40/strict.dtd">

<!DOCTYPE HTML PUBLIC "-//W3C//DTD HTML 4.0 Transitional//EN"
        "http://www.w3.org/TR/REC-html40/loose.dtd">

<!DOCTYPE HTML PUBLIC "-//W3C//DTD HTML 4.0 Frameset//EN"
        "http://www.w3.org/TR/REC-html40/frameset.dtd">
```

The <HEAD> element also includes a read/write profile property as of Netscape Navigator 6 and Internet Explorer 6. This property sets or gets one or more *Uniform Resource Identifiers* (URIs) at which the document's properties and values for those properties are specified. If that sounds vague, it is— no browser uses the PROFILE HTML attribute yet (which corresponds to the JavaScript profile property), and its true purpose has yet to be settled on.

The <TITLE> element also has a read/write text property, as of Netscape Navigator 6 and Internet Explorer 4.0, which holds the text of the document's title. As we'll see in this chapter, that text is traditionally accessed as document.title, but you also can access it with the text property of the <TITLE> element.

And that's it—that gives us the framework we need. Now we're ready to start working with the huge, and important, document object.

The *document* Object Properties

We've worked with the document object ever since Chapter 1, "Essential JavaScript," and we'll take a look at this object's properties here. In Chapter 3, "The JavaScript Language: Loops, Functions, and Errors," we took a look at this code (Listing 03-03.html on the web site) that loops over all the properties of the document object and displays them:

```
<HTML>
    <HEAD>
        <TITLE>
            Using the for...in Loop
        </TITLE>
    </HEAD>

    <BODY>
        <H1>Using the for...in Loop</H1>
        <SCRIPT LANGUAGE="JavaScript">
            <!--
            for (var property in document) {
                document.write(property + ": " + document[property] + "<BR>")
            }
            // -->
        </SCRIPT>
    </BODY>
</HTML>
```

You can see the results of this code in Chapter 3—it's Figure 3.3 for the Netscape Navigator and in Figure 3.4 for the Internet Explorer. In this chapter, it's time to take a look at these properties in detail. You can see the document object properties in overview in Table 9.1, and in depth in Table 9.2.

Table 9.1 **Overview of the Properties of the *document* Object**

Properties		
activeElement	alinkColor	all
anchors	applets	attributes
bgColor	body	charset
characterSet	childNodes	cookie
defaultCharset	designMode	doctype
documentElement	domain	embeds
expando	fgColor	fileCreatedDate
fileModifiedDate	fileSize	firstChild
forms	frames	height
ids	images	implementation

Properties

lastChild	lastModified	layers
linkColor	links	location
mimeType	namespaces	namespaceURI
nextSibling	nodeName	nodeType
ownerDocument	parentNode	parentWindow
plugins	previousSibling	protocol
readyState	referrer	scripts
security	selection	styleSheets
tags	title	uniqueID
URL	URLUnencoded	vlinkColor
width		

Table 9.2   **The Properties of the *document* Object**

Property	NS2	NS3	NS4	NS6	IE3a	IE3b	IE4	IE5	IE5.5	IE6
activeElement							X	X	X	X

Read-only
This property holds the "active element," which either has the focus or will get the focus when the focus is returned to the present window. Useful if you have a multipurpose function that needs to retrieve data from the control the user is working with in another window.

alinkColor	X	X	X	X	X	X	X	X	X	X

Read/write
Holds the active link color in the web page. Set to a valid HTML color—a color triplet or a predefined browser color such as "magenta." See "Setting Colors" in this chapter.

all	See Chapter 5.									
anchors	X	X	X	X	X	X	X	X	X	X

Read-only
Holds the <A> element objects in the web page in an array as JavaScript a objects. See "The document Object Collections" in this chapter.

applets		X	X	X			X	X	X	X

Read-only
Holds the applets as specified in <APPLET> elements in the web page in an array of JavaScript applet objects. See "The document Object Collections" in this chapter.

attributes	See Chapter 5.									

continues ▶

Table 9.2 **Continued**

Property	NS2	NS3	NS4	NS6	IE3a	IE3b	IE4	IE5	IE5.5	IE6
bgColor	x	x	x	x	x	x	x	x	x	x

Read/write
Holds the background color of the web page. Set to a valid HTML color—a color triplet or a predefined browser color such as "cyan." See "Setting Colors" in this chapter.

Property	NS2	NS3	NS4	NS6	IE3a	IE3b	IE4	IE5	IE5.5	IE6
body				x			x	x	x	x

Read/write
Refers to the <BODY> element, as covered later in this chapter. This property holds a JavaScript body object and gives you a handy way to gain access to that object, without needing to assign a name or ID to the <BODY> element first.

Property	NS2	NS3	NS4	NS6	IE3a	IE3b	IE4	IE5	IE5.5	IE6
charset							x	x	x	x

Read/write
Holds the name of the character set used by the Internet Explorer as a string. In the HTML 4.01 specification, the W3C says that you can get a list of the registered character sets at ftp://ftp.isi.edu/in-notes/iana/assignments/character-sets.

Property	NS2	NS3	NS4	NS6	IE3a	IE3b	IE4	IE5	IE5.5	IE6
characterSet				x						

Read/write
Holds the name of the character set used by the Netscape Navigator as a string. In the HTML 4.01 specification, the W3C says that you can get a list of the registered character sets at ftp://ftp.isi.edu/in-notes/iana/assignments/character-sets.

Property	NS2	NS3	NS4	NS6	IE3a	IE3b	IE4	IE5	IE5.5	IE6
childNodes	See Chapter 5.									
cookie	x	x	x	x	x	x	x	x	x	x

Read/write
Enables you to create and access cookies. This is a cool one—see "Creating Cookies" in this chapter for more details, as well as the in-depth coverage in Chapter 23, "Cookies and Creating Your Own Objects."

Property	NS2	NS3	NS4	NS6	IE3a	IE3b	IE4	IE5	IE5.5	IE6
defaultCharset							x	x	x	x

Read/write
Holds the name of the default character set used by the Internet Explorer as a string. In the HTML 4.01 specification, the W3C says that you can get a list of the registered character sets at ftp://ftp.isi.edu/in-notes/iana/assignments/character-sets. You can use this property to restore the charSet property if that property has been changed.

Property	NS2	NS3	NS4	NS6	IE3a	IE3b	IE4	IE5	IE5.5	IE6
designMode								x	x	x

Read/write
Sets or retrieves a value that indicates whether the document can be
edited. It's a string that may be set to "On" to indicate that the docu-
ment can be edited, or "Off | Inherit" (the default) to indicate that the
document cannot be edited.

Property	NS2	NS3	NS4	NS6	IE3a	IE3b	IE4	IE5	IE5.5	IE6
doctype				x						x

Read-only
Holds an object specifying the document type information for the doc-
ument. This property is used more frequently in XML documents; for
HTML documents in both the Netscape Navigator and Internet
Explorer, it is set to null.

Property	NS2	NS3	NS4	NS6	IE3a	IE3b	IE4	IE5	IE5.5	IE6
documentElement				x			x	x		x

Read-only
This property returns the root node of a document—for HTML documents, that's the <HTML> element object itself, and this property gives
you access to that element object.

Property	NS2	NS3	NS4	NS6	IE3a	IE3b	IE4	IE5	IE5.5	IE6
domain	x	x	x		x	x	x	x		x

Read/write
This property starts off holding the host name of the server (as a string)
from which the page came. If a site has multiple servers, the site can
prevent access between frames that were filled from different servers as a
security precaution. However, you can assign a domain suffix to allow
sharing of pages between frames with this property. For example, a
page in one frame from users.starpowder.com and a page from
www.starpowder.com might not be able to communicate with each
other; by setting both page's domain property to "starpowder.com,"
however, both pages are treated as secure and each can access the other.

Property	NS2	NS3	NS4	NS6	IE3a	IE3b	IE4	IE5	IE5.5	IE6
embeds	x	x	x			x	x	x		x

Read-only
Holds an array of the <EMBED> elements in a page as embed objects,
which has the same properties as the <EMBED> elements have attributes.
This element is often used to display or play multimedia files. See "The
document Object Collections" in this chapter.

continues ▶

Table 9.2 **Continued**

Property	NS2	NS3	NS4	NS6	IE3a	IE3b	IE4	IE5	IE5.5	IE6
expando							X	X	X	X

Read/write

This Boolean property indicates whether the document object can support custom ("expando") properties. If set to true, you can store and retrieve data in custom properties like this: document.userNumber = 5. If false, custom properties are ignored.

	NS2	NS3	NS4	NS6	IE3a	IE3b	IE4	IE5	IE5.5	IE6
fgColor	X	X	X	X	X	X	X	X	X	X

Read/write

Holds the foreground (text) color of the web page. Set to a valid HTML color—a color triplet or a predefined browser color such as "blue." See "Setting Colors" in this chapter.

	NS2	NS3	NS4	NS6	IE3a	IE3b	IE4	IE5	IE5.5	IE6
fileCreatedDate							X	X	X	X

Read-only

Holds the date the file was created as a string. (Don't count on this property too heavily; many servers don't give accurate information here.) See "Handling File Dates and Sizes" in this chapter.

	NS2	NS3	NS4	NS6	IE3a	IE3b	IE4	IE5	IE5.5	IE6
fileModifiedDate							X	X	X	X

Read-only

Holds the date the file was last modified as a string. (Don't count on this property too heavily; many servers don't give accurate information here.) See "Handling File Dates and Sizes" in this chapter.

	NS2	NS3	NS4	NS6	IE3a	IE3b	IE4	IE5	IE5.5	IE6
fileSize							X	X	X	X

Read-only

Holds the file size (in bytes) as an integer. (Don't count on this property too heavily; many servers don't give accurate information here.) See "Handling File Dates and Sizes" in this chapter.

Property	NS2	NS3	NS4	NS6	IE3a	IE3b	IE4	IE5	IE5.5	IE6
firstChild	See Chapter 5.									
forms	X	X	X	X	X	X	X	X	X	X

Read-only

Holds an array of form objects corresponding to the <FORM> elements in the page. You can use to access controls in a form like this: document.forms[1].text1.value. See "The document Object Collections" in this chapter.

Property	NS2	NS3	NS4	NS6	IE3a	IE3b	IE4	IE5	IE5.5	IE6
frames							x	x	x	x

Read-only
Holds an array of the `frame` objects corresponding to the `<FRAME>` elements in the page. Each item in the array is really the `window` object in the frame, so to access the document of a particular frame, you can use `document.frames[2].document`. See "The `document` Object Collections" in this chapter. (Personally, I stick with the `window.frames` property, because it feels a little odd to think of a `<FRAMESET>` page as containing a document.)

Property	NS2	NS3	NS4	NS6	IE3a	IE3b	IE4	IE5	IE5.5	IE6
height			x	x						

Read-only
Holds the height of the document in the browser's window. Holds values measured in pixels.

Property	NS2	NS3	NS4	NS6	IE3a	IE3b	IE4	IE5	IE5.5	IE6
ids			x							

Read-only
This Netscape Navigator 4.0-only property was used in this browser's JavaScript-based style sheet syntax, and functions something like the Internet Explorer's `all` collection. However, JavaScript-based style sheets have largely been replaced with CSS style sheets.

Property	NS2	NS3	NS4	NS6	IE3a	IE3b	IE4	IE5	IE5.5	IE6
images		x	x	x			x	x	x	x

Read-only
Holds an array of the `<IMG>` elements in the page as `img` objects. For example, you can access an image's `src` property like this: `document.images[5].src`. See "The `document` Object Collections" in this chapter, and see Chapter 15, "Working with the Mouse, Keyboard, and Images," for more on image handling.

Property	NS2	NS3	NS4	NS6	IE3a	IE3b	IE4	IE5	IE5.5	IE6
implementation				x						x

This property holds an `implementation` object that gives some indication of the HTML and/or XML standards supported by the browser. The `implementation` object supports no properties and only one method, `hasFeature`, which returns true if the browser supports a particular W3C feature and false otherwise. To check for W3C HTML DOM level 2 support, for example, you can call `document.implementation.hasFeature`("HTML," "2.0"). Currently, the features you can check on in the Netscape Navigator 6.0 are "HTML," "XML," "Views," "Stylesheets," "CSS," "Events," "MouseEvents," "HTMLEvents," and "Range." The level you can check on can only be "1.0" or "2.0." In the Internet Explorer, you can check these features only: "HTML" and "XML;" and the level argument is optional and currently only arguments set to "1.0" can return a value of true.

continues ▶

Table 9.2 **Continued**

Property	NS2	NS3	NS4	NS6	IE3a	IE3b	IE4	IE5	IE5.5	IE6
lastChild	See Chapter 5.									
lastModified	x	x	x	x	x	x	x	x	x	x

Read-only
Returns the date the document was last modified, as a string. Not
Internet Explorer-only like `fileModifiedDate`.

layers			x							

Read-only
Holds the layers in a document in an array of `layer` objects. See
Chapter 16, "Dynamic HTML: Changing Web Pages On-the-Fly," for
more on layers and "The `document` Object Collections" in this chapter.

linkColor	x	x	x	x	x	x	x	x	x	x

Read/write
Holds the color for unvisited links in the web page. Set to a valid
HTML color—a color triplet or a predefined browser color such as
"purple." See "Setting Colors" in this chapter.

links	x	x	x	x	x	x	x	x	x	x

Read-only
Holds an array of the links in the document (as link objects)—that is,
`<A>` elements with `HREF` attributes (unlike the `anchors` collection, which
holds all the `<A>` elements). See "The `document` Object Collections" in
this chapter.

location		x	x	x			x	x	x	x

Read/write
Holds the URL of the web page as a string. This is *not* the same as the
`location` object (which is `window.location`, not `document.location`)!
Due to the confusion (especially if you just use `location` without quali-
fying it as `window.location` or `document.location`), this property is
being phased out in favor of `document.URL`.

mimeType								x	x	x

Read-only
Supposed to indicate the MIME (Multipurpose Internet Mail Extension)
type of a document as a string, but in practice very unreliable. May be
better supported in the future as XML becomes more important.

Property	NS2	NS3	NS4	NS6	IE3a	IE3b	IE4	IE5	IE5.5	IE6
namespaces									X	X

Read-only
Holds an array of all namespaces declared in a document as namespace objects. Largely for use with Internet Explorer behaviors. See "The document Object Collections" in this chapter, and see Chapter 17, "Dynamic HTML: Drag and Drop, Data Binding, and Behaviors," for more on behaviors.

namespaceURI	See Chapter 5.
nextSibling	See Chapter 5.
nodeName	See Chapter 5.
nodeType	See Chapter 5.
ownerDocument	See Chapter 5.
parentNode	See Chapter 5.

Property	NS2	NS3	NS4	NS6	IE3a	IE3b	IE4	IE5	IE5.5	IE6
parentWindow							X	X	X	X

Read-only
Holds the window object that contains the current document. In other words, document.parentWindow is the same as just referring to the window object.

Property	NS2	NS3	NS4	NS6	IE3a	IE3b	IE4	IE5	IE5.5	IE6
plugins		X	X				X	X	X	X

Read-only
The same as the embeds property—holds an array of the <EMBED> elements in a page as embed objects (which have the same properties as <EMBED> elements have attributes). This element is often used to display or play multimedia files. This property seems to be used less and less these days—*plugin* is a Netscape Navigator term, and is slowly coming to be replaced by *embed* in the standards.

previousSibling	See Chapter 5.

Property	NS2	NS3	NS4	NS6	IE3a	IE3b	IE4	IE5	IE5.5	IE6
protocol							X	X	X	X

Read/write
Holds a string that contains the full name of the protocol used to retrieve the document. Documents on the Internet report "Hypertext Transfer Protocol" are here; local files on the same machine report "File Protocol."

readyState	See Chapter 5.

continues ▶

Table 9.2   **Continued**

Property	NS2	NS3	NS4	NS6	IE3a	IE3b	IE4	IE5	IE5.5	IE6
referrer	x	x	x	x	x	x	x	x	x	x

Read-only
Holds the URL (as a string) of the web page in which the user clicked a link to get to the current page. (The user must have clicked a link for this property to be filled.) Note that some programmers consider this property is problematic in the Windows version of Internet Explorer 3.0 and 4.0. See "Tracking User Navigation" in this chapter.

Property	NS2	NS3	NS4	NS6	IE3a	IE3b	IE4	IE5	IE5.5	IE6
scripts						x	x	x	x

Read-only
Holds an array of the <SCRIPT> elements in the browser, as script objects. See "The document Object Collections" in this chapter.

Property	NS2	NS3	NS4	NS6	IE3a	IE3b	IE4	IE5	IE5.5	IE6
security									x	x

Read-only
This is actually an undocumented feature of the Internet Explorer (undocumented in both Internet Explorer 5.5 and 6.0), and it seems it'll get more play in the future. For now, the only return value seems to be the string: "This type of document does not have a security certificate."

Property	NS2	NS3	NS4	NS6	IE3a	IE3b	IE4	IE5	IE5.5	IE6
selection	x	x	x	x	x	x	x	x	x	x

Read-only
This property holds the current text selection (as selected by the user) in the page as a selection object. See "Getting Selected Text" in this chapter for an example showing how to use this property.

Property	NS2	NS3	NS4	NS6	IE3a	IE3b	IE4	IE5	IE5.5	IE6
styleSheets				x			x	x	x	x

Read-only
Holds the style sheets in the page as an array of styleSheet objects. See "The document Object Collections" in this chapter.

Property	NS2	NS3	NS4	NS6	IE3a	IE3b	IE4	IE5	IE5.5	IE6
tags			x							

Read-only
This Netscape Navigator 4.0-only property is used with the JavaScript-type style sheets available in this browser, and it works much like the getElementsByTagName method. However, JavaScript-type style sheets are little used today, having been supplanted by CSS style sheets. See "The document Object Collections" in this chapter.

Property	NS2	NS3	NS4	NS6	IE3a	IE3b	IE4	IE5	IE5.5	IE6
title	X	X	X	X	X	X	X	X	X	X

Read/write
Holds the document's title (from the `<TITLE>` element) as a string. In Internet Explorer 4.0 and Netscape Navigator, this property became read/write; before that, it was read-only.

uniqueID	See Chapter 5.

URL		X	X	X			X	X	X	X

Read/write
Holds the document's URL as a string. Note that this property returns an *encoded* URL string—for example, spaces are replaced with %20 (the hexadecimal character code for a space) so that browsers can treat the URL as one unbroken string. To get the unencoded URL, use the `URLUnencoded` property.

URLUnencoded									X	X

Read-only
Holds the document's URL as an unencoded string (which means, for example, that spaces will be spaces and not represented as the hexadecimal character code %20).

vlinkColor	X	X	X	X	X	X	X	X	X	X

Read/write
Holds the color for visited links in the web page. Set to a valid HTML color—a color triplet or a predefined browser color such as "yellow." See "Setting Colors" in this chapter.

width			X	X						

Read-only
Holds the width of the document in the browser's window. Holds values measured in pixels.

The *document* Object Collections

One thing that the `document` object is good for is giving you access to the objects in a web page, organizing things from the top down. Not only does it have the `getElementById`, `getElementsByName`, and `getElementsByTagName` methods, but it also supports the collections (that is, object arrays) you see in Table 9.3. (For the definition of a particular collection, see Table 9.2.)

Table 9.3   **The Collections of the *document* Object**

Properties

all	anchors	applets
childNodes	embeds	forms
frames	images	ids
layers	links	namespaces
scripts	styleSheets	tags

For example, here's how you might use the anchors collection to access a particular anchor's href property:

(Listing 09-01.html on the web site)

```
<HTML>
    <HEAD>
        <TITLE>Using the anchors Collection</TITLE>
    </HEAD>

    <BODY>
        <H1>Using the anchors Collection</H1>
        Take a look at <A HREF="http://www.w3c.org" NAME="W3C">W3C</A>
        <BR>
        <SCRIPT LANGUAGE="JavaScript">
            <!--
            document.write("(The link's URL is " + document.anchors[0].href + ")")
            // -->
        </SCRIPT>
    </BODY>
</HTML>
```

You can see the results in Figure 9.1.

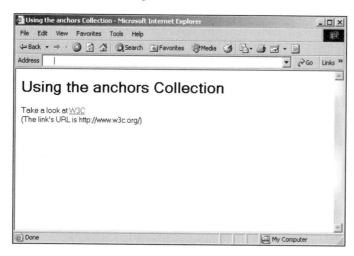

Figure 9.1   Using the anchors collection.

Using the `document` object's collections, you can get a handle on any object in a web page—I recommend you take a look at Table 9.3 to get familiar with what's available. Note also that you don't need to access objects in a collection by numeric index only—if an element has a NAME (not ID) attribute, you can use that name with Netscape Navigator collections like this: `document.anchors["anchor1"].href`. If an element has a NAME or ID attribute, you can use that attribute's value with Internet Explorer collections like this (note parentheses, not square brackets here): `document.anchors("anchor1").href`.

Setting Colors

Another popular use of the `document` object's properties is to set the colors in the page interactively, using the `fgColor`, `bgColor`, `linkColor`, `alinkColor`, and `vlinkColor` properties. Here's an example that puts all five of these properties to use, where I'm using colors predefined in both the Netscape Navigator and the Internet Explorer:

(Listing 09-02.html on the web site)

```html
<HTML>
    <HEAD>
        <TITLE>Setting Colors</TITLE>
        <SCRIPT LANGUAGE="JavaScript">
            <!--
            function setColors()
            {
                document.fgColor = "cyan"
                document.bgColor = "lightyellow"
                document.linkColor = "blue"
                document.alinkColor = "red"
                document.vlinkColor = "orange"
            }
            // -->
        </SCRIPT>
    </HEAD>

    <BODY>
        <H1>Setting Colors</H1>
        Take a look at <A HREF="w3c.org">W3C</A>
        <FORM>
            <INPUT TYPE="button" VALUE="Set Colors" ONCLICK="setColors()">
        </FORM>
    </BODY>
</HTML>
```

You can see the results in Figure 9.2 (in glorious black and white).

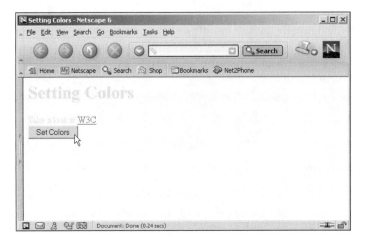

Figure 9.2   Setting colors in the Netscape Navigator.

Creating Cookies

One of the most powerful `document` object properties is the `cookie` property, which enables you to set and read cookies. We'll see how to use cookies in Chapter 23, "Cookies and Creating Your Own Objects," but here's a preview. The `cookie` property holds the text of the cookies in the computer, so you give your cookie a name; I'll just use cookie1 here, and give it an expiration date of one day. When the user clicks a button, the code will set a cookie with the text "Here is the cookie text.", and when the user clicks another button, the code retrieves that cookie's text and displays it. Here's the code—see Chapter 23 for the details on working with cookies:

(Listing 09-03.html on the web site)

```
<HTML>
    <HEAD>
        <TITLE>Working With Cookies</TITLE>
        <SCRIPT LANGUAGE="JavaScript">
            <!--
            function setCookieText()
            {
                var date1 = new Date()
                date1.setTime(date1.getTime() + 24 * 60 * 60 * 1000)
                document.cookie = "cookie1=Here is the cookie text.;expires="
                    + date1.toGMTString()
            }

            function getCookieText()
            {
```

```
        var cookieData = new String(document.cookie)
        var cookieHeader = "cookie1="
        var cookieStart = cookieData.indexOf(cookieHeader)

        if (cookieStart != -1){
            document.form1.text1.value = cookieData.substring(cookieStart
                + cookieHeader.length)
        }
        else{
            document.form1.text1.value = "Could not find the cookie."
        }
    }
    // -->
    </SCRIPT>
</HEAD>

<BODY>
    <H1>Working With Cookies</H1>
    <FORM NAME="form1">
        <INPUT TYPE="TEXT" NAME="text1" SIZE="40">
        <BR>
        <INPUT TYPE="BUTTON" VALUE="Create a cookie" ONCLICK="setCookieText()">
        <BR>
        <INPUT TYPE = BUTTON Value = "Retrieve cookie data"
            ONCLICK="getCookieText()">
    </FORM>
</BODY>
</HTML>
```

You can see the results in Figure 9.3, where I've created a cookie and then retrieved its text. That's just an appetizer—more on cookies is coming up in Chapter 23.

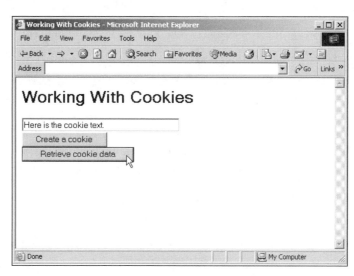

Figure 9.3 Setting and retrieving a cookie.

Handling File Dates and Sizes

The `document` object also gives you access to web page dates and sizes in the Internet Explorer with the `fileCreatedDate`, `fileModifiedDate`, and `fileSize` properties. (Be warned, however—not all servers fill in the information in these properties properly.) Here's an example that puts these properties to work, displaying the dates and size (in bytes) of a document:

(Listing 09-04.html on the web site)

```
<HTML>
    <HEAD>
        <TITLE>Getting File Size and Date</TITLE>
        <SCRIPT LANGUAGE="JavaScript">
            <!--
            function getSizesDates()
            {
                document.writeln("Document created: " + document.fileCreatedDate)
                document.writeln("Last modified: " + document.fileModifiedDate)
                document.writeln("File size: " + document.fileSize)
            }
            // -->
        </SCRIPT>
    </HEAD>

    <BODY ONLOAD="getSizesDates()">
        <H1>Getting File Size and Date</H1>
    </BODY>
</HTML>
```

When you open this document in a browser, it'll display when it was created, when last modified, and what its file size is in bytes—if your server fills those properties in.

Tracking User Navigation

You can use the `document` object's `referrer` property to determine the URL of the page in which the user clicked a link to navigate to the current page. (This property holds a non-empty value only when the user reaches the current page through a link from the previous page.) Here's an example—when you open Listing 09-05.html, you'll see a link to the next page, Listing 09-06.html; clicking that link takes you to the next page, where the URL you came from is displayed:

(Listing 09–05.html on the web site)

```
<HTML>
    <HEAD>
        <TITLE>Here's a Web Page</TITLE>
    </HEAD>

    <BODY>
        <H1>Here's a Web Page</H1>
        <A HREF="09-06.html">Go to the next Web page!</A>
    </BODY>
</HTML>
```

(Listing 09–06.html on the web site)

```
<HTML>
    <HEAD>
        <TITLE>Tracking User Navigation</TITLE>
    </HEAD>

    <BODY>
        <H1>Tracking User Navigation</H1>
        <SCRIPT LANGUAGE="JavaScript">
            <!--
                document.write("You came from:" + document.referrer)
            // -->
        </SCRIPT>
    </BODY>
</HTML>
```

Tip

This property works only when the pages involved have been served from a web server, not on your local hard disk.

The *document* Object Methods

The most famous document object method is the write method, which enables you to write to a web page. However, this object supports many other methods, as you see in Table 9.4 in overview, and in Table 9.5 in depth.

Table 9.4 **Overview of the Methods of the *document* Object**

Methods

attachEvent	captureEvents	clear
clearAttributes	close	createAttribute
createComment	createDocumentFragment	createElement
createEventObject	createRange	createStyleSheet
createTextNode	detachEvent	elementFromPoint
execCommand	focus	getElementById
getElementsByName	getElementsByTagName	getSelection
handleEvent	hasFocus	mergeAttributes
open	queryCommandEnabled	queryCommandIndeterm
queryCommandState	queryCommandSupported	queryCommandValue
recalc	releaseCapture	releaseEvents
routeEvent	setActive	write
writeln		

Table 9.5 **The Methods of the *document* Object**

Method	NS2	NS3	NS4	NS6	IE3a	IE3b	IE4	IE5	IE5.5	IE6
attachEvent	See Chapter 6.									
captureEvents			X							

Returns: Nothing
Lets the `window` object capture events in Netscape Navigator 4.0.
Syntax: `captureEvents(eventTypeList)`. Here, *eventTypeList* holds a
list of events to capture, OR'ed together like this: `Event.CLICK ¦`
`Event.MOUSEUP`. See Chapter 15 for more details.

clear	X	X	X	X	X	X	X	X	X	X

Returns: Nothing
This method clears the current document. Syntax: `document.clear()`.
However, nothing happens after that point, because all elements and
scripts are gone. If you really want to rewrite a document, consider
using the `write` method or the `innerHTML` and `innerText` properties of
the `body` object instead.

| clearAttributes | See Chapter 6. | | | | | | | | | |

Method	NS2	NS3	NS4	NS6	IE3a	IE3b	IE4	IE5	IE5.5	IE6
close	x	x	x	x	x	x	x	x	x	x

Returns: Nothing

This method closes a document that's been opened for writing. Syntax: `document.close()`. See "Writing to a Document" in this chapter for more details on when to use this method.

createAttribute				x						x

Returns: An `attribute` object

This method creates and returns a new `attribute` object. Syntax: `document.createAttribute(name)`, where *name* is the text string holding the attribute's name. See "Creating New Elements and Nodes" in this chapter for an example showing how to create an attribute and connect it to a new element.

createComment				x						x

Returns: A `comment` object

Creates a `comment` object with the specified data. Syntax: `document.createComment(text)`, where *text* is the text in the comment.

createDocumentFragment				x				x	x	x

Returns: A new `document` object

This method actually creates and returns a whole new `document` object. Syntax: `document.createDocumentFragment()`.

createElement				x			x	x	x	x

Returns: A new `element` object

Creates a new HTML element. Syntax: `document.createElement(tagName)`, where *tagName* is the tag name of the new element. In Internet Explorer 4.0, the only new elements you can create are `<IMG>`, `<AREA>`, and `<OPTION>`. As of Internet Explorer 5.0, you can create all elements programmatically, except for `<FRAME>` and `<IFRAME>`. See "Creating New Elements and Nodes" in this chapter for an example showing how to use this method.

createEventObject									x	x

Returns: An `event` object

Generates an `event` object for passing event context information when using the `fireEvent` method (see "The `fireEvent` Method" in Chapter 6). Syntax: `document.createEventObject([eventObject])`. Here, *eventObject* is an existing event object on which to base the new event object.

continues ▶

Table 9.5 **Continued**

Method	NS2	NS3	NS4	NS6	IE3a	IE3b	IE4	IE5	IE5.5	IE6
createRange				x						

Returns: A `Range` object
This method creates a `Range` object, which is the W3C DOM level 2 version of the Internet Explorer's `TextRange` object. Sytnax: `document.createRange()`. More on text ranges in Chapter 11, "Working with HTML Text Elements."

| createStyleSheet | | | | | | | x | x | x | x |

Returns: A `stylesheet` object
This method creates a new style sheet for the document. Syntax: `document.createStyleSheet([URL] [, Index])`, where *URL* is a string. (If you give a filename for the URL, the style information will be added as a `link` object; if the URL contains style information, that information is added to the `style` object). *Index* is an integer that specifies the index showing where the style sheet should be inserted in the `styleSheets` collection. When you create a new style sheet, it's added to the page immediately by default, and so becomes active (unlike other methods such as `createElement`). See Chapter 21, "Cascading Style Sheets and CGI Programming," to see how to create style sheets.

| createTextNode | | | | x | | | x | x | x | x |

Returns: A `text node` object
When you create new elements, you build them piece by piece; and to insert text into an element, you create a text node first. Syntax: `createTextNode(text)`, where *text* is the text you want in the node. See "Creating New Elements and Nodes" in this chapter for an example showing how to use this method.

| detachEvent | See Chapter 6. | | | | | | | | | |

| elementFromPoint | | | | | | | x | x | x | x |

Returns: An element text node
This method returns the element at a specific (x, y) point in the document (measured in pixels). Useful for determining what element the mouse is over. Syntax: `document.elementFromPoint(X, Y)`. See "Finding Elements by Location" in this chapter for an example.

Method	NS2	NS3	NS4	NS6	IE3a	IE3b	IE4	IE5	IE5.5	IE6
ExecCommand							x	x	x	x

Returns: Boolean

This method executes a special command using the current document.
Syntax: execCommand(*Command* [, *UserInterface*] [, *Value*]), where
Command is a string that specifies the command to execute (see "Using
execCommand" in this chapter). This command can be any of the command identifiers that can be executed in script. *UserInterface* is a Boolean
that you set to false (the default) if you do not want to display a user
interface, and true if you do. *Value* is a string or number, or other value
to assign. This method returns true if successful, false otherwise. See
"Using execCommand" in this chapter to learn which commands are possible and to see an example.

Method	NS2	NS3	NS4	NS6	IE3a	IE3b	IE4	IE5	IE5.5	IE6
focus				See Chapter 6.						
getElementById				x			x	x	x	

Returns: An element object

This method finds an element by ID value, which you set with the ID
HTML attribute. Syntax: getElementById(*id*), where *id* is the ID of the
element you're looking for. Discussed in Chapter 4, "Handling the
Browser Environment" (see "Accessing HTML Elements" in that
chapter).

Method	NS2	NS3	NS4	NS6	IE3a	IE3b	IE4	IE5	IE5.5	IE6
getElementsByName				x			x	x	x	

Returns: An array of element objects

This method returns a collection of objects with the same NAME
attribute value. Syntax: getElementsByName(*name*), where *name* is the
name of the element(s) you're looking for. Discussed in Chapter 4 (see
"Accessing HTML Elements" in that chapter).

Method	NS2	NS3	NS4	NS6	IE3a	IE3b	IE4	IE5	IE5.5	IE6
getElementsByTagName			See Chapter 6.							
getSelection			x	x						

Returns: A string

Returns any currently selected text in the web page. Syntax:
getSelection(). See "Getting Selected Text" in this chapter.

Method	NS2	NS3	NS4	NS6	IE3a	IE3b	IE4	IE5	IE5.5	IE6
handleEvent			x							

This Netscape Navigator 4.0 method handles events captured with
setCapture. Syntax: handleEvent(*event*), where *event* is an event type
such as Event.CLICK. See Chapter 15 for more details.

Method	NS2	NS3	NS4	NS6	IE3a	IE3b	IE4	IE5	IE5.5	IE6
hasFocus			See Chapter 6.							

continues ▶

Table 9.5 **Continued**

Method	NS2	NS3	NS4	NS6	IE3a	IE3b	IE4	IE5	IE5.5	IE6
mergeAttributes	See Chapter 6.									
open	x	x	x	x	x	x	x	x	x	x

Returns: Nothing
Opens a document for writing. Syntax: `document.open()`. See "Writing to a Document" in this chapter to see when to use this method.

queryCommandEnabled							x	x	x	x

Returns: Boolean
Checks whether a special command is enabled. Syntax: `queryCommandEnabled(command)`, where *command* is the command you're checking on. See "Using `execCommand`" in this chapter to see what commands you can use this method with.

queryCommandIndeterm							x	x	x	x

Returns: Boolean
Checks whether a special command is in the indeterminate state. Syntax: `queryCommandIndeterm(command)`, where *command* is the command you're checking on. See "Using `execCommand`" in this chapter to see which commands you can use this method with.

queryCommandState							x	x	x	x

Returns: Boolean
Checks whether a special command has been completed—returns true if so. Syntax: `queryCommandState(command)`, where *command* is the command you're checking on. See "Using `execCommand`" in this chapter to see which commands you can use this method with.

queryCommandSupported							x	x	x	x

Returns: Boolean
Checks whether a special command is supported. Syntax: `queryCommandSupported(command)`, where *command* is the command you're checking on. See "Using `execCommand`" in this chapter to see which commands you can use this method with.

queryCommandValue							x	x	x	x

Returns: Strings, numbers
Returns the current value of the document, range, or current selection for the given special command. Syntax: `queryCommandValue(command)`, where *command* is the command you're working with. See "Using `execCommand`" in this chapter to see which commands you can use this method with.

Method	NS2	NS3	NS4	NS6	IE3a	IE3b	IE4	IE5	IE5.5	IE6
recalc								x	x	x

Returns: nothing
Recalculates all dynamic style properties in the current document. You can set dynamic style properties with the setExpression and getExpression methods. Syntax: document.recalc([*forceAll*]), where *forceAll* is a Boolean that you can set to false (the default) to recalculate only those expressions that have changed since the last recalculation, or true to recalculate all expressions in the document. See Chapter 21 on style sheets for more information.

Method	NS2	NS3	NS4	NS6	IE3a	IE3b	IE4	IE5	IE5.5	IE6
releaseCapture	See Chapter 6.									
releaseEvents			x							

Returns: Nothing
This Netscape Navigator method releases event capture. Syntax: Syntax: releaseEvents(*eventTypeList*). Here, *eventTypeList* holds a list of events to release, OR'ed together like this: Event.CLICK ¦ Event.MOUSEUP. See Chapter 15 for more details.

Method	NS2	NS3	NS4	NS6	IE3a	IE3b	IE4	IE5	IE5.5	IE6
routeEvent			x							

Returns: Nothing
If you've turned on event capture in Netscape Navigator 4.0, this method enables you to route an event after you've worked on the event and want to pass it along to the next event handler. Syntax: routeEvent(*event*). See Chapter 15 for more details.

Method	NS2	NS3	NS4	NS6	IE3a	IE3b	IE4	IE5	IE5.5	IE6
setActive	See Chapter 6.									
write	x	x	x	x	x	x	x	x	x	x

Returns: Boolean
Writes text to a document. This is the big one—see "Writing to a Document" in this chapter on how to use this method and for examples. Syntax: write(*text*), where *text* is the text to write to the document.

Method	NS2	NS3	NS4	NS6	IE3a	IE3b	IE4	IE5	IE5.5	IE6
writeln	x	x	x	x	x	x	x	x	x	x

Returns: Boolean
Writes text to a document, followed by a carriage return. Syntax: write(*text*), where *text* is the text to write to the document. See "Writing to a Document" in this chapter.

Getting Selected Text

You can access text the user selected with the mouse in a web page, but the technique you use differs by browser. In the Netscape Navigator, you can use the document.getSelection method; in the Internet Explorer, however, you use the document.selection property, then create a text range from that property using the createRange method, and use the text range's text property to find the selected text. Here's an example, designed for Internet Explorer 6.0 and Netscape Navigator 6.0; this example displays the text the user has selected as soon as the user releases the mouse button:

(Listing 09-07.html on the web site)

```
<HTML>
    <HEAD>
        <TITLE>Reading Selected Text</TITLE>
        <SCRIPT LANGUAGE="JavaScript">
            <!--
            function getSelected()
            {
                if (navigator.appName == "Microsoft Internet Explorer") {
                    document.form1.text1.value = document.selection.createRange().text
                }
                if(navigator.appName == "Netscape") {
                    document.form1.text1.value = document.getSelection()
                }
            }
            // -->
        </SCRIPT>
    </HEAD>

    <BODY ONMOUSEUP="getSelected()">
        <H1>Reading Selected Text</H1>
        Select some of this text!
        <BR>
        <FORM NAME="form1">
            You selected: <INPUT TYPE="TEXT" NAME="text1">
        </FORM>
    </BODY>
</HTML>
```

You can see the results in Figure 9.4, where I'm selecting some text and the code is displaying it.

Tip

Although I've used the document.getSelection method here because this chapter is on the document object, Netscape now looks down on that method, considering it *deprecated*, which means it will eventually stop being supported. The method that is replacing document.getSelection is window.getSelection (covered in Chapter 8, "Using Window and Frame Methods and Events").

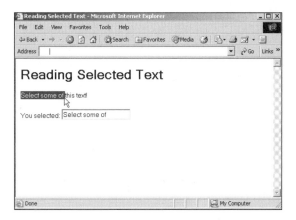

Figure 9.4 Setting and retrieving selected text.

Creating New Elements and Nodes

You can use document methods such as `createElement` and `createTextNode`
(in IE4+ and NS6+) to create and insert new elements in a document, using
methods such as the `insertBefore` method, as we'll see in Chapter 16.
Actually, we've already put these methods to work a while ago in Chapter
6—see "The `insertBefore` Method" in that chapter. There, I created a new
element, created a new text node to hold the text in the element, and then
used `insertBefore` to insert the new element into the web page. Here's what
that code looked like (Listing 06-09.html on the web site):

```
<HTML>
    <HEAD>
        <TITLE>
            Creating New Elements
        </TITLE>

        <SCRIPT LANGUAGE="JavaScript">
            <!--
            function addMore()
            {
                var newDiv, newTextField, newText
                newDiv = document.createElement("DIV")
                newTextField = document.createElement("INPUT")
                newTextField.type = "TEXT"
                newTextField.value = "Hello!"
                newText = document.createTextNode("Here is a new text field: ")
                newDiv.insertBefore(newText, null)
                newDiv.insertBefore(newTextField, null)
                document.body.insertBefore(newDiv, null)
            }
            // -->
```

```
        </SCRIPT>
    </HEAD>

    <BODY>
        <H1>Creating New Elements</H1>
        <FORM>
            <INPUT TYPE=BUTTON VALUE="Click Me!" ONCLICK="addMore()">
        </FORM>
    </BODY>
</HTML>
```

Each time you click the button in this example, a new <DIV> element is created with some text in it, as well as a text field element. You can see the results of this code in Chapter 6, in Figure 6.6.

Using *execCommand*

The Internet Explorer actually supports more methods than are normally available through JavaScript, but you can reach many of them with the execCommand method of the document object. (Some commands are available only through ActiveX programming, for example.) This method works with the document, a current selection, or a text range. (We'll see text ranges in Chapter 11.)

Here's the syntax for this method: execCommand(*Command* [, *UserInterface*] [, *Value*]), where *Command* is a string that specifies the command to execute. *UserInterface* is a Boolean that you set to false (the default) if you do not want to display a user interface, and true if you do. *Value* is a string or number, or other value to assign. This method returns true if successful, false otherwise. You can see the possible commands to use in Table 9.6. (More commands are available, but they're not yet supported by the Internet Explorer.)

Table 9.6 **The Commands of the *execCommand* Method**

Command	Does This
2D-Position	Drags positioned elements.
AbsolutePosition	Sets an element's position to "absolute."
BackColor	Sets or gets the background color of a selection.
Bold	Toggles the current selection between bold and plain (unbold) text.
Copy	Copies the selection to the clipboard.
CreateBookmark	Creates a bookmark anchor.

Command	Does This
CreateLink	Adds a hyperlink to the current selection.
Cut	Deletes the current selection, after copying it to the clipboard.
Delete	Deletes the current selection.
FontName	Sets or gets the font for the current selection.
FontSize	Sets or gets the font size for the current selection.
ForeColor	Sets or gets the text color of the current selection.
Indent	Increases the indent of the current selection by one indentation unit.
InsertButton	Places a button control over a text selection.
InsertHorizontalRule	Places a horizontal line over a text selection.
InsertIFrame	Places an inline frame over a text selection.
InsertImage	Places an image over a text selection.
InsertInputButton	Places an input button over a text selection.
InsertInputCheckbox	Places a check box over a text selection.
InsertInputFileUpload	Places a file input control over a text selection.
InsertInputHidden	Places a hidden HTML control over a text selection.
InsertInputImage	Places an image control over a text selection.
InsertInputPassword	Places a password control over a text selection.
InsertInputRadio	Places a radio button over a text selection.
InsertInputReset	Places a reset button over a text selection.
InsertInputSubmit	Places a submit button over a text selection.
InsertInputText	Places a text field over a text selection.
InsertMarquee	Places an Internet Explorer marquee element (<MARQUEE>) over a text selection.
InsertOrderedList	Changes the format of the current selection from an ordered list and normal text format.
InsertParagraph	Places a paragraph over a text selection.
InsertSelectDropdown	Places a drop-down control over a text selection.
InsertSelectListbox	Places a select box over a text selection.
InsertTextArea	Places a text area over a text selection.
InsertUnorderedList	Places an unordered list over a text selection.
Italic	Toggles the current selection between italic and plain (nonitalic) text.

continues ▶

Table 9.6 **Continued**

Command	Does This
JustifyCenter	Centers the current selection.
JustifyLeft	Left-justifies the current selection.
JustifyRight	Right-justifies the current selection.
MultipleSelection	Enables the user to select more than one element at a time (with the use of the user holds down the Shift or Ctrl keys in Windows, for example).
Outdent	Decreases indentation of the current selection by one increment unit.
OverWrite	Toggles mode between insert and overwrite text-entry mode.
Paste	Pastes the current selection to the clipboard.
Print	Prints the current page.
Refresh	Refreshes the document.
SaveAs	Saves the web page to a file.
SelectAll	Selects an entire document.
UnBookmark	Removes all bookmarks from the current selection.
Underline	Toggles the current selection between underlined and plain (not underlined) text.
Unlink	Removes all hyperlinks from the current selection.
Unselect	Unselects the current selection.

To create a new hyperlink from the current selection in a web page, for example, you can use the "CreateLink" command. Here's an example that does exactly that—when you select some text in this web page and click the button, that text is converted into a hyperlink:

(Listing 09-08.html on the web site)

```
<HTML>
    <HEAD>
        <TITLE>Creating a link</TITLE>
        <SCRIPT LANGUAGE="JavaScript">
            <!--
            function createLink()
            {
                document.execCommand("CreateLink")
            }
            // -->
        </SCRIPT>
    </HEAD>
```

```
<BODY>
    <H1>Creating a link</H1>
    Here's some text. Select some and click the button to turn it into a
    ➥hyperlink.
    <BR>
    <BUTTON ONCLICK="createLink()">Click to create the link</BUTTON>
</BODY>
</HTML>
```

You can see the results in Figure 9.5, where I've selected some text and clicked the button, opening a dialog box where I've filled in information about the hyperlink.

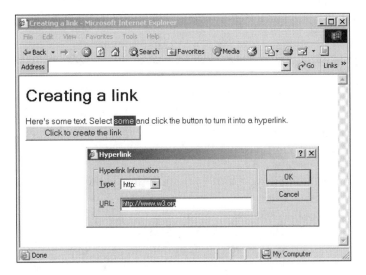

Figure 9.5   Creating a new hyperlink.

When you close the dialog box, the new hyperlink appears, as you see in Figure 9.6—note the URL of the new hyperlink, displayed in the status bar, is the URL I set in the hyperlink dialog box.

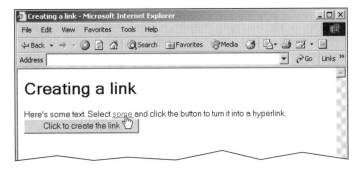

Figure 9.6   A new hyperlink.

Writing to a Document

The most popular `document` object methods are the `write` and `writeln` methods. These methods enable you to write text to a web page; the `writeln` method is the same as the `write` method, except that it adds a carriage return character after the text it writes. Note that carriage returns do not show up in web pages—you need an element such as the `<BR>` element to skip to the next line in a web page displayed in a browser. However, the carriage return can help format the source HTML of an HTML document and make it easier to read. Here's the syntax for these methods:

```
write(text)
writeln(text)
```

In this case, *text* is the text to write to the web page.

Note that although these methods enable you to write to web pages, the `innerHTML`, `innerText`, `outerHTML`, and `outerText` properties we saw in Chapter 5 and will see in more depth in Chapter 16 give you much more precision. That is, it's hard to control just when the browser will write to the web page when you use the `write` methods, because the browser writes to the web page as soon as it encounters a `write` statement (if the body of the web page is available and loaded).

When you're loading a web page, for example, the document is opened, and elements are displayed as they're encountered. When the browser encounters a `write` statement—and the document is open—the browser writes the text in that statement to the web page at once, embedding that text in the web page wherever the browser happens to be writing. Take a look at this code, for example, which asks the user whether he wants a graphics-intensive page, and loads a big or a small image accordingly:

```html
<HTML>
    <HEAD>
        <TITLE>
            Self-modifying Web Pages
        </TITLE>
    </HEAD>

    <BODY>
        <H1>Self-modifying Web Pages</H1>
        <SCRIPT LANGUAGE="JavaScript">
            <!--
            if(confirm("Do you want a graphics intensive page?")) {
                document.write("<BR><IMG WIDTH='2048' HEIGHT='2048' " +
                "SRC='gif/bigimage.jpg'></IMG>")
            }
            else {
                document.write("<BR><IMG WIDTH='100' HEIGHT='100' " +
                "SRC='gif/smallimage.jpg'></IMG>")
```

```
        }
        // -->
      </SCRIPT>
    </BODY>
</HTML>
```

Here, the browser opens the document, writes the <H1> header, and then encounters our `write` statement, so that the image will be embedded in the document after the <H1> header in this case. After the document is complete, the browser closes it.

Because the browser writes to the web page when it encounters the `write` statement during the loading process, it's sometimes a little tricky to get things just right. If we wanted text to follow the image in this web page, for example, the best option would have been to write the text from the <SCRIPT> element instead of embedding it directly into the web page's HTML, because here, the HTML in the page is loaded before the script is run.

When you want to entirely write or rewrite a web page, you have more control, because you control the entire writing process. When you're writing or rewriting a page from scratch, you can use the `document.open` method to open a document (and clear it if it already existed), and then write to the document with `document.write`, and close it with `document.close`. In fact, if a document is closed and you use `document.write` on it, the document is opened automatically (although this wasn't true in the Netscape Navigator before version 4.0—you had to use `document.open` explicitly if a document had been closed)—you don't need to use `document.open`. Here's an example that entirely rewrites a page that has already been loaded (and therefore was already closed) when the user clicks a button:

(Listing 09-09.html on the web site)

```
<HTML>
    <HEAD>
        <TITLE>
            Reopening and Rewriting a Web Page
        </TITLE>
        <SCRIPT LANGUAGE="JavaScript">
            <!--
            function rewrite()
            {
                document.write("You clicked the button!")
                document.close()
            }
            // -->
        </SCRIPT>
    </HEAD>
```

continues ▶

```
<BODY>
    <H1>Reopening and Rewriting a Web Page</H1>
    <FORM>
        <INPUT TYPE="BUTTON" ONCLICK="rewrite()" VALUE="Click Me!">
    </FORM>
</BODY>
</HTML>
```

When you click the button in this example, the code in this example opens and rewrites the entire document to only display the text You clicked the button!, as you see in Figure 9.7.

Figure 9.7 Rewriting a document.

Don't forget to use document.close when you've opened a window yourself and are finished writing to it. (If the browser opened the window, it'll call document.close itself.) Here's an example from Chapter 7, "Using *window* and *frame* Properties," where we're closing a window we opened and wrote to—if you don't use document.close here, the Netscape Navigator will display a wait icon that never goes away, because it considers the window still open for writing (Listing 07-02.html on the web site):

```
<HTML>
    <HEAD>
        <TITLE>Using the closed and opener Properties</TITLE>
        <SCRIPT LANGUAGE="JavaScript">
            <!--
            var window1

            function openWindow()
            {
                window1 = window.open("","window1", "HEIGHT=300, WIDTH=300")
```

```
              window1.document.write("<HTML><BODY><H1>A New Window</H1><BR>" +
                  "<FORM><INPUT TYPE='button' VALUE='Close the original window'" +
                  "ONCLICK='window.opener.close()'>" +
                  "</FORM></BODY></HTML>")
              window1.document.close()
          }

          function closeWindow()
          {
              if (window1 && !window1.closed) {
                  window1.close()
              }
          }
          // -->
      </SCRIPT>
  </HEAD>

  <BODY>
      <H1>Using the closed and opener Properties</H1>
      <FORM>
          <INPUT TYPE="button" VALUE="Open New Window" ONCLICK="openWindow()">
          <INPUT TYPE="button" VALUE="Close New Window" ONCLICK="closeWindow()">
      </FORM>
  </BODY>
</HTML>
```

Finding Elements by Location

A powerful document object method in the Internet Explorer (only) is the
elementFromPoint method. This method enables you to find an element
based on its X and Y position in the browser window (where (0, 0) is at
upper left, and all measurements are in pixels). All you need to do is to pass
the X and Y coordinates, and this method returns the element object
(including the <BODY> element if no other elements are on top of it at the
specific location). Here's an example that enables you to move the mouse
over various elements and displays the ID of the element the mouse is currently over:

(Listing 09-10.html on the web site)

```
<HTML>
    <HEAD>
        <TITLE>Finding Elements by Location</TITLE>
        <SCRIPT LANGUAGE="JavaScript">
            <!--
            function displayID()
            {
                document.form1.text1.value =
                    document.elementFromPoint(window.event.clientX,
                    ➥window.event.clientY).id
```

```
            }
            // -->
        </SCRIPT>
    </HEAD>

<BODY ONMOUSEOVER="displayID()" ID="body1">
    <H1 ID="header1">Finding Elements by Location</H1>
    <FORM NAME="form1">
        <INPUT ID="button1" TYPE="BUTTON" VALUE="Button">
        <BR>
        <INPUT ID="check1" TYPE="CHECKBOX">
        <BR>
        <INPUT ID="radio1" TYPE="RADIO">
        <BR>
        The ID of the button the mouse is over is <INPUT TYPE="TEXT" NAME="text1">
    </FORM>
</BODY>
</HTML>
```

You can see the results in Figure 9.8, where I'm moving the mouse over a button and the button's ID is reported in a text field.

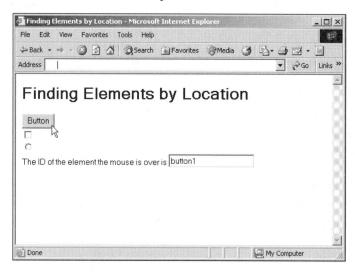

Figure 9.8   Using the `elementFromPoint` method.

The *document* Object Events

The document object also supports many events, as you see in overview in Table 9.7, and in more depth in Table 9.8. As you can see in Table 9.8, we've already covered nearly all the document object's events in Chapter 6.

Table 9.7 **The Events of the *document* Object**

Events		
onactivate	onbeforeactivate	onbeforecut
onbeforedeactivate	onbeforeeditfocus	onbeforepaste
onclick	oncontextmenu	oncontrolselect
oncut	ondblclick	ondeactivate
ondrag	ondragend	ondragenter
ondragleave	ondragover	ondragstart
ondrop	onfocusin	onfocusout
onhelp	onkeydown	onkeypress
onkeyup	onmousedown	onmousemove
onmouseout	onmouseover	onmouseup
onmousewheel	onpaste	onpropertychange
onreadystatechange	onresizeend	onresizestart
onselectionchange	onstop	

Table 9.8 **The Events of the *document* Object**

Event	NS2	NS3	NS4	NS6	IE3a	IE3b	IE4	IE5	IE5.5	IE6
onactivate	See Chapter 6.									
onbeforeactivate	See Chapter 6.									
onbeforecut	See Chapter 6.									
onbeforedeactivate	See Chapter 6.									
onbeforeeditfocus	See Chapter 6.									
onbeforepaste	See Chapter 6.									
onclick	See Chapter 6.									
oncontextmenu	See Chapter 6.									
oncontrolselect	See Chapter 6.									
oncut	See Chapter 6.									
ondblclick	See Chapter 6.									
ondeactivate	See Chapter 6.									
ondrag	See Chapter 6.									
ondragend	See Chapter 6.									
ondragenter	See Chapter 6.									

continues ▶

Table 9.8   **Continued**

Event	NS2	NS3	NS4	NS6	IE3a	IE3b	IE4	IE5	IE5.5	IE6
ondragleave		See Chapter 6.								
ondragover		See Chapter 6.								
ondragstart		See Chapter 6.								
ondrop		See Chapter 6.								
onfocusin		See Chapter 6.								
onfocusout		See Chapter 6.								
onhelp		See Chapter 6.								
onkeydown		See Chapter 6.								
onkeypress		See Chapter 6.								
onkeyup		See Chapter 6.								
onmousedown		See Chapter 6.								
onmousemove		See Chapter 6.								
onmouseout		See Chapter 6.								
onmouseover		See Chapter 6.								
onmouseup		See Chapter 6.								
onmousewheel		See Chapter 6.								
onpaste		See Chapter 6.								
onpropertychange		See Chapter 6.								
onreadystatechange		See Chapter 6.								
onresizeend		See Chapter 6.								
onresizestart		See Chapter 6.								
onselectionchange								x		x

Occurs when the text selection changes when the Internet Explorer is in the edit mode.

| onstop | | | | | | | x | x | | x |

Occurs when the user clicks the browser's Stop button. See "Using onstop" in this chapter.

Using *onstop*

The onstop event occurs when the user clicks the Internet Explorer's Stop button (which usually makes the browser stop loading a document). You can connect a function to this event like this: document.onstop = handlerFunction, like this: <SCRIPT FOR="document" EVENT="onstop">, or using the ONSTOP event attribute in the <BODY> element, which will pass the event on to the document.

Here's an example using this event—in this case, I'll modify Listing 08-08.html, which displayed a clock that updates every second, to stop when the user clicks the Stop button:

(Listing 09-11.html on the web site)

```
<HTML>
    <HEAD>
        <TITLE>
            Using the onstop Method
        </TITLE>
        <SCRIPT LANGUAGE="JavaScript">
            <!--
            document.onstop=stopCounting
            var intervalID = ""

            intervalID = window.setInterval("showTime()", 1000)
            function showTime()
            {
                    var d = new Date()
                    document.form1.text1.value = d.toLocaleTimeString()
            }
            function stopCounting()
            {
                    window.clearInterval(intervalID)
            }
            // -->
        </SCRIPT>
    </HEAD>

    <BODY>
        <H1>Using the onstop Method</H1>
        <FORM NAME="form1">
            <INPUT TYPE="TEXT" NAME="text1">
        </FORM>
    </BODY>
</HTML>
```

And that's all it takes—now this clock works as before, but when you click the Stop button, the clock will stop.

That concludes our look at the `document` object's properties, methods, and events in this chapter—now it's time to turn to the `<BODY>` element.

The *<BODY>* Element

As discussed in the beginning of this chapter, the `document` object came along before the `<BODY>` element, and as a result, many features in the `<BODY>` element—such as web page colors—are also features in the `<BODY>` element, although usually with different names.

The `<BODY>` element didn't become visible in JavaScript until Internet Explorer 4.0, in fact, and it has a lot to offer scripters. You can access the `<BODY>` element either by name or ID (with methods such as `getElementById`), or with the `body` property of the `document` object, which holds the `body` object itself; you use the `body` object like this: `document.body.alink = "cyan"`. I'll take a look at the JavaScript properties, methods, and events of the `<BODY>` element—represented by the `body` object in JavaScript—now.

The Properties of the *<BODY>* Element

You can see the properties of the `<BODY>` element in Table 9.9 in overview, and in depth in Table 9.10. Note that JavaScript's core HTML properties, methods, and events, covered in Chapters 5 and 6, also apply to this element.

Table 9.9 **The Properties of the *<BODY>* Element (See Chapters 5 and 6 for the JavaScript core HTML properties, methods, and events that also apply to this element.)**

Properties			
alink	background	bgColor	bgProperties
blockDirection	bottomMargin	leftMargin	link
noWrap	rightMargin	scroll	scrollLeft
scrollTop	text	topMargin	vLink

Table 9.10 **The Properties of the *<BODY>* Element (See Chapters 5 and 6 for the JavaScript core HTML properties, methods, and events that also apply to this element.)**

Property	NS2	NS3	NS4	NS6	IE3a	IE3b	IE4	IE5	IE5.5	IE6
alink				x			x	x	x	x

Read/write
Holds the color of an active link in the web page (that is, a link as it's being clicked). Set to a browser color value—a color triplet (such as "ff0000") or a predefined browser color (such as "cyan").

Property	NS2	NS3	NS4	NS6	IE3a	IE3b	IE4	IE5	IE5.5	IE6
background				x			x	x	x	x

Read/write
Holds the URL of a background image to display in the browser; set this property to a URL text string. To clear the background to the default, set this property to an empty string.

Property	NS2	NS3	NS4	NS6	IE3a	IE3b	IE4	IE5	IE5.5	IE6
bgColor				x			x	x	x	x

Read/write
Holds the background color of a web page, just like the BGCOLOR attribute. Set to a browser color value—a color triplet (such as "ff0000") or a predefined browser color (such as "green").

Property	NS2	NS3	NS4	NS6	IE3a	IE3b	IE4	IE5	IE5.5	IE6
bgProperties							x	x	x	x

Read/write
Specifies whether the background scrolls with the rest of the page or remains static (giving the impression that the page's content is moving, like a sheet of glass, over the background as you scroll). Set to "scroll" (the default) or "fixed."

Property	NS2	NS3	NS4	NS6	IE3a	IE3b	IE4	IE5	IE5.5	IE6
blockDirection								x	x	x

Read-only
Holds a string value that indicates whether the content in the block element flows from left to right, or from right to left. Set to "ltr" to make the content flow from left to right and "rtl" and right to left.

Property	NS2	NS3	NS4	NS6	IE3a	IE3b	IE4	IE5	IE5.5	IE6
bottomMargin							x	x	x	x

Read/write
Sets or retrieves the bottom margin of the entire body of the page, measured in pixels. Set to an integer. The default value is 15. By default, when you set the value of this property, the opposite margin is set to the same value.

continues ▶

Table 9.10 **Continued**

Property	NS2	NS3	NS4	NS6	IE3a	IE3b	IE4	IE5	IE5.5	IE6
leftMargin							x	x	x	x

Read/write
Sets or retrieves the left margin for the entire body of the page, overriding the default margin. Set to an integer. The default value is 10. By default, when you set the value of this property, the opposite margin is set to the same value.

link				x			x	x	x	x

Read/write
Holds the color of a hyperlink in the web page. Set to a browser color value—a color triplet (such as "ff0000") or a predefined browser color (such as "coral").

noWrap							x	x	x	x

Read/write
This Boolean property gets or sets the value of the <BODY> element's NOWRAP attribute, which specifies whether text wraps at the edge of the displayed area.

rightMargin							x	x	x	x

Read/write
Sets or retrieves the right margin for the entire body of the page. Set to an integer. The default value is 10. By default, when you set the value of this property, the opposite margin is set to the same value.

scroll							x	x	x	x

Read/write
Sets or retrieves a value that indicates whether the scrollbars are turned on or off. Set to "yes" (the default), "no," or "auto" (which means the browser will display scrollbars if needed).

scrollLeft							x	x	x	x

Read/write
Sets or retrieves the distance between the left edge of the body and the leftmost portion of the content currently visible. Set to an integer in pixels.

scrollTop							x	x	x	x

Read/write
Sets or retrieves the distance between the top of the body and the topmost portion of the content currently visible. Set to an integer in pixels.

Property	NS2	NS3	NS4	NS6	IE3a	IE3b	IE4	IE5	IE5.5	IE6
text				X			X	X	X	X

Read/write
Holds the foreground color of a web page (the color used for text).
Set to a browser color value—a color triplet (such as "ff 0000") or a
predefined browser color (such as "magenta").

| topMargin | | | | | | | X | X | X | X |

Read/write
Sets or retrieves the margin for the top of the page. Set to an integer.
The default value is 15. By default, when you set the value of this
property, the opposite margin is set to the same value.

| vLink | | | | X | | | X | X | X | X |

Read/write
Holds the color of an already visited hyperlink in the web page. Set to a
browser color value—a color triplet (such as "ff 0000") or a predefined
browser color (such as "lightyellow").

The Methods of the <*BODY*> Element

You can see the methods of the <BODY> element in Table 9.11 in overview
and in Table 9.12 in depth. Note that JavaScript's core HTML properties,
methods, and events, covered in Chapters 5 and 6, also apply to this element.

Table 9.11 **The Methods of the <*BODY*> Element (See Chapters 5 and
6 for the JavaScript core HTML properties, methods, and events that
also apply to this element.)**

Methods

createControlRange	createTextRange	doScroll

Table 9.12   **The Methods of the *<BODY>* Element (See Chapters 5 and 6 for the JavaScript core HTML properties, methods, and events that also apply to this element.)**

Method	NS2	NS3	NS4	NS6	IE3a	IE3b	IE4	IE5	IE5.5	IE6
createControlRange								x	x	x

Returns: A `controlRange` collection
Creates a `controlRange` collection of selected controls (as opposed to text ranges).
Syntax: `document.body.createControlRange()`.

createTextRange							x	x	x	x

Returns: A `TextRange` object
Creates a `TextRange` object for the body, which gives you a way of working with text.
Syntax: `document.body.createTextRange()`. We'll see more on `TextRange` objects in Chapter 11.

doScroll								x	x	x

Returns: Nothing
This method simulates a click on a scrollbar, enabling you to scroll an object.
Syntax: `document.body.doScroll([scrollAction])`. For the possible values of *scrollAction*, see "Using `doScroll`" in this chapter.

Using *doScroll*

In the Internet Explorer, the `doScroll` method enables you to simulate a mouse click on a scrollbar using this syntax:

`document.body.doScroll([scrollAction])`

Here, *scrollAction* is a string that can take one of these values:

- **`scrollbarDown.`** The default. Same as clicking the down scroll arrow.
- **`scrollbarHThumb.`** Clicks the horizontal scroll thumb/box (no scrolling performed).
- **`scrollbarLeft.`** Same as clicking the left scroll arrow.
- **`scrollbarPageDown.`** Scrolls down one page.
- **`scrollbarPageLeft.`** Scrolls left one page.
- **`scrollbarPageRight.`** Scrolls right one page.
- **`scrollbarPageUp.`** Scrolls up one page.

- **scrollbarRight.** Same as clicking the right scroll arrow.
- **scrollbarUp.** Same as clicking the up scroll arrow.
- **scrollbarVThumb.** Clicks the vertical scroll thumb/box (no scrolling performed).
- **down.** Same as scrollbarDown.
- **left.** Same as scrollbarLeft.
- **pageDown.** Same as scrollbarPageDown.
- **pageLeft.** Same as scrollbarPageLeft.
- **pageRight.** Same as scrollbarPageRight.
- **pageUp.** Same as scrollbarPageUp.
- **right.** Same as scrollbarRight.
- **up.** Same as scrollbarUp.

Here's an example that scrolls a web page downward when the user clicks a button:

(Listing 09-12.html on the web site)

```html
<HTML>
    <HEAD>
        <TITLE>
            Using the doScroll Method
        </TITLE>
        <SCRIPT LANGUAGE="JavaScript">
            <!--
            function scroller()
            {
                document.body.doScroll("scrollbarDown")
            }
            // -->
        </SCRIPT>
    </HEAD>

<BODY>
    <H1>Using the doScroll Method</H1>
    <FORM>
        <INPUT TYPE="BUTTON" ONCLICK="scroller()" VALUE="Click Me!">
    </FORM>
    <BR>
    <BR>
    <BR>
    <BR>
    <BR>
    <BR>
    <BR>
```

```
        <BR>
        <BR>
        <BR>
    </BODY>
</HTML>
```

The Events of the *<BODY>* Element

You can see the events of the <BODY> element in Table 9.13 in overview and in Table 9.14 in depth. Note that JavaScript's core HTML properties, methods, and events, covered in Chapters 5 and 6, also apply to this element.

Table 9.13   **The Events of the *<BODY>* Element (See Chapters 5 and 6 for the JavaScript core HTML properties, methods, and events that also apply to this element.)**

Events		
onAfterPrint	onBeforePrint	onScroll

Table 9.14   **The Events of the *<BODY>* Element (See Chapters 5 and 6 for the JavaScript core HTML properties, methods, and events that also apply to this element.)**

Event				
onafterprint		x	x	x
Occurs immediately after a document prints or previews for printing. See "Printing" in Chapter 8.				
onbeforeprint		x	x	x
Occurs immediately before a document prints or previews for printing. See "Printing" in Chapter 8.				
onscroll	x	x	x	x
Occurs when the user repositions the scroll box (the "thumb") in the scrollbar.				

And that completes our discussion of the document object and the <BODY> element/body object in this chapter. In the next chapter, we'll take a look at using the navigator, location, and history objects.

Using the *navigator*, *location*, and *history* Objects

I̲N THIS CHAPTER, WE'LL TAKE A LOOK at the navigator, location, and
history objects. We've seen all these objects before, but we'll take a look at
them in depth here. These objects give you tremendous power in JavaScript.
I'll start with the navigator object.

The *navigator* Object

The navigator object, also called the clientInformation object in IE4+, refers
to the browser itself. In early versions of the Netscape Navigator, the navigator
object actually functioned as the top-level object, although that role has now
been taken over by the window object. As we've already seen in earlier chapters,
the navigator object is often a very useful one in cross-browser programming.
We've used the navigator object's appName, appVersion, and userAgent properties to get information about the browser as far back as Chapter 1, "Essential
JavaScript," as with this script (Listing 01-07.html on the web site) which
displays the values of those properties:

```
<HTML>
    <HEAD>
        <TITLE>
            Checking Your Browser Type
        </TITLE>
    </HEAD>
```

```
<BODY>
    <SCRIPT LANGUAGE="JavaScript">
        document.write("navigator.appName: " + navigator.appName)
        document.write("<BR><BR>")
        document.write("navigator.appVersion: " + navigator.appVersion)
        document.write("<BR><BR>")
        document.write("navigator.userAgent: " + navigator.userAgent)
    </SCRIPT>

    <H1>Checking Your Browser Type</H1>
</BODY>
</HTML>
```

You can see the results of this script in Chapter 1; Figure 1.12 shows the
results for the Internet Explorer, and Figure 1.13 shows the results for the
Netscape Navigator. Note that even though I'm using Internet Explorer 6.0
in Figure 1.12, the appVersion property shows a value of 4.0; and even
though I'm using Netscape Navigator 6.2 in Figure 1.13, the appVersion
property shows a value of 5.0. As you can see, the appVersion property is not
the one to use to get the actual browser version. You've got to dig that information out of the userAgent property, as we will in this chapter.

You'll find the properties and methods of the navigator object in Table
10.1. (It has no events.) Not all properties and methods are supported in all
browsers, of course.

Table 10.1   **The Properties and Methods of the *navigator* Object**

Properties	Methods
appCodeName	javaEnabled
appMinorVersion	preference
appName	taintEnabled
appVersion	
browserLanguage	
cookieEnabled	
cpuClass	
language	
mimeTypes	
onLine	
oscpu	
platform	
plugins	
product	

Properties	Methods
productSub	
securityPolicy	
systemLanguage	
userAgent	
userLanguage	
userProfile	
vendor	
vendorSub	

It's time to take a look at this object in depth, starting with its properties.

The *navigator* Object's Properties

You'll find the navigator object's properties in overview in Table 10.2, and in depth in Table 10.3.

Table 10.2 **Overview of the Properties of the *navigator* Object**

Properties

appCodeName	appMinorVersion	appName
appVersion	browserLanguage	cookieEnabled
cpuClass	language	mimeTypes
onLine	oscpu	platform
plugins	product	productSub
securityPolicy	systemLanguage	userAgent
userLanguage	userProfile	vendor
vendorSub		

Table 10.3 **The Properties of the *navigator* Object**

Property	NS2	NS3	NS4	NS6	IE3a	IE3b	IE4	IE5	IE5.5	IE6
appCodeName	X	X	X	X	X	X	X	X	X	X

Read-only
This property holds a string that is supposed to hold the browser's name. However, it's less useful than you might think—both the Internet Explorer and Netscape Navigator return "Mozilla" here, the former nickname for the Netscape Navigator and currently the name of its development browser.

continues ▶

Table 10.3 **Continued**

Property	NS2	NS3	NS4	NS6	IE3a	IE3b	IE4	IE5	IE5.5	IE6
appMinorVersion							x	x	x	x

Read-only
Retrieves the application's minor version value. (For example, in the value 6.2, 2 is the minor version.) Unfortunately, this property is not useful, because it returns the minor version of the appVersion property, which does not hold the true browser version. For example, Internet Explorer 5.5 reports version 4.0 in appVersion, which makes the appMinorVersion 0, not 5. Use the userAgent property instead to find this information.

| appName | x | x | x | x | x | x | x | x | x | x |

Read-only
Holds the browser's name, returns "Netscape" or "Microsoft Internet Explorer". See "Detecting Browser and Version" in this chapter.

| appVersion | x | x | x | x | x | x | x | x | x | x |

Read-only
Supposed to return the browser's version, but in fact returns the "Mozilla-compatibility" version. For example, Internet Explorer considers itself compatible with Mozilla (the former nickname for the Netscape Navigator and currently the name of its development browser) 4.0, and so reports 4.0 here (actually returns a string such as `"4.0 (compatible; MSIE 6.0; Windows NT 5.0; COM+ 1.0.2204)"`). It's better to use the userAgent property. See "Detecting Browser and Version" in this chapter.

| browserLanguage | | | | | | | x | x | x | x |

Read-only
Holds the language the browser uses as its default. See "Using the browserLanguage, systemLanguage, and userLanguage Properties" in this chapter.

| cookieEnabled | | | x | | | | x | x | x | x |

Read-only
Returns true if cookies are enabled in the browser, false otherwise.

| cpuClass | | | | | | | x | x | x | x |

Read-only
This Internet Explorer-only property holds a string that specifies the type of CPU on which the browser is running. Holds one of the following values "x86" for an Intel processor, "68K" for a Motorola processor, "Alpha" for a Digital processor, "PPC" for a Motorola-based Power PC, processor, and "Other" for other CPU classes (including such CPUs as Sun SPARC).

Property	NS2	NS3	NS4	NS6	IE3a	IE3b	IE4	IE5	IE5.5	IE6
language			X	X						

Read-only
Holds the language the browser was written for. Applicable only to Netscape Navigator 4+.

| mimeTypes | | X | X | X | | | | | | |

Read-only
Holds the MIME (Multipurpose Internet Mail Extensions) types that the browser can support, such as JPEG, GIF, and so on, in an array of strings. You can find a a list of registered MIME types from `ftp://ftp.isi.edu/in-notes/iana/assignments/media-types/`.

| onLine | | | | | | | X | X | X | X |

Read-only
Indicates whether the system is in global offline mode (in which case `onLine` is false) or global online mode (in which case `onLine` is true). The Internet Explorer uses this property to determine whether the computer is connected to the Internet—even though it's often possible to perform actions in the Internet Explorer that make it think it's offline when in fact it's not. If the Internet Explorer thinks you're offline, it won't even try to access the Internet without first asking you whether it should connect.

| oscpu | | | | X | | | | | | |

Read-only
Similar to the Internet Explorer `cpuClass` property, this property returns a string that holds information about the browser's machine environment. This property can give considerable information, such as what hardware is supporting a particular version of UNIX. However, the information you'll get varies considerably by operating system. On a Windows 2000 machine, for example, this property holds only "Windows NT 5.0," Microsoft's internal designation for Windows 2000.

| platform | | | X | X | | | X | X | X | X |

Read-only
Holds the *operating platform* as a string. An operating platform is like an operating system, but is not necessarily as complete as a full operating system. Windows 3x was considered an operating platform, not an operating system, for example. Here are some possible values: "HP-UX" for HP UNIX-based computers, "MacPPC" for Macintosh PowerPC-based computers, "Mac68K" for Macintosh 68K-based computers, "SunOS" for Solaris-based computers, "Win32" for 32-bit Windows, "Win16" for 16-bit Windows, and "WinCE" for Windows CE.

continues ▶

Table 10.3 **Continued**

Property	NS2	NS3	NS4	NS6	IE3a	IE3b	IE4	IE5	IE5.5	IE6
plugins			X	X	X			X	X	X

Read-only
Holds an array of all `<EMBED>` elements within the document. Currently, this is really the same as the `document` object's `embeds` property, using the Netscape Navigator name *plug-in* instead, and included in the Internet Explorer for compatibility. (Netscape Navigator introduced plug-ins before Internet Explorer introduced `<EMBED>` elements, but W3C has gone with the term *embed*.)

product				X						

Read-only
Netscape Navigator 6.0 was developed as an open-source browser, which means other vendors can adapt the browser engine for themselves. The `product`, `productSub`, `vendor`, and `vendorSub` let other vendors fill in their own identification information. The product and `productSub` (*sub* indicates a secondary information field) hold information about the browser itself, and `vendor` and `vendorSub` hold information about the vendor.

productSub				X						

Read-only
Netscape Navigator 6.0 was developed as an open-source browser, which means other vendors can adapt the browser engine for themselves. The `product`, `productSub`, `vendor`, and `vendorSub` let other vendors fill in their own identification information. The product and `productSub` (*sub* indicates a secondary information field) hold information about the browser itself, and `vendor` and `vendorSub` hold information about the vendor.

securityPolicy			X	X						

Read-only
Holds a string specifying cryptographic information the browser uses. In the Internet Explorer, use the `document.security` property; see Chapter 9, "Using the *document* and *body* Objects."

systemLanguage							X	X	X	X

Read-only
Holds the operating system language as a string. See "Using the `browserLanguage`, `systemLanguage`,l and `userLanguage` Properties" in this chapter.

Property	NS2	NS3	NS4	NS6	IE3a	IE3b	IE4	IE5	IE5.5	IE6
userAgent	X	X	X	X	X	X	X	X	X	X

Read-only
Holds information about the browser in string format. This property is usually the best one for determining browser version information. See "Detecting Browser and Version" and "Using the userAgent Property" in this chapter for the details.

Property	NS2	NS3	NS4	NS6	IE3a	IE3b	IE4	IE5	IE5.5	IE6
userLanguage							X	X	X	X

Read-only
Retrieves the operating system's natural language setting as a string. See "Using the browserLanguage, systemLanguage, and userLanguage Properties" in this chapter

Property	NS2	NS3	NS4	NS6	IE3a	IE3b	IE4	IE5	IE5.5	IE6
userProfile							X	X	X	X

Read-only
Gives you access to a user's profile information stored in the machine. This property holds a userProfile object with methods such as getAttribute(*attr*), which gets the value of the attribute *attr* from the user's profile, and setAttribute(*attr*, *value* [, *flags*]), where *attr* is the name of an attribute, *value* is the value you want to set for this attribute, and *flags* is 1 (the default) if *attr* is case-sensitive and 0 if not.

Property	NS2	NS3	NS4	NS6	IE3a	IE3b	IE4	IE5	IE5.5	IE6
vendor				X						

Read-only
Netscape Navigator 6.0 was developed as an open-source browser, which means other vendors can adapt the browser engine for themselves. The product, productSub, vendor, and vendorSub let other vendors fill in their own identification information. The product and productSub (*sub* indicates a secondary information field) hold information about the browser itself, and vendor and vendorSub hold information about the vendor.

Property	NS2	NS3	NS4	NS6	IE3a	IE3b	IE4	IE5	IE5.5	IE6
vendorSub				X						

Read-only
Netscape Navigator 6.0 was developed as an open-source browser, which means other vendors can adapt the browser engine for themselves. The product, productSub, vendor, and vendorSub let other vendors fill in their own identification information. The product and productSub (*sub* indicates a secondary information field) hold information about the browser itself, and vendor and vendorSub hold information about the vendor.

Using the *browserLanguage, systemLanguage,* and *userLanguage* Properties

In these days of increasing internationalization, you may want to tailor your scripts to use the same language the user is using, which is where the Internet Explorer browserLanguage, systemLanguage, and userLanguage properties come in (see Table 10.3). The possible values for these properties—an abbreviation like "en-us" for U.S. English or "de" for standard German (that is, "Deutsch")—appear in Table 10.4.

Table 10.4 **Language Abbreviations for the *navigator* Object's** *browserLanguage, systemLanguage,* **and** *userLanguage* **Properties**

Language Abbreviations

af Afrikaans	ar-ae Arabic (U.A.E.)
ar-bh Arabic (Bahrain)	ar-dz Arabic (Algeria)
ar-eg Arabic (Egypt)	ar-iq Arabic (Iraq)
ar-jo Arabic (Jordan)	ar-kw Arabic (Kuwait)
ar-lb Arabic (Lebanon)	ar-ly Arabic (Libya)
ar-ma Arabic (Morocco)	ar-om Arabic (Oman)
ar-qa Arabic (Qatar)	ar-sa Arabic (Saudi Arabia)
ar-sy Arabic (Syria)	ar-tn Arabic (Tunisia)
ar-ye Arabic (Yemen)	be Belarusian
bg Bulgarian	ca Catalan
cs Czech	da Danish
de German (Standard)	de-at German (Austria)
de-ch German (Switzerland)	de-li German (Liechtenstein)
de-lu German (Luxembourg)	el Greek
en English	en English (Caribbean)
en-au English (Australia)	en-bz English (Belize)
en-ca English (Canada)	en-gb English (Great Britain)
en-ie English (Ireland)	en-jm English (Jamaica)
en-nz English (New Zealand)	en-tt English (Trinidad)
en-us English (United States)	en-za English (South Africa)
es Spanish (Spain)	es-ar Spanish (Argentina)
es-bo Spanish (Bolivia)	es-cl Spanish (Chile)

Language Abbreviations

es-co Spanish (Colombia)

es-cr Spanish (Costa Rica)

es-do Spanish (Dominican Republic)

es-ec Spanish (Ecuador)

es-gt Spanish (Guatemala)

es-hn Spanish (Honduras)

es-mx Spanish (Mexico)

es-ni Spanish (Nicaragua)

es-pa Spanish (Panama)

es-pe Spanish (Peru)

es-pr Spanish (Puerto Rico)

es-py Spanish (Paraguay)

es-sv Spanish (El Salvador)

es-uy Spanish (Uruguay)

es-ve Spanish (Venezuela)

et Estonian

eu Basque

fa Farsi

fi Finnish

fo Faeroese

fr French (Standard)

fr-be French (Belgium)

fr-ca French (Canada)

fr-ch French (Switzerland)

fr-lu French (Luxembourg)

gd Gaelic (Scotland)

gd-ie Gaelic (Ireland)

he Hebrew

hi Hindi

hr Croatian

hu Hungarian

in Indonesian

is Icelandic

it Italian (Standard)

it-ch Italian (Switzerland)

ja Japanese

ji Yiddish

ko Korean

ko Korean (Johab)

lt Lithuanian

lv Latvian

mk FYRO Macedonian

ms Malaysian

mt Maltese

nl Dutch (Standard)

nl-be Dutch (Belgium)

no Norwegian (Bokmal)

no Norwegian (Nynorsk)

pl Polish

pt Portuguese (Portugal)

pt-br Portuguese (Brazil)

rm Rhaeto-Romanic

ro Romanian

ro-mo Romanian (Moldavia)

ru Russian

ru-mo Russian (Moldavia)

sb Sorbian

sk Slovak

sl Slovenian

sq Albanian

sr Serbian (Cyrillic)

sr Serbian (Latin)

sv Swedish

sv-fi Swedish (Finland)

sx Sutu

sz Sami (Lappish)

continues ▶

Table 10.4 **Continued**

Language Abbreviations

th Thai	tn Tswana
tr Turkish	ts Tsonga
uk Ukrainian	ur Urdu
ve Venda	vi Vietnamese
xh Xhosa	zh-cn Chinese (PRC)
zh-hk Chinese (Hong Kong SAR)	zh-sg Chinese (Singapore)
zh-tw Chinese (Taiwan)	zu Zulu

Using the *userAgent* Property

The most comprehensive information you can get about a browser is usually to be found in the `navigator.userAgent` property. Unfortunately, this string is not standardized, so you must search for the information you want using the JavaScript string methods (which we'll discuss in Chapter 18, "The *Date, Time,* and *String* Objects"). Here are a few possible values for this string and what they mean—note that they always start with "Mozilla" because in the early days, scripts used to search for that word before assuming standard JavaScript compatibility:

- `"Mozilla/5.0 (Windows; U; Windows NT 5.0; en-US; rv:0.9.4) Gecko/20011019 Netscape6/6.2"`. This is the string returned by Netscape Navigator 6.2 for U.S. Windows 2000.

- `"Mozilla/4.0 (compatible; MSIE 5.0; Windows 98; DigExt)"`. This is the string returned by Internet Explorer 5.0 for Windows 98 with digital security enabled.

- `"Mozilla/4.08 — (Win98; I ;Nav)"`. This is the string returned by Netscape Navigator 4.08 for Windows 98.

- `"Mozilla/4.0 (compatible; MSIE 6.0; Windows NT 5.0; COM+ 1.0.2204; .NET CLR 1.0.3512)"`. This is the string returned by Internet Explorer 6.0 for Windows 2000 with .NET installed.

To get what you want from the `userAgent` property, you have to search for it—see the next topic.

Detecting Browser and Version

Because the format of the userAgent property varies so much, it can be hard to know how to extract the browser's version from it. Here's a script we originally saw in Chapter 4, "Handling the Browser Environment." This script was designed to solve that problem, filling a variable named version with the floating-point version of the browser. It's designed to work with all scriptable versions of the two browsers, from version 3.0 to 6.0 of the Internet Explorer and from version 2.0 to 6.2 of the Netscape Navigator, but there are no guarantees. Some odd versions or versions for little-supported operating systems of each browser may use a different format for the userAgent property. Here's the code:

(Listing 10-01.html on the web site)

```html
<HTML>
    <HEAD>
        <TITLE>
            Getting Browser Version
        </TITLE>
    </HEAD>

    <BODY>
        <H1>Getting Browser Version</H1>
        <SCRIPT LANGUAGE="JavaScript">
            <!--
            var start, end, version
            if(navigator.appName == "Netscape") {
                if(navigator.userAgent.indexOf("Netscape") < 0) {
                    start = "Mozilla/".length
                    end = navigator.userAgent.indexOf(" ", start)
                    version = parseFloat(navigator.userAgent.substring(start, end))
                    document.write("You are using Netscape Navigator " + version)
                } else {
                    start = navigator.userAgent.indexOf("Netscape") +
                    "Netscape".length + 2
                    end = navigator.userAgent.length
                    version = parseFloat(navigator.userAgent.substring(start, end))
                    document.write("You are using Netscape Navigator " + version)
                }
            }

            if (navigator.appName == "Microsoft Internet Explorer") {
                start = navigator.userAgent.indexOf("MSIE ") + "MSIE ".length
                if(navigator.userAgent.indexOf(";", start) > 0) {
                    end = navigator.userAgent.indexOf(";", start)
                } else {
```

continues ▶

```
            end = navigator.userAgent.indexOf(")", start)
        }
        version = parseFloat(navigator.userAgent.substring(start, end))
        document.write("You are using Internet Explorer " + version)
      }
    // -->
    </SCRIPT>
  </BODY>
</HTML>
```

You can see the results in the Netscape Navigator in Figure 10.1. In this book, I list the browser support by version of each JavaScript statement, property, method, and event, and using a script something like this one, you can check version information before attempting to put those items to work.

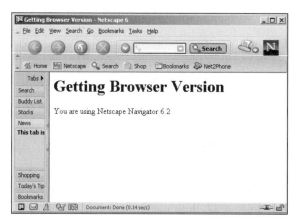

Figure 10.1   Getting browser version.

The *navigator* Object's Methods

You can see the methods of the navigator object in Table 10.5 in overview and in Table 10.6 in depth.

Table 10.5   **Overview of the methods of the navigator object**

Methods		
javaEnabled	preference	taintEnabled

Table 10.6 **The Methods of the *navigator* Object**

Method	NS2	NS3	NS4	NS6	IE3a	IE3b	IE4	IE5	IE5.5	IE6
javaEnabled		x	x	x			x	x	x	x

Returns: Boolean
This method returns true if Java is enabled in the browser, and false otherwise. This method is a good one to use if you want to jump to a non-Java page if needed.
Syntax: `navigator.javaEnabled()`.

preference			x	x						

Returns: Nothing
This method sets browser preferences in the Netscape Navigator.
Syntax: `preference(name [, value])`, where *name* is the name of the preference and *value* is the new value for the preference. See "Setting Netscape Navigator Preferences" in this chapter for the details and an example.

taintEnabled		x	x	x			x	x	x	x

Returns: Nothing
Netscape Navigator 3.0 introduced a feature called *data tainting*, following the lead of languages such as Perl. Tainted data was suspect data, under user control, that could be tampered with by hackers and even run as illicit code. However, this method is no longer used and always returns false now.

Setting Netscape Navigator Preferences

You can use the `preference` method to set Netscape Navigator *preferences*, such as whether the browser should warn the user before accepting cookies and what screen colors to use. Netscape lists about 16 pages of preferences and their possible settings currently at `http://developer.netscape.com/docs/manuals/communicator/preferences/`. Here are a few to give you a sampling:

- **browser.background_color.** Sets the default color for page backgrounds. Set to a browser color triplet.

- **browser.cache.disk_cache_size.** Sets the size of the web page cache on hard disks.

- **browser.foreground_color.** Sets the default color for regular web page text. Set to a browser color triplet.

- **browser.startup.page.** Sets what page, if any, the Netscape Navigator should display when it starts.

- **browser.window_rect.** Specifies the position and dimensions of the browser window, in pixels.

- **network.cookie.warnAboutCookies.** Warns the user before accepting cookies.

For more details and settings, take a look at http://developer.netscape.com/ docs/manuals/communicator/preferences/. Here's an example that toggles whether the browser will warn the user before accepting cookies. Note that to set preferences, this script enables and disables the UniversalPreferencesRead and UniversalPreferencesWrite security privileges. The browser will check with the user—using a dialog box—before changing this privilege level. Note that this example uses getElementById, which is not supported in NS4; if you want to use that browser, you might change this code to write results to a text field rather than a <DIV> element:

(Listing 10-02.html on the web site)

```
<HTML>
    <HEAD>
        <TITLE>Setting Netscape Navigator Preferences</TITLE>
        <SCRIPT LANGUAGE="JavaScript">
            <!--
            function getPref()
            {
                netscape.security.PrivilegeManager.enablePrivilege
                ➥("UniversalPreferencesRead")
                if(navigator.preference('network.cookie.warnAboutCookies')){
                    document.getElementById("div1").innerHTML = "Will warn before
                    accepting cookies."
                } else {
                    document.getElementById("div1").innerHTML = "Will not warn before
                    ➥accepting cookies."
                }
                netscape.security.PrivilegeManager.revertPrivilege
                ➥("UniversalPreferencesRead")
            }
            function warnCookie()
            {
                netscape.security.PrivilegeManager.enablePrivilege
                ➥("UniversalPreferencesWrite")
                navigator.preference('network.cookie.warnAboutCookies', true)
                netscape.security.PrivilegeManager.revertPrivilege
                ➥("UniversalPreferencesWrite")
                getPref()
            }
```

```
function noWarnCookie()
{
    netscape.security.PrivilegeManager.enablePrivilege
    ➥("UniversalPreferencesWrite")
    navigator.preference('network.cookie.warnAboutCookies', false)
    netscape.security.PrivilegeManager.revertPrivilege
    ➥("UniversalPreferencesWrite")
    getPref()
}
// -->
</SCRIPT>
</HEAD>

<BODY ONLOAD="getPref()">
    <H1>Setting Netscape Navigator Preferences</H1>
    <FORM>
        <INPUT TYPE="BUTTON" NAME="warn" ONCLICK="warnCookie()"
            VALUE="Warn before accepting cookies">
        <BR>
        <INPUT TYPE="BUTTON" NAME="nowarn" ONCLICK="noWarnCookie()"
            VALUE="Do not warn when accepting cookies">
    </FORM>
    <BR>
    <DIV ID="div1"></DIV>
</BODY>
</HTML>
```

You can see the results in the Netscape Navigator in Figure 10.2, where I've changed the default behavior of the browser to warn the user before accepting cookies.

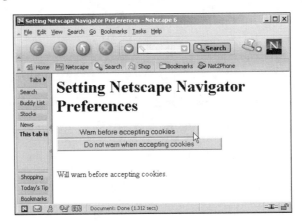

Figure 10.2   Setting Netscape Navigator preferences.

The *location* Object

The location object holds information about the location of the current web page, such as its URL, the domain name, path, server port, and more. This object even enables you to navigate to a new URL just by assigning that URL to the location object's href property—or, in most browsers, even to the location object itself (like this, window.location = "http://www.w3.org").

The location object not only holds the current location in the href property, but also lets you dissect that URL in a handy way, using several properties such as hostname (the www.*name*.com part), host (the same as the hostname property with a port number appended if there is one—for example, in the URL http://www.*name*.com:80/index.html, the hostname is www.*name*.com:80), href (the current URL in full), hash (the part of the URL following the hash mark, #, in the URL if there is one), and pathname (the file name or path specified in the URL). For example, take a look at this URL that discusses the changes in the HTML 4.01 W3C specification:

```
http://www.w3.org/TR/html4/appendix/changes.html#19991224
```

Here are the values of various location properties for this URL:

- **hash:** #19991224
- **host:** www.w3.org
- **hostname:** www.w3.org
- **href:** http://www.w3.org/TR/html4/appendix/changes.html#19991224
- **pathname:** /TR/html4/appendix/changes.html
- **protocol:** http:

We'll see these properties in more detail in a page or two. You'll find the properties and methods (there are no events) of the location object in Table 10.7.

Table 10.7 **The Properties and Methods of the *location* Object**

Properties	Methods
hash	assign
host	reload
hostname	replace
href	
pathname	
port	
protocol	
search	

The `location` object is also a good one when you want to redirect a browser; all you have to do is to assign a new URL to the `location.href` property. Let's take a look at all the properties and methods of this object now, starting with the properties.

The *location* Object's Properties

You can find the properties of the `location` object in Table 10.8.

Table 10.8 **The Properties and Methods of the *location* Object**

Property	NS2	NS3	NS4	NS6	IE3a	IE3b	IE4	IE5	IE5.5	IE6
hash	x	x	x	x	x	x	x	x	x	x

Read/write
Sets or gets the part of the `href` property that follows the hash mark (#), if any, as a string. See "Using the `location` Object's Properties" in this chapter for an example.

host	x	x	x	x	x	x	x	x	x	x

Read/write
The host property just joins the `hostname` and `port` properties, separated by a colon (like this, *hostname:port*), as a string. See "Using the `location` Object's Properties" in this chapter.

hostname	x	x	x	x	x	x	x	x	x	x

Read/write
Sets or gets the host name part of the location or URL as a string. See "Using the `location` Object's Properties" in this chapter.

href	x	x	x	x	x	x	x	x	x	x

Read/write
Sets or gets the entire current URL as a string. See "Using the `location` Object's Properties" in this chapter.

pathname	x	x	x	x	x	x	x	x	x	x

Read/write
Sets or gets the filename or path specified by the object as a string. See "Using the `location` Object's Properties" in this chapter.

port	x	x	x	x	x	x	x	x	x	x

Read/write
Sets or gets the port number of an URL as a string. For example, in the URL `http://www.starpowder.com:80/hello.html`, the port is 80. See "Using the location Object's Properties" in this chapter.

continues ▶

Table 10.8 **Continued**

Property	NS2	NS3	NS4	NS6	IE3a	IE3b	IE4	IE5	IE5.5	IE6
protocol	x	x	x	x	x	x	x	x	x	x

Read/write
Sets or gets the protocol part of a URL, such as http:, ftp:, or file:, as a string. See "Using the `location` Object's Properties" in this chapter.

Property	NS2	NS3	NS4	NS6	IE3a	IE3b	IE4	IE5	IE5.5	IE6
search	x	x	x	x	x	x	x	x	x	x

Read/write
Sets or gets the part of the `href` property following the question mark in that property, if there is one. This property is a string. For example, in the URL `http://www.starpowder.com/inside.html?user=1`, this property will hold "user=1". If there is no question mark in the URL, this property will hold an empty string.

Using the *location* Object's Properties

Let's put the `location` object's properties to work in an example. In this case, the code will let the user open a new window, navigate to a new URL in the new window (using the browser's File | Open Web Location menu item), and then click a button in the original window to display the details of the new window's `location` object.

In this example, I'll navigate to the URL we saw earlier: `http://www.w3.org/TR/html4/appendix/changes.html#19991224`. (I'm choosing this URL because it has a hash part to it.) Usually, browsers won't let you get the properties of the `location` object in another window, but you can enable the `UniversalBrowserRead` privilege in the Netscape Navigator to let you do this, so this script is targeted to that browser:

(Listing 10-03.html on the web site)

```
<HTML>
    <HEAD>
        <TITLE>
            Using the location Object
        </TITLE>
    </HEAD>

    <BODY>
        <H1>Using the location Object</H1>
        <FORM>
            <INPUT TYPE="BUTTON" ONCLICK="openWindow()" VALUE="Open window">
            <INPUT TYPE="BUTTON" ONCLICK="getInfo()" VALUE="Get info">
        </FORM>
```

```
<DIV ID="div1"></DIV>
<SCRIPT LANGUAGE="JavaScript">
    <!--
    var window1
    function openWindow()
    {
        window1 = window.open("","window1", "height=300, width=300,
        ➥menubar=yes")
    }

    function getInfo()
    {
        netscape.security.PrivilegeManager.enablePrivilege
        ➥("UniversalBrowserRead")
        data = "hash: " + window1.location.hash + "<BR>"
        data += "host: " + window1.location.host + "<BR>"
        data += "hostname: " + window1.location.hostname + "<BR>"
        data += "href: " + window1.location.href + "<BR>"
        data += "pathname: " + window1.location.pathname + "<BR>"
        data += "port: " + window1.location.port + "<BR>"
        data += "protocol: " + window1.location.protocol + "<BR>"
        document.getElementById("div1").innerHTML = data
        netscape.security.PrivilegeManager.disablePrivilege
        ➥("UniversalBrowserRead")
    }    // -->
    </SCRIPT>
</BODY>
</HTML>
```

You can see the results in the Netscape Navigator in Figure 10.3, where we're taking a look at the properties of the location object in the newly opened window.

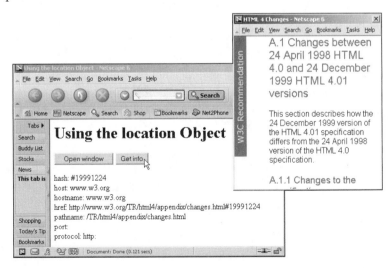

Figure 10.3   Displaying location object properties.

> **Tip**
>
> Note that to make this example work, you must navigate to some URL (such as the one I've used here, http://www.w3.org/TR/html4/appendix/changes.html#19991224) in the new window it opens; use the File | Open Web Location menu item for that.

Navigating to a New URL

The location object is probably best known for enabling you to navigate to a new URL, and we've seen that as long ago as Chapter 4. Here's that example; in this case, we let the user enter a URL and make the browser navigate to that URL when she clicks a button (Listing 04-06.html on the web site):

```html
<HTML>
    <HEAD>
        <TITLE>
            Navigate to an URL
        </TITLE>
        <SCRIPT LANGUAGE = "JavaScript">
            <!--
            function Jump()
            {
                window.location.href = document.form1.text1.value
            }
            // -->
        </SCRIPT>
    </HEAD>

    <BODY>
        <H1>Navigate to an URL</H1>
        <FORM NAME = "form1">
            <BR>
            <INPUT TYPE = TEXT NAME="text1" SIZE = 80>
            <BR>
            <BR>
            <INPUT TYPE = BUTTON Value="Navigate to URL" ONCLICK="Jump()">
        </FORM>
    </BODY>
</HTML>
```

You can see this script at work in Chapter 4, in Figure 4.7, where the user just has to enter a URL into a text field and click a button to navigate to that URL. This is one of the most powerful aspects of JavaScript, in fact—the ability to navigate the browser under programmatic control.

Redirecting a Browser

You also can use the `location` object to redirect a browser as soon as a page loads—for example, to a page with browser-specific code. We saw how to do that in Chapter 4 as well—this is Listing 04-09.html on the web site (note that this code also redirects browsers that don't support scripting using a `<META>` element):

```
<HTML>
    <HEAD>
        <TITLE>Redirecting Browsers</TITLE>
        <SCRIPT LANGUAGE="JavaScript">
            <!--
            if (navigator.appName == "Microsoft Internet Explorer") {
                window.location.href = "IE.html"
            }
            if(navigator.appName == "Netscape") {
                window.location.href = "NS.html"
            }
            //-->
        </SCRIPT>
        <META HTTP-EQUIV="refresh" CONTENT="0; URL=default.html">
    </HEAD>

    <BODY>
        <H1>Redirecting Browsers</H1>
    </BODY>
</HTML>
```

The *location* Object's Methods

You can find the `location` object's methods in Table 10.9.

Table 10.9 **The Properties and Methods of the *location* Object**

Method	NS2	NS3	NS4	NS6	IE3a	IE3b	IE4	IE5	IE5.5	IE6
assign	x	x	x	x	x	x	x	x	x	x

Returns: Nothing
This method performs the same action as assigning a URL to the `href` property.
Syntax: `assign(URL)`, where *URL* is the new URL.

| reload | | x | x | x | | | x | x | x | x |

Reloads the current page.
Syntax: `location.reload([flag])`, where *flag* is true if you want the page to be reloaded from the server, or false (the default) if you want the page reloaded from the browser's cache (if it's still there).

continues ▶

Table 10.9   *Continued*

Method	NS2	NS3	NS4	NS6	IE3a	IE3b	IE4	IE5	IE5.5	IE6
replace		x	x	x			x	x	x	x

Replaces the current document by loading another document from the given URL.

Syntax: `location.replace(URL)`, where *URL* is the new URL.

The *history* Object

The `history` object holds the list of sites the web browser has visited in the current session, called the *history list.* The `history` object gives you access to methods that let you move back and forth in the browser's history list. You can see the properties and methods of the `history` object in Table 10.10.

Table 10.10   **The Properties and Methods of the *history* Object**

Properties	Methods
current	back
length	forward
next	go
previous	

I'll take a look at the `history` object's properties and methods here, starting with its properties.

The *history* Object's Properties

You can find the properties of the `history` object in Table 10.11.

Table 10.11   **The Properties of the *history* Object**

Property	NS2	NS3	NS4	NS6	IE3a	IE3b	IE4	IE5	IE5.5	IE6
current			x	x						

Read-only

Holds the current URL as a string. This property is restricted to Netscape Navigator signed scripts and scripts where the user has explicitly given permission to a script to use.

Property	NS2	NS3	NS4	NS6	IE3a	IE3b	IE4	IE5	IE5.5	IE6
length	x	x	x	x	x	x	x	x	x	x

Read-only
Holds the length of the history list, as an integer. Be careful with this one—the natural tendency is to consider the current page as the most recent one in the history list and navigate from there, using this property as an indication of how far back in the history list you can go. Note, however, that the current page can actually be anywhere in the history list; it's not necessarily the most recent page.

Property	NS2	NS3	NS4	NS6	IE3a	IE3b	IE4	IE5	IE5.5	IE6
next			x	x						

Read-only
Holds the next URL in the history list as a string. This property is restricted to Netscape Navigator signed scripts and scripts where the user has explicitly given permission to a script to use.

Property	NS2	NS3	NS4	NS6	IE3a	IE3b	IE4	IE5	IE5.5	IE6
previous			x	x						

Read-only
Holds the previous URL in the history list as a string. This property is restricted to Netscape Navigator signed scripts and scripts where the user has explicitly given permission to a script to use.

The *history* Object's Methods

You can find the methods of the `history` object in Table 10.12; these methods enable you to navigate around in the history list at will.

Table 10.12 **The Properties of the *history* Object**

Method	NS2	NS3	NS4	NS6	IE3a	IE3b	IE4	IE5	IE5.5	IE6
back	x	x	x	x	x	x	x	x	x	x

Returns: Nothing
Navigates back one place in the history list. Before Netscape Navigator 4.0, you could navigate the contents of a frame back before the beginning of the history list, which was an error; but in Netscape Navigator 4+, that's been fixed. In the Internet Explorer, on the other hand, the `history` object does not store frame URLs, only the URLs of entire pages.
Syntax: `back()`. See "Using the `go`, `forward`, and `back` Methods" in this chapter for an example.

continues ▸

Table 10.12 **Continued**

Method	NS2	NS3	NS4	NS6	IE3a	IE3b	IE4	IE5	IE5.5	IE6
forward	x	x	x	x	x	x	x	x	x	x

Returns: Nothing

Navigates forward one location in the history list, displaying that location in the browser.

Syntax: `forward()`. See "Using the `go`, `forward`, and `back` Methods" in this chapter for an example.

go	x	x	x	x	x	x	x	x	x	x

Loads a URL from the history list.

Syntax: `history.go(location)`, where *location* is an integer that specifies the relative position in the history list you want to go to, or a string holding the URL of the location you want to navigate to. (This must be an URL already in the history list.) To navigate back two locations, for instance, use [ms]2. See "Using the `go`, `forward`, and `back` Methods" in this chapter for an example.

Using the *go, forward,* and *back* Methods

It's easy to put the methods of the `history` object to work. In fact, we've already seen how to do that in Chapter 4. In that example (Listing 04-05.html on the web site), I used the `back`, `forward`, and `go` methods to navigate forward and backward in the browser's history. Here's what the code looks like:

```
<HTML>
    <HEAD>
        <TITLE>Using the history object</TITLE>
        <SCRIPT LANGUAGE="JavaScript">
        <!--
        function back()
        {
            window.history.back()
        }
        function forward()
        {
            window.history.forward()
        }
        function back2()
        {
            window.history.go(-2)
```

```
    }
    function forward2()
    {
        window.history.go(2)
    }
    // -->
  </SCRIPT>
  </HEAD>

  <BODY>
      <H1>Using the history object</H1>
      <FORM>
          <BR>
          Click a button to go forward or back one page:
          <BR>
          <INPUT TYPE = BUTTON VALUE = "< Go back" ONCLICK = "back()">
          <INPUT TYPE = BUTTON VALUE = "Go forward >" ONCLICK = "forward()">
          <BR>
          <BR>
          Click a button to go forward or back two pages:
          <BR>
          <INPUT TYPE = BUTTON VALUE = "<< Go back 2" ONCLICK = "back2()">
          <INPUT TYPE = BUTTON VALUE = "Go forward 2 >>" ONCLICK = "forward2()">
      </FORM>
  </BODY>
</HTML>
```

You can see this code at work in Chapter 4 in Figure 4.6. Clicking the buttons in this example is like clicking the browser's forward and back buttons—except that we're also giving the user the option of moving two pages in either direction.

That's it! That completes our work with the `navigator`, `location`, and `history` objects in this chapter. As you can see, these objects give you control over the inner workings of the browser, determining browser type and version, navigating to new URLs, and moving forward and backward in the history list. In the next chapter, we'll leave the browser objects and start working with the HTML elements in JavaScript, starting with the HTML text elements.

11

Working with HTML
Text Elements

IN THIS CHAPTER, WE'LL TAKE A LOOK at working with various HTML
elements that display text, as well as working with text using text ranges
and text nodes in JavaScript.

In fact, we've already covered many text-handling HTML elements with
JavaScript's core HTML properties, methods, and events we saw in Chapter 5,
"Using Core HTML Properties," and 6, "Using Core HTML Methods and
Events." You can see the core HTML elements already covered in those
chapters in Table 5.3—I'll list the text-handling elements from that table
here in Table 11.1. These are all HTML text elements that we've already
covered.

Table 11.1 **JavaScript Core HTML Text Elements**

Properties			
ACRONYM	ADDRESS	B	BIG
CITE	CODE	DEL	DFN
EM	I	KBD	LISTING
P	PLAINTEXT	PRE	RT
RUBY	S	SAMP	SMALL
STRIKE	STRONG	SUB	SUP
TT	U	VAR	

However, other text-handling elements, such as the Internet Explorer
<MARQUEE> element, have additional capabilities beyond the core properties,
methods, and events; and I'll take a look at them in this chapter in depth.

While on the subject of working with text in web pages, we'll also take a
look at using text ranges in this chapter, including the Internet Explorer
TextRange and selection objects, as well as the Netscape Navigator Range
and selection objects. After you associate a text range with a section of text
in a web page, you can work with that text using JavaScript, much as you
would work with text in your program using String objects. The text range
objects we'll see in this chapter are getting bigger and bigger with each new
browser release, and we'll get a handle on them here. We'll also take a look at
handling text in web pages in terms of W3C text nodes.

I'll start now by taking a look at the text-handling HTML elements that
have capabilities beyond JavaScript's core HTML properties, methods, and
events. Some of these elements, such as <BLOCKQUOTE> coming up next,
aren't the most exciting HTML elements ever, but we'll cover them for
completeness.

The *<BLOCKQUOTE>* Element

You use the <BLOCKQUOTE> element for indented quotations, and most
browsers will indent text in this element automatically. This element object
has two properties beyond the core HTML properties we covered in
Chapter 5—blockDirection and cite—and you can find these properties
in Table 11.2. As with the other HTML elements we cover in this and the
coming chapters, JavaScript's core HTML properties, methods, and events
are also supported by this element. See Chapters 5 and 6 for the details.

Table 11.2 **The Properties of the *<BLOCKQUOTE>* Element (See
Chapters 5 and 6 for the JavaScript core HTML properties, methods,
and events that also apply to this element.)**

Property	NS2	NS3	NS4	NS6	IE3a	IE3b	IE4	IE5	IE5.5	IE6
blockDirection								x	x	x

Read-only
This property indicates whether the content in the block element flows
from left to right, or from right to left. Set to a string: ltr for content that
goes left to right, or rtl for content that goes right to left.

Property	NS2	NS3	NS4	NS6	IE3a	IE3b	IE4	IE5	IE5.5	IE6
cite									x	

Read/write
This property sets or retrieves reference information about the object. You set this to a URL string holding a citation reference. (The browser will not navigate to that URL automatically as it would for a hyperlink.)

The *
* Element

The <BR> element is a favorite for HTML authors, enabling you to insert a line break in a page. This element has only one property beyond the core set—clear—as you can see in Table 11.3.

Table 11.3 **The Properties of the *
* Element (See Chapters 5 and 6 for the JavaScript core HTML properties, methods, and events that also apply to this element.)**

Property	NS2	NS3	NS4	NS6	IE3a	IE3b	IE4	IE5	IE5.5	IE6
clear				x			x	x	x	x

Read/write
This property specifies the side on which floating objects may *not* be placed when a break is inserted into the document. Set this property to a string—here are the possible values: all (break is positioned below any floating object), left (break is positioned below any floating object on the left side), right (break is positioned below any floating object on the right side), and none (floating objects are allowed on any side).

The *<FONT>* Element

The <FONT> element is a popular one, even though it was deprecated in HTML 4.01 in favor of style sheets. This element has a few additional properties beyond the core HTML ones, as you see in Table 11.4.

Table 11.4   **The Properties of the *<FONT>* Element (See Chapters 5 and 6 for the JavaScript core HTML properties, methods, and events that also apply to this element.)**

Property	NS2	NS3	NS4	NS6	IE3a	IE3b	IE4	IE5	IE5.5	IE6
color				x		x	x	x	x	

Read/write
Specifies the color of the font, as a string. Set to a color triplet or a predefined color name the browser understands. In Internet Explorer 5+, you also can set this property to an expression using `setExpression`.

face				x		x	x	x	x	

Read/write
This property holds the requested typeface family. Set this property to a string, such as `"courier"`. You can specify a comma-separated list of typefaces, such as `"courier, arial, times-roman"`, and the browser will select the first one (reading left to right) that it supports.

size				x		x	x	x	x	

Read/write
This property sets or gets the font size used. Set this property to an integer in the range 1 through 7. (The largest font is 7.) You also can specify relative font sizes by using a sign, such as `"+1"`, which increments the font size from the value used in the surrounding text by one. You have more control over font size if you use style sheets.

The *<H1>-<H6>* Heading Elements

The heading elements <H1> to <H6> are block HTML elements, which means they're set off on their own line by browsers. These elements enable you to display headings of various sizes, with <H1> being the largest and <H6> being the smallest. These elements support an `align` property (although note that the ALIGN HTML attribute is actually deprecated in HTML 4.01 in favor of style sheets), as you see in Table 11.5.

Table 11.5   **The Properties of the <H1>-<H6> Elements (See Chapters 5 and 6 for the JavaScript core HTML properties, methods, and events that also apply to these elements.)**

Property	NS2	NS3	NS4	NS6	IE3a	IE3b	IE4	IE5	IE5.5	IE6
align				X			X	X	X	X

Read/write
This property sets or gets the alignment of the heading in its block. Set to "center" (aligns to the center), "justify" (aligns to the left and right edge), "left" (the default—aligns to the left edge), or "right" (aligns to the right edge).

The <HR> Element

The <HR> element displays a horizontal line, or rule, in a web page, visually separating page elements. This object has a few properties beyond the core set, and you can see them in Table 11.6.

Table 11.6   **The Properties of the <HR> Element (See Chapters 5 and 6 for the JavaScript core HTML properties, methods, and events that also apply to this element.)**

Property	NS2	NS3	NS4	NS6	IE3a	IE3b	IE4	IE5	IE5.5	IE6
align				X			X	X	X	X

Read/write
This property sets or gets the alignment of the rule. Set to "center" (aligns to the center), "justify" (aligns to the left and right edge), "left" (the default—aligns to the left edge), or "right" (aligns to the right edge).

Property	NS2	NS3	NS4	NS6	IE3a	IE3b	IE4	IE5	IE5.5	IE6
color				X			X	X	X	X

Read/write
Specifies the color of the rule, as a string. Set to a color triplet or a predefined color name the browser understands. In Internet Explorer 5+, you also can set this property to an expression using setExpression.

Property	NS2	NS3	NS4	NS6	IE3a	IE3b	IE4	IE5	IE5.5	IE6
noShade				X			X	X	X	X

Read/write
This property sets or gets a value indicating whether the rule is drawn with 3D shading. Set to true for no 3D shading or false (the default) for 3D shading.

continues ▶

Table 11.6 **Continued**

Property	NS2	NS3	NS4	NS6	IE3a	IE3b	IE4	IE5	IE5.5	IE6
size				X			X	X	X	X

Read/write

This property sets the height of the rule, in pixels. Set to an integer value.

Property	NS2	NS3	NS4	NS6	IE3a	IE3b	IE4	IE5	IE5.5	IE6
width				X			X	X	X	X

Read/write

This property sets the width of the rule. Set to an integer to specify a width in pixels, or to a string ending with a percent sign (%) to indicate a percentage of the rule's container (usually the browser's client area) width.

The *<LABEL>* Element

You use the <LABEL> element to specify a label for a control in a form such as a text field or a button. This element has two properties not covered by the core list, and you can see those properties in Table 11.7.

Table 11.7 **The Properties of the *<LABEL>* Element (See Chapters 5 and 6 for the JavaScript core HTML properties, methods, and events that also apply to this element.)**

Property	NS2	NS3	NS4	NS6	IE3a	IE3b	IE4	IE5	IE5.5	IE6
form				X						X

Read/write

This property holds a reference to the form object the control is embedded in.

Property	NS2	NS3	NS4	NS6	IE3a	IE3b	IE4	IE5	IE5.5	IE6
htmlFor				X			X	X	X	X

Read/write

This property sets or gets the object to which the label object is assigned.

The <*MARQUEE*> Element

The <MARQUEE> element is a popular one among Internet Explorer program-mers. This element enables you to display scrolling text in an easy way. Here's an example putting a few marquees to work:

(Listing 11-01.html on the web site)

```
<HTML>
    <HEAD>
        <TITLE>
            Using the &lt;MARQUEE&gt; element
        </TITLE>
    </HEAD>

    <BODY>

        <MARQUEE ALIGN="TOP" LOOP="INFINITE" BEHAVIOR="BOUNCE"
            BGCOLOR="#00FF00" DIRECTION="RIGHT">
            <H2>
                Marquee number 1
            </H2>
        </MARQUEE>

        <H1>Using Marquees</H1>

        <MARQUEE ALIGN="LEFT" LOOP="INFINITE" BEHAVIOR="SCROLL"
            BGCOLOR="#FF0000" HEIGHT=40 WIDTH=300 DIRECTION="DOWN">
            <H2>
                Marquee number 2
            </H2>
        </MARQUEE>

        <MARQUEE ALIGN="TOP" LOOP="INFINITE" BEHAVIOR="SLIDE"
            BGCOLOR="#00FFFF" WIDTH=100% DIRECTION="RIGHT">
            <H2>
                Marquee number 3
            </H2>
        </MARQUEE>
    </BODY>
</HTML>
```

You can see the results of this code in Figure 11.1; the various marquees are scrolling different ways and in different colors.

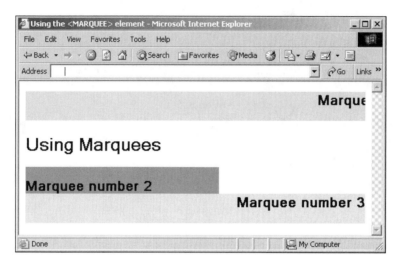

Figure 11.1 Using Internet Explorer marquees.

The <MARQUEE> element has a number of properties, methods, and events beyond the core set, and you can see them in Table 11.8.

Table 11.8 **The Properties, Methods, and Events of the <MARQUEE> Element (See Chapters 5 and 6 for the JavaScript core HTML properties, methods, and events that also apply to this element.)**

Property	Methods	Events
behavior	start	onbounce
bgColor	stop	onfinish
direction		onerrorupdate
height		onstart
hspace		
loop		
scrollAmount		
scrollDelay		
trueSpeed		
vspace		
width		

You can find the details on the <MARQUEE> element's properties in Table 11.9, its methods in Table 11.10, and its events in Table 11.11.

Table 11.9 **The Properties of the <*MARQUEE*> Element (See Chapters 5 and 6 for the JavaScript core HTML properties, methods, and events that also apply to this element.)**

Property	NS2	NS3	NS4	NS6	IE3a	IE3b	IE4	IE5	IE5.5	IE6
behavior							X	X	X	X

Read/write
Sets or gets how the text scrolls in the marquee. May be set to these strings: "`scroll`" (the default—the marquee will scroll in the direction specified by the `direction` property—the text scrolls past the end and then starts over), "`alternate`" (the marquee's scroll action reverses direction when the text reaches the edge), or "`slide`" (the marquee scrolls in the direction specified by the `direction` property, but here the text scrolls to the end and stops).

bgColor							X	X	X	X

Read/write
Specifies the background color of the marquee, as a string. Set to a color triplet or a predefined color name the browser understands. In Internet Explorer 5+, you also can set this property to an expression using `setExpression`.

direction							X	X	X	X

Read/write
Specifies the direction for the marquee to scroll. Set to one of these strings: "`left`" (the default—makes the marquee scroll left), "`right`" (makes the marquee scroll right), "`down`" (makes the marquee scroll down), or "`up`" (makes the marquee scroll up).

height							X	X	X	X

Read/write
Sets the height of the marquee. Set to an integer value measured in pixels, or a string ending in `%` to indicate a percentage of the parent element's height.

hspace							X	X	X	X

Read/write
Sets or gets the horizontal margin for the marquee. Set to an integer value measured in pixels. (The default is 0.)

loop							X	X	X	X

Read/write
Sets or retrieves the number of times a marquee will play. Set to 0, -1, or `INFINITE` to make the marquee play forever, or an integer count to make the marquee play a specific number of times.

continues ▶

Table 11.9 **Continued**

Property	NS2	NS3	NS4	NS6	IE3a	IE3b	IE4	IE5	IE5.5	IE6
scrollAmount							x	x	x	x

Read/write
Sets or gets the number of pixels the text scrolls between each redrawing of the marquee. The default value is 6. Set this property to an integer.

Property	NS2	NS3	NS4	NS6	IE3a	IE3b	IE4	IE5	IE5.5	IE6
scrollDelay							x	x	x	x

Read/write
Sets or gets the speed of the marquee scroll in milliseconds, giving the time in milliseconds between redrawings of the text. Set to an integer; the default value is 85.

Property	NS2	NS3	NS4	NS6	IE3a	IE3b	IE4	IE5	IE5.5	IE6
trueSpeed							x	x	x	x

Read/write
Sets or gets a value indicating whether the position of the marquee is calculated using the scrollDelay and scrollAmount properties and the time from the computer's clock. Set to false (the default) to make the marquee measure times based on 60-millisecond ticks of the clock (meaning every scrollDelay value under 60 is ignored, and the marquee advances the amount of scrollAmount each 60 milliseconds) or to true to make the marquee scroll the text by scrollAmount after the number of milliseconds set in scrollDelay.

Property	NS2	NS3	NS4	NS6	IE3a	IE3b	IE4	IE5	IE5.5	IE6
vspace							x	x	x	x

Read/write
Sets or gets the vertical margin for the marquee. Set to an integer value measured in pixels. (The default is 0.)

Property	NS2	NS3	NS4	NS6	IE3a	IE3b	IE4	IE5	IE5.5	IE6
width							x	x	x	x

Read/write
This property sets the width of the marquee. Set to an integer to specify a width in pixels, or to a string ending with a percent sign (%) to indicate a percentage of the rule's container (usually the browser's client area) width.

Table 11.10   **The Methods of the <*MARQUEE*> Element (See Chapters 5 and 6 for the JavaScript core HTML properties, methods, and events that also apply to this element.)**

Method	NS2	NS3	NS4	NS6	IE3a	IE3b	IE4	IE5	IE5.5	IE6
start							X	X	X	X

Returns: Nothing
Starts scrolling the marquee.
Syntax: *marquee*.start(). Note that this method does not cause the onstart event to occur.

| stop | | | | | | | X | X | X | X |

Returns: Nothing
Stops scrolling the marquee.
Syntax: *marquee*.stop().

Table 11.11   **The Events of the <*MARQUEE*> Element (See Chapters 5 and 6 for the JavaScript core HTML properties, methods, and events that also apply to this element.)**

Event	NS2	NS3	NS4	NS6	IE3a	IE3b	IE4	IE5	IE5.5	IE6
onbounce							X	X	X	X

Occurs when the behavior property of the marquee object is set to "alternate" and the contents of the marquee reach the edge of the marquee.

| onerrorupdate | | | | | | | X | X | X | X |

Occurs in data-bound objects when an error occurs while updating the data in the data source.

| onfinish | | | | | | | X | X | X | X |

Occurs when marquee completes its looping.

| onstart | | | | | | | X | X | X | X |

Occurs at the beginning of every loop of the marquee.

The <Q> Element

The <Q> element is used to set a quotation aside from other text; unlike the <BLOCKQUOTE> element, this element is an inline, not block element (which means it doesn't get its own separate line of text). This element really contains only one property not in the JavaScript core HTML property set—cite, which you can see in Table 11.12.

Table 11.12   **The Properties of the <Q> Element (See Chapters 5 and 6 for the JavaScript core HTML properties, methods, and events that also apply to this element.)**

Property	NS2	NS3	NS4	NS6	IE3a	IE3b	IE4	IE5	IE5.5	IE6
cite										x

Read/write
This property sets or retrieves reference information about the object. You set this to a URL string holding a citation reference. (The browser will not navigate to that URL automatically as it would for a hyperlink.)

And that completes our look at the HTML text elements. Now it's time to start working with text directly, using text ranges.

The *TextRange* Object

The Internet Explorer TextRange object enables you to work with a range of text in a web page. In fact, we've already seen an example using text ranges in Chapter 9, "Using the *document* and *body* Objects"—that example enabled you to access text the user selected with the mouse in a web page. In the Internet Explorer, you use the document.selection property, then create a text range from that property using the createRange method, and use the text range's text property to find the selected text. Here's what that looked like (Listing 09-07.html on the web site):

```
<HTML>
    <HEAD>
        <TITLE>Reading Selected Text</TITLE>
        <SCRIPT LANGUAGE="JavaScript">
            <!--
            function getSelected()
            {
                if (navigator.appName == "Microsoft Internet Explorer") {
                    docum+ent.form1.text1.value = document.selection.createRange().text
                }
                if(navigator.appName == "Netscape") {
```

```
                document.form1.text1.value = document.getSelection()
                }
            }
            // -->
        </SCRIPT>
    </HEAD>

    <BODY ONMOUSEUP="getSelected()">
        <H1>Reading Selected Text</H1>
        Select some of this text!
        <BR>
        <FORM NAME="form1">
            You selected: <INPUT TYPE="TEXT" NAME="text1">
        </FORM>
    </BODY>
</HTML>
```

You can see the results in Chapter 9, in Figure 9.4, where I'm selecting some text and the code is displaying what text was selected.

In this and similar ways, the `TextRange` object gives you access to the text in a web page. You can find the properties and methods of the `TextRange` object in Table 11.13 in overview. You can find the properties of this object in depth in Table 11.14, and its methods in Table 11.15.

Table 11.13 **Overview of the Properties and Methods of the** *TextRange* **Object**

Properties	Methods
boundingHeight	collapse
boundingLeft	compareEndPoints
boundingTop	duplicate
boundingWidth	execCommand
htmlText	expand
offsetLeft	findText
offsetTop	getBookmark
text	getBoundingClientRect
	getClientRects
	inRange
	isEqual
	move
	moveEnd
	moveStart

continues ▶

Table 11.13 **Continued**

Properties	Methods
	moveToBookmark
	moveToElementText
	moveToPoint
	parentElement
	pasteHTML
	queryCommandEnabled
	queryCommandIndeterm
	queryCommandState
	queryCommandSupported
	queryCommandValue
	scrollIntoView
	select
	setEndPoint

Table 11.14 **The Properties of the *TextRange* Object**

Property	NS2	NS3	NS4	NS6	IE3a	IE3b	IE4	IE5	IE5.5	IE6
boundingHeight							x	x	x	x

Read-only
Holds the height of the rectangle that bounds the TextRange object. This is an integer value measured in pixels.

boundingLeft							x	x	x	x

Read-only
Holds the distance between the left edge of the TextRange object and the left side of the object that contains the TextRange. This is an integer value measured in pixels.

boundingTop							x	x	x	x

Read-only
Holds the distance between the top of the TextRange object and the top side of the object that contains the TextRange. This is an integer value measured in pixels.

boundingWidth							x	x	x	x

Read-only
Holds the width of the rectangle that bounds the TextRange object. This is an integer value measured in pixels.

Property	NS2	NS3	NS4	NS6	IE3a	IE3b	IE4	IE5	IE5.5	IE6
htmlText							x	x	x	x

Read-only
Holds the HTML of the text in the TextRange object as a string that is a valid HTML fragment.

Property	NS2	NS3	NS4	NS6	IE3a	IE3b	IE4	IE5	IE5.5	IE6
offsetLeft	See Chapter 5.									
offsetTop	See Chapter 5.									
text							x	x	x	x

Read/write
Sets or gets the text in the range, as a string. See "Creating Text Ranges" in this chapter.

Table 11.15 **The Methods of the *TextRange* Object**

Method	NS2	NS3	NS4	NS6	IE3a	IE3b	IE4	IE5	IE5.5	IE6
collapse							x	x	x	x

Returns: Nothing
Shrinks a text range down to an insertion point.
Syntax: *TextRange*.collapse([*start*]). Here, start can be true (the default) to move the insertion point to the beginning of the text range, or false to move the insertion point to the end of the text range.

Method	NS2	NS3	NS4	NS6	IE3a	IE3b	IE4	IE5	IE5.5	IE6
compareEndPoints							x	x	x	x

Returns: Integer
Compares an end point of a TextRange object with an end point of another range.
Syntax: *TextRange*.compareEndPoints(*type*, *range*), where the possible values of *type* are StartToEnd (compares the start of the *TextRange* object with the end of the *range* parameter), StartToStart (compares the start of the *TextRange* object with the start of the *range* parameter), EndToStart (compares the end of the *TextRange* object with the start of the *range* parameter), EndToEnd (compares the end of the *TextRange* object with the end of the *range* parameter). The *range* parameter holds the range to compare the current one to. Returns ·1 if the comparison point in the *TextRange* object is further to the left than the comparison point in *range*, 0 if the comparison point the *TextRange* object is at the same location as the comparison point in *range*, and 1 if the comparison point in the *TextRange* object is farther to the right than the comparison point in *range*.

continues ▶

Table 11.15 **Continued**

Method	NS2	NS3	NS4	NS6	IE3a	IE3b	IE4	IE5	IE5.5	IE6
duplicate							x	x	x	x

Returns: *TextRange* object
Duplicates and returns a new copy of the text range.
Syntax: *TextRange*.duplicate().

| execCommand | | | | | | | x | x | x | x |

Returns: Boolean
This is a big one—see "Using execCommand" in Chapter 9 for the syntax
and possible parameters (listed in Table 9.6) of this method.

| expand | | | | | | | x | x | x | x |

Returns: Boolean
This method expands a range (even if it was not collapsed) to the next
word, character, and so on.
Syntax: TextRange.expand(*unit*), where *unit* is one of "character"
(expands by a character), "word" (expands by a word), "sentence"
(expands by a sentence), or "textedit" (expands to enclose the entire
range). This method returns true if successful, and false otherwise.

| findText | | | | | | | x | x | x | x |

Returns: Boolean
Searches a range for text. See "Finding and Replacing Text" in this chapter
for the syntax and an example.

| getBookmark | | | | | | | x | x | x | x |

Returns: Bookmark (string)
Gets a bookmark (a string) that you can use with the moveToBookmark
method to move back to the same range.
Syntax: *TextRange*.getBookmark(). Returns a bookmark if successful, or
null otherwise.

getBoundingClientRect   See Chapter 6.

getClientRects   See Chapter 6.

| inRange | | | | | | | x | x | x | x |

Returns: Boolean
Returns a value indicating whether one range is contained within another.
Syntax: *TextRange*.inRange(*range*). Returns true if *range* is in (or is equal
to) *TextRange*, false otherwise.

Method	NS2	NS3	NS4	NS6	IE3a	IE3b	IE4	IE5	IE5.5	IE6
isEqual							X	X	X	X

Returns: Boolean
Indicates whether one range is equal to another.
Syntax: *TextRange*.isEqual(*range*). Returns true if *TextRange* equals *range*. Returns false otherwise.

Method	NS2	NS3	NS4	NS6	IE3a	IE3b	IE4	IE5	IE5.5	IE6
move							X	X	X	X

Returns: Integer
Moves a range a specified number of items, such as characters, words, or sentences.
Syntax: *TextRange*.move(*item* [, *count*]). Here, *item* can be one of "character" (moves by a character), "word" (moves by a word), "sentence" (moves by a sentence), or "textedit" (moves to the start of end of the original range); and *count* is the number of items to move by (can be positive or negative). Returns the number of items the range was moved by.

Method	NS2	NS3	NS4	NS6	IE3a	IE3b	IE4	IE5	IE5.5	IE6
moveEnd							X	X	X	X

Returns: Integer
Moves the end of the range.
Syntax: *TextRange*.moveEnd(*item* [, *count*]). Here, *item* can be one of "character" (moves the end by a character), "word" (moves the end by a word), "sentence" (moves the end by a sentence), or "textedit" (moves to the end of the original range); and *count* is the number of items to move the end by (can be positive or negative). Returns the number of items the end of the range was moved by.

Method	NS2	NS3	NS4	NS6	IE3a	IE3b	IE4	IE5	IE5.5	IE6
moveStart							X	X	X	X

Returns: Integer
Moves the start of the range.
Syntax: *TextRange*.moveStart(*item* [, *count*]). Here, *item* can be one of "character" (moves the start by a character), "word" (moves the start by a word), "sentence" (moves the start by a sentence), or "textedit" (moves to the start of the original range); and *count* is the number of items to move the start by (can be positive or negative). Returns the number of items the start of the range was moved by.

Method	NS2	NS3	NS4	NS6	IE3a	IE3b	IE4	IE5	IE5.5	IE6
moveToBookmark							X	X	X	X

Returns: Boolean
Moves the range to a bookmark set with getBookmark.
Syntax: *TextRange*.moveToBookmark(*bookmark*), where *bookmark* is a string returned by getBookmark. Returns true if successful, false otherwise.

continues ▶

Table 11.15 **Continued**

Method	NS2	NS3	NS4	NS6	IE3a	IE3b	IE4	IE5	IE5.5	IE6
moveToElementText								X	X	X

Returns: Nothing

Moves the text range so that the start and end positions of the range surround the text in the given element.

Syntax: *TextRange*.moveToElementText(*element*), where *element* is the element whose text you want to enclose.

Method	NS2	NS3	NS4	NS6	IE3a	IE3b	IE4	IE5	IE5.5	IE6
moveToPoint							X	X	X	X

Returns: Nothing

Moves the start and end positions of the text range to the given point, collapsing the range to that point.

Syntax: *TextRange*.moveToPoint(*x, y*) where *x* and *y* give the location of the point to move to, measured with respect to the upper left of the browser's client area, in pixels.

Method	NS2	NS3	NS4	NS6	IE3a	IE3b	IE4	IE5	IE5.5	IE6
parentElement							X	X	X	X

Returns: Element

Returns the parent element of the text range if successful, null otherwise.

Syntax: *TextRange*.parentElement().

Method	NS2	NS3	NS4	NS6	IE3a	IE3b	IE4	IE5	IE5.5	IE6
pasteHTML							X	X	X	X

Pastes HTML text into the given text range, replacing any previous text and HTML elements in the range.

Syntax: *TextRange*.pasteHTML(*HTMLText*), where *HTMLText* is the HTML to paste into the range. See "Creating Text Ranges" in this chapter for an example.

Method										
queryCommandEnabled	See Chapter 9 (Table 9.5).									
queryCommandIndeterm	See Chapter 9 (Table 9.5).									
queryCommandState	See Chapter 9 (Table 9.5).									
queryCommandSupported	See Chapter 9 (Table 9.5).									
queryCommandValue	See Chapter 9 (Table 9.5).									
scrollIntoView	See Chapter 6.									

Method	NS2	NS3	NS4	NS6	IE3a	IE3b	IE4	IE5	IE5.5	IE6
select							X	X	X	X

Returns: Nothing

Selects the contents of the text range, making the selection visible in the browser.

Syntax: *TextRange*.select(). See "Selecting Text" in this chapter for an example.

Method	NS2	NS3	NS4	NS6	IE3a	IE3b	IE4	IE5	IE5.5	IE6
setEndPoint							x	x	x	x

Returns: Nothing

Sets the end point of one range based on the end point of another range. Syntax: *TextRange*.setEndPoint(*type, range*), where the possible values of *type* are StartToEnd (moves the start of the *TextRange* object to the end of the *range* parameter), StartToStart (moves the start of the *TextRange* object to the start of the *range* parameter), EndToStart (moves the end of the *TextRange* object to the start of the *range* parameter), EndToEnd (moves the end of the *TextRange* object to the end of the *range* parameter). The *range* parameter holds the range to move with respect to.

These two tables give us the details on text ranges. Now let's put them to work.

Creating Text Ranges

To create a text range, you can use the <BODY> element's createTextRange method (see Table 9.12). After you have a text range, several methods (as you can see in Table 11.15 such as move, moveStart, moveEnd, moveToElementText, expand, and so on) enable you to position the text range as you want it.

Here's an example we've already seen in Chapter 5—it's Listing 05-15.html on the web site. In this case, I create a text range, move it to enclose an element's text, and then use the text range's pasteHTML method to replace the text in the range, all when the user clicks a button:

```
<HTML>
    <HEAD>
        <TITLE>
            Using Text Ranges
        </TITLE>

        <SCRIPT LANGAUGE="JavaScript">
            <!--
            function replaceText()
            {
                if(document.body.isTextEdit){
                    var range = document.body.createTextRange()
                    range.moveToElementText(div1)
                    range.pasteHTML("Here is the replacement text!")
                }
            }
            // -->
        </SCRIPT>
    </HEAD>

    <BODY>
```

continues ▶

```
        <H1>Using Text Ranges</H1>
        <INPUT TYPE=BUTTON VALUE="Click Me!" onclick="replaceText()">
        <BR>
        <BR>
        <DIV ID="div1" STYLE="font-family:Arial, sans-serif; font-weight:bold">
            Click the button to replace all this text.
        </DIV>
    </BODY>
</HTML>
```

You can see the results in Chapter 5, in Figure 5.12, where I've clicked the button and replaced the original text with new text.

You also can create text ranges for controls such as buttons, text fields, text areas, and so on. Here's an example that creates a text range corresponding to the text in the third button in a document, and uses the text range's `text` property to change the button caption to Click Me!:

```
<SCRIPT LANGUAGE="JavaScript">
    var buttons = document.all.tags("BUTTON")
    var range = buttons[2].createTextRange()
    range.text = "Click Me!"
</SCRIPT>
```

Finding and Replacing Text

Another powerful text range technique is to use the `findText` method to search for text. Here's how that method works:

```
TextRange.findText(text [, searchScope] [, flags])
```

Here are the parameters you use with this method:

- **text.** String that holds the text to find.
- **searchScope.** Integer that holds the number of characters to search (starting from the start of the range). A positive integer results in a forward search, and a negative integer results in a backward search.
- **flags.** Integer that holds a flag to indicate the type of search (see the following list.)

Here are the possible values for the `flags` parameter—you can OR these values together with the JavaScript bitwise OR operator, | (see Chapter 2, "The JavaScript Language: Data, Operators, and Branching"), to specify more than one option (such as 2 | 4, which makes `findText` search for whole words only and match case):

- **0** The default. Matches partial words.
- **1** Matches backward.
- **2** Matches whole words only.
- **4** Matches case.
- **131072** Matches bytes.
- **536870912** Matches diacritical marks.
- **1073741824** Matches the Kashida character.
- **2147483648** Matches the AlefHamza character.

This method returns true if the text you're searching for was found, and false otherwise. Here's an example. In this case, I'll search an entire document for the text *Hi* and replace it with the word *Hello*:

(Listing 11-02.html on the web site)

```
<HTML>
    <HEAD>
        <TITLE>Finding text in text ranges</TITLE>
        <SCRIPT LANGUAGE="JavaScript">
            <!--
            function hi()
            {
                var range1 = document.body.createTextRange()
                while(range1.findText("Hi")){
                    range1.text = "Hello"
                }
            }
            // -->
        </SCRIPT>
    </HEAD>

    <BODY ONLOAD="hi()">
    <H1>Finding text in text ranges</H1>
        <P>
            He said, "Hi there!"
        </P>
    </BODY>
</HTML>
```

You can see the results in Figure 11.2, where the code has replaced *Hi* with *Hello* as the page loaded.

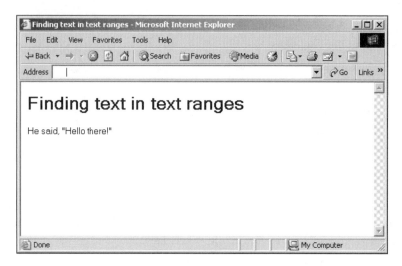

Figure 11.2   Finding and replacing text with text ranges.

Selecting Text

You can use the `select` method to select text in a web browser using text ranges. Here's an example that shows how that works. When you click the button in this web page, the code creates a text range, moves that text range to encompass the text in a `<SPAN>` element, and selects that text:

(Listing 11-03.html on the web site)

```
<HTML>
    <HEAD>
        <TITLE>
            Selecting Text
        </TITLE>

        <SCRIPT LANGAUGE="JavaScript">
            <!--
            function selectRange()
            {
                range = document.body.createTextRange()
                range.moveToElementText(text1)
                range.select()
            }
            // -->
        </SCRIPT>
    </HEAD>

    <BODY>
```

```
<H1>
    Selecting Text
</H1>

<FORM>
    <INPUT TYPE="BUTTON" VALUE="Click Me" ONCLICK="selectRange()">
</FORM>
<BR>
<SPAN ID="text1">Click the button to select this text.</SPAN>
    </BODY>
</HTML>
```

You can see the results in Figure 11.3, where I'm selecting text in a browser with the click of a button.

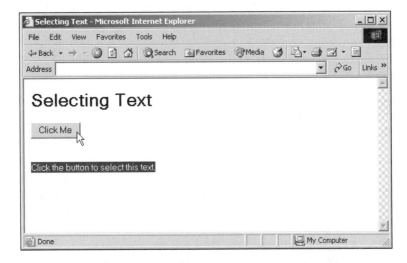

Figure 11.3   Selecting text with text ranges.

Working with selected text is such a common thing to do that you can use a special object—the `selection` object—to handle such tasks.

The *selection* Object

Both the Internet Explorer and the Netscape Navigator support a `selection` object, and, of course, they're different. In fact, no public documentation is available for the Netscape Navigator's `selection` object yet. You can see the properties of the Internet Explorer's `selection` object in Table 11.16, its methods in Table 11.17, and its events in Table 11.18. You can access this object for a document with the `document` object's `selection` property (see Table 9.1).

Tip

Although Netscape has yet to document their selection object, we do know that it contains a getRangeAt method, and I put that method to work in "Using Ranges" later in this chapter.

Table 11.16 **The Properties of the *selection* Object**

Property	NS2	NS3	NS4	NS6	IE3a	IE3b	IE4	IE5	IE5.5	IE6
type							X	X	X	X

Read-only

Retrieves the type of selection, as a string. Possible values: "none" (there is no selection), "text" (the selection is a text selection), or "control" (the selection is a control).

typeDetail									X	X

Read-only

Some nonbrowser applications can provide a custom selections and can set values for this property that indicate the selection type. The implementation of this property in the Internet Explorer returns undefined.

TextRange									X	X

Read-only

Holds an array of the TextRange objects in the selection. An individual text range can be accessed as *selection*.TextRange(*index* [, *subIndex*]). Here, *index* is an integer or string that indicates the element or collection to get. If this parameter is an integer, this method returns the text range at the given position. If this parameter is a string and there is more than one text range with the name or id property equal to that string, this method returns all matching elements as an array. The *subIndex* parameter is used when *index* is a string and more than one text range has the same name or id property, and lets you specify which text range to retrieve.

Table 11.17 **The Methods of the *selection* Object**

Method	NS2	NS3	NS4	NS6	IE3a	IE3b	IE4	IE5	IE5.5	IE6
clear							X	X	X	X

Returns: Nothing

Clears the contents of the selection.

Syntax: *selection*.clear().

Method	NS2	NS3	NS4	NS6	IE3a	IE3b	IE4	IE5	IE5.5	IE6
createRange							x	x	x	x

Returns: `TextRange` object
Creates a `TextRange` object from the current text selection. Sytnax: `selection.createRange()`.

| CreateRangeCollection | | | | | | | | | x | x |

Returns: Collection of `TextRange` objects
Creates a `TextRange` object collection from the current selection—currently, the whole selection is returned in one `TextRange` object. Theoretically, nonbrowser applications can support multiple selections and can return a collection of `TextRange` objects.

| empty | | | | | | | x | x | x | x |

Returns: Nothing
Cancels the current selection, sets the selection type to none, and sets the item property to `null`. Sytnax: `selection.empty()`.

Table 11.18 **The Events of the *selection* Object**

Property	NS2	NS3	NS4	NS6	IE3a	IE3b	IE4	IE5	IE5.5	IE6
ontimeerror	See Chapter 6.									

In fact, we've already seen how to use the Internet Explorer's `selection` object in Chapter 9 (see Listing 09-07.html on the web site). In that example, you could make a selection using the mouse, and as soon as you did, the selected text appeared in a text field.

Here's the code:

```
<HTML>
    <HEAD>
        <TITLE>Reading Selected Text</TITLE>
        <SCRIPT LANGUAGE="JavaScript">
            <!--
            function getSelected()
            {
                if (navigator.appName == "Microsoft Internet Explorer") {
                    document.form1.text1.value = document.selection.createRange().text
                }
                if(navigator.appName == "Netscape") {
                    document.form1.text1.value = document.getSelection()
                }
            }
```

continues ▶

```
        // -->
      </SCRIPT>
  </HEAD>

  <BODY ONMOUSEUP="getSelected()">
      <H1>Reading Selected Text</H1>
      Select some of this text!
      <BR>
      <FORM NAME="form1">
          You selected: <INPUT TYPE="TEXT" NAME="text1">
      </FORM>
  </BODY>
</HTML>
```

You can see the results in Chapter 9, Figure 9.4, where I'm selecting some text and the code is displaying it.

The *Range* Object

The Internet Explorer's TextRange object is a fairly popular one, and the W3C has been working to generalize that object into the Range object—which the Internet Explorer does not (yet) implement. Range objects are more general than text ranges—they can contain ranges of HTML from a Web page, including elements and text. Using this object gives you a way to cut up documents in other ways besides using W3C node trees, which some programmers find hard to work with.

To some extent, the Range object has been implemented in Netscape Navigator 6. You can see the properties and methods of this object in that browser in Table 11.19 in overview, and in Tables 11.20 and 11.21 in depth.

Table 11.19 **Overview of the Properties and Methods of the** *Range* **Object**

Properties	Methods
collapsed	cloneRange
commonAncestorContainer	collapse
endContainer	compareBoundaryPoints
endOffset	createContextualFragment
startContainer	deleteContents
startOffset	detach
	insertNode
	isValidFragment
	selectNode

Properties	Methods
	selectNodeContents
	setEnd
	setEndAfter
	setEndBefore
	setStart
	setStartAfter
	setStartBefore
	toString

Table 11.20 **The Properties of the *Range* Object**

Property	NS2	NS3	NS4	NS6	IE3a	IE3b	IE4	IE5	IE5.5	IE6
collapsed				x						

Read-only
This is a Boolean value that, if true, indicates the start and end of the range are at the same point, which means the range is "collapsed." If false, the range is not collapsed.

commonAncestorContainer				x						

Read-only
Holds a reference to the document tree node that the start and end of the range have in common.

endContainer				x						

Read-only
Holds a reference to the document tree node that contains the end of the range.

endOffset				x						

Read-only
Holds the number of characters or nodes between the end of a range and its containing node.

startContainer				x						

Read-only
Holds a reference to the document tree node that contains the start of the range.

startOffset				x						

Holds the number of characters or nodes between the start of a range and its containing node.

Table 11.21 **The Methods of the *Range* Object**

Method	NS2	NS3	NS4	NS6	IE3a	IE3b	IE4	IE5	IE5.5	IE6
cloneRange				x						

Returns: Range object
Clones a range and returns a new copy of it.
Syntax: *Range*.cloneContents(). Netscape has also announced a cloneContents method, but it's not yet supported in Netscape Navigator 6.

| collapse | | | | x | | | | | | |

Returns: Nothing
Collapses a range down to a single insertion point.
Syntax: Range.collapse(*start*). The *start* parameter is true (the default) if you want the collapsed range to correspond to the beginning of the range, false if you want it to correspond to the end of the range.

| compareBoundaryPoints | | | | x | | | | | | |

Returns: Integer
Compares the start and end positions of two ranges.
Syntax: *Range*.compareBoundaryPoints(*type*, *range*), where *type* can be Range.START_TO_END (compares the start of the *Range* object with the end of the *range* parameter), Range.START_TO_START (compares the start of the *Range* object with the start of the *range* parameter), Range.END_TO_START (compares the end of the *Range* object with the start of the *range* parameter), Range.START_TO_END (compares the end of the *Range* object with the end of the *range* parameter). The *range* parameter holds the range to compare the current one to. Returns -1 if the comparison point in the *Range* object is farther to the left than the comparison point in *range*, 0 if the comparison point in the *Range* object is at the same location as the comparison point in *range*, and 1 if the comparison point in the *Range* object is farther to the right than the comparison point in *range*.

| createContextualFragment | | | | x | | | | | | |

Returns: Document fragment
This method creates an HTML string that you can insert into a node tree, avoiding the need to use createElement, createTextNode, and so on.
Syntax: *Range*.createContextualFragment(*text*), where *text* is the new HTML string.

Method	NS2	NS3	NS4	NS6	IE3a	IE3b	IE4	IE5	IE5.5	IE6
deleteContents				x						

Returns: Nothing
Deletes the contents of a range from the document tree.
Syntax: `Range.deleteContents()`.

| detach | | | | x | | | | | | |

Returns: Nothing
Eliminates a `Range` object from the current document. There's no need to do this, unless you want to save resources. When you detach a `Range` object, it's gone.
Syntax: `Range.detach()`.

| insertNode | | | | x | | | | | | |

Returns: Nothing
This method is the one you use to insert a node at the start of a range. Unfortunately, its implementation in Netscape Navigator 6.0 doesn't work.
Syntax: `Range.insertNode(node)`, where *node* is the node to insert, such as a text of element node.

| isValidFragment | | | | x | | | | | | |

Returns: Boolean
Indicates whether specific text can be converted to a valid document fragment node using the `createContextFragment` method.
Syntax: `Range.isValidFragment(text)`. Returns true if so, false otherwise.

| selectNode | | | | x | | | | | | |

Returns: Nothing
This method enables you to surround a node with a `Range`.
Syntax: `Range.selectNode(node)`, where *node* is the node to select. You can surround element or text nodes with this method. If you surround an element node, the start and end of the new range is the next outer element; if you surround a text node, the start and end of the new range is the parent element of the text node.

| selectNodeContents | | | | x | | | | | | |

Returns: Nothing
This method enables you to surround a node's contents with a `Range`.
Syntax: `Range.selectNodeContents(node)`, where *node* is the node to select. You can surround element or text nodes with this method. If you surround an element node, the start and end of the new range is the same element node you pass to this method; if you surround a text node, the start and end of the new range is the text node itself, and the range is collapsed at the beginning of the text.

continues ▶

Table 11.21 **Continued**

Method	NS2	NS3	NS4	NS6	IE3a	IE3b	IE4	IE5	IE5.5	IE6
setEnd				x						

Returns: Nothing
This method enables you to set the end of a range.
Syntax: *Range*.setEnd(*node, offset*), where *node* is a reference node you're setting the end with respect to, and *offset* is the offset of the new end of the range. If *node* is an element node, *offset* is measured in child elements; if *node* is a text node, *offset* is measured in characters.

Method	NS2	NS3	NS4	NS6	IE3a	IE3b	IE4	IE5	IE5.5	IE6
setEndAfter				x						

Returns: Nothing
Enables you to set the end of a range after an existing node.
Syntax: *Range*.setEndAfter(*node*), where *node* is a node you're setting your position with respect to.

Method	NS2	NS3	NS4	NS6	IE3a	IE3b	IE4	IE5	IE5.5	IE6
setEndBefore				x						

Returns: Nothing
Enables you to set the end of a range before an existing node.
Syntax: *Range*.setEndBefore(*node*), where *node* is a node you're setting your position with respect to.

Method	NS2	NS3	NS4	NS6	IE3a	IE3b	IE4	IE5	IE5.5	IE6
setStart				x						

Returns: Nothing
This method enables you to set the start of a range.
Syntax: *Range*.setStart(*node, offset*), where *node* is a reference node you're setting the start with respect to, and *offset* is the offset of the new start of the range. If *node* is an element node, *offset* is measured in child elements; if *node* is a text node, *offset* is measured in characters.

Method	NS2	NS3	NS4	NS6	IE3a	IE3b	IE4	IE5	IE5.5	IE6
setStartAfter				x						

Returns: Nothing
Enables you to set the start of a range after an existing node.
Syntax: *Range*.setStartAfter(*node*), where *node* is a node you're setting your position with respect to.

Method	NS2	NS3	NS4	NS6	IE3a	IE3b	IE4	IE5	IE5.5	IE6
setStartBefore				x						

Returns: Nothing
Enables you to set the start of a range before an existing node.
Syntax: *Range*.setEndBefore(*node*), where *node* is a node you're setting your position with respect to.

Method	NS2	NS3	NS4	NS6	IE3a	IE3b	IE4	IE5	IE5.5	IE6
toString				x						

Returns: String
Returns the text in the body of a range as a string.
Syntax: *Range*.toString().

Using Ranges

To create a new range in the Netscape Navigator, you can use the document object's createRange method. Then you can use various methods to position the range, such as setStart, setEnd, selectNode, selectNodeContents, and so on. And you can use various properties and methods you see in Table 11.20 and 11.21 to work with the range. (Unfortunately, one of the most attractive methods, insertNode, which lets you insert or replace text in a range, isn't available in the Netscape Navigator yet.)

Here's an example. In this case, I'll display some text in a web page, some of which will be bold, and I'll use createRange to create a range corresponding to the bold text. Next, I'll let the user select some text, and when the user does, create a new range and use the Range object's compareBoundaryPoints method to let the user know whether her selection is before the bold text, after it, or overlaps it. How do we get a Range object corresponding to the current selected text? There's not much known about the Netscape Navigator selection object yet, but it does have a getRangeAt method, and we can get a Range object starting at the beginning of the selection by calling *selection*.getRangeAt(0). Here's what the code looks like (NS6+ only). Note that it creates the first range, range1, which corresponds to the bold text, as soon as the page loads:

(Listing 11-04.html on the web site)

```
<HTML>
    <HEAD>
        <TITLE>Using the Range object</TITLE>
        <SCRIPT LANGUAGE="JavaScript">
            <!--
            var range1

            function display()
            {
                var test11, test2, test3, test4
                var range2 = window.getSelection()
                range2 = range2.getRangeAt(0)
                test1 = range2.compareBoundaryPoints(Range.START_TO_START, range1)
                test2 = range2.compareBoundaryPoints(Range.END_TO_START, range1)
                test3 = range2.compareBoundaryPoints(Range.START_TO_END, range1)
```

continues ▶

```
    test4 = range2.compareBoundaryPoints(Range.END_TO_END, range1)

    if(test1 < 0 && test2 < 0 && test3 < 0 && test4 < 0){
        document.getElementById("p1").innerHTML =
            "Your selection was before the bold text."
    } else if(test1 > 0 && test2 > 0 && test3 > 0 && test4 > 0){
        document.getElementById("p1").innerHTML =
            "Your selection was after the bold text."
    } else {
        document.getElementById("p1").innerHTML =
            "Your selection includes the bold text."
    }
}

function makeRange()
{
    range1 = document.createRange()
    range1.selectNodeContents(document.getElementById("span1").firstChild)
    range1.setEnd(range1.endContainer, 4)
}
// -->
    </SCRIPT>
</HEAD>

<BODY ONLOAD="makeRange()">
<H1>Using the Range object</H1>
    <P ONMOUSEUP="display()">
        Select some <SPAN ID="span1"><B>text</B></SPAN> using the mouse.
    </P>
    <P ID="p1"> </P>
</BODY>
</HTML>
```

You can see the results in Figure 11.4; I've selected some text and the code is accurately identifying where it is.

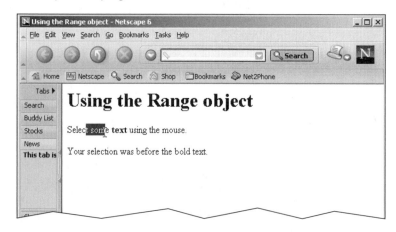

Figure 11.4   Selecting text with ranges.

Text Nodes

You also can handle text in web pages in terms of text nodes. The Netscape Navigator and W3C implement text nodes as `Text` objects, and the Internet Explorer implements them as `TextNode` objects. These objects are similar but, of course, not identical. You can see the properties of the `Text` object in Table 11.22 and its methods in Table 11.23. And you can find the properties of the `TextNode` object in Table 11.24 and its methods in Table 11.25.

Table 11.22 **The Properties of the *Text* Object**

Property	NS2	NS3	NS4	NS6	IE3a	IE3b	IE4	IE5	IE5.5	IE6
attributes	See Chapter 5.									
childNodes	See Chapter 5.									
data				x						
	Read/write									
	This property holds the text in the node, as a string.									
firstChild	See Chapter 5.									
lastChild	See Chapter 5.									
length	See Chapter 5.									
localName	See Chapter 5.									
namespaceURI	See Chapter 5.									
nextSibling	See Chapter 5.									
nodeName	See Chapter 5.									
nodeType	See Chapter 5.									
nodeValue	See Chapter 5.									
ownerDocument	See Chapter 5.									
parentNode	See Chapter 5.									
prefix	See Chapter 5.									
previousSibling	See Chapter 5.									

Table 11.23 **The Methods of the *Text* Object**

Method	NS2	NS3	NS4	NS6	IE3a	IE3b	IE4	IE5	IE5.5	IE6
appendChild	See Chapter 6.									
appendData				x						
	Returns: Nothing									
	Appends text to a text node.									
	Syntax: `appendData(text)`, where *text* is the text to append to the text node.									

continues ▶

Table 11.23 **Continued**

Method	NS2	NS3	NS4	NS6	IE3a	IE3b	IE4	IE5	IE5.5	IE6
cloneNode	See Chapter 6.									
deleteData				x						

Returns: Nothing
Syntax: deleteData(*offset, length*), where *offset* is the offset at which to start deleting, and *length* is the number of characters to delete.

hasChildNodes	See Chapter 6.									
insertBefore	See Chapter 6.									
insertData				x						

Returns: Nothing
Inserts text into a text node.
Syntax: insertData(*offset, text*), where *offset* is the offset (in characters) at which to insert the text, and *text* is the text to insert.

normalize	See Chapter 6.									
removeChild	See Chapter 6.									
replaceChild	See Chapter 6.									
replaceData				x						

Returns: Nothing
Replaces text.
Syntax: replaceData(*offset, length, text*), where *offset* is the offset at which to replace text, *length* is the length of text to replace, and *text* is the new text.

splitText				x						

Returns: Text node
Splits the text in a node.
Syntax: splitText(*offset*), where *offset* gives the location at which to split the text. This method truncates the original text to *offset* in length, and returns the second part of the text.

substringData				x						

Returns: String
Gets a substring.
Syntax: substringData(*offset, length*), where *offset* is the offset at which to get the text, and *length* is the length of the text to get. Returns the substring.

Table 11.24 **The Properties of the *TextNode* Object**

Property	NS2	NS3	NS4	NS6	IE3a	IE3b	IE4	IE5	IE5.5	IE6
data								X	X	X

Read/write
This property holds the text in the node, as a string.

length	See Chapter 5.
nextSibling	See Chapter 5.
nodeName	See Chapter 5.
nodeType	See Chapter 5.
nodeValue	See Chapter 5.
ownerDocument	See Chapter 5.
parentNode	See Chapter 5.
previousSibling	See Chapter 5.

Table 11.25 **The Methods of the *TextNode* Object**

Method	NS2	NS3	NS4	NS6	IE3a	IE3b	IE4	IE5	IE5.5	IE6
appendData										X

Returns: Nothing
Appends text to a text node.
Syntax: appendData(*text*), where *text* is the text to append to the
text node.

deleteData										X

Returns: Nothing
Syntax: deleteData(*offset*, *length*), where *offset* is the offset at which
to start deleting, and *length* is the number of characters to delete.

insertData										X

Returns: Nothing
Inserts text into a text node.
Syntax: insertData(*offset*, *text*), where *offset* is the offset (in
characters) at which to insert the text, and *text* is the text to insert.

replaceData										X

Returns: Nothing
Replaces text.
Syntax: replaceData(*offset*, *length*, *text*), where offset is the offset
at which to replace text, *length* is the length of text to replace, and *text*
is the new text.

continues ▶

Table 11.25 **Continued**

Method	NS2	NS3	NS4	NS6	IE3a	IE3b	IE4	IE5	IE5.5	IE6
splitText										x

Returns: Text node
Splits the text in a node.
Syntax: splitText(*offset*), where *offset* gives the location at which to split the text. This method truncates the original text to *offset* in length, and returns the second part of the text.

| substringData | | | | | | | | | | x |

Returns: String
Gets a substring.
Syntax: substringData(*offset*, *length*), where *offset* is the offset at which to get the text, and *length* is the length of the text to get. Returns the substring.

We've already worked with text nodes as long ago as Chapter 6. You can create text nodes with the document object's createTextNode method (covered in Table 9.5), although you get a Text object in the Netscape Navigator and a TextNode object in the Internet Explorer. In the example in Chapter 6 (Listing 06-09.html on the web site)—which works in both browsers—I'm creating a new <DIV> element using the document object's createElement method (which returns an element object that you also can treat as a node) and adding other objects—text and a text field—to that element using insertBefore:

```
<HTML>
    <HEAD>
        <TITLE>
            Creating New Elements
        </TITLE>

        <SCRIPT LANGUAGE="JavaScript">
            <!--
            function addMore()
            {
                var newDiv, newTextField, newText
                newDiv = document.createElement("DIV")
                newTextField = document.createElement("INPUT")
                newTextField.type = "TEXT"
                newTextField.value = "Hello!"
                newText = document.createTextNode("Here is a new text field: ")
                newDiv.insertBefore(newText, null)
                newDiv.insertBefore(newTextField, null)
                document.body.insertBefore(newDiv, null)
            }
```

```
            // -->
        </SCRIPT>
    </HEAD>

    <BODY>
        <H1>Creating New Elements</H1>
        <FORM>
            <INPUT TYPE=BUTTON VALUE="Click Me!" ONCLICK="addMore()">
        </FORM>
    </BODY>
</HTML>
```

This code gives you the result you see in Figure 6.6—now we're creating new text nodes and inserting them into documents.

That completes our look at HTML text elements and text ranges for this chapter. We've seen quite a bit in this chapter, from elements such as <BLOCKQUOTE> and <MARQUEE> through TextRange and Range objects, all the way to TextNode and Text objects. In the next chapter, I'll start taking a look at the main reasons many JavaScript programmers use JavaScript in the first place—when we start working with forms, buttons, check boxes, and radio buttons.

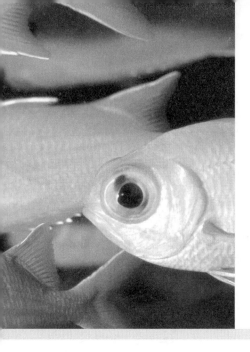

12

Working with Forms, Buttons, Check Boxes, and Radio Buttons

IN THIS CHAPTER, WE'RE GOING TO START WORKING with the HTML controls (the HTML data-entry elements, such as buttons, text fields, and so on) that many JavaScript programmers consider JavaScript to be all about. Here we'll take a look at working with forms, buttons, check boxes, and radio buttons. We'll also take a look at two elements closely allied to working with forms: the <FIELDSET> and <LEGEND> elements.

The <*FORM*> Element

The <FORM> element surrounds the kind of controls the user interacts with in a web page—buttons, radio buttons, check boxes, and so on. Forms not only hold controls you can work with in JavaScript, but also can send the data in those controls back to the server using *Common Gateway Interface* (CGI) programming. On the server, you can use programs to decode that data and construct web pages to send back to the browser using various languages and platforms such as Perl or .NET, or even server-side JavaScript. We'll see more on this topic in Chapter 24, ".NET and Security," but we'll also take a look at a little server-side programming here.

You can see the properties, methods, and events of the <FORM> element in Table 12.1, its properties in depth in Table 12.2, its methods in depth in Table 12.3, and its events in depth in Table 12.4.

Tip

You don't actually need a <FORM> element in the Internet Explorer to work with controls unless you want to divide a web page into separate forms, however, you do need to enclose controls in a <FORM> element in the Netscape Navigator if you want those controls to work. It's a good idea to always enclose all HTML controls in a form.

Table 12.1 **Overview of the Properties, Methods, and Events of the <FORM> Element (See Chapters 5 and 6 for the JavaScript core HTML properties, methods, and events that also apply to this element.)**

Properties	Methods	Events
acceptCharset	handleEvent	onreset
action	reset	onsubmit
autocomplete	submit	
elements		
encoding		
enctype		
length		
method		
name		
target		

Table 12.2 **The Properties of the <FORM> Element**

Property	NS2	NS3	NS4	NS6	IE3a	IE3b	IE4	IE5	IE5.5	IE6
acceptCharset				X				X	X	X

Read/write
Holds the name of the character set, or a comma-separated set of character sets, that the server must accept to use this form. In the HTML 4.01 specification, the W3C says that you can get a list of the registered character sets at ftp://ftp.isi.edu/in-notes/iana/assignments/character-sets.

| action | X | X | X | X | X | X | X | X | X | X |

Read/write
Corresponds to the ACTION attribute of a form, and usually holds the URL of a server-side program to send the form's data to for CGI processing. You can change this property on-the-fly to specify which URL (and therefore CGI program) you want to send the form's data to. Set to a string. See "Submitting Forms" in this chapter for an example.

Property	NS2	NS3	NS4	NS6	IE3a	IE3b	IE4	IE5	IE5.5	IE6
autocomplete								X	X	X

Read/write
Indicates whether the Internet Explorer's AutoComplete feature is turned on. This feature lets the browser prompt for suggested text in controls, such as text fields, based on what the user has entered in the past. Set to on or off.

Property	NS2	NS3	NS4	NS6	IE3a	IE3b	IE4	IE5	IE5.5	IE6
elements	X	X	X	X	X	X	X	X	X	X

Read-only
Holds the elements in a form and gives you access to them. An individual element can be accessed as *form*.elements(*index* [, *subIndex*]). Here, *index* is an integer or string that indicates the element to get. If this parameter is an integer, this method returns the element at the given position. If this parameter is a string and there is more than one element with the name or id property equal to that string, this method returns all matching elements as an array. The *subIndex* parameter, not supported in the Netscape Navigator, is used when *index* is a string and more than one element has the same name or id property, and enables you to specify which element to retrieve. See "Using Radio Buttons" in this chapter for an example.

Property	NS2	NS3	NS4	NS6	IE3a	IE3b	IE4	IE5	IE5.5	IE6
encoding	X	X	X	X	X	X	X	X	X	X

Read/write
Sets or retrieves the MIME encoding for the form's data when it's sent back to the server, corresponding to the ENCTYPE attribute of a form. Set to a string; the default value is "application/x-www-form-urlencoded". See "Emailing Forms" in this chapter for a little more information.

Property	NS2	NS3	NS4	NS6	IE3a	IE3b	IE4	IE5	IE5.5	IE6
enctype				X						X

Read/write
This is the W3C name for the encoding property, and is now supported in the Netscape Navigator 6 and Internet Explorer 6.

Property	NS2	NS3	NS4	NS6	IE3a	IE3b	IE4	IE5	IE5.5	IE6
length	X	X	X	X	X	X	X	X	X	X

Read-only
Holds an integer giving the length of the form's elements array. In other words, this property tells you how many elements are in the form.

Property	NS2	NS3	NS4	NS6	IE3a	IE3b	IE4	IE5	IE5.5	IE6
method	X	X	X	X	X	X	X	X	X	X

Read/write
This property holds the method the form uses to send its data back to the server, and corresponds to the form's METHOD attribute. Set this property to a string—either "GET" or "POST". This property determines how data is relayed back to the server; most CGI programming will require "POST" here. (There is no default value.)

continues ▶

Table 12.2 **Continued**

Property	NS2	NS3	NS4	NS6	IE3a	IE3b	IE4	IE5	IE5.5	IE6
name	x	x	x	x	x	x	x	x	x	x

Read/write
Holds the name of the form, which you can use to access the form's contents in JavaScript. Set to a name string.

	NS2	NS3	NS4	NS6	IE3a	IE3b	IE4	IE5	IE5.5	IE6
target	x	x	x	x	x	x	x	x	x	x

Read/write
This property holds the name of a window or frame that the CGI program on the server should send its results back to if you want to target a specific window or frame. Set to a name string. For information on predefined window/frame names you can use here, such as "_top", see "Opening and Closing New Windows" in Chapter 9, "Using the *document* and *body* Objects."

Table 12.3 **The Methods of the *<FORM>* Element (See Chapters 5 and 6 for the JavaScript core HTML properties, methods, and events that also apply to this element.)**

Method	NS2	NS3	NS4	NS6	IE3a	IE3b	IE4	IE5	IE5.5	IE6
handleEvent			x							

Returns: Nothing
This Netscape Navigator 4.0 method handles events captured with setCapture.
Syntax: handleEvent(*event*), where *event* is an event type such as Event.CLICK. See Chapter 15, "Working with the Mouse, Keyboard, and Images," for more details.

Method	NS2	NS3	NS4	NS6	IE3a	IE3b	IE4	IE5	IE5.5	IE6
reset		x	x	x			x	x	x	x

Returns: Nothing
This method simulates clicking the reset button in a form, which resets the data in the form's controls back to their default values (which you can set with most controls' VALUE attribute). This method causes the onreset event to occur.
Syntax: *form*.reset().

Method	NS2	NS3	NS4	NS6	IE3a	IE3b	IE4	IE5	IE5.5	IE6
submit	x	x	x	x	x	x	x	x	x	x

Returns: Nothing

This method simulates clicking the submit button in a form, which sends the form's data back to the server (depending on the `action` property) for processing. Being able to submit a form through programmatic control like this is great—instead of displaying a submit button and letting the user click it, you can check the user's data before sending it back to the server and send it yourself, for example. This method does *not* cause the `onsubmit` event to occur. See "Submitting Forms" in this chapter for an example. Syntax: *form*.submit().

Table 12.4 **The Events of the <FORM> Element (See Chapters 5 and 6 for the JavaScript core HTML properties, methods, and events that also apply to this element.)**

Event	NS2	NS3	NS4	NS6	IE3a	IE3b	IE4	IE5	IE5.5	IE6
onreset		x	x	x			x	x	x	x

Occurs when the reset button (if there is one) in a form is clicked or the `reset` method is called and the data in the form's controls is set back to its default value(s).

onsubmit	x	x	x	x	x	x	x	x	x	x

Occurs when the user clicks the submit button (if there is one) in a form and the data in the form is about to be sent back to the server. This is a good one to handle yourself if you want to check the user's data before sending it back to the server—returning false from this event's handler cancels the submission back to the server, and returning true allows the submission to happen. See "Submitting Forms" in this chapter for an example.

Using Forms

When you add HTML controls to a web page, they should be in a form, which you create with the <FORM> element. Forms are only HTML constructs. They have no visual representation by themselves (unless you use the <FIELDSET> element; see the discussion on that element at the end of this chapter). We've been using forms since Chapter 1, "Essential JavaScript," as in this example where I've placed an HTML button control into a form; and when the user clicks it, JavaScript calls the `alerter` method to display an alert box.

(Listing 01-03.html on the web site):

```
<HTML>
    <HEAD>
        <TITLE>
            Executing Scripts in Response to User Action
        </TITLE>
        <SCRIPT LANGUAGE="JavaScript">
            <!--
            function alerter()
            {
                window.alert("You clicked the button!")
            }
            // -->
        </SCRIPT>
    </HEAD>

    <BODY>
        <H1>Executing Scripts in Response to User Action</H1>
        <FORM>
            <INPUT TYPE="BUTTON" ONCLICK="alerter()" VALUE="Click Me!">
        </FORM>
    </BODY>
</HTML>
```

So how do you get access to the controls in a form from JavaScript? If you give a form a name using the NAME (not ID) HTML attribute, you can access those controls using syntax like this, as we've seen earlier:

```
document.form1.button1.value = "Clicked!"
```

In this case, I'm setting the `value` property of a button named button1 in a form named form1. That's one way of accessing a control in a form from your code—as document.*formName*.*controlName*. You also can use the `document` object's `forms` array, which enables you to access forms by number or name. Here's an example where the code changes the caption of a button from `Click Me!` to `You clicked the button!` when the user clicks that button (note that the `forms` array isn't available before version 6 in the Netscape Navigator):

(Listing 12-01.html on the web site)

```
<HTML>
    <HEAD>
        <TITLE>
            Executing Scripts in Response to User Action
```

```
        </TITLE>
        <SCRIPT LANGUAGE="JavaScript">
            <!--
            function alerter()
            {
                document.forms[0].text1.value = ("You clicked the button!")
            }
            // -->
        </SCRIPT>
    </HEAD>

    <BODY>
        <H1>Executing Scripts in Response to User Action</H1>
        <FORM>
            <INPUT TYPE="BUTTON" ONCLICK="alerter()" VALUE="Click Me!">
            <INPUT TYPE="TEXT" ID="text1" VALUE="">
        </FORM>
    </BODY>
</HTML>
```

You also can use the form's `elements` array to access the elements in a form; see "Using Radio Buttons" in this chapter for an example. (You also can still access the controls in a form using the `getElementById` method and other methods, of course.)

Submitting Forms

Although you can use JavaScript with controls in a form in the browser and create working, complete programs, forms were originally created to let you send data back to the server. I'll take a look at an example showing how this works here.

In this case, I'll let the user send his name back to a Perl CGI script. (Perl, which stands for *Practical Extraction and Reporting Language*, is one of the popular programming languages for server-side CGI programming, and we'll see more about it in Chapter 24.) Many CGI options are available, such as using Microsoft's .NET framework on the server, or even using server-side JavaScript. That CGI script will create a new web page displaying the user's name and send that web page back to the browser. To make this work, I set the form's `METHOD` attribute to `"POST"` and `ACTION` attribute to the URL of the script (this is a fictitious URL):

(Listing 12-02.html on the web site)

```
<HTML>
    <HEAD>
        <TITLE>CGI Example</TITLE>
    </HEAD>
```

continues ▶

```
<BODY>
    <H1>Sending Data to the Server</H1>
    <FORM METHOD="POST" ACTION="http://www.starpowder.com/12-03.cgi">
        Please enter your name:
        <INPUT TYPE="text" NAME="text" VALUE="">
        <BR>
        <INPUT TYPE="SUBMIT" NAME="Submit" VALUE="Submit">
        <INPUT TYPE="RESET">
    </FORM>
</BODY>
</HTML>
```

Note also that I've included a submit (<INPUT TYPE="SUMIT">) and reset
(<INPUT TYPE="RESET">) button. The user can click the submit button in the
form to send the data in the form—that is, the user's name in the text
field—back to the server, and click the reset button to reset all data in the
form's controls to its default value. Here's what the Perl CGI script, 12-
03.cgi, on the server looks like (more on how Perl scripts like this one work
and how to write them in Chapter 24):

(Listing 12-03.html on the web site)

```perl
#!/usr/local/bin/perl
use CGI;
$co = new CGI;

print $co->header,
$co->start_html(
    -title=>'CGI Example',
    -author=>'Steve',
    -meta=>{'keywords'=>'CGI Perl'},
),
$co->hr;
if ($co->param()) {
    print
        "Your name is: ",$co->em($co->param('text')), ".";
}
print $co->hr;
print $co->end_html;
```

The user can now enter a name in the text field in our web page, as you see
in Figure 12.1.

When the user clicks the submit button in our web page, the data in the
form, including the text in the text field, is sent to the URL I've specified in
the ACTION attribute, which is the URL of our CGI script, 12-03.cgi. That
CGI script processes the data we've sent it and returns the web page you see
in Figure 12.2.

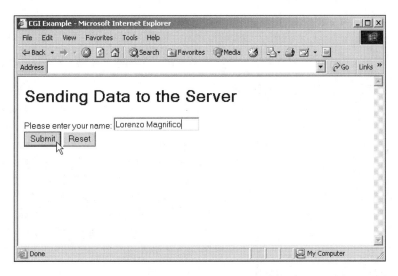

Figure 12.1   Entering data into a form.

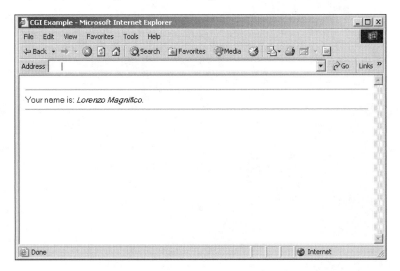

Figure 12.2   Getting a web page back from a server-side script.

So where does JavaScript come in when you're submitting data back to the server? There's plenty of ways that JavaScript can be involved. For example, you can use JavaScript to check the user's data before sending it back to the server, and that's a frequent use of JavaScript.

You can check form data before it's sent back to the server by handling the form's onsubmit event, which occurs when the user clicks the submit button. If you return true from this events handler, the data is submitted to the server; and if you return false, the data is not submitted (and the browser just keeps displaying the same page).

Here's an example; in this case, I'll check whether the user has entered any text into the text field that is supposed to hold their name before sending that data back to the server. I start by connecting a JavaScript function named checkData to the ONSUBMIT attribute of the form like this—note that because the browser needs to use the return value from this function, I assign the text "return checkData()" to the ONSUBMIT attribute, not just "checkData()":

```
<HTML>
    <HEAD>
        <TITLE>CGI Example</TITLE>
        <SCRIPT LANGUAGE="JavaScript">
            <!--
            function checkData()
            {
            .
            .
            .
            }
            // -->
        </SCRIPT>
    </HEAD>

    <BODY>
        <FORM ID="form1" METHOD="POST"
            ACTION="http://www.starpowder.com/steve/12-03.cgi"
            ONSUBMIT="return checkData()">
            Please enter your name:
            <INPUT TYPE="TEXT" ID="text1" VALUE="">
            <BR>
            <INPUT TYPE="SUBMIT" NAME="Submit" VALUE="Submit">
            <INPUT TYPE="RESET">
        </FORM>
    </BODY>
</HTML>
```

Now I just check whether the user has entered any data, prompt the user if she has not, and send the data on to the server or not, as appropriate:

(Listing 12-04.html on the web site)

```
<HTML>
    <HEAD>
        <TITLE>CGI Example</TITLE>
        <SCRIPT LANGUAGE="JavaScript">
```

```
        <!--
        function checkData()
        {
            if(document.form1.text1.value == ""){
                window.alert("Please enter your name.")
                return false
            } else {
                return true
            }
        }
        // -->
    </SCRIPT>
</HEAD>

<BODY>
    <FORM NAME="form1" METHOD="POST"
        ACTION="http://www.starpowder.com/steve/12-03.cgi"
        ONSUBMIT="return checkData()">
        Please enter your name:
        <INPUT TYPE="TEXT" ID="text1" VALUE="">
        <BR>
        <INPUT TYPE="SUBMIT" NAME="Submit" VALUE="Submit">
        <INPUT TYPE="RESET">
    </FORM>
</BODY>
</HTML>
```

You can see how this works in Figure 12.3, where the code is prompting me to enter a name. Checking user data like this before sending it back to the server can save you valuable server time on worthless data—and save the user time waiting for server round trips.

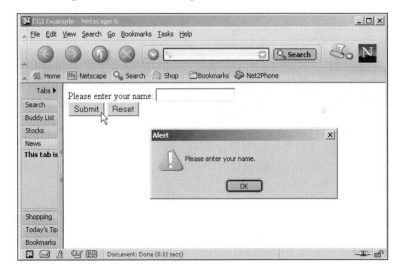

Figure 12.3 Using JavaScript to check form data.

Besides using ONSUBMIT, you also can use ONRESET to warn users that if they click the reset button, they'll be erasing all the form's data. That might look like this:

(Listing 12-05.html on the web site)

```html
<HTML>
    <HEAD>
        <TITLE>CGI Example</TITLE>
        <SCRIPT LANGUAGE="JavaScript">
            <!--
            function checkData()
            {
                if(document.form1.text1.value == ""){
                    window.alert("Please enter your name.")
                    return false
                } else {
                    return true
                }
            }
            function checkReset()
            {
                if(window.confirm("Erase all data and reset to defaults?")){
                    return true
                } else {
                    return false
                }
            }
            // -->
        </SCRIPT>
    </HEAD>

    <BODY>
        <FORM NAME="form1" METHOD="POST"
            ACTION="http://www.starpowder.com/steve/12-03.cgi"
            ONSUBMIT="return checkData()" ONRESET="return checkReset()">
            Please enter your name:
            <INPUT TYPE="TEXT" ID="text1" VALUE="">
            <BR>
            <INPUT TYPE="SUBMIT" NAME="Submit" VALUE="Submit">
            <INPUT TYPE="RESET">
        </FORM>
    </BODY>
</HTML>
```

Submitting Forms Yourself

JavaScript can do more than just check the data in forms; it can submit that data itself using a form's `submit` method. This is good if you want the data-submission process under your control—you don't even have to display a submit button in the form, you can handle it all in JavaScript.

Here's an example. In this case, the submit button in this web page is just a standard HTML button—the form's data is submitted by the JavaScript code after checking with the user:

(Listing 12-06.html on the web site)

```
<HTML>
    <HEAD>
        <TITLE>CGI Example</TITLE>
        <SCRIPT LANGUAGE="JavaScript">
            <!--
            function checkData()
            {
                if(window.confirm("Upload your name?")){
                    document.form1.submit()
                }
            }
            // -->
        </SCRIPT>
    </HEAD>

    <BODY>
        <FORM NAME="form1" METHOD="POST" ACTION="http://www.starpowder.com/steve/
        ➥12-03.cgi">
            Please enter your name:
            <INPUT TYPE="text" NAME="text" VALUE="">
            <BR>
            <INPUT TYPE="BUTTON" VALUE="Submit" ONCLICK="checkData()">
            <INPUT TYPE="RESET">
        </FORM>
    </BODY>
</HTML>
```

Tip

Here's something to know—if you call the submit method, don't execute any code after that method call, because if you do, the form's data is not submitted to the server.

You can see how this works in Figure 12.4, where the code is checking with the user before submitting the form's data.

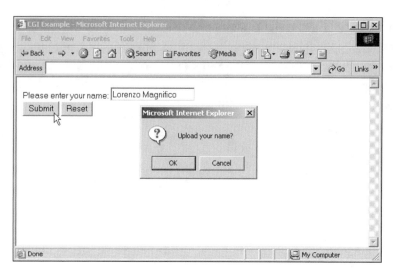

Figure 12.4 Using JavaScript to check with the user.

Emailing Forms

There's another way to handle form data if you don't want to do any CGI programming; and because many readers of this book don't, I'll take a look at this other technique here. You can have the data in a form *emailed* to you if you set the ACTION attribute to a mailto: URL.

Here's an example. In this case, I'll email a form's data to steve@starpowder.com (a fictitious email address). Note also that I set the ENCTYPE attribute—the MIME encoding of the form's data—to "text/plain":

(Listing 12-07.html on the web site)

```
<HTML>
    <HEAD>
        <TITLE>CGI Example</TITLE>
        <SCRIPT LANGUAGE="JavaScript">
            <!--
            function checkData()
            {
                if(document.forms[0].text1.value == ""){
                    window.alert("Please enter your name.")
                    return false
                } else {
                    return true
                }
            }
```

```
            // -->
        </SCRIPT>
    </HEAD>

    <BODY>
        <FORM ID="form1" METHOD="POST"
            ACTION="mailto:steve@starpowder.com?subject=Web%20page%20email"
            ENCTYPE="text/plain"">
            Please enter your name:
            <INPUT TYPE="TEXT" NAME="text">
            <BR>
            <INPUT TYPE="SUBMIT" NAME="Submit" VALUE="Submit">
            <INPUT TYPE="RESET">
        </FORM>
    </BODY>
</HTML>
```

Here's the body of the email that arrives, in plain text because I set the `ENCTYPE` attribute to `"text/plain"`:

```
text=Hello
Submit=Submit
```

That's how the data will arrive in the email—as *name*=value, where *name* is the name of the control and *value* is the data in the control.

Tip

The `submit` method does not work with mailto: URLs for security reasons (so a JavaScript programmer can't get your email address unless you okay it).

Sending form data back to a program on the server is fine; of course you don't need to send a form's data back to the server at all, you can create your entire program in JavaScript and run it all in the browser as we're doing throughout this book.

Passing Forms to Functions

Although you can access data in a form if you know the form's name (like this: `document.form1.button1.value`), what if you have multiple forms in a web page you want to work with? How do you know what form a control called your script from? To let your scripts know which form a control is in when an event occurs in that control, you can pass the control's form to the event handler using the control's `form` property like this: `this.form`. And if you're using an event of the form itself, such as `onsubmit`, you can just use the form's `this` property to refer to itself.

Here's an example. In this case, I have two forms in a web page, form1 and form2, to let the user enter her name and age. I connect both forms' onsubmit event to the same function, checkData, and I pass the form's this property to that function like this:

```
<HTML>
    <HEAD>
        <TITLE>CGI Example</TITLE>
        <SCRIPT LANGUAGE="JavaScript">
            <!--
            function checkData(form)
            {
                .
                .
                .
            }
            // -->
        </SCRIPT>
    </HEAD>

    <BODY>
        <FORM ID="form1" METHOD="POST"
            ACTION="http://www.starpowder.com/steve/12-03.cgi"
            ONSUBMIT="return checkData(this)">
            Please enter your name:
            <INPUT TYPE="TEXT" ID="text1" VALUE="">
            <BR>
            <INPUT TYPE="SUBMIT" NAME="Submit" VALUE="Submit">
            <INPUT TYPE="RESET">
        </FORM>
        <BR>
        <FORM ID="form2" METHOD="POST"
            ACTION="http://www.starpowder.com/steve/12-03.cgi"
            ONSUBMIT="return checkData(this)">
            Please enter your age:
            <INPUT TYPE="TEXT" ID="text1" VALUE="">
            <BR>
            <INPUT TYPE="SUBMIT" NAME="Submit" VALUE="Submit">
            <INPUT TYPE="RESET">
        </FORM>
    </BODY>
</HTML>
```

Now I can tell for which form the onsubmit event occurred by checking the id property of the form passed to the code like this (if you're using Netscape Navigator, you need version 6+ here):

(Listing 12-08.html on the web site)

```
<HTML>
    <HEAD>
        <TITLE>CGI Example</TITLE>
```

```
<SCRIPT LANGUAGE="JavaScript">
    <!--
    function checkData(form)
    {
        if(form.text1.value == ""){
            if(form.id == "form1"){
                window.alert("Please enter your name.")
                return false
            }
            if(form.id == "form2") {
                window.alert("Please enter your age.")
                return false
            }
        } else {
            return true
        }
    }
    // -->
</SCRIPT>
</HEAD>

<BODY>
    <FORM ID="form1" METHOD="POST"
        ACTION="http://www.starpowder.com/steve/12-03.cgi"
        ONSUBMIT="return checkData(this)">
        Please enter your name:
        <INPUT TYPE="TEXT" ID="text1" VALUE="">
        <BR>
        <INPUT TYPE="SUBMIT" NAME="Submit" VALUE="Submit">
        <INPUT TYPE="RESET">
    </FORM>
    <BR>
    <FORM ID="form2" METHOD="POST"
        ACTION="http://www.starpowder.com/steve/12-03.cgi"
        ONSUBMIT="return checkData(this)">
        Please enter your age:
        <INPUT TYPE="TEXT" ID="text1" VALUE="">
        <BR>
        <INPUT TYPE="SUBMIT" NAME="Submit" VALUE="Submit">
        <INPUT TYPE="RESET">
    </FORM>
</BODY>
</HTML>
```

That's it for forms for the moment. Let's turn to HTML buttons next.

Buttons

Along with text fields, buttons are the primary controls you see in web pages. All you need to do is to click them to make something happen. The properties, methods, and events of all buttons are the same in JavaScript. Here are the various button types:

- **Buttons.** `<BUTTON>`, `<BUTTON TYPE="BUTTON">`, `<INPUT TYPE="BUTTON">`.
- **Submit buttons.** `<INPUT TYPE="SUBMIT">` and `<BUTTON TYPE="SUBMIT">`.
- **Reset buttons.** `<INPUT TYPE="RESET">` and `<BUTTON TYPE="RESET">`.

You can see the properties, methods, and events of buttons in Table 12.5 in overview, their properties in depth in Table 12.6, their methods in depth in Table 12.7, and their events in Table 12.8. Note that JavaScript's core HTML properties, methods, and events (such as `onclick`), as covered in Chapters 5, "Using Core HTML Properties," and 6, "Using Core HTML Methods and Events," also apply to buttons.

Table 12.5 **Overview of the Properties, Methods, and Events of the Button Elements (See Chapters 5 and 6 for the JavaScript core HTML properties, methods, and events that also apply to these elements.)**

Properties	Methods	Events
defaultValue	click	onafterupdate
form	createTextRange	onbeforeupdate
name	select	onerrorupdate
size		
type		
value		

Table 12.6 **The Properties of the Button Elements (See Chapters 5 and 6 for the JavaScript core HTML properties, methods, and events that also apply to these elements.)**

Property	NS2	NS3	NS4	NS6	IE3a	IE3b	IE4	IE5	IE5.5	IE6
defaultValue	x	x	x	x	x	x	x	x	x	x

Read/write
Holds the default value of the button as a string. This is the caption the button will display if the form is reset.

form	x	x	x	x	x	x	x	x	x	x

Read-only
This property holds the form that the button is a member of. Useful if you want to access other controls in the same form.

Property	NS2	NS3	NS4	NS6	IE3a	IE3b	IE4	IE5	IE5.5	IE6
name	X	X	X	X	X	X	X	X	X	X

Read/write
This property holds the name of the button as a string, as set with the
NAME attribute. Note that you can change the name of the button in code,
because this property is read/write.

size	X	X	X	X	X	X	X	X	X	X

Read/write
Sets or retrieves the size of the control, measured in characters.

type		X	X	X	X		X	X	X	X

Read-only
This property holds the type of button, as set with the TYPE attribute in an
<INPUT> or <BUTTON> element. Holds the string "button", "submit", or
"reset". For an example, see "Using Radio Buttons" in this chapter. As of
Internet Explorer 5, the type property is read/write, but only once, when
an element is created with the createElement method and before it is
added to the document.

value	X	X	X	X	X	X	X	X	X	X

Read/write
Holds the caption of the button. This is a read/write property, so you can
set it from your code. Set to a string. Note, however, that browsers earlier
than Internet Explorer 4.0 and Netscape Navigator do not resize the button for the new caption. See "Resetting Button Captions" in this chapter.

**Table 12.7   The Methods of the Button Elements (See Chapters 5 and 6
for the JavaScript core HTML properties, methods, and events that also
apply to these elements.)**

Method	NS2	NS3	NS4	NS6	IE3a	IE3b	IE4	IE5	IE5.5	IE6
click	X	X	X	X	X	X	X	X	X	X

Returns: Nothing
Calling this button method is the same as clicking a button, and it causes
the onclick event to occur. See "Clicking a Button from Code" in this
chapter.

createTextRange							X	X	X	X

Returns: TextRange object
Creates a TextRange object for the button.
Syntax: createTextRange(). More on TextRange objects in Chapter 11,
"Working with HTML Text Elements."

continues ▶

Table 12.7   **Continued**

Method	NS2	NS3	NS4	NS6	IE3a	IE3b	IE4	IE5	IE5.5	IE6
select							x	x	x	x

Returns: Nothing
Selects the control.
Syntax: `select()`.

Table 12.8   **The Events of the Button Elements (See Chapters 5 and 6 for the JavaScript core HTML properties, methods, and events that also apply to these elements.)**

Event	NS2	NS3	NS4	NS6	IE3a	IE3b	IE4	IE5	IE5.5	IE6
onafterupdate							x	x	x	x

Occurs in a data-bound object after updating the data in the data source.

| onbeforeupdate | | | | | | | x | x | x | x |

Occurs in a data-bound object before updating the data in the data source.

| onerrorupdate | | | | | | | x | x | x | x |

Occurs in a data-bound object when an error happens while updating data in the data source.

Using Buttons

We've seen buttons since as far back as Chapter 1. Here's an example that displays an alert box using an <INPUT> type button's ONCLICK event attribute that we saw in that chapter:

```
<HTML>
    <HEAD>
        <TITLE>
            Executing Scripts in Response to User Action
        </TITLE>
        <SCRIPT LANGUAGE="JavaScript">
            <!--
            function alerter()
            {
                window.alert("You clicked the button!")
            }
```

```
            // -->
        </SCRIPT>
    </HEAD>

    <BODY>
        <H1>Executing Scripts in Response to User Action</H1>
        <FORM>
            <INPUT TYPE="BUTTON" ONCLICK="alerter()" VALUE="Click Me!">
        </FORM>
    </BODY>
</HTML>
```

Here's the same script using a <BUTTON> type element instead (if you're using Netscape Navigator, you'll need version 6+ to use the <BUTTON> element):

(Listing 12-09.html on the web site)

```
<HTML>
    <HEAD>
        <TITLE>
            Executing Scripts in Response to User Action
        </TITLE>
        <SCRIPT LANGUAGE="JavaScript">
            <!--
            function alerter()
            {
                window.alert("You clicked the button!")
            }
            // -->
        </SCRIPT>
    </HEAD>

    <BODY>
        <H1>Executing Scripts in Response to User Action</H1>
        <FORM>
            <BUTTON ONCLICK="alerter()">Click Me!</BUTTON>
        </FORM>
    </BODY>
</HTML>
```

That's the way most buttons are used in JavaScript, but you can also click a button directly from your code, as we'll see next.

Clicking a Button from Code

Using the `click` method, you can simulate a button click. This method also causes the `onclick` event to occur. Here's an example where I'm simulating a click of one button when the user clicks another (if you're using Netscape Navigator, you'll need version 6+ to use the <BUTTON> element):

(Listing 12-10.html on the web site)

```
<HTML>
    <HEAD>
        <TITLE>
            Executing Scripts in Response to User Action
        </TITLE>
        <SCRIPT LANGUAGE="JavaScript">
            <!--
            function alerter1()
            {
                window.alert("You clicked the button!")
            }
            function alerter2()
            {
                document.form1.button1.click()
            }
            // -->
        </SCRIPT>
    </HEAD>

    <BODY>
        <H1>Executing Scripts in Response to User Action</H1>
        <FORM NAME="form1">
            <INPUT TYPE="BUTTON" ID="button1" ONCLICK="alerter1()" VALUE="Click Me!">
            <BR>
            <INPUT TYPE="BUTTON" ID="button2" ONCLICK="alerter2()" VALUE=
            ➡"Click Me Too!">
        </FORM>
    </BODY>
</HTML>
```

Resetting Button Captions

You also can change button captions on-the-fly, using a button's value property. Here's an example where I change the caption of a button from Click Me! to Clicked! when the user clicks a button:

(Listing 12-11.html on the web site)

```
<HTML>
    <HEAD>
        <TITLE>
            Changing a Button's Caption
        </TITLE>
        <SCRIPT LANGUAGE="JavaScript">
            <!--
            function clicker()
            {
                document.form1.button1.value = "Clicked!"
            }
```

```
            // -->
        </SCRIPT>
    </HEAD>

    <BODY>
        <H1>Changing a Button's Caption</H1>
        <FORM NAME="form1">
            <INPUT TYPE="BUTTON" NAME="button1" ONCLICK="clicker()" VALUE="Click Me!">
        </FORM>
    </BODY>
</HTML>
```

You can see how this works in Figure 12.5; the code has changed the button's caption after I've clicked that button.

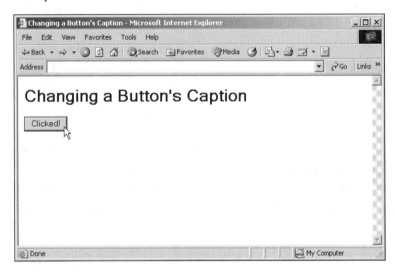

Figure 12.5   Changing a button's caption.

Check Boxes and Radio Buttons

All web users are familiar with check boxes and radio buttons—check boxes enable you to select a number of items in a list, and radio buttons enable you to select one item in a list. You can see the properties, methods, and events of check boxes and radio buttons in Table 12.9 in overview, their properties in depth in Table 12.10, their methods in depth in Table 12.11, and their events in Table 12.12. Note that JavaScript's core HTML properties, methods, and events (such as `onclick`), as covered in Chapters 5 and 6, also apply to these controls.

Table 12.9   **Overview of the Properties, Methods, and Events of the Check Box and Radio Button Elements (See Chapters 5 and 6 for the JavaScript core HTML properties, methods, and events that also apply to this element.)**

Properties	Methods	Events
checked	click	onafterupdate
defaultChecked	createTextRange	onbeforeupdate
defaultValue	select	onerrorupdate
form		
indeterminate		
name		
size		
status		
type		
value		

Table 12.10   **The Properties of the Check Box and Radio Button Elements (See Chapters 5 and 6 for the JavaScript core HTML properties, methods, and events that also apply to this element.)**

Property	NS2	NS3	NS4	NS6	IE3a	IE3b	IE4	IE5	IE5.5	IE6
checked	x	x	x	x	x	x	x	x	x	x

Read/write
This Boolean property is true if a check box or radio button is checked, and false otherwise. You can set this property under programmatic control, which is cool.

| defaultChecked | x | x | x | x | x | x | x | x | x | x |

Read-only
Boolean that indicates whether the check box or radio button appears initially checked.

| defaultValue | x | x | x | x | x | x | x | x | x | x |

Read/write
Holds the default value of the check box or radio button as a string. This is the value that will be used if the reset button (if there is one) is clicked in a form.

Property	NS2	NS3	NS4	NS6	IE3a	IE3b	IE4	IE5	IE5.5	IE6
form	x	x	x	x	x	x	x	x	x	x

Read-only
This property holds the form that the check box or radio button is a member of. Useful if you want to access other controls in the same form.

indeterminate							x	x	x	x

Read/write
Setting the `indeterminate` property to true causes the check box to appear checked *and* dimmed, indicating an "indeterminate" state.

name	x	x	x	x	x	x	x	x	x	x

Read/write
This property holds the name of the check box or radio button as a string, as set with the NAME attribute. Note that you can change the name of the check box or radio button in code, because this property is read/write.

size	x	x	x	x	x	x	x	x	x	x

Read/write
Sets or retrieves the size of the control, in characters. Set to an integer.

status							x	x	x	x

Read/write
Sets or gets a value indicating whether a check box or radio button is selected. May be a Boolean with these values: false (the default—the control is not selected), true (the control is selected), or null (the control is not initialized).

type		x	x	x			x	x	x	x

Read-only
This property holds the control's type, as set with the TYPE attribute in an <INPUT> element. Holds the string `"checkbox"` or `"radio"`. For an example, see "Using Radio Buttons" in this chapter. As of Internet Explorer 5, the `type` property is read/write, but only once, when an element is created with the `createElement` method and before it is added to the document.

continues ▶

Table 12.10 **Continued**

Property	NS2	NS3	NS4	NS6	IE3a	IE3b	IE4	IE5	IE5.5	IE6
value	x	x	x	x	x	x	x	x	x	x

Read/write

Holds a string that you want to associate with the check box or radio button as the value of that control. When the form is sent to a CGI script, this string is sent to the CGI script as the check box's or radio button's value if the check box or radio button is selected. The CGI script is able to access a control's value from the data it is passed, which includes a substring of the form *controlName=value* for each named control. In this way, you can pass data for each check box or radio button (not just true/false values)—for example, if you gave a group of radio buttons the same name (to make them operate as a group) but gave each radio button a different value (such as the days of the week), you can determine which radio button was selected.

Table 12.11 **The Methods of the Check Box and Radio Button Elements (See Chapters 5 and 6 for the JavaScript core HTML properties, methods, and events that also apply to this element.)**

Method	NS2	NS3	NS4	NS6	IE3a	IE3b	IE4	IE5	IE5.5	IE6
click	x	x	x	x	x	x	x	x	x	x

Returns: Nothing
Simulates clicking a check box or radio button.
Syntax: click(). Causes the onclick event to occur.

createTextRange							x	x	x	x

Returns: TextRange object
Creates a TextRange object for the check box or radio button.
Syntax: createTextRange(). More on TextRange objects in Chapter 11.

select							x	x	x	x

Returns: Nothing
Selects the control (does not affect whether the control is checked).
Syntax: select().

Table 12.12   **The Events of the Check Box and Radio Button Elements (See Chapters 5 and 6 for the JavaScript core HTML properties, methods, and events that also apply to these elements.)**

Method	NS2	NS3	NS4	NS6	IE3a	IE3b	IE4	IE5	IE5.5	IE6
onafterupdate							x	x	x	x
Occurs in a data-bound object after updating the data in the data source.										
onbeforeupdate							x	x	x	x
Occurs in a data-bound object before updating the data in the data source.										
onerrorupdate							x	x	x	x
Occurs in a data-bound object when an error happened while updating data in the data source.										

Using Check Boxes

It's fairly easy to handle check boxes in your code. Here's an example that displays a number of check boxes and uses the ONCLICK attribute to display a message when you click a check box, indicating which check box you clicked:

(Listing 12-12.html on the web site)

```
<HTML>
    <HEAD>
        <TITLE>Using Check Boxes</TITLE>
        <SCRIPT LANGUAGE="JavaScript">
            <!--
                function check1Clicked()
                {
                    document.form1.text1.value = "You clicked check box 1."
                }

                function check2Clicked()
                {
                    document.form1.text1.value = "You clicked check box 2."
                }

                function check3Clicked()
                {
                    document.form1.text1.value = "You clicked check box 3."
                }
```

continues ▶

```
        function check4Clicked()
        {
            document.form1.text1.value = "You clicked check box 4."
        }

        function check5Clicked() {
            document.form1.text1.value = "You clicked check box 5."
        }
    // -->
    </SCRIPT>
</HEAD>

<BODY>
    <H1>Using Check Boxes</H1>

    <FORM NAME="form1">
        <TABLE BORDER BGCOLOR = CYAN WIDTH = 200>
            <TR><TD><INPUT TYPE = "CHECKBOX" NAME = "check1" ONCLICK =
            ➥"check1Clicked()">Check 1</TD></TR>
            <TR><TD><INPUT TYPE = "CHECKBOX" NAME = "check2" ONCLICK =
            ➥"check2Clicked()">Check 2</TD></TR>
            <TR><TD><INPUT TYPE = "CHECKBOX" NAME = "check3" ONCLICK =
            ➥"check3Clicked()">Check 3</TD></TR>
            <TR><TD><INPUT TYPE = "CHECKBOX" NAME = "check4" ONCLICK =
            ➥"check4Clicked()">Check 4</TD></TR>
            <TR><TD><INPUT TYPE = "CHECKBOX" NAME = "check5" ONCLICK =
            ➥"check5Clicked()">Check 5</TD></TR>
        </TABLE>
        <BR>
        <BR>
        <INPUT TYPE="TEXT" NAME="text1" SIZE="30">
    </FORM>
</BODY>
</HTML>
```

You can see how this works in Figure 12.6, where I've clicked a check box.

However, this code makes no distinction between check boxes that are selected (displaying a check mark) and those that don't. You can use the checked property to determine whether a check box is checked. In fact, we've already seen an example that does so in Chapter 7, "Using *window* and *frame* Properties," (Listing 07-06.html on the web site) that let the user customize the Netscape Navigator by selecting what elements should be visible using check boxes. To write this example, we used the check boxes' ONCLICK attribute and checked property:

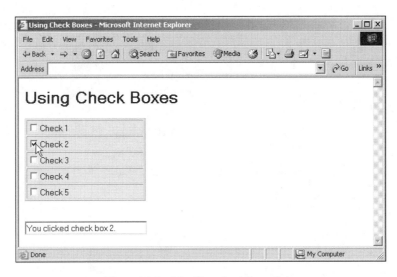

Figure 12.6 Handling check box clicks.

```
<HTML>
    <HEAD>
        <TITLE>Toggling Navigator Bars</TITLE>
        <SCRIPT LANGUAGE="JavaScript">
            <!--
            function handleBar()
            {
netscape.security.PrivilegeManager.enablePrivilege ("UniversalBrowserWrite")
                window.locationbar.visible = document.form1.check01.checked
                window.menubar.visible = document.form1.check02.checked
                window.personalbar.visible = document.form1.check03.checked
                window.scrollbars.visible = document.form1.check04.checked
                window.statusbar.visible = document.form1.check05.checked
                window.toolbar.visible = document.form1.check06.checked
netscape.security.PrivilegeManager.revertPrivilege ("UniversalBrowserWrite")
            }
        // -->
        </SCRIPT>
    </HEAD>

    <BODY>
        <H1>Toggling Navigator Bars</H1>
        <FORM NAME="form1">
            <INPUT TYPE="CHECKBOX" ID="check01" ONCLICK="handleBar()"
            ➥CHECKED>Location Bar
            <BR>
```

continues ▶

```
        <INPUT TYPE="CHECKBOX" ID="check02" ONCLICK="handleBar()" CHECKED>Menu Bar
        <BR>
        <INPUT TYPE="CHECKBOX" ID="check03" ONCLICK="handleBar()"
        ➥CHECKED>Personal Bar
        <BR>
        <INPUT TYPE="CHECKBOX" ID="check04" ONCLICK="handleBar()"
        ➥CHECKED>Scrollbars
        <BR>
        <INPUT TYPE="CHECKBOX" ID="check05" ONCLICK="handleBar()"
        ➥CHECKED>Status Bar
        <BR>
        <INPUT TYPE="CHECKBOX" ID="check05" ONCLICK="handleBar()" CHECKED>Tool Bar
    </FORM>
  </BODY>
</HTML>
```

You can see the results of this code in Chapter 7, in Figures 7.6 and 7.7. Here's another example, which enables the user to select which controls are visible in a web page by clicking a check box to toggle the visibility of two buttons using the style attribute's visibility property and the check boxes' checked property (if you're using Netscape Navigator, you'll need version 6+ here):

(Listing 12-13.html on the web site)

```
<HTML>
  <HEAD>
    <TITLE>Showing and hiding controls</TITLE>
    <SCRIPT LANGUAGE="JavaScript">
        <!--
            function checkClicked(check)
            {
                if(check.checked) {
                    document.form1.button1.style.visibility= "visible"
                    document.form1.button2.style.visibility= "visible"
                } else {
                    document.form1.button1.style.visibility= "hidden"
                    document.form1.button2.style.visibility= "hidden"
                }
            }
        // -->
    </SCRIPT>
  </HEAD>

  <BODY>
    <H1>Showing and hiding controls</H1>

    <FORM NAME="form1">
        <INPUT TYPE="BUTTON" VALUE="Check spelling" NAME="button1"
        ➥STYLE="visibility:hidden">
        <INPUT TYPE="BUTTON" VALUE="Change case" NAME="button2"
        ➥STYLE="visibility:hidden">
```

```
        <BR>
        <INPUT TYPE="TEXT" NAME="text1">
        <INPUT TYPE = "CHECKBOX" NAME = "check1" ONCLICK =
        ➡"checkClicked(this)">Show all options
      </FORM>
  </BODY>
</HTML>
```

You can see how this works in Figure 12.7; I've clicked the check box to make the two buttons visible. In this way, you can let the user set options (such as whether additional controls are visible) using check boxes.

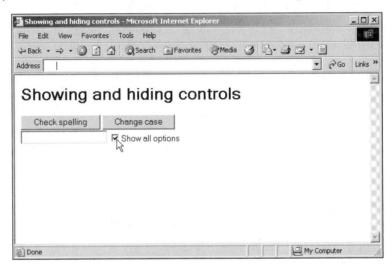

Figure 12.7   Toggling button visibility with a check box.

I'll also take another look at check boxes in the next section on radio buttons, when we use check boxes and radio buttons together.

Using Radio Buttons

Radio buttons are similar to check boxes, except they only let the user select one option from a group (such as day of the week). You group radio buttons into a group by giving them the same name using their NAME attributes. (You can have more than one radio button group in a single web page.) The browser will allow only one radio button in the group to be selected at one time. Here's an example that uses radio buttons' ONCLICK attribute to display a message when you click a radio button:

(Listing 12-14.html on the web site)

```html
<HTML>
    <HEAD>
        <TITLE>Using Radio Buttons</TITLE>
        <SCRIPT LANGUAGE="JavaScript">
            <!--
                function radio1Clicked()
                {
                    document.form1.text1.value = "You clicked radio button 1."
                }

                function radio2Clicked()
                {
                    document.form1.text1.value = "You clicked radio button 2."
                }

                function radio3Clicked()
                {
                    document.form1.text1.value = "You clicked radio button 3."
                }

                function radio4Clicked()
                {
                    document.form1.text1.value = "You clicked radio button 4."
                }

                function radio5Clicked() {
                    document.form1.text1.value = "You clicked radio button 5."
                }
            // -->
        </SCRIPT>
    </HEAD>

    <BODY>
        <H1>Using Radio Buttons</H1>

        <FORM NAME="form1">
            <TABLE BORDER BGCOLOR = CYAN WIDTH = 200>
                <TR><TD><INPUT TYPE="RADIO" NAME = "radios" ONCLICK =
                ➥"radio1Clicked()">Radio 1</TD></TR>
                <TR><TD><INPUT TYPE="RADIO" NAME = "radios" ONCLICK =
                ➥"radio2Clicked()">Radio 2</TD></TR>
                <TR><TD><INPUT TYPE="RADIO" NAME = "radios" ONCLICK =
                ➥"radio3Clicked()">Radio 3</TD></TR>
                <TR><TD><INPUT TYPE="RADIO" NAME = "radios" ONCLICK =
                ➥"radio4Clicked()">Radio 4</TD></TR>
                <TR><TD><INPUT TYPE="RADIO" NAME = "radios" ONCLICK =
                ➥"radio5Clicked()">Radio 5</TD></TR>
            </TABLE>
            <BR>
            <BR>
            <INPUT TYPE="TEXT" NAME="text1" SIZE="30">
```

```
            </FORM>
        </BODY>
</HTML>
```

You can see the results in Figure 12.8.

Tip

You don't need a separate function for each radio button, of course. You could give each radio button a different ID value (*not* a different NAME value, which must be the same for all radio buttons in a group), and then pass the current clicked radio button to the onlick handler (like this: ONCLICK="radioClicked(this)") and use the radio button's id property to discover which button was clicked, as well as its checked property to see whether it's been selected.

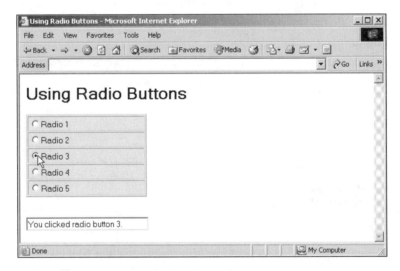

Figure 12.8   Clicking a radio button.

Here's a more involved example. In this case, I'll use both check boxes and radio buttons to let the user make a sandwich, as you see in Figure 12.9. Here the radio buttons on the left select a prebuilt sandwich, and the check boxes on the right display the default items in the sandwich, as you see in Figure 12.9.

When the user clicks a radio button on the left to select a prebuilt sandwich, the code sets the check boxes on the right to show what's in that sandwich. It does that first by calling a function I've named clearSettings to clear all check boxes (by setting their checked property to false), and then selecting the correct check boxes to show the ingredients of the sandwich, and finally calling a function I've named displayCost to examine what ingredient check boxes are checked and to display the corresponding cost, like this:

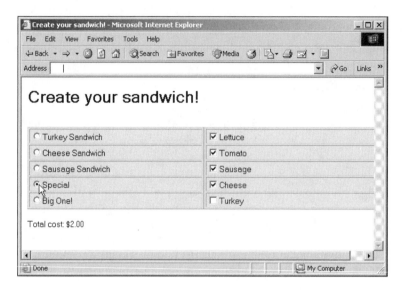

Figure 12.9 Using check boxes and radio buttons together.

```
function radio1Clicked()
{
    clearSettings()                          //Clear the check boxes.
    document.form1.check1.checked = true     //Show the items in this sandwich.
    document.form1.check2.checked = true
    document.form1.check5.checked = true
    displayCost()                            //Display total cost.
}
```

The `displayCost` function works by looping over all the check boxes in the form by looping over all the elements in the form's `elements` array and checking each element's `type` property to make sure it's a check box and that its `checked` property is true like this (this code also uses the `Number` object's `toPrecision` method to format the total cost to two decimal places; this method is available only in Netscape Navigator 6+ and Internet Explorer 5.5+):

```
function displayCost()
{
    var cost = 0

    for (var loopIndex = 0; loopIndex < document.form1.elements.length; loopIndex++) {
        if(document.form1.elements[loopIndex].type=="checkbox"
            && document.form1.elements[loopIndex].checked){
            cost += .50
        }
    }
    document.getElementById("div1").innerHTML = "Total cost: $" + cost.toPrecision(3)
}
```

> **Tip**
>
> There are other ways to set up a loop over all the check boxes in the form. For example, you could use the `getElementsByTagName` method to search for `<INPUT>` elements, and then check the elements' type property to select only check boxes. Or you could give all check boxes the same name and access them using a loop index with the elements array like this: `elements[name, loopIndex]`. (This second index is not supported in the Netscape Navigator.) Or, if you know the numeric positions of the check boxes in the form's `elements` array, you can just set up a loop over the check boxes using a loop index like this: `elements[loopIndex]`.

Besides selecting a whole prebuilt sandwich, the user also can select (or deselect) additional check boxes to customize the sandwich. Doing so uses the check box's ONCLICK attribute to call `displayCost` to recalculate the sandwich's price:

```
<INPUT TYPE="CHECKBOX" NAME="check1" ONCLICK="displayCost()">
```

That's it! Here's the whole code, which uses check boxes together with radio buttons, as well as these controls' ONCLICK attribute, their checked property (both to set check marks and to see what items have been checked), their type property, and the form object's elements property (Netscape Navigator 6+ and Internet Explorer 5.5+):

(Listing 12-15.html on the web site)

```
<HTML>
    <HEAD>
        <TITLE>Create your sandwich!</TITLE>
        <SCRIPT LANGUAGE="JavaScript">
            <!--
                function radio1Clicked()
                {
                    clearSettings()
                    document.form1.check1.checked = true
                    document.form1.check2.checked = true
                    document.form1.check5.checked = true
                    displayCost()
                }

                function radio2Clicked()
                {
                    clearSettings()
                    document.form1.check2.checked = true
                    document.form1.check4.checked = true
                    displayCost()
                }

                function radio3Clicked()
                {
                    clearSettings()
```

continues ▶

```
        document.form1.check1.checked = true
        document.form1.check2.checked = true
        document.form1.check3.checked = true
        displayCost()
    }

    function radio4Clicked()
    {
        clearSettings()
        document.form1.check1.checked = true
        document.form1.check2.checked = true
        document.form1.check3.checked = true
        document.form1.check4.checked = true
        displayCost()
    }

    function radio5Clicked()
    {
        clearSettings()
        document.form1.check1.checked = true
        document.form1.check2.checked = true
        document.form1.check3.checked = true
        document.form1.check4.checked = true
        document.form1.check5.checked = true
        displayCost()
    }

    function clearSettings()
    {
        for (var loopIndex = 0; loopIndex <
    ➥document.form1.elements.length; loopIndex++) {
            if(document.form1.elements[loopIndex].type=="checkbox") {
                document.form1.elements[loopIndex].checked = false
            }
        }
    }

    function displayCost()
    {
        var cost = 0

        for (var loopIndex = 0; loopIndex <
    ➥document.form1.elements.length; loopIndex++) {
            if(document.form1.elements[loopIndex].type=="checkbox"
                && document.form1.elements[loopIndex].checked){
                cost += .50
            }
        }
        document.getElementById("div1").innerHTML = "Total cost: $" +
    ➥cost.toPrecision(3)
```

```
            }
        //-->
    </SCRIPT>
</HEAD>

<BODY>
    <H1>Create your sandwich!</H1>
    <BR>
    <FORM NAME="form1">
        <TABLE NAME="table1" BORDER BGCOLOR="cyan" WIDTH="300" ALIGN="LEFT">
            <TR><TD><INPUT TYPE="RADIO" NAME="radios"
            ➥ONCLICK="radio1Clicked()">Turkey Sandwich</TD></TR>
            <TR><TD><INPUT TYPE="RADIO" NAME="radios"
            ➥ONCLICK="radio2Clicked()">Cheese Sandwich</TD></TR>
            <TR><TD><INPUT TYPE="RADIO" NAME="radios"
            ➥ONCLICK="radio3Clicked()">Sausage Sandwich</TD></TR>
            <TR><TD><INPUT TYPE="RADIO" NAME="radios"
            ➥ONCLICK="radio4Clicked()">Special</TD></TR>
            <TR><TD><INPUT TYPE="RADIO" NAME="radios"
            ➥ONCLICK="radio5Clicked()">Big One!</TD></TR>
        </TABLE>

        <TABLE NAME="table2" BORDER BGCOLOR="cyan" WIDTH="300" ALIGN="RIGHT">
            <TR><TD><INPUT TYPE="CHECKBOX" NAME="check1"
            ➥ONCLICK="displayCost()">Lettuce</TD></TR>
            <TR><TD><INPUT TYPE="CHECKBOX" NAME="check2"
            ➥ONCLICK="displayCost()">Tomato</TD></TR>
            <TR><TD><INPUT TYPE="CHECKBOX" NAME="check3"
            ➥ONCLICK="displayCost()">Sausage</TD></TR>
            <TR><TD><INPUT TYPE="CHECKBOX" NAME="check4"
            ➥ONCLICK="displayCost()">Cheese</TD></TR>
            <TR><TD><INPUT TYPE="CHECKBOX" NAME="check5"
            ➥ONCLICK="displayCost()">Turkey</TD></TR>
        </TABLE>
        <BR CLEAR="ALL">
        <BR>
        <DIV ID="div1"> </DIV>
    </FORM>
</BODY>
</HTML>
```

You can see the results in Figure 12.9. When you click a sandwich radio button, the corresponding ingredients for the sandwich display using the check boxes. You can customize what's in a sandwich by selecting or deselecting check boxes yourself as well. Give it a try! And that's it. This example finishes our work with check boxes and radio buttons in this chapter.

The *<FIELDSET>* and *<LEGEND>* Elements

The <FIELDSET> and <LEGEND> elements enable you to format the appearance of elements in a form, and because you use them with forms, I'll discuss them in this chapter. The <FIELDSET> element draws a rectangle around the form, and a <LEGEND> element nested in that <FIELDSET> element enables you to give the <FIELDSET> element a caption, or legend. You can see the properties of these elements in Table 12.13—note that the properties, methods, and events we saw in Chapters 5 and 6 also apply to these elements. Table 12.14 lists the additional events of <LEGEND> elements.

Table 12.13 **The Properties of the *<FIELDSET>* and *<LEGEND>* Elements (See Chapters 5 and 6 for the JavaScript core HTML properties, methods, and events that also apply to this element.)**

Property	NS2	NS3	NS4	NS6	IE3a	IE3b	IE4	IE5	IE5.5	IE6
align				x				x	x	x

Read/write
This attribute sets the alignment of the <FIELDSET> and <LEGEND> elements. The possible values for the <LEGEND> element are "bottom" (aligns to bottom-center), "center" (aligns to center), "left" (aligns to left), "right" (aligns to right), and "top" (aligns top-center). The Internet Explorer gives you more possible values for the <FIELDSET> element; here they are: "absbottom" (aligns the bottom of the <FIELDSET> with the absolute bottom of the surrounding text), "absmiddle" (aligns the middle of the <FIELDSET> with the middle of the surrounding text), "baseline" (aligns the bottom of the <FIELDSET> with the baseline of the surrounding text), "bottom" (aligns the bottom of the <FIELDSET> with the bottom of the surrounding text), "left" (the default, aligns the <FIELDSET> to the left of the surrounding text), "middle" (aligns the middle of the <FIELD-SET> with the surrounding text), "right" (aligns the <FIELDSET> to the right of the surrounding text), and "top" (aligns the top of the <FIELDSET> with the top of the text).

Property	NS2	NS3	NS4	NS6	IE3a	IE3b	IE4	IE5	IE5.5	IE6
form				x						x

Read-only
Holds the form object for the <FIELDSET> or <LEGEND> element. This property is read-only.

Table 12.14 **The Events of the <*LEGEND*> Element (See Chapters 5 and 6 for the JavaScript core HTML properties, methods, and events that also apply to this element.)**

Event	NS2	NS3	NS4	NS6	IE3a	IE3b	IE4	IE5	IE5.5	IE6
onafterupdate							X	X	X	X
Occurs in a data-bound object after updating the data in the data source.										
onbeforeupdate							X	X	X	X
Occurs in a data-bound object before updating the data in the data source.										
onerrorupdate							X	X	X	X
Occurs in a data-bound object when an error happened while updating data in the data source.										

Here's an example for use in the Internet Explorer that enables you to set the align property of a <LEGEND> element on-the-fly by clicking a button marked Right, Left, or Center:

(Listing 12-16.html on the web site)

```
<HTML>
    <HEAD>
        <TITLE>
            Using &lt;FIELDSET&gt;, &lt;LEGEND&gt;, And &lt;LABEL&gt;
        </TITLE>
        <SCRIPT LANGUAGE="JavaScript">
            <!--
            function left()
            {
                document.getElementById("legend1").align = "left"
            }
            function center()
            {
                document.getElementById("legend1").align = "center"
            }
            function right()
            {
                document.getElementById("legend1").align = "right"
            }
            // -->
        </SCRIPT>
    </HEAD>

    <BODY>

        <H1>Using &lt;FIELDSET&gt;, &lt;LEGEND&gt;, And &lt;LABEL&gt;</H1>
```

continues ▶

```
<FORM>
    <FIELDSET>
        <LEGEND ID="legend1" ACCESSKEY="L" TABINDEX="1"
        ➥ALIGN="right">Answers</LEGEND>
        <LABEL ACCESSKEY="Y">
            <INPUT TYPE="RADIO" NAME="ANSWER" VALUE="YES">Yes
        </LABEL>
        <BR>
        <LABEL ACCESSKEY="N">
            <INPUT TYPE="RADIO" NAME="ANSWER" VALUE="NO">No
        </LABEL>
    </FIELDSET>
    <BUTTON VALUE="Right" ONCLICK="right()">Right</BUTTON>
    <BUTTON VALUE="Left" ONCLICK="center()">Center</BUTTON>
    <BUTTON VALUE="Right" ONCLICK="left()">Left</BUTTON>
</FORM>
</BODY>
</HTML>
```

You can see this example at work in Figure 12.10, where I've clicked the
Right button to realign the legend Answers to the right. (The default is to
align to the left.)

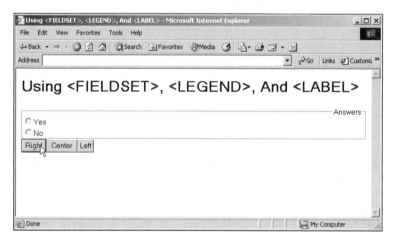

Figure 12.10 Setting the alignment of a <LEGEND> element.

That finishes our work with buttons, check boxes, radio buttons, fieldsets,
and legends in this chapter. We've gotten our start with HTML controls—in
the next chapter, we'll build on that when we take a look at the HTML
text-based and select controls.

13

Working with Text and Select Controls

IN THIS CHAPTER, WE'LL TAKE A LOOK at the HTML text and select controls. That includes more than you might think—text fields, password controls, hidden controls, text areas, select controls, option elements, option group elements, and so on. All these controls are central to any JavaScript programmer's arsenal, so what we see here will be a good part of our JavaScript foundation, just as working with button controls was in the preceding chapter.

For example, it's hard to imagine a substantial JavaScript-based web page that accepts text input from a user without using text fields. We've worked with this basic control since Chapter 1, "Essential JavaScript," both to display and read text, and we're no strangers to code like this, which displays a message, `You clicked the button!`, in a text field when the user clicks a button:

(Listing 13-01.html on the web site)

```
<HTML>
    <HEAD>
        <TITLE>
            Executing Scripts in Response to User Action
        </TITLE>
        <SCRIPT LANGUAGE="JavaScript">
            <!--
            function alerter()
            {
                document.form1.text1.value = "You clicked the button!"
            }
            // -->
        </SCRIPT>
    </HEAD>

    <BODY>
        <H1>Executing Scripts in Response to User Action</H1>
        <FORM NAME="form1">
            <INPUT TYPE="BUTTON" ONCLICK="alerter()" VALUE="Click Me!">
            <INPUT TYPE="TEXT" NAME="text1" SIZE="30">
        </FORM>
    </BODY>
</HTML>
```

You can see this code at work in Figure 13.1. That was easy enough; but what about working with selected text in text controls, or working with text areas? And what about handling user selections in select controls—or even multiple selections? We'll see all of that in this chapter. In fact, besides text fields, password controls, and hidden controls, we'll also see another of the <INPUT> controls—<INPUT TYPE="FILE">, the file upload control—which enables you to upload a file to the server.

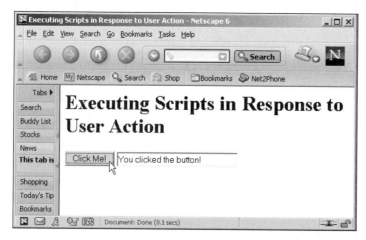

Figure 13.1 Using a text field in the Netscape Navigator.

The *<INPUT TYPE="TEXT">*, *<INPUT TYPE= "PASSWORD">*, and *<INPUT TYPE= "HIDDEN">* Elements

The text controls based on the <INPUT> element share the same properties, methods, and events (except for the hidden control, which doesn't appear in a web page and so can't have visually-oriented events such as onclick). Here are these controls:

- **<INPUT TYPE="TEXT">.** Text fields.
- **<INPUT TYPE="PASSWORD">.** Password controls.
- **<INPUT TYPE="HIDDEN">.** Hidden text controls, which contain text not visible to the user, but available to your code to store text in.

You can see an overview of the properties, methods, and events of these controls in Table 13.1, their properties in depth in Table 13.2, their methods in Table 13.3, and their events in Table 13.4. Note that JavaScript's core HTML properties, methods, and events, which we discussed in Chapters 5, "Using Core HTML Properties," and 6, "Using Core HTML Methods and Events," also apply to these controls.

Table 13.1 **Overview of the Properties, Methods, and Events of the** *<INPUT TYPE="TEXT">*, *<INPUT TYPE="PASSWORD">*, **and** *<INPUT TYPE="HIDDEN">* **Elements (See Chapters 5 and 6 for the JavaScript core HTML properties, methods, and events that also apply to this element.)**

Properties	Methods	Events
defaultValue	select	onafterupdate
form	createTextRange	onbeforeupdate
maxLength		onchange
name		onerrorupdate
readOnly		onselect
size		
type		
value		

Table 13.2 **The Properties of the *<INPUT TYPE="TEXT">*, *<INPUT TYPE="PASSWORD">*, and *<INPUT TYPE="HIDDEN">* Elements (See Chapters 5 and 6 for the JavaScript core HTML properties, methods, and events that also apply to this element.)**

Property	NS2	NS3	NS4	NS6	IE3a	IE3b	IE4	IE5	IE5.5	IE6
defaultValue	x	x	x	x	x	x	x	x	x	x

Read/write
Holds the default value for the control—the value that appears in the control when the control's form is reset. Set to a text string. (In practice, however, this property does not appear to work as it should. Resetting a form, either with a reset button or the reset method does not actually make this property's value appear in text controls.)

	NS2	NS3	NS4	NS6	IE3a	IE3b	IE4	IE5	IE5.5	IE6
form	x	x	x	x	x	x	x	x	x	x

Read-only
Contains a reference to the control's form. This is handy if you pass a control to a function and need access to other controls in the same form.

	NS2	NS3	NS4	NS6	IE3a	IE3b	IE4	IE5	IE5.5	IE6
maxLength				x			x	x	x	x

Read/write
Sets the maximum number of characters the control may contain and display simultaneously. Set to an integer. A very handy property to limit the amount of input you want to accept (and useful to limit hackers from trying to break CGI programs by sending too much data to the server).

	NS2	NS3	NS4	NS6	IE3a	IE3b	IE4	IE5	IE5.5	IE6
name	x	x	x	x	x	x	x	x	x	x

Read/write
Holds the name of the control, as used in code. May be changed in code, because it's read/write. Set to a name string.

	NS2	NS3	NS4	NS6	IE3a	IE3b	IE4	IE5	IE5.5	IE6
readOnly				x			x	x	x	x

Read/write
Specifies whether the control is read-only. Set to true or false. This property is useful to "disable" text controls (although you can also use the disabled property). If you're just using a text control to display text, however, consider using a <DIV> or <SPAN> element with the innerHTML property instead.

	NS2	NS3	NS4	NS6	IE3a	IE3b	IE4	IE5	IE5.5	IE6
size				x			x	x	x	x

Read/write
Sets the width of the control, measured in characters. A very handy property if you want wider text controls than the default.

Property	NS2	NS3	NS4	NS6	IE3a	IE3b	IE4	IE5	IE5.5	IE6
type		x	x	x		x	x	x	x	x

Read-only
Holds the type of the text control, as a string such as "text", "password", or "hidden". This property reflects the TYPE attribute of the control. As of Internet Explorer 5, the type property is read/write, but only once, when an element is created with the createElement method and before it is added to the document.

Property	NS2	NS3	NS4	NS6	IE3a	IE3b	IE4	IE5	IE5.5	IE6
value	x	x	x	x	x	x	x	x	x	x

Read/write
Holds the actual text in the control. Set to a string. You can get or set the text in a text control using this property. See "Using Text Controls" in this chapter.

Table 13.3   **The Methods of the *<INPUT TYPE="TEXT">*, *<INPUT TYPE="PASSWORD">*, and *<INPUT TYPE="HIDDEN">* Elements (See Chapters 5 and 6 for the JavaScript core HTML properties, methods, and events that also apply to this element.)**

Method	NS2	NS3	NS4	NS6	IE3a	IE3b	IE4	IE5	IE5.5	IE6
createTextRange							x	x	x	x

Returns: TextRange object
This method creates a TextRange object for the control.
Syntax: createTextRange(). See Chapter 11, "Working with HTML Text Elements," for more on text ranges.

Method	NS2	NS3	NS4	NS6	IE3a	IE3b	IE4	IE5	IE5.5	IE6
select		x	x	x			x	x	x	x

Returns: Nothing
Selects the text in the control.
Syntax: select(). You can use this method together with the focus method (see Chapter 6) to highlight text and set yourself up for a response from the user.

Table 13.4 **The Events of the** *<INPUT TYPE="TEXT">*, *<INPUT TYPE="PASSWORD">*, **and** *<INPUT TYPE="HIDDEN">* **Elements (See Chapters 5 and 6 for the JavaScript core HTML properties, methods, and events that also apply to this element.)**

Event	NS2	NS3	NS4	NS6	IE3a	IE3b	IE4	IE5	IE5.5	IE6
onafterupdate							X	X	X	X
Occurs in a data-bound object after updating the data in the data source.										
onbeforeupdate							X	X	X	X
Occurs in a data-bound object before updating the data in the data source.										
onchange	X	X	X	X	X	X	X	X	X	X
Occurs when the user has changed the contents of a text control and then leaves the control by setting the focus somewhere else (such as by clicking another control). That is, the user has "committed" the change by moving away from the control—this event does not just happen while the user is entering text. (For that, see onkeydown, onkeypress, and onkeyup in Chapter 6.) See "Using Text Controls" in this chapter.										
onerrorupdate							X	X	X	X
Occurs in a data-bound object when an error happened while updating data in the data source.										
onselect				X	X	X	X	X	X	X
Occurs when text in the control is selected. See "Using Text Areas" in this chapter for an example.										

Using Text Controls

We've already seen a good deal about text controls in this book, so we can skip the elementary aspects of using the value property and so on. The onchange event is a useful one JavaScript programmers should know about. This event occurs when the user has changed the text in a text control and "committed" the change by moving the focus away from the control (as by clicking another control). Here's an example putting onchange to work—when the user enters text into the text field and then clicks outside the text field, the text from the text field is displayed in a <DIV> element (like other examples that use getElementById, you'll need NS6+ if you're using the Netscape Navigator):

(Listing 13-02.html on the web site)

```html
<HTML>
    <HEAD>
        <TITLE>Using the onchange Event</TITLE>
        <SCRIPT LANGUAGE="JavaScript">
            <!--
            function displayText()
            {
                document.getElementById("div1").innerHTML =
                    "The text field holds: " + document.form1.text1.value
            }
            //-->
        </SCRIPT>
    </HEAD>

    <BODY>
        <H1>Using the onchange Event</H1>
        <FORM NAME="form1">
            <INPUT TYPE="TEXT" NAME="text1" ONCHANGE="displayText()">
            <BR>
            <DIV ID="div1">
        </FORM>
    </BODY>
</HTML>
```

Tip

Note that the onchange event does not occur as the user is entering or editing text—for that, see onkeydown, onkeypress, and onkeyup in Chapter 6. Or see the discussion of handling carriage returns, coming up next.

You can see the results of this code in Figure 13.2. If you want to read what the user has entered in a text control when he has just finished entering it, the onchange event is the one to use.

Carriage returns (that is, pressing the Enter key) have a special place in text fields. By tradition, if a form has only one control, a text field, pressing the Enter key when the text field has the focus is the same as clicking a Submit button—even if the form doesn't have one. For that reason, you may be surprised to see the browser attempt to "submit" what's a purely local form when the user presses Enter. (If you haven't specified an URL for the form to be submitted to with the form's ACTION attribute, the browser attempts to send the data back to the URL of the current page with the text data in the text field appended to the URL like this: *URL*?text1=hello!, where I'm assuming the name of the text field was text1, and it held the text "hello!".)

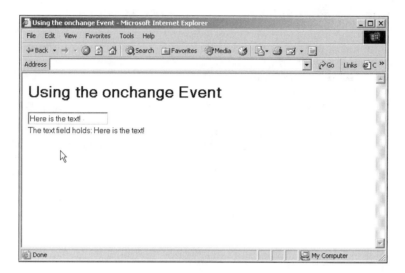

Figure 13.2 Using the onchange event.

You can handle Enter keys in text fields in the same way you can handle any individual keystrokes—with the onkeydown, onkeypress, and onkeyup events. To detect the Enter key, for example, you can check the key code passed to an onkeydown event handler—the key code for the Enter key is 13 (corresponding to the ASCII and Unicode code for a carriage return). If you return false from an onkeydown event handler, the browser will assume you've handled the keystroke yourself and not do any processing on it. That's how you prevent a key from appearing in a text control—return false from the onkeydown event handler. (That's useful, for example, if you only want a user to enter numeric data, because you can check what they type as they type it and prevent any nondigits from appearing.) To prevent the browser from beeping when the user presses Enter in a text field, take a look at this code, which detects the Enter key (and so can initiate some action, such as submitting a form, when the user presses that key) and just displays a message when that key is seen:

(Listing 13-03.html on the web site)

```
<HTML>
    <HEAD>
        <TITLE>Handling the Enter key</TITLE>
        <SCRIPT LANGUAGE="JavaScript">
            <!--
            function checkEnter(e)
            {
                if(navigator.appName == "Netscape") {
                    if(e.which == 13){
```

```
                    document.form1.text2.value = "You pressed Enter"
                    return false
                } else {
                    return true
                }
            }
            if (navigator.appName == "Microsoft Internet Explorer") {
                if(window.event.keyCode == 13){
                    document.form1.text2.value = "You pressed Enter"
                    return false
                } else {
                    return true
                }
            }
        }
        // -->
    </SCRIPT>
</HEAD>

<BODY>
    <H1>Handling the Enter key</H1>
    <BR>
    <FORM NAME="form1">
        <INPUT NAME="text1" TYPE="TEXT" SIZE="20" ONKEYDOWN="return
        ➥checkEnter(event)">
        <BR>
        <INPUT NAME="text2" TYPE="TEXT" SIZE="20">
    </FORM>
</BODY>
</HTML>
```

You can see the results of this code in Figure 13.3.

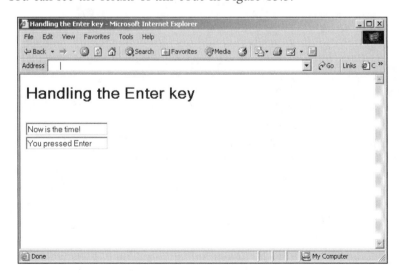

Figure 13.3   Detecting the Enter key.

Here's another text control example, which we first saw in Chapter 6 (Listing 06-16.html on the web site). This example uses the `onfocus` event to display prompts to the user about what kind of data she should enter; it's a web page–based calculator that adds numbers, and each time one of the two text fields the user is supposed to enter an integer into gets the focus, this code uses the `window.status` property to display the prompt `Enter an integer.` in the browser's status bar:

```html
<HTML>
    <HEAD>
        <TITLE>An HTML Calculator</TITLE>
        <SCRIPT LANGUAGE="JavaScript">
            <!--
            function text1Prompt()
            {
                window.status = "Enter an integer."
            }
            function text2Prompt()
            {
                window.status = "Enter an integer."
            }
            function text3Prompt()
            {
                window.status = "The sum is displayed here."
            }
            function Add()
            {
                document.form1.text3.value =
                parseInt(document.form1.text1.value) +
                parseInt(document.form1.text2.value)
            }
            // -->
        </SCRIPT>
    </HEAD>

    <BODY>
        <H1>An HTML Calculator</H1>
        <FORM NAME="form1">
            <INPUT TYPE="TEXT" NAME="text1" ONFOCUS="text1Prompt()">
            +
            <INPUT TYPE="TEXT" NAME="text2" ONFOCUS="text2Prompt()">
            <INPUT TYPE="BUTTON" ONCLICK="Add()" VALUE = " = ">
            <INPUT TYPE="TEXT" NAME="text3" ONFOCUS="text3Prompt()">
        </FORM>
    </BODY>
</HTML>
```

You can see the results in Figure 6.12. (Note the message `Enter an integer.` in the status bar.)

Besides standard text fields, text controls also include the password control, which masks what the user types with a character such as an asterisk ($\star$). The text entered in a password control is masked in this way—the control does not support copying to the clipboard, so someone can't copy the contents of the control and paste it somewhere to see the actual text. However, the text in the control is accessible to your code using the `value` property. Here's an example that reads and displays the actual text in a password control when the user presses the Enter key:

(Listing 13-04.html on the web site)

```html
<HTML>
    <HEAD>
        <TITLE>Using Password Controls</TITLE>
        <SCRIPT LANGUAGE="JavaScript">
            <!--
            function checkEnter(e)
            {
                if(navigator.appName == "Netscape") {
                    if(e.which == 13){
                        document.form1.text2.value = "The password is: " +
                        ➥document.form1.text1.value
                        return false
                    } else {
                        return true
                    }
                }
                if (navigator.appName == "Microsoft Internet Explorer") {
                    if(window.event.keyCode == 13){
                        document.form1.text2.value = "The password is: " +
                        ➥document.form1.text1.value
                        return false
                    } else {
                        return true
                    }
                }
            }
            // -->
        </SCRIPT>
    </HEAD>

    <BODY>
        <H1>Type the password and press Enter</H1>
        <BR>
        <FORM NAME="form1">
            <INPUT NAME="text1" TYPE="PASSWORD" SIZE="20" ONKEYDOWN="return
            ➥checkEnter(event)">
            <BR>
            <INPUT NAME="text2" TYPE="TEXT" SIZE="30">
        </FORM>
    </BODY>
</HTML>
```

You can see the results of this code in Figure 13.4.

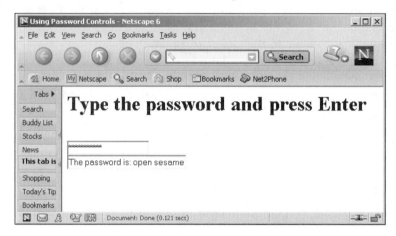

Figure 13.4 Using a password control.

The other standard text control is the hidden control, which does not appear in the web page, but which can hold text. This control is great for holding data about a page you don't want the user to see. For example, you can hold the users' current purchases in a hidden field if their browser has cookies turned off. (Although note that hidden fields are very low security, because users can see the contents of the field if they view the HTML source of the web page.) Hidden controls offer you a good place to hold data in a web page. Here's an example where we're storing some default text in a hidden control and using it to restore the original text in a text field when the user clicks a button:

(Listing 13-05.html on the web site)

```
<HTML>
    <HEAD>
        <TITLE>Using Hidden Controls</TITLE>
        <SCRIPT LANGUAGE = JavaScript>
            <!--
            function restoreData()
            {
                document.form1.text1.value = document.form1.hidden1.value
            }
            //-->
        </SCRIPT>
    </HEAD>

    <BODY>
        <H1>Using Hidden Controls</H1>
        Edit the text, then click the button to restore the original text!
        <FORM NAME="form1">
            <INPUT TYPE="TEXT" VALUE="Hello from JavaScript" NAME="text1" SIZE="25">
```

```
            <BR>
            <INPUT TYPE = BUTTON VALUE="Restore default text" ONCLICK="restoreData()">
            <INPUT TYPE = HIDDEN NAME="hidden1" VALUE = "Hello from JavaScript">
        </FORM>
    </BODY>
</HTML>
```

You can see the results of this code in Figures 13.5 and 13.6. When you load this page, `Hello from JavaScript` appears in the text field, but I've edited that to `Hello from Java!` in Figure 13.5. When I click the button in Figure 13.6, the original text, `Hello from JavaScript`, is restored from the hidden control to the text field.

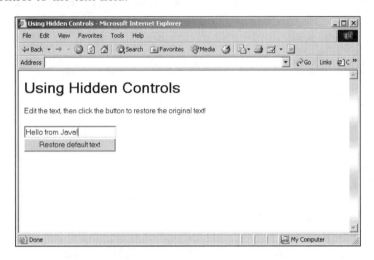

Figure 13.5   Editing text in a text field.

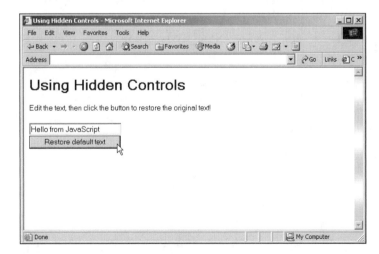

Figure 13.6   Restoring the edited text with data from a hidden control.

The *<TEXTAREA>* Element

Another popular text control is the text area control, which—unlike the other text controls we've seen so far in this chapter—enables you to handle multiple lines of text. You can see the properties, methods, and events of the <TEXTAREA> element in overview in Table 13.5, its properties in depth in Table 13.6, its methods in Table 13.7, and its events in Table 13.8. Also see Chapters 5 and 6 for the JavaScript core HTML properties, methods, and events that also apply to this element.

Table 13.5   **Overview of the Properties, Methods, and Events of the** *<TEXTAREA>* **Element (See Chapters 5 and 6 for the JavaScript core HTML properties, methods, and events that also apply to this element.)**

Properties	Methods	Events
cols	createTextRange	onafterupdate
form	select	onbeforeupdate
name		onchange
readOnly		onerrorupdate
rows		onselect
type		
wrap		

Table 13.6   **The Properties of the** *<TEXTAREA>* **Element (See Chapters 5 and 6 for the JavaScript core HTML properties, methods, and events that also apply to this element.)**

Property	NS2	NS3	NS4	NS6	IE3a	IE3b	IE4	IE5	IE5.5	IE6
cols				x			x	x	x	x

Read/write
Holds the number of columns in the text area, corresponding to the COLS property. Set to an integer.

form	x	x	x	x	x	x	x	x	x	x

Read-only
Contains a reference to the control's form. This is handy if you pass a control to a function and need access to other controls in the same form.

Property	NS2	NS3	NS4	NS6	IE3a	IE3b	IE4	IE5	IE5.5	IE6
name	x	x	x	x	x	x	x	x	x	x

Read/write
Holds the name of the control, as used in code. May be changed in code, because it's read/write. Set to a name string.

readOnly				x			x	x	x	x

Read/write
Specifies whether the control is read-only. Set to true or false. This property is useful to "disable" text controls (although you also can use the disabled property). If you're just using a text control to display text, however, consider using a <DIV> or <SPAN> element with the innerHTML property instead.

rows				x			x	x	x	x

Read/write
Holds the number of rows in the text area, corresponding to the ROWS property. Set to an integer.

type		x	x	x		x	x	x	x	x

Read-only
Holds a string that indicates the type of the control. Holds "textarea" here.

wrap							x	x	x	x

Read/write
Specifies how to handle word wrapping at the ends of lines. Set to a string; the possible values are: "soft" (the default—text displays with word wrapping and is submitted without carriage returns and line feeds), "hard" (text displays with word wrapping and is submitted with returns and line feeds), and "off" (word wrapping is disabled).

Table 13.7 The Methods of the <*TEXTAREA*> Element (See Chapters 5 and 6 for the JavaScript core HTML properties, methods, and events that also apply to this element.)

Method	NS2	NS3	NS4	NS6	IE3a	IE3b	IE4	IE5	IE5.5	IE6
createTextRange							x	x	x	x

Returns: TextRange object
This method creates a TextRange object for the control.
Syntax: createTextRange(). See Chapter 11 for more on text ranges.

continues ▶

Table 13.7 **Continued**

Method	NS2	NS3	NS4	NS6	IE3a	IE3b	IE4	IE5	IE5.5	IE6
select	x	x	x	x	x	x	x	x	x	x

Returns: Nothing

Selects the text in the control.

Syntax: `select()`. You can use this method together with the `focus` method (see Chapter 6) to highlight text and set yourself up for a response from the user.

Table 13.8 **The Events of the <*TEXTAREA*> Element (See Chapters 5 and 6 for the JavaScript core HTML properties, methods, and events that also apply to this element.)**

Event	NS2	NS3	NS4	NS6	IE3a	IE3b	IE4	IE5	IE5.5	IE6
onafterupdate							x	x	x	x

Occurs in a data-bound object after updating the data in the data source.

| onbeforeupdate | | | | | | | x | x | x | x |

Occurs in a data-bound object before updating the data in the data source.

| onchange | x | x | x | x | x | x | x | x | x | x |

Occurs when the user has changed the contents of a text control and then leaves the control by setting the focus somewhere else (such as by clicking another control). In other words, the user has "committed" the change by moving away from the control—this event does not happen while the user is entering text. (For that, see **onkeydown**, **onkeypress**, and **onkeyup** in Chapter 6.) See "Using Text Controls" in this chapter.

| onerrorupdate | | | | | | | x | x | x | x |

Occurs in a data-bound object when an error happened while updating data in the data source.

| onselect | | | x | x | x | x | x | x | x | x |

Occurs when text in the control is selected. See "Using Text Areas" in this chapter for an example.

Using Text Areas

The big difference between text areas and the text controls we've already seen in this chapter is that text areas are two-dimensional, not one-dimensional, and can display multiple lines of text. Here's an example that does exactly that when you click a button. In this case, the text displayed in the text area is Hello\nfrom\nJavaScript!, where \n is the JavaScript newline character (corresponding to ASCII/Unicode code 10), which causes the text to jump to the next line:

(Listing 13-06.html on the web site)

```
<HTML>
    <HEAD>
        <TITLE>Using the &lt;TEXTAREA&gt; Element</TITLE>
        <SCRIPT LANGUAGE="JavaScript">
            <!--
            function DisplayMessage()
            {
                document.form1.textarea1.value = "Hello\nfrom\nJavaScript!"
            }
            //-->
        </SCRIPT>
    </HEAD>

    <BODY>
        <H1>Using the &lt;TEXTAREA&gt; Element</H1>
        <FORM NAME="form1">
            <TEXTAREA NAME="textarea1" COLS="30" ROWS="10"></TEXTAREA>
            <BR>
            <INPUT TYPE="BUTTON" Value = "Display Message" ONCLICK="DisplayMessage()">
        </FORM>
    </BODY>
</HTML>
```

You can see the results of this code in Figure 13.7, including the multiline text.

> **Tip**
>
> The way line endings are actually handled in text areas varies by operating system, so you should prepare for different types of line endings when you read text from text areas. In UNIX, for instance, line endings are handled with a \n JavaScript character (corresponding to ASCII/Unicode code 10), in the Mac as \r (corresponding to ASCII/Unicode code 13), and in Windows as \r\n.

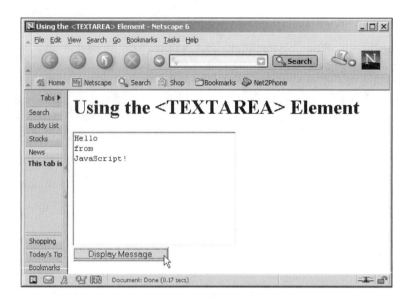

Figure 13.7   Entering multiline text into a text area.

Here's another example using text areas, this time showing how to detect selected text using the `onselect` event. The Internet Explorer enables you to handle this event as the user is selecting text in a text control. In this code, I'll handle the `onselect` event by displaying the text the user is selecting as he is selecting it (the displayed text changes interactively as the user selects text):

(Listing 13-07.html on the web site)

```
<HTML>
    <HEAD>
        <TITLE>Reading Selected Text</TITLE>
        <SCRIPT LANGUAGE="JavaScript">
            <!--
            function getSelected()
            {
                if (navigator.appName == "Microsoft Internet Explorer") {
                    document.form1.text1.value = document.selection.createRange().text
                }
            }
            // -->
        </SCRIPT>
    </HEAD>

    <BODY>
        <H1>Reading Selected Text</H1>
        <FORM NAME="form1">
```

```
<TEXTAREA ONSELECT="getSelected()">Here's some text!</TEXTAREA>
    You selected: <INPUT TYPE="TEXT" NAME="text1">
  </FORM>
 </BODY>
</HTML>
```

You can see the results of this code in Figure 13.8, where the selected text displays and is updated as the user selects text.

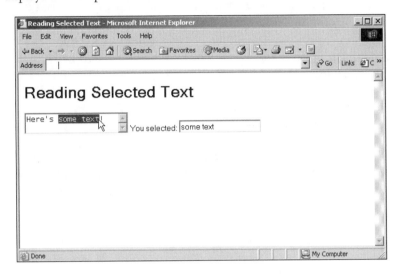

Figure 13.8   Selecting text in a text area.

That completes our look at text controls in this chapter. Now I'll turn to the select control.

The *<SELECT>* Element

<SELECT> elements enable you to display lists of items, as well as drop-down lists of items from which the user can select. You can handle selections in this control, change the displayed items, and more, all under programmatic control. The items displayed in a select control are specified with <OPTION> elements, like this:

```
<SELECT NAME="select1" ONCHANGE="reportSelection()">
    <OPTION>Option 1
    <OPTION>Option 2
    <OPTION>Option 3
    <OPTION>Option 4
    <OPTION>Option 5
</SELECT>
```

Those <OPTION> elements are accessible from your code using the options collection, stored in the options property of a <SELECT> control.

To use select controls, we have to be able to deal with <SELECT> elements, the options collection, and <OPTION> elements. You can see an overview of the <SELECT> element's properties, methods, and events in Table 13.9, its properties in depth in Table 13.10, its methods in depth in Table 13.11, and its events in depth in Table 13.12. Also see Chapters 5 and 6 for the JavaScript core HTML properties, methods, and events that apply to this element.

You can see an overview of the options collection's properties and methods events in Table 13.13, its properties in depth in Table 13.14, and its methods in depth in Table 13.15.

Finally, you can see the <OPTION> element's properties in Table 13.16. Also see Chapters 5 and 6 for the JavaScript core HTML properties, methods, and events that apply to this element.

Table 13.9 **Overview of the Properties, Methods, and Events of the <SELECT> Element (See Chapters 5 and 6 for the JavaScript core HTML properties, methods, and events that also apply to this element.)**

Properties	Methods	Events
form	add	onafterupdate
length	remove	onbeforeupdate
multiple	item	onchange
name	namedItem	onerrorupdate
options		
selectedIndex		
size		
type		
value		

Table 13.10 **The Properties of the <SELECT> Element (See Chapters 5 and 6 for the JavaScript core HTML properties, methods, and events that also apply to this element.)**

Property	NS2	NS3	NS4	NS6	IE3a	IE3b	IE4	IE5	IE5.5	IE6
form	x	x	x	x	x	x	x	x	x	x

Read-only
Contains a reference to the control's form. This is handy if you pass a control to a function and need access to other controls in the same form.

Property	NS2	NS3	NS4	NS6	IE3a	IE3b	IE4	IE5	IE5.5	IE6
length	x	x	x	x	x	x	x	x	x	x

Read/write
Holds the number of <OPTION> elements in the control. Set to an integer.
In NS3+ and IE4+, you can write to this property, but only to set it to its
current value or less. (In which case, <OPTION> elements will disappear
from the end of the list.)

multiple	x	x	x	x	x	x	x	x	x	x

Read/write
Indicates whether multiple selections are allowed, corresponding to the
standalone MULTIPLE attribute. Set to true to allow multiple selections
or false (the default) to disallow multiple selections. See "Using Select
Controls" in this chapter.

name	x	x	x	x	x	x	x	x	x	x

Read/write
Holds the name of the control, as used in code. May be changed in code,
because it's read/write. Set to a name string.

options	x	x	x	x	x	x	x	x	x	x

Read-only
Holds a collection of the <OPTION> elements in the <SELECT> control. The
options collection supports methods such as options[*n*].add()
and options[*n*].remove(). See tables 13.13, 13.14, and 13.15 for more on
the options collection. Also see "Using Select Controls" in this chapter for
an example.

selectedIndex	x	x	x	x	x	x	x	x	x	x

Read/write
Holds the currently selected item's index in the control as an integer
(0-based). You use this property to determine which item is selected in
single-selection select controls.

size				x			x	x	x	x

Read/write
Specifies the number of lines of items visible, corresponding to the SIZE
attribute. Set to an integer. If you don't set a value for the SIZE attribute,
the result is a drop-down list control. See "Using Select Controls" in
this chapter.

continues ▶

Table 13.10 **Continued**

Property	NS2	NS3	NS4	NS6	IE3a	IE3b	IE4	IE5	IE5.5	IE6
type		x	x	x		x	x	x	x	x

Read-only
Specifies the type of <SELECT> control as a string. Will hold "select-one" for single-selection <SELECT> controls and "select-multiple" for multiple selection <SELECT> controls (that is, those <SELECT> controls that include the standalone MULTIPLE HTML attribute).

value					x		x	x	x

Read/write
Holds the contents of the value property of the currently selected <OPTION> element in single-selection select controls. You can associate a value with each <OPTION> element to store data for that <OPTION> element. (For example, the value property can hold a patient ID while the <OPTION> element's text property can hold their name.) Set to a string.

Table 13.11 **The Methods of the** *<SELECT>* **Element (See Chapters 5 and 6 for the JavaScript core HTML properties, methods, and events that also apply to this element.)**

Method	NS2	NS3	NS4	NS6	IE3a	IE3b	IE4	IE5	IE5.5	IE6
add				x						

Returns: Nothing
Adds an item at a specific index to a <SELECT> control.
Syntax: add(*element*, *referenceElement*), where *element* is the new <OPTION> element to add and *referenceElement* is the element to insert the new element before. To insert the new element at the end of the <SELECT> control, set the second parameter to null. See "Creating New Options in a <SELECT> Control" in this chapter for an example.

remove				x						

Returns: Nothing
Removes an item at a specific index in the <SELECT> control.
Syntax: remove(*n*), where *n* is the index of the <OPTION> element to remove. See "Creating New Options in a <SELECT> Control" in this chapter for an example.

item				x						

Returns: <OPTION> element
Returns the <OPTION> element at a specific index in the <SELECT> element.
Syntax: item(*index*), where *index* is a number. This is a recent Netscape-only method; I suggest using the options collection instead.

Method	NS2	NS3	NS4	NS6	IE3a	IE3b	IE4	IE5	IE5.5	IE6
namedItem				x						

Returns: <OPTION> element
Returns the <OPTION> element with a specific ID.
Syntax: item(*ID*), where *ID* is a string holding the <OPTION> element's ID.
This is a recent Netscape-only method; I suggest using the options
collection instead.

Table 13.12   **The Events of the *<SELECT>* Element (See Chapters 5 and 6 for the JavaScript core HTML properties, methods, and events that also apply to this element.)**

Event	NS2	NS3	NS4	NS6	IE3a	IE3b	IE4	IE5	IE5.5	IE6
onafterupdate							x	x	x	x

Occurs in a data-bound object after updating the data in the data source.

| onbeforeupdate | | | | | | | x | x | x | x |

Occurs in a data-bound object before updating the data in the data source.

| onchange | x | x | x | x | x | x | x | x | x | x |

When a new selection is made in the <SELECT> control, this event occurs.
It's the main event you use to handle selections in this control. See "Using
Select Controls" for an example.

| onerrorupdate | | | | | | | x | x | x | x |

Occurs in a data-bound object when an error happened while updating
data in the data source.

Table 13.13   **The Properties and Methods of the *options* Collection**

Properties	Methods
defaultSelected	add
index	remove
selected	
text	
value	

Table 13.14 **The Properties of the *options* Collection**

Property	NS2	NS3	NS4	NS6	IE3a	IE3b	IE4	IE5	IE5.5	IE6
defaultSelected										
	X	X	X	X	X	X	X	X	X	X

Read-only
This property is true for the item in the options collection that is
selected by default when the enclosing <SELECT> control appears. Set to
true or false.
Syntax: options[*n*].defaultSelected.

| index | X | X | X | X | X | X | X | X | X | X |

Read-only
The index of an item in the options collection. (Because you must access
items in this collection by index, however, this property doesn't seem
very useful.)
Syntax: options[*n*].index.

| selected | X | X | X | X | X | X | X | X | X | X |

Read/write
Indicates whether an item in the options collection is selected. You use
this property to determine which options are selected in multiple-
selection <SELECT> controls.
Syntax: options[*n*].selected.

| text | X | X | X | X | X | X | X | X | X | X |

Read/write
Holds the text (caption) of an item in the options collection. Set to
a string.
Syntax: options[*n*].text.

| value | X | X | X | X | X | X | X | X | X | X |

Read/write
Holds the value of an <OPTION> element. You can associate a value with
each <OPTION> element to store data for that <OPTION> element. (For
example, the value property can hold a patient ID while the <OPTION>
element's text property can hold their name.) Set to a string.
Syntax: options[*n*].value. See "The <OPTGROUP> Element" for an
example.

Table 13.15 **The Methods of the *options* Collection**

Method	NS2	NS3	NS4	NS6	IE3a	IE3b	IE4	IE5	IE5.5	IE6
add							X	X	X	X

Returns: Nothing
Adds an new item to the options collection.
Syntax: options.add(*element* [, *index*]), where *element* is the new
<OPTION> element to add and *index* is the index at which to add the item.
If you don't specify an *index* value, the item is added at the end of the
list. See "Creating New Options in a <SELECT> Control" in this chapter
for an example.

Method	NS2	NS3	NS4	NS6	IE3a	IE3b	IE4	IE5	IE5.5	IE6
remove							X	X	X	X

Returns: Nothing
Removes an item from the options collection.
Syntax: options.remove(*n*), where *n* is the index of the item to remove.
See "Creating New Options in a <SELECT> Control" in this chapter for
an example.

Table 13.16 **The Properties of the *<OPTION>* Element (See Chapters 5
and 6 for the JavaScript core HTML properties, methods, and events
that also apply to this element.)**

Property	NS2	NS3	NS4	NS6	IE3a	IE3b	IE4	IE5	IE5.5	IE6
defaultSelected										
	X	X	X	X	X	X	X	X	X	X

Read-only
This property is true if this <OPTION> element is selected by default in a
<SELECT> control. Set to true or false.

Property	NS2	NS3	NS4	NS6	IE3a	IE3b	IE4	IE5	IE5.5	IE6
form	X	X	X	X	X	X	X	X	X	X

Read-only
Contains a reference to the control's form. This is handy if you pass a control to a function and need access to other controls in the same form.

Property	NS2	NS3	NS4	NS6	IE3a	IE3b	IE4	IE5	IE5.5	IE6
label				X						X

Read-only
Sets or gets a value that you can use to implement your own label functionality for the <OPTION> element—there's no standard browser behavior
here yet. Set to a text string.

continues ▶

Table 13.16 **Continued**

Property	NS2	NS3	NS4	NS6	IE3a	IE3b	IE4	IE5	IE5.5	IE6
selected	X	X	X	X	X	X	X	X	X	X

Read/write
This property is true if an <OPTION> element is selected, false otherwise.
You can determine which items are selected in a multiple-select <SELECT>
element using this property.

text	X	X	X	X	X	X	X	X	X	X

Read/write
Holds the text (caption) for the <OPTION> element. Set to a text string.

value	X	X	X	X	X	X	X	X	X	X

Read/write
Holds the value of an <OPTION> element. You can associate a value with
each <OPTION> element to store data for that <OPTION> element. (For example, the value property can hold a patient ID while the <OPTION> element's
text property can hold their name.) Set to a string.
Syntax: options[*n*].value. See "The <OPTGROUP> Element" for an example.

Using *<SELECT>* Controls

When the user makes a selection in a single-selection <SELECT> control
(that is, a <SELECT> control that doesn't include the MULTIPLE standalone
HTML attribute), an onchange event occurs and you can use the
selectedIndex property to get the current selection. Here's an example
that does exactly that:

(Listing 13-08.html on the web site)

```
<HTML>
    <HEAD>
        <TITLE>
            Using Select Controls
        </TITLE>
        <SCRIPT LANGUAGE = JavaScript>
            <!--
            function reportSelection()
            {
                document.form1.text1.value = "You chose item" +
                    (document.form1.select1.selectedIndex + 1)
            }
```

```
            //-->
        </SCRIPT>
    </HEAD>

    <BODY>
        <FORM NAME="form1">
            <H1>Using Select Controls</H1>
            <INPUT NAME="text1" TYPE="TEXT" SIZE = "20">
            <BR>
            <SELECT NAME="select1" ONCHANGE="reportSelection()">
                <OPTION>Option 1
                <OPTION>Option 2
                <OPTION>Option 3
                <OPTION>Option 4
                <OPTION>Option 5
            </SELECT>
        </FORM>
    </BODY>
</HTML>
```

You can see the results of this code in Figure 13.9.

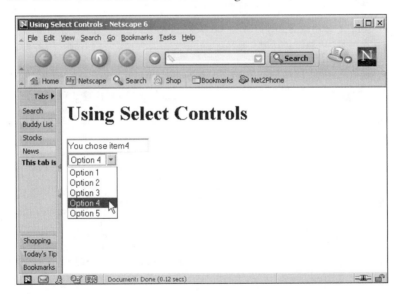

Figure 13.9   Making a selection in a *<SELECT>* control.

Note that this *<SELECT>* control appears as a drop-down list. You can change that into a static list displaying multiple items simultaneously if you use the *SIZE* attribute. For example, here's how to display three items simultaneously:

(Listing 13-09.html on the web site)

```
<HTML>
    <HEAD>
        <TITLE>
            Using Select Controls
        </TITLE>
        <SCRIPT LANGUAGE = JavaScript>
            <!--
            function reportSelection()
            {
                document.form1.text1.value = "You chose item" +
                    (document.form1.select1.selectedIndex + 1)
            }
            //-->
        </SCRIPT>
    </HEAD>

    <BODY>
        <FORM NAME="form1">
            <H1>Using Select Controls</H1>
            <INPUT NAME="text1" TYPE="TEXT" SIZE = "20">
            <BR>
            <SELECT NAME="select1" SIZE="3" ONCHANGE="reportSelection()">
                <OPTION>Option 1
                <OPTION>Option 2
                <OPTION>Option 3
                <OPTION>Option 4
                <OPTION>Option 5
            </SELECT>
        </FORM>
    </BODY>
</HTML>
```

You can see the results of this code in Figure 13.10.

You also can use the MULTIPLE HTML attribute to allow a <SELECT> control to handle multiple selections. (In Windows, for example, the user can
make multiple selections by clicking and using the Shift or Ctrl keys).

When the user makes multiple selections, you can't just use the <SELECT>
element's selectedIndex property anymore, because there is more than one
selection. Instead, you must loop over the items in the options collection,
checking each one's selected property to see whether it's selected. Here's an
example. Note that I'm using the MULTIPLE HTML attribute in the <SELECT>
control to make it a multiselect control:

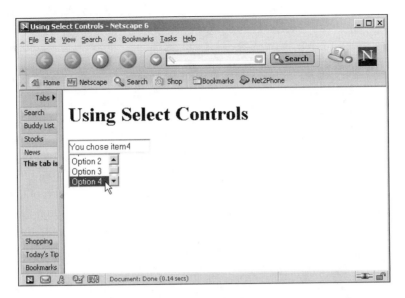

Figure 13.10   Displaying multiple items in a <SELECT> control.

(Listing 13-10.html on the web site)

```
<HTML>
    <HEAD>
        <TITLE>Handling multiple selections</TITLE>
            <SCRIPT LANGUAGE="JavaScript">
                <!--
                function selectionMade()
                {
                    document.form1.textarea1.value = "You selected:\n"

                    with(document.form1.select1){
                        for(var loopIndex = 0; loopIndex < length; loopIndex++){
                            if (options[loopIndex].selected){
                                document.form1.textarea1.value +=
                                ➥options[loopIndex].text + "\n"
                            }
                        }
                    }
                }
                //-->
            </SCRIPT>
    </HEAD>
```

continues ▶

```
<BODY>
    <H1>Handling multiple selections</H1>
    <FORM NAME="form1">
        <SELECT NAME="select1" ONCHANGE="selectionMade()" MULTIPLE>
            <OPTION>Option 1
            <OPTION>Option 2
            <OPTION>Option 3
            <OPTION>Option 4
            <OPTION>Option 5
        </SELECT>
        <BR>
        <TEXTAREA NAME="textarea1" COLS="20" ROWS="10"></TEXTAREA>
    </FORM>
</BODY>
</HTML>
```

You can see the results of this code in Figure 13.11.

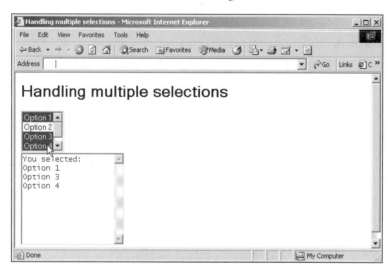

Figure 13.11 Handling multiple selections in a <SELECT> control.

Creating New Options in a *<SELECT>* Control

You can change the items in a <SELECT> control on-the-fly. Not only can you change the text property (and therefore the caption) of each item in a <SELECT> control, you also can add or remove items using the add and remove methods. The catch here is that the add and remove methods are methods of the <SELECT> control itself in the Netscape Navigator (see Table 13.11), and of the options collection in the Internet Explorer (see Table 13.15).

Here's an example that shows how to change the items in a <SELECT> control when the user clicks buttons. The <SELECT> control here will display a list of three colors (red, white, and blue) when it first appears, and when you click the Colors button, or four numbers (1, 2, 3, and 4) when you click the Numbers button. To do this, it has to add and remove items as needed, using both the Netscape Navigator 6+ (earlier versions do not support functions like remove and createElement) and Internet Explorer syntax. Here's what the code looks like:

(Listing 13-11.html on the web site)

```html
<HTML>
    <HEAD>
        <TITLE>Changing Select Options</TITLE>
        <SCRIPT LANGUAGE="JavaScript">
            <!--
            function colors()
            {
                document.form1.select1.options[0].text = "Red"
                document.form1.select1.options[1].text = "White"
                document.form1.select1.options[2].text = "Blue"
                if(navigator.appName == "Netscape") {
                    document.form1.select1.remove(3)
                }
                if (navigator.appName == "Microsoft Internet Explorer") {
                    document.form1.select1.options.remove(3)
                }
            }

            function numbers()
            {
                document.form1.select1.options[0].text = "1"
                document.form1.select1.options[1].text = "2"
                document.form1.select1.options[2].text = "3"
                if(navigator.appName == "Netscape") {
                    var option1 = document.createElement("OPTION")
                    document.form1.select1.add(option1, null)
                    option1.innerHTML = "4"
                }
                if (navigator.appName == "Microsoft Internet Explorer") {
                    var option1 = document.createElement("OPTION")
                    document.form1.select1.options.add(option1)
                    option1.innerHTML = "4"
                }
            }
            //-->
        </SCRIPT>
    </HEAD>
```

continues ▶

```
<BODY>
    <H1>Changing Select Options</H1>
    <FORM NAME="form1">
        <SELECT NAME="select1">
            <OPTION SELECTED>Red
            <OPTION>White
            <OPTION>Blue
        </SELECT>
        <INPUT TYPE="BUTTON" VALUE="Colors" onClick="colors()">
        <INPUT TYPE="BUTTON" VALUE="Numbers" onClick="numbers()">
    </FORM>
</BODY>
</HTML>
```

You can see the results of this code in Figure 13.12, where I've clicked the Numbers button to make the <SELECT> control display the list of numbers.

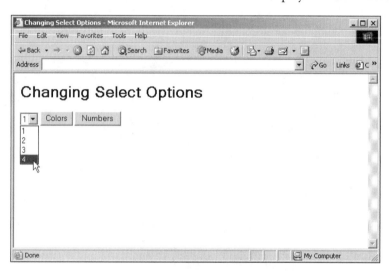

Figure 13.12   Changing items in a <SELECT> control on-the-fly.

The *<OPTGROUP>* Element

The <OPTGROUP> element enables you to divide a <SELECT> control's <OPTION> elements into groups. You can see the properties of the <OPTGROUP> element in Table 13.17.

Table 13.17   **The Properties of the *<OPTGROUP>* Element (See Chapters 5 and 6 for the JavaScript core HTML properties, methods, and events that also apply to this element.)**

Property	NS2	NS3	NS4	NS6	IE3a	IE3b	IE4	IE5	IE5.5	IE6
form				x						x

Read-only
Contains a reference to the control's form. This is handy if you pass a control to a function and need access to other controls in the same form.

| label | | | | x | | | | | | x |

Read/write
Sets or gets the caption for the <OPTGROUP> element. Set to a text string. See "Using the <OPTGROUP> Element" in this chapter.

Using the *<OPTGROUP>* Element

Here's an example using the <OPTGROUP> element. In this case, the code will display three labels to divide a list of <OPTION> elements into groups. You can reset those labels at any time in code, just by assigning text to the label property of the <OPTGROUP> elements. Here's how you can alternate between the old labels and new labels when the user clicks buttons (you'll need NS6+ if using Netscape Navigator here):

(Listing 13-12.html on the web site)

```
<HTML>
    <HEAD>
        <TITLE>Using Option Groups</TITLE>
        <SCRIPT LANGUAGE="JavaScript">
            <!--
            function oldLabels()
            {
                var optionGroupElements = document.getElementsByTagName("OPTGROUP")
                optionGroupElements[0].label = "Old Label 1"
                optionGroupElements[1].label = "Old Label 2"
                optionGroupElements[2].label = "Old Label 3"
            }

            function newLabels()
            {
                var optionGroupElements = document.getElementsByTagName("OPTGROUP")
                optionGroupElements[0].label = "New Label 1"
                optionGroupElements[1].label = "New Label 2"
                optionGroupElements[2].label = "New Label 3"
            }
```

continues ▶

```
    function displaySelection()
    {
        document.getElementById("div1").innerHTML = "The value of the item you
        ➥selected is: " +
            document.form1.select1.options[document.form1.select1
            ➥.selectedIndex].value
    }
    //-->
</SCRIPT>
</HEAD>

<BODY>
    <H1>Using Option Groups</H1>
    <FORM NAME="form1">
        <SELECT NAME="select1" ONCHANGE="displaySelection()">
            <OPTGROUP LABEL="Old Label 1">
                <OPTION value="1:1">Group 1 Item 1
                <OPTION value="1:2">Group 1 Item 2
                <OPTION value="1:3">Group 1 Item 3
            </OPTGROUP>
            <OPTGROUP LABEL="Old Label 2">
                <OPTION value="2:1">Group 2 Item 1
                <OPTION value="2:2">Group 2 Item 2
                <OPTION value="2:3">Group 2 Item 3
            </OPTGROUP>
            <OPTGROUP LABEL="Old Label 3">
                <OPTION value="3:1">Group 3 Item 1
                <OPTION value="3:2">Group 3 Item 2
                <OPTION value="3:3">Group 3 Item 3
            </OPTGROUP>
        </SELECT>
        <BR>
        <INPUT TYPE="BUTTON" VALUE="New labels" ONCLICK="newLabels()">
        <INPUT TYPE="BUTTON" VALUE="Old labels" ONCLICK="oldLabels()">
    </FORM>
    <DIV ID="div1"></DIV>
</BODY>
</HTML>
```

You can see the results of this code in Figure 13.13, where you see the original option group labels, and Figure 13.14, where I've clicked the New labels button and the code displays new option group labels.

This example also uses the value property of <OPTION> elements. This property is valuable because it enables you to store unseen data for each item in a <SELECT> control. For example, an item's caption may display an employee's name, while the value property holds their ID value that your code actually works with. In this example, I'm just assigning a string to each <OPTION> element, indicating its group and item number in the group:

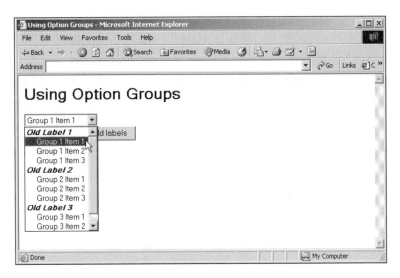

Figure 13.13   Using option groups in a <SELECT> control.

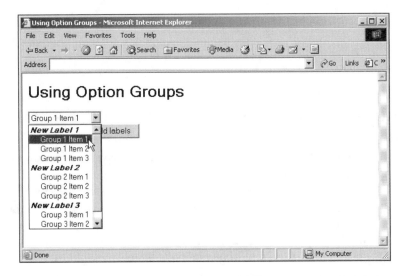

Figure 13.14   Setting new option group labels in a <SELECT> control.

```
<OPTGROUP LABEL="Old Label 1">
    <OPTION value="1:1">Group 1 Item 1
    <OPTION value="1:2">Group 1 Item 2
    <OPTION value="1:3">Group 1 Item 3
</OPTGROUP>
```

When you make a selection in the web page itself, the code in this example displays the string in the `value` property of the selected item, as you see in Figure 13.15.

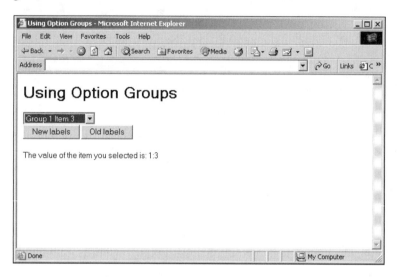

Figure 13.15 Using the `value` property in a `<SELECT>` control.

The File Upload Element *<INPUT TYPE="FILE">*

The last element I'll look at in this chapter is the file upload element, which enables users to upload files to the server—if you have code waiting on the server to read that code. At first glance, it might not be clear how this element fits in with the `<INPUT TYPE="TEXT">`, `<INPUT TYPE="PASSWORD">`, and `<INPUT TYPE="HIDDEN">` elements we've already seen in this chapter, but the file upload element is just another `<INPUT>` element, this time with the `TYPE` attribute set to `"FILE"`: `<INPUT TYPE="FILE">`. You can see the properties, methods, and events of this control in Table 13.18, its properties in depth in Table 13.19, its methods in depth in Table 13.20, and its events in depth in Table 13.21.

Table 13.18 **The Properties and Methods of the File Upload Element**

Properties	Methods	Event
defaultValue	select	onchange
form		
name		
readOnly		
size		
type		
value		

Table 13.19 **The Properties of the *<INPUT TYPE="FILE">* Element (See Chapters 5 and 6 for the JavaScript core HTML properties, methods, and events that also apply to this element.)**

Property	NS2	NS3	NS4	NS6	IE3a	IE3b	IE4	IE5	IE5.5	IE6
defaultValue	x	x	x	x	x	x	x	x	x	x

Read/write
Holds the default value for the control—the value that appears in the control when control's form is reset. Set to a text string. (In practice, however, this property does not appear to work as it should. Resetting a form, either with a reset button or the reset method, does not make this property's value appear.)

	NS2	NS3	NS4	NS6	IE3a	IE3b	IE4	IE5	IE5.5	IE6
form	x	x	x	x	x	x	x	x	x	x

Read-only
Contains a reference to the control's form. This is handy if you pass a control to a function and need access to other controls in the same form.

	NS2	NS3	NS4	NS6	IE3a	IE3b	IE4	IE5	IE5.5	IE6
name	x	x	x	x	x	x	x	x	x	x

Read/write
Holds the name of the control, as used in code. May be changed in code, because it's read/write. Set to a name string.

	NS2	NS3	NS4	NS6	IE3a	IE3b	IE4	IE5	IE5.5	IE6
readOnly				x			x	x	x	x

Read/write
Specifies whether the control is read-only. Set to true or false. This property is useful to "disable" text controls (although you also can use the disabled property).

continues ▶

Table 13.19   **Continued**

Property	NS2	NS3	NS4	NS6	IE3a	IE3b	IE4	IE5	IE5.5	IE6
size				x			x	x	x	x

Read/write
Sets the width of the control, measured in characters. A very handy property if you want wider text controls than the default.

Property	NS2	NS3	NS4	NS6	IE3a	IE3b	IE4	IE5	IE5.5	IE6
type		x	x	x		x	x	x	x	x

Read-only
Holds the type of the file control, as a string: `"file"`. This property reflects the `TYPE` attribute of the control. As of Internet Explorer 5, the `type` property is read/write, but only once, when an element is created with the `createElement` method and before it is added to the document.

Property	NS2	NS3	NS4	NS6	IE3a	IE3b	IE4	IE5	IE5.5	IE6
value	x	x	x	x	x	x	x	x	x	x

Read/write
Holds the name of the file to upload. Set to a string.

Table 13.20   **The Methods of the `<INPUT TYPE="FILE">` Element (See Chapters 5 and 6 for the JavaScript core HTML properties, methods, and events that also apply to this element.)**

Method	NS2	NS3	NS4	NS6	IE3a	IE3b	IE4	IE5	IE5.5	IE6
select		x	x	x			x	x	x	x

Returns: Nothing
Selects the text in the control.
Syntax: `select()`. You can use this method together with the `focus` method (see Chapter 6) to highlight text and set yourself up for a response from the user.

Table 13.21   **The Events of the `<INPUT TYPE="FILE">` Element (See Chapters 5 and 6 for the JavaScript core HTML properties, methods, and events that also apply to this element.)**

Event	NS2	NS3	NS4	NS6	IE3a	IE3b	IE4	IE5	IE5.5	IE6
onchange	x	x	x	x	x	x	x	x	x	x

Occurs when the contents of the control change and the user moves the focus away from the control.

Using the File Upload Element

Here's an example using the file upload element; in this case, I'll upload a file named file.txt with the contents:

```
Here is the text in the file....
```

In this example, the user can select a file to upload and press the Upload button we'll supply. (This button is just a submit button that uploads the form's data, including the file specified in the file control.) When the user does so, the code will ask the user if he is sure that he wants to upload the file, reading the name of the file from the file control's value property. Here's what that code looks like:

(Listing 13-13.html on the web site)

```html
<HTML>
    <HEAD>
        <TITLE>
            CGI File Upload Example
        </TITLE>
        <SCRIPT LANGUAGE="JavaScript">
            <!--
            function dataWarn()
            {
                if (confirm("Are you sure you want to upload " +
                    document.form1.filename.value + "?")) {
                    return true
                } else {
                    return false
                }
            }
            // -->
        </SCRIPT>
    </HEAD>

    <BODY>
        <H1>CGI File Upload Example</H1>
        <FORM METHOD="POST" NAME="form1"
            ACTION="http://www.starpowder.com/steve/cgiupload.cgi"
            ENCTYPE="multipart/form-data" ONSUBMIT="return dataWarn()">
            <INPUT TYPE="FILE" NAME="filename" SIZE="30">
            <BR>
            <INPUT TYPE="SUBMIT" NAME="submit" VALUE="Upload">
            <INPUT TYPE="RESET">
        </FORM>
    </BODY>
</HTML>
```

You can see this page at work in Figure 13.16, where the code is asking the user whether he really wants to upload the file. Clicking OK uploads the file, clicking Cancel cancels the operation.

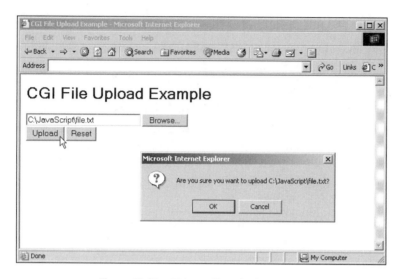

Figure 13.16 Using a file upload control.

To handle the file's data when it arrives on the server, I'll use a Perl CGI script, whose URL is given in the ACTION attribute of the form in our example. (The URL is fictitious.) Here's the Perl code that will read the file and display its contents by sending a web page back to the browser (more on Perl CGI scripts in Chapter 24, ".NET and Security"):

(Listing 13-14.cgi on the web site)

```perl
#!/usr/local/bin/perl
use CGI;
$co = new CGI;

print $co->header,
$co->start_html(
    -title=>'CGI Example',
    -author=>'Steve',
    -meta=>{'keywords'=>'CGI Perl'},
);

$file = $co->param('filename');
@data = <$file>;

foreach (@data) {
    s/\n/<br>/g;
}

print
    $co->center($co->h2("Here's what was in $file:")),
    "@data";
print $co->end_html;
```

You can see the results in Figure 13.17, where you see the uploaded text from the file.

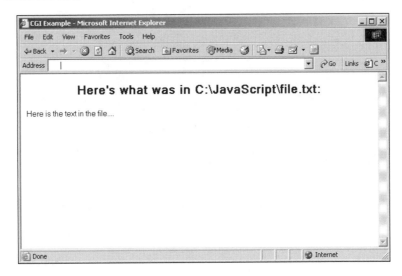

Figure 13.17 The text of an uploaded file.

And that's it. That completes our chapter. We've come far in this chapter, handling text controls such as text fields, password controls, hidden controls, text areas, select controls and option elements, and now file upload controls. In the next chapter, we'll get the details on links, lists, and working with tables in JavaScript.

14

Working with Links, Lists, and Tables

I N THIS CHAPTER, WE'LL START WORKING with hyperlinks, lists, and tables. Of these, tables are the biggest, with plenty of JavaScript capabilities. HTML tables are popular because they enable you to format text as well as images in a page. Theoretically, you also can use style sheets to do the same thing, but many older browsers won't understand style sheets well; even if they do, there'll be differences between browsers, so tables are very popular. We'll see how to work with tables in depth in this chapter. We're also going to take a look at two other popular HTML constructs—hyperlinks and lists—starting with hyperlinks. I'll start with hyperlinks.

The *<A>* Element: Hyperlinks and Anchors

You create hyperlinks with the <A> element, of course, as well as HTML anchors that can serve as hyperlink targets. Like the location object (see Chapter 10, "Using the *navigator*, *location*, and *history* Objects"), this element not only holds the target of the hyperlink in the href property, but also enables you to dissect that URL in a handy way, using several properties such as hostname (the www.*name*.com part), host (the same as the hostname property with a port number appended if there is one—for example, in the URL http://www.*name*.com:80/index.html, the hostname is www.*name*.com:80), href (the current URL in full), hash (the part of the URL following the hash mark (#) in the URL if there is one), and pathname (the filename or path specified in the URL). Here's the URL we dissected when looking at the `location` object in Chapter 10 (it discusses the changes in the HTML 4.01 W3C specification):

`http://www.w3.org/TR/html4/appendix/changes.html#19991224`

Here are the values of various location properties for this URL:

- **hash** `"#19991224"`.
- **host** `"www.w3.org"`.
- **hostname** `"www.w3.org"`.
- **href** `"http://www.w3.org/TR/html4/appendix/changes.html#19991224"`.
- **pathname** `"/TR/html4/appendix/changes.html"`.
- **protocol** `"http:"`.

For more on these properties, take a look at Table 10.8. Let's turn to the <A> element in detail now. You can find its properties in Table 14.1, and its events in Table 14.2. As usual, note also that JavaScript's core HTML properties, methods, and events that we covered in Chapters 5, "Using Core HTML Properties," and 6, "Using Core HTML Methods and Events," apply to this element as well.

Table 14.1 **The Properties of the <*A*> Element (See Chapters 5 and 6 for the JavaScript core HTML properties, methods, and events that also apply to this element.)**

Property	NS2	NS3	NS4	NS6	IE3a	IE3b	IE4	IE5	IE5.5	IE6
charset				x						x

Read/write
Holds the name of the character set used by the document to which the hyperlink points. In the HTML 4.01 specification, the W3C says that you can get a list of the registered character sets at `ftp://ftp.isi.edu/in-notes/iana/assignments/character-sets`. Not in wide use yet.

coords				x						x

Read/write
This property is used in creating image maps with given coordinates in an image. Although listed as supported, this property does not actually seem to work in Netscape Navigator 6.0. In the Internet Explorer, set to a string with the coordinates for the image map.

Property	NS2	NS3	NS4	NS6	IE3a	IE3b	IE4	IE5	IE5.5	IE6
hash	x	x	x	x	x	x	x	x	x	x

Read/write
See Table 10.8.

host	x	x	x	x	x	x	x	x	x	x

Read/write
See Table 10.8.

hostname	x	x	x	x	x	x	x	x	x	x

Read/write
See Table 10.8.

href	x	x	x	x	x	x	x	x	x	x

Read/write
This property holds the target of the hyperlink; Set it to a URL string. You can change this property on-the-fly, which is cool, enabling you to configure the hyperlinks in your page in response to user action (such as selecting between web pages written in different languages). See "Using Hyperlinks" in this chapter for an example, including using a JavaScript URL.

hreflang				x						x

Read/write
This property holds the language of the target document pointed to by this element. Set to a string; see "Using the browserLanguage, systemLanguage, and userLanguage Properties" in Chapter 10 for possible values.

Methods							x	x	x	x

Read/write
Sets or retrieves the list of HTTP methods supported by the object. The uppercase *M* is not an error here. This is one of the few properties that start with an uppercase letter, and it's also a rare HTML 4.01 attribute that is not part of the W3C DOM. This property corresponds to the METHODS attribute of the <A> element. Set to a string containing an HTTP method that the browser should use to access the target document. Note that the Internet Explorer doesn't actually use this information yet.

name			x	x			x	x	x	x

Read/write
This property corresponds to the NAME attribute of an <A> element. You need to set the NAME attribute to make an <A> element function as an anchor. Set to a name string.

continues ▶

Table 14.1 **Continued**

Property	NS2	NS3	NS4	NS6	IE3a	IE3b	IE4	IE5	IE5.5	IE6
nameProp							x	x	x	x

Read-only
This property holds the name of the HTML document, as extracted from the URL to which the hyperlink (taken from the href property) points. (Note that if there is a port number, however, that number is returned as part of the name!) This property is a string.

pathname	x	x	x	x	x	x	x	x	x	x

Read/write
See Table 10.8.

port	x	x	x	x	x	x	x	x	x	x

Read/write
See Table 10.8.

protocol	x	x	x	x	x	x	x	x	x	x

Read/write
See Table 10.8.

rel				x			x	x	x	x

Read/write
This property sets or gets the relationship between the link and its destination, corresponding to the REL attribute. Set to a string containing "Alternate", "Appendix", "Bookmark", "Chapter", "Contents", "Copyright", "Glossary", "Help", "Index", "Next", "Offline", "Prev", "Section", "Shortcut Icon", "Start", "Stylesheet", or "Subsection". The rev and rel properties are similar, but they specify relationships in opposite directions—a relationship given by rev from A to B is the same as a relationship given by rel from B to A.

rev				x			x	x	x	x

Read/write
This property sets or gets the relationship between the link and its destination, corresponding to the REV attribute. Set to a string containing "Alternate", "Appendix", "Bookmark", "Chapter", "Contents", "Copyright", "Glossary", "Help", "Index", "Next", "Offline", "Prev", "Section", "Shortcut Icon", "Start", "Stylesheet", or "Subsection". The rev and rel properties are similar, but they specify relationships in opposite directions—a relationship given by rev from A to B is the same as a relationship given by rel from B to A.

Property	NS2	NS3	NS4	NS6	IE3a	IE3b	IE4	IE5	IE5.5	IE6
search	x	x	x	x	x	x	x	x	x	x

Read/write
See Table 10.8.

Property	NS2	NS3	NS4	NS6	IE3a	IE3b	IE4	IE5	IE5.5	IE6
shape				x						x

Read/write
This property is used in creating image maps with different shapes, such as polygons, circles, and rectangles. Although listed as supported, this property does not actually seem to work in Netscape Navigator 6.0.

Property	NS2	NS3	NS4	NS6	IE3a	IE3b	IE4	IE5	IE5.5	IE6
target	x	x	x	x	x	x	x	x	x	x

Read/write
Holds the window or frame name that represents the target of this link—that is, where the document pointed to by this link should be loaded. This property holds a string and corresponds to the TARGET attribute of the <A> element.

Property	NS2	NS3	NS4	NS6	IE3a	IE3b	IE4	IE5	IE5.5	IE6
text			x							

Read/write
Navigator 4.0 enables you to read the text for the hyperlink in a web page using this property (that is, the text between the <A> and </A> tags that the user clicks to navigate to the hyperlink's target). Set to a string. I recommend you use the innerHTML property in recent browsers instead.

Property	NS2	NS3	NS4	NS6	IE3a	IE3b	IE4	IE5	IE5.5	IE6
type				x						x

Read/write
Holds the *Multipurpose Internet Mail Extension* (MIME) type of the target document pointed to by the hyperlink. This property corresponds to the <A> element's TYPE attribute, which is not widely used—although your scripts can access this property in case you need to handle the target document in some special way. Set to a string containing a MIME type (such as "text/plain").

Property	NS2	NS3	NS4	NS6	IE3a	IE3b	IE4	IE5	IE5.5	IE6
urn							x	x	x	x

Read/write
Sets or gets the *Uniform Resource Name* (URN) for a target document; URNs indicate the identity of a document (rather than URLs, which indicate a document's location). Set to a string. URNs aren't in general use at this time.

continues ▶

Table 14.1 **Continued**

Property	NS2	NS3	NS4	NS6	IE3a	IE3b	IE4	IE5	IE5.5	IE6
x				x						

Read-only
Holds the X coordinate of the hyperlink in a page—in NS6 and IE4+, you use the `offsetLeft` property instead. Set to a pixel measurement. See "The `offsetHeight`, `offsetWidth`, `offsetLeft`, `offsetRight`, and `offsetParent` Properties" in Chapter 5.

Property	NS2	NS3	NS4	NS6	IE3a	IE3b	IE4	IE5	IE5.5	IE6
y				x						

Read-only
Holds the Y coordinate of the hyperlink in a page—in NS6 and IE4+, you use the `offsetTop` property instead. Set to a pixel measurement. See "The `offsetHeight`, `offsetWidth`, `offsetLeft`, `offsetRight`, and `offsetParent` Properties" in Chapter 5.

Table 14.2 **The Events of the `<A>` Element (See Chapters 5 and 6 for the JavaScript core HTML properties, methods, and events that also apply to this element.)**

Event	NS2	NS3	NS4	NS6	IE3a	IE3b	IE4	IE5	IE5.5	IE6
onafterupdate							x	x	x	x

Occurs in a data-bound object after updating the data in the data source.

Event	NS2	NS3	NS4	NS6	IE3a	IE3b	IE4	IE5	IE5.5	IE6
onbeforeupdate							x	x	x	x

Occurs in a data-bound object before updating the data in the data source.

Event	NS2	NS3	NS4	NS6	IE3a	IE3b	IE4	IE5	IE5.5	IE6
onerrorupdate							x	x	x	x

Occurs in a data-bound object when an error happened while updating data in the data source.

Using Hyperlinks

Using JavaScript, you can manipulate hyperlinks in a page easily. For example, take a look at this script, which changes a hyperlink's destination URL when the user clicks a button (if you're using JavaScript, you need NS6+ to use `getElementById` like this):

(Listing 14-01.html on the web site)

```
<HTML>
    <HEAD>
        <TITLE>
            Changing a link's URL
        </TITLE>
        <SCRIPT LANGUAGE="JavaScript">
            <!--
            function changeURL()
            {
                document.getElementById("link1").href = "http://www.w3c.org"
            }
            // -->
        </SCRIPT>
    </HEAD>

    <BODY>
        <H1>Changing a link's URL</H1>
        Want more information? <A ID="link1" HREF="http://www.microsoft.com">Click
here.</A>
        <FORM>
            <INPUT TYPE="BUTTON" ONCLICK="changeURL()" VALUE="Click me to change the
            ➥link's URL">
        </FORM>
    </BODY>
</HTML>
```

This is useful if, for example, you want to change the URLs in a page to point to different language versions of web pages on your site.

Note that the ONCLICK attribute overrides the HREF attribute if scripting is enabled. This means, for example, that you can have an <A> element send the user to a JavaScript-enabled or non-enabled page as appropriate, like this:

```
<SCRIPT LANGUAGE="JavaScript">
    <!--
    function goTo()
    {
        location.href = "JSPage.html"
    }
    // -->
</SCRIPT>
        .
        .
        .
<A HREF="nonJSPage.html" ONCLICK="goTo()">Click here to see my page.</A>
```

Alternatively, you can just automatically change a hyperlink's URL for JavaScript-enabled browsers when a page loads, and use a default URL for non-enabled browsers:

```
<SCRIPT LANGUAGE="JavaScript">
    <!--
    document.getElementById("link1").href = "JSPage.html"
    // -->
</SCRIPT>
        .
        .
        .
<A HREF="nonJSPage.html" ID="link1">Click here to see my page.</A>
```

Using JavaScript URLs

As we saw in Chapter 7, "Using *window* and *frame* Properties," you also can use *JavaScript URLs*. A JavaScript URL is actually a JavaScript function that the browser treats as a URL—you just preface the function name with `"javascript:"`. When the browser jumps to that URL, it just runs the JavaScript function. You can connect the HREF attribute of <A> elements to JavaScript URLs (just as we did with the SRC attribute of <FRAME> elements in Chapter 7—see "Creating Frames in JavaScript: JavaScript URLs" in that chapter), which means you're able to execute JavaScript when the user clicks a link, just as if they had clicked a button.

Here's a useful example. This code opens a URL in a new window when the user clicks a hyperlink, which means the user doesn't have to leave the current page even when he clicks a hyperlink:

```
<HTML>
    <HEAD>
        <TITLE>
            Opening New Windows Using Hyperlinks
        </TITLE>
        <SCRIPT LANGUAGE="JavaScript">
            <!--
            function opener()
            {
                window.open("http://www.w3.org")
            }
            // -->
        </SCRIPT>
    </HEAD>

    <BODY>
        <H1>Opening New Windows Using Hyperlinks</H1>
        <FORM>
            Take a look at <A HREF="javascript:opener()">W3C</A>.
        </FORM>
    </BODY>
</HTML>
```

Here's another example. This one uses a navigation bar with hyperlinks and frames. In this case, I'll load existing documents into a target frame when the user clicks hyperlinks in the navigation bar for the most part. When the user clicks the link for Page 3 in the navigation bar, however, a JavaScript function will create a new document from scratch instead of loading a preexisting document, and load that new document into the target frame. You can see what this looks like in Figure 14.1, where the navigation bar is on the left and I've clicked the Page 3 link to create and display a new document in the frame on the right.

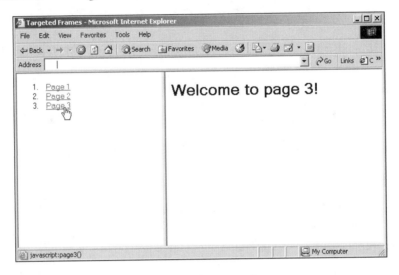

Figure 14.1   Creating a new document.

Here's what the <FRAMESET> document (which is what you're looking at in Figure 14.1) looks like for this example—14-03.html is the navigation bar, and the frame named "display" is the target frame that will display documents:

(Listing 14-02.html on the web site)

```
<HTML>
    <HEAD>
        <TITLE>
            Targeted Frames
        </TITLE>
    </HEAD>

    <FRAMESET COLS="40%, 60%">
        <FRAME SRC="14-03.html">
        <FRAME NAME="display">
    </FRAMESET>
</HTML>
```

And here's the navigation bar page, 14-03.html, that does all the work. Note the JavaScript URL for the HREF attribute for page 3 here:

(Listing 14-03.html on the web site)

```
<HTML>
    <HEAD>
        <SCRIPT LANGUAGE="JavaScript">
            <!--
            function page3()
            {
                top.frames[1].document.write("<HTML><HEAD><TITLE>Frame</TITLE></HEAD>" +
                    "<BODY><H1>Welcome to page 3!</H1></BODY></HTML>")
                parent.frames[1].document.close()
            }
            //-->
        </SCRIPT>
    </HEAD>

    <BODY>
        <OL>
            <LI>
                <A HREF="frame1.html" TARGET="display">
                Page 1
                </A>
            </LI>
            <LI>
                <A HREF="frame2.html" TARGET="display">
                Page 2
                </A>
            </LI>
            <LI>
                <A HREF="javascript:page3()">
                Page 3
                </A>
            </LI>
        </OL>
    </BODY>
</HTML>
```

Tip

As of NS3 and IE4, you also can preface the JavaScript function's name with the keyword void to guarantee that the function does not inadvertently navigate the browser somewhere, like this: HREF="javascript: void function1()". The void keyword discards any return value from the function.

In fact, there's a simpler way to do this: Instead of executing a function to write a new document to the display frame, you could just have that function return the HTML for the new document. Using the TARGET attribute of the

<A> element, the browser will place that HTML in the named frame automatically. Here's what the <FRAMESET> document would look like in this case (you'll need NS6+ if using the Netscape Navigator here):

(Listing 14-04.html on the web site)

```
<HTML>
    <HEAD>
        <TITLE>
            Targeted Frames
        </TITLE>
        <SCRIPT LANGUAGE="JavaScript">
            <!--
            function page3()
            {
                return "<HTML><HEAD><TITLE>Frame</TITLE></HEAD>" +
                    "<BODY><H1>Welcome to page 3!</H1></BODY></HTML>"
            }
            //-->
        </SCRIPT>
    </HEAD>

    <FRAMESET COLS="40%, 60%">
        <FRAME SRC="14-05.html">
        <FRAME NAME="display">
    </FRAMESET>
</HTML>
```

And here's what the navigation bar page would look like. Note that I've set the TARGET attribute of the <A> element with the JavaScript URL to the display frame:

(Listing 14-05.html on the web site)

```
<HTML>
    <HEAD>
        <TITLE>Frame</TITLE>
    </HEAD>
    <BODY>
        <OL>
            <LI>
                <A HREF="frame1.html" TARGET="display">
                Page 1
                </A>
            </LI>
            <LI>
                <A HREF="frame2.html" TARGET="display">
                Page 2
                </A>
            </LI>
            <LI>
```

continues ▶

```
        <A HREF="javascript:parent.page3()" TARGET="display">
        Page 3
        </A>
      </LI>
    </OL>
  </BODY>
</HTML>
```

That's all it takes.

Keep in mind that the hyperlinks in a document also are available using the document object's `links` and `anchors` collections. The `links` collection holds all `<A>` elements with HREF attributes, and the `anchors` collection holds all `<A>` elements with NAME attributes. For example, we could have written `document.getElementById("link1").href = "http://www.w3c.org"` in Listing 14.1 as `document.links[0].href = "http://www.w3c.org"`. See Table 9.2 and "The document Object Collections" in Chapter 9, "Using the *document* and *body* Objects," for more information on these collections.

> **Tip**
>
> Keep in mind that hyperlinks don't just have to hold URLs; they also can hold `mailto:` URLs, such as `"mailto:steve@starpowder.com?subject=hello"`.

The *<OL>* Element: Ordered Lists

You create ordered lists, which display numbered or lettered items, with the `<OL>` element. (Note that we just saw such a list in Listing 14.3.) You create each item in the list with an `<LI>` element. Here's an example that displays such a list:

(Listing 14-06.html on the web site)

```
<HTML>
  <HEAD>
    <TITLE>
      An Ordered List
    </TITLE>
  </HEAD>

  <BODY>
    <H1>
      Creating An Ordered List
    </H1>
    Buying a computer? Let's consider:
    <OL>
      <LI> Price
      <LI> CPU Speed
      <LI> Memory
```

```
            <LI> Disk space
            <LI> CD-ROM/DVD speed
         </OL>
      </BODY>
</HTML>
```

You can see the results in Figure 14.2.

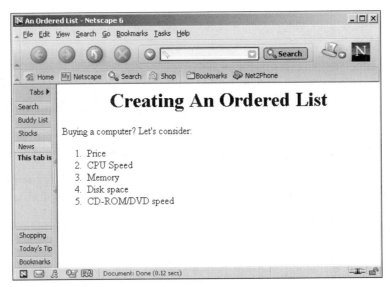

Figure 14.2 Using an ordered list.

You can find the JavaScript properties for the `<OL>` element in Table 14.3. Remember that JavaScript's core HTML properties, methods, and events, which we covered in Chapters 5 and 6, apply to this element as well.

Table 14.3 **The Properties of the *<OL>* Element (See Chapters 5 and 6 for the JavaScript core HTML properties, methods, and events that also apply to this element.)**

Property	NS2	NS3	NS4	NS6	IE3a	IE3b	IE4	IE5	IE5.5	IE6
compact				X			X	X	X	X

Read/write
Supposedly affects the spacing of the text and the list numbering/bulleting, but in fact has no effect. The COMPACT attribute is deprecated in HTML 4.01.

continues ▶

Table 14.3 **Continued**

Property	NS2	NS3	NS4	NS6	IE3a	IE3b	IE4	IE5	IE5.5	IE6
start				x			x	x	x	x

Read/write

Sets or gets the starting number for an ordered list. This is the number you want the list numbering to begin with. Set to a string.

| type | | | | x | | | x | x | x | x |

Read/write

Specifies the type of list item label; set to "A" (capital letters), "a" (lower-case letters), "I" (large roman numerals), "i" (small roman numerals), "1" (default numbering scheme). Deprecated in HTML 4.01.

The *<UL>* Element: Unordered Lists

You use the <UL> element to create unordered lists that usually have some visual element, such as a bullet in front of every item. Here's an example:

(Listing 14-07.html on the web site)

```
<HTML>
    <HEAD>
        <TITLE>
            An Unordered List
        </TITLE>
    </HEAD>

    <BODY>
        <H1>
            Creating An Unordered List
        </H1>
        Buying a computer? Let's consider:
        <UL>
            <LI> Price
            <LI> CPU Speed
            <LI> Memory
            <LI> Disk space
            <LI> CD-ROM/DVD speed
        </UL>
    </BODY>
</HTML>
```

You can see this page in Figure 14.3.

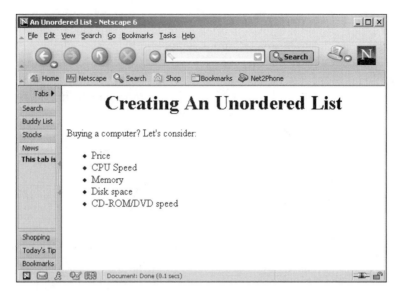

Figure 14.3 Using an unordered list.

You can find the JavaScript properties for the <UL> element in Table 14.4. Remember that JavaScript's core HTML properties, methods, and events, which we covered in Chapters 5 and 6, apply to this element as well.

Table 14.4 **The Properties of the *<UL>* Element (See Chapters 5 and 6 for the JavaScript core HTML properties, methods, and events that also apply to this element.)**

Property	NS2	NS3	NS4	NS6	IE3a	IE3b	IE4	IE5	IE5.5	IE6
compact				X			X	X	X	X
	Read/write Supposedly affects the spacing of the text and the list numbering/ bulleting, but in fact has no effect. The COMPACT attribute is deprecated in HTML 4.01.									
type				X			X	X	X	X
	Read/write Specifies the type of list item label; set to "disc" (default solid bullet), "square" (solid square), or "circle" (hollow bullet). Deprecated in HTML 4.01.									

The *<LI>* Element: List Items

You use <LI> elements to create list items; you place <LI> elements inside <OL> and <UL> elements, one for each item in the list. You can find the JavaScript properties for the <LI> element in Table 14.5. Remember that JavaScript's core HTML properties, methods, and events, which we covered in Chapters 5 and 6, apply to this element as well.

Table 14.5 **The Properties of the *<LI>* Elements (See Chapters 5 and 6 for the JavaScript core HTML properties, methods, and events that also apply to this element.)**

Property	NS2	NS3	NS4	NS6	IE3a	IE3b	IE4	IE5	IE5.5	IE6
type				x			x	x	x	x

Read/write
This property specifies the label for the list item, and can be set to any type value for <OL> and <UL> elements. See Tables 14.3 and 14.4.

Property	NS2	NS3	NS4	NS6	IE3a	IE3b	IE4	IE5	IE5.5	IE6
value				x			x	x	x	x

Read/write
In an ordered list, the value is the number or letter that labels the list item. Note that changing the value of an item also changes the numbering/lettering of all following items.

The *<DL>*, *<DT>*, *<DD>*, *<DIR>*, and *<MENU>* Elements

The <DL>, <DT>, and <DD> elements enable you to set up definition lists, which list terms and their definitions in pairs. You create a definition list with the <DL> element, and create items in this list using both the <DT> element to define a term and the <DD> element to give the term's definition. The definition usually appears indented under the term being defined. Here's an example:

(Listing 14-08.html on the web site)

```
<HTML>
    <HEAD>
        <TITLE>
            A Definition List
        </TITLE>
    </HEAD>
```

```
<BODY>
    <H1>
        Creating A Definition List
    </H1>

    Buying a computer? Let's consider:
    <DL>
        <DT>Price<DD>Keep this low!
        <DT>CPU Speed<DD>Processor speed
        <DT>RAM<DD>Random access memory
        <DT>Disk space<DD>Get plenty!
        <DT>CD-ROM/DVD speed<DD>Access speed for your CDs
    </DL>
</BODY>
</HTML>
```

You can see this page in Figure 14.4.

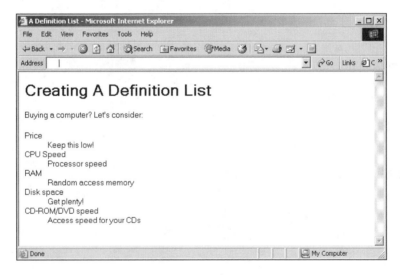

Figure 14.4   Using a definition list.

There are even more list elements—the <DIR> and <MENU> elements—but
they are deprecated in HTML 4.01 and are just treated as <UL> elements. You
can see the properties of the <DL>, <DT>, and <DD> elements in Table 14.6.
Remember that JavaScript's core HTML properties, methods, and events,
which we covered in Chapters 5 and 6, apply to the <DL>, <DT>, and <DD>
elements as well.

Table 14.6 **The Properties of the *<DL>*, *<DT>*, *<DD>*, *<DIR>*, and *<MENU>* Elements (See Chapters 5 and 6 for the JavaScript core HTML properties, methods, and events that also apply to these elements.)**

Property	NS2	NS3	NS4	NS6	IE3a	IE3b	IE4	IE5	IE5.5	IE6
compact				x			x	x	x	x

Read/write

Sets or gets a Boolean value indicating whether the list should be compacted by removing extra space between list objects. The COMPACT attribute is deprecated in HTML 4.01. In the Internet Explorer, this property was added for <DIR> and <MENU> elements in version 6.0.

Using Lists

Lists don't actually have specific methods that enable you to configure them on-the-fly; but using methods that apply to all HTML elements, such as appendChild and replaceChild, you can change them yourself. Here's an example that we saw in Chapter 6 (Listing 06-03.html on the web site) that uses the appendChild method to add a new item to an unordered list, and the replaceChild method to replace the first item in the list (you'll need NS6+ if using Netscape Navigator for methods such as appendChild and replaceChild):

```
<HTML>
    <HEAD>
        <TITLE>
            Using the appendChild and replaceChild Methods
        </TITLE>

        <SCRIPT LANGUAGE="JavaScript">
            <!--
            function adder()
            {
                var item1 = document.createElement("LI")
                item1.innerHTML = "Next item"
                document.getElementById("list1").appendChild(item1)
            }

            function replacer(form)
            {
                var item1 = document.createElement("LI")
                item1.innerHTML = "Newer First Item"
                var lastItem = document.getElementById("list1").firstChild
                document.getElementById("list1").replaceChild(item1, lastItem)
            }
```

```
            -->
        </SCRIPT>
    </HEAD>
    <BODY>
        <H1>Using the appendChild and replaceChild Methods</H1>
        <FORM>
            <INPUT TYPE=BUTTON VALUE="Add New Item" ONCLICK="adder()">
            <INPUT TYPE=BUTTON VALUE="Replace First Item" ONCLICK="replacer()">
        </FORM>
        <UL ID="list1">
            <LI>First Item
            <LI>Second Item
        <UL>
    </BODY>
</HTML>
```

Using this code, the user can add new items and replace the first item in a list, all just using buttons. You can see the results of this code in Chapter 6, in Figure 6.4.

The *<TABLE>* Element: Creating Tables

As mentioned in the beginning of the chapter, tables are great for letting you format text. Tables started off just as rectangular grids of cells containing text, but they've taken off from there, and now support images, column groups, footers, headers, and so on. Here's a basic table to get us started. You create the table with the <TABLE> element, create the rows in the table with the <TR> element, the headers for columns with <TH> elements, and display the actual data in each cell with the <TD> element:

(Listing 14-09.html on the web site)

```
<HTML>
    <HEAD>
        <TITLE>
            HTML Tables
        </TITLE>
    </HEAD>

    <BODY>
        <H1>
            HTML Tables
        </H1>
        <TABLE BORDER="1">
            <TR>
                <TH ROWSPAN="3">Tic<BR>Tac<BR>Toe</TH>
                <TD>X</TD>
                <TD>O</TD>
```

continues ▶

```
                <TD>X</TD>
            </TR>
            <TR>
                <TD>O</TD>
                <TD>X</TD>
                <TD>O</TD>
            </TR>
            <TR>
                <TD>X</TD>
                <TD>O</TD>
                <TD>X</TD>
            </TR>
        </TABLE>
    </BODY>
</HTML>
```

You can see the results in Figure 14.5.

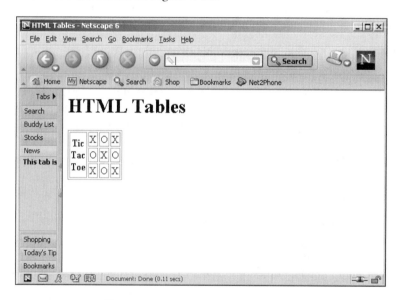

Figure 14.5 Creating an HTML table.

I'll start with the <TABLE> element. You can see an overview of the properties, methods, and events of this element in Table 14.7, its properties in depth in Table 14.8, its methods in Table 14.9, and its events in Table 14.10. Remember that JavaScript's core HTML properties, methods, and events, which we covered in Chapters 5 and 6, apply to the <TABLE> element as well.

Table 14.7 **Overview of the Properties, Methods, and Events of the *<TABLE>* Element (See Chapters 5 and 6 for the JavaScript core HTML properties, methods, and events that also apply to this element.)**

Properties	Methods	Events
align	createCaption	onscroll
background	createTFoot	
bgColor	createTHead	
border	deleteCaption	
borderColor	deleteRow	
borderColorDark	deleteTFoot	
borderColorLight	deleteTHead	
caption	firstPage	
cellPadding	insertRow	
cellSpacing	lastPage	
cells	moveRow	
cols	nextPage	
dataPageSize	previousPage	
frame	refresh	
height		
rows		
rules		
summary		
tBodies		
tFoot		
tHead		
width		

Table 14.8 **The Properties of the *<TABLE>* Element (See Chapters 5 and 6 for the JavaScript core HTML properties, methods, and events that also apply to this element.)**

Property	NS2	NS3	NS4	NS6	IE3a	IE3b	IE4	IE5	IE5.5	IE6
align				X			X	X	X	X

Read/write
Sets the alignment of the table in the page. Set to `"right"`, `"left"`, or `"center"`. The <TABLE> element's ALIGN attribute is deprecated in HTML.

background							X	X	X	X

Read/write
Sets or gets the background picture behind the text and graphics in the table. Set to the URL of an image.

bgColor				X			X	X	X	X

Read/write
Sets or gets the background color for the table. Set to a color triplet (such as `"ffffff"`) or a predefined color the browser understands (such as `"magenta"`).

border				X			X	X	X	X

Read/write
Corresponds to the BORDER attribute. Sets or gets the border width. Set this property to an integer value, in pixels; setting it to zero or omitting the BORDER attribute removes the border.

borderColor							X	X	X	X

Read/write
Sets or gets the border color. Set to a color triplet (such as `"ffffff"`) or a predefined color the browser understands (such as `"coral"`).

borderColorDark							X	X	X	X

Read/write
Holds a color used for shading effects to make the table look "raised." Set to a color triplet (such as `"ffffff"`) or a predefined color the browser understands (such as `"cyan"`).

borderColorLight							X	X	X	X

Read/write
Holds a color used for shading effects to make the table look "raised." Set to a color triplet (such as `"ffffff"`) or a predefined color the browser understands (such as `"paleblue"`).

Property	NS2	NS3	NS4	NS6	IE3a	IE3b	IE4	IE5	IE5.5	IE6
caption				X			X	X	X	X
cellPadding				X			X	X	X	X
cellSpacing				X			X	X	X	X
cells								X	X	X
cols							X	X	X	X
dataPageSize							X	X	X	X
frame				X			X	X	X	X
height				X			X	X	X	X

caption

Read/write
Holds the table's caption, set to a text string.

cellPadding

Read/write
Holds the cell padding between a cell's contents and the cell walls. Set to
an integer value, in pixels.

cellSpacing

Read/write
Holds the spacing between cells. Set to an integer value, in pixels.

cells

Read-only
Holds a collection of all cells in the table (that is, all <TD> and <TH> elements). This collection enables you to address each cell individually.

cols

Read/write
Holds the number of columns in the table, corresponding to the COLS
attribute. This property holds an integer.

dataPageSize

Read/write
Sets or gets the number of records displayed in a table bound to a data
source. Holds an integer.

frame

Read/write
Sets or gets the way the border frame around the table is displayed. Holds
"void" (the default— all outside table borders are removed), "above"
(border on the top side of the border displays), "below" (border on the
bottom side of the table displays), "border" (borders on all sides of the
table display), "box" (borders on all sides of the table display), "hsides"
(borders on the top and bottom sides of the table display), "lhs" (border
on the left side of the table displays), "rhs" (border on the right side of
the table displays), or "vsides" (borders on the left and right sides of the
table display).

height

Read/write
The height of the table, measured in pixels. Set to an integer value.

continues ▶

Table 14.8 **Continued**

Property	NS2	NS3	NS4	NS6	IE3a	IE3b	IE4	IE5	IE5.5	IE6
rows				x			x	x	x	x

Read-only
Holds a collection of all rows in the table (that is, all `<TR>` elements). This property enables you to address each row individually. See "Using Tables" in this chapter for an example. You can access rows by number or name. In the Internet Explorer, you can access rows with the same name using a second, numeric index like this: `rows["row1", 2]`.

rules				x			x	x	x	x

Read/write
Sets or gets which inner borders are displayed. Set to `"all"` (borders display on all rows and columns), `"cols"` (borders display between all table columns), `"groups"` (horizontal borders display between all `<THEAD>`, `<TBODY>`, and `<TFOOT>` elements), `"vertical"` (borders display between all `<COLGROUP>` objects), `"none"` (no interior table borders), or `"rows"` (horizontal borders display between every table row).

summary				x						x

Read/write
Sets or gets a description of the table. Set to a text string. Intended for use in nonvisual media.

tBodies				x			x	x	x	x

Read-only
Holds a collection of all `<TBODY>` elements objects in the table.

tFoot				x			x	x	x	x

Read-only
Holds the `<TFOOT>` element of the table, if there is one.

tHead				x			x	x	x	x

Read-only
Holds the `<THEAD>` element of the table, if there is one.

width				x			x	x	x	x

Read/write
Holds the width of the table, in pixels. Set to an integer.

Table 14.9 **The Methods of the <*TABLE*> Element (See Chapters 5 and 6 for the JavaScript core HTML properties, methods, and events that also apply to this element.)**

Method	NS2	NS3	NS4	NS6	IE3a	IE3b	IE4	IE5	IE5.5	IE6
createCaption				X			X	X	X	X

Returns: <CAPTION> object
If no caption exists, the createCaption method creates an empty table caption, adds it to the table, and returns it.
Syntax: *table*.createCaption().

createTFoot				X			X	X	X	X

Returns: <TFOOT> object
Creates an empty <TFOOT> element for the table.
Syntax: *table*.createTFoot().

createTHead				X			X	X	X	X

Returns: <THEAD> object
Creates an empty <THEAD> element for the table.
Syntax: *table*.createTHead().

deleteCaption				X			X	X	X	X

Returns: Nothing
Deletes the caption of a table.
Syntax: *table*.deleteCaption().

deleteRow				X			X	X	X	X

Returns: Nothing
Removes the specified row from the table and from the rows collection.
Syntax: *table*.deleteRow([*index*]), where *index* is the index of the row in the rows collection.

deleteTFoot				X			X	X	X	X

Returns: Nothing
Deletes the <TFOOT> element of this table.
Syntax: *table*.deleteTFoot().

deleteTHead				X			X	X	X	X

Returns: Nothing
Deletes the <THEAD> element of this table.
Syntax: *table*.deleteTHead().

continues ▶

Table 14.9 **Continued**

Method	NS2	NS3	NS4	NS6	IE3a	IE3b	IE4	IE5	IE5.5	IE6
firstPage								X	X	X

Returns: Nothing
Displays the first page of records in the data set to which the table is bound.
Syntax: *table*.firstPage().

insertRow			X			X	X	X	X

Returns: new row
Inserts a new row into a table.
Syntax: *table*.insertRow(*index*), where *index* is the position at which
to insert the row in the rows collection. Set *index* to –1 to append a row
to the end of the table. See "Using Tables" in this chapter for an example.

lastPage								X	X	X

Returns: Nothing
Displays the last page of records in the data set to which the table is bound.
Syntax: *table*.lastPage().

moveRow								X	X	X

Returns: <ROW> element
Moves a row to a new position.
Syntax: *table*.moveRow(*source*, *target*), where *source* is the index in
the rows collection of the table row you want to move and *target* is
the index that specifies where the row should be moved to in the rows
collection.

nextPage							X	X	X	X

Returns: Nothing
Displays the next page of records in the data set to which the table
is bound.
Syntax: *table*.nextPage().

previousPage							X	X	X	X

Returns: Nothing
Displays the previous page of records in the data set to which the table
is bound.
Syntax: *table*.previousPage().

refresh							X	X	X	X

Returns: Nothing
Refreshes the contents of the table, redisplaying them.
Syntax: *table*.refresh().

Table 14.10 **The Event of the *<TABLE>* Elements (See Chapters 5 and 6 for the JavaScript core HTML properties, methods, and events that also apply to this element.)**

Event	NS2	NS3	NS4	NS6	IE3a	IE3b	IE4	IE5	IE5.5	IE6
onscroll				x			x	x	x	x

Occurs when the user moves the thumb/scroll box in the scrollbar.

The *<TR>* Element

You create rows in tables with the <TR> element; you can see an overview of the properties and methods of this element in Table 14.11, its properties in depth in Table 14.12, and its methods in Table 14.13. Remember that JavaScript's core HTML properties, methods, and events, which we covered in Chapters 5 and 6, apply to the <TR> element as well.

Table 14.11 **Overview of the Properties and Methods of the *<TR>* Element (See Chapters 5 and 6 for the JavaScript core HTML properties, methods, and events that also apply to this element.)**

Properties	Methods
align	deleteCell
bgColor	insertCell
borderColor	
borderColorDark	
borderColorLight	
cells	
ch	
chOff	
height	
rowIndex	
sectionRowIndex	
vAlign	

Table 14.12 **The Properties of the *<TR>* Element (See Chapters 5 and 6 for the JavaScript core HTML properties, methods, and events that also apply to this element.)**

Property	NS2	NS3	NS4	NS6	IE3a	IE3b	IE4	IE5	IE5.5	IE6
align				X			X	X	X	X

Read/write
Sets or gets the alignment of the row relative to the table. Set to `"center"` (aligns to the center), `"justify"` (aligns to the left and right edge), `"left"` (the default—aligns to the left edge), or `"right"` (aligns to the right edge).

bgColor				X			X	X	X	X

Read/write
Sets or gets the background color for the table row. Set to a color triplet (such as `"ffffff"`) or a predefined color the browser understands (such as `"magenta"`).

borderColor							X	X	X	X

Read/write
Sets or gets the border color. Set to a color triplet (such as `"ffffff"`) or a predefined color the browser understands (such as `"coral"`).

borderColorDark							X	X	X	X

Read/write
Holds a color used for shading effects to make the table look "raised." Set to a color triplet (such as `"ffffff"`) or a predefined color the browser understands (such as `"cyan"`).

borderColorLight							X	X	X	X

Read/write
Holds a color used for shading effects to make the table look "raised." Set to a color triplet (such as `"ffffff"`) or a predefined color the browser understands (such as `"paleblue"`).

cells				X			X	X	X	

Read-only
Holds a collection of all cells in the row (that is, all `<TD>` and `<TH>` elements). This property enables you to address each cell individually.

ch				X					X	

Read/write
Corresponds to the CHAR attribute in `<TR>` elements, but doesn't actually do anything in either browser yet.

Property	NS2	NS3	NS4	NS6	IE3a	IE3b	IE4	IE5	IE5.5	IE6
chOff				x						x

Read/write
Corresponds to the CHAROFF attribute in <TR> elements, but doesn't actually do anything in either browser yet.

| height | | | | | | | x | x | x | x |

Read/write
The height of the row, measured in pixels. Set to an integer value.

| rowIndex | | | | x | | | x | x | x | x |

Read-only
Holds the position of the row in the rows collection. Set to an integer.

| sectionRowIndex | | | | x | | | x | x | x | x |

Read-only
Holds the position of the object in the <TBODY>, <THEAD>, <TFOOT> elements, or rows collection as an integer.

| vAlign | | | | x | | | x | x | x | x |

Read/write
Sets or gets how row contents are aligned within the row that contains them. Set to "middle" (the default—aligns the text in the middle), "baseline" (aligns the base line of the first line of text with the base lines in adjacent objects), "bottom" (aligns the text at the bottom of the row), or "top" (aligns the text at the top of the row).

Table 14.13 **The Methods of the <*TR*> Element (See Chapters 5 and 6 for the JavaScript core HTML properties, methods, and events that also apply to this element.)**

Method	NS2	NS3	NS4	NS6	IE3a	IE3b	IE4	IE5	IE5.5	IE6
deleteCell				x			x	x	x	x

Returns: Nothing
Deletes a cell.
Syntax: *tr*.deleteCell([*index*]), where *index* is the index of the cell in the cells collection. If *index* is omitted, this method deletes the last cell in the cells collection.

| insertCell | | | | x | | | x | x | x | x |

Returns: New cell
Inserts a cell.
Syntax: *tr*.insertCell([*index*]), where *index* is the index of the cell to insert in the cells collection. If *index* is omitted, this method inserts a new cell at the end of the cells collection.

The *<TD>* and *<TH>* Elements

The actual data in tables is contained in <TD> and <TH> elements. You can find the properties of the <TD> and <TH> elements in Table 14.14. Remember that JavaScript's core HTML properties, methods, and events, which we covered in Chapters 5 and 6, apply to the <TD> and <TH> elements as well.

Table 14.14 The Properties of the *<TH>* and *<TD>* Elements (See Chapters 5 and 6 for the JavaScript core HTML properties, methods, and events that also apply to these elements.)

Property	NS2	NS3	NS4	NS6	IE3a	IE3b	IE4	IE5	IE5.5	IE6
abbr				x						x

Read/write
Sets or gets the abbreviated text for the element. Set to a string.

align	x	x	x	x	x	x	x	x	x	x

Sets or gets the alignment of the cell. Set to "center" (aligns to the center), "justify" (aligns to the left and right edge), "left" (the default—aligns to the left edge), or "right" (aligns to the right edge).

axis				x						x

Read/write
Sets or gets a comma-delimited list of categories associated with the cell, as text. This information can be used for nonvisual media or Braille.

background							x	x	x	x

Read/write
Sets or gets the background picture behind the cell. Set to the URL of an image.

bgColor				x			x	x	x	x

Read/write
Sets or gets the background color for the cell. Set to a color triplet (such as "ffffff") or a predefined color the browser understands (such as "green").

borderColor							x	x	x	x

Read/write
Sets or gets the border color. Set to a color triplet (such as "ffffff") or a predefined color the browser understands (such as "lightgreen").

Property	NS2	NS3	NS4	NS6	IE3a	IE3b	IE4	IE5	IE5.5	IE6
borderColorDark							X	X	X	X

Read/write
Holds a color used for shading effects to make the table look "raised." Set to a color triplet (such as `"ffffff"`) or a predefined color the browser understands (such as `"purple"`).

borderColorLight							X	X	X	X

Read/write
Holds a color used for shading effects to make the table look "raised." Set to a color triplet (such as `"ffffff"`) or a predefined color the browser understands (such as `"rose"`).

cellIndex				X			X	X	X	X

Read-only
The index of this cell in the `cells` collection. Set to an integer.

ch				X						X

Read/write
Corresponds to the `CHAR` attribute in the cell, but doesn't actually do anything in either browser yet.

chOff				X						X

Read/write
Corresponds to the `CHAROFF` attribute in the `cell`, but doesn't actually do anything in either browser yet.

colSpan				X			X	X	X	X

Read/write
Corresponds to the `COLSPAN` attribute, and indicates how many columns the cell spans. Set to an integer.

headers				X						X

Read/write
Sets or gets a list of header cells that provide information for the object. This information can be used for nonvisual media or Braille.

height				X			X	X	X	X

Read/write
Holds the height of the cell, in pixels. Set to an integer.

continues ▶

Table 14.14 **Continued**

Property	NS2	NS3	NS4	NS6	IE3a	IE3b	IE4	IE5	IE5.5	IE6
noWrap				X			X	X	X	X

Read/write
Indicates whether the text in a cell wraps automatically. Set to true (text wraps) or false (the default—text does not wrap).

rowSpan				X			X	X	X	X

Read/write
Corresponds to the ROWSPAN attribute, and indicates how many rows the cell spans. Set to an integer.

vAlign				X			X	X	X	X

Read/write
Sets or gets how cell contents are aligned. Set to "middle" (the default—aligns the text in the middle), "baseline" (aligns the base line of the first line of text with the base lines in adjacent objects), "bottom" (aligns the text at the bottom of the row), or "top" (aligns the text at the top of the row).

width				X			X	X	X	X

Read/write
The width of the cell, in pixels. Set to an integer.

The *<TBODY>*, *<TFOOT>*, and *<THEAD>* Elements

Since the early days, tables have become more elaborate, adding header, body, and footer elements, as well as column and row groups. The details of all of HTML are beyond the scope of this book, but here's an example putting these elements to work (note that all the features used here are supported fully only in the Internet Explorer):

(Listing 14-10.html on the web site)

```
<HTML>
    <HEAD>
        <TITLE>
            Tables with bodies, captions, and groups
        </TITLE>
    </HEAD>
```

```
<BODY>
    <CENTER>
        <H1>Tables with bodies, captions, and groups</H1>
        <TABLE BORDER="2" WIDTH="90%" FRAME="HSIDES" RULES="GROUPS">
            <CAPTION>Racing Times</CAPTION>
            <COLGROUP WIDTH="25%">
            <COLGROUP ALIGN="CENTER">
                <COL SPAN="2" WIDTH="30%">
                <COL SPAN="1" WIDTH="15%"
            </COLGROUP>

            <THEAD>
                <TR>
                    <TH>Car</TH>
                    <TH>Race</TH>
                    <TH>Owner</TH>
                    <TH>Time</TH>
                </TR>
            </THEAD>

            <TFOOT>
                <TR>
                    <TH>Car</TH>
                    <TH>Race</TH>
                    <TH>Owner</TH>
                    <TH>Time</TH>
                </TR>
            </TFOOT>

            <TBODY>
            <TR>
                <TD ALIGN="CENTER">69</TD>
                <TD>Chicago Trials</TD>
                <TD>Johnson</TD>
                <TD>5:33</TD>
            </TR>
            <TR>
                <TD ALIGN="CENTER">73</TD>
                <TD>Chicago Trials</TD>
                <TD>Chalmo</TD>
                <TD>6:41</TD>
            </TR>
            </TBODY>

            <TBODY>
            <TR>
                <TD ALIGN="CENTER">99</TD>
                <TD>Lotus Bowl</TD>
                <TD>Preston</TD>
                <TD>9:29</TD>
```

continues ▶

```
            </TR>
            <TR>
                <TD ALIGN="CENTER">21</TD>
                <TD>Lotus Bowl</TD>
                <TD>Liston</TD>
                <TD>12:23</TD>
            </TR>
            </TBODY>
        </TABLE>
    </BODY>
</HTML>
```

You can see the results in Figure 14.6.

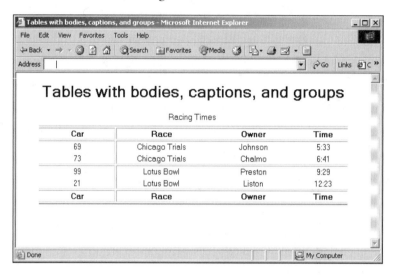

Figure 14.6 Using table bodies, captions, and groups.

You can find an overview of the properties and methods of the <TBODY>, <TFOOT>, and <THEAD> elements in Table 14.15, their properties in depth in Table 14.16, and their methods in Table 14.16. JavaScript's core HTML properties, methods, and events, which we covered in Chapters 5 and 6, also apply to the <TBODY>, <TFOOT>, and <THEAD> elements as well.

Table 14.15 **Overview of the Properties and Methods of the *<TBODY>*, *<TFOOT>*, and *<THEAD>* Elements (See Chapters 5 and 6 for the JavaScript core HTML properties, methods, and events that also apply to these elements.)**

Properties	Methods
align	deleteRow
bgColor	insertRow
ch	moveRow
chOff	
rows	
vAlign	

Table 14.16 **The Properties of the *<TBODY>*, *<TFOOT>*, and *<THEAD>* Elements (See Chapters 5 and 6 for the JavaScript core HTML properties, methods, and events that also apply to these elements.)**

Property	NS2	NS3	NS4	NS6	IE3a	IE3b	IE4	IE5	IE5.5	IE6
align				X			X	X	X	X

Read/write
Sets or gets the alignment of the element. Set to "center" (aligns to the center), "justify" (aligns to the left and right edge), "left" (the default—aligns to the left edge), or "right" (aligns to the right edge).

bgColor				X			X	X	X	X

Read/write
Sets or gets the background color for the element. Set to a color triplet (such as "ffffff") or a predefined color the browser understands (such as "blue").

ch				X						X

Read/write
Corresponds to the CHAR attribute, but doesn't actually do anything in either browser yet.

chOff				X						X

Read/write
Corresponds to the CHAROFF attribute, but doesn't actually do anything in either browser yet.

continues ▶

Table 14.16 **Continued**

Property	NS2	NS3	NS4	NS6	IE3a	IE3b	IE4	IE5	IE5.5	IE6
rows				X			X	X	X	X

Read-only
Holds a collection of all rows in the element (that is, all `<TR>` elements).
This collection enables you to address each row individually.

Property	NS2	NS3	NS4	NS6	IE3a	IE3b	IE4	IE5	IE5.5	IE6
vAlign				X			X	X	X	X

Read/write
Sets or gets how contents are aligned within the row that contains them.
Set to `"middle"` (the default—aligns the text in the middle), `"baseline"`
(aligns to the base line), `"bottom"` (aligns the text at the bottom), or `"top"`
(aligns the text at the top).

Table 14.17 **The Methods of the `<TBODY>`, `<TFOOT>`, and `<THEAD>`**
Elements (See Chapters 5 and 6 for the JavaScript core HTML properties,
methods, and events that also apply to these elements.)

Method	NS2	NS3	NS4	NS6	IE3a	IE3b	IE4	IE5	IE5.5	IE6
deleteRow				X			X	X	X	X

Returns: Nothing
Removes the specified row from the table and from the rows collection.
Syntax: `element.deleteRow([index])`, where *index* is the index of the
row in the rows collection.

Method	NS2	NS3	NS4	NS6	IE3a	IE3b	IE4	IE5	IE5.5	IE6
insertRow				X			X	X	X	X

Returns: New row
Inserts a new row into a table.
Syntax: `element.insertRow(index)`, where *index* is the position at which
to insert the row in the rows collection. Set *index* to -1 to append a row
to the end of the table. See "Using Tables" in this chapter for an example.

Method	NS2	NS3	NS4	NS6	IE3a	IE3b	IE4	IE5	IE5.5	IE6
moveRow								X	X	X

Returns: `<ROW>` element
Moves a row to a new position.
Syntax: `element.moveRow(source, target)`, where *source* is the index
in the rows collection of the table row you want to move and *target* is
the index that specifies where the row should be moved to in the rows
collection.

The *<CAPTION>* Element

You use the `<CAPTION>` element to add a caption to a table (see Listing 14.10 for an example). As you would expect, this element has its own properties (see Table 14.18). JavaScript's core HTML properties, methods, and events, which we covered in Chapters 5 and 6, also apply to the `<CAPTION>` element as well.

Table 14.18 **The Properties of the *<CAPTION>* Element (See Chapters 5 and 6 for the JavaScript core HTML properties, methods, and events that also apply to this element.)**

Property	NS2	NS3	NS4	NS6	IE3a	IE3b	IE4	IE5	IE5.5	IE6
align				x			x	x	x	x

Read/write
Sets or gets the alignment of the element. Set to `"center"` (aligns to the center), `"justify"` (aligns to the left and right edge), `"left"` (the default—aligns to the left edge), or `"right"` (aligns to the right edge).

| vAlign | | | | x | | | x | x | x | x |

Read/write
Sets or gets how contents are aligned within the row that contains them. Set to `"middle"` (the default—aligns the text in the middle), `"baseline"` (aligns the base line), `"bottom"` (aligns the text at the bottom), or `"top"` (aligns the text at the top).

The *<COL>* and *<COLGROUP>* Elements

The `<COL>` and `<COLGROUP>` elements create and group columns together. Although the in-depth HTML for these elements is beyond the scope of this book, you can see an example using the `<COL>` and `<COLGROUP>` elements in Listing 14.10, where I've created a few columns with the `<COL>` element and grouped them together with the `<COLGROUP>` element. You can find the properties of these elements in Table 14.19. JavaScript's core HTML properties, methods, and events, which we covered in Chapters 5 and 6, also apply to these elements as well.

Table 14.19 **The Properties of the <COL> and <COLGROUP> Elements (See Chapters 5 and 6 for the JavaScript core HTML properties, methods, and events that also apply to this element.)**

Property	NS2	NS3	NS4	NS6	IE3a	IE3b	IE4	IE5	IE5.5	IE6
align				x			x	x	x	x

Read/write
Sets or gets the alignment of the element. Set to `"center"` (aligns to the center), `"justify"` (aligns to the left and right edge), `"left"` (the default—aligns to the left edge), or `"right"` (aligns to the right edge).

Property	NS2	NS3	NS4	NS6	IE3a	IE3b	IE4	IE5	IE5.5	IE6
ch				x						x

Read/write
Corresponds to the CHAR attribute, but doesn't actually do anything in either browser yet.

Property	NS2	NS3	NS4	NS6	IE3a	IE3b	IE4	IE5	IE5.5	IE6
chOff				x						x

Read/write
Corresponds to the CHAROFF attribute, but doesn't actually do anything in either browser yet.

Property	NS2	NS3	NS4	NS6	IE3a	IE3b	IE4	IE5	IE5.5	IE6
span				x			x	x	x	x

Read/write
Sets or gets the number of columns in the group.

Property	NS2	NS3	NS4	NS6	IE3a	IE3b	IE4	IE5	IE5.5	IE6
vAlign				x			x	x	x	x

Read/write
Sets or gets how contents are aligned. Set to `"middle"` (the default—aligns the text in the middle), `"baseline"` (aligns to the base line), `"bottom"` (aligns the text at the bottom), or `"top"` (aligns the text at the top).

Property	NS2	NS3	NS4	NS6	IE3a	IE3b	IE4	IE5	IE5.5	IE6
width				x			x	x	x	x

Read/write
Sets or gets the width of the element, in pixels. Set to an integer.

Using Tables

As you can see in Tables 14.7 to 14.19, there's a lot of JavaScript support for working with tables. Let's take a look at some examples showing what JavaScript is good for here.

Here's an example where the user is buying an item and can specify the number of the item she wants to buy using a <SELECT> control in a table cell, and the code in the page will automatically update the total price in another table cell. You can see this code at work in Figure 14.7. When you select a number in the <SELECT> control control>, the code multiplies that number by the price per item and displays the result in the table cell on the right.

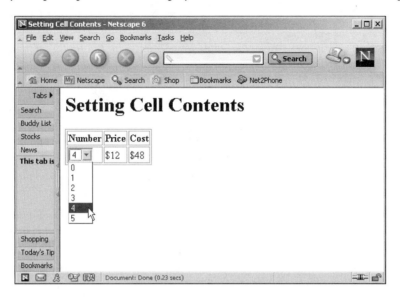

Figure 14.7 Updating table cell content on-the-fly.

This example is pretty easy to put together. You just use the <SELECT> control's ONCHANGE attribute to call a JavaScript function (named calculate here), and that gets the number selected in the <SELECT> control, performs the multiplication, and rewrites the content of the result table cell using the innerHTML property (to manipulate table cells such as this, you'll need NS6+ if using Netscape Navigator):

(Listing 14–11.html on the web site)

```
<HTML>
    <HEAD>
        <TITLE>Setting Cell Contents</TITLE>
        <SCRIPT LANGUAGE="JavaScript">
            <!--
            function calculate(select1)
            {
                document.getElementById("td1").innerHTML = "$" +
                select1.options[select1.selectedIndex].value * 12
            }
            // -->
        </SCRIPT>
    </HEAD>
```

continues ▶

```
<BODY>
    <H1>Setting Cell Contents</H1>
    <FORM>
        <TABLE BORDER=1>
            <TR>
                <TH>Number</TH>
                <TH>Price</TH>
                <TH>Cost</TH>
            </TR>
            <TR>
                <TD>
                    <SELECT ONCHANGE="calculate(this)">
                        <OPTION VALUE="0">0
                        <OPTION VALUE="1">1
                        <OPTION VALUE="2">2
                        <OPTION VALUE="3">3
                        <OPTION VALUE="4">4
                        <OPTION VALUE="5">5
                    </SELECT>
                </TD>
                <TD>
                    $12
                </TD>
                <TD ID="td1">
                     
                </TD>
            </TR>
        </TABLE>
    </FORM>
</BODY>
</HTML>
```

Tip

Note that I put a nonbreaking HTML space character ( ) into the results table cell in the preceding code; that's so this cell is not totally empty and so has a border like other cells when the table first appears.

Here's another example. This one shows how to build and alter tables on-the-fly using code that both the Netscape Navigator and Internet Explorer can execute. In this example, you can click buttons to add new rows, delete rows, add new columns, delete columns, add a caption, and so on, all using table methods.

When working with a table like this, the useful table properties and methods are the rows and cells collections, which give you access to the rows and cells in the table, and the insertRow, insertCell, deleteRow, and deleteCell methods, which enable you to alter tables on-the-fly. For this example, I'll create an empty table named table1:

```
<TABLE COLS="3" ID="table1"BORDER="1">
</TABLE>
```

When the page first loads, I'll insert a row of three cells into this table using the `insertRow` method and then insert three cells using the `insertCell` method into that row like this in a function named `init` (here, I'm filling the new cells with alternating x's and o's):

```
function init()
{
    var table1 = document.getElementById("table1")
    var row1 = table1.insertRow(0)
    var cell1
    for (var loopIndex = 0; loopIndex < 3; loopIndex++) {
        cell1 = row1.insertCell(loopIndex)
        cell1.style.backgroundColor = "cyan"
        cell1.innerHTML = loopIndex % 2 ? "o" : "x"
    }
    numberCols = 3
}
```

This example uses similar code to insert new rows into the table when the user clicks a button. To delete a row, we can just use the `deleteRow` method:

```
function deleteRow()
{
    document.getElementById("table1").deleteRow(0)
}
```

There is no `insertColumn` method, so to insert a new column, we can loop over all the rows using the `rows` collection, and insert a new cell in each row with the `insertCell` method (we also increment the number of columns, which we're storing in the global variable `numberCols`—the Internet Explorer `<TABLE>` element has a `cols` property that holds the number of columns, but the Netscape Navigator does not support this property, so we've got to keep track of the number of columns ourselves):

```
function insertColumn()
{
    var row1, cell1
    var table1 = document.getElementById("table1")
    for (var loopIndex = 0; loopIndex < table1.rows.length; loopIndex++) {
        row1 = table1.rows[loopIndex]
        cell1 = row1.insertCell(0)
        cell1.style.backgroundColor = "cyan"
        cell1.innerHTML = loopIndex % 2 ? "o" : "x"
        }
    numberCols++
}
```

As you can see, tables are completely open to you in JavaScript. Here's the whole code for this example (note that to use methods such as `insertRow` and `insertCell`, you'll need NS6+ if using Netscape Navigator):

(Listing 14-12.html on the web site)

```
<HTML>
    <HEAD>
        <TITLE>
            Inserting and Altering Rows and Columns
        </TITLE>
        <SCRIPT LANGUAGE="JavaScript">
            <!--
            var numberCols
            function init()
            {
                var table1 = document.getElementById("table1")
                var row1 = table1.insertRow(0)
                var cell1
                for (var loopIndex = 0; loopIndex < 3; loopIndex++) {
                    cell1 = row1.insertCell(loopIndex)
                    cell1.style.backgroundColor = "cyan"
                    cell1.innerHTML = loopIndex % 2 ? "o" : "x"
                  }
                numberCols = 3
            }

            function createRow()
            {
                var table1 = document.getElementById("table1")
                var row1 = table1.insertRow(0)
                var cell1
                for (var loopIndex = 0; loopIndex < numberCols; loopIndex++) {
                    cell1 = row1.insertCell(loopIndex)
                    cell1.style.backgroundColor = "cyan"
                    cell1.innerHTML = loopIndex % 2 ? "o" : "x"
                  }
            }

            function insertRow()
            {
                var table1 = document.getElementById("table1")
                var row1 = table1.insertRow(1)
                var cell1
                for (var loopIndex = 0; loopIndex < numberCols; loopIndex++) {
                    cell1 = row1.insertCell(loopIndex)
                    cell1.style.backgroundColor = "cyan"
                    cell1.innerHTML = loopIndex % 2 ? "x" : "o"
                }
            }

            function deleteRow()
            {
                document.getElementById("table1").deleteRow(0)
            }
```

```
        function createCaption()
        {
            var newCaption = document.getElementById("table1").createCaption()
            newCaption.innerHTML = "Here is a Caption"
        }

        function deleteCaption()
        {
            document.getElementById("table1").deleteCaption()
        }

        function insertColumn()
        {
            var row1, cell1
            var table1 = document.getElementById("table1")
            for (var loopIndex = 0; loopIndex < table1.rows.length; loopIndex++) {
                row1 = table1.rows[loopIndex]
                cell1 = row1.insertCell(0)
                cell1.style.backgroundColor = "cyan"
                cell1.innerHTML = loopIndex % 2 ? "o" : "x"
            }
            numberCols++
        }

        function deleteColumn(form)
        {
            var row1
            var table1 = document.getElementById("table1")
            for (var loopIndex = 0; loopIndex < table1.rows.length; loopIndex++) {
                row1 = table1.rows[loopIndex]
                row1.deleteCell(0)
            }
            numberCols--
        }
        // -->
    </SCRIPT>
</HEAD>

<BODY ONLOAD="init()">
    <H1>Inserting and Altering Rows and Columns</H1>
    <FORM>
        <INPUT TYPE="BUTTON" ONCLICK="createRow()" VALUE="Create a row">
        <INPUT TYPE="BUTTON" ONCLICK="insertRow()" VALUE="Insert new row 1">
        <INPUT TYPE="BUTTON" ONCLICK="deleteRow()" VALUE="Delete a row">
        <BR>
        <INPUT TYPE="BUTTON" ONCLICK="createCaption()" VALUE="Create a caption">
        <INPUT TYPE="BUTTON" ONCLICK="deleteCaption()" VALUE="Remove the caption">
        <BR>
        <INPUT TYPE="BUTTON" ONCLICK="insertColumn()" VALUE="Insert a column">
        <INPUT TYPE="BUTTON" ONCLICK="deleteColumn()" VALUE="Remove a column">
```

continues ▶

```
          </FORM>
          <TABLE COLS="3" ID="table1"BORDER="1">
          </TABLE>
     </BODY>
</HTML>
```

You can see this code at work in Figure 14.8, where I've clicked a button to add a new row to the table, and in Figure 14.9, where I've clicked a button to add a new column to the table. You can delete rows and columns as well, just by clicking buttons. For that matter, you also can add and remove a new table caption using the buttons in this example.

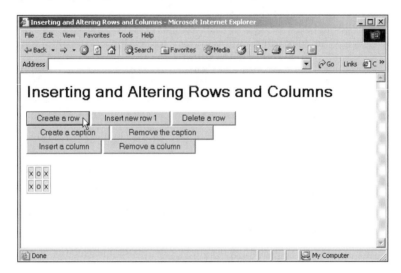

Figure 14.8   Adding a new table row.

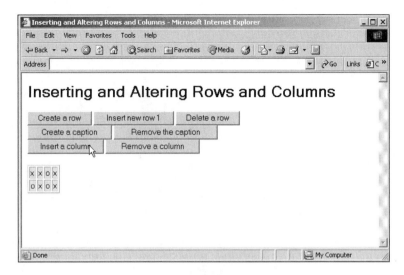

Figure 14.9 Adding a new table column.

And that's it for our work with hyperlinks, lists, and tables in this chapter. As we've seen, there's a lot of power here when you're using JavaScript. In the next chapter, we'll start working with the mouse, keyboard, images—and in-depth event handling.

15

Working with the Mouse, Keyboard, and Images

IN THIS CHAPTER, WE'RE GOING TO SEE some favorite JavaScript topics—working with the mouse, keyboard, images, and handling events in depth. Most visual elements support mouse and keyboard events; to see how they work, we'll enable the document object's mouse and keyboard events in this chapter so that you can use the keyboard and mouse anywhere in the entire page.

As we work with the mouse and keyboard, we'll find that the real keynote for this chapter is event handling. The event handling we'll see in this chapter has changed radically as browser versions have changed, and we'll have to take several different event object models into account in our code. In fact, that's the best place to start this discussion—with an overview of working with events in depth.

Working with Events

We've been using events since Chapter 1, "Essential JavaScript." However, one often uses events as simple notifications that an event—such as a mouse click—occurred so that you can execute your own code. On the other hand, when you're reading keys or detecting which mouse button was clicked, you need to know more—you need to use the properties of the event object.

The event object has changed a great deal as browsers developed. Chapter 6, "Using Core HTML Methods and Events," discussed in overview the three major event object models. I reproduce that information in Table 15.1 here, because we need it in this chapter. As you can see, the three major event object models correspond to Netscape Navigator version 4.0, Internet Explorer 4+, and Netscape Navigator 6.0. To read a keystroke in Netscape Navigator 4.0, for example, you use the which property, but to read a keystroke in Internet Explorer 4.0, you use the keyCode property.

Table 15.1 **Core *event* Object Properties**

NS4	NS6	IE4+	Means
–	clientX	clientX	X location in a window
–	clientY	clientY	Y location in a window
layerX	layerX	x	X location in a positioned item
layerY	layerY	y	Y location in a positioned item
modifiers	shiftKey	shiftKey	Keyboard modifier keys
	altKey	altKey	
	ctrlKey	ctrlKey	
–	–	offsetX	X location in a container
–	–	offsetY	Y location in a container
pageX	pageX	–	X location in the page
pageY	pageY	–	Y location in the page
screenX	screenX	screenX	X location in the screen
screenY	screenY	screenY	Y location in the screen
target	target	srcElement	Element the event was targeted to
type	type	type	Type of event that occurred
–	–	wheelDelta	The distance the wheel button rolled
which	keyCode	keyCode	Keyboard key that caused the event
which	button	button	Mouse button that caused the event

We're going to take a look at the properties of the event object for all three models in depth in this chapter, which will enable us to work with devices such as the mouse and the keyboard. Let's start by taking a look at working with the mouse.

The Mouse

We saw the available mouse events, such as the available keyboard events, in Chapter 6, including which browser supports which events. (For example, the onmousewheel event is currently supported only by Internet Explorer 6.0.) Here's an overview of these events:

- **onmousedown.** Occurs when the primary mouse button mouse is pressed.

- **onmouseenter.** Occurs when the mouse enters an object. This event was new in Internet Explorer 5.5 and is an alternative to onmouseover.

- **onmouseleave.** Occurs when the mouse leaves an object. This event was new in Internet Explorer 5.5 and is an alternative to onmouseout.

- **onmousemove.** Occurs when the mouse moves.

- **onmouseout.** Occurs when the mouse leaves an object (just like onmouseleave).

- **onmouseover.** Occurs when the mouse enters an object (just like onmouseenter).

- **onmouseup.** Occurs when the primary mouse button is released.

- **onmousewheel.** Occurs when the mouse wheel button is rotated.

Let's take a look at an example. Connecting the mouse to your code isn't all that hard; in this case, we'll connect the mouse-down event to the document object with the code document.onmousedown = mouseDownHandler. You can connect event handlers for this event to other elements as well, of course; for example, you can use the ONMOUSEDOWN attribute of a button element like this:
`<INPUT TYPE="BUTTON" ONMOUSEDOWN="mouseDownHandler()">`.

Tip
Although I'll take a look at the mouse-down event here, the event object properties you use are virtually the same in the mouse up and mouse move events.

The difficulty comes in the details—each of the three major event models works differently with the mouse. I'll try to include all possibilities in this example to make how this works clear, including using the Shift, Ctrl, and Alt keys with the left and right mouse buttons.

In the NS4 model, for example, you use the `event` object's `which` property to determine which mouse button was pressed, and the `modifiers` property to determine which of the Shift, Ctrl, and Alt keys were pressed, if any. In the NS6 and IE4+ event object models, you use the `button` property to determine which mouse button was pressed, and the `shiftKey`, `altKey`, and `ctrlKey` properties to check which modifier keys were also pressed—but the `button` property holds different values for the mouse buttons in each browser. Determining where the mouse was actually pressed is also different.

Note

For coverage of all these properties, see the discussion of the three event objects at the end of this chapter.

As you can see, it's pretty chaotic. As discussed in Chapter 6, however, the W3C has been bringing some sanity to this picture by introducing its own event object, and that object is the one that the NS6 event model tries to implement, as we'll see later in this chapter. Meanwhile, however, we're stuck with three different event models, and we have to handle them all. Here's the code for this example, which indicates which mouse button was pressed (left or right), which modifier keys were pressed (Shift, Ctrl, or Alt), and where the mouse button was pressed in the page:

(Listing 15-01.html on the web site)

```
<HTML>
    <HEAD>
        <TITLE>Working with the mouse</TITLE>
    </HEAD>

    <BODY>
        <H1>Working with the mouse</H1>

        <FORM name="form1">
            <H2>Press a mouse button and Shift, Ctrl, or Alt</H2>
            <BR>
            <INPUT TYPE="text" NAME="text1" SIZE = 60>
        </FORM>

        <SCRIPT LANGUAGE= "JavaScript">
            <!--
            document.onmousedown = mouseDownHandler
            document.oncontextmenu = noclick
```

```
function noclick()
{
    return false
}

function mouseDownHandler(e)
{
    var x, y, button

    if(navigator.appName == "Netscape" &&
        parseInt(navigator.appVersion) == 4) {

        switch(e.which){
            case 1:
                button = "left"
                break
             case 3:
                button = "right"
                break
        }

        switch(e.modifiers){
            case 0:
                document.form1.text1.value = button +
                " mouse button down at: " + e.pageX + ", " +
                e.pageY
                break
            case 1:
                document.form1.text1.value = "Alt key and " + button +
                " mouse button down at: " +
                e.pageX + ", " + e.pageY
                break
            case 2:
                document.form1.text1.value = "Ctrl key and " + button +
                " mouse button down at: " +
                e.pageX + ", " + e.pageY
                break
            case 4:
                document.form1.text1.value = "Shift key and " + button +
                " mouse button down at: " +
                e.pageX + ", " + e.pageY
                break
            case 6:
                document.form1.text1.value =
                document.form1.text1.value = "Shift and Ctrl keys and " +
                button + " mouse button down at: " +
                e.pageX + ", " + e.pageY
                break
        }
```

continues ▶

```
            } else {
                if(!e){
                    e = window.event
                }

                x = e.clientX
                y = e.clientY

                if(navigator.appName == "Netscape" &&
                    parseInt(navigator.appVersion) > 4) {
                    switch(e.button){
                        case 0:
                            button = "left"
                            break
                        case 2:
                            button = "right"
                            break
                    }
                }

                if (navigator.appName == "Microsoft Internet Explorer") {
                    switch(e.button){
                        case 1:
                            button = "left"
                            break
                        case 2:
                            button = "right"
                            break
                    }
                }

                if(e.shiftKey && e.ctrlKey){
                    document.form1.text1.value = "Shift and Ctrl keys and " +
                    button + " mouse button down at: " + x + ", " + y
                    return
                }

                if(e.shiftKey){
                    document.form1.text1.value = "Shift key and " + button +
                    " mouse button down at: " + x + ", " + y
                    return
                }

                if(e.ctrlKey){
                    document.form1.text1.value = "Ctrl key and " + button +
                    " mouse button down at: " + x + ", " + y
                    return
                }
```

```
                    if(e.altKey){
                        document.form1.text1.value = "Alt key and " + button +
                        " mouse button down at: " + x + ", " + y
                        return
                    }

                    document.form1.text1.value = button +
                    " mouse button down at: " + x + ", " + y
                }
            }
            //-->
        </SCRIPT>
    </BODY>
</HTML>
```

Yes, this is a large amount of code just to handle mouse clicks; the issue, of course, is detecting which event object you're using and providing code for them all. You can see the results of this code in Figure 15.1 in the Netscape Navigator and in Figure 15.2 in the Internet Explorer.

My hope in introducing this example is that you can adapt it as needed for your own mouse handling—there's nothing like some working code to get you started on a project.

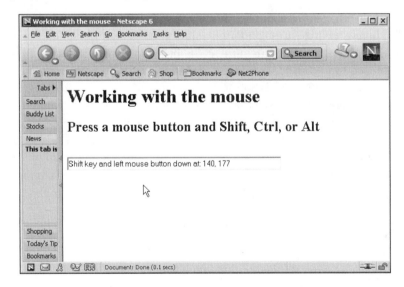

Figure 15.1   Using the mouse in the Netscape Navigator.

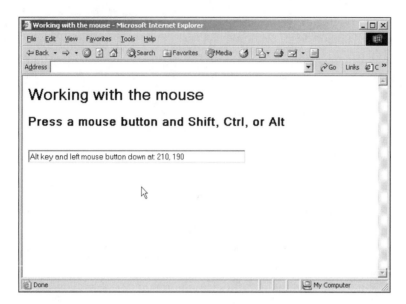

Figure 15.2   Using the mouse in the Internet Explorer.

Here's another popular use for mouse handling: disabling right-clicks. The idea here is that the user can't right-click your page to download images using the popup context menu that the browser normally displays. There's a lot of this code already around for the NS4 and IE4+ event models, but I haven't seen any for the NS6 model, which seems to have programmers stymied; even if you handle the mouse-down and mouse-up events, returning false from the event handler to stop further processing of the event, the context menu still appears in NS6. (It didn't in NS4.) To get rid of that menu, you must handle the oncontextmenu event in Netscape Navigator 6.0. This code does that, and will work for all three event models, disabling right mouse clicks and displaying an alert box with an error message if the user does right-click the mouse:

(Listing 15-02.html on the web site)

```
<HTML>
    <HEAD>
        <TITLE>Disabling Right Clicks</TITLE>
    </HEAD>

    <BODY>
        <H1>Disabling Right Clicks</H1>
        <IMG ID="img1" SRC="image1.jpg">
        <SCRIPT LANGUAGE= "JavaScript">
            <!--
```

```
                    document.oncontextmenu=noclick
                    document.onmousedown = mouseDownHandler

                    if(navigator.appName == "Netscape" &&
                        parseInt(navigator.appVersion) == 4) {
                        document.captureEvents(Event.MOUSEDOWN)
                    }

                    function noclick()
                    {
                        return false
                    }

                    function mouseDownHandler(e)
                    {
                        if (navigator.appName == "Netscape"){
                            if (parseInt(navigator.appVersion) == 4 && e.which == 3) {
                                alert("Sorry, right clicking is disabled.")
                                return false
                            }
                            if (parseInt(navigator.appVersion) > 4 && e.button == 2) {
                                alert("Sorry, right clicking is disabled.")
                                return false
                            }
                        }

                        if (navigator.appName == "Microsoft Internet Explorer") {
                            if (event.button == 2){
                                alert("Sorry, right clicking is disabled.")
                                return false
                            }
                        }
                    }
                //-->
            </SCRIPT>
        </BODY>
</HTML>
```

Once again, the difficulty in this code is in the details; we have to handle all three event models here. You can see the results of this code in Figure 15.3 in the Netscape Navigator 6.0.

Tip

Before you rely on this code, there are some things you should know: There's no guarantee it will work with future browsers, of course. In addition, note that it cannot really prevent users from saving your images; users can just turn off scripting, or, because they have the URLs of your images, they can download them directly. I created this example mostly because it's a widespread use of JavaScript, but it's not really a secure technique for protecting your images.

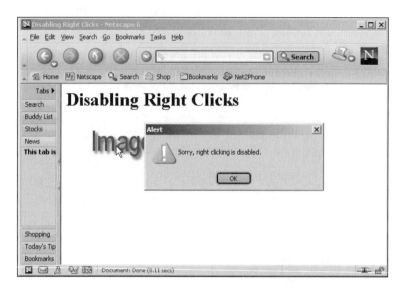

Figure 15.3 Disabling right-clicks in the Netscape Navigator 6.0.

The Keyboard

Working with the keyboard is much like working with the mouse—the difficulty is in handling the different event models. There are only three keystroke events. Here they are, in the order in which they occur, and what they do:

- **onkeydown.** Occurs when a key is struck or is held down and repeats (along with onkeyup) when you hold it down. Internet Explorer: event.keyCode holds the key's key code. Netscape Navigator: event.keyCode holds the key code and event.charCode holds zero.

- **onkeypress.** Occurs after the onkeydown and before the onkeyup event when you press an alphanumeric key, as well as ! @ # $ % ^ & * ( ) _ - + = < [ ] { } , . / ? \ | ' ` " ~ Esc, Spacebar, and Enter. Internet Explorer: event.keyCode holds the key's character code. Netscape Navigator: event.charCode holds the character code and event.keyCode holds zero.

- **onkeyup.** Occurs when a key is released or is held down and repeats (along with onkeydown) when you hold a key down. Internet Explorer: event.keyCode holds the key's key code. Netscape Navigator: event.keyCode holds the key code and event.charCode holds zero.

As discussed in Chapter 6, when you're handling alphanumeric keys, you should use the `onkeypress` event. When you're handling nonalphanumeric keys (such as arrow keys), use `onkeydown` and/or `onkeyup`. The reason for this is that in the `onkeydown` and `onkeyup` events, you get key codes (corresponding to the key's location in the keyboard) and modifier keys (such as the Shift key) that haven't been applied to the key you're reading, and you have to check properties such as `event.shiftKey` yourself (see Table 15.1) to determine whether a character should be capitalized. In the `onkeypress` event, you get the actual character code (an ASCII/Unicode code corresponding to the character as it appears on the screen), which holds an uppercase or lowercase character as appropriate.

To handle nonprinting keys such as arrow keys, you use the key codes you get in the `onkeydown` and `onkeyup` events. The key code, which you can read in the `keyCode` property in the `onkeydown` and `onkeyup` events, holds a code for the key corresponding to its location in the keyboard. Be aware, however, that the key code varies by operating system and machine type (for instance, PC versus Mac). So how do you find key codes? The easiest technique is just to write a short script that displays the key code when you press a key. (For example, here's a text field that will display key codes in an alert box in both the Internet Explorer and the Netscape Navigator when you enter text: `<INPUT TYPE="TEXT" ONKEYDOWN="alert(event.keyCode)">`.) Then you just press the keys for which you want to know the key codes.

Most key-handling JavaScript code uses the `onkeypress` event and character codes. Note, however, that the character codes (and key codes) you get are just numbers—you still have to translate them into characters. We saw an example in Chapter 6 that did exactly that (Listing 06-17.html on the web site)—that is, enabled users to just type; then what they typed was inserted into a text field when we handled the `document` object's `onkeypress` event (make sure the document has the focus when you're using this example—click it if necessary):

```
<HTML>
    <HEAD>
        <TITLE>Reading Keys</TITLE>
        <SCRIPT LANGUAGE="JavaScript">
            <!--
            document.onkeypress = keyPress

            var instring = ""

            function keyPress(e)
```

continues ▶

```
    {
        if(navigator.appName == "Netscape") {
            if(parseInt(navigator.appVersion) == 4) {
                instring += unescape("%" + e.which.toString(16))
                document.form1.text1.value = instring
            }
            if(parseInt(navigator.appVersion) > 4) {
                instring += unescape("%" + e.charCode.toString(16))
                document.form1.text1.value = instring
            }
        }
        if (navigator.appName == "Microsoft Internet Explorer") {
            instring += String.fromCharCode(window.event.keyCode)
            document.form1.text1.value = instring
        }
    }
    // -->
    </SCRIPT>
</HEAD>

<BODY>
    <H1>Reading Keys Directly (Type some text!)</H1>
    <BR>
    <FORM NAME="form1">
        <INPUT NAME="text1" TYPE="TEXT" SIZE="20">
    </FORM>
</BODY>
</HTML>
```

You can see the results of this code in Figure 15.4.

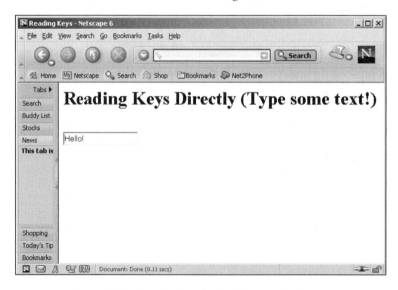

Figure 15.4 Reading keys in the Netscape Navigator.

What if you want to cancel an event such as a keystroke? Here's an example that does exactly that; if you try to enter text into the text field in this example, nothing will appear (you can get the details on the preventDefault method, available in NS6+ only, and the returnValue property in Tables 15.6 and 15.8 at the end of this chapter):

(Listing 15-03.html on the web site)

```
<HTML>
    <HEAD>
        <TITLE>
            Canceling Keystrokes
        </TITLE>
        <SCRIPT LANGUAGE="JavaScript">
            <!--
            function cancelKey(e)
            {
                if(navigator.appName == "Netscape"){
                    e.preventDefault()
                }
                if (navigator.appName == "Microsoft Internet Explorer") {
                    event.returnValue = false
                }
                return false
            }
            // -->
        </SCRIPT>
    </HEAD>

    <BODY>
        <H1>Canceling Keystrokes</H1>
        <FORM>
            <INPUT TYPE="TEXT" ONKEYPRESS="return cancelKey(event)">
        </FORM>
    </BODY>
</HTML>
```

Tip

Note that you're free to change a typed key by changing the keyCode and charCode properties in an event handler.

Next I'll turn to a topic near and dear to many JavaScript programmers: working with images.

The *<IMG>* Element

The `<IMG>` displays images in HTML, and, like all other HTML elements, this tag is active in HTML. You can see the properties and events of this element in Table 15.2 in overview, its properties in depth in Table 15.3, and its events in depth in Table 15.4. Note that JavaScript's core HTML properties, methods, and events that we discussed in Chapters 5, "Using Core HTML Properties," and 6, "Using Core HTML Methods and Events," also apply to this element.

Table 15.2 **Overview of the Properties and Events of the *<IMG>* Element (See Chapters 5 and 6 for the JavaScript core HTML properties, methods, and events that also apply to this element.)**

Properties	Events
align	onabort
alt	onafterupdate
border	onerror
complete	onerrorupdate
dynsrc	onload
fileCreatedDate	
fileModifiedDate	
fileSize	
fileUpdatedDate	
galleryImg	
height	
hspace	
isMap	
longDesc	
loop	
lowsrc	
name	
nameProp	
protocol	
src	
start	

Properties	Events
useMap	
vspace	
width	
x	
y	

Table 15.3 The Properties of the <*IMG*> Element (See Chapters 5 and 6 for the JavaScript core HTML properties, methods, and events that also apply to this element.)

Property	NS2	NS3	NS4	NS6	IE3a	IE3b	IE4	IE5	IE5.5	IE6
align				X			X	X	X	X

Read/write
This attribute sets the alignment of the <IMG> element. The possible values are "absbottom" (aligns the bottom with the absolute bottom of the surrounding text), "absmiddle" (aligns the middle with the middle of the surrounding text), "baseline" (aligns the bottom with the baseline of the surrounding text), "bottom" (aligns the bottom with the bottom of the surrounding text), "left" (the default, aligns to the left of the surrounding text), "middle" (aligns the middle with the surrounding text), "right" (aligns to the right of the surrounding text), and "top" (aligns the top with the top of the text).

alt				X			X	X	X	X

Read/write
Sets or gets alternate text for the graphic, displayed on mouse-over events or if the image can't load.

border		X	X	X			X	X	X	X

Read/write
Sets the thickness of the border in pixels. Set this property to zero if you're using the image in an <A> hyperlink element and don't want a border to appear. See "Mouse Rollovers" in this chapter for an example.

complete		X	X	X			X	X	X	X

Read-only
This property is true if the image has fully loaded and is false otherwise. If you specify a LOWSRC image, that's the one that's used; otherwise, the SRC image is used. (So don't rely on this property to make sure the SRC image is loaded if you're using both the SRC and LOWSRC properties.)

continues ▶

Table 15.3 **Continued**

Property	NS2	NS3	NS4	NS6	IE3a	IE3b	IE4	IE5	IE5.5	IE6
dynsrc							x	x	x	x

Read/write
Sets or gets the address of a video clip or VRML world to display in the element.

| fileCreatedDate | | | | | | | x | x | x | x |

Read-only
Holds the file's creation date in text form, such as "Sunday, December 07, 1997". Don't rely on this property; many web servers won't supply this information.

| fileModifiedDate | | | | | | | x | x | x | x |

Read-only
Holds the date the file was last modified, in text form, such as "Saturday, December 06, 1997". Don't rely on this property; many web servers won't supply this information.

| fileSize | | | | | | | x | x | x | x |

Read-only
Holds the size of the image file, in bytes.

| fileUpdatedDate | | | | | | | x | x | x | x |

Read-only
Holds the date the file was last updated in text form, such as "Friday, December 05, 1997". Don't rely on this property; many web servers won't supply this information.

| galleryImg | | | | | | | | | x | |

Sets or gets whether the My Pictures Photo Support image toolbar is visible for the current image. Set to yes (or true; this is the default) to enable the Image toolbar for the image, or no (or false) to disable this toolbar for the image.

| height | | x | x | x | | | x | x | x | x |

Read/write
Holds the height of the image, in pixels. Set this property to stretch an image; see "Using Images" in this chapter for an example.

| hspace | | x | x | x | | | x | x | x | x |

Read/write
Holds the width of the invisible margin around the image, in pixels.

Property	NS2	NS3	NS4	NS6	IE3a	IE3b	IE4	IE5	IE5.5	IE6
isMap				X			X	X	X	X

Read/write
This property is true if the image is part of an image map, and false otherwise. Corresponds to the ISMAP attribute.

longDesc				X						X

Read/write
Meant to provide a long description of the image, or the URL at which such a description may be found. Not in common use. Holds text.

loop					X	X	X	X	X	X

Read/write
Holds the number of times a video clip should play. The default value is 1, setting this value to –1 makes the loop play over and over.

lowsrc		X	X	X			X	X	X	X

Read/write
Holds the URL of a low-resolution version of the image to be displayed as the higher-resolution version (specified by the SRC attribute) loads. Set to a URL string.

name	X	X	X	X			X	X	X	X

Read/write
Holds the name of the control as a name string.

nameProp								X	X	X

Read-only
Holds the filename of the image file (unlike the lowsrc and src properties, which hold complete URLs). Contains a name string.

protocol							X	X	X	X

Read-only
Holds the protocol used to get the file—"HyperText Transfer Protocol" (for HTTP) or "File Protocol" (for FTP).

src		X	X	X			X	X	X	X

Read/write
Holds the source URL for the image. Set to a URL string. See "Using Images" in this chapter. This property is also good for use with precaching images—see "Precaching Images and the Image Object" in this chapter.

continues ▶

Table 15.3 **Continued**

Property	NS2	NS3	NS4	NS6	IE3a	IE3b	IE4	IE5	IE5.5	IE6
start							x	x	x	x

Read/write
Specifies when a video clip should start playing. Set to `"fileopen"` (the default) to make the video begin as soon as it finishes loading, or `"mouseover"` to begin the video when the user moves the mouse over it.

useMap				x			x	x	x	x

Read/write
Sets or gets the URL (often with a hash extension, such as #name) to use as a client-side image map.

vspace		x	x	x			x	x	x	x

Read/write
Holds the height of the invisible margin around the image, in pixels.

width		x	x	x			x	x	x	x

Read/write
Sets or gets the width of the image, in pixels. See "Using Images" in this chapter.

x				x						

Read-only
Holds the X coordinate of the upper-left of the `<IMG>` element, in pixels.

y				x						

Read-only
Holds the Y coordinate of the upper-left of the `<IMG>` element, in pixels.

Table 15.4 **The Events of the *<IMG>* Element (See Chapters 5 and 6 for the JavaScript core HTML properties, methods, and events that also apply to this element.)**

Event	NS2	NS3	NS4	NS6	IE3a	IE3b	IE4	IE5	IE5.5	IE6
onabort		x	x	x			x	x	x	x

Occurs when the user stops loading the image, as by clicking the Stop button.

Event	NS2	NS3	NS4	NS6	IE3a	IE3b	IE4	IE5	IE5.5	IE6
onafterupdate							X	X	X	X

Occurs in a data-bound object after updating the data in the data source.

onbeforeupdate							X	X	X	X

Occurs in a data-bound object before updating the data in the data source.

onerror	X	X	X				X	X	X	X

Occurs when there's been an error loading the image.

onerrorupdate							X	X	X	X

Occurs in a data-bound object when an error happened while updating data in the data source.

onload	X	X	X				X	X	X	X

Occurs when the LOWSRC image finishes loading; if there is no LOWSRC image, this event occurs when the SRC image finishes loading. Also occurs when each frame of an animated GIF image displays.

Using Images

Let's see some examples using images and JavaScript. The most basic type of image work is where you just swap images using the src property; here's an example where the image displays when the page loads displays the text Image 1; but when you click a button, the code loads a new image, which displays Image 2:

(Listing 15-04.html on the web site)

```
<HTML>
    <HEAD>
        <TITLE>
            Reloading Images
        </TITLE>

        <SCRIPT LANGUAGE="JavaScript">
            <!--
            function newImage()
```

continues ▶

```
        {
            document.form1.img1.src = "image2.jpg"
        }
        //-->
    </SCRIPT>
</HEAD>

<BODY>
    <H1>Reloading Images</H1>
    <FORM NAME="form1">
        <IMG NAME="img1" SRC="image1.jpg"
            WIDTH="216" HEIGHT="72">
        <BR>
        <INPUT TYPE="BUTTON" Value="Load new image"
            ONCLICK="newImage()">
    </FORM>
</BODY>
</HTML>
```

You can see the results of this code in Figure 15.5, where I've clicked the button to load a new image into the `<IMG>` element. Being able to reload images such as this (as well as being able to load and display banner ads) is one of the primary attractions of JavaScript for many programmers.

Figure 15.5   Loading a new image into an `<IMG>` element.

You also can access the images in a document with the document object's images collection (see "The document Object Collections" in Chapter 9, "Using the *document* and *body* Objects," and see Table 9.2). Here's an example that loads an image into all the <IMG> elements in a document by looping over the images collection:

(Listing 15-05.html on the web site)

```html
<HTML>
    <HEAD>
        <TITLE>
            Reloading Images
        </TITLE>

        <SCRIPT LANGUAGE="JavaScript">
            <!--
            function newImages()
            {
                for(var loopIndex = 0; loopIndex < document.images.length;
                ➥loopIndex++){
                    document.images[loopIndex].src = "image2.jpg"
                }
            }
            //-->
        </SCRIPT>
    </HEAD>

    <BODY>
        <H1>Reloading Images</H1>
        <FORM NAME="form1">
            <IMG NAME="img1" SRC="image1.jpg"
                WIDTH="216" HEIGHT="72">
            <BR>
            <IMG NAME="img1" SRC="image1.jpg"
                WIDTH="216" HEIGHT="72">
            <BR>
            <IMG NAME="img1" SRC="image1.jpg"
                WIDTH="216" HEIGHT="72">
            <BR>
            <INPUT TYPE="BUTTON" Value="Load new images"
                ONCLICK="newImages()">
        </FORM>
    </BODY>
</HTML>
```

You can see the results of this code in Figure 15.6.

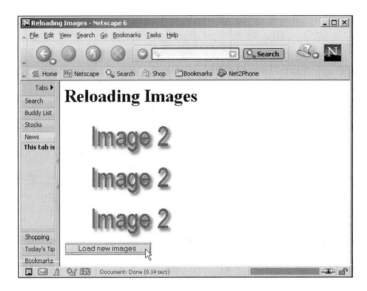

Figure 15.6 Loading new images into <IMG> elements.

You also can use the width and height properties to change the dimensions of an image on-the-fly, stretching it. Here's an example that doubles the width of an image when you click a button (you'll need version 6+ if you're using Netscape Navigator):

(Listing 15-06.html on the web site)

```
<HTML>
    <HEAD>
        <TITLE>Stretching Images</TITLE>
        <SCRIPT LANGUAGE="JavaScript">
            <!--
            function stretcher()
            {
                document.getElementById("img1").width = 432
            }
            // -->
        </SCRIPT>
    </HEAD>

    <BODY>
        <H1>Stretching Images</H1>
        <IMG ID="img1" HEIGHT = "72" WIDTH="216" SRC="image1.jpg">
        <FORM>
            <INPUT TYPE="BUTTON" ONCLICK="stretcher()" VALUE="Click Me!">
        </FORM>
    </BODY>
</HTML>
```

You can see the results of this code in Figure 15.7.

Figure 15.7 Stretching an image.

TIP

You can create composite images using JavaScript, to an extent, by placing <IMG> elements right next to each other to form a single image. If you want to create a web page hit counter, for example, you could use the HTML <IMG ID="img1"><IMG ID="img2"><IMG ID="img3"> and JavaScript like:

```
document.getElementById("img1").src="1.jpg"
document.getElementById("img2").src="2.jpg"
document.getElementById("img3").src="3.jpg"
```

(where 1.jpg displays 1, 2.jpg displays 2, and so on, to display the number 123).

Mouse Rollovers

One of the main reasons JavaScript became popular was its capability to swap images in the browser in real time when the mouse moved over an image. Here's an example that shows how that works, using the mouse-over and mouse events. You can handle these events in the <IMG> element itself, or in an element that encloses the <IMG> element. For example, here I'm enclosing an image in a hyperlink <A> element. Note that I've set the BORDER property of the <IMG> element to "0" so that no hyperlink border appears. When the page loads, the image displayed shows the text Image 1, but when the mouse moves over the image, it's swapped for an image that displays the text Image 2:

(Listing 15-07.html on the web site)

```
<HTML>
    <HEAD>
        <TITLE>Mouse Rollovers</TITLE>
        <SCRIPT LANGUAGE= JavaScript>
            <!--
            function ImgOver()
            {
                document.form1.img1.src="image2.jpg"
            }

            function ImgOut()
            {
                document.form1.img1.src="image1.jpg"
            }
            //-->
        </SCRIPT>
    </HEAD>

    <BODY>
        <H1>Mouse Rollovers</H1>
        <FORM NAME="form1">
            <A HREF="http://www.w3.org" NAME="link1"
                ONMOUSEOVER="ImgOver()" ONMOUSEOUT="ImgOut()">
                <IMG BORDER="0" NAME="img1" SRC="image1.jpg" WIDTH="216" HEIGHT="72">
            </A>
        </FORM>
    </BODY>
</HTML>
```

You can see the results of this code in Figure 15.8. Handling mouse rollovers by swapping images such as this is one of the favorite aspects of JavaScript for many programmers. We'll also take a look at handling mouse rollovers for text in Chapter 21, "Cascading Style Sheets and CGI Programming."

Note that when you swap images such as this quickly, it's a good idea to have the new image already downloaded and in memory. You can do that by *precaching* the image.

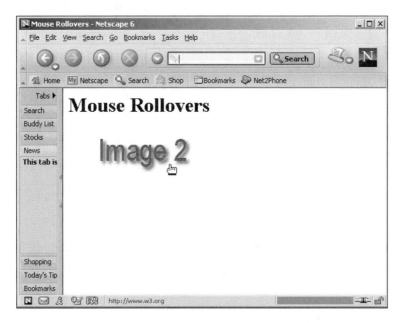

Figure 15.8   Handling mouse rollovers.

Precaching Images and the *Image* Object

JavaScript supports an `Image` object that enables you to hold images in memory and work with them using many of the same properties of the `<IMG>` element. One use for the `Image` object is to download images you'll use later to avoid download delays, precaching those images. You do that by creating an `Image` object, setting its `height` and `width` properties for the image you want to pre-cache, and then setting the `Image` object's `src` property to load the image into the `Image` object. When you want to display the precached image in a web page, just set the `src` property of an image to the `Image` object's `src` property. Here's an example showing how this works. Note that the second image is precached as soon as the page loads, but only displayed when the user clicks a button (you'll need version 6+ if you're using Netscape Navigator):

(Listing 15-08.html on the web site)

```
<HTML>
    <HEAD>
        <TITLE>
            Precaching Images
```

continues ▶

```
        </TITLE>
        <SCRIPT LANGUAGE="JavaScript">
            <!--
            var precache = new Image(216, 72)
            precache.src = "image2.jpg"
            function display()
            {
                document.getElementById("img1").src = precache.src
            }
            // -->
        </SCRIPT>
    </HEAD>

    <BODY>
        <H1>Precaching Images</H1>
        <IMG ID="img1" WIDTH="216" HEIGHT="72" SRC="image1.jpg">
        <FORM>
            <INPUT TYPE="BUTTON" ONCLICK="display()" VALUE="Click Me!">
        </FORM>
    </BODY>
</HTML>
```

In this way, using the `Image` object, you can store images in memory and use them when you're ready for them. This is particularly useful for JavaScript-supported animation.

Moving Images

Here's another way to work with images—you can move them around in a web page, repositioning them where you want them. Normally, the browser handles the flow and placement of images in the page, but you can specify the exact location of images using cascading styles (which we'll see more of in Chapter 21). Here's an example that changes the left and top styles of an image when you click a button, moving the image (again, you'll need version 6+ if you're using Netscape Navigator to work with styles this way):

(Listing 15-09.html on the web site)

```
<HTML>
    <HEAD>
        <TITLE>Moving Images</TITLE>
        <SCRIPT LANGUAGE="JavaScript">
            <!--
            function mover()
            {
                document.getElementById("div1").style.left = "150"
                document.getElementById("div1").style.top = "200"
            }
```

```
            // -->
        </SCRIPT>
    </HEAD>

    <BODY>
        <H1>Moving Images</H1>
        <DIV ID="div1" STYLE="POSITION:ABSOLUTE; LEFT:10; TOP:180; WIDTH:240;
        ➥HEIGHT:300">
            <IMG HEIGHT = "72" WIDTH="216" SRC="image2.jpg">
        </DIV>
        <DIV STYLE="POSITION:ABSOLUTE; LEFT:120; TOP:100; WIDTH:240; HEIGHT:250">
            <IMG HEIGHT = "72" WIDTH="216" SRC="image1.jpg">
        </DIV>
        <FORM>
            <INPUT TYPE="BUTTON" ONCLICK="mover()" VALUE="Click Me!">
        </FORM>
    </BODY>
</HTML>
```

You can see the results of this code in Figure 15.9, where I've clicked the button to move the second image. This is another technique good for JavaScript-supported animation.

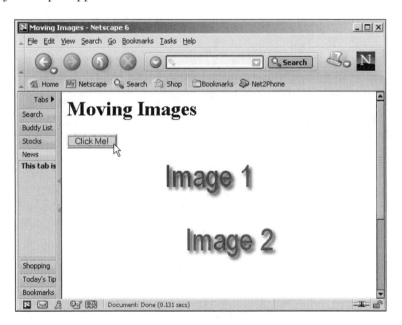

Figure 15.9   Moving an image.

You can extend this example to create "mouse trails," where a set of images follows the mouse around; just use the onmousemove event and the setInterval method and move an image to follow the mouse cursor. Here's some code that does just that (this is just intended as a simple demo, and it's targeted at Internet Explorer 4+ and Netscape Navigator 6; if you want to use this example in earlier browser versions, you'll have to replace methods like getElementById with their earlier counterparts):

(Listing 15-10.html on the web site)

```
<HTML>
    <HEAD>
        <TITLE>Mouse Trails!</TITLE>
        <SCRIPT LANGUAGE="JavaScript">
            <!--
            var xData, yData
            var oldX, oldY, timeout, counter
            var timer = setInterval("draw()", 20);

            function init()
            {
                xData = new Array(-1, -1, -1, -1, -1, -1)
                yData = new Array(-1, -1, -1, -1, -1, -1)
                timeout = 0
                counter = 0
                oldX = -1
                oldY = -1
            }

            document.onmousemove = mouseMove

            function draw()
            {
                var id
                for (loopIndex = 0; loopIndex  < 6; loopIndex++) {
                    id = "img" + parseInt(loopIndex)
                    if((xData[0] == oldX) && (yData[0] == oldY)) {
                        timeout++
                    } else {
                        timeout = 0
                    }

                    if(timeout > 20) {
                        document.getElementById(id).style.visibility = "hidden"
                        document.getElementById(id).style.left = 0
                        document.getElementById(id).style.top = 2000
                    } else {
                        if((xData[loopIndex] > 0) && (yData[loopIndex] > 0)) {
                            document.getElementById(id).style.visibility = "visible"
                            document.getElementById(id).style.left = xData[loopIndex]
                            document.getElementById(id).style.top = yData[loopIndex]
```

```
                    }
                }
                oldX = xData[0]
                oldY = yData[0]
            }
        }

        function mouseMove(e)
        {
            counter++
            if(counter < 4) {
                return
            }
            counter = 0

            var newx, newy

            if(window.event){
                e = window.event
            }

            newx = e.clientX - 10
            newy = e.clientY - 10

            for(var loopIndex = 5; loopIndex >= 0; loopIndex--){
                xData[loopIndex + 1] = xData[loopIndex]
                yData[loopIndex + 1] = yData[loopIndex]
            }
            xData[0] = newx
            yData[0] = newy
        }
        //-->
    </SCRIPT>
</HEAD>

<BODY BGCOLOR="BLACK" TEXT="ffffff" ONLOAD="init()">
    <H1>Mouse Trails!</H1>
    <DIV ID="img0" STYLE="POSITION:ABSOLUTE; LEFT:0; TOP:2000; VISIBILTY:hidden">
        <IMG SRC="star.gif">
    </DIV>
    <DIV ID="img1" STYLE="POSITION:ABSOLUTE; LEFT:0; TOP:2000; VISIBILTY:hidden">
        <IMG SRC="star.gif">
    </DIV>
    <DIV ID="img2" STYLE="POSITION:ABSOLUTE; LEFT:0; TOP:2000; VISIBILTY:hidden">
        <IMG SRC="star.gif">
    </DIV>
    <DIV ID="img3" STYLE="POSITION:ABSOLUTE; LEFT:0; TOP:2000; VISIBILTY:hidden">
        <IMG SRC="star.gif">
    </DIV>
    <DIV ID="img4" STYLE="POSITION:ABSOLUTE; LEFT:0; TOP:2000; VISIBILTY:hidden">
        <IMG SRC="star.gif">
    </DIV>
```

continues ▶

```
    <DIV ID="img5" STYLE="POSITION:ABSOLUTE; LEFT:0; TOP:2000; VISIBILTY:hidden">
        <IMG SRC="star.gif">
    </DIV>
  </BODY>
</HTML>
```

You can see the results of this code in Figure 15.10, where you can see a trail of stars following the mouse around.

Figure 15.10   Mouse trails.

Tip

Want to make an image appear to move *under* other page elements? Just include the style `"z-index:-1"` for the `<IMG>` element for a cool effect.

Image Maps

Another use for JavaScript with images is to handle image maps. As we know, you can use JavaScript URLs with HREF attributes, and the `<AREA>` elements you use in image maps support the HREF attribute. Usually, the HREF attribute of `<AREA>` elements points to URLs the browser navigates to when the corresponding area in the image map is clicked, but you also can execute JavaScript code instead. Here's an example showing how this works. When the user clicks the Guest Book label in the following code, a JavaScript function displays an alert box with the text `The guest book is unavailable.`:

(Listing 15-11.html on the web site)

```html
<HTML>
    <HEAD>
        <TITLE>
            JavaScript and Image Maps
        </TITLE>

        <SCRIPT LANGUAGE="JavaScript">
            <!--
            function notify()
            {
                window.alert("The guest book is unavailable.")
            }
            //-->
        </SCRIPT>
    </HEAD>

<BODY BGCOLOR="BLACK">
    <IMG WIDTH="528" HEIGHT="137" SRC="mainmenu.jpg"
        BORDER="0" ALT="Image Map" USEMAP="#MAP" ALIGN="CENTER">
        <MAP NAME="MAP">
            <AREA SHAPE="RECT" COORDS="16,39 127,61"
                HREF="http://www.reuters.com" ALT="News">
            <AREA SHAPE="RECT" COORDS="62,71 173,93"
                HREF="http://www.starpowder.com/steve/search.html"
                ALT="Web search">
            <AREA SHAPE="RECT" COORDS="98,104 209,126"
                HREF="http://www.nnic.noaa.gov" ALT="Weather">
            <AREA SHAPE="RECT" COORDS="411,35 522,57"
                HREF="javascript:notify()"
                ALT="Guest book">
            <AREA SHAPE="RECT" COORDS="360,67 471,89"
                HREF="http://www.yahoo.com/Guides_and_Tutorials/"
                ALT="Create a Web page">
            <AREA SHAPE="RECT" COORDS="328,98 439,120"
                HREF="http://www.web21.com/services/hot100/index.html"
                "Hottest 100 sites">
            <AREA NAME="DEFAULT" SHAPE="DEFAULT"
                HREF=
                "http://www.starpowder.com/steve/index.html#mainmenu"
                ALT="Image map">
        </MAP>
    </BODY>
</HTML>
```

You can see the results of this code in Figure 15.11 (the image for this example, mainmenu.jpg, is on the web site), where I've clicked the Guest Book label.

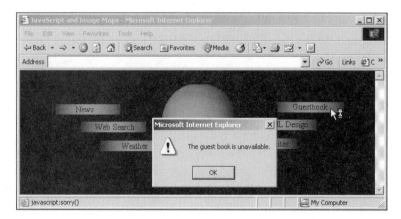

Figure 15.11   Using JavaScript in an image map.

That completes our work with images in this chapter. Next I'll take a look at working with events in depth.

Handling Events

Working with events in JavaScript has grown complicated over the years as event object models have changed and more functionality has been added. There are all kinds of things you can do in event handling in JavaScript. Here's an example that reassigns event handlers on-the-fly (you'll need version 6+ if you're using Netscape Navigator):

(Listing 15-12.html on the web site)

```
<HTML>
    <HEAD>
        <TITLE>
            Reassigning Event Handlers
        </TITLE>
        <SCRIPT LANGUAGE="JavaScript">
            <!--
            function alerter()
            {
                window.alert("You clicked the button!")
            }

            function reassign()
            {
                document.getElementById("button1").onclick=alerter2
            }

            function alerter2()
```

```
            {
                window.alert("Here's a new message!")
            }
            // -->
        </SCRIPT>
    </HEAD>

    <BODY>
        <H1>Reassigning Event Handlers</H1>
        <FORM>
            <INPUT TYPE="BUTTON" ID="button1" ONCLICK="alerter()" VALUE="Click Me!">
            <INPUT TYPE="BUTTON" ONCLICK="reassign()" VALUE="Reassign event handler">
        </FORM>
    </BODY>
</HTML>
```

Most of the complexity involved in event handling comes from dealing with the different event object models, as we saw in the beginning of this chapter when we worked with the keyboard and the mouse. There are three event models—the NS4, NS6, and IE4+ event models; I'll take a look at all of them here.

Tip

See Chapter 6 for the basics on event handling, such as making sure event objects are passed to event handlers and so on. For the syntax of JavaScript's core properties and methods that you can use with events, such as captureEvents and addEventListener, see Chapters 5 and 6. We'll see many of these properties and methods in use in this chapter.

The NS4 *event* Object

You can see the properties of the event object used in Netscape Navigator 4.0 in Table 15.5.

Table 15.5   **The Properties of the NS4 *event* Object**

Property	NS2	NS3	NS4	NS6	IE3a	IE3b	IE4	IE5	IE5.5	IE6
data			x							

Read-only
Holds the text data associated with a drag-and-drop operation. Using this property, you can drag and drop text data.

continues ▶

Table 15.5 **Continued**

Property	NS2	NS3	NS4	NS6	IE3a	IE3b	IE4	IE5	IE5.5	IE6
layerX			x							

Read-only
Holds the X coordinate in the layer where the event (usually a mouse event) occurred. Holds a pixel value, an integer.

layerY			x							

Read-only
Holds the Y coordinate in the layer where the event (usually a mouse event) occurred. Holds a pixel value, an integer.

modifiers			x							

Read-only
Holds the modifier keys that were pressed when the event occurred, such as the Shift, Ctrl, Meta, or Option keys. To check whether these keys were pressed, you can use an expression such as *event*.modifiers & Event.SHIFT_MASK, which is true if the Shift key was down, or *event*.modifiers & Event.ALT_MASK, which is true if the Alt key was down, and so on.

pageX			x							

Read-only
Holds the X coordinate in the page where the event (usually a mouse event) occurred. Holds a pixel value, an integer.

pageY			x							

Read-only
Holds the Y coordinate in the page where the event (usually a mouse event) occurred. Holds a pixel value, an integer.

screenX			x							

Read-only
Holds the X coordinate in the screen where the event (usually a mouse event) occurred. Holds a pixel value, an integer.

screenY			x							

Read-only
Holds the Y coordinate in the screen where the event (usually a mouse event) occurred. Holds a pixel value, an integer.

target			x							

Read-only
Holds the target of the event, such as a button object. Contains an object reference.

Property	NS2	NS3	NS4	NS6	IE3a	IE3b	IE4	IE5	IE5.5	IE6
type			X							

Read-only

Holds the type of event, such as `"click"`. Contains a text string.

which			X							

Read-only

Contains the mouse button for the mouse event or key code for the keyboard event that occurred. Contains 1 for the left/primary mouse button or 3 for the right/secondary mouse button. Contains 2 for the middle mouse button, if there is one.

Using the NS4 *event* Object

In Netscape Navigator 4.0, you can capture and release events with methods such as `captureEvents`, `disableExternalCapture`, `enableExternalCapture`, `handleEvent`, `releaseEvents`, and `routeEvent` (see Chapter 6).

Here's an example targeted to that browser that shows how to capture events. By default, when you click a button labeled Click Me! in this example, an alert box appears with the message `Button saw the event`. On the other hand, events in this browser start at the top of the object hierarchy and move downward; so if we capture the event in the `document` object with the `captureEvent` method, that event won't get down to the button. You can do that by clicking the Enable Document Capture button; after you do and when you click the Click Me! button, all you'll see is an alert box with the message `Captured by the document.`:

(Listing 15-13.html on the web site)

```
<HTML>
    <HEAD>
        <TITLE>Capturing and releasing events in NS4</TITLE>
        <SCRIPT LANGUAGE="JavaScript">
            <!--
                document.onclick=click

                function capture()
                {
                    document.captureEvents(Event.CLICK)
                }

                function click(e)
```

continues ▶

```
            {
                if (e.target.type == "button") {
                    alert("Captured by the document.")
                    document.releaseEvents(Event.CLICK)
                }
            }
        //-->
    </SCRIPT>
</HEAD>

<BODY>
    <H1>Capturing and releasing events in NS4</H1>
    <FORM>
        <INPUT TYPE="BUTTON" ONCLICK="capture()" VALUE="Enable Document Capture">
        <BR>
        <INPUT TYPE="BUTTON" VALUE="Click Me!" ONCLICK="alert('Button saw the
        ➥event.')">
    </FORM>
</BODY>
</HTML>
```

In this way, you can capture events that start at the top of the object hierarchy before they can move down to their intended target. To stop capturing events, you use the `releaseCapture` method.

The IE4+ *event* Object

You can see the properties of the event object used in Internet Explorer 4+ in Table 15.6.

Table 15.6   **The Properties of the IE4+ *event* Object**

Property	NS2	NS3	NS4	NS6	IE3a	IE3b	IE4	IE5	IE5.5	IE6
Abstract										x

Read-only
Holds the content of a banner in an *Advanced Stream Redirector* (ASX) file. Contains text.

altKey							x	x	x	x

Read-only
True if the Alt key was pressed when the event occurred, false otherwise.

altLeft									x	x

Read-only
True if the left Alt key was pressed when the event occurred, false otherwise.

Property	NS2	NS3	NS4	NS6	IE3a	IE3b	IE4	IE5	IE5.5	IE6
Banner										X

Read-only
Gets the banner content of an entry in an ASX file.

bookmarks							X	X	X	X

Read-only
Holds a collection of *ActiveX Data Objects* (ADO) bookmarks.

boundElements							X	X	X	X

Read-only
Holds a collection of all elements in the document bound to a data set.

button							X	X	X	X

Read-only
Indicates what mouse button was pressed or released. Holds 0 (the default, no button is pressed), 1 (left button is pressed), 2 (right button is pressed), 3 (left and right buttons are both pressed), 4 (middle button is pressed), 5 (left and middle buttons both are pressed), 6 (right and middle buttons are both pressed), or 7 (all three buttons are pressed).

cancelBubble							X	X	X	X

Read/write
Sets or gets whether the current event should bubble up the hierarchy of event handlers. Set to false (the default, bubbling is enabled, allowing the next event handler in the hierarchy to get the event) or true (bubbling is disabled for this event, preventing the next event handler in the hierarchy from getting the event).

clientX							X	X	X	X

Read/write
Holds the X coordinate of the event in client area coordinates. To get the actual position in a page if the page has been scrolled, add `document.body.scrollLeft` to this value.

clientY							X	X	X	X

Read/write
Holds the Y coordinate of the event in client area coordinates. To get the actual position in a page if the page has been scrolled, add `document.body.scrollTop` to this value.

contentOverflow									X	X

Read-only
Holds a value that indicates whether the document contains additional content beyond the current layout. Contains true if so, false if not.

continues ▶

Table 15.6 **Continued**

Property	NS2	NS3	NS4	NS6	IE3a	IE3b	IE4	IE5	IE5.5	IE6
ctrlKey							X	X	X	X

Read-only
True if the Ctrl key was pressed when the event occurred, false otherwise.

ctrlLeft									X	X

Read-only
True if the left Ctrl key was pressed when the event occurred, false otherwise.

dataTransfer								X	X	X

Read-only
Gives you access to predefined clipboard formats for use in drag-and-drop operations. This property holds a `dataTransfer` object. See Chapter 17, "Dynamic HTML: Drag and Drop, Data Binding, and Behaviors," for more on this property and the `dataTransfer` object.

fromElement							X	X	X	X

Read-only
Holds the object the mouse came from before entering the object that caused the event.

keyCode							X	X	X	X

Read/write
Holds the key code or character code associated with a keyboard event. See "The Keyboard" in this chapter for more information and an example.

moreInfo									X	

Read-only
Holds the MoreInfo content of a banner in an ASX file.

nextPage									X	X

Read-only
Holds the position of the next page within a print template.

offsetX							X	X	X	X

Read/write
Holds the X coordinate of the event inside the target element. Set to a pixel measurement, an integer.

offsetY							X	X	X	X

Read/write
Holds the Y coordinate of the event inside the target element. Set to a pixel measurement, an integer.

Property	NS2	NS3	NS4	NS6	IE3a	IE3b	IE4	IE5	IE5.5	IE6
propertyName								X	X	X

Read-only
Contains a string that holds the name of the property whose value will change in this event.

qualifier							X	X	X	X

Read-only
Holds the name of the data member provided by a data source object.

reason							X	X	X	X

Read-only
Holds the result of the data transfer for a data source object. This value is an integer holding 0 (data transmitted successfully), 1 (data transfer aborted), or 2 (data transferred in error).

recordset							X	X	X	X

Read-only
Holds a reference to the current recordset.

repeat								X	X	X

Read-only
Indicates whether the onkeydown event is being repeated. Holds true if so, false otherwise.

returnValue							X	X	X	X

Read/write
Sets or gets the return value from the event. Set to true (the default— continue normal processing) or false (the default action of the event on the source object is canceled). You can also return false from an event handler to cancel an event's normal processing.

saveType									X	X

Read-only
Holds the type of data in the clipboard for oncontentsave events. Holds "HTML" or "TEXT".

screenX							X	X	X	X

Read/write
Holds the X coordinate of the event in screen coordinates. Set to a pixel measurement, an integer.

continues ▶

Table 15.6 **Continued**

Property	NS2	NS3	NS4	NS6	IE3a	IE3b	IE4	IE5	IE5.5	IE6
screenY							x	x	x	x

Read/write
Holds the Y coordinate of the event in screen coordinates. Set to a pixel measurement, an integer.

| shiftKey | | | | | | | x | x | x | x |

Read-only
True if the Shift key was pressed when the event occurred, false otherwise.

| shiftLeft | | | | | | | | | x | x |

Read-only
True if the left Shift key was pressed when the event occurred, false otherwise.

| srcElement | | | | | | | x | x | x | x |

Read-only
Holds the object that cause the event. Contains an object reference.

| srcFilter | | | | | | | x | x | x | x |

Read/write
Sets or gets the filter object that caused the `onfilterchange` event to occur.

| srcUrn | | | | | | | | x | x | x |

Read-only
Holds the *Uniform Resource Name* (URN) of the Internet Explorer behavior that caused the event. See Chapter 17 for more on behaviors.

| toElement | | | | | | | x | x | x | x |

Read-only
Holds a reference to the object the mouse is over now.

| type | | | | | | x | x | x | x |

Read-only
Contains the event name from the `event` object. For example, holds the text `"click"` for a click event.

| wheelDelta | | | | | | | | | | x |

Read-only
Holds the distance and direction the wheel button has rolled. This property holds an integer that indicates the distance that the wheel has rotated, expressed in multiples of 120. For an example, see "The `onmousedown`, `onmouseenter`, `onmouseleave`, `onmousemove`, `onmouseout`, `onmouseover`, `onmouseup`, and `onmousewheel` Events" in Chapter 6.

Property	NS2	NS3	NS4	NS6	IE3a	IE3b	IE4	IE5	IE5.5	IE6
x							X	X	X	X

Read/write
Sets or gets the X coordinate, in pixels, of the mouse pointer's position relative to a positioned parent element.

Property	NS2	NS3	NS4	NS6	IE3a	IE3b	IE4	IE5	IE5.5	IE6
y							X	X	X	X

Read/write
Sets or gets the Y coordinate, in pixels, of the mouse pointer's position relative to a positioned parent element.

Using the IE4+ *event* Object

Unlike the Netscape Navigator 4.0 event model, where events move down to their intended target from the top of the object hierarchy, events in the Internet Explorer move up from their target in a process called *bubbling*.

Here's an example that shows how bubbling works. In this case, I'll attach event handlers to the button, form, body, <HTML>, and document objects to handle onclick events. When you click the button in this example, you'll see alert boxes showing how the event is bubbling up the object hierarchy, from the button all the way up to the document object. Here's the code:

(Listing 15-14.html on the web site)

```
<HTML ONCLICK="alert('HTML element level')">
    <HEAD>
        <TITLE>Event Bubbling</TITLE>
        <SCRIPT LANGUAGE="JavaScript">
            <!--
            document.onclick = documentLevel

            function documentLevel()
            {
                alert("document level")
            }

            function bodyLevel()
            {
                alert("body level")
            }
            //-->
        </SCRIPT>
    </HEAD>

    <BODY ONCLICK="alert('body level')">
```

continues ▶

```
        <H1>Event Bubbling</H1>
        <FORM ONCLICK="alert('form level')">
            <INPUT TYPE="BUTTON" VALUE="Click Me!" ONCLICK="alert('button level')">
        </FORM>
    </BODY>
</HTML>
```

You can see the results of this code in Figure 15.12. When you click the button, you can watch the click event bubble up through the button, form, body, <HTML> element, and document levels.

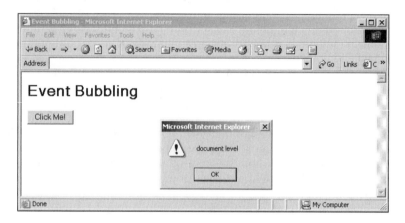

Figure 15.12   Event bubbling.

Tip
You can cancel event bubbling with the event object's `cancelBubble` property. See Table 15.6.

The NS6+ *event* Object

The event object used in Netscape Navigator 6 is based on the W3C DOM level 2 event object, with a number of properties thrown in from Netscape Navigator 4. Now that W3C is in the act, we'll see more sanity in event handling in the future. You can see the properties of the event object used in Netscape Navigator 6 in Table 15.7, and its methods in Table 15.8.

Table 15.7 **The Properties of the NS6 *event* Object**

Property	NS2	NS3	NS4	NS6	IE3a	IE3b	IE4	IE5	IE5.5	IE6
altKey				X						

Read-only
True if the Alt key was pressed when the event occurred, false otherwise.

| bubbles | | | | X | | | | | | |

Read-only
Indicates whether an event bubbles; true if so, false otherwise.

| button | | | | X | | | | | | |

Read-only
Holds 1 if the left/primary mouse button was used, and 3 if the right/secondary mouse button was used. Holds a value of 2 if the middle button was used in a three-button mouse.

| cancelBubble | | | | X | | | | | | |

Read/write
Setting this property to true prevents the event from bubbling further.

| cancelable | | | | X | | | | | | |

Read-only
This property is true if you can cancel an event's default action from occurring. To actually cancel the event's default action, use the `preventDefault` method.

| charCode | | | | X | | | | | | |

Read-only
Holds the character code for a keyboard event. See "The Keyboard" in this chapter for more information and an example.

| clientX | | | | X | | | | | | |

Read-only
The X coordinate of the event in the client area of the browser, in pixels. Relative to the browser window.

| clientY | | | | X | | | | | | |

Read-only
The Y coordinate of the event in the client area of the browser, in pixels. Relative to the browser window.

| ctrlKey | | | | X | | | | | | |

Read-only
True if the Ctrl key was pressed when the event occurred, false otherwise.

continues ▶

Table 15.7 **Continued**

Property	NS2	NS3	NS4	NS6	IE3a	IE3b	IE4	IE5	IE5.5	IE6
currentTarget				x						

Read-only
Holds a reference to the object whose event listener is processing the event.

| detail | | | | x | | | | | | |

Read-only
Not used currently; may be used in the future to hold information about the event.

| eventPhase | | | | x | | | | | | |

Read-only
Indicates the event's "phase." A listener function can determine how the event is being processed using this property. The possible values are 1 (the event was captured), 2 (the event is at its intended target), and 3 (the event is bubbling).

| isChar | | | | x | | | | | | |

Read-only
This property is true if a key is a character key on the keyboard (as opposed to a noncharacter key such as an arrow key).

| keyCode | | | | x | | | | | | |

Read-only
Holds the key code associated with a keyboard event. See "The Keyboard" in this chapter for more information and an example.

| layerX | | | | x | | | | | | |

Read-only
The X coordinate of the event in a Netscape Navigator layer, in pixels.

| layerY | | | | x | | | | | | |

Read-only
The Y coordinate of the event in a Netscape Navigator layer, in pixels.

| metaKey | | | | x | | | | | | |

Read-only
True if the Meta key was pressed when the event occurred, false otherwise.

| pageX | | | | x | | | | | | |

Read-only
The X coordinate of the event in the document, in pixels.

Property	NS2	NS3	NS4	NS6	IE3a	IE3b	IE4	IE5	IE5.5	IE6
pageY				x						

Read-only
The Y coordinate of the event in the document, in pixels.

| relatedTarget | | | | x | | | | | | |

Read-only
In the onmouseover event, this property holds a reference to the previous element the mouse was over. In the onmouseout event, this property holds a reference to the element the mouse is over now.

| screenX | | | | x | | | | | | |

Read-only
The X coordinate of the event in screen coordinates, in pixels.

| screenY | | | | x | | | | | | |

Read-only
The X coordinate of the event in screen coordinates, in pixels.

| shiftKey | | | | x | | | | | | |

Read-only
True if the Shift key was pressed when the event occurred, false otherwise.

| target | | | | x | | | | | | |

Read-only
Holds the object that was the original target of the event.

| timeStamp | | | | x | | | | | | |

Read-only
Holds an integer value recording the time of the event in the same format as the JavaScript Date object.

| type | | | | x | | | | | | |

Read-only
Holds the type of the event as a string, such as "click" or "mouseup".

| view | | | | x | | | | | | |

Read-only
Holds a reference to the window object in which the event occurred.

Table 15.8 **The Methods of the NS6 *event* Object**

Method	NS2	NS3	NS4	NS6	IE3a	IE3b	IE4	IE5	IE5.5	IE6
preventDefault				x						

Returns: Nothing
Although you can cancel an event by returning false from the event handler, you also can cancel an event with this method, which prevents the browser from performing the default action for the event (such as displaying a struck key in a text field).
Syntax: *event*.preventDefault().

| stopPropagation | | | | x | | | | | | |

Returns: Nothing
Stops further bubbling of the event and stops further event listeners from being informed of the event. In other words, ends further processing of the event following the current event handler.
Syntax: *event*.stopPropagation().

In Netscape Navigator 6, events bubble by default, just as in the Internet Explorer (and unlike Netscape Navigator 4). You also can use the addEventListener method (see the sections "Handling Events in the W3C DOM" and "The *addEventListener* Method" in Chapter 6) to add event listeners for specific events to objects of your choice and so configure how events are routed in your code.

Here's an example. In this case, I'll add onclick event handlers to the window, document, body, and button objects in this code that will indicate whether the event has been captured by a listener or is bubbling. Then I'll add click listeners to the document and form objects, in that order. Here's what the code looks like:

(Listing 15-15.html on the web site)

```
<HTML>
    <HEAD>
        <TITLE>W3C Capture and Bubbling</TITLE>
    </HEAD>

    <BODY>
        <H1>W3C Capture and Bubbling</H1>
        <FORM NAME="form1">
            <INPUT TYPE="BUTTON" VALUE="Click Me!" ONCLICK="buttonClick(event)">
        </FORM>

        <SCRIPT LANGUAGE="JavaScript">
            <!--
```

```
window.onclick = windowClick
document.onclick = documentClick
document.body.onclick = bodyClick

document.addEventListener("click", documentClick, true)
document.form1.addEventListener("click", formCapture, true)
document.form1.addEventListener("click", formBubble, false)

function buttonClick(e)
{
    switch (e.eventPhase) {
        case 1:
            text = "Captured"
            break
        case 2:
            text = "Seen"
            break
        case 3:
            text = "Bubbling"
            break
        }
    alert(text + " at the button level.")
}

function windowClick(e)
{
    switch (e.eventPhase) {
        case 1:
            text = "Captured"
            break
        case 2:
            text = "Seen"
            break
        case 3:
            text = "Bubbling"
            break
        }
    alert(text + " at the window level.")
}

function documentClick(e)
{
    switch (e.eventPhase) {
        case 1:
            text = "Captured"
            break
        case 2:
            text = "Seen"
            break
        case 3:
            text = "Bubbling"
```

continues ▶

```
                    break
                }
            alert(text + " at the document level.")
        }

        function bodyClick(e)
        {
            switch (e.eventPhase) {
                case 1:
                    text = "Captured"
                    break
                case 2:
                    text = "Seen"
                    break
                case 3:
                    text = "Bubbling"
                    break
                }
            alert(text + " at the body level.")
        }

        function formCapture(e)
        {
            alert("Captured at the form level.")
        }

        function formBubble(e)
        {
            alert("Bubbling at the form level.")
        }
    //-->
    </SCRIPT>
  </BODY>
</HTML>
```

When you click the button in this example, you can watch the progress of the event with alert boxes. The event is first captured by the document and form objects because of the event listeners we've added to those objects, and then bubbles from the button up through the form, body, document, window objects. You can see this example at work in Figure 15.13.

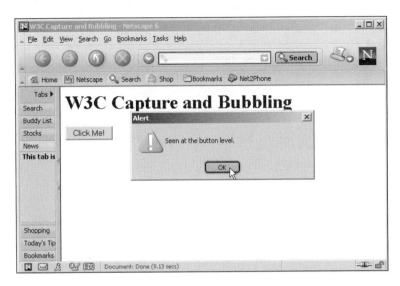

Figure 15.13   Event handling in Netscape Navigator 6.

As you can see, you can use event bubbling in Netscape Navigator 6, as well as event listeners to track events as you want.

And that's it for this chapter. You've seen a lot of JavaScript, including the mouse, keyboard, images, and in-depth event handling. In the next chapter, we'll start taking a look at another favorite JavaScript topic: Dynamic HTML.

16

Dynamic HTML: Changing Web Pages On-the-Fly

MUCH OF JAVASCRIPT IS ALL ABOUT MAKING your web pages "come alive," and in this chapter we're going to focus on that, using a variety of dynamic effects to change your web pages on-the-fly. Here's an overview of the techniques we'll see here:

- Changing visual properties on-the-fly
- Rewriting documents with the `document.write` method
- Using the `insertAdjacentHTML` and `insertAdjacentText` methods
- Rewriting documents with the `innerHTML`, `innerText`, `outerHTML`, and `outerText` properties
- Creating new elements
- Rewriting documents with text ranges
- Moving elements using Netscape Navigator layers
- Setting element visibility on-the-fly
- Adding visual effects with filters
- Using Internet Explorer visual transitions
- Changing pages with dynamic styles
- Drawing graphics with *Vector Markup Language* (VML)
- Using Internet Explorer Direct Animation

Many of these topics are part of what's been called *Dynamic HTML*, which has become a catch-all term for dynamic visual effects. There's a lot to Dynamic HTML, and we'll take a look at this topic in this and the next chapter—some of which we've already seen, most of which we haven't.

The W3C hasn't gotten around to standardizing Dynamic HTML yet; you can find what W3C has to say about Dynamic HTML at www.w3.org/DOM, and here it is:

> "Dynamic HTML" is a term used by some vendors to describe the combination of HTML, style sheets and scripts that allows documents to be animated. W3C has received several submissions from members companies on the way in which the object model of HTML documents should be exposed to scripts. These submissions do not propose any new HTML tags or style sheet technology. The W3C DOM WG is working hard to make sure interoperable and scripting-language neutral solutions are agreed upon.

That's as far as W3C has gotten in this area, however, which means that the browser manufacturers have been free to develop in different directions. And they have. The Dynamic HTML implementation in the Internet Explorer is far larger than what you'll find in the Netscape Navigator, for example. I'll take a look at what Dynamic HTML means in the Internet Explorer first, and then take a look at what it means in the Netscape Navigator.

Dynamic HTML in Internet Explorer

You can find information about Microsoft's Dynamic HTML at http://msdn.microsoft.com/library/default.asp?url=/workshop/author/ dhtml/dhtml_node_entry.asp. Dynamic HTML in the Internet Explorer is extensive and can nearly turn web pages into entire applications that run without round trips back to the server. Here are the key features of Dynamic HTML in the Internet Explorer:

- **Document Object Model (DOM).** As we know, all the elements in the Microsoft DOM can be accessed at runtime and changed. That alone brings your web pages alive.

- **Dynamic content.** Using Dynamic HTML in the Internet Explorer, you can create new elements and attributes on-the-fly, modifying your pages by inserting and deleting elements.

- **Dynamic styles.** You can change *any* style sheet attribute, including color and font, in your code. As you'll see in this chapter, for example, you can change text's color or size when a cursor moves over it.

- **Absolute positioning.** You also can use style sheet positioning to move elements and even create animated effects.

- **Special ActiveX controls.** As we'll see in this chapter, the Internet Explorer comes with ActiveX controls that support visual effects such as animation, visual filters, and visual transitions.

- **Data binding.** As we'll discuss in the next chapter, you can create data-bound documents that display, manipulate (for example, sort or filter), and update data in the browser.

- **Behaviors.** As we'll also see in the next chapter, behaviors represent HTML applications that enable you to separate code from data in web pages, and that enable you add new "behaviors" to the elements in your web page work.

As you can see, the support for Dynamic HTML is extensive in the Internet Explorer. I'll take a look at what's available in the Netscape Navigator next.

Dynamic HTML in Netscape Communicator

Netscape's implementation of Dynamic HTML is more limited than Microsoft's, and you can find information about it at http:// developer.netscape.com/docs/manuals/communicator/dynhtml/index.htm. Here are the key elements of Netscape's version of Dynamic HTML:

- **Document Object Model (DOM).** Microsoft's DOM is more extensive than Netscape's is, as we've seen in the previous chapters. Although you can access many elements in code, the support is not as full as in the Internet Explorer.

- **Dynamic content.** Like the Internet Explorer, you can change the content of elements in the Netscape Navigator—but the options are more limited. Instead of using methods such as insertAdjacentHTML and insertAdjacentText, as well as properties such as innerText, innerHTML, outerText, and outerHTML, Netscape Navigator supports only the innerHTML property.

- **Absolute positioning.** As in the Internet Explorer, you can use style sheet positioning to move elements and even create animated effects.

- **Downloadable fonts.** In the Netscape Navigator, you can download fonts from the Internet and install them in your web pages, using downloadable fonts. However, these are not in widespread use.

As you can see, Netscape's implementation of Dynamic HTML is more restricted than Microsoft's. That means that many of the topics in this and the next chapter will apply to the Internet Explorer only.

Changing Properties

Making your web pages dynamic can be as easy as setting visual properties at runtime—browsers didn't used to change their displays when you did so, but since IE4, they do. Here's an example that changes the background color of a web page to green when the user clicks it (you'll need version 6+ if you're using Netscape Navigator):

(Listing 16-01.html on the web site)

```
<HTML>
    <HEAD>
        <TITLE>
            Setting Background Color
        </TITLE>
    </HEAD>

    <BODY ONMOUSEDOWN="document.bgColor='green'">
        <H1>
            Click this page to turn it green.
        </H1>
    </BODY>
</HTML>
```

That's the most basic level of Dynamic HTML—changing visual properties, such as a page's title or text color, on-the-fly.

Dynamic Styles

Styles have become more important as time has gone on (we'll cover working with styles in Chapter 21, "Cascading Style Sheets and CGI Programming"), now even replacing the beloved HTML <CENTER> element (according to W3C, you're supposed to center elements with styles starting with HTML 4), and, in many ways, the Netscape <LAYER> element we'll see later in this chapter.

Using the style property, you can change the appearance of a page at runtime in browsers such as IE4+ and NS6+; you also can position elements on-the-fly. Here's an example showing how to create text mouse rollovers (also see graphic mouse rollovers in Chapter 15, "Working with the Mouse, Keyboard, and Images"). In this case, the code makes some text bigger when the mouse rolls over it:

(Listing 16-02.html on the web site)

```
<HTML>
    <HEAD>
        <TITLE>
            Text Mouse Rollovers
        </TITLE>
    </HEAD>

    <BODY>
        <CENTER>
            <H1>
                Text Mouse Rollovers
            </H1>
            <SPAN ONMOUSEOVER="this.style.fontSize='48'"
                ONMOUSEOUT="this.style.fontSize='12'"
                STYLE="fontSize:36">
                This text gets big when the mouse is over it.
            </SPAN>
        </CENTER>
    </BODY>
</HTML>
```

You can see the results in Figure 16.1.

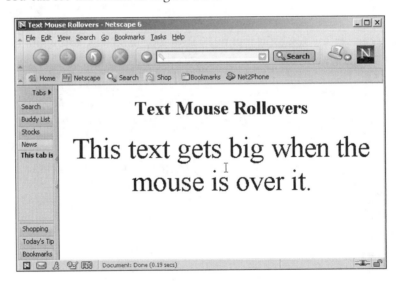

Figure 16.1   Using dynamic styles to make text big.

Making text grow was probably the most common use for dynamic styles with mouse rollovers early on, but it's a little disconcerting to see text grow and squirm around in reaction to mouse movements. More recently, web pages are just changing the color of text when the mouse moves over that text. Here's an example that changes the color of text to red when the mouse moves over it (you'll need version 6+ if you're using Netscape Navigator):

(Listing 16-03.html on the web site)

```
<HTML>
    <HEAD>
        <TITLE>
            Text Mouse Rollovers
        </TITLE>
    </HEAD>

    <BODY>
        <CENTER>
            <H1>
                Text Mouse Rollovers
            </H1>
            <SPAN ONMOUSEOVER="this.style.color='red'"
                ONMOUSEOUT="this.style.color='black'">
                This text changes color when the mouse is over it.
            </SPAN>
        </CENTER>
    </BODY>
</HTML>
```

You can see the results in Figure 16.2, in glorious black and white (although the text really is red).

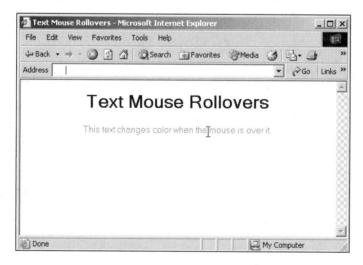

Figure 16.2   Using dynamic styles to change text color.

You also can use styles to position elements at runtime to make your web pages come alive; see "Moving Images" in Chapter 15 for examples, including a mouse trail example where a trail of stars follows the mouse as you move it around.

Self-Modifying Pages Using *document.write*

We've used the `document.write` method (see in Table 9.5) to change documents on-the-fly throughout this book, but it's important to include it in our Dynamic HTML chapters. This method is limited in precision, because it's hard to specify exactly when the writing should start to a document. (Note that relying on a certain loading order of elements to estimate when the `<SCRIPT>` element containing the `document.write` method will execute is not reliable.) As a result, programmers usually use `document.write` only when a document is loading or when they're creating a new document. Here's an example from Chapter 9, "Using the *document* and *body* Objects," that writes different HTML to a document, letting users indicate with a confirm dialog box whether they want to see the large image or a smaller one:

```
<HTML>
    <HEAD>
        <TITLE>
            Self-modifying Web Pages
        </TITLE>
    </HEAD>

    <BODY>
        <H1>Self-modifying Web Pages</H1>
        <SCRIPT LANGUAGE="JavaScript">
            <!--
            if(confirm("Do you want a graphics intensive page?")) {
                document.write("<BR><IMG WIDTH='2048' HEIGHT='2048' " +
                "SRC='gif/bigimage.jpg'></IMG>")
            }
            else {
                document.write("<BR><IMG WIDTH='100' HEIGHT='100' " +
                "SRC='gif/smallimage.jpg'></IMG>")
            }
            // -->
        </SCRIPT>
    </BODY>
</HTML>
```

Here's another example. This one—the JavaScript Café—responds to the local time of day on the user's computer to display one of three menus: breakfast, lunch, or dinner:

(Listing 16-04.html on the web site)

```
<HTML>
    <HEAD>
        <TITLE>
            Welcome to the JavaScript Café
        </TITLE>
        <SCRIPT LANGUAGE="JavaScript">
            <!--
            var currentDate = new Date()
            var currentHour = currentDate.getHours()
            document.write( "<CENTER>")
            document.write( "<H1>")
            document.write( "Welcome to the JavaScript Café")
            document.write( "</H1>")
            document.write( "</CENTER>")

            if (currentHour < 5 || currentHour > 23){
                document.write( "<CENTER>")
                document.write( "<H1>")
                document.write( "Sorry, we're closed now." )
                document.write( "</H1>")
                document.write( "</CENTER>")
            }

            if (currentHour > 6 && currentHour < 12 ) {
                document.write( "<CENTER>")
                document.write( "<TABLE BORDER BGCOLOR='CYAN'>")
                document.write(
                    "<TR><TH COLSPAN = 2>Breakfast Menu</TH></TR>")
                document.write(
                    "<TR><TD>Two eggs</TD><TD>$2.50</TD></TR>")
                document.write(
                    "<TR><TD>Three eggs</TD><TD>$3.50</TD></TR>")
                document.write(
                    "<TR><TD>Pancakes</TD><TD>$2.00</TD></TR>")
                document.write(
                    "<TR><TD>Cereal</TD><TD>$1.00</TD></TR>")
                document.write( "</TABLE>")
                document.write( "</CENTER>")
                document.write( "</TABLE>")
                document.write( "</CENTER>")
            }

            if ( currentHour >= 12 && currentHour < 17 ) {
                document.write( "<CENTER>")
```

```
                document.write( "<TABLE BORDER BGCOLOR='CYAN'>")
                document.write(
                    "<TR><TH COLSPAN = 2>Lunch Menu</TH></TR>")
                document.write(
                    "<TR><TD>Lobster</TD><TD>$5.00</TD></TR>")
                document.write(
                    "<TR><TD>Frog legs</TD><TD>$3.50</TD></TR>")
                document.write(
                    "<TR><TD>Brie rollups</TD><TD>$3.00</TD></TR>")
                document.write(
                    "<TR><TD>Peacock flambé</TD><TD>$4.50</TD></TR>")
                document.write(
                    "<TR><TD>Chili</TD><TD>$2.00</TD></TR>")
                document.write(
                    "<TR><TD>Octopus Soup</TD><TD>$1.50</TD></TR>")
                document.write( "</TABLE>")
                document.write( "</CENTER>")
            }

        if ( currentHour >= 17 && currentHour < 22 ) {
            document.write( "<CENTER>")
            document.write( "<TABLE BORDER BGCOLOR='CYAN'>")
            document.write(
                "<TR><TH COLSPAN = 2>Dinner Menu</TH></TR>")
            document.write(
                "<TR><TD>Lobster Newburg</TD><TD>$9.50</TD></TR>")
            document.write(
                "<TR><TD>Filet mignon</TD><TD>$9.00</TD></TR>")
            document.write(
                "<TR><TD>Strip steak</TD><TD>$8.00</TD></TR>")
            document.write(
                "<TR><TD>House salad</TD><TD>$2.50</TD></TR>")
            document.write(
                "<TR><TD>Garlic potato</TD><TD>$1.50</TD></TR>")
            document.write(
                "<TR><TD>Broccoli alfredo</TD><TD>$1.50</TD></TR>")
            document.write("</TABLE>")
            document.write("</CENTER>")
        }
        //-->
    </SCRIPT>
</HEAD>

<BODY>
</BODY>
</HTML>
```

You can see what's for lunch in Figure 16.3. Using code like this, you can make your web pages respond to the time of day.

Figure 16.3   Rewriting a page in response to the time of day.

The *insertAdjacentHTML* and *insertAdjacentText* Methods

The Internet Explorer `insertAdjacentHTML` and `insertAdjacentText` methods (see "The `insertAdjacentHTML` and `insertAdjacentText` Methods" in Chapter 6, "Using Core HTML Methods and Events," for their syntax) give you finer control over where the HTML you insert in pages goes than `document.write` provides.

The `insertAdjacentHTML` method enables you to insert HTML next to an element that exists already, and the `insertAdjacentText` method enables you to insert text (which will *not* be treated as HTML, but just as plain text). You can determine where the new text or HTML will go with respect to the already existing element by passing the constants `"BeforeBegin"`, `"AfterBegin"`, `"BeforeEnd"`, or `"AfterEnd"` to `insertAdjacentHTML` and `insertAdjacentText`, as discussed in Chapter 6.

These methods are useful to change web pages on-the-fly; we've seen these methods in Chapter 6. Here's an example (it's Listing 6.8) that inserts text and a text field when the user clicks a button in the Internet Explorer:

```
<HTML>
    <HEAD>
        <TITLE>
            Using the insertAdjacentHTML Method
        </TITLE>
```

```
<SCRIPT LANGUAGE="JavaScript">
    <!--
    function addMore()
    {
        div1.insertAdjacentHTML("afterEnd",
        "<P>Here is a new text field: <input type=text VALUE='Hello!'>");
    }
    // -->
</SCRIPT>
</HEAD>

<BODY>
    <H1>Using the insertAdjacentHTML Method</H1>
    <DIV ID="div1">
        <INPUT TYPE=BUTTON VALUE="Click Me!" onclick="addMore()">
    </DIV>
</BODY>
</HTML>
```

You can see the results in Chapter 6, in Figure 6.6.

The *innerHTML*, *innerText*, *outerHTML*, and *outerText* Properties

One of the most precise ways to rewrite a web page is with the innerHTML, innerText, outerHTML, and outerText properties. (See "The innerHTML, innerText, outerHTML, and outerText Properties" in Chapter 5, "Using Core HTML Properties.") Here's what those properties do. Note that innerHTML is the only one supported by Netscape Navigator so far:

- **innerHTML** changes contents of element *between* start and end tags, which may include HTML.

- **innerText** enables you change the text *between* the start and end tags of an element.

- **outerHTML** changes contents of an element, *including* start and end tags, treats text as HTML.

- **outerText** enables you to change all the element's text, *including* the start and end tags.

The innerHTML property (available in NS6+ and IE4+) has been our constant companion throughout the book. We've used it to display the results of a script in a <DIV> or <SPAN> element, but it's important to mention it in our Dynamic HTML chapters. Here's an example that shows how to use the onchange event in a text field:

(Listing 16-05.html on the web site)

```
<HTML>
    <HEAD>
        <TITLE>Using the onchange Event</TITLE>
        <SCRIPT LANGUAGE="JavaScript">
            <!--
            function displayText()
            {
                document.getElementById("div1").innerHTML =
                    "The text field holds: " + document.form1.text1.value
            }
            //-->
        </SCRIPT>
    </HEAD>

    <BODY>
        <H1>Using the onchange Event</H1>
        <FORM NAME="form1">
            <INPUT TYPE="TEXT" NAME="text1" ONCHANGE="displayText()">
            <BR>
            <DIV ID="div1">
        </FORM>
    </BODY>
</HTML>
```

Here's an example using the outerHTML property in the Internet Explorer, which enables you to rewrite the HTML for an element entirely. In this case, I'm changing an <H1> header to a scrolling <MARQUEE> element when the user clicks that header:

(Listing 16-06.html on the web site)

```
<HTML>
    <HEAD>
        <TITLE>
            Using the outerHTML Property
        </TITLE>

        <SCRIPT LANGUAGE = "JavaScript">
            <!--
            function rewriteHeader()
            {
                h1.outerHTML =
                    "<MARQUEE BGCOLOR='cyan' STYLE='font-size:54;text-decoration:
                    ➥underline'>" +
                    "Here's the new marquee!</MARQUEE>"
                span1.innerText = "You changed the header."
            }
            //-->
        </SCRIPT>
    </HEAD>
```

```
    <BODY>
        <H1 ID="h1" ONCLICK="rewriteHeader()">Using the outerHTML Property</H1>
        <SPAN ID="span1">Click the header to change it to a marquee</SPAN>
    </BODY>
</HTML>
```

You can see the results in Figure 16.4.

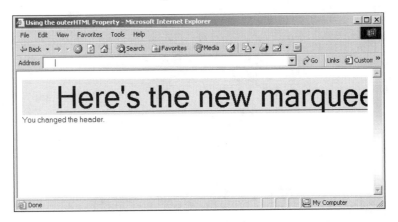

Figure 16.4   Using the `outerHTML` property.

Using Text Ranges

Another way to modify a web page in the Internet Explorer on-the-fly is to use a `TextRange` object, which we saw in Chapter 11, "Working with HTML Text Elements." In this chapter, I'll take a look at the `pasteHTML` method, which enables you to change text ranges on-the-fly. Here's an example in which I create a text range with the `createTextRange` method, select the text of an element ("No problem.") with the `moveToElementText` method, and replace that text with the `pasteHTML` method (to "No worries!"):

(Listing 16-07.html on the web site)

```
<HTML>
    <HEAD>
        <TITLE>
            Using Text Ranges
        </TITLE>

        <SCRIPT LANGUAGE="JavaScript">
            <!--
```

continues ▶

```
        function replaceText()
        {
            if(document.body.isTextEdit){
                var range = document.body.createTextRange()
                range.moveToElementText(div1)
                range.pasteHTML("No worries!")
            }
        }
        // -->
    </SCRIPT>
</HEAD>

<BODY>
    <H1>Using Text Ranges</H1>
    <INPUT TYPE=BUTTON VALUE="Click Me!" ONCLICK="replaceText()">
    <BR>
    <BR>
    <DIV ID="div1" STYLE="font-family:Arial, sans-serif; font-weight:bold">
        No problem.
    </DIV>
</BODY>
</HTML>
```

You can see the results in Figure 16.5. As you can see, text ranges provide you with another way to rewrite web page content on-the-fly.

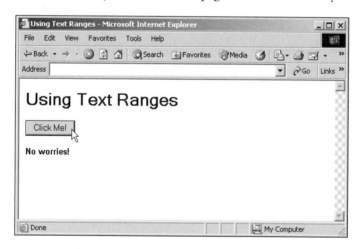

Figure 16.5   Using the `pasteHTML` method.

The *<LAYER>* Element

Netscape Navigator 4.0 introduced the <LAYER> element, which enables you to create positionable layers of content in a web page. Today that role has largely been taken over by style sheets and elements such as <DIV>, but layers were quite popular for a while. (They're no longer supported in Netscape Navigator 6.) Layers are often used to position and move elements in a page, so I'll take a look at them here in our dynamic pages chapter. You can see an overview of the properties, methods, and events of the <LAYER> element in Table 16.1, its properties in depth in Table 16.2, its methods in Table 16.3, and its events in Table 16.4.

Table 16.1 **Overview of the Properties, Methods, and Events of the *<LAYER>* Element**

Properties	Methods	Events
above	captureEvents	onblur
background	handleEvent	onfocus
below	load	onload
bgcolor	moveAbove	onmouseout
clip	moveBelow	onmouseover
document	moveBy	
left	moveTo	
name	moveToAbsolute	
pageX	releaseEvents	
pageY	resizeBy	
parentLayer	resizeTo	
siblingAbove	routeEvent	
siblingBelow		
src		
top		
visibility		
zIndex		

Table 16.2 **The Properties of the *<LAYER>* Element**

Property	NS2	NS3	NS4	NS6	IE3a	IE3b	IE4	IE5	IE5.5	IE6
above			x							

Read-only
Holds the layer above this one.

| background | | | x | | | | | | | |

Read/write
Holds a background image. Set to an `Image` object (see "Precaching Images and the `Image` Object" in Chapter 15).

| below | | | x | | | | | | | |

Read-only
Holds the layer below this one.

| bgcolor | | | x | | | | | | | |

Read/write
Holds the background color of the layer, set to a predefined browser color (such as `"coral"`) or a color triplet (such as `"ffffff"`). See "Layers and the Mouse" in this chapter for an example.

| clip | | | x | | | | | | | |

Read/write
Enables you to specify rectangular areas in a layer. The `clip` object supports these pixel measurement properties: `clip.bottom`, `clip.left`, `clip.right`, and `clip.top`.

| document | | | x | | | | | | | |

Read-only
Each layer has its own `document` object, and this property holds the `document` object for the layer.

| left | | | x | | | | | | | |

Read/write
Corresponds to the `LEFT` attribute of the `<LAYER>` element relative to its parent, giving the X coordinate of the layer's upper-point. Set to a pixel measurement. See "Moving Layers On-the-Fly" in this chapter for an example.

| name | | | x | | | | | | | |

Read/write
Holds the name of the layer, used in code. Set to a name string.

Property	NS2	NS3	NS4	NS6	IE3a	IE3b	IE4	IE5	IE5.5	IE6
pageX			x							

Read-only
Corresponds to the X coordinate of the layer's upper-left point relative to the document's upper-left point. Set to a pixel measurement.

Property	NS2	NS3	NS4	NS6	IE3a	IE3b	IE4	IE5	IE5.5	IE6
pageY			x							

Read-only
Corresponds to the Y coordinate of the layer's upper-left point relative to the document's upper-left point. Set to a pixel measurement.

Property	NS2	NS3	NS4	NS6	IE3a	IE3b	IE4	IE5	IE5.5	IE6
parentLayer			x							

Read-only
The layer that contains the current one, if there is one. Set to a <LAYER> object.

Property	NS2	NS3	NS4	NS6	IE3a	IE3b	IE4	IE5	IE5.5	IE6
siblingAbove			x							

Read-only
Holds the sibling layer (in the same parent layer container) above this one.

Property	NS2	NS3	NS4	NS6	IE3a	IE3b	IE4	IE5	IE5.5	IE6
siblingBelow			x							

Read-only
Holds the sibling layer (in the same parent layer container) below this one.

Property	NS2	NS3	NS4	NS6	IE3a	IE3b	IE4	IE5	IE5.5	IE6
src			x							

Read/write
Document to be displayed in the current layer. Set to a URL.

Property	NS2	NS3	NS4	NS6	IE3a	IE3b	IE4	IE5	IE5.5	IE6
top			x							

Read/write
Corresponds to the TOP attribute of the <LAYER> element relative to its parent, giving the Y coordinate of the layer's upper-left point. Set to a pixel measurement.

Property	NS2	NS3	NS4	NS6	IE3a	IE3b	IE4	IE5	IE5.5	IE6
visibility			x							

Read/write
Sets the layer's visibility—can hold "show", "hide", or "inherit" (which means inherit this setting from the parent layer).

Property	NS2	NS3	NS4	NS6	IE3a	IE3b	IE4	IE5	IE5.5	IE6
zIndex			x							

Read/write
Sets the stacking level with regard to other layers. (That is, specifies which layers this layer is on top of or under.) Set to a positive integer.

Table 16.3 **The Methods of the *<LAYER>* Element**

Method	NS2	NS3	NS4	NS6	IE3a	IE3b	IE4	IE5	IE5.5	IE6
captureEvents			x							

Returns: Nothing
Lets the window object capture events in Netscape Navigator 4.0.
Syntax: captureEvents(*eventTypeList*). Here, *eventTypeList* holds
a list of events to capture, OR'ed together like this: Event.CLICK ¦
Event.MOUSEUP.

handleEvent			x							

Returns: Nothing
This Netscape Navigator 4.0 method handles events captured with
setCapture.
Syntax: handleEvent(*event*), where *event* is an event type such as
Event.CLICK.

load			x							

Returns: Nothing
Loads a new document into the layer.
Syntax: load(*URL*, *width*), where *URL* is the URL of the new document
and *width* is the width in pixels of the new layer.

moveAbove			x							

Returns: Nothing
Moves the current layer above another.
Syntax: moveAbove(*layer*), where *layer* is the layer to move the current
layer above.

moveBelow			x							

Returns: Nothing
Moves the current layer below another.
Syntax: moveBelow(*layer*), where *layer* is the layer to move the current
layer below.

moveBy			x							

Returns: Nothing
Moves a layer by a specified amount.
Syntax: moveBy(*changeInX*, *changeInY*), where *changeInX* is the change in
the X coordinate and *changeInY* is the change in the Y coordinate.

Method	NS2	NS3	NS4	NS6	IE3a	IE3b	IE4	IE5	IE5.5	IE6
moveTo			x							

Returns: Nothing
Moves a layer to a specified location relative to its container's coordinate system.
Syntax: `moveBy(X, Y)`, where *X* is the new X coordinate and *Y* is the new Y coordinate.

Method	NS2	NS3	NS4	NS6	IE3a	IE3b	IE4	IE5	IE5.5	IE6
moveToAbsolute			x							

Returns: Nothing
Moves a layer to a specified location relative to the page coordinate system.
Syntax: `moveToAbsolute(X, Y)`, where *X* is the new X coordinate and *Y* is the new Y coordinate.

Method	NS2	NS3	NS4	NS6	IE3a	IE3b	IE4	IE5	IE5.5	IE6
releaseEvents			x							

Returns: Nothing
This Netscape Navigator method releases event capture.
Syntax: `releaseEvents(eventTypeList)`. Here, *eventTypeList* holds a list of events to release, OR'ed together like this: `Event.CLICK ¦ Event.MOUSEUP`.

Method	NS2	NS3	NS4	NS6	IE3a	IE3b	IE4	IE5	IE5.5	IE6
resizeBy			x							

Returns: Nothing
Resizes a layer by a specified amount.
Syntax: `resizeBy(changeInX, changeInY)`, where *changeInX* is the change in the width and *changeInY* is the change in height.

Method	NS2	NS3	NS4	NS6	IE3a	IE3b	IE4	IE5	IE5.5	IE6
resizeTo			x							

Returns: Nothing
Resizes a layer.
Syntax: `resizeBy(X, Y)`, where *X* is the new width and *Y* is the new height.

Method	NS2	NS3	NS4	NS6	IE3a	IE3b	IE4	IE5	IE5.5	IE6
routeEvent			x							

Returns: Nothing
If you've turned on event capture in Netscape Navigator 4.0, this method enables you to route an event after you've worked on the event and want to pass it along to the next event handler.
Syntax: `routeEvent(event)`.

Table 16.4   **The Events of the <LAYER> Element**

Event	NS2	NS3	NS4	NS6	IE3a	IE3b	IE4	IE5	IE5.5	IE6
onblur			x							
Occurs when the layer loses the focus.										
onfocus			x							
Occurs when the layer gets the focus.										
onload			x							
Occurs when the layers and its contents are fully loaded.										
onmouseout			x							
Occurs when the mouse leaves a layer.										
onmouseover			x							
Occurs when the mouse moves over a layer.										

Layers and the Mouse

A popular use for layers is to create mouseover effects. Here's an example that changes the background behind some text pink when the mouse moves over that text (Netscape Navigator 4.0 only, in order to use layers):

(Listing 16-08.html on the web site)

```
<HTML>
    <HEAD>
        <TITLE>
            Using layers and the mouse
        </TITLE>
    </HEAD>

    <BODY>
        <LAYER BGCOLOR="white" TOP="40" LEFT="40"
            ONMOUSEOVER="this.bgColor='pink'" ONMOUSEOUT="this.bgColor='white'" >
            <H1>
                Using layers and the mouse
            </H1>
        </LAYER>
    </BODY>
</HTML>
```

You can see the results in Figure 16.6 in Netscape Navigator 4.0.

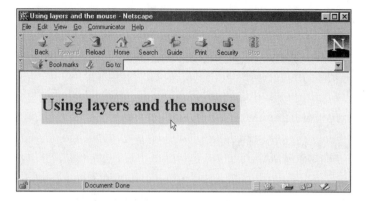

Figure 16.6 Using layers in Netscape Navigator 4.0.

Moving Layers On-the-Fly

Besides optical effects, you also can use layers to move specific elements in real time. Here's an example for Netscape Navigator 4.0 that steadily increments the left property of a layer, moving it to the right, when the user clicks a button:

(Listing 16-09.html on the web site)

```html
<HTML>
    <HEAD>
        <TITLE>
            Moving layers
        </TITLE>
        <SCRIPT LANGUAGE="JavaScript">
            <!--
            function moveLayer()
            {
                document.layers['layer1'].left = document.layers['layer1'].left + 5

                if (document.layers['layer1'].left < 1000) {
                    setTimeout('moveLayer()', 40)
                }
            }
            //-->
        </SCRIPT>
    </HEAD>

    <BODY>
        <H1>
            Moving layers
        </H1>
```

continues ▶

```
<DIV STYLE="POSITION:absolute; TOP:60; LEFT:0">
    <IMG SRC="image1.jpg">
</DIV>

<LAYER NAME=layer1 left="0" top="60">
    <IMG SRC="image2.jpg">
</LAYER>

<DIV STYLE="POSITION:absolute; TOP:140; LEFT:40">
    <FORM>
    <INPUT TYPE="BUTTON" VALUE="Move the layer"
        ONCLICK="moveLayer()">
    </FORM>
</DIV>
    </BODY>
</HTML>
```

You can see the results in Figure 16.7, where, although you can't see it, image 2 is moving to the right.

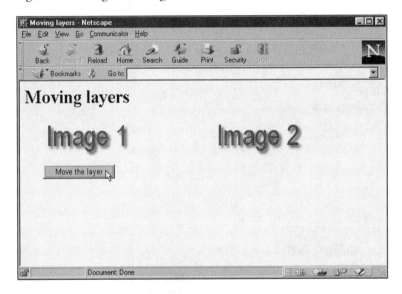

Figure 16.7 Moving layers in Netscape Navigator 4.0.

Setting Element Visibility On-the-Fly

Another way to make the elements in your pages dynamic is by using the visibility style property, which you can set to "visible" or "hidden" to show or hide elements. Here's an example that does exactly that, showing or hiding some text when the user clicks a button:

(Listing 16-10.html on the web site)

```
<HTML>
    <HEAD>
        <TITLE>
            Making elements visible using the visibility property
        </TITLE>

        <SCRIPT LANGUAGE="JAVASCRIPT">
            <!--
            function showAll()
            {
                document.getElementById("div1").style.visibility = "visible"
            }
            //-->
        </SCRIPT>
    </HEAD>

    <BODY>
        <H1>
            Making elements visible using the visibility property
        </H1>

        <FORM NAME="form1">
            <INPUT TYPE="BUTTON" VALUE="Click Me" ONCLICK="showAll()">
            <BR>
            <BR>
            <DIV ID="div1" STYLE="visibility:hidden">
                Here's some additional text!
            </DIV>
        </FORM>
    </BODY>
</HTML>
```

You can see the results in Figure 16.8.

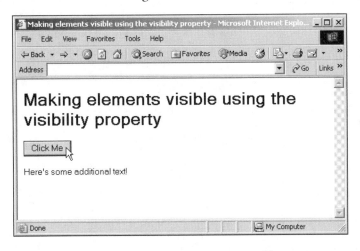

Figure 16.8 Making invisible text visible.

In fact, you also can use the display style property to do the same thing. Here's an example showing how to show or hide the same text using this property, not the visibility property (you'll need version 6+ if you're using Netscape Navigator):

(Listing 16-11.html on the web site)

```
<HTML>
    <HEAD>
        <TITLE>
            Making elements visible using the display property
        </TITLE>

        <SCRIPT LANGUAGE="JAVASCRIPT">
            <!--
            function showAll()
            {
                document.getElementById("div1").style.display = ""
            }
            //-->
        </SCRIPT>
    </HEAD>

    <BODY>
        <H1>
            Making elements visible using the display property
        </H1>

        <FORM>
            <INPUT TYPE="BUTTON" VALUE="Click Me" ONCLICK="showAll()">
            <BR>
            <BR>
            <DIV ID="div1" STYLE="display: none">
                Here's some additional text!
            </DIV>
        </FORM>
    </BODY>
</HTML>
```

You can see the results in Figure 16.9.

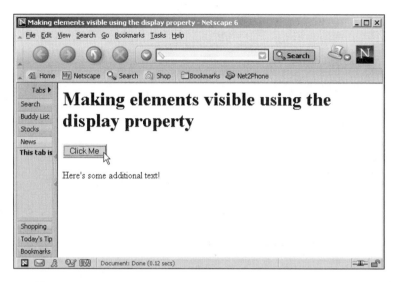

Figure 16.9 Using the display property in the Netscape Navigator.

Creating New Elements

You also can create new elements with the document object's createElement
method (see Table 9.5) and insert them into a document on-the-fly with
methods such as insertBefore (see "The insertBefore Method" in Chapter 6)
after configuring them.

We've seen createElement in passing before, but we haven't taken a systematic look at this process. The important thing to realize is that the mere creation of a new element does not insert that element into the document.
Instead, you first configure the new element using various properties such as
name and value. When the element is ready for use, you can insert it into the
document using methods such as insertBefore. (This method was introduced
in Internet Explorer 5.0 and is now supported in Netscape Navigator 6.0.)

Here's an example where I'm creating a new button, and then configuring
that button with the name, type, value, and onclick properties to connect
that button to an event handler that displays an alert box. Then I insert the
button into a web page just before another button by passing that other button as the reference node to insertBefore (you'll need version 6+ if you're
using Netscape Navigator to use the createElement method):

(Listing 16-12.html on the web site)

```
<HTML>
    <HEAD>
        <TITLE>
            Creating New Elements
        </TITLE>

        <SCRIPT LANGUAGE="JavaScript">
            <!--
            function addMore()
            {
                var newButton
                newButton = document.createElement("INPUT")
                newButton.name = "button2"
                newButton.type = "BUTTON"
                newButton.value = "Click Me Too!"
                newButton.onclick = alerter
                document.form1.insertBefore(newButton, document.form1.button1)
            }

            function alerter()
            {
                alert("You clicked the button!")
            }
            // -->
        </SCRIPT>
    </HEAD>

    <BODY>
        <H1>Creating New Elements</H1>
        <FORM NAME="form1">
            <INPUT TYPE="BUTTON" NAME="button1" VALUE="Click Me!" ONCLICK="addMore()">
        </FORM>
    </BODY>
</HTML>
```

You can see the results in Figure 16.10. In that figure, I've clicked the Click Me! button, which creates and displays the new Click Me Too! button, which, when clicked, displays an alert box.

You also can use the Internet Explorer method insertAdjacentElement (see "The insertAdjacentElement Method" in Chapter 6) to insert elements; here's what the addMore function would look like with that method:

Figure 16.10   Adding new elements on-the-fly.

```
function addMore()
{
    var newDiv, newTextField, newText
    newButton = document.createElement("INPUT")
    newButton.name = "button2"
    newButton.type = "BUTTON"
    newButton.value = "Click Me Too!"
    newButton.onclick = alerter
    document.form1.button1.insertAdjacentElement("beforeBegin", newButton)
}
```

Here's another example, this one from Chapter 13, "Working with Text and Select Controls" (Listing 13.11); in this case, we're adding and removing <SELECT> items when the user clicks buttons (you'll need version 6+ if you're using Netscape Navigator to use the createElement method):

```
<HTML>
    <HEAD>
        <TITLE>Changing Select Options</TITLE>
        <SCRIPT LANGUAGE="JavaScript">
            <!--
            function colors()
            {
                document.form1.select1.options[0].text = "Red"
                document.form1.select1.options[1].text = "White"
                document.form1.select1.options[2].text = "Blue"
                if(navigator.appName == "Netscape") {
                    document.form1.select1.remove(3)
                }
```

continues ▸

```
            if (navigator.appName == "Microsoft Internet Explorer") {
                document.form1.select1.options.remove(3)
            }
        }

        function numbers()
        {
            document.form1.select1.options[0].text = "1"
            document.form1.select1.options[1].text = "2"
            document.form1.select1.options[2].text = "3"
            if(navigator.appName == "Netscape") {
                var option1 = document.createElement("OPTION")
                document.form1.select1.add(option1, null)
                option1.innerHTML = "4"
            }
            if (navigator.appName == "Microsoft Internet Explorer") {
                var option1 = document.createElement("OPTION")
                document.form1.select1.options.add(option1)
                option1.innerHTML = "4"
            }
        }
        //-->
    </SCRIPT>
</HEAD>

<BODY>
    <H1>Changing Select Options</H1>
    <FORM NAME="form1">
        <SELECT NAME="select1">
            <OPTION SELECTED>Red
            <OPTION>White
            <OPTION>Blue
        </SELECT>
        <INPUT TYPE="BUTTON" VALUE="Colors" onClick="colors()">
        <INPUT TYPE="BUTTON" VALUE="Numbers" onClick="numbers()">
    </FORM>
</BODY>
</HTML>
```

You can see the results in Chapter 13, in Figure 13.12.

That's how creating new elements and inserting them into web pages on-the-fly works: You create the new element, configure it, and insert it into the document. That's all it takes!

Filters

The Internet Explorer has a number of built-in Dynamic HTML features, such as *filters*. Filters enable you to support various visual effects; you assign a filter with the `filter` property of an object's `style` object.

Here's an example showing the available Internet Explorer filters and what they do. When you select a filter using radio buttons and click a button, the filter is applied to some text:

(Listing 16–13.html on the web site)

```
<HTML>
    <HEAD>
        <TITLE>
            Using Filters
        </TITLE>

        <SCRIPT LANGUAGE="JavaScript">
            <!--
            function applyFilter()
            {
                div1.style.filter=""

                if (document.form1.radio01.checked) {
                    div1.style.filter = "fliph(enabled=1)"
                }
                if (document.form1.radio02.checked) {
                    div1.style.filter = "flipv(enabled=1)"
                }
                if (document.form1.radio03.checked) {
                    div1.style.filter = "gray(enabled=1)"
                }
                if (document.form1.radio04.checked) {
                    div1.style.filter = "invert(enabled=1)"
                }
                if (document.form1.radio05.checked) {
                    div1.style.filter = "xray(enabled=1)"
                }
                if (document.form1.radio06.checked){
                    var opacityValue = document.form1.opacity.value
                    div1.style.filter = "alpha(opacity=" + opacityValue +
                        ", enabled=1)"
                }
                if (document.form1.radio07.checked) {
                    div1.style.filter =
                        "blur(direction=45, strength=15, add=0, enabled=1)"
                }
                if (document.form1.radio08.checked) {
                    div1.style.filter = "chroma(color=#FFFF00, enabled=1)"
                }
                if (document.form1.radio09.checked) {
                    div1.style.filter = "dropshadow(offx=5, offy=9, " +
                        "color=#008fff, enabled=1)"
                }
                if (document.form1.radio10.checked) {
```

continues ▶

```
                    div1.style.filter = "glow(strength=5, color=#ffff00, "
                    + "enabled=1) "
                }
                if (document.form1.radio11.checked) {
                    div1.style.filter = "mask(color=#FF0000 ,enabled=1)"
                }
                if (document.form1.radio12.checked) {
                    div1.style.filter =
                    "shadow(color=#FF0088, direction=320, enabled=1)"
                }
                if (document.form1.radio13.checked) {
                    div1.style.filter = "wave(freq=2, strength=6, phase=0, " +
                    "lightstrength=0, add=0, enabled=1)"
                }
            }
            // -->
        </SCRIPT>
    </HEAD>

    <BODY>
        <H1>Using Filters</H1>
        <FORM NAME="form1">
            <INPUT TYPE="RADIO" NAME="radiobuttons" ID="radio01">Flip Horizontal
            <INPUT TYPE="RADIO" NAME="radiobuttons" ID="radio02">Flip Vertical
            <INPUT TYPE="RADIO" NAME="radiobuttons" ID="radio03">Gray
            <INPUT TYPE="RADIO" NAME="radiobuttons" ID="radio04">Invert
            <INPUT TYPE="RADIO" NAME="radiobuttons" ID="radio05">XRay
            <BR>
            <BR>
            <INPUT TYPE="RADIO" NAME="radiobuttons" ID="radio07">Blur
            <INPUT TYPE="RADIO" NAME="radiobuttons" ID="radio08">Chroma
            <INPUT TYPE="RADIO" NAME="radiobuttons" ID="radio09">Drop Shadow
            <INPUT TYPE="RADIO" NAME="radiobuttons" ID="radio10">Glow
            <INPUT TYPE="RADIO" NAME="radiobuttons" ID="radio11">Mask
            <BR>
            <BR>
            <INPUT TYPE="RADIO" NAME="radiobuttons" ID="radio12">Shadow
            <INPUT TYPE="RADIO" NAME="radiobuttons" ID="radio13">Wave
            <INPUT TYPE="RADIO" NAME="radiobuttons" ID="radio06">
                Alpha   Opacity: 
            <INPUT TYPE="TEXT" ID="opacity" VALUE="60" SIZE="3" MAXLENGTH="3">
            <BR>
            <INPUT TYPE="BUTTON" NAME="startFilter" VALUE="Apply Filter"
                ONCLICK="applyFilter()">
        </FORM>
        <DIV ID="div1" STYLE="POSITION:absolute; WIDTH:250; HEIGHT:100;
            TOP:220; LEFT:30; font-size:24pt;font-family:arial;
            font-style:bold; color:red;">
            Here is the text!
        </DIV>
    </BODY>
</HTML>
```

You can see the results in Figure 16.11, where the code is displaying the glow filter. It's useful to play around with this example to see what kinds of filters there are and what kinds of effects they produce.

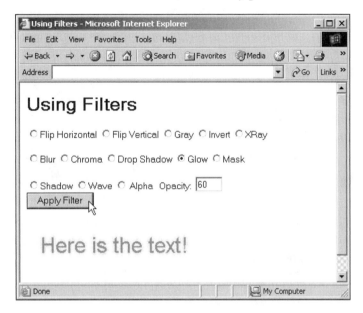

Figure 16.11   Using filters in the Internet Explorer.

Vector Markup Language

In the Internet Explorer, you can also use *Vector Markup Language* (VML) to draw graphics in your web pages. VML is supported by an Internet Explorer *behavior*, and we'll see more about behaviors in the next chapter. Here's an example that draws two figures, an oval and a rectangle, using VML:

(Listing 16-14.html on the web site)

```
<HTML xmlns:v="urn:schemas-microsoft-com:vml">
    <HEAD>
        <TITLE>
            Working With VML
        </TITLE>
        <STYLE>
            v\:* {behavior: url(#default#VML);}
        </STYLE>
    </HEAD>
```

continues ▶

```
<BODY>
    <H1>
        Working With VML
    </H1>
    <BR>
    <v:oval STYLE="width:100pt; height:75pt"
        FILLCOLOR="red" STROKECOLOR="blue" STROKEWEIGHT="4pt"> </v:oval>
    <BR>
    <v:rect STYLE="width:100pt; height:75pt" FILLCOLOR="green"
        STROKECOLOR="red" STROKEWEIGHT="2pt"/>
</BODY>
</HTML>
```

You can see the results in Figure 16.12.

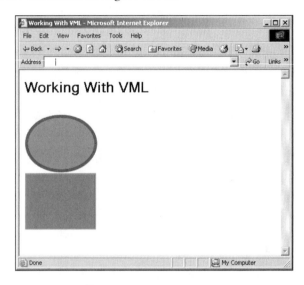

Figure 16.12   Using VML.

Tip
You can find more on VML at http://msdn.microsoft.com/library/default.asp?url=/workshop/
author/vml/ref/default.asp.

Visual Transitions

The Internet Explorer also supports visual transitions to help make your web page come alive. There are 24 transitions, and they enable you to fade one element out and another in using effects such as "circle in" and "wipe down" and so on. Here's an example that will enables you to play with all the transitions. In this example, the code toggles between a red square and a blue square, using the transition you select from the drop-down list to move between them:

(Listing 16-15.html on the web site)

```
<HTML>
    <HEAD>
        <TITLE>
            Handling Visual Transitions
        </TITLE>
        <SCRIPT LANGUAGE="JavaScript">
            <!--
            var duration
            var direction
            var transitioning
            direction = 0
            duration = 4

            function filterChange()
            {
                transitioning = false
            }

            function doTransition()
            {
                if (transitioning){
                    return
                }

                div1.filters.item(0).apply()

                if (direction == 1){
                    direction = 2
                    image2.style.visibility = "visible"
                    image1.style.visibility = "hidden"
                }
                else {
                    direction = 1
                    image1.style.visibility = "visible"
                    image2.style.visibility = "hidden"
                }

                div1.filters.item(0).Transition = document.form1.select1.selectedIndex
                div1.filters(0).play(duration)
                transitioning = true
            }
            //-->
        </SCRIPT>
    </HEAD>
```

continues ▶

```
<BODY>
    <H1>
        Handling Visual Transitions
    </H1>
    <DIV STYLE="POSITION:absolute;TOP:150;LEFT:320">
        <FORM NAME="form1">
        <SELECT ID="select1">
            <OPTION>Box in</OPTION>
            <OPTION>Box out</OPTION>
            <OPTION>Circle in</OPTION>
            <OPTION>Circle out</OPTION>
            <OPTION>Wipe up</OPTION>
            <OPTION>Wipe down</OPTION>
            <OPTION>Wipe right</OPTION>
            <OPTION>Wipe left</OPTION>
            <OPTION>Vertical blinds</OPTION>
            <OPTION>Horizontal blinds</OPTION>
            <OPTION>Checker board across</OPTION>
            <OPTION>Checker board down</OPTION>
            <OPTION>Random dissolve</OPTION>
            <OPTION>Split vertical in</OPTION>
            <OPTION>Split vertical out</OPTION>
            <OPTION>Split horizontal in</OPTION>
            <OPTION>Split horizontal out</OPTION>
            <OPTION>Strips left down</OPTION>
            <OPTION>Strips left up</OPTION>
            <OPTION>Strips right down</OPTION>
            <OPTION>Strips right up</OPTION>
            <OPTION>Random bars horizontal</OPTION>
            <OPTION>Random bars vertical</OPTION>
            <OPTION>Random</OPTION>
        </SELECT>
        <INPUT TYPE="BUTTON" VALUE="Do transition" ONCLICK="doTransition()">
        </FORM>
    </DIV>

    <DIV ID="div1"
        STYLE="POSITION:absolute; WIDTH:300;
HEIGHT:300;FILTER:revealTrans(Duration=1.0, Transition=1)"
            ONFILTERCHANGE="filterChange()">
        <IMG ID="image1" STYLE=
            "Position:absolute;width:300;height:300;visibility:hidden"
            SRC="blue.jpg" WIDTH="300" HEIGHT="300">
        <IMG ID="image2" STYLE=
            "Position:absolute;width:300;height:300"
            SRC="red.jpg" WIDTH="300" HEIGHT="300">
    </DIV>
</BODY>
</HTML>
```

You can see the results in Figure 16.13, where I'm using the vertical blinds transition. If you want to use transitions, take a look at this code, which shows how to handle the direction of the transition and set the duration and so on.

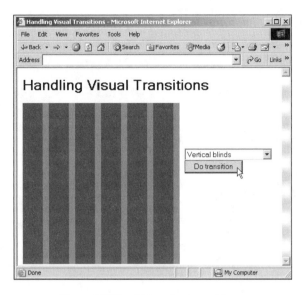

Figure 16.13 Using visual transitions.

Internet Explorer Direct Animation

The Internet Explorer comes with even more powerful tools, such as *Direct Animation*. Direct Animation enables you to create and move graphics and image objects of great complexity. In fact, many people find Direct Animation pretty complex to use, which may account for the fact that it's not in widespread use. (I've never seen a web page "in the wild" that uses it.) What it does can also be done in many cases with styles or other applications such as Macromedia Flash.

Here's an example that uses Direct Animation. In this case, the code creates a figure made of three boxes with various colors—purple, red, green, and blue—and then makes that figure slowly revolve and move above the other elements on the page, making it appear that it's floating above them. Note that this example uses the Direct Animation ActiveX control that is installed with Internet Explorer and that you access with the <OBJECT> element:

(Listing 16-16.html on the web site)

```
<HTML>
    <HEAD>
        <TITLE>
            Using Direct Animation
        </TITLE>
```

continues ▶

```
<SCRIPT LANGUAGE="JavaScript">
    <!--
    function animate()
    {
        var library = DAControl1.MeterLibrary
        var surface = library.NewDrawingSurface()

        surface.FillColor(library.ColorRgb(1, 0, 1))
        surface.FillPath(library.Polyline(Array(0, 0, 400, 0,
            400, 400, 0, 400, 0, 0)))

        surface.FillColor(library.ColorRgb(1, 0, 0))
        surface.FillPath(library.Polyline(Array(200, 0, 0,
            400, 400, 400, 200, 0)))

        surface.FillColor(library.ColorRgb(1, 0, 1))
        surface.FillPath(library.Polyline(Array(0, 0, -400,
            0, -400, -400, 0, -400, 0, 0)))

        surface.FillColor(library.ColorRgb(0, 1, 0))
        surface.FillPath(library.Polyline(Array(-200, -400,
            -400, 0, 0, 0, -200, -400)))

        surface.FillColor(library.ColorRgb(1, 0, 1))
        surface.FillPath(library.Polyline(Array(-400, -400, -800,
            -400, -800, -800, -400, -800, -400, -400)))

        surface.FillColor(library.ColorRgb(0, 0, 1))
        surface.FillPath(library.Polyline(Array(-600, -800,
            -800, -400, -400, -400, -600, -800)))

        var axis = library.Vector3(40, 40, 40)
        var startPoint = library.Point2(-2000, 0)
        var endPoint = library.Point2(4000, 0)

        var path = library.FollowPath(library.Line(startPoint,
            endPoint), 10)

        var twist = library.Rotate3RateDegrees(axis,
            180).Duration(10).ParallelTransform2()

        DAControl1.Image =
            surface.Image.Transform(twist).
            Transform(path).Transform(library.Scale2(1./30000., 1./30000.))

        DAControl1.Start()
    }
    //-->
    </SCRIPT>
</HEAD>

<BODY>
    <H1>
```

```
            Using Direct Animation
        </H1>

        <FORM>
            <INPUT TYPE="BUTTON" VALUE="Click me!" ONCLICK="animate()">
        </FORM>

        <OBJECT ID="DAControl1"
            STYLE="position:absolute; left:10%; top:10%; width:90%; height:90%"
            CLASSID="CLSID:B6FFC24C-7E13-11D0-9B47-00C04FC2F51D">
        </OBJECT>
        <BR>
        <BR>
        Animated graphics that can move over page elements...
    </BODY>
</HTML>
```

You can see the results in Figure 16.14, where the figure I've created is twisting and turning and moving to the right over the underlying text. Note that it's not clear whether Microsoft will continue to support Direct Animation in the future (in fact, there are indications that it will not), now that .NET has been introduced. However, Direct Animation has been around since Internet Explorer 5.0 and is still shipping with the most recent versions of Internet Explorer 6.0.

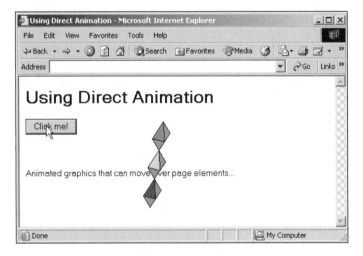

Figure 16.14   Using direct animation.

That completes our look at making web page content dynamic, in this chapter. In the next chapter, we're going to take a look at some related topics: drag and drop, data binding, and behaviors, as we continue our exploration of Dynamic HTML.

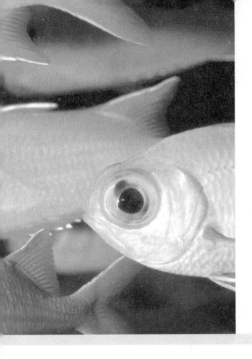

17

Dynamic HTML: Drag and Drop, Data Binding, and Behaviors

IN THIS CHAPTER, WE'RE GOING TO KEEP WORKING on making our web pages come alive, this time by supporting drag and drop, data binding, and Internet Explorer behaviors.

You can implement drag and drop in two primary ways: implementing visual dragging, and implementing data transfer. Visual dragging involves moving objects around in a web page, and data transfer means dragging and dropping actual data, from text to images, that you can work with in code. Naturally, we'll see both ways.

Data binding is a big topic in the Internet Explorer, and we'll take a look at it here. You can store data in a variety of formats—plain text, HTML format, and even XML documents (we'll see all of these formats here)—and display that data in the browser. We'll let the user move through the various records and fields of our data using buttons, and we'll also see how to display our data in tables.

Internet behaviors represent Microsoft's attempt to separate data from code, which is a big programming topic these days. When you separate code from data, the resulting application is cleaner and easier to maintain. Behaviors enable you to place JavaScript code in external files with the extension .htc, and you can associate a behavior with an HTML element using styles (as we'll see in this chapter). You can give a behavior custom properties, methods, and events, just as HTML elements have (as we'll also see in this chapter).

> **Tip**
>
> These database solutions are read-only, which means you can't edit the displayed data in the Internet Explorer. If you want to edit the data in the original database file, you've got to have some software installed on the server, such as *Remote Data Server* (RDS) support, CGI scripts, or the Microsoft .NET framework. Although these topics are beyond the scope of this book as far as database-handling goes, we will take a look at .NET programming and CGI scripting in Chapter 24, ".NET and Security."

> **Note**
>
> More on styles is coming up in our style sheet chapter, Chapter 21, "Cascading Style Sheets and CGI Programming."

Dragging and Dropping Visual Elements

To drag and drop visual elements, you can write the code yourself; it's not difficult. Here's an example targeted at IE4+ and NS6+. This example enables us to drag and drop an image. When the mouse goes down, we'll start the dragging operation; in the mouse move event, we can move the image to correspond to the mouse location, and in the mouse up event, we can drop the image.

When the mouse goes down, I'll record the location of the mouse in the image itself, and start the dragging operation by setting a variable named dragging to true:

```
var xDown, yDown, dragging = false

function mouseDown(e)
{
    if(window.event){
        e = window.event
    }
    xDown = e.clientX - document.getElementById("img1").offsetLeft
    yDown = e.clientY - document.getElementById("img1").offsetTop
    dragging = true

    return false
}
```

To handle the mouse move event, I first check whether a dragging operation is going on, and if so, adjust the position of the image to correspond to the mouse pointer, taking into account the location of the mouse in the image, like this:

```
function mouseMove(e)
{
    if (!dragging){
        return
    }

    var newx, newy

    if(window.event){
        e = window.event
    }

    newx = e.clientX - xDown
    newy = e.clientY - yDown

    document.getElementById("img1").style.left = newx
    document.getElementById("img1").style.top = newy

    return false
}
```

Finally, when the mouse goes up, we can stop the drag operation by setting dragging to false:

```
function mouseUp(e)
{
    dragging = false

    return false
}
```

That's all it takes. Here's the whole code:

(Listing 17-01.html on the web site)

```
<HTML>
    <HEAD>
        <TITLE>Dragging and Dropping</TITLE>
        <SCRIPT LANGUAGE="JavaScript">
            <!--
            var xDown, yDown, dragging = false

            document.onmousemove = mouseMove
            document.onmouseup = mouseUp

            function mouseDown(e)
            {
                if(window.event){
                    e = window.event
                }
                xDown = e.clientX - document.getElementById("img1").offsetLeft
                yDown = e.clientY - document.getElementById("img1").offsetTop
```

continues ▶

```
            dragging = true

            return false
        }

        function mouseMove(e)
        {
            if (!dragging){
                return
            }

            var newx, newy

            if(window.event){
                e = window.event
            }

            newx = e.clientX - xDown
            newy = e.clientY - yDown

            document.getElementById("img1").style.left = newx
            document.getElementById("img1").style.top = newy

            return false
        }

        function mouseUp(e)
        {
            dragging = false

            return false
        }
        //-->
    </SCRIPT>
  </HEAD>

  <BODY>
    <H1>Dragging and Dropping</H1>
    <DIV ID="img1" STYLE="POSITION:ABSOLUTE; LEFT:100; TOP:100">
        <IMG SRC="image1.jpg" ONMOUSEDOWN="return mouseDown(event)">
    </DIV>
  </BODY>
</HTML>
```

You can see the results of this code in Figure 17.1. When you use the mouse, the image follows the cursor smoothly, until you drop the image by releasing the cursor.

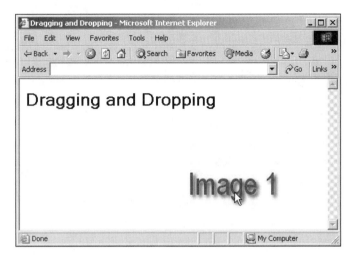

Figure 17.1   Dragging and dropping an image.

Dragging and Dropping Data

Besides dragging and dropping visual elements, you also can drag and drop
data. This is already implemented in both Netscape Navigator 4+ and
Internet Explorer 4+ to some extent. For example, you can select and drag
page text in both browsers and drop it into another application (such as a
word processor) or a text-oriented control in the same page. Here's an example that just displays text and a text field:

(Listing 17-02.html on the web site)

```
<HTML>
    <HEAD>
        <TITLE>Dragging Selected Text</TITLE>
    </HEAD>

    <BODY>
        <H1>Dragging Selected Text</H1>
        Select some of this text and drag it to the text field!
        <BR>
        <INPUT TYPE="TEXT" NAME="text1">
    </BODY>
</HTML>
```

You can see the results of this code in Figure 17.2, where I've selected some
text and am about to drop it. You can see the standard drag-and-drop mouse
cursor in that figure, showing that a drag-and-drop operation is occurring. In
Figure 17.3, I've dropped the text into the text field.

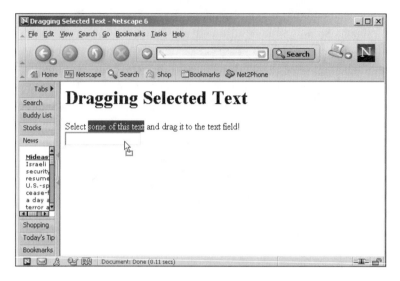

Figure 17.2 Dragging text in the Netscape Navigator.

Figure 17.3 Dropping text in the Netscape Navigator.

You also can implement this kind of operation yourself in the Internet Explorer, using the dataTransfer object (not available in the Netscape Navigator, and available in the Internet Explorer as of version 5.0). The dataTransfer object has two properties; the first is dropEffect, which sets or gets the type of drag-and-drop operation and the type of cursor to display. Here are the possible values:

- **"copy"**. Copy cursor is displayed.
- **"link"**. Link cursor is displayed.
- **"move"**. Move cursor is displayed.
- **"none"**. This is the default. The no-drop cursor is displayed.

The second property is effectAllowed, which sets or gets which data transfer operations are allowed for the object. Here are the possible values:

- **"copy"**. The selection is copied.
- **"link"**. The selection is linked to the drop target.
- **"move"**. The selection is moved to the target when dropped.
- **"copyLink"**. The selection is copied or linked, depending on the target's default.
- **"copyMove"**. The selection is copied or moved, depending on the target's default.
- **"linkMove"**. The selection is linked or moved, depending on the target's default.
- **"all"**. All drop effects are supported.
- **"none"**. Dropping is not enabled, and the no-drop cursor is displayed.
- **"uninitialized"**. This is the default. No value has been set through the effectAllowed property. The default effect still works in this case.

The dataTransfer object also supports these methods:

- **clearData.** Clears the current data in the clipboard for a particular data format.
  Syntax: dataTransfer.clearData([*format*]), where *format* is one of "Text" (text data), "URL" (URL data), "File" (file data), "HTML" (HTML data), or "Image" (image data). Returns: Nothing.
- **getData.** Gets the current data in the clipboard for a particular data format.
  Syntax: dataTransfer.getData(*format*), where *format* is one of "Text" (text data) or "URL" (URL data). Returns: A string holding the data.
- **setData.** clears the current data in the clipboard for a particular data format.
  Syntax: dataTransfer.setData(*format*, *data*); where *format* is one of "Text" (text data) or "URL" (URL data), and *data* is the data to place in the clipboard. This information can be text, a source path to an image, or a URL. When you pass "URL" as the *format* parameter, you must use the *data* parameter to specify the location of the object to transfer. Returns: true if successful; false otherwise.

Let's look at an example to make how this works clear. In this case, I'll associate some text data with an image, and when the user drags the image to a <DIV> element, I'll transfer the text data to that <DIV>. We start with the ONDRAGSTART attribute of the image, calling a function we'll name beginDrag:

```
<IMG SRC="image1.jpg" ONDRAGSTART="beginDrag()">
```

In the beginDrag function, I'll use the dataTransfer property of the event object, setting the allowed drag-and-drop operation to "copy" (which sets the mouse cursor), and adding the text data "This is the text data for the drag operation." to the dataTransfer object:

```
function beginDrag()
{
    event.dataTransfer.effectAllowed = "copy"
    event.dataTransfer.setData("Text",
        "This is the text data for the drag operation.")
}
```

We'll use a <DIV> element as the drop target in this example. To do that, I'll use the ONDRAGENTER (occurs when the mouse first enters the object), ONDRAGOVER (occurs as the mouse moves over the object), and ONDROP (occurs when the data is dropped) attributes. Here's what the <DIV> element looks like:

```
<DIV ID="droptarget"
    STYLE="background:cyan; width:200; height:50;"
    ONDRAGENTER="dragEnter()" ONDROP="endDrag()"
    ONDRAGOVER="dragEnter()">
    Drag the image and drop it here...
</DIV>
```

For the ONDRAGENTER and ONDRAGOVER events, I'll use the same function, dragEnter, to indicate that the <DIV> is a working drop target by setting the dropEffect property of the event object to "copy". This changes the mouse cursor from a circle and bar "no-drop" symbol to the cursor you see in Figure 17.4:

```
function dragEnter()
{
    event.dataTransfer.dropEffect = "copy"
    event.returnValue = false
    return false
}
```

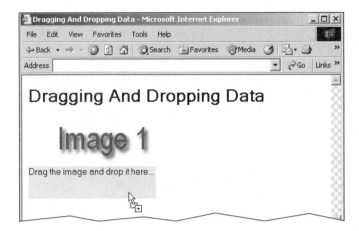

Figure 17.4   Dragging data in the Internet Explorer.

When the data is dropping into the `<DIV>` element, the code calls a function I'll name endDrag. In that function, I use the dataTransfer object's getData method to get the text associated with the drag-and-drop operation and display it in the `<DIV>` element:

```
function endDrag()
{
    event.dataTransfer.dropEffect = "copy"
    droptarget.innerHTML = event.dataTransfer.getData("Text")
    event.returnValue = false
    return false
}
```

That's all there is to it. You can see the dropped data in Figure 17.5. Now we're dragging and dropping data in the Internet Explorer.

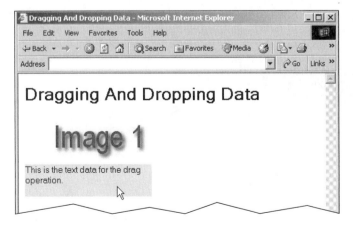

Figure 17.5   Dropping data in the Internet Explorer.

Here's the whole code for this example:

(Listing 17-03.html on the web site)

```html
<HTML>
    <HEAD>
        <TITLE>
            Dragging And Dropping Data
        </TITLE>
        <SCRIPT>
            <!--
            function beginDrag()
            {
                event.dataTransfer.effectAllowed = "copy"
                event.dataTransfer.setData("Text",
                    "This is the text data for the drag operation.")
            }

            function dragEnter()
            {
                event.dataTransfer.dropEffect = "copy"
                event.returnValue = false
                return false
            }

            function endDrag()
            {
                event.dataTransfer.dropEffect = "copy"
                droptarget.innerHTML = event.dataTransfer.getData("Text")
                event.returnValue = false
                return false
            }
            //-->
        </SCRIPT>
    </HEAD>

    <BODY>
        <H1>Dragging And Dropping Data</H1>
        <IMG SRC="image1.jpg" ONDRAGSTART="beginDrag()">
        <DIV ID="droptarget"
            STYLE="background:cyan; width:200; height:50;"
            ONDRAGENTER="dragEnter()" ONDROP="endDrag()"
            ONDRAGOVER="dragEnter()">
            Drag the image and drop it here...
        </DIV>
    </BODY>
</HTML>
```

Dragging and Dropping Using Layers

You also can implement dragging and dropping using layers in Netscape Navigator 4.0. Here's an example that does exactly that. This example works by capturing the mouse down, mouse move, and mouse up events in a layer with the captureEvents method, and moves the layer (which contains the image to be dragged) in response to mouse movements:

(Listing 17-04.html on the web site)

```
<HTML>
    <HEAD>
        <TITLE>
            Dragging and Dropping Using Layers
        </TITLE>
        <SCRIPT LANGUAGE="JavaScript">
            <!--

            function init()
            {
                document.layers.layer1.captureEvents(Event.MOUSEDOWN);
                document.layers.layer1.onmousedown = mouseDown
            }

            function mouseDown(e)
            {
                document.layers.layer1.offX = e.pageX-document.layers.layer1.pageX
                document.layers.layer1.offY = e.pageY-document.layers.layer1.pageY
                window.captureEvents(Event.MOUSEMOVE¦Event.MOUSEUP)
                window.onmousemove = mouseDrag
                window.onmouseup = mouseUp
                return false
            }

            function mouseDrag(e)
            {
                document.layers.layer1.pageX = e.pageX-document.layers.layer1.offX
                document.layers.layer1.pageY = e.pageY-document.layers.layer1.offY
                return false
            }

            function mouseUp ()
            {
                window.releaseEvents(Event.MOUSEMOVE ¦ Event.MOUSEUP)
                return false
            }
            //-->
        </SCRIPT>
    </HEAD>
```

continues ▶

```
<BODY ONLOAD="init()">
    <H1>
        Dragging and Dropping Using Layers
    </H1>
    <LAYER NAME="layer1" LEFT="100" TOP="100">
        <IMG SRC="image1.jpg">
    </LAYER>
</BODY>
</HTML>
```

You can see the results of this code in Figure 17.6 in the Netscape Navigator 4.0, where I'm dragging an image using layers.

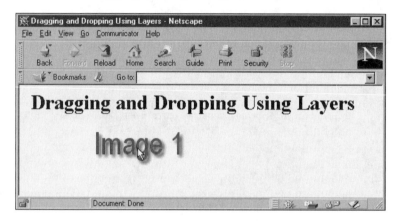

Figure 17.6 Dragging and dropping using layers in the Netscape Navigator 4.0.

Data Binding

The Internet Explorer supports several *data source objects* (DSOs) that you can use to bind data in various formats to elements in a web page. To bind a DSO to an element, you can use the `DATASRC`, `DATAFLD`, and `DATAFORMATAS` attributes we saw in Chapter 5, "Using Core HTML Properties." (See "The `dataFld`, `dataFormatAs`, and `dataSrc` Properties" in Chapter 5.) You can then treat the data bound to those elements as a *recordset*, which has methods that enable you to navigate through your data using JavaScript, as we'll see.

The three Internet Explorer DSOs we'll take a look at are the MSHTML control, the Tabular Data Control (TDC), and the XML DSO. They all come built in to the Internet Explorer.

Using the MSHTML Control

Using the MSHTML control, you can read data in HTML format into a recordset. Here's an example, which I'll call data.html. This document holds data in HTML format; the data we're using here represents a set of employees. I've divided the data into *records*, one for each employee. Each record has several *fields*, such as Name to hold the employee's name, ID to hold their ID number, and so on. You can create a record just by storing multiple fields, and you create a field by giving a <SPAN> element a name and then storing the data as that <SPAN> element's text. Here's what the data document looks like, with five employee records:

(data.html on the web site)

```
<HTML>
    <HEAD>
        <TITLE>
            A Data Document
        </TITLE>
    </HEAD>

    <BODY>
        <H1>
            This page holds data.
        </H1>
        Name: <SPAN ID="NAME">Frank</SPAN><BR>
        ID: <SPAN ID="ID">2314</SPAN><BR>
        Hire Date: <SPAN ID="HIRE_DATE">
            9-2-2003</SPAN><BR>
        Department: <SPAN ID="DEPARTMENT">
            Shipping</SPAN><BR>
        Title: <SPAN ID="TITLE">Packer</SPAN><BR>

        Name: <SPAN ID="NAME">Martin</SPAN><BR>
        ID: <SPAN ID="ID">2315</SPAN><BR>
        Hire Date: <SPAN ID="HIRE_DATE">
            9-2-2003</SPAN><BR>
        Department: <SPAN ID="DEPARTMENT">
            Packing</SPAN><BR>
        Title: <SPAN ID="TITLE">Programmer</SPAN><BR>

        Name: <SPAN ID="NAME">Tom</SPAN><BR>
        ID: <SPAN ID="ID">2316</SPAN><BR>
        Hire Date: <SPAN ID="HIRE_DATE">
            9-2-2003</SPAN><BR>
        Department: <SPAN ID="DEPARTMENT">
            Shipping</SPAN><BR>
        Title: <SPAN ID="TITLE">Packer</SPAN><BR>

        Name: <SPAN ID="NAME">Henry</SPAN><BR>
```

continues ▶

```
        ID: <SPAN ID="ID">2317</SPAN><BR>
        Hire Date: <SPAN ID="HIRE_DATE">
            9-2-2003</SPAN><BR>
        Department: <SPAN ID="DEPARTMENT">
            Shipping</SPAN><BR>
        Title: <SPAN ID="TITLE">Packer</SPAN><BR>

        Name: <SPAN ID="NAME">Paula</SPAN><BR>
        ID: <SPAN ID="ID">2318</SPAN><BR>
        Hire Date: <SPAN ID="HIRE_DATE">
            9-2-2003</SPAN><BR>
        Department: <SPAN ID="DEPARTMENT">
            Shipping</SPAN><BR>
        Title: <SPAN ID="TITLE">Packer</SPAN><BR>
    </BODY>
</HTML>
```

To use the MSHTML DSO, you just use the `<OBJECT>` element and the `DATA` attribute to point to the HTML data document. Here's how I create an MSHTML DSO named `dso1` that uses data.html for its data:

```
<HTML>
    <HEAD>
        <TITLE>
            Using the MSHTML Control
        </TITLE>
    </HEAD>

    <BODY>
        <H1>
            Using The MSHTML Control
        </H1>
        <OBJECT ID="dso1" DATA="data.html" HEIGHT="0" WIDTH="0"></OBJECT>
        .
        .
        .
```

Now you can bind the data in this DSO to various elements, such as `<SPAN>`, `<DIV>`, or text field elements, setting the `DATASRC` attribute to `"dso1"` and the `DATAFLD` attribute to the data field whose data you want to display in the element.

If the bound element can display only a single item, such as `<SPAN>`, `<DIV>`, or text field elements, the data from the field you've specified will appear in that element. The data is taken from that field in the *current record* in the DSO. What's the current record? When the DSO first loads, the first record is the current record, but you can use methods such as `MoveNext` and `MovePrevious` to move to different records, as we'll see. When you move to a new record, that record becomes the current record. If the bound element can display multiple items, such as a table, the data from all records will display simultaneously, as we'll also see.

Here's how I bind a <SPAN> element to the Name data field of the current record in dso1:

```
Name: <SPAN DATASRC="#dso1" DATAFLD="NAME"></SPAN>
```

In the same way, you can bind text fields, buttons, and more to a field in the DSO, using the DATASRC and DATAFLD attributes.

So how do you let the user navigate from record to record (which will automatically update the data in any bound elements)? You access the recordset object of the DSO, giving you direct access to the data in the DSO, and then use methods such as MoveFirst (move to the first record), MoveNext (move to the next record), MovePrevious (move to the previous record), and MoveLast (move to the last record). Here's how you can do that in a web page. In this case, I'll create four navigation buttons with captions like <<, <, >, and >> to move through the data in data.html:

```
<BUTTON ONCLICK="dso1.recordset.MoveFirst()">&lt;&lt;</BUTTON>
<BUTTON ONCLICK="if (!dso1.recordset.BOF)
    dso1.recordset.MovePrevious()">&lt;</BUTTON>
<BUTTON ONCLICK="if (!dso1.recordset.EOF)
    dso1.recordset.MoveNext()">&gt;</BUTTON>
<BUTTON ONCLICK="dso1.recordset.MoveLast()">&gt;&gt;</BUTTON>
```

Here's what the whole code looks like for this example. This program binds the data in data.html to various elements and enables you to move from record to record using navigation buttons, displaying the data from each record's fields in bound elements:

(Listing 17-05.html on the web site)

```
<HTML>
    <HEAD>
        <TITLE>
            Using the MSHTML Control
        </TITLE>
    </HEAD>

    <BODY>
        <H1>
            Using The MSHTML Control
        </H1>
        <OBJECT ID="dso1" DATA="data.html" HEIGHT="0" WIDTH="0"></OBJECT>

        Name: <SPAN DATASRC="#dso1" DATAFLD="NAME"></SPAN>
        <BR>
        ID: <SPAN DATASRC="#dso1" DATAFLD="ID"></SPAN>
        <BR>
        Department: <SELECT DATASRC="#dso1"
            DATAFLD="DEPARTMENT" SIZE=1>
```

continues ▶

```
                <OPTION VALUE="Shipping">Shipping
                <OPTION VALUE="Packing">Packing
                <OPTION VALUE="Accounting">Accounting
                <OPTION VALUE="Billing">Billing
        </SELECT>
        <BR>
        Title: <SPAN DATASRC="#dso1" DATAFLD="TITLE"></SPAN>
        <BR>
        Date hired: <SPAN DATASRC="#dso1" DATAFLD="HIRE_DATE"></SPAN><P>
        <BR>

        <BUTTON ONCLICK="dso1.recordset.MoveFirst()">&lt;&lt;</BUTTON>
        <BUTTON ONCLICK="if (!dso1.recordset.BOF)
            dso1.recordset.MovePrevious()">&lt;</BUTTON>
        <BUTTON ONCLICK="if (!dso1.recordset.EOF)
            dso1.recordset.MoveNext()">&gt;</BUTTON>
        <BUTTON ONCLICK="dso1.recordset.MoveLast()">&gt;&gt;</BUTTON>
    </BODY>
</HTML>
```

You can see the results of this code in Figure 17.7, where I've bound the data in data.html to various elements, and can use the navigation buttons you see to navigate through the records in data.html.

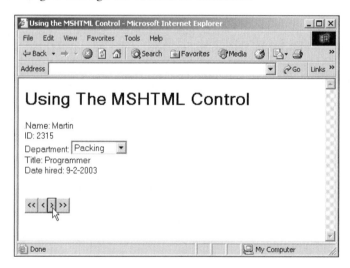

Figure 17.7   Using the MSHTML DSO.

You also can bind an MSHTML DSO to an HTML table, which enables you to display data from all the records in a recordset simultaneously. To connect a DSO to a table, you use the DATASRC attribute of the <TABLE> element:

```
<TABLE DATASRC="#dso1" CELLSPACING="10">
```

Now the data in the DSO is available throughout the table. To display the data from the various fields in a record, for example, you can use <SPAN> elements in table cells (here, I'm specifying the format of the data we're binding to as HTML, using the DATAFORMATAS attributes because we're binding to data.html—in fact, HTML is the default format, so you don't actually have to use the DATAFORMATAS attributes in this case):

```
<TR>
    <TD><SPAN DATAFLD="NAME" DATAFORMATAS="HTML"></SPAN></TD>
    <TD><SPAN DATAFLD="ID" DATAFORMATAS="HTML"></SPAN></TD>
    <TD><SPAN DATAFLD="DEPARTMENT"
        DATAFORMATAS="HTML"></SPAN></TD>
    <TD><SPAN DATAFLD="TITLE"
        DATAFORMATAS="HTML"></SPAN></TD>
    <TD><SPAN DATAFLD="HIRE_DATE"
        DATAFORMATAS="HTML"></SPAN></TD>
</TR>
```

Now the Internet Explorer will automatically create a row in the table for each record in data.html. Here's what the code looks like:

(Listing 17-06.html on the web site)

```
<HTML>
    <HEAD>
        <TITLE>
            Using The MSHTML Control and a Table
        </TITLE>
    </HEAD>

    <BODY>
        <H1>
            Using The MSHTML Control and a Table
        </H1>

        <OBJECT ID="dso1" DATA="data.html" HEIGHT=0 WIDTH=0></OBJECT>

        <TABLE DATASRC="#dso1" CELLSPACING="10">
            <THEAD>
                <TR>
                    <TH>Name</TH>
                    <TH>ID</TH>
                    <TH>Department</TH>
                    <TH>Title</TH>
                    <TH>Date Hired</TH>
                </TR>
            </THEAD>
            <TBODY>
                <TR>
                    <TD><SPAN DATAFLD="NAME" DATAFORMATAS="HTML"></SPAN></TD>
                    <TD><SPAN DATAFLD="ID" DATAFORMATAS="HTML"></SPAN></TD>
```

continues ▶

```
                    <TD><SPAN DATAFLD="DEPARTMENT"
                        DATAFORMATAS="HTML"></SPAN></TD>
                    <TD><SPAN DATAFLD="TITLE"
                        DATAFORMATAS="HTML"></SPAN></TD>
                    <TD><SPAN DATAFLD="HIRE_DATE"
                        DATAFORMATAS="HTML"></SPAN></TD>
                </TR>
            </TBODY>
        </TABLE>
    </BODY>
</HTML>
```

You can see the results of this code in Figure 17.8, where all the data from data.html is displayed simultaneously.

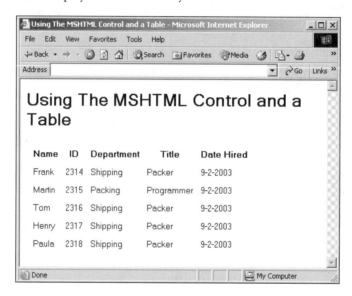

Figure 17.8 Binding the MSHTML DSO to a table.

Using the Tabular Data Control

Besides the MSHTML DSO, another DSO in the Internet Explorer is the *Tabular Data Control* (TDC). The TDC enables you to read data in text format. Let's take a look at how that works by placing our employee data in a text file, data.txt. You start that file by indicating the name of each field and its type like this:

```
NAME:String;ID:Int;HIRE_DATE:Date;DEPARTMENT:String;TITLE:String
```

Then you can store the data for each record, field by field, like this:

(data.txt on the web site)

```
NAME:String;ID:Int;HIRE_DATE:Date;DEPARTMENT:String;TITLE:String
Frank;2314;9-2-2003;Shipping;Packer
Martin;2315;9-2-2003;Packing;Programmer
Tom;2316;9-2-2003;Shipping;Packer
Henry;2317;9-2-2003;Shipping;Packer
Paula;2318;9-2-2003;Shipping;Packer
```

To use the TDC, you have to refer to its class ID in the `<OBJECT>` element, using the `CLASSID` attribute. (Every type of ActiveX control has a unique class ID.) In this example, I'll create a TDC named dso1. You then configure the TDC with `<PARAM>` elements in the `<OBJECT>` element. Here I'm setting the TDC DSO's `DataURL` property to data.txt, its `FieldDelim` property—which gives the character or characters you've used to delimit data in the data file—to ";", setting the `UseHeader` property to `"True"` to indicate that the DSO can get field names from the first line of data.txt, and telling the DSO to sort the data with the ID field using the `Sort` property:

```
<OBJECT CLASSID="clsid:333C7BC4-460F-11D0-BC04-0080C7055A83"
    ID="dso1" WIDTH=0 HEIGHT=0>
    <PARAM NAME="DataURL" VALUE="data.txt">
    <PARAM NAME="FieldDelim" VALUE=";">
    <PARAM NAME="UseHeader" VALUE="True">
    <PARAM NAME="Sort" VALUE="ID">
</OBJECT>
```

Now, as we did with the MSHTML DSO, I can bind the Name field of the current record in the TDC DSO to a `<SPAN>` element like this:

```
Name: <SPAN DATASRC="#dso1" DATAFLD="NAME"></SPAN>
```

And the rest is just the same as with the MSHTML control. You can use the TDC DSO's `recordset` property to gain access to the data, and methods such as `MoveFirst` and `MoveNext` to navigate as before:

(Listing 17-07.html on the web site)

```
<HTML>
    <HEAD>
        <TITLE>
            Using the Tabular Data Control
        </TITLE>
    </HEAD>

    <BODY>
        <H1>
            Using the Tabular Data Control
```

continues ▶

```
        </H1>

        <OBJECT CLASSID="clsid:333C7BC4-460F-11D0-BC04-0080C7055A83"
            ID="dso1" WIDTH=0 HEIGHT=0>
            <PARAM NAME="DataURL" VALUE="data.txt">
            <PARAM NAME="FieldDelim" VALUE=";">
            <PARAM NAME="UseHeader" VALUE="True">
            <PARAM NAME="Sort" VALUE="ID">
        </OBJECT>

        Name: <SPAN DATASRC="#dso1" DATAFLD="NAME"></SPAN>
        <BR>
        ID: <SPAN DATASRC="#dso1" DATAFLD="ID"></SPAN>
        <BR>
        Department: <SELECT DATASRC="#dso1"
            DATAFLD="DEPARTMENT" SIZE=1>

            <OPTION VALUE="Shipping">Shipping
            <OPTION VALUE="Packing">Packing
            <OPTION VALUE="Accounting">Accounting
            <OPTION VALUE="Billing">Billing
        </SELECT>
        <BR>
        Title: <SPAN DATASRC="#dso1" DATAFLD="TITLE"></SPAN>
        <BR>
        Date hired: <SPAN DATASRC="#dso1" DATAFLD="HIRE_DATE"></SPAN><P>
        <BR>

        <BUTTON ONCLICK="dso1.recordset.MoveFirst()">&lt;&lt;</BUTTON>
        <BUTTON ONCLICK="if (!dso1.recordset.BOF)
            dso1.recordset.MovePrevious()">&lt;</BUTTON>
        <BUTTON ONCLICK="if (!dso1.recordset.EOF)
            dso1.recordset.MoveNext()">&gt;</BUTTON>
        <BUTTON ONCLICK="dso1.recordset.MoveLast()">&gt;&gt;</BUTTON>
    </BODY>
</HTML>
```

When you run this code in the Internet Explorer, it looks just like the results you see in Figure 17.7—even though we're using an entirely different DSO, and reading our data in an entirely different format.

You also can bind the TDC DSO to HTML tables, just as with the MSHTML DSO. Here's an example that shows how to do that:

(Listing 17-08.html on the web site)

```
<HTML>
    <HEAD>
        <TITLE>
            Using the Tabular Data Control and a Table
        </TITLE>
    </HEAD>
```

```
<BODY>
    <H1>
        Using the Tabular Data Control and a Table
    </H1>

    <OBJECT CLASSID="clsid:333C7BC4-460F-11D0-BC04-0080C7055A83"
        ID="dso1" WIDTH=0 HEIGHT=0>
        <PARAM NAME="DataURL" VALUE="data.txt">
        <PARAM NAME="FieldDelim" VALUE=";">
        <PARAM NAME="UseHeader" VALUE="True">
        <PARAM NAME="Sort" VALUE="ID">
    </OBJECT>

    <TABLE DATASRC="#dso1" CELLSPACING="10">
        <THEAD>
            <TR>
                <TH>Name</TH>
                <TH>ID</TH>
                <TH>Department</TH>
                <TH>Title</TH>
                <TH>Date hired</TH>
            </TR>
        </THEAD>

        <TBODY>
            <TR>
                <TD><SPAN DATAFLD="NAME" DATAFORMATAS="HTML">
                    </SPAN></TD>
                <TD><SPAN DATAFLD="ID" DATAFORMATAS="HTML">
                    </SPAN></TD>
                <TD><SPAN DATAFLD="DEPARTMENT"
                    DATAFORMATAS="HTML"></SPAN></TD>
                <TD><SPAN DATAFLD="TITLE"
                    DATAFORMATAS="HTML"></SPAN></TD>
                <TD><SPAN DATAFLD="HIRE_DATE" DATAFORMATAS="HTML">
                    </SPAN></TD>
            </TR>
        </TBODY>
    </TABLE>
</BODY>
</HTML>
```

Just as with our navigation button example, when you run this code in the Internet Explorer, it looks just like the results we saw for the MSHTML DSO, which you can see in Figure 17.8. Although the results appear the same, we're using an entirely different DSO and reading our data in an entirely different format.

Using the XML DSO

You also can use the XML DSO that comes with Internet Explorer to handle data in XML format. We'll see more on XML in Chapter 22, "XML and XSLT." In XML documents, you create your own tags and elements. In this case, I'll enclose all our data in an element I'll call <EMPLOYEES>, and enclose each record in an element I'll name <ITEM>. To name the fields in each record, you create elements of the same name, such as <NAME> for the Name field, <ID> for the ID field, and so on. Given all that, here's how I store our employee data as an XML document, data.xml:

(data.xml on the web site)

```
<?xml version="1.0"?>
<EMPLOYEES>
    <ITEM>
        <NAME>Frank</NAME>
        <ID>2314</ID>
        <DEPARTMENT>Shipping</DEPARTMENT>
        <TITLE>Packer</TITLE>
        <HIRE_DATE>9-2-2003</HIRE_DATE>
    </ITEM>
    <ITEM>
        <NAME>Martin</NAME>
        <ID>2315</ID>
        <DEPARTMENT>Packing</DEPARTMENT>
        <TITLE>Programmer</TITLE>
        <HIRE_DATE>9-2-2003</HIRE_DATE>
    </ITEM>
    <ITEM>
        <NAME>Tom</NAME>
        <ID>2316</ID>
        <DEPARTMENT>Shipping</DEPARTMENT>
        <TITLE>Packer</TITLE>
        <HIRE_DATE>9-2-2003</HIRE_DATE>
    </ITEM>
    <ITEM>
        <NAME>Henry</NAME>
        <ID>2317</ID>
        <DEPARTMENT>Shipping</DEPARTMENT>
        <TITLE>Packer</TITLE>
        <HIRE_DATE>9-2-2003</HIRE_DATE>
    </ITEM>
    <ITEM>
        <NAME>Paula</NAME>
        <ID>2318</ID>
        <DEPARTMENT>Shipping</DEPARTMENT>
        <TITLE>Packer</TITLE>
        <HIRE_DATE>9-2-2003</HIRE_DATE>
    </ITEM>
</EMPLOYEES>
```

The XML DSO is actually a Java applet that comes with the Internet Explorer. You can create a DSO with that applet using the <APPLET> element like this, where I'm creating an XML DSO named dso1 and filling that DSO with the data in data.xml:

```
<APPLET CODE="com.ms.xml.dso.XMLDSO.class"
    ID="dso1" WIDTH="0" HEIGHT="0" MAYSCRIPT="true">
    <PARAM NAME="URL" VALUE="data.xml">
</APPLET>
```

Now we can use this DSO as we have the MSHTML and TDC DSOs. Here's some code that puts the XML DSO to work, binding the data in data.xml to elements in a web page:

(Listing 17-09.html on the web site)

```
<HTML>
    <HEAD>
        <TITLE>
            Using the XML Data Source Control
        </TITLE>
    </HEAD>

    <BODY>
        <H1>
            Using the XML Data Source Control
        </H1>

        <APPLET CODE="com.ms.xml.dso.XMLDSO.class"
            ID="dso1" WIDTH="0" HEIGHT="0" MAYSCRIPT="true">
            <PARAM NAME="URL" VALUE="data.xml">
        </APPLET>

        Name: <SPAN DATASRC="#dso1" DATAFLD="NAME"></SPAN>
        <BR>
        ID: <SPAN DATASRC="#dso1" DATAFLD="ID"></SPAN>
        <BR>
        Department: <SELECT DATASRC="#dso1"
            DATAFLD="DEPARTMENT" SIZE=1>

            <OPTION VALUE="Shipping">Shipping
            <OPTION VALUE="Packing">Packing
            <OPTION VALUE="Accounting">Accounting
            <OPTION VALUE="Billing">Billing
        </SELECT>
        <BR>
        Title: <SPAN DATASRC="#dso1" DATAFLD="TITLE"></SPAN>
        <BR>
        Date hired: <SPAN DATASRC="#dso1" DATAFLD="HIRE_DATE"></SPAN><P>
        <BR>

        <BUTTON ONCLICK="dso1.recordset.MoveFirst()">&lt;&lt;</BUTTON>
```

continues ▶

```
        <BUTTON ONCLICK="if (!dso1.recordset.BOF)
            dso1.recordset.MovePrevious()">&lt;</BUTTON>
        <BUTTON ONCLICK="if (!dso1.recordset.EOF)
            dso1.recordset.MoveNext()">&gt;</BUTTON>
        <BUTTON ONCLICK="dso1.recordset.MoveLast()">&gt;&gt;</BUTTON>
    </BODY>
</HTML>
```

The results in the Internet Explorer are just like what you see in Figure 17.7, except that we're using a different DSO; and in this case, we've stored our data in XML format, not text and not HTML.

You also can bind the XML DSO to an HTML table, just as with the MSHTML and TDC DSOs. Here's an example that does that in the Internet Explorer:

(Listing 17-10.html on the web site)

```
<HTML>
    <HEAD>
        <TITLE>
            Using the XML Data Source Control and a Table
        </TITLE>
    </HEAD>

    <BODY>
        <H1>
            Using the XML Data Source Control and a Table
        </H1>

        <APPLET CODE="com.ms.xml.dso.XMLDSO.class"
            ID="dso1" WIDTH="0" HEIGHT="0" MAYSCRIPT="true">
            <PARAM NAME="URL" VALUE="data.xml">
        </APPLET>

        <TABLE DATASRC="#dso1" CELLSPACING="10">
            <THEAD>
                <TR>
                    <TH>Name</TH>
                    <TH>ID</TH>
                    <TH>Department</TH>
                    <TH>Title</TH>
                    <TH>Date hired</TH>
                </TR>
            </THEAD>

            <TBODY>
                <TR>
                    <TD><SPAN DATAFLD="NAME" DATAFORMATAS="HTML">
                        </SPAN></TD>
                    <TD><SPAN DATAFLD="ID" DATAFORMATAS="HTML">
                        </SPAN></TD>
```

```
            <TD><SPAN DATAFLD="DEPARTMENT"
                    DATAFORMATAS="HTML"></SPAN></TD>
            <TD><SPAN DATAFLD="TITLE"
                    DATAFORMATAS="HTML"></SPAN></TD>
            <TD><SPAN DATAFLD="HIRE_DATE" DATAFORMATAS="HTML">
                    </SPAN></TD>
        </TR>
    </TBODY>
    </TABLE>
    </BODY>
</HTML>
```

As before, the results are just like what you see in Figure 17.8, except that we're using a different DSO; and in this case, we've stored our data in XML format, not text and not HTML.

Internet Explorer Behaviors

Internet Explorer behaviors were introduced in version 5.0 of that browser, and they enable you to separate your JavaScript code from the data in a web page. Your code can still access elements in the web page and work with them, but that code resides in a separate file, with the extension .htc.

Tip

You can learn more about Internet Explorer behaviors at http://msdn.microsoft.com/library/ default.asp?url=/workshop/author/behaviors/reference/reference.asp.

Attaching Behaviors to Events

An example will make how Internet Explorer behaviors work clearer. In this example, I'll use an Internet Explorer behavior to make the text in a <DIV> element glow when you pass the over it, as you see in Figure 17.9.

To make this happen, I'll give the <DIV> element a style class, class1, that will have a behavior associated with it (we'll see how this works in Chapter 21):

```
<DIV CLASS="class1" STYLE="top:100; left:40">
    Move the mouse over this text.
</DIV>
```

I use the glow filter (see Chapter 16, "Dynamic HTML: Changing Web Pages On-the-Fly," for more on filters) in this style class, class1, but disable it at first by setting its enabled property to 0. I also associate a behavior I'll call glower.htc with this style class, as you see here:

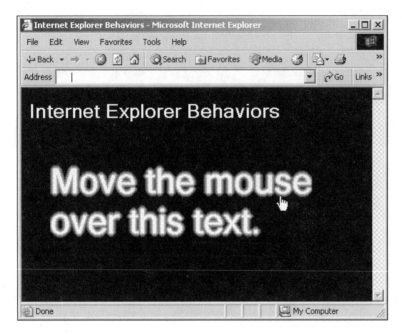

Figure 17.9 Using an Internet Explorer behavior.

```
<STYLE>
    .class1 {font-size:36pt; font-weight:bold;
    color:white; position:absolute; cursor:hand;
    filter:glow(enabled=0);behavior:url(glower.htc)}
</STYLE>
```

In glower.htc, I start with the behavior `<PUBLIC:COMPONENT>` element to indicate that I'm creating a behavior:

```
<PUBLIC:COMPONENT>
        .
        .
        .
</PUBLIC:COMPONENT>
```

Then I attach event handlers to the element this behavior is connected to, which is the `<DIV>` element, using the behavior `<ATTACH>` element. In this case, I'll connect the JavaScript function `doGlow` to the `onmouseover` event and the function `noGlow` to the `onmouseout` event like this (the `<ATTACH>` element uses the XML style end tags, which means you can end a tag with /> and not need a closing tag):

```
<PUBLIC:COMPONENT>
    <ATTACH EVENT="onmouseover" FOR="element" HANDLER="doGlow" />
    <ATTACH EVENT="onmouseout" FOR="element" HANDLER="noGlow" />
        .
        .
        .
</PUBLIC:COMPONENT>
```

All that's left is to write the JavaScript to enable and disable the glow filter in the functions `doGlow` and `noGlow`, where I can just refer to the element the behavior is working on as `element`. Here's what those functions look like:

(glower.htc on the web site)

```
<PUBLIC:COMPONENT>
    <ATTACH EVENT="onmouseover" FOR="element" HANDLER="doGlow" />
    <ATTACH EVENT="onmouseout" FOR="element" HANDLER="noGlow" />

    <SCRIPT LANGUAGE="JavaScript">
    <!--
    function doGlow()
    {
        element.filters.glow.enabled = true
        element.filters.glow.color = 256 * 255 + 255      //Cyan
    }

    function noGlow()
    {
        element.filters.glow.enabled = false
    }
    //-->
    </SCRIPT>
</PUBLIC:COMPONENT>
```

That's all you need for glower.htc. Now you can use it in the Internet Explorer web page you see in Figure 17.9, turning the glow on and off as the cursor rolls over the text in the `<DIV>`:

(Listing 17-11.html on the web site)

```
<HTML>
    <HEAD>
        <TITLE>
            Internet Explorer Behaviors
        </TITLE>

        <STYLE>
            .class1 {font-size:36pt; font-weight:bold;
            color:white; position:absolute; cursor:hand;
            filter:glow(enabled=0);behavior:url(glower.htc)}
        </STYLE>
    </HEAD>
```

continues ▶

```
<BODY BGCOLOR="BLACK">
    <H1 STYLE="color:white">
        Internet Explorer Behaviors
    </H1>
    <DIV CLASS="class1" STYLE="top:100; left:40">
        Move the mouse over this text.
    </DIV>
</BODY>
</HTML>
```

Creating Behavior Properties, Methods, and Events

You also can add properties, methods, and events to behaviors. Here's an example. In this case, the behavior enlarges text as you watch. You can use the behavior's `text` property to set the text to enlarge, its `enlargements` property to determine the number of times to enlarge the text, and its `enlarge` method to enlarge the text. When the text has been enlarged `enlargements` times, the behavior will make its event, which I'll call `oncomplete`, occur; and we can handle that event in the main web page.

You can see this behavior at work in the main web page in Figure 17.10, where it's enlarging the text `Hello!` 20 times, making that text appear to grow as you watch. When the enlargements are done, we can handle the `oncomplete` event, displaying the text `How's that?` in the main web page, as you see in Figure 17.11.

Figure 17.10 Using a behavior with properties.

Figure 17.11 Using a behavior's event.

Here's the main web page. Note that I'm connecting this new behavior, behavior.htc, to the style class class1, and then connecting that class to a <DIV> element. Now we can use the properties, methods, and events of the behavior as properties, methods, and events of the <DIV> element. Here's what the main web page looks like. Note that I'm using the JavaScript setInterval function to repeatedly call the behavior's enlarge method to keep enlarging the text:

(Listing 17-12.html on the web site)

```
<HTML>
    <HEAD>
        <TITLE>
            Creating Internet Explorer Behaviors
        </TITLE>

        <STYLE>
            .class1 {font-size:12pt; behavior:url(behavior.htc);}
        </STYLE>

        <SCRIPT Language="JavaScript">
            <!--
            var timerID1
            var object1
```

continues ▶

```
        function doBehavior()
        {
            object1 = document.all("div1")
            object1.text = document.all("text1").value
            object1.enlargements = document.all("text2").value
            timerID1 = setInterval("object1.enlarge()", 100)
        }

        function finished()
        {
            timerID1 = null
            document.all("div2").innerText = "How's that?"
        }
        //-->
    </SCRIPT>
</HEAD>

<BODY>
    <H1>
        Creating Internet Explorer Behaviors
    </H1>
    Text to enlarge:
    <INPUT TYPE="TEXT" ID="text1" VALUE="Hello!">
    <BR>
    Number of enlargements:
    <INPUT TYPE="TEXT" ID="text2" VALUE="20" SIZE=4>
    <BR>
    <DIV CLASS="class1" ID="div1" ONCOMPLETE="finished()"></DIV>
    <BR>
    <DIV ID="div2"></DIV>
    <BR>
    <INPUT TYPE="BUTTON" VALUE="Enlarge Text" ONCLICK="doBehavior()">
</BODY>
</HTML>
```

You can see how we use the behavior here, how we can handle its oncomplete event with the ONCOMPLETE attribute, how to call its enlarge method, and how to use its properties.

All that's left is to create the behavior, behavior.htc, itself, and support its properties, methods, and events. I can create the text and enlargements properties with the behavior <PUBLIC:PROPERTY> element, naming the property with the NAME attribute. When a property value is set, the function specified by the PUT attribute is called and the new value passed to that function; when its value is read, the function specified by the GET attribute is called and you return the value of the property. Here's how I implement the text and enlargements properties in behavior.htc, storing the values for those properties in JavaScript variables:

```
<PUBLIC:COMPONENT>
    <PUBLIC:PROPERTY NAME="text" PUT="setText"/>
    <PUBLIC:PROPERTY NAME="enlargements" PUT="setEnlargements"/>

    <SCRIPT LANGUAGE="JavaScript">
        <!--
        var loopIndex, loopMax, text

        function setText(value)
        {
            text = value
        }

        function setEnlargements(value)
        {
            loopIndex = 1
            loopMax = value
        }
        .
        .
        .
        //-->
    </SCRIPT>
</PUBLIC:COMPONENT>
```

Each time the `enlarge` method is called, we want to enlarge the text, so I implement the `enlarge` method with the behavior `<PUBLIC:METHOD>` element this way:

```
<PUBLIC:COMPONENT>
    <PUBLIC:PROPERTY NAME="text" PUT="setText"/>
    <PUBLIC:PROPERTY NAME="enlargements" PUT="setEnlargements"/>
    <PUBLIC:METHOD NAME="enlarge"/>

    <SCRIPT LANGUAGE="JavaScript">
        <!--
        var loopIndex, loopMax, text

        function setText(value)
        {
            text = value
        }

        function setEnlargements(value)
        {
            loopIndex = 1
            loopMax = value
        }

        function enlarge()
        {
```

continues ▶

```
            if (loopIndex < loopMax)
            {
                loopIndex++
                element.innerHTML = text
                element.style.fontSize = 5 * loopIndex
            }
            else {
                raiseEvent()
            }
        }
        .
        .
        .
        //-->
    </SCRIPT>
</PUBLIC:COMPONENT>
```

Note that in the code for this method, we check whether the number of
enlargements we're supposed to execute have already been performed; if so,
we call the raiseEvent function. That function makes causes the behavior's
event, oncomplete, to occur, which we make happen with the event's
fireEvent method:

(behavior.htc on the web site)

```
<PUBLIC:COMPONENT>
    <PUBLIC:PROPERTY NAME="text" PUT="setText"/>
    <PUBLIC:PROPERTY NAME="enlargements" PUT="setEnlargements"/>
    <PUBLIC:METHOD NAME="enlarge"/>
    <PUBLIC:EVENT NAME="oncomplete" ID="completeEvent"/>

    <SCRIPT LANGUAGE="JavaScript">
        <!--
        var loopIndex, loopMax, text

        function setText(value)
        {
            text = value
        }

        function setEnlargements(value)
        {
            loopIndex = 1
            loopMax = value
        }

        function enlarge()
        {
            if (loopIndex < loopMax)
            {
                loopIndex++
```

```
            element.innerHTML = text
            element.style.fontSize = 5 * loopIndex
        }
        else {
            raiseEvent()
        }
    }

    function raiseEvent()
    {
        var event1 = createEventObject()
        completeEvent.fire(event1)
    }
    //-->
</SCRIPT>
</PUBLIC:COMPONENT>
```

That's all we need. Now we've added properties, methods, and events to a behavior and put them to work in a web page. Take a look at this example in some detail if you want to work with behaviors; it's not difficult to figure out.

Using Default Behaviors

A number of default behaviors come with the Internet Explorer, and you can use them with a little JavaScript coding. To use a default behavior, you specify a URL of the form #default#*behaviorName* in a style class, where *behaviorName* is the name of the default behavior you want to use. You can find how to use the various default behaviors at http://msdn.microsoft.com/workshop/author/behaviors/reference/reference.asp. Here are those behaviors in overview:

- **anchor.** Lets the browser navigate to a folder.
- **anim.** Creates a Microsoft Direct Animation viewer in an HTML document.
- **animation.** Creates a timed animation element in an HTML document.
- **audio.** Creates a timed audio element in an HTML document.
- **clientCaps.** Holds information about the capabilities supported by the current version of the Microsoft Internet Explorer.
- **download.** Downloads a file and calls a given function when the download has finished.
- **event.** Creates a custom event.
- **excl.** Creates a timed object that allows a child element to play at any given time.
- **homePage.** Holds information about a user's home page.

- **httpFolder.** Holds scripting features that enable browser navigation.

- **img.** Creates a timed image element.

- **media.** Creates a generic, timed media element in an HTML document.

- **par.** Creates a timeline container for independently timed elements.

- **saveFavorite.** Lets an object store data in the Favorites folder.

- **saveHistory.** Lets an object save some data in the browser history.

- **saveSnapshot.** Lets the object to save data when a web page is saved.

- **seq.** Creates a new timeline container in an HTML document that will be used for sequentially timed elements.

- **time.** Creates an active timeline for a single HTML element.

- **time2.** Creates an active timeline for a single HTML element or a group of elements.

- **userData.** Lets the object save data.

- **Video.** Creates a timed video element in an HTML document.

Here's an example. In this case, I'll use the userData behavior to store and retrieve temporary text data. The data I store with this behavior is stored in the browser's own temporary storage, because that's exactly what this behavior does—give us access to that temporary storage. In this case, I'll create a style class named class1 that uses this behavior:

```
<HTML>
    <HEAD>
        <TITLE>
            Using Default Behaviors
        </TITLE>

        <STYLE>
            .class1 {behavior:url(#default#USERDATA);}
        </STYLE>
        .
        .
        .
```

Then I connect this style class, class1, to a text field:

```
<INPUT CLASS="class1" TYPE="TEXT" ID="text1" VALUE="Hello!">
```

Now I can add two buttons to save the data in temporary storage and retrieve it, connecting these buttons to two JavaScript methods, setData and getData:

```
<INPUT TYPE="BUTTON" VALUE="Save the text" ONCLICK="setData()">
<BR>
<INPUT TYPE="BUTTON" VALUE="Get the text" ONCLICK="getData()">
```

In the setData function, I store the text in the text field in the browser's temporary data store, using methods of the userData behavior, and then delete the text in the text field:

```
function setData()
{
    document.all("text1").setAttribute("savedText", document.all("text1").value)
    document.all("text1").save("savedData")
    document.all("text1").value = ""
}
```

In the getData function, I retrieve that text and display it in the text field like this:

(Listing 17-13.html on the web site)

```
<HTML>
    <HEAD>
        <TITLE>
            Using Default Behaviors
        </TITLE>

        <STYLE>
            .class1 {behavior:url(#default#USERDATA);}
        </STYLE>

        <SCRIPT LANGUAGE="JavaScript">
            <!--
            function getData()
            {
                document.all("text1").load("savedData")
                document.all("text1").value = document.all("text1").getAttribute
                ➥("savedText")
            }

            function setData()
            {
                document.all("text1").setAttribute("savedText",
                ➥document.all("text1").value)
                document.all("text1").save("savedData")
                document.all("text1").value = ""
            }
            //-->
        </SCRIPT>
    </HEAD>

    <BODY>
```

continues ▶

```
        <H1>
            Using Default Behaviors
        </H1>
        <INPUT CLASS="class1" TYPE="TEXT" ID="text1" VALUE="Hello!">
        <BR>
        <INPUT TYPE="BUTTON" VALUE="Save the text" ONCLICK="setData()">
        <BR>
        <INPUT TYPE="BUTTON" VALUE="Get the text" ONCLICK="getData()">
    </BODY>
</HTML>
```

You can see the results in Figure 17.12, where the text entered into the text field is stored when the user clicks the Save the text button, and then the text field is blanked. The text is read from the browser's temporary data store and restored to the text field when the user clicks the Get the text button. That's it; now we're using a default behavior.

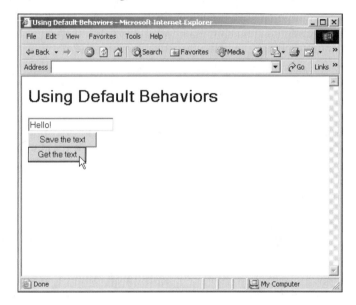

Figure 17.12   Using a default behavior.

That's it for this chapter. Here we've added a great deal to our JavaScript arsenal, including dragging and dropping, data binding, and behaviors. In the next chapter, we'll take a look at the JavaScript Date, Time, and String objects.

18

The *Date, Time,* and *String* Objects

IN THIS CHAPTER, WE'LL TAKE A LOOK at two important JavaScript objects: the Date and String objects. Both are fairly extensive, and both are useful. As you can guess from their names, the Date object enables you to work with dates, and the String object enables you to work with strings. I'll discuss the Date object in detail first.

The *Date* Object

Date objects store dates and provide many methods to extract the hours, minutes, and so on parts of dates. There are a number of different ways to create Date objects, such as the following:

```
var date1 = new Date()
var date1 = new Date(dateVal)
var date1 = new Date(year, month, date[, hours[, minutes[, seconds[, ms]]]])
```

Note the use of the keyword new here. Both the Date and String types are object types, and you use the new keyword to create objects, as discussed in Chapter 2, "The JavaScript Language: Data, Operators, and Branching." As you see here, you can pass values to the Date type's constructor (constructors were discussed in Chapter 2; they're methods that create objects and have the same name as the object you're creating, such as Date) to indicate how to configure the new object. Here are what the parameters mean in this case:

- **dateVal.** If a number, *dateVal* is the number of milliseconds in *Universal Coordinated Time* (UTC) between the date you want to use and midnight January 1, 1970. If a string, *dateVal* is parsed using the Date object's parse method.

- **year.** The four-digit year.

- **month.** The month (as an integer between 0 and 11, where January = 0).

- **date.** The day of the month (as an integer between 1 and 31).

- **hours.** The hour as an integer from (0 to 23, which corresponds to midnight to 11 p.m.).

- **minutes.** The minutes as an integer (from 0 to 59).

- **seconds.** The seconds as an integer (from 0 to 59).

- **ms.** An integer from 0 to 999 that gives the milliseconds (one-thousandths of a second).

If you don't pass any parameters to the Date constructor, the created Date object will correspond to the current date. When you create a new date, you can use the various Date object methods to get the parts of the date, such as the number of hours:

```
var date1 = new Date()
var hours1 = date1.getHours()
```

You can see the methods of the Date object in Table 18.1.

Table 18.1 **The Methods of the *Date* Object**

Method	NS2	NS3	NS4	NS6	IE3a	IE3b	IE4	IE5	IE5.5	IE6
getDate	X	X	X	X	X	X	X	X	X	X
	Returns: Integer Returns the day of the month, 1–31. Syntax: *date*.getDate().									
getDay	X	X	X	X	X	X	X	X	X	X
	Returns: Integer Returns the day of the week, 0–6 (where Sunday = 0, and Saturday = 6). Syntax: *date*.getDay().									
getFullYear			X	X		X	X	X	X	X
	Returns: Integer Gets the full, four-digit year. Syntax: *date*.getFullYear().									

Method	NS2	NS3	NS4	NS6	IE3a	IE3b	IE4	IE5	IE5.5	IE6
getHours	X	X	X	X	X	X	X	X	X	X

Returns: Integer
Gets the hour of the day since midnight, 0–]23.
Syntax: *date*.getHours().

getMilliseconds			X	X		X	X	X	X	X

Returns: Integer
Returns the milliseconds value in a **Date** object using local time.
Syntax: *date*.getMilliseconds().

getMinutes	X	X	X	X	X	X	X	X	X	X

Returns: Integer
Returns the minutes value in a **Date** object using local time.
Syntax: *date*.getMinutes().

getMonth	X	X	X	X	X	X	X	X	X	X

Returns: Integer
Returns the month value, 0–11 (January = 0) in the **Date** object using local time.
Syntax: *date*.getMonth().

getSeconds	X	X	X	X	X	X	X	X	X	X

Returns: Integer
Returns the seconds value in a **Date** object using local time. Returns 0–59.
Syntax: *date*.getSeconds().

getTime	X	X	X	X	X	X	X	X	X	X

Returns: Integer
Returns an integer value representing the number of milliseconds between midnight, January 1, 1970 and the time value in the **Date** object. In the Internet Explorer, the range of dates is approximately 285,616 years from either side of midnight, January 1, 1970. Negative numbers mean dates before 1970.
Syntax: *date*.getTime().

getTimezoneOffset

	X	X	X	X	X	X	X	X	X	X

Returns: Integer
Returns the difference in minutes between the time on the computer and UTC.
Syntax: *date*.getTimezoneOffset().

continues ▶

Table 18.1 **Continued**

Method	NS2	NS3	NS4	NS6	IE3a	IE3b	IE4	IE5	IE5.5	IE6
getUTCDate			X	X		X	X	X	X	X

Returns: Integer
Returns the day of the month in a `Date` object using UTC. Returns 1–31.
Syntax: *date*.getUTCDate().

getUTCDay			X	X		X	X	X	X	X

Returns: Integer
Returns the day of the week value in a `Date` object using UTC. Returns
0–6 (where 0 = Sunday).
Syntax: *date*.getUTCDay().

getUTCFullYear			X	X		X	X	X	X	X

Returns: Integer
Returns the four-digit year value in a `Date` object using UTC.
Syntax: *date*.getUTCFullYear().

getUTCHours			X	X		X	X	X	X	X

Returns: Integer
Returns the hours value in a `Date` object using UTC. returns 0–23.
Syntax: *date*.getUTCHours().

getUTCMilliseconds			X	X		X	X	X	X	X

Returns: Integer
Returns the milliseconds value in a `Date` object using UTC.
Returns 0–999.
Syntax: *date*.getUTCMilliseconds().

getUTCMinutes			X	X		X	X	X	X	X

Returns: Integer
Returns the minutes value in a `Date` object using UTC. Returns 0–59.
Syntax: *date*.getUTCMinutes().

getUTCMonth			X	X		X	X	X	X	X

Returns: Integer
Returns the month value in a `Date` object using UTC. Returns 0–11
(January = 0).
Syntax: *date*.getUTCMonth().

getUTCSeconds			X	X		X	X	X	X	X

Returns: Integer
Returns the month value in a `Date` object using UTC. Returns 0–59.
Syntax: *date*.getUTCSeconds().

Method	NS2	NS3	NS4	NS6	IE3a	IE3b	IE4	IE5	IE5.5	IE6
getVarDate							X	X	X	X

Returns: Date object
Returns the date using VT_DATE format, which you use when interacting with COM objects, ActiveX objects, or other objects that accept and return date values in VT_DATE format in the Internet Explorer.
Syntax: *date*.getVarDate().

| getYear | X | X | X | X | X | X | X | X | X | X |

Returns: Integer
This method is considered obsolete; use the getFullYear method instead. In the Internet Explorer, for the years 1900 though 1999, the year is a 2-digit integer value returned as the difference between the stored year and 1900. For dates outside that period, the 4-digit year is returned. In the Netscape Navigator, the year is returned as the difference between the stored year and 1900.
Syntax: *date*.getYear().

| parse | X | X | X | X | X | X | X | X | X | X |

Returns: Integer
Parses a string containing a date, and returns the number of milliseconds between that date and midnight, January 1, 1970. The acceptable date formats vary by browser, such as "December 15, 2003 11:20 AM".
Syntax: Date.parse("dateString"). Note that you don't need a Date *object* here, just the name Date.

| setDate | X | X | X | X | X | X | X | X | X | X |

Returns: Nothing
Sets the day of the month.
Syntax: *date*.setDate(*value*), where *value* is 1–31.

| setDay | X | X | X | X | X | X | X | X | X | X |

Returns: Nothing
Sets the day of the week.
Syntax: *date*.setDay(*value*), where *value* is 0–6 (Sunday = 0).

| setFullYear | | | X | X | | X | X | X | X | X |

Returns: Integer
Sets the four-digit year.
Syntax: *date*.setFullYear(*year*), where *year* is the four-digit year.

continues ▶

Table 18.1 **Continued**

Method	NS2	NS3	NS4	NS6	IE3a	IE3b	IE4	IE5	IE5.5	IE6
setHours	x	x	x	x	x	x	x	x	x	x

Returns: Nothing

Sets the hour of the day in 24-hour time.

Syntax: *date*.setHours(*value*), where *value* is 0–23.

setMilliseconds			x	x		x	x	x	x	x

Returns: Nothing

Sets the number of milliseconds.

Syntax: *date*.setMilliseconds(*value*) where *value* is 0–999.

setMinutes	x	x	x	x	x	x	x	x	x	x

Returns: Nothing

Sets the number of minutes.

Syntax: *date*.setMinutes(*value*), where *value* is 0–59.

setMonth	x	x	x	x	x	x	x	x	x	x

Returns: Nothing

Sets the month in the date.

Syntax: *date*.setMonth(*value*), where *value* is 0–11 (January = 0).

setSeconds	x	x	x	x	x	x	x	x	x	x

Returns: Nothing

Sets the seconds in the date.

Syntax: *date*.setSeconds(*value*), where *value* is 0–59.

setTime	x	x	x	x	x	x	x	x	x	x

Returns: Nothing

Sets the date and time using a millisecond value.

Syntax: *date*.setTime(*value*), where *value* is an integer value representing the number of elapsed seconds since midnight, January 1, 1970 *Greenwich Mean Time* (GMT).

setUTCDate			x	x		x	x	x	x	x

Returns: Nothing

Sets the day of the month in the **Date** object using UTC.

Syntax: *date*.setUTCDate(*value*), where *value* is 1–31.

setUTCDay			x	x		x	x	x	x	x

Returns: Nothing

Sets the day of the week in the **Date** object using UTC.

Syntax: *date*.setUTCDay(*value*), where *value* is 0–6 (Sunday = 0).

Method	NS2	NS3	NS4	NS6	IE3a	IE3b	IE4	IE5	IE5.5	IE6
setUTCFullYear			X	X		X	X	X	X	X

Returns: Nothing
Sets the full year in the Date object using UTC.
Syntax: *date*.setUTCFullYear(*value*), where *value* is the four-digit year.

| setUTCHours | | | X | X | | X | X | X | X | X |

Returns: Nothing
Sets the hour in the Date object using UTC.
Syntax: *date*.setUTCHours(*value*), where *value* is 0–23 in 24-hour time.

| setUTC Milliseconds | | | X | X | | X | X | X | X | X |

Returns: Nothing
Sets the milliseconds value in the Date object using UTC.
Syntax: *date*.setUTCMilliseconds(*value*), where *value* is 0–999.

| setUTCMinutes | | | X | X | | X | X | X | X | X |

Returns: Nothing
Sets the minutes value in the Date object using UTC.
Syntax: *date*.setUTCMinutes(*value*), where *value* is 0–59.

| setUTCMonth | | | X | X | | X | X | X | X | X |

Returns: Nothing
Sets the minutes value in the Date object using UTC.
Syntax: *date*.setUTCMonth(*value*), where *value* is 0–11 (January = 0).

| setUTCSeconds | | | X | X | | X | X | X | X | X |

Returns: Nothing
Sets the seconds value in the Date object using UTC.
Syntax: *date*.setUTCSeconds(*value*), where *value* is 0–59.

| setYear | X | X | X | X | X | X | X | X | X | X |

Returns: Nothing
This method is considered obsolete; use setFullYear instead. Sets the year value in the Date object.
Syntax: *date*.setYear(*value*), where *value* is the year.

| toDateString | | | | | | | | | X | X |

Returns: String
Returns a (browser-dependent) string holding the date.
Syntax: *date*.toDateString().

continues ▶

Table 18.1 **Continued**

Method	NS2	NS3	NS4	NS6	IE3a	IE3b	IE4	IE5	IE5.5	IE6
toGMTString	x	x	x	x	x	x	x	x	x	x

Returns: String
Returns a (browser-dependent) string holding the GMT date.
Syntax: *date*.toGMTString().

Method	NS2	NS3	NS4	NS6	IE3a	IE3b	IE4	IE5	IE5.5	IE6
toLocaleString				x					x	x

Returns: String
Returns a (browser-dependent) string holding the local date in local format.
Syntax: *date*.toLocaleString().

Method	NS2	NS3	NS4	NS6	IE3a	IE3b	IE4	IE5	IE5.5	IE6
toLocaleDateString				x					x	x

Returns: String
Returns a (browser-dependent) string holding the local date in
UTC format.
Syntax: *date*.toLocaleDateString().

Method	NS2	NS3	NS4	NS6	IE3a	IE3b	IE4	IE5	IE5.5	IE6
toLocaleTimeString				x					x	x

Returns: String
Returns a (browser-dependent) string holding the local time in local
format.
Syntax: *date*.toLocaleTimeString().

Method	NS2	NS3	NS4	NS6	IE3a	IE3b	IE4	IE5	IE5.5	IE6
toString	x	x	x	x	x	x	x	x	x	x

Returns: String
Returns a (browser-dependent) string holding the local time.
Syntax: *date*.toString().

Method	NS2	NS3	NS4	NS6	IE3a	IE3b	IE4	IE5	IE5.5	IE6
toTimeString				x					x	x

Returns: String
Returns a (browser-dependent) string holding the time.
Syntax: *date*.toTimeString().

Method	NS2	NS3	NS4	NS6	IE3a	IE3b	IE4	IE5	IE5.5	IE6
toUTCString			x	x		x	x	x	x	x

Returns: String
Returns the date converted to a string using UTC.
Syntax: *date*.toUTCString().

Method	NS2	NS3	NS4	NS6	IE3a	IE3b	IE4	IE5	IE5.5	IE6
UTC	x	x	x	x	x	x	x	x	x	x

Returns: Integer
Returns the number of milliseconds between midnight, January 1, 1970 UTC (or GMT) and the given date.
Syntax: `Date.UTC(year, month, day[, hours[, minutes[, seconds[,ms]]]])`. Note that you don't need a `Date` object here, just the `Date` name.

Method	NS2	NS3	NS4	NS6	IE3a	IE3b	IE4	IE5	IE5.5	IE6
valueOf		x	x	x			x	x	x	x

Returns: String
Returns the date converted to a string using UTC.
Syntax: `date.valueOf()`.

> **Tip**
>
> Note that days of the month are stored in 1–31 values in `Date` objects, but that days of the week are stored as 0–6 values, not 1–7.

Working with the *Date* Object

You can see the various methods of the `Date` object in Table 18.1, and they're great for working with dates. In fact, we've already used the `Date` object in Chapter 16, "Dynamic HTML: Changing Web Pages On-the-Fly"—in the JavaScript Café, which responds to the local time of day on the user's computer to display one of three menus: breakfast, lunch, or dinner, using a `Date` object. Here's how that works. When you create a `Date` object without any parameters, the created date corresponds to the current date:

```
<HTML>
    <HEAD>
        <TITLE>
            Welcome to the JavaScript Café
        </TITLE>
        <SCRIPT LANGUAGE="JavaScript">
            <!--
            var currentDate = new Date()
            var currentHour = currentDate.getHours()
            document.write( "<CENTER>")
            document.write( "<H1>")
            document.write( "Welcome to the JavaScript Café")
            document.write( "</H1>")
            document.write( "</CENTER>")
```

continues ▶

```
if (currentHour < 5 || currentHour > 23){
    document.write( "<CENTER>")
    document.write( "<H1>")
    document.write( "Sorry, we're closed now." )
    document.write( "</H1>")
    document.write( "</CENTER>")
}
    .
    .
    .
```

Here's another example. In this case, I'll use the various methods of a `Date` object to get the month, day, and year of the current date, using `getMonth`, `getDay`, and `getYear`. This causes a problem, however, because the Internet Explorer and Netscape Navigator report the year differently for `getYear` (see Table 18.1), so we have to treat them differently. The year 2003 is reported as 2003 from Internet Explorer's `getYear`, but is reported as 103 (the number of years from 1900) from Netscape Navigator's `getYear`. That makes the code look like this:

(Listing 18-01.html on the web site)

```
<HTML>
    <HEAD>
        <TITLE>Getting Today's Date</TITLE>
        <SCRIPT LANGUAGE="JavaScript">
            <!--
                function getDate()
                {
                    alert(dateString())
                }

            function dateString()
            {
                var date, text = "Today is "
                date = new Date()
                text += (date.getMonth() + 1) + "/"
                text += date.getDate() + "/"
                if (navigator.appName == "Netscape") {
                    text += date.getYear() + 1900
                }
                if (navigator.appName == "Microsoft Internet Explorer") {
                    text += date.getYear()
                }
                return(text)
            }
            //-->
        </SCRIPT>
    </HEAD>
```

```
    <BODY>
        <H1>Getting Today's Date</H1>
        <FORM NAME="form1">
            <INPUT TYPE="BUTTON" VALUE="Get Date" ONCLICK="getDate()">
        </FORM>
    </BODY>
</HTML>
```

You can see the results in Figure 18.1.

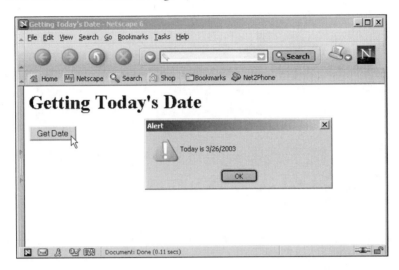

Figure 18.1   Displaying the date.

You can fix the problem with `getYear` by using `getFullYear` instead, which returns the full four-digit year. In fact, `getYear` is considered obsolete because of Y2K issues, so you should use `getFullYear`:

```
<HTML>
    <HEAD>
        <TITLE>Getting Today's Date</TITLE>
        <SCRIPT LANGUAGE="JavaScript">
            <!--
                function getDate()
                {
                    alert(dateString())
                }

            function dateString()
            {
                var date, text = "Today is "
                date = new Date()
                text += (date.getMonth() + 1) + "/"
                text += date.getDate() + "/"
```

continues ▶

```
                    text += date.getFullYear()
                    return(text)
                }
                //-->
            </SCRIPT>
        </HEAD>

        <BODY>
            <H1>Getting Today's Date</H1>
            <FORM NAME="form1">
                <INPUT TYPE="BUTTON" VALUE="Get Date" ONCLICK="getDate()">
            </FORM>
        </BODY>
    </HTML>
```

In this example, I've used methods such as `getMonth` to extract data from a `Date` object, but you also can just use a method such as `toString` to get the date in text string format:

```
function dateString()
{
    var date
    date = new Date()
    return(date.toString())
}
```

However, the format of this text string varies by browser. Here's what you get from the Netscape Navigator:

```
Tue Mar 26 14:20:18 GMT-0500 (Eastern Standard Time) 2003
```

And here's what you get from the Internet Explorer:

```
Tue Mar 26 14:20:07 EST 2003
```

Creating an Alarm Clock

`Date` objects are useful for many applications that need to keep track of the time, as you can imagine. Here's an alarm clock program, for example, which you can see at work in Figure 18.2.

This example is just a demo, so it's not written to understand the difference between a.m. and p.m., but it will display the current time and has a useable "alarm," which you can toggle on and off with the radio buttons at the lower left. When the alarm is on and the current time is after the time set in the text field at left for the alarm setting, the alarm goes off by making the page flash, alternating between a red and white background, until you turn the alarm off.

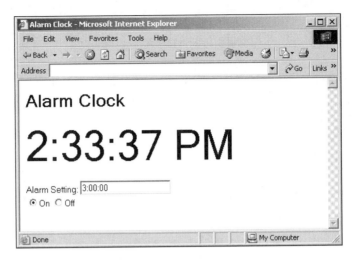

Figure 18.2   An alarm clock.

Here's how this example works. I use `setInterval` to call a function named `showTime` every half second:

```
var intervalID = window.setInterval("showTime()", 500)
```

In the `showTime` function, we get the time and display it like this in a `<DIV>` element whose style I've set to 48-point font:

```
function showTime()
{
    var d = new Date()
    document.getElementById("div1").innerHTML = d.toLocaleTimeString()
        .
        .
        .
}
```

We can then compare the time to the alarm setting using `getHour`, `getMinute`, and so on; but in this example, I'm going to do a simple string comparison (which is why you shouldn't trust this demo to know the difference between a.m. and p.m.) to see whether we should turn on the alarm:

```
function showTime()
{
    var d = new Date()
    document.getElementById("div1").innerHTML = d.toLocaleTimeString()

    if(on && d.toLocaleTimeString() > document.form1.text1.value){
        if(color == "white"){
            color = "red"
        } else {
```

continues ▶

```
        color = "white"
    }
document.body.bgColor = color
    }
}
```

That's it. Here's the whole code, including the support for the radio buttons that turn the alarm on and off (if you're using Netscape Navigator, you have to use version 6 or later):

(Listing 18-02.html on the web site)

```
<HTML>
    <HEAD>
        <TITLE>
            Alarm Clock
        </TITLE>
        <SCRIPT LANGUAGE="JavaScript">
            <!--
            var intervalID = window.setInterval("showTime()", 500), on = false,
            ➥color="white"

            function showTime()
            {
                    var d = new Date()
                    document.getElementById("div1").innerHTML = d.toLocaleTimeString()

                    if(on && d.toLocaleTimeString() > document.form1.text1.value){
                        if(color == "white"){
                            color = "red"
                        } else {
                            color = "white"
                        }
                        document.body.bgColor = color
                    }
            }

            function alarmOn()
            {
                    on = true
            }

            function alarmOff()
            {
                    on = false
                    document.body.bgColor = "white"
            }
            // -->
        </SCRIPT>
    </HEAD>

    <BODY>
        <H1>Alarm Clock</H1>
        <FORM NAME="form1">
```

```
            <DIV ID="div1" STYLE="font-size:48pt"></DIV>
            <BR>
            Alarm Setting: <INPUT TYPE="TEXT" NAME="text1">
            <BR>
            <INPUT TYPE="RADIO" NAME="onoff" ONCLICK="alarmOn()">On</INPUT>
            <INPUT TYPE="RADIO" NAME="onoff" ONCLICK="alarmOff()" CHECKED>Off</INPUT>
        </FORM>
    </BODY>
</HTML>
```

Adding and Subtracting Dates

Another useful aspect of using the `Date` object is to add and subtract dates. That's usually done by converting both dates to milliseconds (with `getTime`, which returns a millisecond count measured in total milliseconds since 1/1/70) and working with those values, and then converting the resulting number of milliseconds back to a time.

To subtract dates, you just have to subtract the millisecond values to find the time difference in milliseconds. To add a specified amount of time to a date, you can convert the date to milliseconds, add the number of milliseconds you want to it, and then convert the result back to a date by creating a new `Date` object (`var date1 = new Date(`*`milliseconds`*`)`) or setting the date in an existing `Date` object (`date1.setTime(`*`milliseconds`*`)`).

Here's an example—the Date Subtractor—which enables you to subtract one date from another and gives you the number of intervening days. You can see this program at work in Figure 18.3, where I subtracting two dates and get the resulting time difference in days.

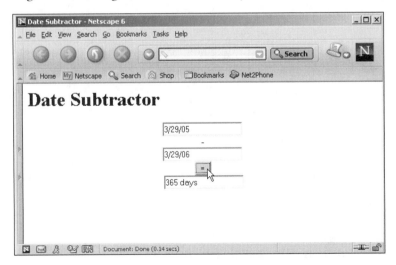

Figure 18.3   Subtracting dates.

All we have to do in this case is to convert the two dates into milliseconds since 1/1/1970. I then subtract those millisecond values (using the `Math.abs` absolute value method we'll see in the next chapter to get a positive value) and convert the result to days (using the `Math.floor` method we'll also see in the next chapter to round off the result):

(Listing 18-03.html on the web site)

```
<HTML>
    <HEAD>
        <TITLE>
            Date Subtractor
        </TITLE>
        <SCRIPT LANGUAGE="JavaScript">
            <!--

            function showTime()
            {
                var date1, date2
                date1 = new Date(document.form1.text1.value)
                date2 = new Date(document.form1.text2.value)
                var difference
                difference = Math.abs(date1.getTime() - date2.getTime())

                document.form1.text3.value =
                    Math.floor(difference / (1000 * 60 * 60 * 24)) + " days"
            }
            // -->
        </SCRIPT>
    </HEAD>

    <BODY>
        <H1>Date Subtractor</H1>
        <FORM NAME="form1">
            <CENTER>
            <INPUT TYPE="TEXT" NAME="text1">
            <BR>
                -
            <BR>
            <INPUT TYPE="TEXT" NAME="text2">
            <BR>
            <INPUT TYPE="BUTTON" ONCLICK="showTime()"
VALUE="  =  ">
            <BR>
            <INPUT TYPE="TEXT" NAME="text3">
            </CENTER>
        </FORM>
    </BODY>
</HTML>
```

That's all there is to it.

Handling Date Strings

Some JavaScript properties, such as `fileCreatedDate`, `lastModified`, and `fileModifiedDate` (see Table 9.2) hold date strings in `Date` object format. You can use those date strings when you create a new `Date` object, like this:

```
var lastUpdated = new Date(document.fileCreatedDate)
```

Here's an example that does that for the last-modified date of a document. In this case, the code just displays when the document was last modified:

(Listing 18-04.html on the web site)

```
<HTML>
    <HEAD>
        <TITLE>Getting Last Updated Dates</TITLE>
    </HEAD>

    <BODY>
        <H1>Getting Last Updated Dates</H1>
        <FORM NAME="form1">
            <INPUT NAME="text1" SIZE="50"></INPUT>
        </FORM>
        <SCRIPT LANGUAGE="JavaScript">
            <!--
                var lastUpdated = new Date(document.lastModified)
                month = lastUpdated.getMonth() + 1
                date = lastUpdated.getDate()
                year = lastUpdated.getFullYear()
                document.form1.text1.value =
                    "This document was last updated " + month + "/" + date + "/"
                ➥+ year
            //-->
        </SCRIPT>
    </BODY>
</HTML>
```

You can see the results in Figure 18.4, where the document's last-modified time appears.

Checking Date Format

Before using date strings when you create `Date` objects (such as `var date1 = new Date(dateString)`), it's worth remembering that not all date strings in all formats are acceptable to JavaScript. One good way to check the format of date strings is with *regular expressions*, which we'll see in Chapter 20, "The *RegExp* Object: Working with Regular Expressions." Regular expressions enable you to specify patterns that match or don't match text, letting you know whether the text conforms to what you want.

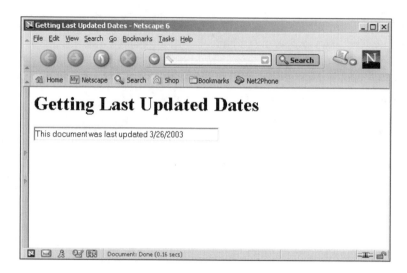

Figure 18.4   Displaying a document's last-modified time.

Here, for example, I'm only allowing the user to enter date strings made up of one or two digits, followed by a slash (/), followed by one or two digits, followed by a slash, followed by two or four digits for the year:

(Listing 18-05.html on the web site)

```html
<HTML>
    <HEAD>
        <TITLE>Checking Dates</TITLE>
        <SCRIPT LANGUAGE="JavaScript">
            <!--
            function checker()
            {
                var regExp1 = /^(\d{1,2})\/(\d{1,2})\/(\d{2})$/
                var regExp2 = /^(\d{1,2})\/(\d{1,2})\/(\d{4})$/
                var resultArray1 = document.form1.text1.value.match(regExp1)
                var resultArray2 = document.form1.text1.value.match(regExp2)
                if (resultArray1 == null && resultArray2 == null) {
                    alert("Sorry, that's not in valid date format.")
                } else {
                    alert("That's in valid date format.")
                }
            }
            //-->
        </SCRIPT>
    </HEAD>

    <BODY>
```

```
        <H1>Checking Dates</H1>
        <FORM NAME="form1">
            <INPUT TYPE="TEXT" NAME="text1"></INPUT>
            <INPUT TYPE="BUTTON" VALUE="Check Date" ONCLICK="checker()">
        </FORM>
    </BODY>
</HTML>
```

You can see the results in Figure 18.5, where the code is indicating that the user has not entered a valid date. (Note that this example doesn't check whether a date is completely valid—it doesn't check whether the user entered 13 for the month, and so on).

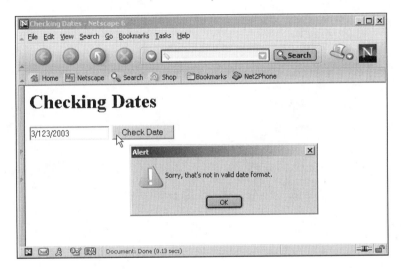

Figure 18.5   Checking date format.

Creating Custom Date Strings

Although you can use `Date` object methods such as `toString` to get the date in string format, that format varies between browsers. It's usually easier to put together date strings yourself if you want to be consistent across all browsers. The following example puts together a date string representing the current date:

(Listing 18-06.html on the web site)

```
<HTML>
    <HEAD>
        <TITLE>Getting Today's Date</TITLE>
        <SCRIPT LANGUAGE="JavaScript">
```

continues ▶

```
<!--
function getDate()
{
    month = new Array(12)
    day = new Array(7)
    month[0] = "January"
    month[1] = "February"
    month[2] = "March"
    month[3] = "April"
    month[4] = "May"
    month[5] = "June"
    month[6] = "July"
    month[7] = "August"
    month[8] = "September"
    month[9] = "October"
    month[10] = "November"
    month[11] = "December"
    day[0] = "Sunday"
    day[1] = "Monday"
    day[2] = "Tuesday"
    day[3] = "Wednesday"
    day[4] = "Thursday"
    day[5] = "Friday"
    day[6] = "Saturday"
    var date = new Date()
    document.form1.text1.value = "Today is " + day[date.getDay()] + ", "
        + month[date.getMonth()] + " "
        + date.getDate() + ", " + date.getFullYear()
}
//-->
</SCRIPT>
</HEAD>

<BODY>
    <H1>Getting Today's Date</H1>
    <FORM NAME="form1">
        <INPUT TYPE="TEXT" NAME="text1" SIZE="60"></INPUT>
        <BR>
        <INPUT TYPE="BUTTON" VALUE="Get Date" ONCLICK="getDate()">
    </FORM>
</BODY>
</HTML>
```

You can see the results of this code in Figure 18.6, where the code displays the date in a standard format.

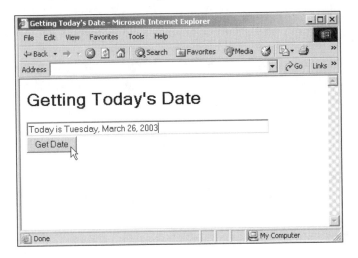

Figure 18.6   Formatting a date string.

The *String* Object

We've worked with strings throughout the book, but we haven't dealt with the `String` object formally yet. In fact, when you use strings in variables, they're automatically converted into `String` objects in JavaScript:

```
var text = "Now is the time."
```

You also can use the `String` constructor to create a `String` object:

```
var text = new String("Now is the time.")
```

> **Tip**
>
> The strings you assign to simple variables in JavaScript aren't actually treated as full `String` objects—you can't add properties and methods to them, for example, which you can with full `String` objects. More on that in Chapter 23, "Cookies and Creating Your Own Objects."

You can find the properties and methods of the `String` object in Table 18.2, its properties in depth in Table 18.3, and its methods in depth in Table 18.4.

Table 18.2 **The Properties and Methods of the *String* Object**

Properties	Methods
constructor	anchor
length	big
prototype	blink
	bold
	charAt
	charCodeAt
	concat
	fixed
	fontcolor
	fontsize
	fromCharCode
	indexOf
	italics
	lastIndexOf
	link
	localeCompare
	match
	replace
	search
	slice
	small
	split
	strike
	sub
	substr
	substring
	sup
	toLocaleLowerCase
	toLocaleUpperCase
	toLowerCase
	toString
	toUpperCase
	valueOf

Table 18.3 **The Properties of the *String* Object**

Property	NS2	NS3	NS4	NS6	IE3a	IE3b	IE4	IE5	IE5.5	IE6
constructor			X	X			X	X	X	X

Read/write
This property specifies the function that creates an object.

length	X	X	X	X	X	X	X	X	X	X

Read-only
This property holds the length of the text in the string, measured in characters.

prototype		X	X	X			X	X	X	X

Read/write
This property holds a reference to the `String` object's prototype.

Table 18.4 **The Methods of the *String* Object**

Method	NS2	NS3	NS4	NS6	IE3a	IE3b	IE4	IE5	IE5.5	IE6
anchor	X	X	X	X	X	X	X	X	X	X

Returns: String
This method returns a string with an HTML anchor with a `NAME` attribute around specified text in the object.
Syntax: *string*.`anchor(`*text*`)`, where *text* is the text you want to place in the `NAME` attribute of the HTML anchor.

big	X	X	X	X	X	X	X	X	X	X

Returns: String
This method changes the text to big text by surrounding it with HTML `<BIG>` tags.
Syntax: *string*.`big()`. See "Formatting Text" in this chapter.

blink	X	X	X	X	X	X	X	X	X	X

This method changes the text to blinking text by surrounding it with HTML `<BLINK>` tags.
Syntax: *string*.`blink()`. See "Formatting Text" in this chapter.

bold	X	X	X	X	X	X	X	X	X	X

This method changes the text to big text by surrounding it with HTML `<B>` tags.
Syntax: *string*.`bold()`. See "Formatting Text" in this chapter.

continues ▶

Table 18.4 **Continued**

Method	NS2	NS3	NS4	NS6	IE3a	IE3b	IE4	IE5	IE5.5	IE6
charAt	x	x	x	x	x	x	x	x	x	x

Returns: Single character
This method returns the character at the specified index of a String object.
Syntax: *string*.charAt(*index*), where *index* is the index of the character you want.

Method	NS2	NS3	NS4	NS6	IE3a	IE3b	IE4	IE5	IE5.5	IE6
charCodeAt			x	x			x	x	x	x

Returns: Integer character code
This method returns the character code of the character at the specified index of a String object.
Syntax: *string*.charCodeAt(*index*), where *index* is the index of the character whose code you want.

Method	NS2	NS3	NS4	NS6	IE3a	IE3b	IE4	IE5	IE5.5	IE6
concat			x	x			x	x	x	x

Returns: String
Returns a string value containing the concatenation of the current string with any given string(s). Sytnax: *string*.concat([*string1* [, ... [, *stringN*]]]]).

Method	NS2	NS3	NS4	NS6	IE3a	IE3b	IE4	IE5	IE5.5	IE6
fixed	x	x	x	x	x	x	x	x	x	x

This method changes the text to fixed-width text by surrounding it with HTML <TT> tags.
Syntax: *string*.fixed(). See "Formatting Text" in this chapter.

Method	NS2	NS3	NS4	NS6	IE3a	IE3b	IE4	IE5	IE5.5	IE6
fontcolor	x	x	x	x	x	x	x	x	x	x

This method sets font color by adding <FONT> tags.
Syntax: *string*.fontcolor(*color*), where *color* is the new color (either a color triplet or a color name recognized by the browser).

Method	NS2	NS3	NS4	NS6	IE3a	IE3b	IE4	IE5	IE5.5	IE6
fontsize	x	x	x	x	x	x	x	x	x	x

This method sets font size by adding <FONT> tags.
Syntax: *string*.fontsize(*size*), where *size* is the an integer for the <FONT> tag's SIZE attribute.

Method	NS2	NS3	NS4	NS6	IE3a	IE3b	IE4	IE5	IE5.5	IE6
fromCharCode			x	x			x	x	x	x

Returns: String
This method returns a string from a number of character values.
Syntax: *string*.fromCharCode([*code1* [, ... [, *codeN*]]]]).

Method	NS2	NS3	NS4	NS6	IE3a	IE3b	IE4	IE5	IE5.5	IE6
indexOf	x	x	x	x	x	x	x	x	x	x

Returns: Integer
This method the character position where the first occurrence of a sub-string occurs within a String object.
Syntax: *string*.indexOf(*subString*), where *subString* is the string you're searching for. See "Searching Strings" in this chapter.

Method	NS2	NS3	NS4	NS6	IE3a	IE3b	IE4	IE5	IE5.5	IE6
italics	x	x	x	x	x	x	x	x	x	x

This method changes the text to italics by surrounding it with HTML
<I> tags.
Syntax: *string*.italics(). See "Formatting Text" in this chapter.

Method	NS2	NS3	NS4	NS6	IE3a	IE3b	IE4	IE5	IE5.5	IE6
lastIndexOf	x	x	x	x	x	x	x	x	x	x

Returns: Integer
This method the character position where the last occurrence of a sub-string occurs within a String object.
Syntax: *string*.lastIndexOf(*subString*), where *subString* is the string for which you're searching. See "Searching Strings" in this chapter.

Method	NS2	NS3	NS4	NS6	IE3a	IE3b	IE4	IE5	IE5.5	IE6
link	x	x	x	x	x	x	x	x	x	x

This method returns as string with an HTML anchor and an HREF attribute around the text in a String object.
Syntax: *string*.link(*href*), where *href* is the URL the hyperlink should point to.

Method	NS2	NS3	NS4	NS6	IE3a	IE3b	IE4	IE5	IE5.5	IE6
localeCompare				x					x	x

Returns: Integer
This method performs a locale-sensitive string comparison of strings. Returns −1, 0, or +1, depending on the sort order of the system default locale.
Syntax: *string1*.localeCompare(*string2*). If *string1* sorts before *string2*, returns −1; if *string1* sorts after *string2*, returns 1. Returning 0 means that the two strings are equal.

Method	NS2	NS3	NS4	NS6	IE3a	IE3b	IE4	IE5	IE5.5	IE6
match	x	x	x	x	x	x	x	x	x	x

Returns: Array of strings
This method executes a regular expression match on the string.
Syntax: *string*.match(*regExp*). Returns an array of matches or null if there were no matches. See Chapter 20 for more on regular expressions.

continues ▶

Table 18.4 **Continued**

Method	NS2	NS3	NS4	NS6	IE3a	IE3b	IE4	IE5	IE5.5	IE6
replace			X	X			X	X	X	X

Returns: New string
This method replaces substrings with a new string.
Syntax: `string.replace(`*regExp, replacementText*`)`, where *regExp* is a regular expression and *replacementText* replaces matches to *regExp* (all matches are replaced if *regExp* includes the /g modifier). See "Searching and Replacing" in this chapter for an example.

Method	NS2	NS3	NS4	NS6	IE3a	IE3b	IE4	IE5	IE5.5	IE6
search			X	X			X	X	X	X

Returns: Integer
This method returns the position of the first substring match in a regular expression search.
Syntax: `string.search(`*regExp*`)`, where *regExp* is the regular expression to match.

Method	NS2	NS3	NS4	NS6	IE3a	IE3b	IE4	IE5	IE5.5	IE6
slice			X	X			X	X	X	X

Returns: String
This method returns a slice—that is, a section—of a string.
Syntax: `string.slice(`*start, end*`)`, where *start* and *end* are the indices of the start and end points of the slice.

Method	NS2	NS3	NS4	NS6	IE3a	IE3b	IE4	IE5	IE5.5	IE6
small	X	X	X	X	X	X	X	X	X	X

This method changes the text to small text by surrounding it HTML `<SMALL>` tags.
Syntax: `string.small()`. See "Formatting Text" in this chapter.

Method	NS2	NS3	NS4	NS6	IE3a	IE3b	IE4	IE5	IE5.5	IE6
split		X	X	X			X	X	X	X

Returns: Array of strings
This method splits a string. Returns the array of strings that results when a string is separated into substrings.
Syntax: `string.split(`*separator* `[,` *max*`])`, where *separator* is the delimiter (such as `","`) or regular expression to split into substrings, and *max* is the maximum number of substrings to create. See "Splitting Strings" in this chapter.

Method	NS2	NS3	NS4	NS6	IE3a	IE3b	IE4	IE5	IE5.5	IE6
strike	X	X	X	X	X	X	X	X	X	X

This method changes the text to struck-out text by surrounding it with HTML `<STRIKE>` tags.
Syntax: `string.strike()`. See "Formatting Text" in this chapter.

Method	NS2	NS3	NS4	NS6	IE3a	IE3b	IE4	IE5	IE5.5	IE6
sub	X	X	X	X	X	X	X	X	X	X

This method changes the text to subscript text by surrounding it with HTML <SUB> tags.

Syntax: *string*.sub(). See "Formatting Text" in this chapter.

Method	NS2	NS3	NS4	NS6	IE3a	IE3b	IE4	IE5	IE5.5	IE6
substr			X	X			X	X	X	X

Returns: String

This method returns a substring beginning at a specified location and having a given length.

Syntax: *string*.substr(*start* [, *length*); where *start* is the beginning index of the substring, and *length* is the length of the substring.

Method	NS2	NS3	NS4	NS6	IE3a	IE3b	IE4	IE5	IE5.5	IE6
substring	X	X	X	X	X	X	X	X	X	X

Returns: String

This method returns the substring at the specified location within a String object.

Syntax: *string*.substring(*start* [, *end*); where *start* is the beginning index of the substring, and *end* is the ending index of the substring.

Method	NS2	NS3	NS4	NS6	IE3a	IE3b	IE4	IE5	IE5.5	IE6
sup	X	X	X	X	X	X	X	X	X	X

This method changes the text to superscript text by surrounding it with HTML <SUP> tags.

Syntax: *string*.sup(). See "Formatting Text" in this chapter.

Method	NS2	NS3	NS4	NS6	IE3a	IE3b	IE4	IE5	IE5.5	IE6
toLocaleLowerCase				X					X	X

Returns: String

This method converts the string to locale-sensitive lower case.

Syntax: *string*.toLocaleLowerCase().

Method	NS2	NS3	NS4	NS6	IE3a	IE3b	IE4	IE5	IE5.5	IE6
toLocaleUpperCase				X					X	X

Returns: String

This method converts the string to locale-sensitive upper case.

Syntax: *string*.toLocaleUpperCase().

Method	NS2	NS3	NS4	NS6	IE3a	IE3b	IE4	IE5	IE5.5	IE6
toLowerCase	X	X	X	X	X	X	X	X	X	X

Returns: String

This method converts the string to lower case.

Syntax: *string*.toLowerCase(). See "Changing Case" in this chapter.

continues ▶

Table 18.4 **Continued**

Method	NS2	NS3	NS4	NS6	IE3a	IE3b	IE4	IE5	IE5.5	IE6
toString			X	X			X	X	X	X

Returns: String
This method just returns the string itself.
Syntax: *string*.toString().

Method	NS2	NS3	NS4	NS6	IE3a	IE3b	IE4	IE5	IE5.5	IE6
toUpperCase	X	X	X	X	X	X	X	X	X	X

Returns: String
This method converts the string to upper case.
Syntax: *string*.toUpperCase(). See "Changing Case" in this chapter.

Method	NS2	NS3	NS4	NS6	IE3a	IE3b	IE4	IE5	IE5.5	IE6
valueOf			X	X			X	X	X	X

Returns: String
This method just returns the string itself.
Syntax: *string*.valueOf().

Working with the *String* Object

Working with strings is not difficult, and we'll see several examples here. It's worth noting that you can use "escaped" codes to stand for special characters in a string. Here are a few of those codes, all of which start with a backslash (\):

- \" Double quote
- \' Single quote
- \\ Backslash
- \b Backspace
- \t Tab
- \n New line
- \r Carriage return
- \f Form feed

To embed a tab in a string, for instance, you can do something like this: "Here\tThere." (which translates as "Here[TAB]There."). Let's take a look at a few of the String methods now.

Changing Case

You can change the case of text using the String toUpperCase and toLowerCase methods. Here's an example that enables you to change the case of text just by clicking buttons:

(Listing 18-07.html on the web site)

```
<HTML>
    <HEAD>
        <TITLE>
            Changing Case
        </TITLE>
        <SCRIPT LANGUAGE="JavaScript">
            <!--
            function lower()
            {
                document.form1.text1.value = document.form1.text1.value.toLowerCase()
            }

            function upper()
            {
                document.form1.text1.value = document.form1.text1.value.toUpperCase()
            }
            // -->
        </SCRIPT>
    </HEAD>

    <BODY>
        <H1>Changing Case</H1>
        <FORM NAME="form1">
            <INPUT TYPE="TEXT" NAME="text1" VALUE="Text">
            <BR>
            <INPUT TYPE="BUTTON" ONCLICK="lower()" VALUE="Lower case">
            <INPUT TYPE="BUTTON" ONCLICK="upper()" VALUE="Upper case">
        </FORM>
    </BODY>
</HTML>
```

You can see the results of this code in Figure 18.7, where I've capitalized some text by clicking a button.

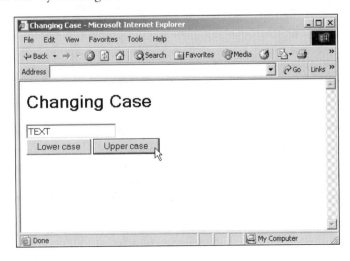

Figure 18.7   Changing text case.

Formatting Text

The `String` object contains many methods for formatting text by surrounding that text with HTML tags. Here's an example where I'm using the `bold`, `italics`, `strike`, and `big` `String` methods to work on some text and display it (if you're using the Netscape Navigator, you'll need version 6+ here to handle the `getElementById` function):

(Listing 18-08.html on the web site)

```
<HTML>
    <HEAD>
        <TITLE>
            Searching Strings
        </TITLE>
        <SCRIPT LANGUAGE="JavaScript">
            <!--
            function formatter()
            {
                document.getElementById("div1").innerHTML = "Now ".bold() +
                    "is ".italics() + "the ".strike() + "time.".big()
            }
            // -->
        </SCRIPT>
    </HEAD>

    <BODY>
        <H1>Searching Strings</H1>
        <FORM NAME="form1">
            <DIV ID="div1">Now is the time.</DIV>
            <BR>
            <INPUT TYPE="BUTTON" ONCLICK="formatter()" VALUE="Format Text">
        </FORM>
    </BODY>
</HTML>
```

You can see the results of this code in Figure 18.8, where I've formatted some text just by clicking a button.

Splitting Strings

You can also split strings into an array of substrings, which is useful, for example, if the user enters a series of commands all in the same text string. To do this, you use the `split` `String` method and specify the character(s) (or regular expression) that you want to split the string on. For example, splitting the string `"Now is the time"` on spaces will create an array of strings whose elements are `"Now"`, `"is"`, `"the"`, and `"time"`. Here's an example, where I'm doing exactly that and displaying the resulting substrings in a text area:

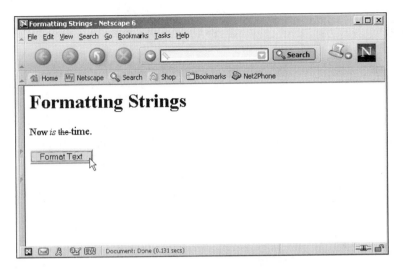

Figure 18.8   Formatting text.

(Listing 18-09.html on the web site)

```
<HTML>
    <HEAD>
        <TITLE>
            Splitting Strings
        </TITLE>
        <SCRIPT LANGUAGE="JavaScript">
            <!--
            function split()
            {
                var stringArray = document.form1.text1.value.split(" ")
                var text = "You typed: \n"
                for (var loopIndex = 0; loopIndex < stringArray.length; loopIndex++){
                    text += stringArray[loopIndex] + "\n"
                }
                document.form1.textarea1.value = text
            }
            // -->
        </SCRIPT>
    </HEAD>

    <BODY>
        <H1>Splitting Strings</H1>
        <FORM NAME="form1">
            <INPUT TYPE="TEXT" NAME="text1" VALUE="Now is the time">
            <BR>
            <INPUT TYPE="BUTTON" ONCLICK="split()" VALUE="Split String">
            <BR>
```

continues ▶

```
          <TEXTAREA ROWS="6" NAME="textarea1"></TEXTAREA>
      </FORM>
   </BODY>
</HTML>
```

You can see the results of this code in Figure 18.9, where I've split the text and the code displays the results.

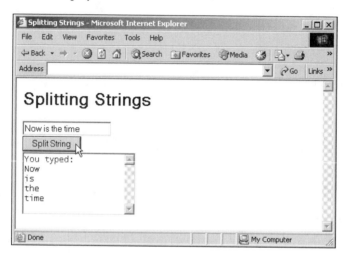

Figure 18.9   Splitting strings.

Searching Strings

You also can search strings using the `indexOf` and `lastIndexOf` methods. The `indexOf` method returns first index of a substring in the main string, and the `lastIndexOf` method returns last index of a substring in the main string. Here's an example, which searches for the letter *t* in the text `"Now is the time"`:

(Listing 18-10.html on the web site)

```
<HTML>
    <HEAD>
        <TITLE>
            Searching Strings
        </TITLE>
        <SCRIPT LANGUAGE="JavaScript">
            <!--
            function findT()
            {
                var firstT = document.form1.text1.value.indexOf("t")
                var text = "First 't' found at index " + firstT + "\n"
```

```
            var lastT = document.form1.text1.value.lastIndexOf("t")
            text += "Last 't' found at index " + lastT + "\n"
            document.form1.textarea1.value = text
        }
        // -->
    </SCRIPT>
</HEAD>

<BODY>
    <H1>Searching Strings</H1>
    <FORM NAME="form1">
        <INPUT TYPE="TEXT" NAME="text1" VALUE="Now is the time">
        <BR>
        <INPUT TYPE="BUTTON" ONCLICK="findT()" VALUE="Find the letter 't'">
        <BR>
        <TEXTAREA ROWS="2" COLS = "30" NAME="textarea1"></TEXTAREA>
    </FORM>
</BODY>
</HTML>
```

You can see the results of this code in Figure 18.10, where the code has found the first and last *t* in the text.

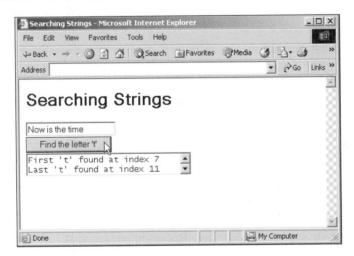

Figure 18.10   Searching strings.

Searching and Replacing

You can search a string and replace matches with another string using the `String` object's `replace` method. In such a case, you have to supply a regular expression (see Chapter 20) that matches the substring(s) you want to replace, and the replacement string.

Here's an example. In this case, we'll search for the text *is* in the phrase "Now is the time" and replace it with the text *isn't*. Here's what the code looks like (the g modifier in the regular expression makes the search-and-replace operation global, which makes it match all occurrences of *is*):

(Listing 18-11.html on the web site)

```
<HTML>
    <HEAD>
        <TITLE>
            Replacing Text
        </TITLE>
        <SCRIPT LANGUAGE="JavaScript">
            <!--
            function replacer()
            {
                var regExp = /is/g
                var text = document.form1.text1.value.replace(regExp, "isn't")
                document.form1.text1.value = text
            }
            // -->
        </SCRIPT>
    </HEAD>

    <BODY>
        <H1>Replacing Text</H1>
        <FORM NAME="form1">
            <INPUT TYPE="TEXT" NAME="text1" VALUE="Now is the time">
            <BR>
            <INPUT TYPE="BUTTON" ONCLICK="replacer()" VALUE="Replace Text">
        </FORM>
    </BODY>
</HTML>
```

You can see the results of this code in Figure 18.11, where the code has changed *is* to *isn't*. That's all there is to it.

That completes our look at the Date and String objects in this chapter. As you can see, there's a lot of programming power here. In the next chapter, we'll keep going in the same direction as we take a look at the Math, Number, Boolean, and Array objects.

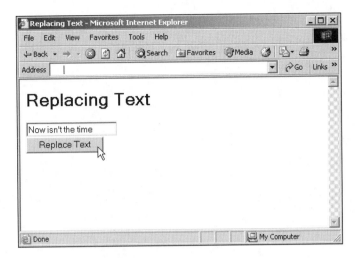

Figure 18.11   Replacing text.

19

The *Math, Number, Boolean,* and *Array* Objects

IN THIS CHAPTER, WE'LL TAKE A LOOK AT THE `Math`, `Number`, `Boolean`, and `Array` JavaScript objects. Except for the `Boolean` object, we've seen all these objects already, but we've never taken a systematic look at them and listed all their properties and methods. We'll do that in this chapter, starting with the `Math` object.

The *Math* Object

The `Math` object gives you access to powerful math routines, such as `log`, `sqrt`, and `pow` (which raises values to various powers). We've already seen the `Math` object in the book every now and then when we had to round off numbers or find absolute values. You can see the properties (actually, they're read-only constants, which is why they're all in capital letters) and methods of the `Math` object in Table 19.1, its properties in depth in Table 19.2, and its methods in Table 19.3.

Tip

The trig methods of the `Math` object take or return radian values. To convert an angle in degrees to radians, multiply that angle by pi and divide by 180.

Table 19.1 **Overview of the Properties and Methods of the *Math* Object**

Properties	Methods
E	abs
LN2	acos
LN10	asin
LOG2E	atan
LOG10E	atan2
PI	ceil
SQRT1_2	cos
SQRT2	exp
	floor
	log
	max
	min
	pow
	random
	round
	sin
	sqrt
	tan

Table 19.2 **The Properties of the *Math* Object**

Property	NS2	NS3	NS4	NS6	IE3a	IE3b	IE4	IE5	IE5.5	IE6
E	x	x	x	x	x	x	x	x	x	x
	Read-only The natural log constant e, stored in JavaScript as 2.718281828459045091.									
LN2	x	x	x	x	x	x	x	x	x	x
	Read-only The natural log of 2, stored in JavaScript as 0.6931471805599452862.									
LN10	x	x	x	x	x	x	x	x	x	x
	Read-only The natural log of 10, stored in JavaScript as 2.302585092994045901.									

Property	NS2	NS3	NS4	NS6	IE3a	IE3b	IE4	IE5	IE5.5	IE6
LOG2E	x	x	x	x	x	x	x	x	x	x

Read-only
The base 2 log of e, stored in JavaScript as 1.442695040888963387.

	NS2	NS3	NS4	NS6	IE3a	IE3b	IE4	IE5	IE5.5	IE6
LOG10E	x	x	x	x	x	x	x	x	x	x

Read-only
The base 10 log of e, stored in JavaScript as 0.4342944819032518167.

	NS2	NS3	NS4	NS6	IE3a	IE3b	IE4	IE5	IE5.5	IE6
PI	x	x	x	x	x	x	x	x	x	x

Read-only
Pi, stored in JavaScript as 3.141592653589793116.

	NS2	NS3	NS4	NS6	IE3a	IE3b	IE4	IE5	IE5.5	IE6
SQRT1_2	x	x	x	x	x	x	x	x	x	x

Read-only
The square root of one half, stored in JavaScript as
0.7071067811865475727.

	NS2	NS3	NS4	NS6	IE3a	IE3b	IE4	IE5	IE5.5	IE6
SQRT2	x	x	x	x	x	x	x	x	x	x

Read-only
The square root of 2, stored in JavaScript as 1.414213562373095145.

Table 19.3 **The Methods of the *Math* Object**

Method	NS2	NS3	NS4	NS6	IE3a	IE3b	IE4	IE5	IE5.5	IE6
Eabs	x	x	x	x	x	x	x	x	x	x

Returns: Number
Returns the absolute value of a number.
Syntax: `Math.abs(value)`, where *value* is the number for which you
want the absolute value.

	NS2	NS3	NS4	NS6	IE3a	IE3b	IE4	IE5	IE5.5	IE6
acos	x	x	x	x	x	x	x	x	x	x

Returns: Number
Returns the arc cosine of a value, in radians.
Syntax: `Math.acos(value)`, where *value* is the value for which you
want the arc cosine.

	NS2	NS3	NS4	NS6	IE3a	IE3b	IE4	IE5	IE5.5	IE6
asin	x	x	x	x	x	x	x	x	x	x

Returns: Number
Returns the arc sine of a value, in radians.
Syntax: `Math.asin(value)`, where *value* is the value for which you
want the arc sine.

continues ▶

Table 19.3 **Continued**

Method	NS2	NS3	NS4	NS6	IE3a	IE3b	IE4	IE5	IE5.5	IE6
atan	X	X	X	X	X	X	X	X	X	X

Returns: Number
Returns the arc tangent of a value, in radians.
Syntax: `Math.atan(value)`, where *value* is the value for which you want the arc tangent.

Method	NS2	NS3	NS4	NS6	IE3a	IE3b	IE4	IE5	IE5.5	IE6
atan2	X	X	X	X	X	X	X	X	X	X

Returns: Number
Returns the angle (in radians) from the X axis to a point (y, x).
Syntax: `Math.atan2(y, x)`.

Method	NS2	NS3	NS4	NS6	IE3a	IE3b	IE4	IE5	IE5.5	IE6
ceil	X	X	X	X	X	X	X	X	X	X

Returns: Number
Returns the smallest integer greater than or equal to the value you pass.
Syntax: `Math.ceil(value)`, where *value* is the value you want to round up.

Method	NS2	NS3	NS4	NS6	IE3a	IE3b	IE4	IE5	IE5.5	IE6
cos	X	X	X	X	X	X	X	X	X	X

Returns: Number
Returns the cosine of a value.
Syntax: `Math.cos(value)`, where *value* is the value, in radians, for which you want the cosine.

Method	NS2	NS3	NS4	NS6	IE3a	IE3b	IE4	IE5	IE5.5	IE6
exp	X	X	X	X	X	X	X	X	X	X

Returns: Number
Returns e to the power you specify.
Syntax: `Math.exp(value)`, where *value* is the value for which you want e to the power.

Method	NS2	NS3	NS4	NS6	IE3a	IE3b	IE4	IE5	IE5.5	IE6
floor	X	X	X	X	X	X	X	X	X	X

Returns: Number
Returns the greatest integer less than or equal to the value you pass.
Syntax: `Math.floor(value)`, where *value* is the value you want to round down.

Method	NS2	NS3	NS4	NS6	IE3a	IE3b	IE4	IE5	IE5.5	IE6
log	X	X	X	X	X	X	X	X	X	X

Returns: number
Returns the natural log, base e, of a value.
Syntax: `Math.log(value)`, where *value* is the value for which you want the natural log.

Method	NS2	NS3	NS4	NS6	IE3a	IE3b	IE4	IE5	IE5.5	IE6
max	x	x	x	x	x	x	x	x	x	x

Returns: Number
Returns the greater of the two values you pass to it.
Syntax: `Math.max(value1, value2)`, where *value1* and *value2* are the values you're comparing.

min	x	x	x	x	x	x	x	x	x	x

Returns: Number
Returns the lesser of the two values you pass to it.
Syntax: `Math.min(value1, value2)`, where *value1* and *value2* are the values you're comparing.

pow	x	x	x	x	x	x	x	x	x	x

Returns: Number
Returns the value of a base expression raised to a given power.
Syntax: `Math.pow(base, exponent)`.

random	x	x	x	x	x	x	x	x	x	x

Returns: Number
Returns a random number between 0 and 1.
Syntax: `Math.random()`.

round	x	x	x	x	x	x	x	x	x	x

Returns: Number
Returns an numeric expression rounded to the nearest integer.
`Math.round(value)`. If the decimal part of *value* is 0.5 or greater, the return value is the smallest integer that is still greater than *value*. Otherwise, the return value is the largest integer less than or equal to *value*.

sin	x	x	x	x	x	x	x	x	x	x

Returns: Number
Returns the sine of a value.
Syntax: `Math.sin(value)`, where *value* is the value, in radians, for which you want the sine.

sqrt	x	x	x	x	x	x	x	x	x	x

Returns: Number
Returns the square root of a value.
Syntax: `Math.sqrt(value)`, where *value* is the value, in radians, for which you want the square root.

continues ▶

Table 19.3 **Continued**

Method	NS2	NS3	NS4	NS6	IE3a	IE3b	IE4	IE5	IE5.5	IE6
tan	x	x	x	x	x	x	x	x	x	x

Returns: Number

Returns the tangent of a value.

Syntax: `Math.tan(value)`, where *value* is the value, in radians, for which you want the tangent.

Using the *Math* Object

You don't need to create an object of the `Math` type before you use it, you can just use the precreated `Math` object like this, where I'm using the `pow` method to create various powers of 2:

```
dim var1 = Math.pow(2, 10)
dim var2 = Math.pow(2, 11)
dim var3 = Math.pow(2, 12)
```

If you're doing a lot of math calculations, you might want to use the `with` statement (see "The `with` Statement" in Chapter 3, "The JavaScript Language: Loops, Functions, and Errors") so that you don't have to preface the `Math` object's methods with the name `Math`; here's how that might look:

```
with (Math)
{
    dim var1 = pow(2, 10)
    dim var2 = pow(2, 11)
    dim var3 = pow(2, 12)
}
```

I'll take a look at some of the ways of using the `Math` object now.

Performing Calculations

When you need to perform math calculations in JavaScript, you turn to the `Math` object. As you can see in Table 19.3, plenty of math methods built in to this object, from `log` to `exp`, go far beyond the standard JavaScript operators. (See Table 2.3 for the JavaScript operators and what they do.) Here's an example, a simple calculator, which enables the user to calculate all kinds of quantities, from absolute values to cosines at the click of a button:

(Listing 19-01.html on the web site)

```html
<HTML>
    <HEAD>
        <TITLE>
            The Easy Calculator
        </TITLE>
        <SCRIPT LANGUAGE="JavaScript">
            <!--
            function abs()
            {
                document.form1.text1.value = Math.abs(document.form1.text1.value)
            }
            function cos()
            {
                document.form1.text1.value = Math.cos(document.form1.text1.value)
            }
            function exp()
            {
                document.form1.text1.value = Math.exp(document.form1.text1.value)
            }
            function floor()
            {
                document.form1.text1.value = Math.floor(document.form1.text1.value)
            }
            function log()
            {
                document.form1.text1.value = Math.log(document.form1.text1.value)
            }
            function sqrt()
            {
                document.form1.text1.value = Math.sqrt(document.form1.text1.value)
            }
            // -->
        </SCRIPT>
    </HEAD>

    <BODY>
        <H1>The Easy Calculator</H1>
        <FORM NAME="form1">
            <INPUT TYPE="TEXT" NAME="text1">
            <BR>
            <INPUT TYPE="BUTTON" ONCLICK="abs()" VALUE=" Abs ">
            <INPUT TYPE="BUTTON" ONCLICK="cos()" VALUE=" Cos ">
            <INPUT TYPE="BUTTON" ONCLICK="exp()" VALUE=" Exp ">
            <BR>
            <INPUT TYPE="BUTTON" ONCLICK="floor()" VALUE="Floor">
            <INPUT TYPE="BUTTON" ONCLICK="log()" VALUE=" Log ">
            <INPUT TYPE="BUTTON" ONCLICK="sqrt()" VALUE=" Sqrt">
        </FORM>
    </BODY>
</HTML>
```

You can see the results in Figure 19.1.

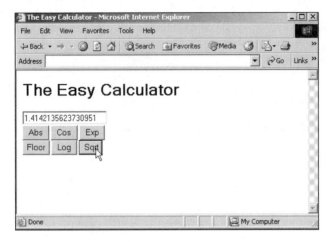

Figure 19.1 The easy calculator.

Random Numbers

You can use the `random` method to create random numbers from 0 to 1, which is great for all kinds of uses, from statistics to games.

> **Tip**
>
> If you need a random number between a and b, you can use the expression a + Math.random() *
> (b - a).

Here's an example. In this case, I'll create a fictitious bar graph that displays a stock projection for several years. I'll assemble the bar graph using a single red piece of a bar, piece.jpg, over and over—the number of times the piece displays in each bar will be set by `Math.random`.

I'll display the bar graph in a `<DIV>` element, `div1`, using the `innerHTML` property of that element (note that this example is targeted to NS6+ and IE4+ because I'm using the `getElementById` method here):

```
function draw()
{
    html = "2003: " + doPieces()
    html += "2004: " + doPieces()
    html += "2005: " + doPieces()
    html += "2006: " + doPieces()
    document.getElementById("div1").innerHTML = html
}
```

The `doPieces` function just assembles each bar in the graph, using `<IMG>` elements, using `Math.random` to determine how many pieces to assemble in each bar:

```
function doPieces()
{
    var piece = "<IMG SRC='piece.jpg'>", text = ""
    var number = Math.floor(5 * Math.random()) + 1
    for (var loopIndex = 0; loopIndex < number; loopIndex++){
        text += piece
    }
    return text + "<BR>"
}
```

You can see the results in Figure 19.2. Click the button a few times to see an entirely different stock projection.

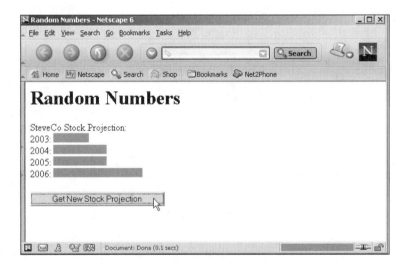

Figure 19.2   Generating a random graph.

Here's the full code for this example:

(Listing 19-02.html on the web site)

```
<HTML>
    <HEAD>
        <TITLE>
            Random Numbers
        </TITLE>
        <SCRIPT LANGUAGE="JavaScript">
            <!--
            function draw()
            {
```

```
                    html = "2003: " + doPieces()
                    html += "2004: " + doPieces()
                    html += "2005: " + doPieces()
                    html += "2006: " + doPieces()
                    document.getElementById("div1").innerHTML = html
                }

            function doPieces()
            {
                var piece = "<IMG SRC='piece.jpg'>", text = ""
                var number = Math.floor(5 * Math.random()) + 1
                for (var loopIndex = 0; loopIndex < number; loopIndex++){
                    text += piece
                }
                return text + "<BR>"
            }
            // -->
        </SCRIPT>
    </HEAD>

    <BODY>
        <H1>Random Numbers</H1>
        SteveCo Stock Projection:
        <FORM NAME="form1">
            <DIV ID="div1"></DIV>
            <BR>
            <INPUT TYPE="BUTTON" ONCLICK="draw()" VALUE="Get New Stock Projection">
        </FORM>
    </BODY>
</HTML>
```

Finding Absolute Values and Rounding Down

Two of the biggest uses for the Math object are finding absolute values and rounding values down, for which you use the abs and floor methods. In fact, we've already seen these methods at work in Chapter 18, "The Date, Time, and String Objects" (Listing 18-03.html), where we subtracted two dates to find the number of days between them:

```
<HTML>
    <HEAD>
        <TITLE>
            Date Subtractor
        </TITLE>
        <SCRIPT LANGUAGE="JavaScript">
            <!--

            function showTime()
            {
                var date1, date2
```

```
                date1 = new Date(document.form1.text1.value)
                date2 = new Date(document.form1.text2.value)
                var difference
                difference = Math.abs(date1.getTime() - date2.getTime())

                document.form1.text3.value =
                    Math.floor(difference / (1000 * 60 * 60 * 24)) + " days"
            }
            // -->
        </SCRIPT>
    </HEAD>

    <BODY>
        <H1>Date Subtractor</H1>
        <FORM NAME="form1">
            <CENTER>
            <INPUT TYPE="TEXT" NAME="text1">
            <BR>
            -
            <BR>
            <INPUT TYPE="TEXT" NAME="text2">
            <BR>
            <INPUT TYPE="BUTTON" ONCLICK="showTime()"
            VALUE="  =  ">
            <BR>
            <INPUT TYPE="TEXT" NAME="text3">
            </CENTER>
        </FORM>
    </BODY>
</HTML>
```

The *Number* Object

As you can guess from its name, the Number object handles numbers. Mostly, there's little need to use this object, because you can just use simple numbers instead, and JavaScript is good at that. In fact, JavaScript creates Number objects from simple numbers automatically as it needs them. It's useful to know the properties and methods of the Number object, however, and you can find them in Table 19.4 in overview, its properties in depth in Table 19.5, and its methods in depth in Table 19.6.

Table 19.4 **Overview of the Properties and Methods of the *Number* Object**

Properties	Methods
constructor	toExponential
MAX_VALUE	toFixed
MIN_VALUE	toLocaleString
NaN	toPrecision
NEGATIVE_INFINITY	toString
POSITIVE_INFINITY	valueOf
Prototype	

Table 19.5 **The Properties of the *Number* Object**

Property	NS2	NS3	NS4	NS6	IE3a	IE3b	IE4	IE5	IE5.5	IE6
constructor			x	x			x	x	x	x

Read/write
This property specifies the function that creates an object.

MAX_VALUE		x	x	x		x	x	x	x	x

Read-only
This property holds the maximum possible numeric value JavaScript can handle, typically about 1.79E+308.

MIN_VALUE		x	x	x		x	x	x	x	x

Read-only
This property holds the minimum possible numeric value JavaScript can handle, typically about 5.00E-324.

NaN		x	x	x		x	x	x	x	x

Read-only
This property, "Not a Number," is a special value that indicates an arithmetic expression returned a value that was not a number.

NEGATIVE_INFINITY x		x	x	x		x	x	x	x	x

Read-only
This property is how JavaScript refers to negative infinity.

POSITIVE_INFINITY x		x	x	x		x	x	x	x	x

Read-only
This property is how JavaScript refers to positive infinity.

Property	NS2	NS3	NS4	NS6	IE3a	IE3b	IE4	IE5	IE5.5	IE6
prototype			x	x			x	x	x	x

Read/write
This property returns a reference to the object's prototype. You use the prototype property to provide base functionality to a class of objects. See "Using the prototype Property" in this chapter.

Table 19.6 **The Methods of the *Number* Object**

Method	NS2	NS3	NS4	NS6	IE3a	IE3b	IE4	IE5	IE5.5	IE6
toExponential				x					x	x

Returns: String
This method returns a string containing a number in exponential form.
Syntax: *number*.toExponential(*digits*), where *digits* is the number of digits after the decimal point.

| toFixed | | | | x | | | | | x | x |

Returns: String
This method returns a string containing the number in fixed-point notation.
Syntax: *number*.toFixed(*digits*), where *digits* is the number of digits after the decimal point.

| toLocaleString | | | | x | | | | | x | x |

Returns: String
This method returns a number converted to a string using the current locale.
Syntax: *number*.toLocaleString().

| toPrecision | | | | x | | | | | x | x |

Returns: String
This method returns a string containing a number in either exponential or fixed-point form with a specified number of digits.
Syntax: *number*.toPrecision(*digits*), where *digits* is the number of significant (total) digits.

| toString | | x | x | x | | | x | x | x | x |

Returns: String
This method returns the number as a string.
Syntax: *number*.toString().

continues ▶

Table 19.6 **Continued**

Method	NS2	NS3	NS4	NS6	IE3a	IE3b	IE4	IE5	IE5.5	IE6
valueOf			x	x			x	x	x	x

Returns: Number

This method returns the value of the number contained by the `Number` object.

Syntax: *number*`.valueOf()`.

Using the *Number* Object

You can create a new `Number` object with the `Number` constructor like this:

```
var number1 = new Number(5)
```

That's all it takes, now you can use the `Number` object's properties and methods. I'll take a look at a few of them here.

Setting Precision

You can set the precision of numeric values with the `setPrecision` method, which sets the total number of significant digits (before and after the decimal place). We've already seen this method at work in Chapter 12, "Working with Forms, Buttons, Check Boxes, and Radio Buttons," when we let the user click radio buttons and check boxes to select the price of a sandwich. All prices were of the form *n.nn*—that is, three significant digits; so to make sure the price had two decimal places, we used `setPrecision(3)`, as you can see (Listing 12-14.html):

```
function displayCost()
{
    var cost = 0

    for (var loopIndex = 0; loopIndex < document.form1.elements.length;
    ➥loopIndex++) {
        if(document.form1.elements[loopIndex].type=="checkbox"
            && document.form1.elements[loopIndex].checked){
            cost += .50
        }
    }
    document.getElementById("div1").innerHTML = "Total cost: $" + cost.toPrecision(3)
}
```

This worked because every price had three significant digits. If the price could be any number of digits, however, we can ensure two decimal places with the toFixed method, which explicitly sets the number of decimal places, like this:

```
function displayCost()
{
    var cost = 0

    for (var loopIndex = 0; loopIndex < document.form1.elements.length;
    ➥loopIndex++) {
        if(document.form1.elements[loopIndex].type=="checkbox"
            && document.form1.elements[loopIndex].checked){
            cost += .50
        }
    }
    document.getElementById("div1").innerHTML = "Total cost: $" + cost.toFixed(2)
}
```

Determining Maximum and Minimum Possible Values

JavaScript is implemented on many different machines and a number of different platforms. If you need to know how big or how small the numbers you can handle in your code can be, check the MAX_VALUE and MIN_VALUE properties of the Number object. (These properties are in capital letters to explicitly indicate that they're constants.) Here's an example that does that, displaying the maximum and minimum numbers you can handle in JavaScript for a particular browser:

(Listing 19-03.html on the web site)

```
<HTML>
    <HEAD>
        <TITLE>
            Maximum and Minimum Values
        </TITLE>
    </HEAD>

    <BODY>
        <H1>Maximum and Minimum Values</H1>
        <FORM NAME="form1">
            <INPUT TYPE="TEXT" NAME="text1" SIZE="40">
            <BR>
            <INPUT TYPE="TEXT" NAME="text2" SIZE="40">
        </FORM>
        <SCRIPT LANGUAGE="JavaScript">
            <!--
            document.form1.text1.value = "Max value = " + Number.MAX_VALUE
            document.form1.text2.value = "Min value = " + Number.MIN_VALUE
            // -->
```

```
        </SCRIPT>
    </BODY>
</HTML>
```

You can see the results in Figure 19.3, where you see the maximum and minimum possible values for the Internet Explorer's JScript implementation.

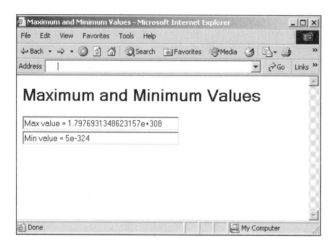

Figure 19.3   Ascertaining maximum and minimum possible numeric values.

Using the *prototype* Property

One of the most useful properties of the `Number` object is the `prototype` property, which enables you to add your own methods to `Number` objects (just like the `prototype` property of `String` objects). When you add a method to a `Number` object in this way, it's added to all `Number` objects.

Here's an example. Suppose that I want to add a method named `sqrt` to all `Number` objects that returned the square root of the number. In this case, you could use that method like this:

```
var n = new Number(5)
var squareRoot = n.sqrt()
```

Here's how to do that. I start by adding a prototype named `sqrt` to all `Number` objects and tying that prototype to a function named `sqRoot`:

```
Number.prototype.sqrt = sqRoot
    .
    .
    .
```

In the `sqRoot` function, I can refer to the current `Number` object with the `this` keyword, and the value stored in the current `Number` object as `this.valueOf()`. That means I can return the square root of the current number like this in the `sqRoot` function:

```
Number.prototype.sqrt = sqRoot

function sqRoot()
{
    return Math.sqrt(this.valueOf())
}
```

Here's how that looks in an example, where the user can enter a number in a text field and click a button to see the square root of that number:

(Listing 19-04.html on the web site)

```
<HTML>
    <HEAD>
        <TITLE>
            Using the prototype Property
        </TITLE>
        <SCRIPT LANGUAGE="JavaScript">
            <!--
            Number.prototype.sqrt = sqRoot

            function sqRoot()
            {
                return Math.sqrt(this.valueOf())
            }

            function display()
            {
                var n = new Number(document.form1.text1.value)
                document.form1.text1.value = n.sqrt()
            }
            // -->
        </SCRIPT>
    </HEAD>

    <BODY>
        <H1>Using the prototype Property</H1>
        <FORM NAME="form1">
            <INPUT TYPE="TEXT" NAME="text1">
            <INPUT TYPE="BUTTON" ONCLICK="display()" VALUE="Get the Square Root">
        </FORM>
    </BODY>
</HTML>
```

You can see the results in Figure 19.4, where I'm finding the square root of 5.

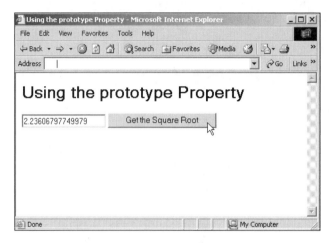

Figure 19.4   Using the `prototype` property.

As you can imagine, the `prototype` property is very useful when you want to augment objects such as `String` or `Number`.

The *Boolean* Object

As its name makes clear, the `Boolean` object handles Boolean values. There's not really a great deal to this object, but we should cover it for the sake of completeness. You can see the properties of the Boolean object in Table 19.7 and its methods in Table 19.8.

Table 19.7   **The Properties of the *Boolean* Object**

Property	NS2	NS3	NS4	NS6	IE3a	IE3b	IE4	IE5	IE5.5	IE6
constructor		x	x	x		x	x	x	x	x

Read/write
This property specifies the function that creates an object.

prototype		x	x	x		x	x	x	x	x

Read/write
This property returns a reference to the object's prototype. You use the `prototype` property to provide base functionality to a class of objects. See "Using the `prototype` Property" in this chapter.

Table 19.8 **The Methods of the *Boolean* Object**

Method	NS2	NS3	NS4	NS6	IE3a	IE3b	IE4	IE5	IE5.5	IE6
toString		X	X	X		X	X	X	X	X

Returns: String
This method returns the string "true" or "false" to match the
Boolean value of the object.
Syntax: *boolean*.toString().

valueOf		X	X	X		X	X	X	X	X

Returns: Number
This method returns a Boolean value of true or false to match the
Boolean value of the object.
Syntax: *boolean*.valueOf().

Using the *Boolean* Object

You can create Boolean objects with the Boolean constructor, passing a value
of true or false to initialize the object, like this:

```
var boolean1 = new Boolean(true)
```

You can then assign new true or false values to the Boolean object:

```
var boolean1 = new Boolean(true)
boolean1 = false
```

Here's an example. In this case, I'll create a new Boolean object and toggle it
between true and false when the user clicks a button using the JavaScript not
operator, ! (see Table 2.3 and the section "Logical Operators" in Chapter 2,
"The JavaScript Language: Data, Operators, and Branching," for more on the
! operator), which flips the logical sense of its argument:

```
var boolean1 = new Boolean(true)

function toggler()
{
    document.form1.text1.value = "boolean1 = " + boolean1.valueOf()
    boolean1 = !boolean1
}
```

Here's what this code looks like in the full example:

(Listing 19-05.html on the web site)

```
<HTML>
    <HEAD>
        <TITLE>
```

continues ▶

```
        Toggling Boolean Values
      </TITLE>
      <SCRIPT LANGUAGE="JavaScript">
        <!--
        var boolean1 = new Boolean(true)

        function toggler()
        {
            document.form1.text1.value = "boolean1 = " + boolean1.valueOf()
            ➡boolean1 = !boolean1
        }
        // -->
      </SCRIPT>
    </HEAD>

    <BODY>
      <H1>Toggling Boolean Values</H1>
      <FORM NAME="form1">
          <INPUT TYPE="TEXT" NAME="text1">
          <INPUT TYPE="BUTTON" ONCLICK="toggler()" VALUE="Click Me!">
      </FORM>
    </BODY>
</HTML>
```

You can see the results in Figure 19.5, where the value of the Boolean variable flips logical sense from true to false and back again each time you click the button.

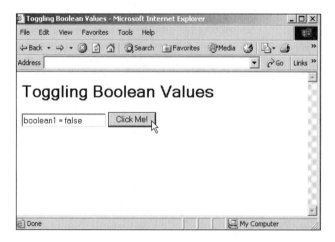

Figure 19.5 Toggling a Boolean object's logical value.

The *Array* Object

We've already seen the `Array` object in Chapter 2 (see the section "Arrays" in Chapter 2), but we haven't taken an in-depth look at the `Array` object itself. We'll do that here. You can see an overview of the properties and methods of the `Array` object in Table 19.9, its properties in depth in Table 19.10, and its methods in depth in Table 19.11.

Table 19.9 Overview of the Properties and Methods of the *Array* Object

Properties	Methods
constructor	concat
length	join
prototype	pop
	push
	reverse
	shift
	slice
	sort
	splice
	toLocaleString
	toString
	unshift

Table 19.10 The Properties of the *Array* Object

Property	NS2	NS3	NS4	NS6	IE3a	IE3b	IE4	IE5	IE5.5	IE6
constructor		x	x	x		x	x	x	x	x

Read/write
This property specifies the function that creates an object.

length		x	x	x		x	x	x	x	x

Read/write
This property holds an integer value one higher than the index of the highest element in an array. Note that because elements don't have to be contiguous, this property does not technically have to reflect the total number of elements in an array!

continues ▶

Table 19.10 **Continued**

Property	NS2	NS3	NS4	NS6	IE3a	IE3b	IE4	IE5	IE5.5	IE6
prototype		X	X	X		X	X	X	X	X

Read/write
This property returns a reference to the object's prototype. You use the
prototype property to provide base functionality to a class of objects.
See "Using the prototype Property" in this chapter.

Table 19.11 **The Methods of the *Array* Object**

Method	NS2	NS3	NS4	NS6	IE3a	IE3b	IE4	IE5	IE5.5	IE6
concat			X	X			X	X	X	X

Returns: Array object
This method concatenates (joins) two arrays together and returns
the result.
Syntax: *array1*.concat(*array2*).

join		X	X	X		X	X	X	X	X

Returns: String
This method returns a string holding all the elements of an array joined
together, separated by a separator string.
Syntax: *array*.join(*separator*), where *separator* is the separator string
you want to appear between elements in the returned string.

pop			X	X					X	X

Returns: Array entry
This method "pops" the array by removing the last element from an
array and returning it. See "Pushing and Popping" in this chapter.
Syntax: *array*.pop().

push			X	X					X	X

Returns: Array entry
This method "pushes" a new element or elements onto an array by
appending them to the end of the array and returning the new length
of the array.
Syntax: *array*.push(*item1* [, *item2* ... [, *itemN*]]). See "Pushing
and Popping" in this chapter.

reverse		X	X	X		X	X	X	X	X

Returns: Array object
This method returns the array with the order of the elements reversed.
Syntax: *array*.reverse().

Method	NS2	NS3	NS4	NS6	IE3a	IE3b	IE4	IE5	IE5.5	IE6
shift			X	X					X	X

Returns: Array entry
This method removes the first element of an array and returns that element.
Syntax: *array*.shift().

| slice | | | X | X | | | X | X | X | X |

Returns: Array object
This method returns a slice, or section, of an array.
Syntax: *array*.slice(*start*, *end*); where *start* is the beginning index of the slice, and *end* is the ending index of the slice.

| sort | X | X | X | | X | X | X | X | X | X |

Returns: Array object
This method sorts an array.
Syntax: *array*.sort([*function*]); where *function* is a function that returns a negative value if the first argument passed to it is less than the second argument (according to the way you want to sort the items), zero if the two arguments are equal, and a positive value if the first argument is greater than the second argument. If you omit *function*, the array is sorted in ascending text order. See "Sorting Arrays" in this chapter.

| splice | | | X | X | | | | | X | X |

Returns: Array object
This method removes elements from an array and can also insert new elements. This method returns the deleted elements.
Syntax: *array*.splice(*start*, *count* [,*item1* [, *item2* [, ... [, *itemN*]]]]); where *start* is the location at which to start deleting elements, *count* is the number of elements to delete, and *item1* to *itemN* are elements to insert to replace the deleted elements.

| toLocaleString | | | | X | | | | | X | X |

Returns: String
This method returns the array in locale-sensitive string form.
Syntax: *array*.toLocaleString().

| toString | X | X | X | | X | X | X | X | X | X |

Returns: String
This method returns the array in string form.
Syntax: *array*.toString().

continues ▶

Table 19.11   **Continued**

Method	NS2	NS3	NS4	NS6	IE3a	IE3b	IE4	IE5	IE5.5	IE6
unshift			X	X					X	X

Returns: Array entry

This method returns the array with the given elements inserted at the beginning.

Syntax: *array*.unshift((*[item1*[, *item2* [, ... [, *itemN*]]]])),
where *item1* to *itemN* are elements to insert at the start of the array.

Using the *Array* Object

You can create a new array in a variety of ways using the Array constructor:

```
var array1 = new Array()             //Creates an empty array
var array1 = new Array([size])
var array1 = new Array([element0 [, element1[, ... [, elementN]]]])
```

Here are the arguments I'm using in this code:

- **size.** The size of the new array.

- **element0 to elementN.** The elements to put into the array, initializing it. This creates an array with N + 1 elements.

We've seen how to work with arrays in Chapter 2, but I'm going to take a look at working with Array objects in more detail now.

Initializing Arrays

You can initialize an array by providing a list of elements that you want in the array, like this:

```
var array1 = new Array([element0 [, element1[, ... [, elementN]]]])
```

This initializes element 0 through element N of the array. In fact, as of NS4+ and IE4+, you can just use the [] array constructor, which is just a pair of square brackets, like this:

```
var array1 = [element0, element1, ... elementN]
```

As mentioned in Chapter 2, you also can use names to refer to elements in an array, like this:

```
array1["name"] = "Ralph"
```

In fact, you can even use this syntax:

```
array1.name = "Ralph"
```

Or this syntax to store `"Ralph"` as element 4 in an array:

```
array1.4 = "Ralph"
```

> **Tip**
>
> What if you try to create a new array with the expression new `Array(1)`? Up to NS3 and IE4, that expression created an array of length 1, where the single element was undefined. Now it creates an array of length 1, where the single element is set to 1.

Sorting Arrays

You can use the `sort` method to sort arrays. Here's an example, where I'm sorting an array containing the names `"Ralph"`, `"Ed"`, `"Alice"`, and `"Trixie"`:

(Listing 19-06.html on the web site)

```html
<HTML>
    <HEAD>
        <TITLE>
            Sorting Arrays
        </TITLE>
    </HEAD>

    <BODY>
        <H1>Sorting Arrays</H1>
        <FORM NAME="form1">
            <TEXTAREA NAME="textarea1" ROWS="4"></TEXTAREA>
        </FORM>
        <SCRIPT LANGUAGE="JavaScript">
            <!--
            var array1 = new Array("Ralph", "Ed", "Alice", "Trixie")

            array1.sort()

            for(var loopIndex = 0; loopIndex < array1.length; loopIndex++){
                document.form1.textarea1.value += array1[loopIndex] + "\n"
            }
            // -->
        </SCRIPT>
    </BODY>
</HTML>
```

You can see the results in Figure 19.6, where the elements `"Ralph"`, `"Ed"`, `"Alice"`, and `"Trixie"` have been sorted in ascending text order.

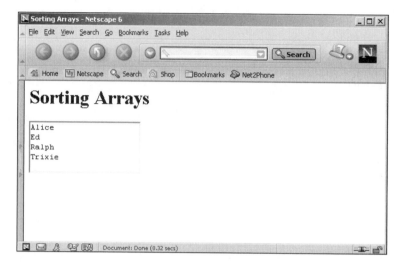

Figure 19.6 Sorting an array.

You also can define the sort order yourself if you supply a custom sorting function. If you use a sorting function, it must return one of the following values:

- A negative value if the first value passed to the function is less than the second value in the sorting order you want.

- A positive value if the first value passed to the function is greater than the second value.

- Zero if the two values are equal.

Using the values you return from this sorting function, JavaScript can sort the elements in the array in the order you want.

Instead of sorting the elements in an array in ascending text order, for example, I could sort them in reverse order by supplying a sorting function, which I'll call reverser:

```
array1.sort(reverser)
```

Here's the reverser function, which reverses the normal sort order:

```
function reverser(a, b)
{
    if(a < b) return 1
    if(a > b) return -1
    return 0
}
```

You can see the results in Figure 19.7, where you see the array sorted in reverse order. Using sort functions like this, you can create all kinds of sorts on all kinds of data items, including objects.

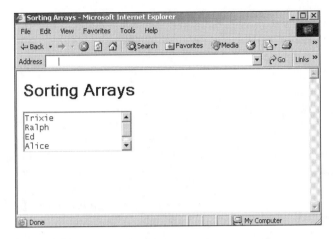

Figure 19.7   Sorting an array in reverse order.

Here's the code for this example:

(Listing 19-07.html on the web site)

```
<HTML>
    <HEAD>
        <TITLE>
            Sorting Arrays
        </TITLE>
    </HEAD>

    <BODY>
        <H1>Sorting Arrays</H1>
        <FORM NAME="form1">
            <TEXTAREA NAME="textarea1" ROWS="4"></TEXTAREA>
        </FORM>
        <SCRIPT LANGUAGE="JavaScript">
            <!--
            var array1 = new Array("Ralph", "Ed", "Alice", "Trixie")

            array1.sort(reverser)

            for(var loopIndex = 0; loopIndex < array1.length; loopIndex++){
                document.form1.textarea1.value += array1[loopIndex] + "\n"
            }
```

continues ▶

```
function reverser(a, b)
{
    if(a < b) return 1
    if(a > b) return -1
    return 0
}
// -->
</SCRIPT>
</BODY>
</HTML>
```

Multidimensional Arrays

Inherently, JavaScript `Array` objects are one-dimensional—that is, all the elements in the array are indexed with one index value alone. However, you can create multidimensional arrays by creating an *array of arrays.*

What does that mean? Let's see an example. Suppose that I want to create an array that's 4-by-3 (that is, four rows and three columns). Each row can store a first name, a last name, and an ID number. We can create such an array by making each element in that array an array itself. Here's how you can do that, where we're creating an array of arrays:

```
var array1 = [new Array("Ralph",  "Kramden", 1),
    new Array("Ed",     "Norton",  2),
    new Array("Alice",  "Kramden", 3),
    new Array("Trixie", "Norton",  4)]
```

If you're using a recent browser (NS4+ and IE4+), you can use the `[]` array constructor like this:

```
var array1 = [["Ralph",  "Kramden", 1],
    ["Ed",     "Norton",  2],
    ["Alice",  "Kramden", 3],
    ["Trixie", "Norton",  4]]
```

That makes it clear how we're setting up and initializing this two-dimensional array—as four rows of three columns each. Each row is itself a subarray of the main array.

So how do you address an element in a multidimensional array like this? You can use the syntax `array[row][column];` where *row* is the row, and *column* is the column of the element you're addressing. If we want to load the first and last names from the array `array1` we just created into a `<SELECT>` control, `select1`, for example, the code to do so might look like this:

```
document.form1.select1.options[0].text = array1[0][0] +
    " " + array1[0][1]
document.form1.select1.options[1].text = array1[1][0] +
    " " + array1[1][1]
```

```
document.form1.select1.options[2].text = array1[2][0] +
    " " + array1[2][1]
document.form1.select1.options[3].text = array1[3][0] +
    " " + array1[3][1]
```

Here's an example that uses this code and loads the first and last names from our array into a <SELECT> control; when the user clicks one of the items in the <SELECT> control, we can display that person's ID value in a text field like this:

(Listing 19-08.html on the web site)

```
<HTML>
    <HEAD>
        <TITLE>
            Creating Multi-dimensional Arrays
        </TITLE>
    </HEAD>

    <BODY>
        <H1>Creating Multi-dimensional Arrays</H1>
        <FORM NAME="form1">
            <SELECT NAME="select1" ONCHANGE="reportID(this.selectedIndex)">
                <OPTION NAME="option1">
                <OPTION NAME="option2">
                <OPTION NAME="option3">
                <OPTION NAME="option4">
            </SELECT>
            <BR>
            <INPUT TYPE="TEXT" NAME="text1">
        </FORM>
        <SCRIPT LANGUAGE="JavaScript">
            <!--
            var array1 = [["Ralph",  "Kramden", 1],
                          ["Ed",     "Norton",  2],
                          ["Alice",  "Kramden", 3],
                          ["Trixie", "Norton",  4]]

            document.form1.select1.options[0].text = array1[0][0] +
                " " + array1[0][1]
            document.form1.select1.options[1].text = array1[1][0] +
                " " + array1[1][1]
            document.form1.select1.options[2].text = array1[2][0] +
                " " + array1[2][1]
            document.form1.select1.options[3].text = array1[3][0] +
                " " + array1[3][1]

            function reportID(id)
            {
                document.form1.text1.value = "That person's ID is " + (id + 1)
            }
            // -->
        </SCRIPT>
    </BODY>
</HTML>
```

You can see the results in Figure 19.8.

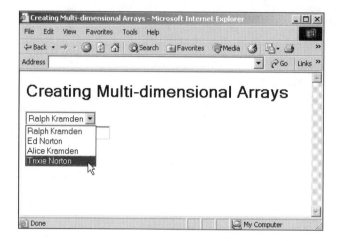

Figure 19.8   Creating multidimensional arrays.

Pushing and Popping

Another popular programming operation when handling arrays is to *push* and *pop* elements. Pushing an element appends it to the end of the array, and popping it removes it from the end of the array.

Here's an example. In this case, I'll just push six numbers, 0 to 5, onto an array with the push method:

```
document.form1.text1.value = "Pushing "
for(var loopIndex = 0; loopIndex <= 5; loopIndex++){
    document.form1.text1.value += loopIndex + ", "
    array1.push(loopIndex)
}
```

Next I'll pop them off the array with pop. Note that they'll come off the array in reverse order, because you push elements onto the end of the array and also pop them from the end of the array:

```
document.form1.text2.value = "Popping "
for(var loopIndex = 0; loopIndex <= 5; loopIndex++){
    document.form1.text2.value += array1.pop() + ", "
}
```

Tip

Pushing and popping like this enables you to simulate programming constructions called *stacks*. Want to work with the start of the array rather than the end? Use shift and unshift, not push and pop. See Table 19.10.

Here's the full code for this example, which pushes elements onto an array and displays the pushed elements, and then pops them and displays them in the order they come off the array. All operations are displayed in text fields:

(Listing 19-09.html on the web site)

```html
<HTML>
    <HEAD>
        <TITLE>
            Pushing and Popping
        </TITLE>
    </HEAD>

    <BODY>
        <H1>Pushing and Popping</H1>
        <FORM NAME="form1">
            <INPUT TYPE="TEXT" NAME="text1">
            <BR>
            <INPUT TYPE="TEXT" NAME="text2">
        </FORM>
        <SCRIPT LANGUAGE="JavaScript">
            <!--
            var array1 = new Array()

            document.form1.text1.value = "Pushing "
            for(var loopIndex = 0; loopIndex <= 5; loopIndex++){
                document.form1.text1.value += loopIndex + ", "
                array1.push(loopIndex)
            }

            document.form1.text2.value = "Popping "
            for(var loopIndex = 0; loopIndex <= 5; loopIndex++){
                document.form1.text2.value += array1.pop() + ", "
            }
            // -->
        </SCRIPT>
    </BODY>
</HTML>
```

You can see the results in Figure 19.9.

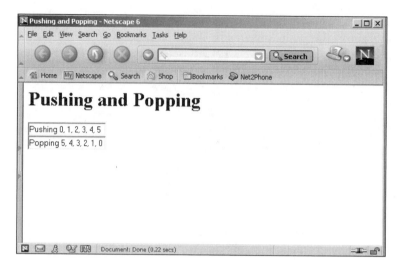

Figure 19.9 Pushing and popping elements in an array.

That's it for our work with the Math, Number, Boolean, and Array objects in this chapter. As you can see, there's plenty of programming support in these utility objects. In the next chapter, we're going to work with something we've already come across in the preceding chapter: regular expressions, which enable you to search through and handle text expressions.

20

The *RegExp* Object: Working with Regular Expressions

O NE OF THE POWERFUL ASPECTS OF JAVASCRIPT is its capability to work with text. Ever since Internet Explorer 4.0 and Netscape Navigator 4.0, that has been augmented by being able to work with *regular expressions*. Regular expressions enable you to handle not only text strings as variables, but also work with the text content of those strings.

Using a regular expression, you can specify what kind of text substrings you want to match and work with. For example, here's how I'm using the regular expression /[aeiou]/ to search text in a text field for vowels, and if any vowels are found, to display the message Yes, we got vowels! in a text field:

(Listing 20-01.html on the web site)

```
<HTML>
    <HEAD>
        <TITLE>Checking for Vowels</TITLE>
        <SCRIPT LANGUAGE="JavaScript">
            <!--
            function checkVowels()
            {
                var regexp = /[aeiou]/

                var matches = regexp.exec(document.form1.text1.value)

                if (matches) {
                    document.form1.text2.value = "Yes, we got vowels!"
                } else {
```

```
            document.form1.text2.value = "Sorry, no vowels!"
        }
    }
    //-->
    </SCRIPT>
</HEAD>

<BODY>
    <H1>Checking for Vowels</H1>
    <FORM NAME="form1">
        Type some text:
        <BR>
        <INPUT TYPE="TEXT" NAME="text1">
        <BR>
        <INPUT TYPE="BUTTON" VALUE="Check for Vowels" ONCLICK="checkVowels()">
        <BR>
        <INPUT TYPE="text" NAME="text2" SIZE="30">
    </FORM>
</BODY>
</HTML>
```

You can see the results of this code in Figure 20.1, where the code has determined that there are indeed vowels present.

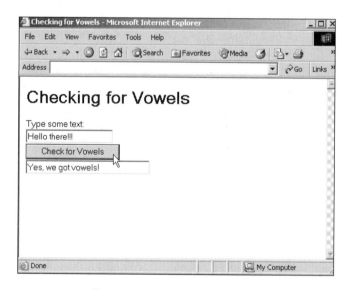

Figure 20.1   Checking for vowels.

This chapter shows you how to work with regular expressions such as /[aeiou]/ in JavaScript. There are two primary ways to use regular expressions: to find matches and to replace text. I'll cover both of them first, and then we'll take a look at how to create regular expressions themselves (which can get pretty involved).

Finding Matches

Finding matches is all about searching text. You create a regular expression, also called a *pattern*, and then see whether that pattern matches any of the text you're searching. You can use regular expressions in JavaScript to find matches in several ways:

- **The String object's match method.** This method finds regular expression matches in a string.
  Syntax: *string*.match(*regExp*). Returns an array of matches or null if there were no matches. See Chapter 18, "The Date, Time, and String Objects," for more information.

- **The String object's search method.** This method returns the position of the *first* substring match in a regular expression search.
  Syntax: *string*.search(*regExp*), where *regExp* is the regular expression to match. See Chapter 18 for more information.

- **The regular expression's exec method.** Like the String object's match method, this method finds regular expression matches in a string.
  Syntax: *regularExpression*.exec(*string*), where *string* is the string you're searching. Returns an array of matches or null if there were no matches.

For example, we've already seen the match method at work in Chapter 18 (in Listing 18-05.html). In that example, I only allowed the user to enter date strings that are made up of one or two digits, followed by a slash (/), followed by one or two digits, followed by a slash, followed by two or four digits for the year. To do that, I used two regular expressions (we'll see how to create these regular expressions later in the chapter) and the match method; if both match expressions returned null, no valid dates were found:

```
<HTML>
    <HEAD>
        <TITLE>Checking Dates</TITLE>
        <SCRIPT LANGUAGE="JavaScript">
            <!--
            function checker()
            {
```

continues ▶

```
var regExp1 = /^(\d{1,2})\/(\d{1,2})\/(\d{2})$/
var regExp2 = /^(\d{1,2})\/(\d{1,2})\/(\d{4})$/
var resultArray1 = document.form1.text1.value.match(regExp1)
var resultArray2 = document.form1.text1.value.match(regExp2)
if (resultArray1 == null && resultArray2 == null) {
    alert("Sorry, that's not in valid date format.")
} else {
    alert("That's in valid date format.")
}
        }
        //-->
    </SCRIPT>
</HEAD>

<BODY>
    <H1>Checking Dates</H1>
    <FORM NAME="form1">
        <INPUT TYPE="TEXT" NAME="text1"></INPUT>
        <INPUT TYPE="BUTTON" VALUE="Check Date" ONCLICK="checker()">
    </FORM>
</BODY>
</HTML>
```

You can see the results in Chapter 18, in Figure 18.5. This brings up a question: If there were indeed matches to a regular expression, how do you get the matching text? In other words, how do you find out which substrings in the text you're searching for matched your regular expression?

If your regular expression matches any substring in the searched string, you get an array holding of those matches. To search for words that use only lower case letters, for example, you can use the regular expression /\b[^A-Z]+\b/ (which means "word boundary followed by one or more characters that don't include any upper case letters, followed by a word boundary"). We'll see how to create this regular expression in this chapter. Here's an example that puts this regular expression to work, using the `exec` method, returning an array of the lower case words in the text `JavaScript is the subject.`:

(Listing 20-02.html on the web site)

```
<HTML>
    <HEAD>
        <TITLE>Getting Lower Case Words</TITLE>
        <SCRIPT LANGUAGE="JavaScript">
            <!--
            function getLowers()
            {
                var regexp = /\b[^A-Z]+\b/

                var matches = regexp.exec(document.form1.text1.value)
```

```
        if (matches) {
            for (var loopIndex = 0; loopIndex < matches.length; loopIndex++){
                document.form1.text2.value += matches[loopIndex] + " "
            }
        } else {
            document.form1.text2.value = "Sorry, no lower case words."
        }
    }
    //-->
  </SCRIPT>
</HEAD>

<BODY>
    <H1>Getting Lower Case Words</H1>
    <FORM NAME="form1">
        <INPUT TYPE="TEXT" NAME="text1" VALUE="JavaScript is the subject."
        ➥SIZE="30">
        <BR>
        <INPUT TYPE="BUTTON" VALUE="Get Lower Case Words" ONCLICK="getLowers()">
        <BR>
        <INPUT TYPE="text" NAME="text2" SIZE="30">
    </FORM>
</BODY>
</HTML>
```

You can see the results of this code in Figure 20.2, where the code is display-ing all the lower case words by looping over the array returned by the exec method.

That technique is fine if your regular expression is intended to be used over and over to find a number of matches, as was the case in this example. However, you also can use regular expressions that have various *submatches*.

Suppose, for example, that you want to extract the month, day, and year from a "MM/DD/YYYY" string. You can use one regular expression to match each of those three items. In this case, I'll match the date in "MM/DD/YYYY" format using the regular expression (we'll see how to create regular expres-sions like this in this chapter):

```
var regexp = /^(0?[1-9]|1[0-2])\/(0?[1-9]|[12][0-9]|3[01])\/((18|19|20)\d{2})$/
```

Note the parentheses, which I've placed around parts of the regular expression that I want to treat as submatches. The first expression in parentheses is (0?[1-9]|1[0-2]), which will match the month; the next is (0?[1-9]|[12] [0-9]|3[01]), which matches the day; and the last is ((18|19|20)\d{2}), which matches the year. (The parentheses around (18|19|20) are to match either 18, 19, or 20 as the first two digits of the year, and are not used for submatches, as discussed later in this chapter.) Because these expressions are enclosed in paren-theses, we can access the text they matched. (Such text is called a *submatch*.)

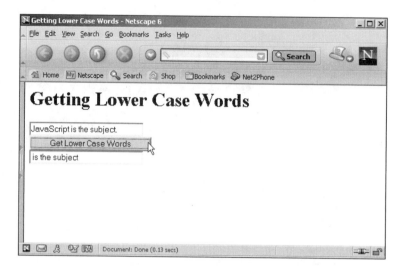

Figure 20.2   Getting matches to a regular expression.

Suppose, for example, that I use this regular expression with the date "09/02/1957". The exec method will return an array with the matches to our regular expression. The first element in the array will be the match to the entire regular expression ("09/02/1957"), the next will be the match to the expression in the first set of parentheses ("09"), the next will be the match to the expression in the second set of parentheses ("02"), and the last will be the match to the expression in the third set of parentheses ("1957"). Here's an example putting this all to work by extracting the parts of a date the user has entered:

(Listing 20-03.html on the web site)

```
<HTML>
    <HEAD>
        <TITLE>Getting Match Data</TITLE>
        <SCRIPT LANGUAGE="JavaScript">
            <!--
            function getDate()
            {
                var regexp = /^(0?[1-9]|1[0-2])\/(0?[1-9]|[12]
            ➥[0-9]|3[01])\/((18|19|20)\d{2})$/

                var matches = regexp.exec(document.form1.text1.value)

                if (matches) {
                    var month = matches[1]
                    var date = matches[2]
                    var year = matches[3]
```

```
                    document.form1.text2.value = "Month: " + month +
                        " Day: " + date + " Year: " + year

                }
            }
            //-->
        </SCRIPT>
    </HEAD>

    <BODY>
        <H1>Getting Match Data</H1>
        <FORM NAME="form1">
            Type a date (MM/DD/YYYY):
            <BR>
            <INPUT TYPE="TEXT" NAME="text1">
            <BR>
            <INPUT TYPE="BUTTON" VALUE="Get Date" ONCLICK="getDate()">
            <BR>
            <INPUT TYPE="text" NAME="text2" SIZE="30">
        </FORM>
    </BODY>
</HTML>
```

You can see the results of this code in Figure 20.3, where we're able to dissect a date into its component parts using parenthesized submatches.

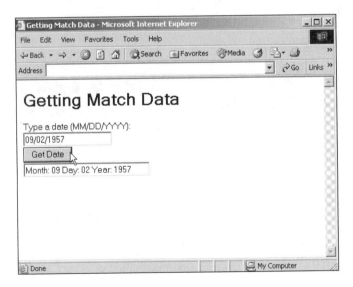

Figure 20.3 Dissecting a date.

Replacing Text

Besides searching for matches to regular expressions, you also can use them
to replace text, using the String object's replace method:

- **The String object's replace method.** This method replaces substrings
  with a new string. Syntax: string.replace(*regExp*, *replacementText*);
  where *regExp* is a regular expression, and *replacementText* replaces
  matches to *regExp*. (All matches are replaced if *regExp* includes the g
  modifier.) See Chapter 18 for more information.

We saw an example of this method in Chapter 18. In that example, we
searched for the text *is* in the phrase "Now is the time" and replaced it with
the text *isn't*. Here's what the code looked like (Listing 18-11.html on the
web site); the g modifier in the regular expression makes the search-and-
replace operation global, which makes it match all occurrences of *is* in the
searched string:

```
<HTML>
    <HEAD>
        <TITLE>
            Replacing Text
        </TITLE>
        <SCRIPT LANGUAGE="JavaScript">
            <!--
            function replacer()
            {
                var regExp = /is/g
                var text = document.form1.text1.value.replace(regExp, "isn't")
                document.form1.text1.value = text
            }
            // -->
        </SCRIPT>
    </HEAD>

    <BODY>
        <H1>Replacing Text</H1>
        <FORM NAME="form1">
            <INPUT TYPE="TEXT" NAME="text1" VALUE="Now is the time">
            <BR>
            <INPUT TYPE="BUTTON" ONCLICK="replacer()" VALUE="Replace Text">
        </FORM>
    </BODY>
</HTML>
```

You can see the results of this code in Chapter 18, in Figure 18.11, where
we've changed "Now is the time" to "Now isn't the time".

Those are the two ways to use regular expressions in JavaScript: to search text and to replace text. However, the actual syntax of regular expressions is still mysterious at this point. How on earth do you actually create—much less understand—an expression such as `/^(0?[1-9]|1[0-2])\/(0?` `[1-9]|[12][0-9]|3[01])\/((18|19|20)\d{2})$/`? I'll take a look at how you create regular expressions now.

Creating Regular Expressions

In JavaScript, regular expressions are expressions enclosed between forward slashes (/), such as the ones we've already seen (for instance, `/\b[^A-Z]+\b/`); they also can be followed by modifier characters outside the last slash (for instance, `/\b[^A-Z]+\b/g`, which uses the g modifier to make a search global). In general, such regular expressions can be made up of these parts:

- Characters
- Character classes
- Alternative match patterns
- Quantifiers
- Assertions
- Backreferences
- Regular expression extensions

The following sections discuss all of these parts. Note that regular expressions can get very complex very quickly, and that they're very, very compact. They'll often take some patience to work with until you become an expert. I'll start by taking a look at characters in regular expressions.

Regular Expressions: Characters

In a regular expression, any single character matches itself (unless it is a special character such as $ or ^, as we'll see later, because those characters have special meaning). For example, I can check whether the user has typed the word *exit*, by matching to the regular expression `/exit/`—and if so, display a message:

```
function checker()
{
    var regexp = /exit/
    var matches = document.form1.text1.value.match(regexp)
    document.form1.text2.value = "You typed exit."
}
```

In fact, it may be a good idea to make sure that the user typed only *exit*, and not, for example, *Don't exit!!!*. We can do that by making sure that the text we're checking contains *exit* and nothing else. We can do that with the regular expression /^exit$/i. The special character ^ matches the beginning of a line of text, the character $ matches the end of a line of text, and the i modifier makes the match non-case-sensitive (so the user could type *exit*, *EXIT*, *ExIt*, and so on). In this way, you see how to build a regular expression—piece by piece, left to right. Here's how we match the beginning of the line, followed by *exit*, followed by the end of the line:

```
function checker()
{
    var regexp = /^exit$/i
    var matches = document.form1.text1.value.match(regexp)
    document.form1.text2.value = "You typed exit."
}
```

Besides normal characters, JavaScript defines these special characters that you can use in regular expressions. Note that you "escape" these characters by starting them with a backslash:

- **\077** Octal character code
- **\a** Alarm (bell)
- **\cX** Control character (\cX is ^X, \cC is ^C, and so on)
- **\d** Match a digit character
- **\D** Match a non-digit character
- **\f** Form feed
- **\n** Newline
- **\r** Return
- **\S** Match a non-whitespace character
- **\s** Match a whitespace character
- **\t** Tab
- **\w** Match a word character (alphanumeric characters and "_")
- **\W** Match a non-word character
- **\x1A** Hex character code 1A

In general, if you preface a character with a backslash, JavaScript will treat the character as itself and not try to interpret it as a special code of any kind. If you really want to match a dollar sign and not the end of a line, for example, use \$, not $.

Note some of the useful characters here—such as \w, which matches a word character. Note that a \w matches only *one* alphanumeric character, not a whole word. To match a word, you need to match one or more word characters with the expression \w+; here, the plus sign (+) means "one or more match." (See the section, "Regular Expressions: Quantifiers," for more on how to use the plus sign.). For example, here is how we can match the first word in the text "Here is the text." and replace that word (that is, *Here*) with *There*:

(Listing 20-04.html on the web site)

```
<HTML>
    <HEAD>
        <TITLE>Replacing Words</TITLE>
        <SCRIPT LANGUAGE="JavaScript">
            <!--
                function displayer()
                {
                    var regexp = /\w+/
                    document.form1.text2.value =
                    ↵document.form1.text1.value.replace(regexp, "There")
                }
            //-->
        </SCRIPT>
    </HEAD>

    <BODY>
        <H1>Replacing Words</H1>
        <FORM NAME="form1">
            <INPUT TYPE="TEXT" NAME="text1" VALUE="Here is the text.">
            <BR>
            <INPUT TYPE="BUTTON" VALUE="Replace First Word" ONCLICK="displayer()">
            <BR>
            <INPUT TYPE="TEXT" NAME="text2">
        </FORM>
    </BODY>
</HTML>
```

You can see the results of this code in Figure 20.4, where we're replacing the first word in the typed text (from *Here* to *There*).

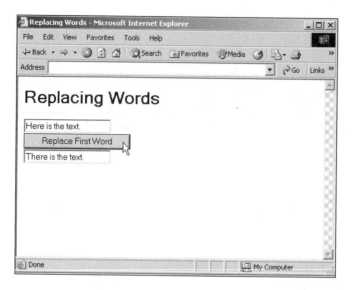

Figure 20.4   Replacing a word.

Matching Any Character

A very powerful character that you can use in regular expressions is the dot (.). This character matches *any* character except a newline (\n). For example, I can substitute an asterisk (*) for all the characters in the string "JavaScript is the subject." like this, where I'm making the substitution operation global with the g modifier:

(Listing 20-05.html on the web site)

```
<HTML>
    <HEAD>
        <TITLE>Replacing Characters</TITLE>
        <SCRIPT LANGUAGE="JavaScript">
            <!--
                function replacer()
                {
                    var regexp = /./g
                    document.form1.text2.value =
                    ➥document.form1.text1.value.replace(regexp, "*")
                }
            //-->
        </SCRIPT>
    </HEAD>

    <BODY>
        <H1>Replacing Characters</H1>
        <FORM NAME="form1">
```

```
                <INPUT TYPE="TEXT" NAME="text1" VALUE="JavaScript is the subject."
                ➥SIZE="30">
                <BR>
                <INPUT TYPE="BUTTON" VALUE="Replace All Text" ONCLICK="replacer()">
                <BR>
                <INPUT TYPE="TEXT" NAME="text2" SIZE="30">
            </FORM>
        </BODY>
    </HTML>
```

You can see the results of this code in Figure 20.5, where we're replacing all the text "JavaScript is the subject." with asterisks.

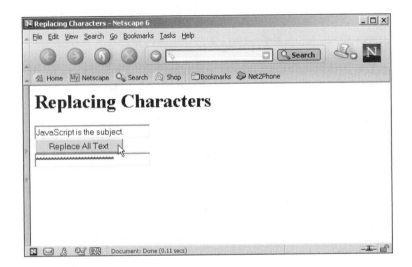

Figure 20.5   Replacing text.

What if you really want to match a dot (that is, a period)? Characters that have special meaning, such as the dot, are called *metacharacters* (the metacharacters are: \ | ( ) [{ ^ $ ★ + ? .), and you can preface any of them with a backslash to make them be interpreted literally and not as a metacharacter. Here's an example where I remove the period at the beginning of a sentence by actually matching the period at the beginning of the text ".Now is the time.":

(Listing 20-06.html on the web site)

```
<HTML>
    <HEAD>
        <TITLE>Replacing Characters</TITLE>
        <SCRIPT LANGUAGE="JavaScript">
            <!--
                function displayer()
                {
```

continues ▶

```
                        var regexp = /^\./
                        document.form1.text2.value =
                        ➥document.form1.text1.value.replace(regexp, "")
                    }
                // -->
            </SCRIPT>
        </HEAD>

        <BODY>
            <H1>Replacing Characters</H1>
            <FORM NAME="form1">
                <INPUT TYPE="TEXT" NAME="text1" VALUE=".Now is the time." SIZE="30">
                <BR>
                <INPUT TYPE="BUTTON" VALUE="Replace Leading Period" ONCLICK="displayer()">
                <BR>
                <INPUT TYPE="TEXT" NAME="text2">
            </FORM>
        </BODY>
    </HTML>
```

Regular Expressions: Character Classes

You also can put a number of characters into a *character class*. Such a class will match any single character in it. To create a character class, you enclose a number of characters in square brackets. We've already seen this example, in which we're searching for any vowel:

```
<HTML>
    <HEAD>
        <TITLE>Checking for Vowels</TITLE>
        <SCRIPT LANGUAGE="JavaScript">
            <!--
            function checkVowels()
            {
                var regexp = /[aeiou]/

                var matches = regexp.exec(document.form1.text1.value)

                if (matches) {
                    document.form1.text2.value = "Yes, we got vowels!"
                } else {
                    document.form1.text2.value = "Sorry, no vowels!"
                }
            }
            // -->
        </SCRIPT>
    </HEAD>

    <BODY>
        <H1>Checking for Vowels</H1>
```

```
    <FORM NAME="form1">
        Type some text:
        <BR>
        <INPUT TYPE="TEXT" NAME="text1">
        <BR>
        <INPUT TYPE="BUTTON" VALUE="Check for Vowels" ONCLICK="checkVowels()">
        <BR>
        <INPUT TYPE="text" NAME="text2" SIZE="30">
    </FORM>
    </BODY>
</HTML>
```

You also can specify a range of characters in a character class, using a hyphen (–), as in this case, where I'm matching any upper case letter: [A-Z]. (If you actually want to match a hyphen, you should escape it as \-].)

In addition, you can use ^ as the first character in a character class—if you do, that character stands for "not" (and not the beginning of a line, which is what ^ matches outside a character class), meaning that the character class matches anything *not* in the character class. Here's an example that we saw at the beginning of the chapter that uses that technique, and which we can now understand (the \b stands for "word boundary," which matches the boundary between whitespace and a word character, or the boundary between a word character and following whitespace):

```
<HTML>
    <HEAD>
        <TITLE>Getting Lower Case Words</TITLE>
        <SCRIPT LANGUAGE="JavaScript">
            <!--
            function getLowers()
            {
                var regexp = /\b[^A-Z]+\b/

                var matches = regexp.exec(document.form1.text1.value)

                if (matches) {
                    for (var loopIndex = 0; loopIndex < matches.length; loopIndex++){
                        document.form1.text2.value += matches[loopIndex] + " "
                    }
                } else {
                    document.form1.text2.value = "Sorry, no lower case words."
                }
            }
            //-->
        </SCRIPT>
    </HEAD>

    <BODY>
        <H1>Getting Lower Case Words</H1>
```

```
        <FORM NAME="form1">
            <INPUT TYPE="TEXT" NAME="text1" VALUE="JavaScript is the subject."
            ➥SIZE="30">
            <BR>
            <INPUT TYPE="BUTTON" VALUE="Get Lower Case Words" ONCLICK="getLowers()">
            <BR>
            <INPUT TYPE="text" NAME="text2" SIZE="30">
        </FORM>
    </BODY>
</HTML>
```

Regular Expressions: Alternative Match Patterns

You also can use *alternative match patterns,* which enable you to specify a number of different patterns as possible matches. You can specify alternatives by using a bar (|) to separate them. Here's an example—the user can type *exit,* or *quit,* or *stop* to match this pattern:

```
function checker()
{
    var regexp = /exit|quit|stop/
    var matches = document.form1.text1.value.match(regexp)
    document.form1.text2.value = "You want to quit?"
}
```

> **Tip**
>
> Alternative match patterns are checked from left to right, and the first one that matches is used. Note, therefore, that a pattern that could match may not be used if an earlier pattern has already matched (which is important to know if, for example, the later, unused, pattern uses parentheses to return various substrings and the earlier, matching, pattern doesn't).

To make it more clear that a number of patterns make up various alternatives, it's customary to put them in parentheses so that they don't interfere with the rest of the regular expression. When you're specifying alternate match patterns using the | character, enclosing parentheses are treated just as enclosing alternative match patterns, not creating submatches (as parentheses normally do in a match pattern):

```
function checker()
{
    var regexp = /(exit|quit|stop)/
    var matches = document.form1.text1.value.match(regexp)
    document.form1.text2.value = "You want to quit?"
}
```

Now we can understand more of this match pattern that we saw earlier in this chapter (Listing 20-03.html) to match dates—the parentheses around 18|19|20 are really just to group alternative match patterns so that we can match years starting with 18, 19, or 20:

```
var regexp = /^(0?[1-9]|1[0-2])\/(0?[1-9]|[12][0-9]|3[01])\/((18|19|20)\d{2})$/
```

> **Tip**
>
> Note that you can use | to specify alternative matches inside parentheses, but not inside square brackets, which create character classes. The character class [18|19|20] is the same as [01289|], for example, because all characters in it are treated as literal, not special, characters.

Regular Expressions: Quantifiers

What if you want to match an unknown number of characters? For example, what if you're trying to match words that can vary in length? You can do that with *quantifiers*.

For example, the pattern \w matches a single-word character (any alphanumeric character and "_"). To match one or more word characters in succession (that is, a whole word), you can use the expression \w+, because + is a quantifier that means "one or more of."

Here's another example. In this case, I want to replace one or more *a* characters with a single *a* character, changing the word *JaaaaaavaScript* to *JavaScript*. I can match all those *a* characters with the pattern a+:

(Listing 20-07.html on the web site)

```
<HTML>
    <HEAD>
        <TITLE>Replacing Characters</TITLE>
        <SCRIPT LANGUAGE="JavaScript">
            <!--
            function replacer()
            {
                var regexp = /a+/g
                document.form1.text2.value =
                ➥document.form1.text1.value.replace(regexp, "a")
            }
            //-->
        </SCRIPT>
    </HEAD>

    <BODY>
        <H1>Replacing Characters</H1>
        <FORM NAME="form1">
```

continues ▶

```
            <INPUT TYPE="TEXT" NAME="text1" VALUE="JaaaaaavaScript is the subject."
            ↪SIZE="30">
            <BR>
            <INPUT TYPE="BUTTON" VALUE="Replace Characters" ONCLICK="replacer()">
            <BR>
            <INPUT TYPE="TEXT" NAME="text2" SIZE="30">
        </FORM>
    </BODY>
</HTML>
```

You can see the results of this code in Figure 20.6.

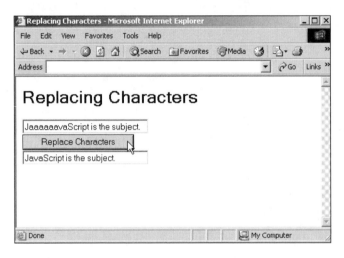

Figure 20.6 Replacing characters.

So which quantifiers are available? Here they are:

- *****   Match zero or more times

- **+**   Match one or more times

- **?**   Match one or zero times

- **{n}**   Match *n* times

- **{n,}**   Match at least *n* times

- **{n,m}** Match at least *n*—but not more than *m*—times

Here's another example where I'm making sure the user types lines of at least 20 characters, matching any character with the dot (.) special character and using the quantifier {20,}:

(Listing 20-08.html on the web site)

```
<HTML>
    <HEAD>
        <TITLE>Checking Text Length</TITLE>
        <SCRIPT LANGUAGE="JavaScript">
            <!--
            function checkText()
            {
                var regexp = /.{20,}/

                var matches = regexp.exec(document.form1.text1.value)

                if (!matches) {
                    alert("Please type longer sentences...")
                }
            }
            //-->
        </SCRIPT>
    </HEAD>

    <BODY>
        <H1>Checking Text Length</H1>
        <FORM NAME="form1">
            <INPUT TYPE="TEXT" NAME="text1">
            <BR>
            <INPUT TYPE="BUTTON" VALUE="Check Text" ONCLICK="checkText()">
        </FORM>
    </BODY>
</HTML>
```

Regular expression quantifiers are "greedy," which means they'll return the longest match possible. What does that mean? Here's an example. Suppose we want to change `"That is some text, isn't it?"` to `"That's some text, isn't it?"` by replacing the *That is* with *That's*. You might try it this way, searching for any number of characters followed by *is* like this: `".*is"`, hoping it'll match *That is* so that you can replace the match with *That's*:

```
<HTML>
    <HEAD>
        <TITLE>Replacing Characters</TITLE>
        <SCRIPT LANGUAGE="JavaScript">
            <!--
            function displayer()
            {
                var regexp = /.*is/
                document.form1.text2.value =
                ➥document.form1.text1.value.replace(regexp, "That's")
            }
            //-->
        </SCRIPT>
```

```
    </HEAD>

    <BODY>
        <H1>Replacing Characters</H1>
        <FORM NAME="form1">
            <INPUT TYPE="TEXT" NAME="text1" VALUE="That is some text, isn't it?"
            ➥SIZE="30">
            <BR>
            <INPUT TYPE="BUTTON" VALUE="Find First Word" ONCLICK="displayer()">
            <BR>
            <INPUT TYPE="TEXT" NAME="text2">
        </FORM>
    </BODY>
</HTML>
```

The problem is that because quantifiers are greedy, they will try to match as much as they can, which means JavaScript will use the `.*` preceding *is* to match all the characters up to the last *is* in the text. That makes the result of the preceding code `"That'sn't it?"`—not what we expected. However, you *can* fix the problem by making quantifiers less greedy; see the section, "Quantifier Greediness," later in this chapter.

Regular Expressions: Assertions

You use regular expression assertions (sometimes called *anchors*) to match a condition in some text, not actual text. For example, the `^` assertion matches the beginning of a line, as we've already seen. Assertions are "zero-width," which means they do not extend the matched string at all. (In other words, you're matching a condition in the text, not specific characters.) Here are the possible assertions, some of which we've already seen:

- `^`   Match the beginning of the line
- `$`   Match the end of the line (or before newline at the end)
- `\b`   Match a word boundary
- `\B`   Match a non-word boundary

One of the most commonly used assertions is `\b`, which matches word boundaries. For example, here's how we matched words consisting of only lower case words:

```
var regexp = /\b[^A-Z]+\b/
```

Regular Expressions: Backreferences

You can refer to the submatches resulting from searching a string (that is, the text returned when a section of a regular expression is enclosed in parentheses) as $1, $2, $3, up to $9 in your code, where $1 holds the text of the first submatch, $2 holds the text of the second submatch, and so on. These values, $1 to $9, are called *backreferences*. (They're actually properties of the RegExp object, as discussed at the end of this chapter.)

Here's an example to show how you can use $1, $2, $3, and so on. In this case, I'm matching three words separated by spaces (spaces are matched with the \s code) using the regular expression /(\w+)\s*(\w+)\s*(\w+)/. Because I've surrounded the match to each of the three words in parentheses, I can refer to those words in code just as $1, $2, and $3, which means that to reverse the order of those words, I could just assemble a replacement string using those matches in reverse order:

(Listing 20-09.html on the web site)

```
<HTML>
    <HEAD>
        <TITLE>The Reverser</TITLE>
        <SCRIPT LANGUAGE="JavaScript">
            <!--
            function reversem()
            {
                var regexp =/(\w+)\s*(\w+)\s*(\w+)/
                document.form1.text1.value =
                ➥document.form1.text1.value.replace(regexp, "$3 $2 $1")
            }
            //-->
        </SCRIPT>
    </HEAD>

    <BODY>
        <H1>The Reverser</H1>
        <FORM NAME="form1">
            Type three words:
            <BR>
            <INPUT TYPE="TEXT" NAME="text1">
            <BR>
            <INPUT TYPE="BUTTON" VALUE="Reverse Order" ONCLICK="reversem()">
        </FORM>
    </BODY>
</HTML>
```

You can see the results of this code in Figure 20.7. Note that you don't have to use $1, $2, $3, up to $9 to refer to submatches at all of course—you can use the array returned by the exec or match methods (which can hold many more than nine submatches). However, $1, $2, and $3 match the original regular expression syntax in languages such as Perl, and that syntax is available in JavaScript as well.

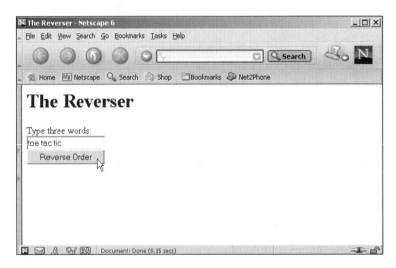

Figure 20.7   Reversing word order.

Regular Expressions: Regular Expression Extensions

Regular expressions also support an "extension" syntax that uses parentheses with a question mark (these are not yet supported in the Netscape Navigator):

- **(?:pattern)** Groups subexpressions as with (and), but doesn't make submatches as (and) would.

- **(?=*EXPR*)** Positive lookahead assertion; matches if *EXPR* would match next.

- **(?!*EXPR*)** Negative lookahead assertion; matches if *EXPR* would match next.

The (?=...) and (?!...) assertions are called *lookahead* assertions. These assertions work with matches that *could* happen next, although the match is not actually made. That is, the results of these assertions are not added to any ongoing match; their conditions are just tested.

Because these assertions do not become part of an ongoing match, they can prove very useful. Suppose, for example, that you're looking for the names *Rome*, *Paris*, and *London*, but you don't know what order they will appear in. That could be a problem with a standard pattern—for example, if you're searching "I'm going to Rome, London, and Paris.", the pattern /.*Rome.*Paris.*London/ will fail, because after it finds *Paris*, it's already past *London* and can't go back, so it won't match the three cities:

```html
<HTML>
    <HEAD>
        <TITLE>Find Cities</TITLE>
        <SCRIPT LANGUAGE="JavaScript">
            <!--
            function findThem()
            {
                var regexp = /.*Rome.*Paris.*London/

                var matches = regexp.exec(document.form1.text1.value)

                if (matches) {
                    document.form1.text2.value = "Found them all!"
                }
            }
            //-->
        </SCRIPT>
    </HEAD>

    <BODY>
        <H1>Getting Match Data</H1>
        <FORM NAME="form1">
            <INPUT TYPE="TEXT" NAME="text1" VALUE="I'm going to Rome, London, and
            ➥Paris." SIZE="40">
            <BR>
            <INPUT TYPE="BUTTON" VALUE="Find Cities" ONCLICK="findThem()">
            <BR>
            <INPUT TYPE="text" NAME="text2">
        </FORM>
    </BODY>
</HTML>
```

Lookahead assertions, however, do not become part of (and therefore extend) the match, so they can be used to repeatedly search the same string from its beginning. That means that this regular expression will work with the same search (not supported in Netscape Navigator):

(Listing 20-10.html on the web site)

```
<HTML>
    <HEAD>
        <TITLE>Find Cities</TITLE>
        <SCRIPT LANGUAGE="JavaScript">
            <!--
            function findThem()
            {
                var regexp = /(?=.*Rome)(?=.*Paris)(?=.*London)/

                var matches = regexp.exec(document.form1.text1.value)

                if (matches) {
                    document.form1.text2.value = "Found them all!"
                }
            }
            //-->
        </SCRIPT>
    </HEAD>

    <BODY>
        <H1>Getting Match Data</H1>
        <FORM NAME="form1">
            <INPUT TYPE="TEXT" NAME="text1" VALUE="I'm going to Rome, London, and
            ↵Paris." SIZE="40">
            <BR>
            <INPUT TYPE="BUTTON" VALUE="Find Cities" ONCLICK="findThem()">
            <BR>
            <INPUT TYPE="text" NAME="text2">
        </FORM>
    </BODY>
</HTML>
```

You can see the results of this code in Figure 20.8, where we've found all three cities.

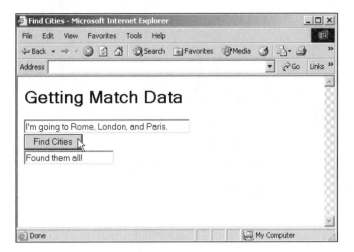

Figure 20.8 Using lookahead assertions.

Using Modifiers

JavaScript supports a number of modifiers you can use with regular expressions. These modifiers are single characters, such as the g modifier, that you place at the end of a regular expression, like this: /\bHello\b/g. Here are the modifiers supported so far in JavaScript:

- **i** Ignore alphabetic case
- **g** Globally perform all possible operations
- **m** Let ^ and $ match embedded \n characters to handle multiline text (**m** means "multiline")

Here's an example we've already seen (Listing 20-05.html), but now can make sense of; in this case, we're replacing all characters in a string with an asterisk by using the global g modifier:

```
<HTML>
    <HEAD>
        <TITLE>Replacing Characters</TITLE>
        <SCRIPT LANGUAGE="JavaScript">
            <!--
                function displayer()
                {
                    var regexp = /./g
                    document.form1.text2.value =
                    ➥document.form1.text1.value.replace(regexp, "*")
```

continues ▶

```
                    }
                //-->
            </SCRIPT>
    </HEAD>

    <BODY>
        <H1>Replacing Characters</H1>
        <FORM NAME="form1">
            <INPUT TYPE="TEXT" NAME="text1" VALUE="JavaScript is the subject."
            ↪SIZE="30">
            <BR>
            <INPUT TYPE="BUTTON" VALUE="Find First Word" ONCLICK="displayer()">
            <BR>
            <INPUT TYPE="TEXT" NAME="text2">
        </FORM>
    </BODY>
</HTML>
```

If we had used the regular expression /./ rather than /./g, only the first character would have been replaced.

Tip

In JavaScript, you usually only have to use the g modifier with the replace method—the exec and match methods apply regular expressions globally by default, returning as many matches as they can find.

Matching Words

It's worth taking a look at a common task—matching whole words—because there are several ways to do that. For example, you can match a word using \S, which matches non-white space characters. Here's an example that does that, matching and displaying the first word in some text:

```
<HTML>
    <HEAD>
        <TITLE>Finding Words</TITLE>
        <SCRIPT LANGUAGE="JavaScript">
            <!--
                function displayer()
                {
                    var regexp = /\S+/
                    var matches = document.form1.text1.value.match(regexp)
                    document.form1.text2.value = matches[0]
                }
            //-->
        </SCRIPT>
    </HEAD>
```

```
    <BODY>
        <H1>Finding Words</H1>
        <FORM NAME="form1">
            <INPUT TYPE="TEXT" NAME="text1" VALUE="JavaScript is the subject."
            ↩SIZE="30">
            <BR>
            <INPUT TYPE="BUTTON" VALUE="Find First Word" ONCLICK="displayer()">
            <BR>
            <INPUT TYPE="TEXT" NAME="text2">
        </FORM>
    </BODY>
</HTML>
```

On the other hand, \s can match many non–alphanumeric characters, which you might not be interested in. You can avoid them if you match using \w, which matches all alphanumeric characters and underscores (_):

```
<HTML>
    <HEAD>
        <TITLE>Finding Words</TITLE>
        <SCRIPT LANGUAGE="JavaScript">
            <!--
            function displayer()
            {
                var regexp = /\w+/
                var matches = document.form1.text1.value.match(regexp)
                document.form1.text2.value = matches[0]
            }
            //-->
        </SCRIPT>
    </HEAD>

    <BODY>
        <H1>Finding Words</H1>
        <FORM NAME="form1">
            <INPUT TYPE="TEXT" NAME="text1" VALUE="JavaScript is the subject."
            ↩SIZE="30">
            <BR>
            <INPUT TYPE="BUTTON" VALUE="Find First Word" ONCLICK="displayer()">
            <BR>
            <INPUT TYPE="TEXT" NAME="text2">
        </FORM>
    </BODY>
</HTML>
```

There are other options as well. For example, you can use a character class to match only words made up of upper or lower case letters:

```
<HTML>
    <HEAD>
        <TITLE>Finding Words</TITLE>
        <SCRIPT LANGUAGE="JavaScript">
```

continues ▶

```
                    <!--
                        function displayer()
                        {
                            var regexp = /([A-Za-z]+)/
                            var matches = document.form1.text1.value.match(regexp)
                            document.form1.text2.value = matches[0]
                        }
                    //-->
                </SCRIPT>
        </HEAD>

    <BODY>
        <H1>Finding Words</H1>
        <FORM NAME="form1">
            <INPUT TYPE="TEXT" NAME="text1" VALUE="JavaScript is the subject."
            ➥SIZE="30">
            <BR>
            <INPUT TYPE="BUTTON" VALUE="Find First Word" ONCLICK="displayer()">
            <BR>
            <INPUT TYPE="TEXT" NAME="text2">
        </FORM>
    </BODY>
</HTML>
```

Actually, to be even safer, you also should straddle your match with word boundary assertions with \b:

(Listing 20-11.html on the web site)

```
<HTML>
    <HEAD>
        <TITLE>Finding Words</TITLE>
        <SCRIPT LANGUAGE="JavaScript">
            <!--
                function displayer()
                {
                    var regexp = /\b([A-Za-z]+)\b/
                    var matches = document.form1.text1.value.match(regexp)
                    document.form1.text2.value = matches[0]
                }
            //-->
        </SCRIPT>
    </HEAD>

    <BODY>
        <H1>Finding Words</H1>
        <FORM NAME="form1">
            <INPUT TYPE="TEXT" NAME="text1" VALUE="JavaScript is the subject."
            ➥SIZE="30">
            <BR>
            <INPUT TYPE="BUTTON" VALUE="Find First Word" ONCLICK="displayer()">
            <BR>
```

```
            <INPUT TYPE="TEXT" NAME="text2">
        </FORM>
    </BODY>
</HTML>
```

The \b assertion matches the zero-width transition (not an actual character) between a word character (that is, \w, which matches all alphanumeric and "_" characters) and a non-word character (\W, which matches every character *except* word characters).

Tip

A non-word boundary assertion, \B, also exists, which matches everything but word boundaries.

As you can see, there are several ways to match words when using regular expressions.

Matching Numbers

Another big use for regular expressions in JavaScript is to let you extract numbers (including dates, as we've already done in this chapter) from text. You can use the \d and \D assertions to check for digits, for example, to check user input to make sure that input is a number. The \D special character matches any character *except* digits, so you can check whether a string doesn't represent a valid number this way:

(Listing 20-12.html on the web site)

```
<HTML>
    <HEAD>
        <TITLE>Checking Numbers</TITLE>
        <SCRIPT LANGUAGE="JavaScript">
            <!--
            function checkNumber()
            {
                var regexp = /\D/

                var matches = regexp.exec(document.form1.text1.value)

                if (matches) {
                    document.form1.text2.value = "That's not a number."
                } else {
                    document.form1.text2.value = "OK."
                }
            }
            //-->
        </SCRIPT>
    </HEAD>
```

continues ▶

```
<BODY>
    <H1>Checking Numbers</H1>
    <FORM NAME="form1">
        Type a number:
        <BR>
        <INPUT TYPE="TEXT" NAME="text1">
        <BR>
        <INPUT TYPE="BUTTON" VALUE="Check Number" ONCLICK="checkNumber()">
        <BR>
        <INPUT TYPE="text" NAME="text2" SIZE="30">
    </FORM>
</BODY>
</HTML>
```

You can see the results of this code in Figure 20.9.

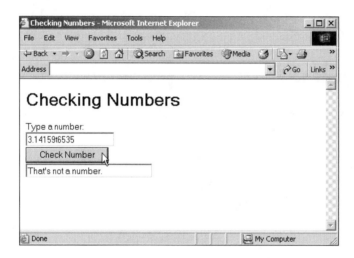

Figure 20.9 Checking for valid numbers.

The \d special character matches individual digits, as in this pattern that matches dates in the form 12/31/1960 that we've already seen:

```
var regexp = /^(\d{1,2})\/(\d{1,2})\/(\d{4})$/
```

You also can create custom formats. For example, you may want to handle numbers of at least one digit followed by a decimal point and some optional digits after the decimal point. Here's how that would look:

```
var regexp =  /^\d+\.\d*$/
```

What about numeric signs, such as + or -? You can handle those with a character class:

```
var regexp = /^[+-]\d+\.\d*$/
```

Want to match hexadecimal numbers? Try this one:

```
var regexp = /^[\da-f]+$/i
```

Quantifier Greediness

As we've already seen, JavaScript quantifiers are "greedy" by default. That means they match the most characters they can, consistent with the regular expression they're in. For example, we tried to change the text `"That is some text, isn't it?"` to `"That's some text, isn't it?"` by replacing matches to the regular expression `/.*is/` with *That's*. However, `/.*is/` didn't match *That is*; it matched *That is some text, is* instead, because quantifiers are greedy. That made the result of our code `"That'sn't it?"`, which is not what we wanted.

To fix the problem, you can make quantifiers less greedy. In fact, to match the *minimum* number of times possible, you follow the quantifier with a question mark (?):

- ***?**   Match 0 or more times
- **+?**   Match 1 or more times
- **??**   Match 0 or 1 time
- **{n}?**   Match *n* times
- **{n,}?**   Match at least *n* times
- **{n,m}?**   Match at least *n* but not more than *m* times

That means that we should use the regular expression `/.*?is/` in our example to match *That is* rather than *That is some text, is*. Here's what that looks like in code:

(Listing 20-13.html on the web site)

```
<HTML>
    <HEAD>
        <TITLE>Handling Quantifier Greediness</TITLE>
        <SCRIPT LANGUAGE="JavaScript">
            <!--
                function displayer()
                {
                    var regexp = /.*?is/
                    document.form1.text2.value =
                    ➥document.form1.text1.value.replace(regexp, "That's")
                }
            //-->
        </SCRIPT>
    </HEAD>
```

continues ▶

```
<BODY>
    <H1>Handling Quantifier Greediness</H1>
    <FORM NAME="form1">
        <INPUT TYPE="TEXT" NAME="text1" VALUE="That is some text, isn't it?"
        ⇒SIZE="30">
        <BR>
        <INPUT TYPE="BUTTON" VALUE="Replace Text" ONCLICK="displayer()">
        <BR>
        <INPUT TYPE="TEXT" NAME="text2">
    </FORM>
</BODY>
</HTML>
```

You can see the results of this code in Figure 20.10, where we've matched just the text we want.

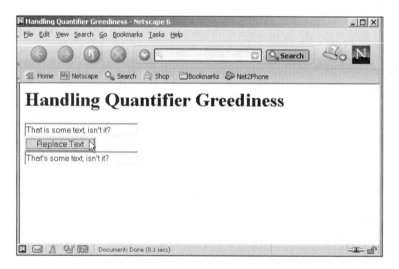

Figure 20.10   Making quantifiers less greedy.

Removing Leading and Trailing White Space

Here's another use for regular expressions—to trim leading or trailing white space. For example, I can match leading white space with the regular expression /^\s+/ and delete it with replace like this:

(Listing 20-14.html on the web site)

```
<HTML>
    <HEAD>
        <TITLE>Trimming Leading White Space</TITLE>
        <SCRIPT LANGUAGE="JavaScript">
            <!--
            function trimmer()
            {
                var regexp = /^\s+/
                document.form1.text2.value =
                document.form1.text1.value.replace(regexp, "")
            }
            //-->
        </SCRIPT>
    </HEAD>

    <BODY>
        <H1>Trimming Leading White Space</H1>
        <FORM NAME="form1">
            <INPUT TYPE="TEXT" NAME="text1" VALUE="   JavaScript is the subject."
            SIZE="30">
            <BR>
            <INPUT TYPE="BUTTON" VALUE="Trim White Space" ONCLICK="trimmer()">
            <BR>
            <INPUT TYPE="TEXT" NAME="text2" SIZE="30">
        </FORM>
    </BODY>
</HTML>
```

You can see the results of this code in Figure 20.11.

Figure 20.11   Trimming white space.

To trim trailing white space, you can use a regular expression like this:

(Listing 20-15.html on the web site)

```
<HTML>
    <HEAD>
        <TITLE>Trimming Trailing White Space</TITLE>
        <SCRIPT LANGUAGE="JavaScript">
            <!--
            function trimmer()
            {
                var regexp = /\s+$/
                document.form1.text2.value =
                ➥document.form1.text1.value.replace(regexp, "")
            }
            //-->
        </SCRIPT>
    </HEAD>

    <BODY>
        <H1>Trimming Trailing White Space</H1>
        <FORM NAME="form1">
            <INPUT TYPE="TEXT" NAME="text1" VALUE="JavaScript is the subject.     "
            ➥SIZE="30">
            <BR>
            <INPUT TYPE="BUTTON" VALUE="Trim White Space" ONCLICK="trimmer()">
            <BR>
            <INPUT TYPE="TEXT" NAME="text2" SIZE="30">
        </FORM>
    </BODY>
</HTML>
```

That's all there is to it.

Regular Expression Objects

The regular expressions we've been using are actually treated as *regular expression objects* in JavaScript. There are two ways to create such objects—by just assigning a pattern to a variable (as we've been doing), or by explicitly creating a new regular expression object with the new operator:

```
var regexp = /pattern/[modifiers]
var regexp = new RegExp("pattern",["modifiers"])
```

We've already seen that you can pass regular expression objects to methods such as match, or use the methods of such objects, such as exec. Let's take a more systematic look at regular expression objects now. You can find their properties and methods in Table 20.1 in overview, their properties in depth in Table 20.2, and their methods in overview in Table 20.3.

Table 20.1 **The Properties and Methods of Regular Expression Objects**

Properties	Methods
constructor	compile
global	exec
ignoreCase	test
lastIndex	
multiline	
source	

Table 20.2 **The Properties of Regular Expression Objects**

Property	NS2	NS3	NS4	NS6	IE3a	IE3b	IE4	IE5	IE5.5	IE6
constructor		x	x				x		x	x
Read-only This property specifies the function that creates an object.										
global		x	x						x	x
Read-only This property holds the Boolean setting of the g modifier.										
ignoreCase		x	x						x	x
Read-only This property holds the Boolean setting of the i modifier.										
lastIndex		x	x						x	x
Read/write This property holds the position where the next match begins in a searched string.										
multiline		x	x						x	x
Read-only This property holds a Boolean value indicating the state of the multiline modifier m used with a regular expression. The default is false.										
source		x	x			x	x	x	x	x
Read-only This property holds the text of the regular expression pattern itself.										

Table 20.3   **The Methods of Regular Expression Objects**

Method	NS2	NS3	NS4	NS6	IE3a	IE3b	IE4	IE5	IE5.5	IE6
compile			x	x			x	x	x	x

Returns: Regular expression object
This method compiles a regular expression into an internal format for faster execution.
Syntax: *regexp*.compile(*pattern*, [*modifiers*]); where *pattern* is the regular expression pattern, and *modifiers* are the modifiers you want to use (such as "ig").

Method	NS2	NS3	NS4	NS6	IE3a	IE3b	IE4	IE5	IE5.5	IE6
exec			x	x			x	x	x	x

Returns: Array of matches
Returns an array of matches to a regular expression, or null if there were no matches. If you're using parentheses for matches, the first element in the array is the entire match, and the subsequent elements are the submatches to the sections of the regular expression enclosed in parentheses.
Syntax: *regexp*.exec(*string*), where *string* is the text you want to work on. Note that the array returned by the exec method has three properties: input, index and lastIndex. The input property holds the searched string, the index property holds the position of the matched substring within the searched string, and the lastIndex property is the position following the last character in the match.

Method	NS2	NS3	NS4	NS6	IE3a	IE3b	IE4	IE5	IE5.5	IE6
test			x	x			x	x	x	x

Returns: Boolean
Returns a Boolean value that indicates whether a pattern exists in a searched string.
Syntax: *regexp*.test(*string*), where *string* is the text you want to search. Returns true if there was a match, false otherwise.

The *RegExp* Object

Besides regular expression objects, there is also a global object named RegExp that holds data about the most recent regular expression operation. This object always exists—don't confuse it with regular expression objects of the kind just covered. The global RegExp object holds data about the most recent regular expression operation, whereas regular expression objects hold data about their particular regular expression operations. You can find the properties of the RegExp object in Table 20.4.

Table 20.4 **The Properties of the *RegExp* Object**

Property	NS2	NS3	NS4	NS6	IE3a	IE3b	IE4	IE5	IE5.5	IE6
index							x	x	x	x

Read-only
This property holds the character position where the first successful match began in the string you're searching.

	NS2	NS3	NS4	NS6	IE3a	IE3b	IE4	IE5	IE5.5	IE6
input		x	x						x	x

Read/write
This property holds the string on which a regular expression search was performed. There's a shortcut for this property, following the Perl language: $_. (That is, you can reach this property's value as `RegExp.input` or `RegExp.$_`.)

	NS2	NS3	NS4	NS6	IE3a	IE3b	IE4	IE5	IE5.5	IE6
lastIndex							x	x	x	x

Read-only
Returns the character position where the next match begins in a searched string.

	NS2	NS3	NS4	NS6	IE3a	IE3b	IE4	IE5	IE5.5	IE6
lastMatch		x	x						x	x

Read-only
This property holds the last matched characters from any regular expression search.

	NS2	NS3	NS4	NS6	IE3a	IE3b	IE4	IE5	IE5.5	IE6
lastParen		x	x						x	x

Read-only
This property holds the last parenthesized submatch from any regular expression search.

	NS2	NS3	NS4	NS6	IE3a	IE3b	IE4	IE5	IE5.5	IE6
leftContext		x	x						x	x

Read-only
This property holds the characters from the beginning of the string up to the position before the beginning of the last match.

	NS2	NS3	NS4	NS6	IE3a	IE3b	IE4	IE5	IE5.5	IE6
rightContext		x	x						x	x

Read-only
This property holds the characters from the position following the last match to the end of a string.

	NS2	NS3	NS4	NS6	IE3a	IE3b	IE4	IE5	IE5.5	IE6
$1...$9		x	x				x	x	x	x

Read-only
These properties hold the various back matches to submatches that matched sections of the regular expression in parentheses.

The `RegExp` object is a global one, and to use properties such as $1 through $9, which refer to parenthesized submatches, you can just use $1 through $9 in your code. In fact, we've already seen that when we used those properties to reverse the order of three words (from Listing 20-09.html):

```
<HTML>
    <HEAD>
        <TITLE>The Reverser</TITLE>
        <SCRIPT LANGUAGE="JavaScript">
            <!--
            function reversem()
            {
                var regexp =/(\w+)\s*(\w+)\s*(\w+)/
                document.form1.text1.value =
                ➥document.form1.text1.value.replace(regexp, "$3 $2 $1")
            }
            //-->
        </SCRIPT>
    </HEAD>
        .
        .
        .
</HTML>
```

That's it for our look at regular expressions in this chapter. As you can see, there's a terrific amount of power—and complexity—available if you need to work with matching and extracting text. In the next chapter, we'll keep going with text handling—and handling other elements such as images—as we start working with *Cascading Style Sheets* (CSS) in depth.

21

Cascading Style Sheets and CGI Programming

I<small>N THIS CHAPTER, I'LL TAKE A LOOK AT WORKING</small> with *Cascading Style Sheets* (CSS). CSS and JavaScript connect well because styles are dynamic these days, which means you can change them on-the-fly, as we'll see in this chapter.

You set styles using *style attributes*—for example, here's how I use the `color` style attribute to set the text color in a document to coral:

```
<BODY STYLE="color: coral">
        .
        .
        .
</BODY>
```

The exciting thing is that you can access style properties from JavaScript. We've already seen this at work to some extent. For example, here's Listing 16-01.html, which turns the color of text red when the cursor moves over it (if using Netscape Navigator, you'll need version 6.0 or later):

```
<HTML>
    <HEAD>
        <TITLE>
            Text Mouse Rollovers
        </TITLE>
    </HEAD>

    <BODY>
        <H1>
            Text Mouse Rollovers
        </H1>
```

```
<SPAN ONMOUSEOVER="this.style.color='red'"
    ONMOUSEOUT="this.style.color='black'">
    This text changes color when the mouse is over it.
</SPAN>
    </BODY>
</HTML>
```

This works because, using JavaScript, we have access to the CSS `color` style attribute of the `<SPAN>` element that encloses the text whose color we want to change. Just like HTML attributes, we also can work with style attributes, which become properties in JavaScript. You use style *attributes* in style sheets and inline HTML `STYLE` attributes, and you use the corresponding style *properties* in JavaScript code.

Here's an example. Suppose that we have a `<SPAN>` element and that we want to make sure the color of text in the element is black. We can set that color with the style `color` *attribute* like this:

```
<SPAN NAME="span1" STYLE="color: black">Hello from JavaScript!</SPAN>
```

The `color` style attribute becomes the `color` *property* of the `<SPAN>` element's `style` object in JavaScript. To access this property, you can use JavaScript syntax with the `color` property like this, turning the text red:

```
document.all.span1.style.color = "red"
```

In this way, you can access the individual style attributes in JavaScript as style properties—in this case, the `color` style attribute became the `color` style property in code. It's almost that easy for all CSS style attributes, except for one thing—many style attributes have hyphenated names, such as `text-decoration` (which sets text "decoration" such as underlining—setting this property to "none" for hyperlinks will remove their underlining, for example). JavaScript, however, does not allow names with hyphens, so the style attribute `text-decoration` becomes the style property `textDecoration` property in JavaScript. That's how it works—it you want to use a hyphenated style attribute in code, change it by removing the hyphen(s) and using the standard JavaScript capitalization scheme.

CSS is a specification of the *World Wide Consortium* (W3C), and we're going to take a look at both Cascading Style Sheets specification 1 (named CSS1) and 2 (named CSS2) here. Parts of both specifications are supported by both browsers, and of course, I'll list which style attributes are supported in which browser. (You also can find more information online, such as at `http://www.webreview.com/style/css1/charts/mastergrid.shtml`.) Note, however, that there are far too many style attributes to cover them all here, so I'll be looking at only the most common, and the most powerful, style sheet attributes in this chapter.

Using CSS is something that many JavaScript programmers are not very familiar with, so in this chapter I'll take a brief look at the ways you connect styles to elements first, then what style attributes there are, and then dig into many examples to make what you can do clear.

Inline Styles

One way of using styles is to use *inline* styles, where you apply styles to one HTML element only. To create an inline style, you use the STYLE attribute that most HTML elements have. Here's an example we saw in Chapter 6, "Using Core HTML Methods and Events," (Listing 06-15.html) for the Internet Explorer, where we used inline styles to color and size a <DIV> element that we used as a drop target:

```
<HTML>
    <HEAD>
        <TITLE>
            Dragging and Dropping Data
        </TITLE>

        <SCRIPT LANGUAGE="JavaScript">
            <!--
            function startDrag()
            {
                event.dataTransfer.setData("Text",
                    "The data was passed to the target!");
                event.dataTransfer.effectAllowed = "copy"
            }

            function endDrag()
            {
                event.returnValue = false
                event.dataTransfer.dropEffect = "copy"
                droptarget.innerHTML =
                    event.dataTransfer.getData("Text")
            }

            function dragOver()
            {
                event.returnValue = false
                event.dataTransfer.dropEffect = "copy"
            }
            // -->
```

continues ▶

```
        </SCRIPT>
    </HEAD>

<BODY>
    <H1>Dragging and Dropping Data</H1>
    <IMG SRC="dragger.jpg" ondragstart="startDrag()">
    <DIV ID="droptarget"
        STYLE="background:pink; width:300; height:100;"
        ONDRAGENTER="dragOver()" ondrop="endDrag()"
        ONDRAGOVER="dragOver()">
        Drop the data here...
    </DIV>
    </BODY>
</HTML>
```

That's how you set style attributes using inline styles, with the HTML STYLE attribute like this: STYLE="style-attribute: value; style-attribute: value; ...". This text, made up of style-attribute: value pairs, is called a style *rule*. You can assign a style rule to the STYLE attribute of individual elements like this, or you can group all style rules for a document together into a <STYLE> element, as we'll see next.

Embedded Style Sheets

Besides inline styles, you also can use the HTML <STYLE> element to set styles for a document, creating an *embedded style sheet*. This element usually goes in a web page's head; here's an example, where I'm setting the style of the <BODY>, making it display white text on a black background, and <P> elements, making them display italicized text, in a document:

(Listing 21-01.html on the web site)

```
<HTML>
    <HEAD>
        <TITLE>Using the &lt;STYLE&gt; Element</TITLE>
        <STYLE TYPE="text/css">
            BODY {background: black; color: white}
            P {font-style: italic}
        </STYLE>
    </HEAD>

    <BODY>
        <H1>
            Using the &lt;STYLE&gt; Element
        </H1>
        <P>
            This text is italic.
        </P>
    </BODY>
</HTML>
```

You can see the results in Figure 21.1.

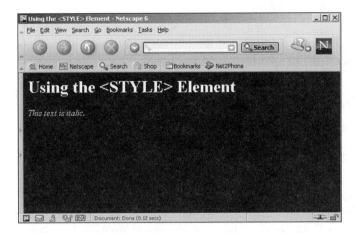

Figure 21.1   Using the <STYLE> element.

External Style Sheets

You can specify styles using external style sheets, which you connect to a page using the <LINK> element like this:

(Listing 21-02.html on the web site)

```
<HTML>
    <HEAD>
        <TITLE>Using the &lt;STYLE&gt; Element</TITLE>
        <LINK REL="stylesheet" HREF="21-03.css"
    </HEAD>

    <BODY>
        <H1>
            Using the &lt;STYLE&gt; Element
        </H1>
        <P>
            This text is italic.
        </P>
    </BODY>
</HTML>
```

This HTML links the web page to an external style sheet, 21-03.css. Here's what that style sheet looks like:

(Listing 21-03.css on the web site)

```
BODY {background: black; color: white}
P {font-style: italic}
```

As you can see, this file contains just the style sheet rules that would have appeared in an embedded <STYLE> element.

Style Classes

You also can create style *classes*, which contain all kinds of style rules. You can then apply those styles to elements by using the CLASS attribute of those elements.

Here's an example where I'm creating a style class named underlinedText that underlines the text of elements to which you apply it. To indicate I'm creating a class, I start the class name with a dot (.) in the <STYLE> element, and then I can use that class with the CLASS attribute of a <SPAN> element:

(Listing 21-04.html on the web site)

```
<HTML>
    <HEAD>
        <TITLE>
            Style Classes
        </TITLE>
        <STYLE>
            .underlinedText {text-decoration: underline}
        </STYLE>
    </HEAD>

    <BODY>
        <H1>
            Style Classes
        </H1>
        <SPAN CLASS="underlinedText">
            This text is underlined.
        </SPAN>
    </BODY>
</HTML>
```

In fact, we've already put style classes to work in Chapter 17, "Dynamic HTML: Drag and Drop, Data Binding, and Behaviors," when we used Internet Explorer behaviors. Here's Listing 17-11, which creates a style class named class1 that uses the behavior glower.htc:

```
<HTML>
    <HEAD>
        <TITLE>
            Internet Explorer Behaviors
        </TITLE>
```

```
        <STYLE>
            .class1 {font-size:36pt; font-weight:bold;
            color:white; position:absolute; cursor:hand;
            filter:glow(enabled=0);behavior:url(glower.htc)}
        </STYLE>
    </HEAD>

    <BODY BGCOLOR="BLACK">
        <H1 STYLE="color:white">
            Internet Explorer Behaviors
        </H1>
        <DIV CLASS="class1" STYLE="top:100; left:40">
            Move the mouse over this text.
        </DIV>
    </BODY>
</HTML>
```

There are other ways to assign styles to HTML elements, but we've seen the principal ways here—using inline styles with the HTML STYLE attribute, using embedded style sheets with the <STYLE> element, using external style sheets with the <LINK> element, and creating style classes you use with the HTML CLASS attribute.

The next step is to see what style attributes are available. There are hundreds of them; and instead of just listing them after another, it's a good idea to get some overview first; so I'll do that now. Note that this is just an overview. We'll see the possible values you can set these style attributes to later in this chapter.

Using Font Styles: Font, Font Size, Font Weight, Font Style

Here are some of the properties you can use with fonts:

- **font-family** specifies a font, such as Arial or Helvetica. You can list alternative fonts in case the host computer doesn't support your first choice. To do that, specify font names as a comma-separated list, like this: {font-family: Arial, Helvetica}.

- **font-style** indicates whether the text is to display using a normal, italic, or oblique face.

- **font-variant** indicates whether the text is to display using the normal letters for lowercase characters or using small capitals instead.

- **font-weight** specifies the boldness or lightness of the characters.

- **font-stretch** specifies whether text should be expanded.

- **line-height** specifies the height of a line.

- **font-size** refers to the size of a font.

Here's an example using some of these style attributes to display italic, bold, and underlined text:

(Listing 21-05.html on the web site)

```
<HTML>
    <HEAD>
        <TITLE>
            Text Styles
        </TITLE>
        <STYLE>
            P {font-size:12pt; font-style:italic; font-family:
                Arial; text-align:center}
        </STYLE>
    </HEAD>

    <BODY>
        <H1>
            Text Styles
        </H1>
        <P>
            Here is some
            <SPAN STYLE="font-weight: bold">bold</SPAN>
            and
            <SPAN STYLE="text-decoration: underline">
            underlined</SPAN> text.
        </P>
    </BODY>
</HTML>
```

Using Colors and Backgrounds

Here are the style properties you use to set color and backgrounds:

- **color** specifies the foreground color.

- **background-color** specifies the background color.

- **background-image** specifies a background image.

- **background-repeat** specifies whether the background image should be tiled.

- **background-attachment** specifies whether the background scrolls with the rest of the document.

- **background-position** specifies the initial position of the background.

Here's an example. In this case, I'm styling both the background and fore-ground colors of a document:

(Listing 21-06.html on the web site)

```
<HTML>
    <HEAD>
        <TITLE>
            Color Styles
        </TITLE>
    </HEAD>

    <BODY STYLE="background-color: cyan">
        <H1>
            Color Styles
        </H1>

        <DIV STYLE="color: red">
            Using Color Styles!
        </DIV>
    </BODY>
</HTML>
```

You can see the results in Figure 21.2.

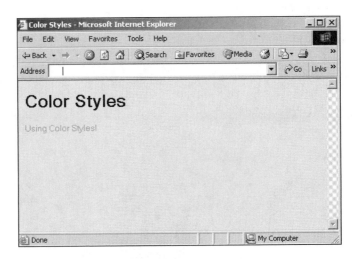

Figure 21.2 Using color styles.

Using Margin, Indentation, and Alignment Styles

Here are some of the properties you use to work with margins, indentations, and alignments:

- **margin-left** specifies the left margin.

- **margin-right** specifies the right margin.

- **margin-top** specifies the top margin.

- **text-indent** specifies the indentation of text.

- **text-align** specifies the alignment of text.

Here's an example showing how to put some of these properties to work:

(Listing 21-07.html on the web site)

```
<HTML>
    <HEAD>
        <TITLE>
            Margin And Alignment Styles
        </TITLE>

        <STYLE type="text/css">
            BODY {margin-left: 15px}
            P {text-indent: 30px}
            H1 {text-align: center}
        </STYLE>
    </HEAD>

    <BODY>
        <H1>
            Margin And Alignment Styles
        </H1>
        <P>
            Here is an indented paragraph.
        </P>
    </BODY>
</HTML>
```

You can see the results in Figure 21.3.

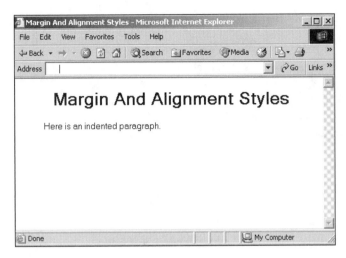

Figure 21.3   Using margin styles.

Using Hyperlink Styles

You can set the colors of hyperlinks using these *pseudo-classes*:

- `A:link` refers to hyperlinks as they originally appear, before they've been visited.
- `A:visited` refers to hyperlinks that have been visited.
- `A:hover` refers to hyperlinks that have the cursor over them.
- `A:active` refers to hyperlinks that are active—that is, being clicked.

A pseudo-class works something like a class; you set it up in a `<STYLE>` element. To set the color of visited hyperlinks to purple, for example, you assign the color property of the `A:visited` to `"purple"`.

Tip

Note in particular the hover pseudo-class, which enables you to set the color of a hyperlink as the cursor moves over it without any additional programming.

Here's an example. In this case, I'm setting the color of hyperlinks to green, visited links to yellow, links with the cursor over them to red, and active links (as they're being clicked) to blue:

(Listing 21-08.html on the web site)

```
<HTML>
    <HEAD>
        <TITLE>Setting Hyperlink Colors</TITLE>
        <STYLE type="text/css">
            A:link {color: green}
            A:visited {color: yellow}
            A:hover {color: red}
            A:active {color: blue}
        </STYLE>
    </HEAD>

    <BODY>
        <H1>
            Setting Hyperlink Colors
        </H1>
        Here's a link: <A HREF="http://www.w3c.org">W3C</A>.
    </BODY>
</HTML>
```

Using Absolute Positioning

Here's a powerful one. You can use the position property to set the position of elements in a web page. I'll take a look at positioning items absolutely in this section and relatively in the next section. Here are the properties you usually use when you work with positioning:

- **position** specifies what type of positioning you want: absolute or relative.

- **top** specifies the offset of the top of the element.

- **bottom** specifies the offset of the bottom of the element.

- **left** specifies the offset of the left edge of the element.

- **right** specifies the offset of the right edge of the element.

Here's an example where I'm setting position to absolute, and then specifying the top and left properties for two <DIV> elements, each of which contains an image:

(Listing 21-09.html on the web site)

```
<HTML>
    <HEAD>
        <TITLE>
            Absolute Positioning With Styles
        </TITLE>
    </HEAD>
```

```
<BODY>
    <H1>
        Absolute Positioning With Styles
    </H1>
    <DIV STYLE="position:absolute; left:10; top:60; border-width:thick">
        <IMG SRC="image1.jpg" WIDTH="216" HEIGHT="72">
    </DIV>
    <DIV STYLE="position:absolute; left:300; top:160; border-width:thick">
        <IMG SRC="image2.jpg" WIDTH="216" HEIGHT="72">
    </DIV>
</BODY>
</HTML>
```

You can see the results in Figure 21.4, where we've positioned the two images as we want them.

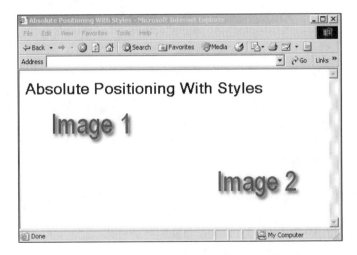

Figure 21.4   Using absolute positioning.

You can set the position of elements in code, moving them as you want, using properties such as `left` and `top`. We did that in the mouse trails example in Chapter 15, "Working with the Mouse, Keyboard, and Images," (Listing 15-10.html); here's the code that moved a trail of stars to follow the mouse:

```
function draw()
{
    var id
    for (loopIndex = 0; loopIndex  < 6; loopIndex++) {
        id = "img" + parseInt(loopIndex)
        if((xData[0] == oldX) && (yData[0] == oldY)) {
            timeout++
        } else {
            timeout = 0
        }
```

```
        if(timeout > 20) {
            document.getElementById(id).style.visibility = "hidden"
            document.getElementById(id).style.left = 0
            document.getElementById(id).style.top = 2000
        } else {
            if((xData[loopIndex] > 0) && (yData[loopIndex] > 0)) {
                document.getElementById(id).style.visibility = "visible"
                document.getElementById(id).style.left = xData[loopIndex]
                document.getElementById(id).style.top = yData[loopIndex]
            }
        }
        oldX = xData[0]
        oldY = yData[0]
    }
}
```

Using Relative Positioning

You also can position elements in a relative way, where they're positioned relative to the location they would have had in the normal flow of elements in the web browser. To position items in a relative way, you set the `position` style attribute to `relative`, and then you set properties such as `left` and `top` to specify the new relative position. What is the element being positioned relative to? It's positioned with respect to the place the browser would normally display the element if you didn't move it yourself.

Here's an example. In this case, I'm moving some text up six pixels and other text down six pixels from the normal position at which the browser would place that text:

(Listing 21-10.html on the web site)

```
<HTML>
    <HEAD>
        <TITLE>
            Relative Positioning With Styles
        </TITLE>
    </HEAD>

    <BODY>
        <H1>
            Relative Positioning With Styles
        </H1>
        I like
        <SPAN STYLE="position:relative; top:-6">roller</SPAN>
        <SPAN STYLE="position:relative; top:6">coasters,</SPAN> don't you?
    </BODY>
</HTML>
```

You can see the results in Figure 21.5, where we've positioned the two words as we want them—above other text, and below other text.

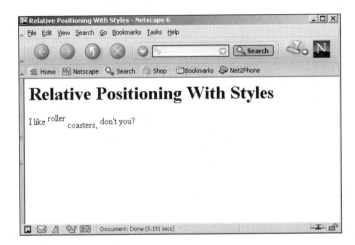

Figure 21.5   Using relative positioning.

Style Specifications

We've seen a number of style attributes in overview now, and it's time to take a look at what attributes are available in a more systematic way. We'll see many such attributes in tables, and it's going to be important to know how to understand those tables. For example, take a look at the single-item Table 21.1, showing the `background-color` attribute.

Table 21.1   **Style Specification Example**

Attribute	NS2	NS3	NS4	NS6	IE3a	IE3b	IE4	IE5	IE5.5	IE6
`background-color`				x	x		x	x	x	x

CSS1: `<color>` | `transparent`
CSS2: `inherit`
Default: `transparent`
Applies to: All elements
Specifies the background color of an element, either a `<color>` value or the keyword `transparent`, which makes the underlying color shine through.

As you can see in Table 21.1, I'm going to list which browsers you can use the style attribute in, as well as the possible values each style attribute can take in CSS1 and the values added in CSS2. (You don't have to pay attention to CSS version if you just want to use the browser version information instead.) In Table 21.1, for example, you see that CSS1 supported `<color>` | `transparent` for the `background-color` attribute and CSS2 adds `inherit` (which means the `background-color` attribute will *inherit* its setting from its enclosing element). Note that I'll also list the default value of the style attribute, if there is one, and which HTML elements the style attribute applies to.

Note also that in the upcoming style attribute tables, I'll use the same syntax that W3C uses when describing style attributes. (You might recognize some of this syntax from our discussion of regular expressions in the previous chapter.)

- Terms in angle brackets, <>, indicate a specific data format listed in Table 21.2.

- Values separated with a pipe symbol, |, give alternatives, but only one may be used at a time.

- Values separated with double pipe symbols, ||, give alternatives, one or more of which must be used.

- Square brackets, [], group statements together.

- An asterisk, *, means the preceding term should be present zero or more times.

- A plus sign, +, means the preceding term should be present one or more times.

- A question mark, ?, means the preceding term is optional.

- Curly braces, {}, surround the minimum and maximum number of times a term may occur (such as {1, 4}).

Table 21.1 lists the possible values for the `background-color` attribute as `<color>` | `transparent`, which we now know means `<color>` or transparent. But what do the angle brackets around `<color>` mean? They indicate a data format, and you can find the possible data formats in Table 21.2, where we learn that `<color>` can be a predefined color value (such as `"cyan"`) or RGB triplet color value (such as `"ffffff"`). You can assign all kinds of different data from integers to percentages to style attributes, and you'll find the possible data formats in Table 21.2.

Table 21.2 **Style Attribute Data Formats**

Data Format	Means
`<absolute-size>`	Absolute font sizes. May be `xx-small`, `x-small`, `small`, `medium`, `large`, `x-large`, `xx-large`.
`<angle>`	Angles. May be `deg`, `grad`, or `rad`.
`<border-style>`	A box's border. May be `none`, `dotted`, `dashed`, `solid`, `double`, `groove`, `ridge`, `inset`, or `outset`.
`<border-width>`	Sets the width of a border. May be `thin`, `medium`, `thick`, or an explicit length.
`<color>`	Color. May be specified with a predefined color value or RGB triplet color value.
`<family-name>`	Font family name, such as Arial, Times New Roman, or Courier.
`<frequency>`	Frequency values, units may be Hz or KHz.
`<generic-family>`	Generic names for fonts that you use as a last resort if the browser can't find a specific font. Examples are `serif`, `sans-serif`, and `monospace`.
`<generic-voice>`	Voices. May be `male`, `female`, or `child`.
`<integer>`	Integer values.
`<length>`	Length. May start with a + or -, followed by a number (may include a decimal point) followed by a unit identifier, which may be `em` (font size of the relevant font), `ex` (the x-height of the font), `px` (pixels as specified relative to the viewing device), `pt` (points, 1/72nds of an inch), `in` (inches), `cm` (centimeters), `mm` (millimeters), or `pc` (picas, 1/6th of an inch).
`<number>`	A number. May include a sign and a decimal point.
`<percentage>`	A percentage measurement. A number (may include a sign) followed by a percentage sign (%).
`<relative-size>`	A font size relative to the parent element. May be `larger` or `smaller`.
`<shape>`	May specify a rectangle, such as this: `rect(<top> <right> <bottom> <left>)`.
`<time>`	Time. Specified as a number followed by `ms` (for milliseconds) or `s` (for seconds).
`<uri>`	*Uniform Resource Indicator* (URI). This is the web address of a page element, such as an image.

Before we begin looking at the formal uses for various style attributes, you should also know the term *box*. When working with styles, an element's box is the invisible rectangle that encloses that element, and which it's drawn in. Because many style attributes have to do with margins and borders, they will refer to the element's box. Another term to know is *block*. A block-level HTML element takes up its own line—or block—by default in a browser, such as <BR> or <H1>. Some style attributes (such as clear) apply only to block-level elements, as I'll indicate.

Now we're ready to take a look at style attributes in depth, including what values you can set them to and which elements they apply to.

Background and Color Attributes

Many style attributes enable you to work with backgrounds and colors, and you'll find a sample of them in Table 21.3.

Table 21.3 **Background and Color Style Attributes**

Attribute	NS2	NS3	NS4	NS6	IE3a	IE3b	IE4	IE5	IE5.5	IE6
background			x	x	x	x	x	x	x	x

CSS1: [<background-color> || <background-image> || <background-repeat> || <background-attachment> || <background-position>]
CSS2: inherit
Applies to: All elements

This is a shorthand attribute for setting background properties including background-color, background-image, background-repeat, background-attachment, and background-position at once.

background-attachment				x			x	x	x	x

CSS1: scroll | fixed
CSS2: inherit
Default: scroll
Applies to: All elements

Specifies whether a background image is fixed, or scrolls when the user scrolls the rest of the page.

Attribute	NS2	NS3	NS4	NS6	IE3a	IE3b	IE4	IE5	IE5.5	IE6
background-color			X	X		X	X	X	X
background-image		X	X			X	X	X	X
background-position			X			X	X	X	X
background-repeat		X	X			X	X	X	X
color		X	X	X	X	X	X	X	X

background-color

CSS1: `<color>` | `transparent`
CSS2: `inherit`
Default: `transparent`
Applies to: All elements

Indicates the background color of an element.

background-image

CSS1: `<uri>` | `none`
CSS2: `inherit`
Default: `none`
Applies to: All elements

Indicates the background image of an element.

background-position

CSS1: `[ [<percentage>` | `<length> ]{1,2}` | `[ [top` | `center` |
`bottom]` || `[left` | `center` | `right] ] ]`
CSS2: `inherit`
Default: `0% 0%`
Applies to: Block-level elements

Sets the initial position of a background image.

background-repeat

CSS1: `repeat` | `repeat-x` | `repeat-y` | `no-repeat`
CSS2: `inherit`
Default: `repeat`
Applies to: All elements

Indicates how a background image should be tiled (repeated).

color

CSS1: `<color>`
CSS2: `inherit`
Default: Depends on the browser
Applies to: All elements

Sets the foreground color of text elements.

Positioning and Block Attributes

A popular use of style sheets is to position elements in pages, and we've already discussed relative and absolute positioning in this chapter. You can find some positioning and block style attributes in Table 21.4.

Table 21.4 **Positioning and Block Style Attributes**

Attribute	NS2	NS3	NS4	NS6	IE3a	IE3b	IE4	IE5	IE5.5	IE6
bottom, top, left, right			X	X	X	X	X	X	X	X

CSS2: `<length>` | `<percentage>` | `auto` | `inherit`
Default: `auto`
Applies to: All elements

You position a box with these properties, which specify how far a box's bottom, top, left, or right content edge should be set from the box's containing area.

direction								X	X	X

CSS1: `ltr` | `rtl`
CSS2: `inherit`
Default: `ltr`
Applies to: All elements

Gives the writing direction of HTML blocks for the Unicode bi-directional algorithm (left-to-right or right-to-left).

display			X	X			X	X	X	X

CSS1: `inline` | `block` | `list-item` CSS2: `run-in` | `compact` | `marker` | `table` | `inline-table` | `table-row-group` | `table-header-group` | `table-footer-group` | `table-row` | `table-column-group` | `table-column` | `table-cell` | `table-caption` | `none` | `inherit`
Default: `inline`
Applies to: All elements

Indicates how various elements should be displayed. Note that implementation of this attribute is spotty as of yet.

float			X	X			X	X	X	X

CSS1: `left` | `right` | `none`
CSS2: `inherit`
Default: `none`
Applies to: All but positioned elements

Specifies whether a box should float to the left or right as needed.

Attribute	NS2	NS3	NS4	NS6	IE3a	IE3b	IE4	IE5	IE5.5	IE6
position			x	x			x	x	x	x

CSS2: `static` | `relative` | `absolute` | `fixed` | `inherit`
Default: `static`
Applies to: All elements

Specifies how to position an element (which affects how the browser uses attributes such as `left` and `top`).

Attribute	NS2	NS3	NS4	NS6	IE3a	IE3b	IE4	IE5	IE5.5	IE6
z-index			x	x			x	x	x	x

CSS2: `auto` | `<integer>` | `inherit`
Default: `auto`
Applies to: Positioned elements

Sets the stacking level of the box in the stacking order for positioned boxes. Enables you to specify which elements appear on top of which other elements.

HTML Element Box Attributes

A number of style attributes enables you to work with the box an element are drawn in, such as border, which enables you to draw a border around an element. You can see a sampling of such attributes in Table 21.5.

Table 21.5 **HTML Element Box Style Attributes**

Attribute	NS2	NS3	NS4	NS6	IE3a	IE3b	IE4	IE5	IE5.5	IE6
border			x	x			x	x	x	x

CSS1: [`<border-width>` || `<border-style>` || `<color>`]
CSS2: `inherit`
Default: Varies
Applies to: All elements

This attribute is a shorthand attribute enabling you to set the width, color, and style for all four borders of a box at one time.

border-top, border-right, border-bottom, border-left	NS2	NS3	NS4	NS6	IE3a	IE3b	IE4	IE5	IE5.5	IE6
				x			x	x	x	x

CSS1: [`<border-top/right/bottom/left-width>` || `<border-style>` || `<color>`]
CSS2: `inherit`
Default: Varies
Applies to: All elements

Sets the width, style, and color of the top, right, bottom, and left border of a box.

continues ▶

Table 21.5 **Continued**

Attribute	NS2	NS3	NS4	NS6	IE3a	IE3b	IE4	IE5	IE5.5	IE6
`border-color`			X	X			X	X	X	X

CSS1: `<color>{1,4}` | `transparent`
CSS2: `inherit`
Default: Varies
Applies to: All elements

Sets the color of the borders of a box.

Attribute	NS2	NS3	NS4	NS6	IE3a	IE3b	IE4	IE5	IE5.5	IE6
`border-top-color`, `border-right-color`, `border-bottom-color`, `border-left-color`			X	X			X	X	X	X

CSS1: `<color>`
CSS2: `inherit`
Default: Varies
Applies to: All elements

Specifies the color of a border of a box.

Attribute	NS2	NS3	NS4	NS6	IE3a	IE3b	IE4	IE5	IE5.5	IE6
`border-style`			X	X			X	X	X	X

CSS1: `<border-style>{1,4}`
CSS2: `inherit`
Default: Varies
Applies to: All elements

Specifies the style of the four borders of a box. You can give from one to four values at the same time.

Attribute	NS2	NS3	NS4	NS6	IE3a	IE3b	IE4	IE5	IE5.5	IE6
`border-top-style`, `border-right-style`, `border-bottom-style`, `border-left-style`			X	X			X	X	X	X

CSS1: `<border-style>`
CSS2: `inherit`
Default: `none`
Applies to: All elements

Specifies the style of a specific border of a box.

Attribute	NS2	NS3	NS4	NS6	IE3a	IE3b	IE4	IE5	IE5.5	IE6
`border-width`			X	X			X	X	X	X

CSS1: `<border-width>{1,4}`
CSS2: `inherit`
Default: Not defined
Applies to: All elements
Inherited: No

This is a shorthand attribute for setting the `border-top-width`, `border-right-width`, `border-bottom-width`, and `border-left-width` attributes at once.

Attribute	NS2	NS3	NS4	NS6	IE3a	IE3b	IE4	IE5	IE5.5	IE6
`border-top-width`, `border-right-width`, `border-bottom-width`, `border-left-width`										
		X	X			X	X	X	X

CSS1: `<border-width>`
CSS2: `inherit`
Default: `medium`
Applies to: All elements

Sets the border widths of the sides of a box.

| clear | | X | X | | | X | X | X | X |

CSS1: `none | left | right | both`
CSS2: `inherit`
Default: `none`
Applies to: Block–level elements

This attribute specifies to the browser that the sides of an element's box should not be next to a previous floating box.

| height, width | | X | X | | | X | X | X | X |

CSS1: `<length> | <percentage> | auto`
CSS2: `inherit`
Default: `auto`
Applies to: All elements except inline elements, table columns, and column groups

Sets the height or width of boxes.

| margin | | X | X | X | X | X | X | X | X |

CSS1: `<margin-width>{1,4}`
CSS2: `inherit`
Default: Not defined
Applies to: All elements

This attribute is a shorthand attribute for specifying the `margin-top`, `margin-right`, `margin-bottom`, and `margin-left` attributes all at once.

| `margin-top`, `margin-right`, `margin-bottom`, `margin-left` | | | | | | | | | | |
| | | X | X | X | X | X | X | X | X |

CSS1: `<margin-width>`
CSS2: `inherit`
Default: `0`
Applies to: All elements

Correspond to the top, right, bottom, and left margin of a box.

continues ▶

Table 21.5   **Continued**

Attribute	NS2	NS3	NS4	NS6	IE3a	IE3b	IE4	IE5	IE5.5	IE6
`max-height, max-width`							X	X	X	X

CSS2: `<length>` | `<percentage>` | `none` | `inherit`
Default: `none`
Applies to: All elements except non-replaced inline elements and table elements

Set constraints on box heights and widths.

Attribute	NS2	NS3	NS4	NS6	IE3a	IE3b	IE4	IE5	IE5.5	IE6
`min-height, min-width`							X	X	X	X

CSS2: `<length>` | `<percentage>` `inherit`
Default: `0`
Applies to: All elements except non-replaced inline elements and table elements

Enables you to set minimum box heights and widths.

Attribute	NS2	NS3	NS4	NS6	IE3a	IE3b	IE4	IE5	IE5.5	IE6
`padding`			X	X			X	X	X	X

CSS1: `<length>` | `<percentage>`
CSS2: `inherit`
Default: Not defined
Applies to: All elements

This is a shorthand attribute for setting the `padding-top`, `padding-right`, `padding-bottom`, and `padding-left` attributes all at once.

Attribute	NS2	NS3	NS4	NS6	IE3a	IE3b	IE4	IE5	IE5.5	IE6
`padding-top, padding-right, padding-bottom, padding-left`			X	X			X	X	X	X

CSS1: `<length>` | `<percentage>`
CSS2: `inherit`
Default: `0`
Applies to: All elements

Specifies the top, right, bottom, and left box padding.

Font Attributes

You also can work with plenty of font style attributes—see Table 21.6 for a sample.

Table 21.6 **Font Style Attributes**

Attribute	NS2	NS3	NS4	NS6	IE3a	IE3b	IE4	IE5	IE5.5	IE6
font		X	X	X	X	X	X	X	X	X

CSS1: [[<font-style> || <font-variant> || <font-weight>
]? <font-size> [/ <line-height>]? <font-family>
CSS2: caption | icon | menu | message-box | small-caption |
status-bar | inherit
Default: Varies
Applies to: All elements

This is a shorthand attribute that enables you to set the font-style,
font-variant, font-weight, font-size, line-height, and font-
family attributes all at once. You specify values for those attributes in
that order, and without commas.

Attribute	NS2	NS3	NS4	NS6	IE3a	IE3b	IE4	IE5	IE5.5	IE6
font-family		X	X	X	X	X	X	X	X	X

CSS1: [[<family-name> | <generic-family>],]* [<family-
name> | <generic-family>]
CSS2: inherit
Default: Depends on the browser
Applies to: All elements

Indicates a list of font family names and/or generic family names.
Separate the names of the fonts you want to use with commas; the
browser will use the first one it can find, starting from the first font in
the list.

Attribute	NS2	NS3	NS4	NS6	IE3a	IE3b	IE4	IE5	IE5.5	IE6
font-size		X	X	X	X	X	X	X	X	X

CSS1: <absolute-size> | <relative-size> | <length> |
<percentage>
CSS2: inherit
Default: medium
Applies to: All elements

Sets the size of a font.

Attribute	NS2	NS3	NS4	NS6	IE3a	IE3b	IE4	IE5	IE5.5	IE6
font-stretch							X	X	X	X

CSS2: normal | wider | narrower | ultra-condensed | extra-
condensed | condensed | semi-condensed | semi-expanded |
expanded | extra-expanded | ultra-expanded | inherit
Default: normal
Applies to: All elements

Sets normal, condensed, or extended font face.

continues ▶

Table 21.6 **Continued**

Attribute	NS2	NS3	NS4	NS6	IE3a	IE3b	IE4	IE5	IE5.5	IE6
font-style			x	x	x	x	x	x	x	x

CSS1: normal | italic | oblique
CSS2: inherit
Default: normal
Applies to: All elements

Enables you to select from normal (also called Roman or upright), italic, and oblique font faces.

font-variant							x	x	x	x

CSS1: normal | small-caps
CSS2: inherit
Default: normal
Applies to: All elements

Indicates whether a font is a small-caps font (which is made up of small capital letters).

font-weight			x	x	x	x	x	x	x	x

CSS1: normal | bold | bolder | lighter | 100 | 200 | 300 | 400 | 500 | 600 | 700 | 800 | 900
CSS2: inherit
Default: normal
Applies to: All elements

Gives the "weight" of a font, such as normal or bold.

Text Attributes

A number of style attributes also are available to use with text, and you can see a sample of them in Table 21.7.

Table 21.7 **Text Style Attributes**

Attribute	NS2	NS3	NS4	NS6	IE3a	IE3b	IE4	IE5	IE5.5	IE6
letter-spacing			x				x	x	x	x

CSS1: normal | <length>
CSS2: inherit
Default: normal
Applies to: All elements

This property enables you to set the spacing between text characters.

Attribute	NS2	NS3	NS4	NS6	IE3a	IE3b	IE4	IE5	IE5.5	IE6
line-height		x	x	x	x	x	x	x	x	

CSS1: `normal` | `<number>` | `<length>` | `<percentage>`
CSS2: `inherit`
Default: `normal`
Applies to: All elements

Gives the minimum height of an element's box.

text-align		x	x	x	x	x	x	x	x	

CSS1: `left` | `right` | `center` | `justify`
CSS2: `<string>` | `inherit`
Default: Varies
Applies to: Block-level elements

Sets alignment for the content of a block: left, right, center, or justify. CSS2 enables you to specify a string to align the text with respect to.

text-decoration		x	x	x	x	x	x	x	x	

CSS1: `none` | `[ underline || overline || line-through || blink ]`
CSS2: `inherit`
Default: `none`
Applies to: All elements

Gives the "decorations" for the text in an element, such as underlining, overlining, and line-through (also called strike-through).

text-indent		x	x	x	x	x	x	x	x	

CSS1: `<length>` | `<percentage>`
CSS2: `inherit`
Default: `0`
Applies to: Block-level elements

Specifies the indentation of the first line of text in a block element.

text-shadow								x	x	x

CSS2: `none` | `[<color> || <length> <length> <length>? ,]*`
`[<color> || <length> <length> <length>?] | inherit`
Default: `none`
Applies to: All elements
Inherited: No

Enables you to give a comma-separated list of shadow effects to apply to text in the element.

continues ▶

Table 21.7   **Continued**

Attribute	NS2	NS3	NS4	NS6	IE3a	IE3b	IE4	IE5	IE5.5	IE6
vertical-align				x			x	x	x	x

CSS1: `baseline` | `sub` | `super` | `top` | `text-top` | `middle` |
`bottom` | `text-bottom` | `<percentage>` | `<length>`
CSS2: `inherit`
Default: `baseline`
Applies to: Inline-level and table-cell elements

Indicates the vertical position of text in an element.

Attribute	NS2	NS3	NS4	NS6	IE3a	IE3b	IE4	IE5	IE5.5	IE6
white-space			x	x						x

CSS1: `normal` | `pre` | `nowrap`
CSS2: `inherit`
Default: `normal`
Applies to: Block-level elements

Indicates how whitespace in an element displays.

Visual Effect Attributes

CSS2 supports some new visual effects, such as making elements visible or invisible. You can see a sample in Table 21.8.

Table 21.8   **Visual Effect Style Attributes**

Attribute	NS2	NS3	NS4	NS6	IE3a	IE3b	IE4	IE5	IE5.5	IE6
clip								x	x	x

CSS2: `<shape>` | `auto` | `inherit`
Default: `auto`
Applies to: Block-level and replaced elements

Specifies what part of an element is visible by setting the "clipping" region of an element.

Attribute	NS2	NS3	NS4	NS6	IE3a	IE3b	IE4	IE5	IE5.5	IE6
overflow								x	x	x

CSS2: `visible` | `hidden` | `scroll` | `auto` | `inherit`
Default: `visible`
Applies to: Block-level and replaced elements

Specifies whether the contents in a block-level element are clipped if the contents overflows the element's box.

Attribute	NS2	NS3	NS4	NS6	IE3a	IE3b	IE4	IE5	IE5.5	IE6
visibility				x				x	x	x

CSS2: visible | hidden | collapse | inherit
Default: inherit
Applies to: All elements

Sets whether the element is displayed or hidden.

Now let's put some of the style attributes we've seen to work using JavaScript.

Text Mouse Rollovers

Styles can be changed dynamically, and that's where JavaScript comes in. We've seen, for example, that you can change the style of text when the mouse rolls over it. Here's Listing 16-02.html—and now we know how this works (dynamic styles such as this won't work in Netscape Navigator before version 6.):

```
<HTML>
    <HEAD>
        <TITLE>
            Text Mouse Rollovers
        </TITLE>
    </HEAD>

    <BODY>
        <CENTER>
            <H1>
                Text Mouse Rollovers
            </H1>
            <SPAN ONMOUSEOVER="this.style.fontSize='48'"
                ONMOUSEOUT="this.style.fontSize='12'"
                STYLE="fontSize:36">
                This text gets big when the mouse is over it.
            </SPAN>
        </CENTER>
    </BODY>
</HTML>
```

You also can change other style properties when the mouse rolls over text, such as the color of that text as in this case, where we're changing the text color to red:

```
<HTML>
    <HEAD>
        <TITLE>
            Text Mouse Rollovers
        </TITLE>
```

continues ▶

```
    </HEAD>

    <BODY>
        <CENTER>
            <H1>
                Text Mouse Rollovers
            </H1>
            <SPAN ONMOUSEOVER="this.style.color='red'"
                ONMOUSEOUT="this.style.color='black'">
                This text changes color when the mouse is over it.
            </SPAN>
        </CENTER>
    </BODY>
</HTML>
```

Changing Style Classes On-the-Fly

In the preceding two examples, we changed individual style attributes. But what if you have dozens of style attributes you've set up in a style class?

It turns out that you can change the style class of an element on-the-fly in JavaScript. You might expect that you use a property named class for that to match the HTML CLASS attribute, but the word *class* is already reserved in JavaScript, so you use a property called className instead. Here's an example showing how that works. In this case, I'll change the style class of a <DIV> element from blue to red text when the mouse moves over the element:

(Listing 21-11.html on the web site)

```
<HTML>
    <HEAD>
        <TITLE>
            Text Mouse Rollovers Using Style Classes
        </TITLE>
        <STYLE>
            .red {color:red}
            .blue {color:blue}
        </STYLE>
    </HEAD>

    <BODY>
        <H1>
            Text Mouse Rollovers Using Style Classes
        </H1>
        <DIV CLASS=blue ONMOUSEOVER="this.className='red'"
            ONMOUSEOUT="this.className='blue'">
            Change this text's color with the mouse!
        </DIV>
    </BODY>
</HTML>
```

You can see the results in Figure 21.6.

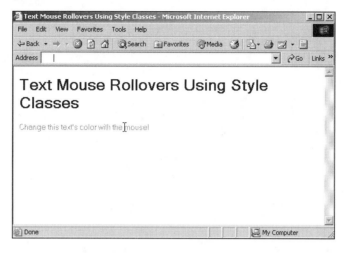

Figure 21.6 Using dynamic style classes.

Changing Style Sheets On-the-Fly

In the Internet Explorer, the `document` object contains a collection of the available style sheets in the `styleSheets` collection. You can select which style sheet is active with the style sheet `disabled` property. (Set this property to false for the style sheet you want to make active, and true for all the others.) Here's an example that enables you to toggle between two style sheets for a document just by clicking buttons:

(Listing 21-12.html on the web site)

```
<HTML>
    <HEAD>
        <TITLE>
            Dynamic Style Sheets
        </TITLE>

        <STYLE ID="WOW">
            body {font-family:verdana; color:white; background-color:black}
        </STYLE>

        <STYLE ID="NORMAL" DISABLED="TRUE">
            body {font-family:'times new roman'; color:black;
                background-color:white}
        </STYLE>
```

continues ▶

```
<SCRIPT LANGUAGE="JavaScript">
    <!--
    function style1()
    {
        document.styleSheets["NORMAL"].disabled = false
        document.styleSheets["WOW"].disabled = true
    }
    function style2()
    {
        document.styleSheets["NORMAL"].disabled = true
        document.styleSheets["WOW"].disabled = false
    }
    //-->
</SCRIPT>
</HEAD>

<BODY>
    <H1>
        Dynamic Style Sheets
    </H1>
        <INPUT TYPE=BUTTON VALUE="Style 1" ONCLICK="style1()">
        <INPUT TYPE=BUTTON VALUE="Style 2" ONCLICK="style2()">
    <BR>
        Set the style sheet for this document with the above buttons!
</BODY>
</HTML>
```

You can see the results in Figure 21.7, where I've toggled the "WOW" style sheet on.

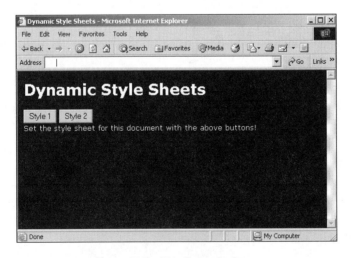

Figure 21.7   Toggling style sheets.

Changing Mouse Cursors

Here's another good one to know: You can change the mouse cursor in the Internet Explorer with the cursor property. Here's an example that makes that browser display a hand cursor rather than the default cursor when the mouse moves over some text:

(Listing 21-13.html on the web site)

```
<HTML>
    <HEAD>
        <TITLE>
            Setting Mouse Cursors
        </TITLE>
    </HEAD>

    <BODY>
        <H1>
            Setting Mouse Cursors
        </H1>
        <DIV ONMOUSEOVER="this.style.cursor = 'hand'"
            ONMOUSEOUT="this.style.cursor = 'default'">
            Change the cursor with the mouse.
        </DIV>
    </BODY>
</HTML>
```

You can see the results in Figure 21.8.

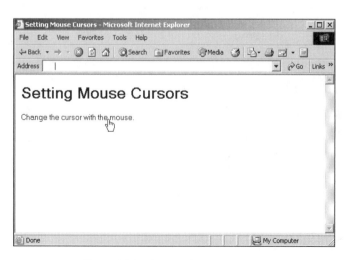

Figure 21.8   Setting the mouse cursor.

Showing and Hiding Elements

JavaScript programmers also find a lot of use for the visibility property, which enables you to toggle the visibility of elements. Here's how we used that property in Chapter 12, "Working with Forms, Buttons, Check Boxes, and Radio Buttons," (Listing 12-13.html) to show and hide some extra controls (if using Netscape Navigator, you'll need version 6.0 or later):

```html
<HTML>
    <HEAD>
        <TITLE>Showing and hiding controls</TITLE>
        <SCRIPT LANGUAGE="JavaScript">
            <!--
                function checkClicked(check)
                {
                    if(check.checked) {
                        document.form1.button1.style.visibility= "visible"
                        document.form1.button2.style.visibility= "visible"
                    } else {
                        document.form1.button1.style.visibility= "hidden"
                        document.form1.button2.style.visibility= "hidden"
                    }
                }

                function hideButtons()
                {
                    document.form1.button1.style.visible = false
                    document.form1.button2.style.visible = false
                }
            // -->
        </SCRIPT>
    </HEAD>

    <BODY>
        <H1>Showing and hiding controls</H1>

        <FORM NAME="form1">
            <INPUT TYPE="BUTTON" VALUE="Check spelling" NAME="button1" ➥
            ➥STYLE="visibility:hidden">
            <INPUT TYPE="BUTTON" VALUE="Change case" NAME="button2"
            ➥STYLE="visibility:hidden">
            <BR>
            <INPUT TYPE="TEXT" NAME="text1">
            <INPUT TYPE = "CHECKBOX" NAME = "check1" ONCLICK =
            ➥"checkClicked(this)">Show all options
        </FORM>
    </BODY>
</HTML>
```

Menus

You can even put together a menu system displayed inside a web page using styles. To do that, you need a browser that supports the visibility style property (although it's possible to make menus "appear" and "disappear" with their left and top properties, moving them on- or off-screen).

Here's a demo menu program, targeted at IE5+. (Earlier versions didn't support the CSS2 visibility property.) Here the menu is actually a <DIV> that encloses a <TABLE> element (which I use to make sure the menu items appear one on top of the other). When the user clicks the menu name (File), the menu opens by making the <DIV> containing the menu visible. (And if the user clicks outside the menu without making a selection, the menu will close.) Each item in the menu is actually a hyperlink (with its TEXT-DECORATION style attribute set to none to remove underlining) to a JavaScript URL, enabling you to place code to execute when the user clicks that menu item in a JavaScript function.

In this example, the code just displays a message indicating which menu item you selected. Here's what the code looks like:

(Listing 21-14.html on the web site)

```
<HTML>
    <HEAD>
        <TITLE>Menus</TITLE>
        <SCRIPT LANGUAGE="JavaScript">
            <!--
            function showMenu(e)
            {
               document.getElementById("div2").style.visibility = "visible"
            }
            function hideMenu(e)
            {
               var id = e.srcElement.id
               if(id != "div1"){
                   document.getElementById("div2").style.visibility = "hidden"
               }
            }
            function open()
            {
               document.getElementById("div3").innerText = "You clicked the open item."
            }
            function save()
            {
               document.getElementById("div3").innerText = "You clicked the save item."
            }
            function close()
            {
              document.getElementById("div3").innerText = "You clicked the close item."
            }
```

continues ▶

```
        //-->
      </SCRIPT>
  </HEAD>

<BODY ONCLICK="hideMenu(event)">
    <H1>Menus</H1>
    <FORM NAME="form1">
        <DIV ID="div1" ONMOUSEDOWN="showMenu(event)"
      ➥ONMOUSEOVER="this.style.cursor = 'hand'"
          ONMOUSEOUT="this.style.cursor = 'default'"
          STYLE="FONT-FAMILY:Arial; FONT-SIZE:12; POSITION:ABSOLUTE; LEFT:10;
            TOP:100; WIDTH:25; HEIGHT:18; BACKGROUND-COLOR:YELLOW">
          File
        </DIV>
        <DIV ID="div2"
          STYLE="POSITION:ABSOLUTE; LEFT:15; TOP:118; WIDTH:60; HEIGHT:40;
            BACKGROUND-COLOR:YELLOW; VISIBILITY:HIDDEN">
          <TABLE BORDER="0">
            <TR>
              <TD><A HREF="javascript:save()" STYLE="FONT-FAMILY:Arial;
                FONT-SIZE:12; TEXT-DECORATION:NONE;
                ➥COLOR:BLACK">Save</A></TD>
            </TR>
            <TR>
              <TD><A HREF="javascript:open()" STYLE="FONT-FAMILY:Arial;
                FONT-SIZE:12; TEXT-DECORATION:NONE;
                ➥COLOR:BLACK">Open</A></TD>
            </TR>
            <TR>
              <TD><A HREF="javascript:close()" STYLE="FONT-FAMILY:Arial;
                FONT-SIZE:12; TEXT-DECORATION:NONE;
                ➥COLOR:BLACK">Close</A></TD>
            </TR>
          </TABLE>
        </DIV>
        <DIV ID="div3">
        </DIV>
    </FORM>
  </BODY>
</HTML>
```

You can see the results in Figure 21.9, where clicking the File item has opened the menu, and Figure 21.10, where I've selected the Close item, and the code is reporting that fact. Pretty cool, and all made possible with dynamic styles and JavaScript.

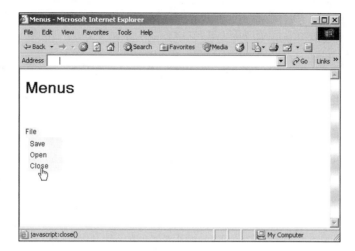

Figure 21.9   Creating JavaScript-based menus.

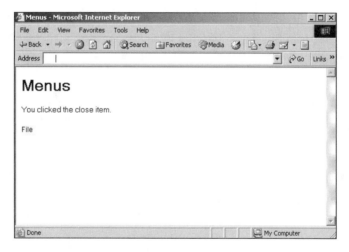

Figure 21.10   Creating JavaScript-based menus.

That's it for our work with CSS in this chapter. As you can see, there's a terrific amount of power here for the JavaScript programmer's arsenal. In the next chapter, we'll take a look at working with JavaScript together with XML and XSLT.

22

XML and XSLT

I N THIS CHAPTER, WE'RE GOING TO TAKE A LOOK at using JavaScript with XML and XSLT. You're probably familiar with XML, *Extensible Markup Language*, at least in name. In XML, you can create your own markup tags, such as `<PERSON>` or `<PHONE_NUMBER>`. You may not be so familiar with XSLT, *Extensible Style Sheet Language Transformations*, however. Using XSLT, you can transform XML documents into other formats such as HTML or plain text—or other HTML documents with a different organization. We'll take a look at both in this chapter.

Note that although the Netscape Navigator can work with XML to some extent, the Internet Explorer already lets you handle both XML and XSLT using JavaScript in an advanced way, so this chapter is only going to be applicable to Internet Explorer.

The in-depth details of both XML and XSLT are beyond the scope of this book—there just isn't space in a book on JavaScript to discuss all the ins and outs of XML and XSLT. Even if you're completely unfamiliar with these topics, however, you can probably catch the gist of what's going on just by reading this chapter—although the details, such as how to construct an XML *Document Type Definition* (DTD), will still be elusive. Both XML and XSLT are standardized by the W3C, and you can check out the W3C recommendations for XML at www.w3.org/TR/REC-xml and XSLT at www.w3.org/TR/xslt20.

> **Tip**
>
> For more information on XML, see New Rider's *Inside XML*. For more information on XSLT, see New Rider's *Inside XSLT*.

XML

Unlike HTML, in XML documents, you're free to create your own tags—you're not restricted to the tags that an HTML browser already understands, such as `<P>` and `<INPUT>`. That's both liberating and constricting—although you're now free to structure your own documents from top to bottom, it's also true that browsers such as the Internet Explorer will have no idea what to do with the elements in your XML document. The browser can't know, for example, that you mean the tag `<RED>` to indicate red text—not unless you handle the document in code with JavaScript (or transform the document into HTML using XSLT and JavaScript as we'll do later in the chapter). To really work with XML documents in the Internet Explorer, therefore, you have to use a scripting language such as JavaScript to interpret the XML and work with it.

Let's take a look at an XML document to get us started. You start off such documents with the XML declaration `<?xml version="1.0"?>`, and all the rest of the elements in the document must be enclosed in a single element, called the *document element*. In HTML, the document element is `<HTML>`; but in XML, that element can be anything you want. Here's what our example XML document looks like—I'll make this part of a publicist's schedule book, keeping track of various publicity events and who went to them:

```
<?xml version="1.0"?>
<EVENTS>
    <EVENT TYPE="informal">
        <EVENT_TITLE>15th Award Ceremony</EVENT_TITLE>
        <EVENT_NUMBER>1207</EVENT_NUMBER>
        <SUBJECT>Gala Event</SUBJECT>
        <DATE>7/4/2003</DATE>
        <PEOPLE>
            <PERSON ATTENDANCE="present">
                <FIRST_NAME>Sam</FIRST_NAME>
                <LAST_NAME>Edwards</LAST_NAME>
            </PERSON>
            <PERSON ATTENDANCE="absent">
                <FIRST_NAME>Sally</FIRST_NAME>
                <LAST_NAME>Jackson</LAST_NAME>
            </PERSON>
            <PERSON ATTENDANCE="present">
                <FIRST_NAME>Cary</FIRST_NAME>
```

```
                    <LAST_NAME>Grant</LAST_NAME>
                </PERSON>
            </PEOPLE>
        </EVENT>
    </EVENTS>
```

Note that this looks very much like an HTML document, with elements that can enclose other elements. When the nesting of elements is correct (for example, no element overlaps another element like this `<ELEM1><ELEM2>text</ELEM1></ELEM2>`), the document is called *well-formed*.

Besides being well-formed, the other usual requirement for XML documents is that they be *valid*. Because you can create the entire tag syntax for an XML document, the browser you're displaying it in can't check that syntax as it can for an HTML document—unless you tell the browser what that syntax is. You can tell the browser, for example, what elements can contain what other elements, what order elements must appear in, what elements can have which attributes, and so on. There are several ways to do that, and we'll look at the most common way here—using a DTD. Using a DTD, the browser can check your XML document and make sure that it adheres to the syntax rules you've specified. We'll see how the Internet Explorer can do this near the end of this chapter.

The details of setting up a DTD are involved and beyond the scope of this book, but here's a DTD I'll add to our sample XML document which accurately defines its syntax:

(Listing 22-01.xml on the web site)

```
<?xml version="1.0"?>
<!DOCTYPE EVENTS [
<!ELEMENT EVENTS (EVENT*)>
<!ELEMENT EVENT (EVENT_TITLE, EVENT_NUMBER, SUBJECT, DATE, PEOPLE*)>
<!ELEMENT EVENT_TITLE (#PCDATA)>
<!ELEMENT EVENT_NUMBER (#PCDATA)>
<!ELEMENT SUBJECT (#PCDATA)>
<!ELEMENT DATE (#PCDATA)>
<!ELEMENT FIRST_NAME (#PCDATA)>
<!ELEMENT LAST_NAME (#PCDATA)>
<!ELEMENT PEOPLE (PERSON*)>
<!ELEMENT PERSON (FIRST_NAME,LAST_NAME)>
<!ATTLIST EVENT
    TYPE CDATA #IMPLIED>
<!ATTLIST PERSON
    ATTENDENCE CDATA #IMPLIED>
]>
<EVENTS>
    <EVENT TYPE="informal">
        <EVENT_TITLE>15th Award Ceremony</EVENT_TITLE>
        <EVENT_NUMBER>1207</EVENT_NUMBER>
```

continues ▶

```
        <SUBJECT>Gala Event</SUBJECT>
        <DATE>7/4/2003</DATE>
        <PEOPLE>
            <PERSON ATTENDENCE="present">
                <FIRST_NAME>Sam</FIRST_NAME>
                <LAST_NAME>Edwards</LAST_NAME>
            </PERSON>
            <PERSON ATTENDENCE="absent">
                <FIRST_NAME>Sally</FIRST_NAME>
                <LAST_NAME>Jackson</LAST_NAME>
            </PERSON>
            <PERSON ATTENDENCE="present">
                <FIRST_NAME>Cary</FIRST_NAME>
                <LAST_NAME>Grant</LAST_NAME>
            </PERSON>
        </PEOPLE>
    </EVENT>
</EVENTS>
```

In fact, the Internet Explorer enables you to view such XML documents directly, as you can see in Figure 22.1. You can click small plus (+) and minus (–) signs that appear on the left in XML documents to expand and collapse XML elements.

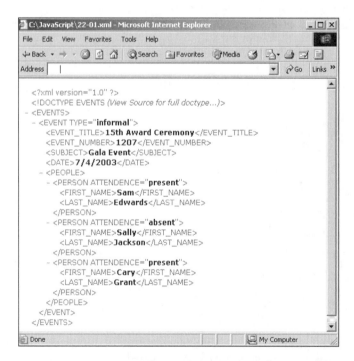

Figure 22.1 Displaying an XML document in the Internet Explorer.

Although it's good to see our XML document in the Internet Explorer, that's of limited utility. XML documents are meant to store data, and the first step in working with that data is to access it—which you can do with JavaScript.

Accessing XML Documents

You can access data in XML documents using JavaScript in several ways, and I'll take a look at them here. The idea is that you load the XML document in behind the scenes, work with it by extracting the data you want, and then display your results using HTML.

To see how this works, I'll use our XML document, 22-01.xml, throughout this chapter. The data I'll extract is the first and last name of the third person attending the event, who we'll consider the main guest—in our case, that's Cary Grant:

```
<EVENTS>
    <EVENT TYPE="informal">
        <EVENT_TITLE>15th Award Ceremony</EVENT_TITLE>
        <EVENT_NUMBER>1207</EVENT_NUMBER>
        <SUBJECT>Gala Event</SUBJECT>
        <DATE>7/4/2003</DATE>
        <PEOPLE>
            <PERSON ATTENDANCE="present">
                <FIRST_NAME>Sam</FIRST_NAME>
                <LAST_NAME>Edwards</LAST_NAME>
            </PERSON>
            <PERSON ATTENDANCE="absent">
                <FIRST_NAME>Sally</FIRST_NAME>
                <LAST_NAME>Jackson</LAST_NAME>
            </PERSON>
            <PERSON ATTENDANCE="present">
                <FIRST_NAME>Cary</FIRST_NAME>
                <LAST_NAME>Grant</LAST_NAME>
            </PERSON>
                .
                .
                .
```

One way to load this document into the Internet Explorer is with the Internet Explorer ActiveX object named Microsoft.XMLDOM. (More recent ActiveX XML objects are available too; see the discussion at the end of this chapter about XSLT.) First, I create an object of this kind and then use its load method to load our XML document, 22-01.xml (you can pass any URL to the load method):

```
var document1
document1 = new ActiveXObject("Microsoft.XMLDOM")
document1.load("22-01.xml")
    .
    .
    .
```

That loads the XML document into memory. The next step is to get access to the document element in our XML document, which is the all-enclosing `<EVENTS>` element. You can refer to that element with the `documentElement` property—and when you have access to the document element, you have access to the whole document. For example, we can now use the W3C node-navigation properties we saw in Chapter 5, "Using Core HTML Properties," such as `firstChild`, `lastChild`, `nextSibling`, and so on, to navigate through the XML document to the nodes from which we want to extract data:

```
var document1, eventsNode, eventNode, peopleNode
var firstNameNode, lastNameNode, displayText
document1 = new ActiveXObject("Microsoft.XMLDOM")
document1.load("22-01.xml")

eventsNode = document1.documentElement
eventNode = eventsNode.firstChild
peopleNode = eventNode.lastChild
personNode = peopleNode.lastChild
firstNameNode = personNode.firstChild
lastNameNode = firstNameNode.nextSibling
    .
    .
    .
```

To actually get the data we want from the nodes we now have access to, you just use the `nodeValue` property:

(Listing 22-02.html on the web site)

```
<HTML>
    <HEAD>
        <TITLE>
            Accessing XML Elements
        </TITLE>

        <SCRIPT LANGUAGE="JavaScript">
            <!--
            function reader()
            {
```

```
                    var document1, eventsNode, eventNode, peopleNode
                    var firstNameNode, lastNameNode, displayText
                    document1 = new ActiveXObject("Microsoft.XMLDOM")
                    document1.load("22-01.xml")

                    eventsNode = document1.documentElement
                    eventNode = eventsNode.firstChild
                    peopleNode = eventNode.lastChild
                    personNode = peopleNode.lastChild
                    firstNameNode = personNode.firstChild
                    lastNameNode = firstNameNode.nextSibling

                    displayText = "The main guest was: " +
                            firstNameNode.firstChild.nodeValue + ' '
                        + lastNameNode.firstChild.nodeValue
                    div1.innerHTML=displayText
                }
                //-->
            </SCRIPT>
        </HEAD>

        <BODY>
            <H1>
                Accessing XML Elements
            </H1>

            <INPUT TYPE="BUTTON" VALUE="Get the name of the main guest"
                ONCLICK="reader()">
            <BR>
            <DIV ID="div1"></DIV>
        </BODY>
    </HTML>
```

And that's all it takes—when the user clicks the button with the caption "Get the name of the main guest," our JavaScript code will load in the XML document, navigate to the data we want, and display that data in a <DIV> element.

You can see this code at work in the Internet Explorer in Figure 22.2. When the user clicks the button, the XML document 22-01.xml is read, parsed, and we retrieve and display the third person's name. Now we're accessing the data in XML documents.

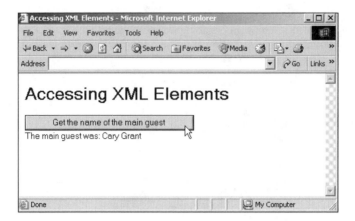

Figure 22.2   Reading data from an XML element.

Using XML Data Islands

As of version 5 in the Internet Explorer, you also can use *XML data islands* to actually embed XML inside HTML pages. The Internet Explorer supports an HTML <XML> element (which is not part of the HTML standard) that you can just enclose an XML document inside, like this:

```
<XML ID="message1">
    <DOCUMENT>
        <MESSAGE>Hello XML!</MESSAGE>
    </DOCUMENT>
</XML>
```

The Internet Explorer <XML> element has some attributes worth noting:

- **ID.** The ID you can use to refer to the <XML> element in code. Set to an alphanumeric string.
- **NS.** The URI of the XML namespace used by the XML content. Set to an URL.
- **SRC.** Source for the XML document, if that XML document is external. Set to an URL.

When you use this element, you access it using its ID value in code. To reach the element, for example, you can use the all collection, passing it the ID you gave the element like this for the preceding example: document.all("message"). To get the document object corresponding to the XML document, you can then use the XMLDocument property. Here's how I convert the previous example to use a data island instead of the Microsoft.XMLDOM object:

(Listing 22-03.html on the web site)

```
<HTML>
    <HEAD>
        <TITLE>
            Getting XML Elements Using XML Data Islands
        </TITLE>

        <XML ID="xml1" SRC="22-01.xml"></XML>

        <SCRIPT LANGUAGE="JavaScript">
            <!--
            function reader()
            {
                var document1, eventsNode, eventNode, peopleNode
                var firstNameNode, lastNameNode, displayText

                document1= document.all("xml1").XMLDocument

                eventsNode = document1.documentElement
                eventNode = eventsNode.firstChild
                peopleNode = eventNode.lastChild
                personNode = peopleNode.lastChild
                firstNameNode = personNode.firstChild
                lastNameNode = firstNameNode.nextSibling

                displayText = "The main guest was: " +
                    firstNameNode.firstChild.nodeValue + ' '
                   + lastNameNode.firstChild.nodeValue
                div1.innerHTML=displayText
            }
            //-->
        </SCRIPT>
    </HEAD>

    <BODY>
        <CENTER>
            <H1>
                Getting XML Elements Using XML Data Islands
            </H1>

        <INPUT TYPE="BUTTON" VALUE="Get the name of the main guest"
            ONCLICK="reader()">
            <P>
            <DIV ID="div1"></DIV>
        </CENTER>
    </BODY>
</HTML>
```

This example works as the previous example did (Listing 22-02.html).

Here's something else to know. In this example, I used an external XML document, 22-01.xml, which I accessed with the <XML> element's SRC attribute; but you also can enclose the entire XML document in the <XML> element like this:

(Listing 22-04.html on the web site)

```
<HTML>
    <HEAD>
        <TITLE>
            Creating An XML Data Island
        </TITLE>

        <XML ID="xml1">
            <?xml version="1.0"?>
            <EVENTS>
                <EVENT TYPE="informal">
                    <EVENT_TITLE>15th Award Ceremony</EVENT_TITLE>
                    <EVENT_NUMBER>1207</EVENT_NUMBER>
                    <SUBJECT>Gala Event</SUBJECT>
                    <DATE>7/4/2003</DATE>
                    <PEOPLE>
                        <PERSON ATTENDENCE="present">
                            <FIRST_NAME>Sam</FIRST_NAME>
                            <LAST_NAME>Edwards</LAST_NAME>
                        </PERSON>
                        <PERSON ATTENDENCE="absent">
                            <FIRST_NAME>Sally</FIRST_NAME>
                            <LAST_NAME>Jackson</LAST_NAME>
                        </PERSON>
                        <PERSON ATTENDENCE="present">
                            <FIRST_NAME>Cary</FIRST_NAME>
                            <LAST_NAME>Grant</LAST_NAME>
                        </PERSON>
                    </PEOPLE>
                </EVENT>
            </EVENTS>
        </XML>

        <SCRIPT LANGUAGE="JavaScript">
            <!--
            function reader()
            {
                var document1, eventsNode, eventNode, peopleNode
                var firstNameNode, lastNameNode, displayText

                document1= document.all("xml1").XMLDocument

                eventsNode = document1.documentElement
                eventNode = eventsNode.firstChild
```

```
                    peopleNode = eventNode.lastChild
                    personNode = peopleNode.lastChild
                    firstNameNode = personNode.firstChild
                    lastNameNode = firstNameNode.nextSibling

                    displayText = "The main guest was: " +
                          firstNameNode.firstChild.nodeValue + ' '
                        + lastNameNode.firstChild.nodeValue
                    div1.innerHTML=displayText
                }
                //-->
            </SCRIPT>
    </HEAD>

    <BODY>
        <CENTER>
            <H1>
                Getting XML Elements Using XML Data Islands
            </H1>

        <INPUT TYPE="BUTTON" VALUE="Get the name of the main guest"
            ONCLICK="reader()">
            <P>
            <DIV ID="div1"></DIV>
        </CENTER>
    </BODY>
</HTML>
```

So far, I've used the XMLDocument property of the object corresponding to the
XML data island to get the document object, but you also can use the
documentElement property of the data island directly to get the root element
of the XML document, like this:

```
<HTML>
    <HEAD>
        <TITLE>
            Reading XML Data Values
        </TITLE>

        <XML ID="xml1" SRC="22-01.xml"></XML>

        <SCRIPT LANGUAGE="JavaScript">
            <!--
            function reader()
            {
                var document1, eventsNode, eventNode, peopleNode
                var firstNameNode, lastNameNode, displayText

                eventsNode = xml1.documentElement
                eventNode = eventsNode.firstChild
```

continues ▶

```
              peopleNode = eventNode.lastChild
              personNode = peopleNode.lastChild
              firstNameNode = personNode.firstChild
              lastNameNode = firstNameNode.nextSibling
                 .
                 .
                 .

</HTML>
```

Accessing XML Elements by Name

We've used properties such as `nextSibling` and `nextChild` to navigate through XML documents. However, you also can get individual elements by searching for them by name using methods such as `getElementsByTagName`.

Here's an example. In this case, I'll do the same thing that we did using properties such as `nextSibling` and `nextChild`—find the third person's name in Listing 22-01.xml. I'll start by getting a `document` object for that XML document:

```
document1 = new ActiveXObject("Microsoft.XMLDOM")
document1.load("22-01.xml")
     .
     .
     .
```

Now we can use `getElementsByTagName` on this `document` object. In this case, we want to extract information from the `<FIRST_NAME>` and `<LAST_NAME>` elements in the document, so that I get an array of those elements like this:

```
document1 = new ActiveXObject("Microsoft.XMLDOM")
document1.load("22-01.xml")

firstNameNodes = document1.getElementsByTagName("FIRST_NAME")
lastNameNodes = document1.getElementsByTagName("LAST_NAME")
     .
     .
     .
```

We're looking for data about the third person in the XML document, so that corresponds to element 2 in the 0-based array. And we can do that like this:

```
document1 = new ActiveXObject("Microsoft.XMLDOM")
document1.load("22-01.xml")

firstNameNodes = document1.getElementsByTagName("FIRST_NAME")
lastNameNodes = document1.getElementsByTagName("LAST_NAME")
```

```
var displayText = "The main guest was: " +
    firstNameNodes(2).firstChild.nodeValue + ' '
    + lastNameNodes(2).firstChild.nodeValue
div1.innerHTML = displayText
```

Here's the whole code:

(Listing 22-05.html on the web site)

```
<HTML>
    <HEAD>
        <TITLE>
            Accessing XML Element Values
        </TITLE>

        <SCRIPT LANGUAGE="JavaScript">
            <!--
            function reader()
            {
                var document1, firstNameNodes, lastNameNodes

                document1 = new ActiveXObject("Microsoft.XMLDOM")
                document1.load("22-01.xml")

                firstNameNodes = document1.getElementsByTagName("FIRST_NAME")
                lastNameNodes = document1.getElementsByTagName("LAST_NAME")

                var displayText = "The main guest was: " +
                        firstNameNodes(2).firstChild.nodeValue + ' '
                    + lastNameNodes(2).firstChild.nodeValue
                div1.innerHTML = displayText
            }
            //-->
        </SCRIPT>
    </HEAD>

    <BODY>
        <H1>
            Accessing XML Element Values
        </H1>

        <INPUT TYPE="BUTTON" VALUE="Get the name of the main guest"
            ONCLICK="reader()">
        <BR>
        <DIV ID="div1"></DIV>
    </BODY>
</HTML>
```

This gives the same result we've already seen (see Figure 22.2, for example).

So far, we've seen a number of ways of accessing XML element content, but there's more to the story. What about an XML element's *attributes*? I'll take a look at that next.

Accessing Attribute Values in XML Elements

Like HTML elements, XML elements can have attributes. To show how to read attribute values from an XML document, I'll create a new example to read the value of the ATTENDENCE attribute of the third person in the XML document 22-01.xml:

```
<?xml version="1.0"?>
<EVENTS>
    <EVENT TYPE="informal">
        <EVENT_TITLE>15th Award Ceremony</EVENT_TITLE>
        <EVENT_NUMBER>1207</EVENT_NUMBER>
        <SUBJECT>Gala Event</SUBJECT>
        <DATE>7/4/2003</DATE>
        <PEOPLE>
            <PERSON ATTENDENCE="present">
                <FIRST_NAME>Sam</FIRST_NAME>
                <LAST_NAME>Edwards</LAST_NAME>
            </PERSON>
            <PERSON ATTENDENCE="absent">
                <FIRST_NAME>Sally</FIRST_NAME>
                <LAST_NAME>Jackson</LAST_NAME>
            </PERSON>
            <PERSON ATTENDENCE="present">
                <FIRST_NAME>Cary</FIRST_NAME>
                <LAST_NAME>Grant</LAST_NAME>
            </PERSON>
            .
            .
            .
```

How do you read attribute values? You start by getting the attributes collection of the current element using that element's attributes property. In this case, we want the attributes of the third <PERSON> element, and we get the attributes collection like this by navigating to that element:

```
var document1, eventsNode, eventNode, peopleNode

var firstNameNode, lastNameNode, displayText
var attributes, attendencePerson

document1= document.all("xml1").XMLDocument

eventsNode = document1.documentElement
eventNode = eventsNode.firstChild
peopleNode = eventNode.lastChild
personNode = peopleNode.lastChild
firstNameNode = personNode.firstChild
lastNameNode = firstNameNode.nextSibling
```

```
attributes = personNode.attributes
        .
        .
        .
```

Now we can get the value of the ATTENDENCE attribute with the attribute collection's getNamedItem method, passing it the name of the attribute. This
returns, not the value of the attribute as you might hope, but an attribute
object, and you must use that object's value property to get the value of the
attribute:

```
var document1, eventsNode, eventNode, peopleNode
var firstNameNode, lastNameNode, displayText
var attributes, attendencePerson

document1= document.all("xml1").XMLDocument

eventsNode = document1.documentElement
eventNode = eventsNode.firstChild
peopleNode = eventNode.lastChild
personNode = peopleNode.lastChild
firstNameNode = personNode.firstChild
lastNameNode = firstNameNode.nextSibling

attributes = personNode.attributes
attendencePerson = attributes.getNamedItem("ATTENDENCE")
displayText = firstNameNode.firstChild.nodeValue
    + ' ' + lastNameNode.firstChild.nodeValue
    + " was " + attendencePerson.value
div1.innerHTML=displayText
```

Here's what the entire code looks like:

(Listing 22-06.html on the web site)

```
<HTML>
    <HEAD>
        <TITLE>
            Reading XML Element Attribute Values
        </TITLE>

        <XML ID="xml1" SRC="22-01.xml"></XML>

        <SCRIPT LANGUAGE="JavaScript">
            <!--
            function readXMLDocument()
            {
                var document1, eventsNode, eventNode, peopleNode
                var firstNameNode, lastNameNode, displayText
                var attributes, attendencePerson
```

continues ▶

```
                document1= document.all("xml1").XMLDocument

                eventsNode = document1.documentElement
                eventNode = eventsNode.firstChild
                peopleNode = eventNode.lastChild
                personNode = peopleNode.lastChild
                firstNameNode = personNode.firstChild
                lastNameNode = firstNameNode.nextSibling
                attributes = personNode.attributes
                attendencePerson = attributes.getNamedItem("ATTENDANCE")
                displayText = firstNameNode.firstChild.nodeValue
                    + ' ' + lastNameNode.firstChild.nodeValue
                    + " was " + attendencePerson.value
                div1.innerHTML=displayText
            }
            //-->
        </SCRIPT>
    </HEAD>

    <BODY>
        <H1>
            Reading XML Element Attribute Values
        </H1>

        <INPUT TYPE="BUTTON" VALUE="Get Attendence of the Main Guest"
            ONCLICK="readXMLDocument()">
        <BR>
        <DIV ID="div1"></DIV>
    </BODY>
</HTML>
```

You can see the results in Figure 22.3, where we're displaying an attribute's value.

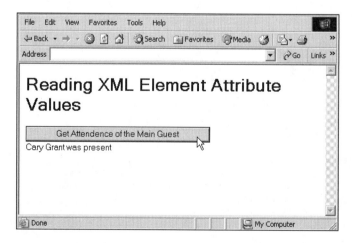

Figure 22.3   Displaying attribute values from an XML document.

Parsing XML Documents in Code

We've seen how to access an individual element in an XML document now, so let's take the next step—parsing (that is, reading and interpreting) an entire XML document at once.

To do that, I'll create a new example, which will display the whole structure of an XML document. In this case, I'll name the function that parses the document parse. You pass a node to this function, and it will navigate through all of that node's contained nodes automatically. To parse the entire document, then, you just pass the document element to parse like this, where we're working on our XML document, 22-01.xml:

```
<HTML>
    <HEAD>
        <TITLE>
            Parsing XML Documents
        </TITLE>

        <XML ID="xml1" SRC="22-01.xml"></XML>

        <SCRIPT LANGUAGE="JavaScript">
            <!--
            function parseDocument()
            {
                documentXML = document.all("xml1").XMLDocument
                div1.innerHTML = parse(documentXML, "")
            }
            .
            .
            .
        <INPUT TYPE="BUTTON" VALUE="Parse XML document"
            ONCLICK="parseDocument()">
        <DIV ID="div1"></DIV>
    </BODY>
</HTML>
```

The parse function itself will create a string, giving all the details of each node in the XML document. I'll also indent the output to show which nodes are contained by other nodes.

That's how it will work. I'll pass a node to parse to work through all the node's contained nodes, and also pass an indentation string, incrementing that string each time we go deeper into a set of nested nodes to indent the output further. To get the current node's name, we can use the nodeName property; and to get its value, we can use the nodeValue property (both of these properties are covered in Chapter 5—also in this code, you'll see the HTML code for a non-breaking space— —to make sure that the browser preserves our indentation as we want it):

```html
<HTML>
    <HEAD>
        <TITLE>
            Parsing XML Documents
        </TITLE>

        <XML ID="xml1" SRC="22-01.xml"></XML>

        <SCRIPT LANGUAGE="JavaScript">
            <!--
            function parseDocument()
            {
                documentXML = document.all("xml1").XMLDocument
                div1.innerHTML = parse(documentXML, "")
            }

            function parse(node1, indent)
            {
                var text

                if (node1.nodeValue != null) {
                    text = indent + node1.nodeName
                    + "  = " + node1.nodeValue
                } else {
                    text = indent + node1.nodeName
                }

                text += "<BR>"

                if (node1.childNodes.length > 0) {
                    for (var loopIndex = 0; loopIndex <
                        node1.childNodes.length; loopIndex++) {
                        text += parse(node1.childNodes(loopIndex),
                        indent + "    ")
                    }
                }
                return text
            }
            //-->
        </SCRIPT>
    </HEAD>

    <BODY>
        .
        .
        .
    </BODY>
</HTML>
```

Note that at the end of the code, we check whether there are any child nodes (using the `childNodes` property; see "The `childNodes` Property" in Chapter 5) and, if so, call `parse` again on each of those child nodes. In this way, the `parse` function will parse not only each child node, but also each child node's children, if there are any. In this way, we're calling parse *recursively* (see "Handling Recursion" in Chapter 3, "The JavaScript Language: Loops, Functions, and Errors") to navigate through an entire XML document without having to know that document's structure beforehand.

So far, we've indicated each node's type and value, but we can do more. We also can indicate the type of each node we display by checking the `nodeType` property (see Chapter 5). Here are the possible values for this property in an XML document:

- 1—Element
- 2—Attribute
- 3—Text
- 4—CDATA section
- 5—Entity reference
- 6—Entity
- 7—Processing instruction
- 8—Comment
- 9—Document
- 10—Document type
- 11—Document fragment
- 12—Notation

Now we can determine the type of each node using a `switch` statement, and display that information like this:

```
<HTML>
    <HEAD>
        <TITLE>
            Parsing XML Documents
        </TITLE>

        <XML ID="xml1" SRC="22-01.xml"></XML>

        <SCRIPT LANGUAGE="JavaScript">
            <!--
                .
                .
                .
```

continues ▶

```
function parse(node1, indent)
{
    var type

    switch (node1.nodeType) {
        case 1:
            type = "element"
            break
        case 2:
            type = "attribute"
            break
        case 3:
            type = "text"
            break
        case 4:
            type = "CDATA section"
            break
        case 5:
            type = "entity reference"
            break
        case 6:
            type = "entity"
            break
        case 7:
            type = "processing instruction"
            break
        case 8:
            type = "comment"
            break
        case 9:
            type = "document"
            break
        case 10:
            type = "document type"
            break
        case 11:
            type = "document fragment"
            break
        case 12:
            type = "notation"
    }
    var text

    if (node1.nodeValue != null) {
        text = indent + node1.nodeName
        + "  = " + node1.nodeValue
        + "  (Node type: " + type
        + ")"
    } else {
        text = indent + node1.nodeName
```

```
                                + "  (Node type: " + type
                                + ")"
                    }

                text += "<BR>"
                    .
                    .
                    .
                return text
            }
            //-->
        </SCRIPT>
    </HEAD>

    <BODY>
        .
        .
        .
    </BODY>
</HTML>
```

We can also display the attributes of each node, if there are any, and we've seen how to use the `attributes` collection for that:

```
<HTML>
    <HEAD>
        <TITLE>
            Parsing XML Documents
        </TITLE>

        <XML ID="xml1" SRC="22-01.xml"></XML>

        <SCRIPT LANGUAGE="JavaScript">
            <!--
                .
                .
                .
            function parse(node1, indent)
            {
                var type
                    .
                    .
                    .
                if (node1.nodeValue != null) {
                    text = indent + node1.nodeName
                    + "  = " + node1.nodeValue
                    + "  (Node type: " + type
                    + ")"
                } else {
                    text = indent + node1.nodeName
                    + "  (Node type: " + type
                    + ")"
                }
```

continues ▶

```
        if (node1.attributes != null) {
            if (node1.attributes.length > 0) {
                for (var loopIndex = 0; loopIndex <
                    node1.attributes.length; loopIndex++) {
                    text += " (Attribute: " +
                        node1.attributes(loopIndex).nodeName +
                        " = \"" +
                        node1.attributes(loopIndex).nodeValue
                        + "\")"
                }
            }
        }
        .
        .
        .
        return text
    }
    //-->
    </SCRIPT>
</HEAD>

<BODY>
    .
    .
    .
</BODY>
</HTML>
```

And that's it! You can see the results in Figure 22.4, where we're laying bare the entire structure of our XML document.

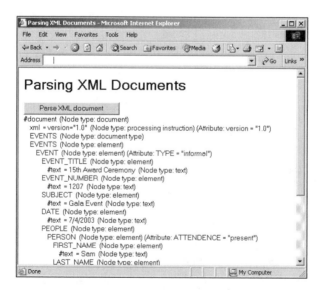

Figure 22.4   Parsing an XML document.

Here's the entire code:

(Listing 22-07.html on the web site)

```html
<HTML>
    <HEAD>
        <TITLE>
            Parsing XML Documents
        </TITLE>

        <XML ID="xml1" SRC="22-01.xml"></XML>

        <SCRIPT LANGUAGE="JavaScript">
            <!--
            function parseDocument()
            {
                documentXML = document.all("xml1").XMLDocument
                div1.innerHTML = parse(documentXML, "")
            }

            function parse(node1, indent)
            {
                var type

                switch (node1.nodeType) {
                    case 1:
                        type = "element"
                        break
                    case 2:
                        type = "attribute"
                        break
                    case 3:
                        type = "text"
                        break
                    case 4:
                        type = "CDATA section"
                        break
                    case 5:
                        type = "entity reference"
                        break
                    case 6:
                        type = "entity"
                        break
                    case 7:
                        type = "processing instruction"
                        break
                    case 8:
                        type = "comment"
                        break
                    case 9:
                        type = "document"
                        break
```

continues ▶

```
                    case 10:
                        type = "document type"
                        break
                    case 11:
                        type = "document fragment"
                        break
                    case 12:
                        type = "notation"
            }
            var text

            if (node1.nodeValue != null) {
                text = indent + node1.nodeName
                + "  = " + node1.nodeValue
                + "  (Node type: " + type
                + ")"
            } else {
                text = indent + node1.nodeName
                + "  (Node type: " + type
                + ")"
            }

        if (node1.attributes != null) {
            if (node1.attributes.length > 0) {
                for (var loopIndex = 0; loopIndex <
                    node1.attributes.length; loopIndex++) {
                    text += " (Attribute: " +
                        node1.attributes(loopIndex).nodeName +
                        " = \"" +
                        node1.attributes(loopIndex).nodeValue
                        + "\")"
                }
            }
        }

        text += "<BR>"

        if (node1.childNodes.length > 0) {
            for (var loopIndex = 0; loopIndex <
                node1.childNodes.length; loopIndex++) {
                text += parse(node1.childNodes(loopIndex),
                indent + "    ")
            }
        }
    }
    return text
    }
    //-->
    </SCRIPT>
</HEAD>

<BODY>
    <H1>
```

```
        Parsing XML Documents
    </H1>

    <INPUT TYPE="BUTTON" VALUE="Parse XML document"
        ONCLICK="parseDocument()">
    <DIV ID="div1"></DIV>
    </BODY>
</HTML>
```

At this point, then, we have a good handle on working with the contents of
XML documents. When you know how to access those contents, you can
read all the data you need from an XML document, and you can use
JavaScript to work with that data. An XML document might tell you what
HTML elements to create in a page and where to place them, for example,
or it might give you data to fill controls such as select controls with.

> **Tip**
>
> You also can write XML documents, but not directly with Internet Explorer (which can't write data to the user's
> disk from code). Instead, you should send the data back to the server using HTML forms and create or install soft-
> ware on the server to write the XML documents and send them back.

Handling XML Document Events

As with HTML documents, it can be important to know when an XML
document loads and its data is available. The Internet Explorer actually
enables you to track the progress of an XML document as it's being loaded.
In this case, you can use the onreadystatechange and ondataavailable
events. The ondataavailable event occurs when the data from the XML
document is available for use, and you can connect an event handler to this
event like this:

```
document1.ondataavailable = dataAvailable
    .
    .
    .
function dataAvailable()
{
    div1.innerHTML = "The data is now available!"
}
```

The `readyState` property in the `onreadystatechange` event lets you know about the current status of a document's data. You also can connect an event handler to this event, and check the `readyState` property to see what's going on:

```
document1.onreadystatechange = stateChange
    .
    .
    .
function stateChange()
{
    switch (document1.readyState)
    {
        case 1:
            div1.innerHTML = "The data is uninitialized."
            break
        case 2:
            div1.innerHTML = "The data is being loaded."
            break
        case 3:
            div1.innerHTML = "The data is loaded."
            break
        case 4:
            div1.innerHTML = "The data loading process is done."
            if (document1.parseError.errorCode != 0) {
                div1.innerHTML = "Error."
            }
            else {
                div1.innerHTML = "The data loaded OK."
            }
        break
    }
}
```

Here's an example putting this kind of code to work, enabling us to watch the loading progress of an XML document:

(Listing 22-08.html on the web site)

```
<HTML>
    <HEAD>
        <TITLE>
            Loading XML Documents
        </TITLE>

        <SCRIPT LANGUAGE="JavaScript">
            <!--
            var document1

            function loader()
            {
                document1 = new ActiveXObject("microsoft.XMLDOM")
```

```
            document1.ondataavailable = dataAvailable
            document1.onreadystatechange = stateChange

            document1.load('22-01.xml')
        }

        function dataAvailable()
        {
            div1.innerHTML += "The data is now available!<BR>"
        }

        function stateChange()
        {
            switch (document1.readyState)
            {
                case 1:
                    div1.innerHTML += "The data is uninitialized.<BR>"
                    break
                case 2:
                    div1.innerHTML += "The data is being loaded.<BR>"
                    break
                case 3:
                    div1.innerHTML += "The data is loaded.<BR>"
                    break
                case 4:
                    div1.innerHTML += "The data loading process is done.<BR>"
                    if (document1.parseError.errorCode != 0) {
                        div1.innerHTML += "Error.<BR>"
                    }
                    else {
                        div1.innerHTML += "The data loaded OK.<BR>"
                    }
                    break
            }
        }
        //-->
    </SCRIPT>
</HEAD>

<BODY>
    <H1>
        Loading XML Documents
    </H1>

    <INPUT TYPE="BUTTON" VALUE="Load XML Document"
        ONCLICK="loader()">
    <DIV ID="div1"></DIV>
</BODY>
</HTML>
```

The results of this web page appear in Figure 22.5, and you can see the progress that the Internet Explorer made in loading our XML document in that page.

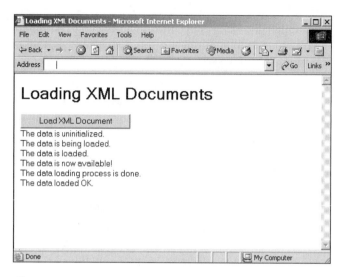

Figure 22.5   Loading an XML document in the Internet Explorer.

Validating XML Documents

As mentioned in the beginning of this chapter, you can specify the syntax of an XML document yourself. You can do that typically with a DTD or an XML schema (which we won't cover here; see www.w3.org/TR/xmlschema-0/ for more information). The Internet Explorer does try to validate XML documents as it loads them, checking them against the syntax you've specified; but you won't see any validation errors unless you check the parseError object. Let's take a look at how that works.

> **Tip**
>
> You can also turn validation on or off with the document object's validateOnParse property. This property is set to true by default, but if you set it to false, validation is turned off.

Here's an example where I'll purposely introduce an error into our sample XML document, 22-01.xml. That document has a DTD that specifies the syntax for the document's contents; for example, the DTD entry for the <EVENT> element indicates that this element should contain an <EVENT_TITLE>

element, an <EVENT_NUMBER> element, a <SUBJECT> element, and a <DATE>
element, followed by zero or more <PEOPLE> elements, in that order:

```
<?xml version="1.0"?>
<!DOCTYPE EVENTS [
<!ELEMENT EVENTS (EVENT*)>
<!ELEMENT EVENT (EVENT_TITLE, EVENT_NUMBER, SUBJECT, DATE, PEOPLE*)>
<!ELEMENT EVENT_TITLE (#PCDATA)>
<!ELEMENT EVENT_NUMBER (#PCDATA)>
<!ELEMENT SUBJECT (#PCDATA)>
<!ELEMENT DATE (#PCDATA)>
<!ELEMENT FIRST_NAME (#PCDATA)>
<!ELEMENT LAST_NAME (#PCDATA)>
<!ELEMENT PEOPLE (PERSON*)>
<!ELEMENT PERSON (FIRST_NAME,LAST_NAME)>
<!ATTLIST EVENT
    TYPE CDATA #IMPLIED>
<!ATTLIST PERSON
    ATTENDENCE CDATA #IMPLIED>
]>
<EVENTS>
    <EVENT TYPE="informal">
        <EVENT_TITLE>15th Award Ceremony</EVENT_TITLE>
        <EVENT_NUMBER>1207</EVENT_NUMBER>
        <SUBJECT>Gala Event</SUBJECT>
          .
          .
          .
```

Now I'll alter the DTD by removing the <EVENT_NUMBER> element from the
<EVENT> element's specification, creating this new XML document, 22-
09.xml:

(Listing 22-09.xml on the web site)

```
<?xml version="1.0"?>
<!DOCTYPE EVENTS [
<!ELEMENT EVENTS (EVENT*)>
<!ELEMENT EVENT (EVENT_TITLE, SUBJECT, DATE, PEOPLE*)>
<!ELEMENT EVENT_TITLE (#PCDATA)>
<!ELEMENT EVENT_NUMBER (#PCDATA)>
<!ELEMENT SUBJECT (#PCDATA)>
<!ELEMENT DATE (#PCDATA)>
<!ELEMENT FIRST_NAME (#PCDATA)>
<!ELEMENT LAST_NAME (#PCDATA)>
<!ELEMENT PEOPLE (PERSON*)>
<!ELEMENT PERSON (FIRST_NAME,LAST_NAME)>
<!ATTLIST EVENT
    TYPE CDATA #IMPLIED>
<!ATTLIST PERSON
    ATTENDENCE CDATA #IMPLIED>
]>
<EVENTS>
```

continues ▶

```
<EVENT TYPE="informal">
    <EVENT_TITLE>15th Award Ceremony</EVENT_TITLE>
    <EVENT_NUMBER>1207</EVENT_NUMBER>
    <SUBJECT>Gala Event</SUBJECT>
    <DATE>7/4/2003</DATE>
    <PEOPLE>
        <PERSON ATTENDENCE="present">
            <FIRST_NAME>Sam</FIRST_NAME>
            <LAST_NAME>Edwards</LAST_NAME>
        </PERSON>
        <PERSON ATTENDENCE="absent">
            <FIRST_NAME>Sally</FIRST_NAME>
            <LAST_NAME>Jackson</LAST_NAME>
        </PERSON>
        <PERSON ATTENDENCE="present">
            <FIRST_NAME>Cary</FIRST_NAME>
            <LAST_NAME>Grant</LAST_NAME>
        </PERSON>
    </PEOPLE>
</EVENT>
</EVENTS>
```

With this new XML document, the Internet Explorer will expect a
<SUBJECT> element to follow <EVENT_TITLE> elements, not an
<EVENT_NUMBER> element, as is actually the case in the data.

So how can we get all the details of the validation error that will occur?
We can check whether there's been an error by checking whether the
readyState property is set to 4, and if so, we can get all the details of the
error with the parseError object's errorCode, url, line, linepos,
errorString, and reason properties:

```
if(document1.readyState == 4){
    var errorString = document1.parseError.srcText
    if (document1.parseError.errorCode != 0) {
        div1.innerText = "Error in " +
        document1.parseError.url +
        " line " + document1.parseError.line +
        " position " + document1.parseError.linepos +
        ".\nError source: " + errorString +
        "\n" + document1.parseError.reason +
        "\n" + "Error: " +
        document1.parseError.errorCode
    }
    else {
        div1.innerText = "The document loaded OK.\n"
    }
}
```

Here's how we can use this code in an example that reads in the XML document with the DTD error, 22-09.xml:

(Listing 22-10.xml on the web site)

```html
<HTML>
    <HEAD>
        <TITLE>
            Validating an XML Document
        </TITLE>

        <SCRIPT LANGUAGE="JavaScript">
            <!--
            var document1

            function loader()
            {
                document1 = new ActiveXObject("microsoft.XMLDOM")
                document1.onreadystatechange = stateChange
                document1.ondataavailable = dataAvailable
                document1.load('22-09.xml')
            }

            function dataAvailable()
            {
                div1.innerHTML += "The data is available.<BR>"
            }

            function stateChange()
            {
                if(document1.readyState == 4){
                    var errorString = document1.parseError.srcText
                    if (document1.parseError.errorCode != 0) {
                        div1.innerText = "Error in " +
                        document1.parseError.url +
                        " line " + document1.parseError.line +
                        " position " + document1.parseError.linepos +
                        ".\nError source: " + errorString +
                        "\n" + document1.parseError.reason +
                        "\n" + "Error: " +
                        document1.parseError.errorCode
                    }
                    else {
                        div1.innerText = "The document loaded OK.\n"
                    }
                }
            }
            //-->
        </SCRIPT>
    </HEAD>
```

continues ▸

```
<BODY>
    <H1>
        Validating an XML Document
    </H1>

    <INPUT TYPE="BUTTON" VALUE="Check the Document"
        ONCLICK="loader()">
    <DIV ID="div1"></DIV>
    </BODY>
</HTML>
```

You can see the results of in Figure 22.6, where the validation error is reported in detail.

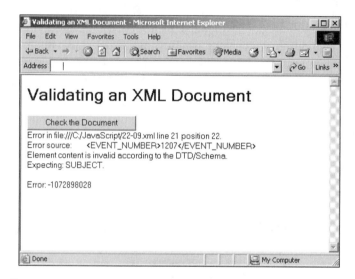

Figure 22.6   Displaying XML validation errors in the Internet Explorer.

That completes our look at standard XML in this chapter; I'll take a look at XSLT next.

XSLT

Extensible Style Language Extensions Transformations provide you with a way to transform XML documents into other formats, including (but not limited to) HTML, XHTML (W3C's XML-based version of HTML, which you can find all about at www.w3.org/TR/xhtml1), plain text, RTF (*Rich Text Format*, which word processors such as Microsoft Word can use), or even reformatted XML.

The internal workings of XSLT are beyond the scope of this book, but we can still take a look at an example. In this example, I'll transform an XML document's data into HTML form, displaying it in an HTML table. Here's the HTML document that does this in the Internet Explorer. Note that I load the XML document and XSL *style sheet*, and then use the `transformNode` method to transform the XML to HTML:

(Listing 22-11.html on the web site)

```
<HTML>
    <HEAD>
        <TITLE>Working With XSLT</TITLE>

        <SCRIPT LANGUAGE="JavaScript">
            <!--
            function xslt()
            {
                var XMLdocument1 = new ActiveXObject("Microsoft.XMLDOM")
                var XSLdocument1 = new ActiveXObject("Microsoft.XMLDOM")
                var div1 = document.all['div1']

                XMLdocument1.load('22-12.xml')
                XSLdocument1.load('22-13.xsl')
                div1.innerHTML = XMLdocument1.transformNode(XSLdocument1)
            }
            //-->
        </SCRIPT>
    </HEAD>

    <BODY ONLOAD="xslt()">
        <DIV ID="div1">
        </DIV>
    </BODY>
</HTML>
```

Here's the XML document that holds the data. In this case, this document just holds data for a few planets—how far from the sun they are, their radius, and so on:

(Listing 22-12.xml on the web site)

```
<?xml version="1.0"?>
<PLANETS>
    <PLANET>
        <NAME>Mercury</NAME>
        <MASS UNITS="(Earth = 1)">.0553</MASS>
        <DAY UNITS="days">58.65</DAY>
        <RADIUS UNITS="miles">1516</RADIUS>
        <DENSITY UNITS="(Earth = 1)">.983</DENSITY>
        <DISTANCE UNITS="million miles">43.4</DISTANCE><!--At perihelion-->
    </PLANET>
```

continues ▶

```
    <PLANET>
        <NAME>Venus</NAME>
        <MASS UNITS="(Earth = 1)">.815</MASS>
        <DAY UNITS="days">116.75</DAY>
        <RADIUS UNITS="miles">3716</RADIUS>
        <DENSITY UNITS="(Earth = 1)">.943</DENSITY>
        <DISTANCE UNITS="million miles">66.8</DISTANCE><!--At perihelion-->
    </PLANET>

    <PLANET>
        <NAME>Earth</NAME>
        <MASS UNITS="(Earth = 1)">1</MASS>
        <DAY UNITS="days">1</DAY>
        <RADIUS UNITS="miles">2107</RADIUS>
        <DENSITY UNITS="(Earth = 1)">1</DENSITY>
        <DISTANCE UNITS="million miles">128.4</DISTANCE><!--At perihelion-->
    </PLANET>
</PLANETS>
```

And here's the XSLT style sheet that the Internet Explorer uses to do the XML-to-HTML transformation. XSLT style sheets work by setting up style sheet rules named templates, which match various XML elements, enable you to access their data, and reformat that data:

(Listing 22-13.xsl on the web site)

```
<?xml version="1.0"?>
<xsl:stylesheet version="1.1"
xmlns:xsl="http://www.w3.org/1999/XSL/Transform">
    <xsl:template match="/PLANETS">
        <HTML>
            <HEAD>
                <TITLE>
                    Working With XSLT
                </TITLE>
            </HEAD>
            <BODY>
                <H1>
                    Working With XSLT
                </H1>
                <TABLE BORDER="2">
                    <TR>
                        <TD>Name</TD>
                        <TD>Mass</TD>
                        <TD>Radius</TD>
                        <TD>Day</TD>
                    </TR>
                    <xsl:apply-templates/>
                </TABLE>
            </BODY>
        </HTML>
```

```
      </xsl:template>

   <xsl:template match="PLANET">
      <TR>
         <TD><xsl:value-of select="NAME"/></TD>
         <TD><xsl:apply-templates select="MASS"/></TD>
         <TD><xsl:apply-templates select="RADIUS"/></TD>
         <TD><xsl:apply-templates select="DAY"/></TD>
      </TR>
   </xsl:template>

   <xsl:template match="MASS">
      <xsl:value-of select="."/>
      <xsl:text> </xsl:text>
      <xsl:value-of select="@UNITS"/>
   </xsl:template>

   <xsl:template match="RADIUS">
      <xsl:value-of select="."/>
      <xsl:text> </xsl:text>
      <xsl:value-of select="@UNITS"/>
   </xsl:template>

   <xsl:template match="DAY">
      <xsl:value-of select="."/>
      <xsl:text> </xsl:text>
      <xsl:value-of select="@UNITS"/>
   </xsl:template>

</xsl:stylesheet>
```

And that's it! You can see the results in Figure 22.7. Now we're using XSLT with JavaScript to reformat XML as HTML.

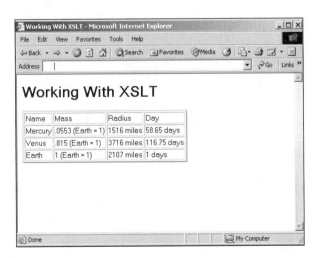

Figure 22.7 Transforming an XML document to HTML in the Internet Explorer.

Tip

If this example doesn't work, you may need to install a more recent version of the Microsoft XML parser. The MS XML parser version 3.0 has full support for XSLT, and you can download it from `http://msdn.microsoft.com/downloads/default.asp?URL=/code/sample.asp?url=/msdn-files/027/001/469/msdncompositedoc.xml`. Then replace the lines var `XMLdocument1 = new ActiveXObject("Microsoft.XMLDOM")` and var `XSLdocument1 = new ActiveXObject("Microsoft.XMLDOM")` in Listing 22-11.html with var `XMLdocument1 = new ActiveXObject("MSXML2.DOMDocument.3.0")` and var `XSLdocument1 = new ActiveXObject("MSXML2.DOMDocument.3.0")`.

That completes our look at XML and XSLT with JavaScript in this chapter. As you can tell, we've just scratched the surface here. For more information on Microsoft's coverage of these topics, take a look at `http://msdn.microsoft.com` and search for "XML" and "XSLT," or take a look at books like *Inside XML* and *Inside XSLT*. In the next chapter, we'll take a look at working with cookies and creating your own objects in JavaScript.

23

Cookies and Creating Your Own Objects

IN THIS CHAPTER, WE'LL TAKE A LOOK AT TWO topics near and dear to the JavaScript programmer's heart: using cookies and creating your own objects.

Everyone knows about *cookies*—they're those data items that you can store on someone's computer. You can store everything from the users' name (if they give it to you) to the current items they've purchased and how much their total is. Using cookies is easier than you might think in JavaScript, and we'll take a look at how to work with them in this chapter. We'll see not only how to create and store a cookie, but also what's involved in reading them at a later time. We'll also see how to specify when a cookie expires—that is, when the browser should delete it. And we'll see how to delete a cookie ourselves.

We'll also take a look at creating custom objects in this chapter. JavaScript uses objects, but it's not truly object-oriented, because it doesn't support all those elements that are necessary for true *object-oriented programming* (OOP), such as classes, inheritance, polymorphism, and more.

Instead, some people consider JavaScript *object-based*. That is, instead of supporting all the OOP formality, JavaScript enables you to work with many preexisting objects, such as the built-in objects such as `String`, `Array`, `Boolean`, and so on, as well as gives you access to browser objects such as the `document`, `navigator`, and `window` objects.

Nonetheless, you can create your own objects in JavaScript, and we'll see how to do so here. We'll create new objects that support not only properties, but methods as well. We'll even see how to create constructors to which you can pass data to initialize your objects.

That's the program for this chapter then—working with cookies and custom objects. These are both favorite topics for the JavaScript programmer, and we'll get all the details in this chapter.

Cookies

Cookies—you either love them or hate them. Programmers are not usually on the hate-them side, because cookies help the programming process a great deal by enabling you to store data that the browser environment—a notoriously ephemeral environment—can use. You can customize the appearance of your web site for particular users with cookies—fetching and displaying economic data, for example, or setting background color—or store the data associated with a single session but multiple pages.

From the users' point of view, however, you're storing data on their computer. Worse, they have no control over that data. Although cookies have largely been accepted now, there continue to be security issues, including cases of hackers being able to store code in cookies that is executed by the browser (although security holes like this are patched vigorously by browser manufacturers when discovered).

The actual cookie stored by JavaScript code is just text, and it's stored in the `document.cookie` property. This makes accessing cookies very easy, as we'll see. The actual cookie text itself is made up of `name=value;` pairs. (Each pair is sometimes called a *crumb*, and each should end with a semicolon.) If you want to store a value of 555 as a cookie's ID, for example, you might use a pair like this `id=555;`. In JavaScript, you can store up to 20 such pairs in a single cookie string.

Some pairs are already interpreted by the browser, including the following:

- `expires=date;` sets the expiration date for the cookie. Use GMT format to specify the date. Note that not setting expiration date for a cookie will make it to expire when the browser is closed. On the other hand, if you set an expiration date for sometime in the future, the cookie is saved until then. If you set an expiration date in the past, however, the cookie is deleted.

- `domain=domainname;` sets a cookie's domain. This isn't often used—setting the domain of the cookie lets pages from one domain that is made up of multiple servers share a cookie.

- **path=path;** sets a cookie's path. Setting a path for the cookie allows the current page to share cookie information with other pages from the same domain, because cookies are stored according to path.
- **secure;** makes a cookie secure. Making a cookie secure means the cookie information can be read or set only in a secure environment.

The browser stores only one cookie per page. When you reload that page, the browser determines which cookie to give you access to by seeing what page (including the path of that page) you've loaded, and you'll get the whole cookie text for that page in the `document.cookie` property. You have to search that cookie text for the data pair you want yourself.

Let's take a look at an example.

Creating Cookies

In this case, I'll create an example that will enable us to store a cookie, retrieve it, and delete it. With a great burst of originality, I'll call this cookie `cookie1`, and give it the text `Here is the cookie data!`. To set this cookie, I'll create a function named `setCookie`, and just assign the cookie data pair to `document.cookie`:

```
function setCookie()
{
    document.cookie =
        "cookie1=Here is the cookie data!;"
        .
        .
        .

}
```

Now when I want to search for the cookie's data (as when the page is reloaded later), all I have to do is to search the `document.cookie` for `cookie1=`, and I know that the data for that cookie follows.

In fact, it's rare that you set a cookie this way, because it'll expire as soon as the browser closes. Instead, you usually set an expiration date yourself using an `expires=date;` pair. For example, I can make the cookie expire in 24 hours by adding 24 * 60 * 60 * 1000 milliseconds to the current time and setting that as the expiration date (after converting it to GMT time with the `toGMTString` method). Here's how that looks in code. Note that I'm also displaying an alert box to indicate that the cookie has been created:

```
function setCookie()
{
```

continues ▶

```
var cookieDate = new Date()
cookieDate.setTime(cookieDate.getTime() + 24 * 60 * 60 *
    1000)
document.cookie =
    "cookie1=Here is the cookie data!;expires="
    + cookieDate.toGMTString()
alert("Cookie created!")
}
```

Here's an example that uses this code to set cookie1 when the user clicks a button:

(Listing 23-01.html on the web site)

```
<HTML>
    <HEAD>
        <TITLE>
            Working With Cookies
        </TITLE>
        <SCRIPT LANGUAGE="JavaScript">
            <!--
            function setCookie()
            {
                var cookieDate = new Date()
                cookieDate.setTime(cookieDate.getTime() + 24 * 60 * 60 *
                    1000)
                document.cookie =
                    "cookie1=Here is the cookie data!;expires="
                    + cookieDate.toGMTString()
                alert("Cookie created!")
            }
            //-->
        </SCRIPT>
    </HEAD>

    <BODY>
        <H1>
            Working With Cookies
        </H1>
        <FORM NAME="form1">
            <INPUT TYPE = BUTTON Value = "Create the cookie"
                ONCLICK = "setCookie()">
        </FORM>
    </BODY>
</HTML>
```

You can see the results in Figure 23.1, where I've clicked the button and created the cookie.

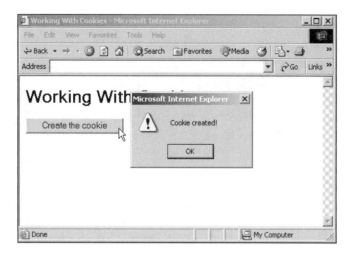

Figure 23.1 Creating a cookie.

The next step is to read the cookie data back in, and I'll take a look at that now.

Reading Cookies

Now that we've set a cookie, we can read its data back in. That involves using the document.cookie property—the browser will fill that property with the cookie text for the page that was set earlier automatically.

In the preceding section, we used the setCookie function to set a cookie named cookie1. When we check that property again (even after reloading the same page), we'll see that document.cookie holds "cookie1=Here is the cookie data!". Note that this text does not contain the expires=date; pair that we set in the cookie in setCookie, because that pair was intended for the browser itself.

In this example, document.cookie only holds one data pair ("cookie1=Here is the cookie data!"), but I'll show how one extracts cookie data in general, even if your cookie contains many such pairs. To retrieve the cookie's data, I'll create a function named getCookie. I start by making a copy of document.cookie so we don't inadvertently change that property. Next I determine the start and end positions of the text that's been assigned to cookie1 (that is, Here is the cookie data!) by searching for the terminating semicolon that ends cookie data pairs like this (note that if the data you're searching for is at the very end of the cookie string, some browsers omit the final semicolon, which I'm also taking care of in this code):

```
function getCookie()
{
    var cookieData = new String(document.cookie)
    var cookieHeader = "cookie1="
    var cookieStart = cookieData.indexOf(cookieHeader) + cookieHeader.length
    var cookieEnd = cookieData.indexOf(";", cookieStart)
    if(cookieEnd == -1 ) {
        cookieEnd = cookieData.length
    }
         .
         .
         .
}
```

Now we have the starting and ending indices of our data in the cookie string; all that remains is to extract that data itself using the substring method. Here's what that looks like. Note that I'm also handling the case where the cookie was not found (presumably because it was not set or expired):

```
function getCookie()
{
    var cookieData = new String(document.cookie)
    var cookieHeader = "cookie1="
    var cookieStart = cookieData.indexOf(cookieHeader) + cookieHeader.length
    var cookieEnd = cookieData.indexOf(";", cookieStart)
    if(cookieEnd == -1 ) {
        cookieEnd = cookieData.length
    }

    if (cookieData.indexOf(cookieHeader) != -1){
        document.form1.text1.value =
            cookieData.substring(cookieStart, cookieEnd)
    }
    else{
        document.form1.text1.value = "Could not find the cookie."
    }
}
```

Here's an example that puts this code to work, enabling us to retrieve and display the cookie's text in a text field:

(Listing 23-02.html on the web site)

```
<HTML>
    <HEAD>
        <TITLE>
            Working With Cookies
        </TITLE>
        <SCRIPT LANGUAGE="JavaScript">
            <!--
            function setCookie()
            {
```

```
        var cookieDate = new Date()
        cookieDate.setTime(cookieDate.getTime() + 24 * 60 * 60 *
            1000)
        document.cookie =
            "cookie1=Here is the cookie data!;expires="
            + cookieDate.toGMTString()
        alert("Cookie created!")
    }

    function getCookie()
    {
        var cookieData = new String(document.cookie)
        var cookieHeader = "cookie1="
        var cookieStart = cookieData.indexOf(cookieHeader) +
        ➥cookieHeader.length
        var cookieEnd = cookieData.indexOf(";", cookieStart)
        if(cookieEnd == -1 ) {
            cookieEnd = cookieData.length
        }

        if (cookieData.indexOf(cookieHeader) != -1){
            document.form1.text1.value =
                cookieData.substring(cookieStart, cookieEnd)
        }
        else{
            document.form1.text1.value = "Could not find the cookie."
        }
    }
    //-->
    </SCRIPT>
</HEAD>

<BODY>
    <H1>
        Working With Cookies
    </H1>
    <FORM NAME="form1">
        <INPUT TYPE = BUTTON Value = "Create the cookie"
            ONCLICK = "setCookie()">
        <BR>
        <INPUT TYPE="text1" NAME="text1" SIZE="30">
        <BR>
        <INPUT TYPE = BUTTON Value = "Get the cookie"
            ONCLICK = "getCookie()">
    </FORM>
</BODY>
</HTML>
```

You can see the results in Figure 23.2, where we're reading the text we've assigned to the cookie. Now we're using cookies. Note that you can set the cookie in one session, close the browser, open it again, load the same page, and click the "Get the cookie" button to read and see the cookie's data (so long as the cookie hasn't expired, of course).

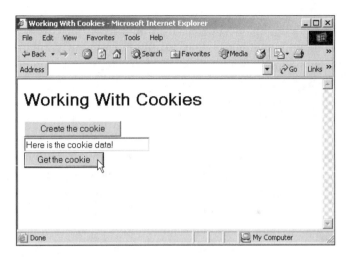

Figure 23.2 Reading cookie data.

Now we've set a cookie and read it back in, deciphering its data. But what about cookie maintenance? Can you delete cookies when you want to? I'll take a look at that in the next section.

Deleting Cookies

The browser will delete cookies when they're expired (although it might take the browsers a little time to do so). That means we can delete `cookie1` just by resetting its expiration time. Here's a function, `deleteCookie`, which does exactly that, setting the cookie's expiration date to some time in the past:

```
function deleteCookie()
{
    document.cookie =
        "cookie1=Here is the cookie data!;expires=Fri, 31 Dec 1999 23:00:00 GMT;"
        document.form1.text1.value = ""
        window.alert("Cookie will be deleted!")
}
```

That's all it takes. Here's how we can add this function to our cookie example:

(Listing 23-03.html on the web site)

```html
<HTML>
    <HEAD>
        <TITLE>
            Working With Cookies
        </TITLE>
        <SCRIPT LANGUAGE="JavaScript">
            <!--
            function setCookie()
            {
                var cookieDate = new Date()
                cookieDate.setTime(cookieDate.getTime() + 24 * 60 * 60 *
                    1000)
                document.cookie =
                    "cookie1=Here is the cookie data!;expires="
                    + cookieDate.toGMTString()
                alert("Cookie created!")
            }

            function getCookie()
            {
                var cookieData = new String(document.cookie)
                var cookieHeader = "cookie1="
                var cookieStart = cookieData.indexOf(cookieHeader) +
                ➡cookieHeader.length
                var cookieEnd = cookieData.indexOf(";", cookieStart)
                if(cookieEnd == -1 ) {
                    cookieEnd = cookieData.length
                }

                if (cookieData.indexOf(cookieHeader) != -1){
                    document.form1.text1.value =
                        cookieData.substring(cookieStart, cookieEnd)
                }
                else{
                    document.form1.text1.value = "Could not find the cookie."
                }
            }

            function deleteCookie()
            {
                document.cookie =
                    "cookie1=Here is the cookie data!;expires=Fri, 31 Dec 1999
                    ➡23:00:00 GMT;"
                document.form1.text1.value = ""

                window.alert("Cookie will be deleted!")
            }
```

continues ▶

```
                    //-->
            </SCRIPT>
    </HEAD>

    <BODY>
        <H1>
            Working With Cookies
        </H1>
        <FORM NAME="form1">
            <INPUT TYPE = BUTTON Value = "Create the cookie"
                ONCLICK = "setCookie()">
            <BR>
            <INPUT TYPE="text1" NAME="text1" SIZE="30">
            <BR>
            <INPUT TYPE = BUTTON Value = "Get the cookie"
                ONCLICK = "getCookie()">
            <BR>
            <INPUT TYPE = BUTTON Value = "Delete the cookie"
                ONCLICK = "deleteCookie()">
            <BR>
            <INPUT TYPE = BUTTON Value = "Get the cookie"
                ONCLICK = "getCookie()">
        </FORM>
    </BODY>
</HTML>
```

You can see the results in Figure 23.3. In this case, I've clicked the "Delete the cookie" button, followed by the "Get the cookie" button. As you can see in the figure, the cookie has indeed been deleted.

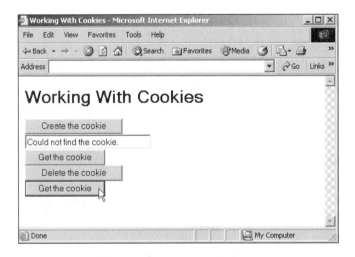

Figure 23.3 Deleting a cookie.

Now we've gotten a good introduction to the whole topic of working with cookies. We've seen how to set, read, and delete cookies at will. In the next section, I'll take a look at how to use cookies with self-modifying pages that read and use data stored in cookies.

Self-Modifying Pages That Respond to Cookie Data

Here's another cookie example. This time, you'll see two different pages depending on whether a cookie was set. The page will modify itself to ask the user for his name if the cookie was not set, and will display a welcome message using his name if the cookie containing that name was set.

Here's how it works. We'll start by checking whether the cookie, which I'll call name1, is set, and if so, write a welcoming message to our web page using that name:

```
var cookieData = new String(document.cookie)
var cookieHeader = "name1="
var cookieStart = cookieData.indexOf(cookieHeader) + cookieHeader.length
var cookieEnd = cookieData.indexOf(";", cookieStart)
if(cookieEnd == -1 ) {
    cookieEnd = cookieData.length
}

if (cookieData.indexOf(cookieHeader) != -1){
    var name = cookieData.substring(cookieStart, cookieEnd)
    document.write("<BR><H1>Welcome " + name + "!</H1>")
}
        .
        .
        .
```

On the other hand, if the cookie does not exist, we'll display a page inviting the user to set the cookie by showing a prompt, a text field in which to enter his name, and a button:

```
if (cookieData.indexOf(cookieHeader) != -1){
    var name = cookieData.substring(cookieStart, cookieEnd)
    document.write("<BR><H1>Welcome " + name + "!</H1>")
}
else{
    document.write("<BR>")
    document.write("<H1>")
    document.write("Enter your name and click the button.")
    document.write("</H1>")
    document.write("<BR>")
    document.write("<FORM NAME='form1'>")
    document.write("<INPUT TYPE='TEXT' NAME='text1' SIZE='40'>")
```

continues ▶

```
document.write("<BR><BR>")
document.write("<INPUT TYPE='BUTTON' VALUE='Store Name' ONCLICK='setCookie()'>")
document.write("</FORM>")
}
```

When the user enters his name and clicks the button, the `setCookie` function is called, and we just set a temporary cookie that will expire in one day, using the name name1:

```
function setCookie()
{
    var then = new Date()
    then.setTime(then.getTime() + 24 * 60 * 60 * 1000)
    document.cookie = "name1=" + document.form1.text1.value + ";expires="
    + then.toGMTString()
    alert("The cookie was set!")
}
```

Here's the whole code for this page, which modifies itself depending on whether a cookie was set:

(Listing 23-04.html on the web site)

```
<HTML>
    <HEAD>
        <TITLE>Self-Modifying Pages That Respond to Cookies</TITLE>
    </HEAD>
    <BODY>
        <SCRIPT LANGUAGE="JavaScript">
            <!--
                var cookieData = new String(document.cookie)
                var cookieHeader = "name1="
                var cookieStart = cookieData.indexOf(cookieHeader) +
                ➥cookieHeader.length
                var cookieEnd = cookieData.indexOf(";", cookieStart)
                if(cookieEnd == -1 ) {
                    cookieEnd = cookieData.length
                }

                if (cookieData.indexOf(cookieHeader) != -1){
                    var name = cookieData.substring(cookieStart, cookieEnd)
                    document.write("<BR><H1>Welcome " + name + "!</H1>")
                }
                else{
                    document.write("<BR>")
                    document.write("<H1>")
                    document.write("Enter your name and click the button.")
                    document.write("</H1>")
                    document.write("<BR>")
                    document.write("<FORM NAME='form1'>")
                    document.write("<INPUT TYPE='TEXT' NAME='text1' SIZE='40'>")
                    document.write("<BR><BR>")
```

```
                document.write("<INPUT TYPE='BUTTON' VALUE='Store Name'
                ➥ONCLICK='setCookie()'>")
                document.write("</FORM>")
            }

            function setCookie()
            {
                var then = new Date()
                then.setTime(then.getTime() + 24 * 60 * 60 * 1000)
                document.cookie = "name1=" + document.form1.text1.value +
                ➥";expires="
                + then.toGMTString()
                alert("The cookie was set!")
            }
        //-->
        </SCRIPT>
    </BODY>
</HTML>
```

You can see the results in Figure 23.4 when you first load the page. In that figure, you can see the code asking for a name to store. When I store my name and reload the page at a later time (up until the cookie expires), the page displays a welcoming message using my name, as you see in Figure 23.5.

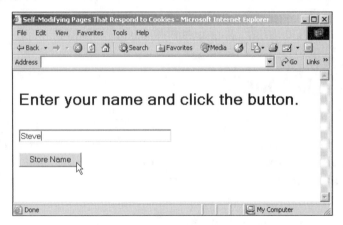

Figure 23.4 Setting a cookie in a self-modifying page.

Figure 23.5 Modifying a page based on cookie content.

That's it for our work on cookies in this chapter. As you can see, it's not difficult in theory; you just add data pairs to a cookie string, and that cookie string is made available to you later in the document.cookie property each time that page is loaded again and the cookie is still available. Keep in mind that not all users tolerate cookies, and may even have to browser set not to accept them, in which case you should offer an alternative, such as storing data in hidden HTML fields.

Accessing the Disk

Here's a quick one that I'm putting right after cookies because it involves accessing information from the user's hard disk. It's just a small topic that doesn't really fit anywhere else in the book, but it's a nice trick to know.

By setting the ACTION attribute to a file: URL in the Internet Explorer, you can get access to the user's hard disk in Windows, displaying the file structure. Here's an example:

(Listing 23-05.html on the web site)

```
<HTML>
    <HEAD>
        <TITLE>Accessing the Disk</TITLE>
    </HEAD>

    <BODY>
        <H1>Accessing the Disk</H1>
        <FORM ACTION="file:///c¦/">
            <INPUT TYPE="submit" VALUE="See C: Drive">
        </FORM>
    </BODY>
</HTML>
```

You can see the results in Figure 23.6, where the file structure of the C: drive is displayed.

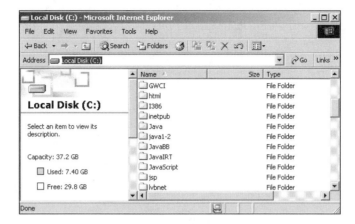

Figure 23.6 Accessing the disk.

It's time to turn to the other topic we're going to cover in this chapter: creating custom objects. As mentioned at the beginning of this chapter, some programmers say that JavaScript isn't object-oriented so much as object-based. And that's also true when you want to create your own objects—you can put them together object by object. You don't create the OOP classes that genuine OOP languages such as Java or C++ use. Instead, you add can add properties one at a time to objects just by assigning values to them. You also can add methods the same way—by assigning a method to an object—as we'll see.

That's not to say that you can't add a new property or method to a whole set of objects at the same time—using prototypes, you can, as we'll see here. However, you still don't start with classes and then create objects as you do in true OOP languages; you work with objects from the very beginning.

Let's take a look at this now, starting by creating custom objects and giving them properties.

Creating Custom Objects: Properties

Suppose that we want to keep track of some friends, including their names, phone numbers, and our own personal ranking of them. Unfortunately, JavaScript doesn't come with a `friend` object built in with these properties, but we can create one.

So how do you create a custom object? One way is to create a function with the same name as the object type you want to create, and to treat that function as the object's constructor, which you use to create objects of that type. (We discussed constructors as far back as Chapter 2, "The JavaScript Language: Data, Operators, and Branching.") For example, here's how we might create a constructor for friend objects, where we're passing the friend's name, phone, and our ranking of that friend:

```
function friend(name, phone, rank)
{
        .
        .
        .

}
```

You can then store the friend's name, phone, and your ranking of that friend in the object like this:

```
function friend(name, phone, rank)
{
    this.name = name
    this.phone = phone
    this.rank = rank
}
```

That's all it takes. Now you can create objects using this constructor when you use the new keyword. Here's an example where I'm creating an array, array1, of friend objects:

```
var array1 = new Array(4)
array1[0] = new friend("Ed", "555-1111", 4)
array1[1] = new friend("Harold", "555-2222", 1)
array1[2] = new friend("Nancy", "555-3333", 3)
array1[3] = new friend("Sandy", "555-4444", 2)
```

Here's some code that brings this together. In this case, I'll create the array of friend objects and then loop over that array, displaying each property of each friend object in a text area. Note that I can now refer to each property using the standard syntax, *object.property*:

(Listing 23-06.html on the web site)

```
<HTML>
    <HEAD>
        <TITLE>
            Creating Custom Objects
        </TITLE>
    </HEAD>

    <BODY>
        <H1>Creating Custom Objects</H1>
```

```
<FORM NAME="form1">
    <TEXTAREA NAME="textarea1" ROWS="5" COLS="40"></TEXTAREA>
</FORM>
<SCRIPT LANGUAGE="JavaScript">
    <!--
    function friend(name, phone, rank)
    {
        this.name = name
        this.phone = phone
        this.rank = rank
    }

    var array1 = new Array(4)
    array1[0] = new friend("Ed", "555-1111", 4)
    array1[1] = new friend("Harold", "555-2222", 1)
    array1[2] = new friend("Nancy", "555-3333", 3)
    array1[3] = new friend("Sandy", "555-4444", 2)

    for(var loopIndex = 0; loopIndex < array1.length; loopIndex++){
        document.form1.textarea1.value += "Name: " + array1[loopIndex].name
        ➥+ " "
        document.form1.textarea1.value += "Phone: " + array1[loopIndex].phone
        ➥+ " "
        document.form1.textarea1.value += "Rank: " + array1[loopIndex].rank
        ➥+ "\n"
    }
    // -->
</SCRIPT>
</BODY>
</HTML>
```

You can see the results in Figure 23.7, where all the objects in the array are initialized, created, and then displayed, object by object and property by property.

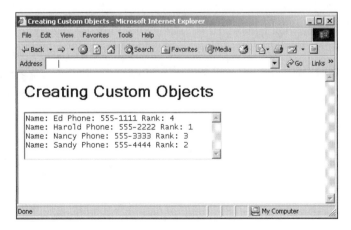

Figure 23.7 Adding properties to custom objects.

> **Tip**
>
> So far, we've added properties one by one to objects, but you also can add properties to an entire set of objects at once using prototypes; see "Adding Methods to Existing Objects" later in this chapter.

Here's another thing to know: You also can set default values for properties in a constructor of the type we're using here.

Setting Default Property Values

In NS4+ and IE4+, you can specify default values for properties in a constructor using this syntax, where the default value appears as the second term in each OR expression (which uses the JavaScript || operator):

```
function friend(name, phone, rank)
{
    this.name = name || "George"
    this.phone = phone || "555-1212"
    this.rank = rank || 10
}
```

Now you can pass an empty string or null as an argument to this constructor, and the appropriate default value will be used instead. In fact, you can even omit arguments, and the constructor will apply the default value instead, as long as the default arguments are at the very end of the argument list you pass (so the constructor knows which arguments have been omitted). Here's an example where I'm omitting the "rank" argument in a call to this constructor when creating one object:

(Listing 23-07.html on the web site)

```
<HTML>
    <HEAD>
        <TITLE>
            Creating Custom Objects
        </TITLE>
    </HEAD>

    <BODY>
        <H1>Creating Custom Objects</H1>
        <FORM NAME="form1">
            <TEXTAREA NAME="textarea1" ROWS="5" COLS="40"></TEXTAREA>
        </FORM>
        <SCRIPT LANGUAGE="JavaScript">
            <!--
            function friend(name, phone, rank)
            {
```

```
            this.name = name || "George"
            this.phone = phone || "555-1212"
            this.rank = rank || 10
        }

        var array1 = new Array(4)
        array1[0] = new friend("Ed", "555-1111", 4)
        array1[1] = new friend("Harold", "555-2222", 1)
        array1[2] = new friend("Nancy", "555-3333", 3)
        array1[3] = new friend("Sandy", "555-4444")

        for(var loopIndex = 0; loopIndex < array1.length; loopIndex++){
            document.form1.textarea1.value += "Name: " + array1[loopIndex].name
            ➥+ " "
            document.form1.textarea1.value += "Phone: " + array1[loopIndex].phone
            ➥+ " "
            document.form1.textarea1.value += "Rank: " + array1[loopIndex].rank
            ➥+ "\n"
        }
        // -->
    </SCRIPT>
  </BODY>
</HTML>
```

You can see the results in Figure 23.8. Note the last entry for Sandy—you can see the default value for the rank property, 10, is set in that object.

Figure 23.8   Using default properties.

Besides adding properties to custom objects, you also can add methods. I'll take a look at that next.

Creating Custom Objects: Methods

To create a custom method, you just add it to an object as you would a property. Suppose, for example, that you wanted to add a method named `display` that displayed the person's name in an alert box to a `friend` object; you could do that like this:

```
function friend(name, phone, rank)
{
    this.name = name
    this.phone = phone
    this.rank = rank
    this.display = display
}
```

In the `display` method, you can refer to the current object with the `this` keyword; so here's how you can display an object's name in an alert box:

```
function display()
{
    window.alert("Name: " + this.name)
}
```

To put this new method to work, I'll add a text field to the example that enables the user to enter a friend's rank to look up, and when the user clicks a button, we can use this function to get the friend with that rank, and use the `display` method to display the person's name:

```
function getName()
{
    for(var loopIndex = 0; loopIndex < array1.length; loopIndex++){
        if(array1[loopIndex].rank == document.form1.text1.value) {
            array1[loopIndex].display()
        }
    }
}
```

Here's what that looks like in code:

(Listing 23-08.html on the web site)

```
<HTML>
    <HEAD>
        <TITLE>
            Creating Custom Objects
        </TITLE>
    </HEAD>

    <BODY>
        <H1>Creating Custom Objects</H1>
        <FORM NAME="form1">
            <TEXTAREA NAME="textarea1" ROWS="5" COLS="40"></TEXTAREA>
            <BR>
```

```
        Friend Rank: <INPUT TYPE="TEXT" NAME="text1">
        <INPUT TYPE="BUTTON" ONCLICK="getName()" VALUE="Get Name">
    </FORM>
    <SCRIPT LANGUAGE="JavaScript">
        <!--
        function friend(name, phone, rank)
        {
            this.name = name
            this.phone = phone
            this.rank = rank
            this.display = display
        }

        function display()
        {
            window.alert("Name: " + this.name)
        }

        var array1 = new Array(4)
        array1[0] = new friend("Ed", "555-1111", 4)
        array1[1] = new friend("Harold", "555-2222", 1)
        array1[2] = new friend("Nancy", "555-3333", 3)
        array1[3] = new friend("Sandy", "555-4444", 2)

        for(var loopIndex = 0; loopIndex < array1.length; loopIndex++){
            document.form1.textarea1.value += "Name: " + array1[loopIndex].name + " "
            document.form1.textarea1.value += "Phone: " + array1[loopIndex].phone + " "
            document.form1.textarea1.value += "Rank: " + array1[loopIndex].rank + "\n"
        }

        function getName()
        {
            for(var loopIndex = 0; loopIndex < array1.length; loopIndex++){
                if(array1[loopIndex].rank == document.form1.text1.value) {
                    array1[loopIndex].display()
                }
            }
        }
        // -->
    </SCRIPT>
    </BODY>
</HTML>
```

You can see the results in Figure 23.9, where I've entered a rank of 1, and the code displays the name of the corresponding friend: Harold.

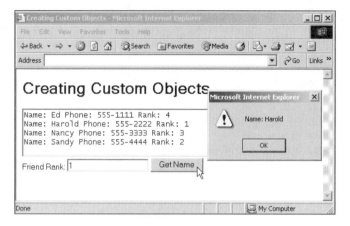

Figure 23.9 Creating custom object methods.

Sorting Arrays of Custom Objects

Say that you want to sort the array of custom friend objects that we've created by the rank you've assigned to each object. You can do that easily enough in JavaScript using a sorting function (see "Sorting Arrays" in Chapter 19, "The *Math, Number, Boolean*, and *Array* Objects"). In this case, I'll add a button with the caption "Sort by Rank" that calls this function, which sorts the array of objects, array1, with a sorting function named sorter, and displays the sorted array of objects in the text area:

```
function sort()
{
    array1.sort(sorter)
    document.form1.textarea1.value = ""
    for(var loopIndex = 0; loopIndex < array1.length; loopIndex++){
        document.form1.textarea1.value += "Name: " + array1[loopIndex].name + " "
        document.form1.textarea1.value += "Phone: " + array1[loopIndex].phone + " "
        document.form1.textarea1.value += "Rank: " + array1[loopIndex].rank + "\n"
    }
}
```

Here's the sorting function, sorter (see the topic "Sorting Arrays" in Chapter 19 for the details on string functions) that lets JavaScript sort our objects based on the rank property:

```
function sorter(a, b)
{
    if(a.rank < b.rank) return -1
    if(a.rank > b.rank) return 1
    return 0
}
```

Here's the new code:

(Listing 23-09.html on the web site)

```html
<HTML>
    <HEAD>
        <TITLE>
            Creating Custom Objects
        </TITLE>
    </HEAD>

    <BODY>
        <H1>Creating Custom Objects</H1>
        <FORM NAME="form1">
            <TEXTAREA NAME="textarea1" ROWS="5" COLS="40"></TEXTAREA>
            <BR>
            Friend Rank: <INPUT TYPE="TEXT" NAME="text1">
            <INPUT TYPE="BUTTON" ONCLICK="getName()" VALUE="Get Name">
            <BR>
            <INPUT TYPE="BUTTON" ONCLICK="sort()" VALUE="Sort by Rank">
        </FORM>
        <SCRIPT LANGUAGE="JavaScript">
            <!--
            function friend(name, phone, rank)
            {
                this.name = name
                this.phone = phone
                this.rank = rank
                this.display = display
            }

            function display()
            {
                window.alert("Name: " + this.name)
            }

            var array1 = new Array(4)
            array1[0] = new friend("Ed", "555-1111", 4)
            array1[1] = new friend("Harold", "555-2222", 1)
            array1[2] = new friend("Nancy", "555-3333", 3)
            array1[3] = new friend("Sandy", "555-4444", 2)

            for(var loopIndex = 0; loopIndex < array1.length; loopIndex++){
                document.form1.textarea1.value += "Name: " + array1[loopIndex].name + " "
                document.form1.textarea1.value += "Phone: " + array1[loopIndex].phone + " "
                document.form1.textarea1.value += "Rank: " + array1[loopIndex].rank + "\n"
            }

            function getName()
            {
                for(var loopIndex = 0; loopIndex < array1.length; loopIndex++){
                    if(array1[loopIndex].rank == document.form1.text1.value) {
```

continues ▶

```
                        array1[loopIndex].display()
                  }
            }
      }

      function sort()
      {
            array1.sort(sorter)
            document.form1.textarea1.value = ""
            for(var loopIndex = 0; loopIndex < array1.length; loopIndex++){
                  document.form1.textarea1.value += "Name: " +
                  ➥array1[loopIndex].name + " "
                  document.form1.textarea1.value += "Phone: " +
                  ➥array1[loopIndex].phone + " "
                  document.form1.textarea1.value += "Rank: " +
                  ➥array1[loopIndex].rank + "\n"
            }
      }

      function sorter(a, b)
      {
            if(a.rank < b.rank) return -1
            if(a.rank > b.rank) return 1
            return 0
      }
      // -->
    </SCRIPT>
  </BODY>
</HTML>
```

You can see the results in Figure 23.10, where you can click the "Sort by Rank" button to sort and display the friends by rank.

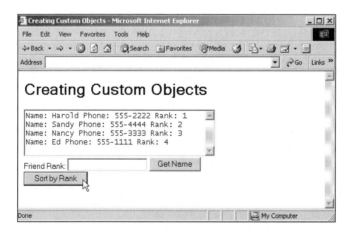

Figure 23.10 Sorting an array of custom objects.

The JavaScript *Object* Object

Here's another way to create custom objects, as of Netscape Navigator 3 and Internet Explorer 4: You can base them on the JavaScript `Object` object explicitly. In fact, all JavaScript objects are based on the `Object` object now, and that means any object you create with the `new` operator.

For example, here's how I create a new object, `object1`, and add a property to it, `value`, and then store a number in that property and display the stored value:

(Listing 23-10.html on the web site)

```html
<HTML>
    <HEAD>
        <TITLE>
            Creating a Custom Object
        </TITLE>
        <SCRIPT LANGUAGE="JavaScript">
            <!--
            function creator()
            {
                var object1 = new Object()
                object1.value = 5
                document.form1.text1.value = "object1.value = " + object1.value
            }
            // -->
        </SCRIPT>
    </HEAD>

    <BODY>
        <H1>Creating a Custom Object</H1>
        <FORM NAME="form1">
            <INPUT TYPE="BUTTON" ONCLICK="creator()" VALUE="Click Me!">
            <BR>
            <INPUT TYPE="TEXT" NAME="text1">
        </FORM>
    </BODY>
</HTML>
```

You can see the results in Figure 23.11, where we've created a new object using the JavaScript `Object` object, added a property to it, stored a value in that property, and displayed the stored value.

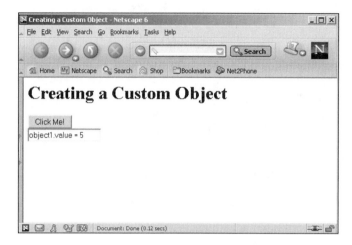

Figure 23.11 Creating a new object using the JavaScript `Object` object.

You can find the properties and methods of the `Object` object in Table 23.1 in overview, its properties in depth in Table 23.2, and its methods in Table 23.3 in depth.

Table 23.1 Overview of the Properties and Methods of the *Object* Object

Properties	Methods
constructor	hasOwnProperty
propertyIsEnumerable	isPrototypeOf
prototype	toLocaleString
	toString
	valueOf

Table 23.2 The Properties of the *Object* Object

Property	NS2	NS3	NS4	NS6	IE3a	IE3b	IE4	IE5	IE5.5	IE6
constructor		x	x	x			x	x	x	x

Read/write
This property specifies the function that creates an object.

propertyIsEnumerable				x					x	x

Read/write
You use this property like this: *object*.propertyIsEnumerable
(*property*). (It looks more like a method, but Microsoft calls it a property.) This property is true if *property* exists in *object* and can be looped over using a `for...in` loop, and false otherwise.

Property	NS2	NS3	NS4	NS6	IE3a	IE3b	IE4	IE5	IE5.5	IE6
prototype		x	x	x			x	x	x	x

Read/write
This property returns a reference to the object's prototype. You use the `prototype` property to provide base functionality to a set of objects. See "Adding Methods to Existing Objects" in this chapter for more information.

Table 23.3 The Methods of the *Object* Object

Method	NS2	NS3	NS4	NS6	IE3a	IE3b	IE4	IE5	IE5.5	IE6
hasOwnProperty				x					x	x

Returns: Boolean
This method returns true if an object has a property of the specified name, false if it does not. Syntax: `object.hasOwnProperty(name)`, where *name* is the name of the property you're checking.

isPrototypeOf				x					x	x

Returns: Boolean
This method returns true if an object has the current object in its prototype set.
Syntax: `object.isPrototypeOf(name)`, where *name* is the name of the object you're checking.

toLocaleString				x					x	x

Returns: String
Returns an object's data converted to a string using the current locale.
Syntax: *object*`.toLocaleString()`.

toString				x					x	x

Returns: String
Returns an object's data converted to a string.
Syntax: *object*`.toString()`.

valueOf				x					x	x

Returns: Object
Returns an object's data.
Syntax: *object*`.valueOf()`.

Using the JavaScript *Object* Object

We can convert our previous example (Listing 23-08) to use the Object object. Here's how that looks. Note that each time we create a new object in the constructor now, we use the new operator to create a new Object object, and then add properties to the object and return the new object:

(Listing 23-11.html on the web site)

```
<HTML>
    <HEAD>
        <TITLE>
            Creating Custom Objects
        </TITLE>
    </HEAD>

    <BODY>
        <H1>Creating Custom Objects</H1>
        <FORM NAME="form1">
            <TEXTAREA NAME="textarea1" ROWS="5" COLS="40"></TEXTAREA>
            <BR>
            Friend Rank: <INPUT TYPE="TEXT" NAME="text1">
            <INPUT TYPE="BUTTON" ONCLICK="getName()" VALUE="Get Name">
            <BR>
            <INPUT TYPE="BUTTON" ONCLICK="sort()" VALUE="Sort by Rank">
        </FORM>
        <SCRIPT LANGUAGE="JavaScript">
            <!--
            function friend(name, phone, rank)
            {
                var object1 = new Object()
                object1.name = name
                object1.phone = phone
                object1.rank = rank
                object1.display = display
                return object1
            }

            function display()
            {
                window.alert("Name: " + this.name)
            }

            var array1 = new Array(4)
            array1[0] = friend("Ed", "555-1111", 4)
            array1[1] = friend("Harold", "555-2222", 1)
            array1[2] = friend("Nancy", "555-3333", 3)
            array1[3] = friend("Sandy", "555-4444", 2)
```

```
        for(var loopIndex = 0; loopIndex < array1.length; loopIndex++){
            document.form1.textarea1.value += "Name: " + array1[loopIndex].name + " "
            document.form1.textarea1.value += "Phone: " + array1[loopIndex].phone + " "
            document.form1.textarea1.value += "Rank: " + array1[loopIndex].rank + "\n"
        }

        function getName()
        {
            for(var loopIndex = 0; loopIndex < array1.length; loopIndex++){
                if(array1[loopIndex].rank == document.form1.text1.value) {
                    array1[loopIndex].display()
                }
            }
        }

        function sort()
        {
            array1.sort(sorter)
            document.form1.textarea1.value = ""
            for(var loopIndex = 0; loopIndex < array1.length; loopIndex++){
                document.form1.textarea1.value += "Name: " +
                ➥array1[loopIndex].name + " "
                document.form1.textarea1.value += "Phone: " +
                ➥array1[loopIndex].phone + " "
                document.form1.textarea1.value += "Rank: " +
                ➥array1[loopIndex].rank + "\n"
            }
        }

        function sorter(a, b)
        {
            if(a.rank < b.rank) return -1
            if(a.rank > b.rank) return 1
            return 0
        }
        // -->
    </SCRIPT>
  </BODY>
</HTML>
```

That's all it takes. Now our objects are created explicitly using the JavaScript Object object. This code gives the same results as Figures 23.7 through 23.10 (except for default property values, which it doesn't implement).

Adding Properties to Existing Objects

You also can add properties to existing objects in JavaScript, just by assigning such properties values as if those properties existed. To do this, the object you're working with must be a real object, which means you must create it with the new operator.

Here's an example. In this case, I'll create a new string with a greeting in it, add a new property named purpose to the string, and set the string's purpose to "greeting":

```
var string1 = new String("Hello from JavaScript!")
string1.purpose = "greeting"
       .
       .
       .
```

Here's an example that uses this code and displays the value of the new property in a text field:

(Listing 23-12.html on the web site)

```
<HTML>
    <HEAD>
        <TITLE>
            Creating Custom Properties for Existing Objects
        </TITLE>
        <SCRIPT LANGUAGE="JavaScript">
            <!--
            function display()
            {
                var string1 = new String("Hello from JavaScript!")
                string1.purpose = "greeting"
                document.form1.text1.value = "The string's purpose is to be a " +
                ➥string1.purpose
            }
            // -->
        </SCRIPT>
    </HEAD>

    <BODY>
        <H1>Creating Custom Properties for Existing Objects</H1>
        <FORM NAME="form1">
            <INPUT TYPE="TEXT" NAME="text1" SIZE="40">
            <BR>
            <INPUT TYPE="BUTTON" ONCLICK="display()" VALUE="Get Custom Property Value">
        </FORM>
    </BODY>
</HTML>
```

You can see the results of this code in Figure 23.12, where we've added a property to an existing object.

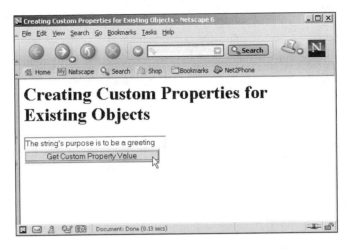

Figure 23.12 Adding a property to an existing object.

Adding Methods to Existing Objects

You also can add methods to existing objects in the same way as we just added properties in the preceding topic; you just assign a function name to the name of the method you want, like this: *object*.method = *function*.

We've been adding properties and methods to objects one at a time, but you also can use prototypes to add properties or methods to all objects of a particular type simultaneously. We saw an example of this in Chapter 19. In that example, I wanted to add a method named sqrt to all Number objects that returned the square root of the number. For example, you could use that method like this:

```
var n = new Number(5)
var squareRoot = n.sqrt()
```

To make this work, I added a prototype named sqrt to all Number objects. In addition, I connected that prototype to a function named sqRoot like this:

```
Number.prototype.sqrt = sqRoot
    .
    .
    .
```

As with any other method, in the `sqRoot` method, I can get access to the
current `Number` object with the `this` keyword, and the value stored in
the current `Number` object as `this.valueOf()`. To return the square root
of the number, then, I can use this code in the `sqRoot` function:

```
Number.prototype.sqrt = sqRoot

function sqRoot()
{
    return Math.sqrt(this.valueOf())
}
```

We saw this at work in Chapter 19, in Listing 19-04.html. In that example,
the user can enter a number in a text field and click a button to see the
square root of that number displayed in a text field:

```
<HTML>
    <HEAD>
        <TITLE>
            Using the prototype Property
        </TITLE>
        <SCRIPT LANGUAGE="JavaScript">
            <!--
            Number.prototype.sqrt = sqRoot

            function sqRoot()
            {
                return Math.sqrt(this.valueOf())
            }

            function display()
            {
                var n = new Number(document.form1.text1.value)
                document.form1.text1.value = n.sqrt()
            }
            // -->
        </SCRIPT>
    </HEAD>

    <BODY>
        <H1>Using the prototype Property</H1>
        <FORM NAME="form1">
            <INPUT TYPE="TEXT" NAME="text1">
            <INPUT TYPE="BUTTON" ONCLICK="display()" VALUE="Get the Square Root">
        </FORM>
    </BODY>
</HTML>
```

You can see the results in Chapter 19, in Figure 19.4, where the code is finding the square root of 5 and displaying that value in a text field.

As you can imagine, the `prototype` property is very useful when you want to augment objects such as `String` or `Number` objects, or any other custom objects that you've created. When you use the prototype property, you can automatically add properties and methods to all such objects simultaneously.

That's it for cookies and custom objects in this chapter. In the next chapter, we'll take a look at the server side of things when we examine server-side programming, such as writing scripts in Perl that can interact with JavaScript.

24

.NET and Security

IN THIS CHAPTER, WE'LL TAKE A LOOK AT THE SERVER-SIDE of things. JavaScript is great in the browser, but it's also used to communicate to the server. For example, we've been using HTML forms to support the HTML controls we use in JavaScript, but those forms were originally intended to send data back to the server. Here, we'll see how to work with data when it is sent back to the server.

There are plenty of ways to install your code on the server. In this chapter, we'll take a look at two of those ways: Microsoft's .NET initiative; and Perl (which stands for *Practical Extraction and Reporting Language*), one of the most popular *Common Gateway Interface* (CGI) programming languages.

Microsoft's .NET initiative is a huge affair, involving many programming packages and a fundamental change to Microsoft Windows. Usually, the code you use in .NET web applications stays on the server, and everything needs a round trip to the server in order to be processed. However, there's a way to add JavaScript to .NET pages that enables you to avoid that round trip—a way not many .NET programmers know about. We'll see how to use JavaScript in .NET in this chapter.

Perl is one of the popular programming languages for server-side CGI programming. It's both free and already installed on most UNIX-based web servers, so the chances are good that you already have access to it. We'll get an introduction to Perl in this chapter, sufficient to enable you to write Perl code, to read data from JavaScript-enabled web pages, and to return new web pages based on data the user enters.

Tip

As of this writing, the Tripod network, `www.tripod.lycos.com`, offers free web sites that include access to Perl.

I'll start by taking a look at using JavaScript with .NET programming.

.NET and JavaScript

Among other things, the Microsoft .NET initiative is an effort to make server-side programming easier. For example, Visual Basic .NET provides you with a programming environment that enables you to stay connected to the server as you develop your code. You can see the Visual Basic .NET development environment in Figure 24.1, where I'm developing a .NET web application. There are two main kinds of .NET applications—Windows applications and web applications—and JavaScript programming can help with the web applications of the kind we'll see here.

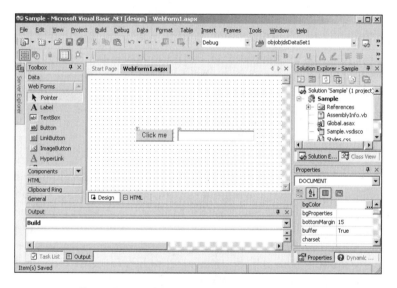

Figure 24.1   The Visual Basic .NET environment.

In Figure 24.1, I've created a new Visual Basic .NET project on a web server—although I'm working locally on my own machine—and I'm adding controls to a .NET web form. In this case, I'm adding a button and a text field. Note the small icons at the upper left in each control, which indicate that they are server-side controls—their code is on the server, and every time you click the button, all the data in the web form will be sent back to the server and processed there.

You add controls such as text fields and buttons to a web form in Visual Basic .NET using the "toolbox" at left, where I'm selecting controls from the Web Forms tab; these controls are handled on the server—that is, their code resides on the server, not in the browser. If you double-click the button, the Visual Basic code that stays on the server to support the web page, Webform1.aspx.vb, appears (see Figure 24.2).

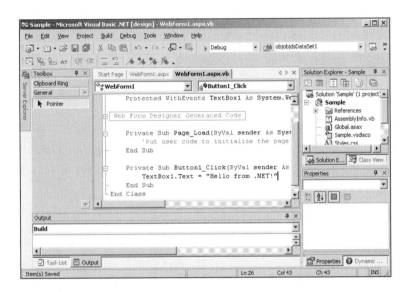

Figure 24.2   The server-side code for a .NET web page.

Double-clicking the button as we have makes Visual Basic .NET create a click event handler for that button in the server-side code for this web form, as you see in Figure 24.2:

```
Private Sub Button1_Click(ByVal sender As System.Object, ByVal e As System.EventArgs)
    Handles Button1.Click

End Sub
```

We can make the text field, which is named TextBox1 by default, display the message Hello from .NET! by adding this code, as you see in Figure 24.2:

```
Private Sub Button1_Click(ByVal sender As System.Object, ByVal e As System.EventArgs)
    Handles Button1.Click
    TextBox1.Text = "Hello from .NET!"
End Sub
```

That's all we need to make this web application complete. Here's the server-side Visual Basic code for this web page:

(Listing 24-01.aspx.vb on the web site)

```
Public Class WebForm1
    Inherits System.Web.UI.Page
    Protected WithEvents Button1 As System.Web.UI.WebControls.Button
    Protected WithEvents TextBox1 As System.Web.UI.WebControls.TextBox

#Region " Web Form Designer Generated Code "

    'This call is required by the Web Form Designer.
    <System.Diagnostics.DebuggerStepThrough()> Private Sub InitializeComponent()

    End Sub

    Private Sub Page_Init(ByVal sender As System.Object, ByVal e As System.EventArgs)
        Handles MyBase.Init
        'CODEGEN: This method call is required by the Web Form Designer
        'Do not modify it using the code editor.
        InitializeComponent()
    End Sub

#End Region

    Private Sub Page_Load(ByVal sender As System.Object, ByVal e As System.EventArgs)
        Handles MyBase.Load
        'Put user code to initialize the page here
    End Sub

    Private Sub Button1_Click(ByVal sender As System.Object, ByVal e As
    ➥System.EventArgs)
        Handles Button1.Click
        TextBox1.Text = "Hello from .NET!"
    End Sub
End Class
```

You can see the results in Figure 24.3, where I've run the application on the server, and you can see the newly created web page in the Internet Explorer. When you click the button, the message Hello from .NET! appears in the text field, as you see in Figure 24.3.

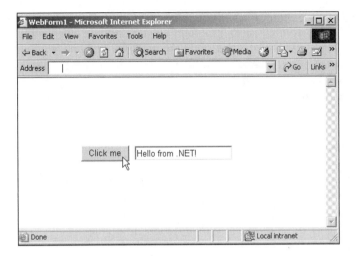

Figure 24.3 Running a .NET application.

Note that all this code works fine; to place some text into a text field, however, we've had to send all the data back to the server. The code we've placed on the server executes, creates a new web page, and sends that page back to the browser. And that can be a problem in .NET applications, because it all takes time. If the user is expecting more immediate results, a server round trip can be very annoying.

That's where JavaScript can help. Many .NET programmers don't realize that you can use JavaScript in .NET applications; but you can—and it can help speed things up, because JavaScript code is executed in the browser. That's not to say you want to write an entire .NET application using JavaScript—there's no reason to have any server-side .NET code in that case—but JavaScript can help perform many tasks that don't need a server round trip. And the data JavaScript places into controls will be sent back to the server when the user uses server-side control.

Let's take a look at an example. In this example, we'll create the same results you see in Figure 24.3; this time, however, we'll do it with JavaScript.

You can see this new application being developed in Figure 24.4. I've added a button and text field to the new web form in this new application; but this time, I'm using controls in the toolbox's HTML (not Web Forms) tab. The controls you add with this tab are straight HTML controls and are not intended to be handled on the server. As you see in the figure, there is no small icon at the upper left in these controls; they're not meant to be handled back on the server.

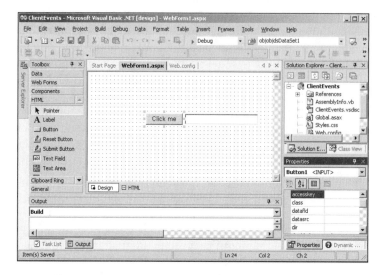

Figure 24.4 Adding HTML controls to a .NET application.

So how do you work with these controls? You can give the HTML controls names using the Properties window you see at the lower right in Figure 24.4; in this case, I'll name the text field Text1 and the button Button1.

Now we can connect a JavaScript function named clicker to the button by editing the HTML for the web form itself. To do that, just click the HTML tab you see in Figure 24.5. This opens the HTML code for the web form, Webform1.aspx, as you see in Figure 24.5.

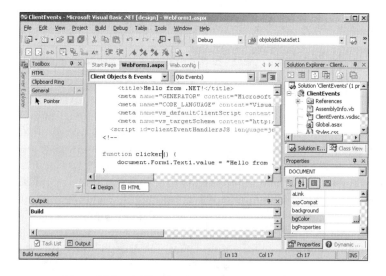

Figure 24.5 Adding JavaScript to a .NET application.

This code file, Webform1.aspx, is an *Active Server Pages* (ASP) page. (You need an ASP server to run web forms.) You can embed HTML directly into this file, and it'll appear in the HTML page the browser displays. Here's the way our button looks now in Webform1.aspx:

```
<INPUT ID="Button1" STYLE="Z-INDEX: 101; LEFT: 125px; POSITION: absolute; TOP: 85px"
TYPE="button" VALUE="Click me">
```

We can connect it to a JavaScript function named `clicker` like this:

```
<INPUT ID="Button1" STYLE="Z-INDEX: 101; LEFT: 125px; POSITION: absolute; TOP: 85px"
TYPE="button" VALUE="Click me" LANGUAGE="JavaScript" ONCLICK="return clicker()">
```

Here's what the `clicker` function looks like. You can just add this function to Webform1.aspx directly by typing in the code for this function like this:

```
function clicker()
{
    document.Form1.Text1.value = "Hello from .NET!"
}
```

That's all it takes. Here's the code for the new application, complete with the JavaScript we've added:

(Listing 24-02.aspx on the web site)

```
<%@ Page Language="vb" AutoEventWireup="false"
    Codebehind="WebForm1.aspx.vb" Inherits="ClientEvents.WebForm1"%>
<!DOCTYPE HTML PUBLIC "-//W3C//DTD HTML 4.0 Transitional//EN">
<HTML>
    <HEAD>
        <title>Hello from .NET!</title>
        <meta name="GENERATOR" content="Microsoft Visual Studio.NET 7.0">
        <meta name="CODE_LANGUAGE" content="Visual Basic 7.0">
        <meta name=vs_defaultClientScript content="JavaScript">
        <meta name=vs_targetSchema
        content="http://schemas.microsoft.com/intellisense/ie5">
        <script id=clientEventHandlersJS language=javascript>
            <!--
            function clicker()
            {
                document.Form1.Text1.value = "Hello from .NET!"
            }
            //-->
        </script>
    </HEAD>

    <body MS_POSITIONING="GridLayout">
        <form id="Form1" method="post" runat="server">
            <INPUT id="Button1"
                style="Z-INDEX: 101; LEFT: 125px; POSITION: absolute; TOP: 85px"
                TYPE="button" VALUE="Click me" LANGUAGE="JavaScript"
                ONCLICK="return clicker()">
```

continues ▶

```
                <INPUT id="Text1"
                    style="Z-INDEX: 102; LEFT: 208px; WIDTH: 155px;
                    POSITION: absolute; TOP: 86px; HEIGHT: 22px" type=text>
        </form>
    </body>
</HTML>
```

Now we can run this new JavaScript-enabled application, as you see in Figure 24.6. When you click the button in this application, the message Hello from .NET! appears in the text field—no round trip to the server needed. This time, everything is handled in the browser, using JavaScript.

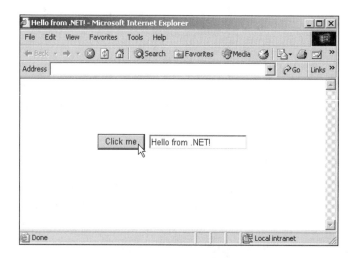

Figure 24.6   Using JavaScript in a .NET application.

The data you put into controls using JavaScript goes back to the server when you use server-side controls. Therefore, knowing you can use JavaScript gives the .NET programmer options. You can use server-side controls for much of a .NET web application; when time is of the essence, however, JavaScript is there for you.

Next I'll take a look at another—and free—option for server-side option: using Perl.

Perl and JavaScript

We've taken a brief look at using JavaScript and Perl in Chapter 12, "Working with Forms, Buttons, Check Boxes, and Radio Buttons." In an example in that chapter, we enable the user to send his name back to a Perl CGI script. You can see the web page we'll use in Figure 24.7.

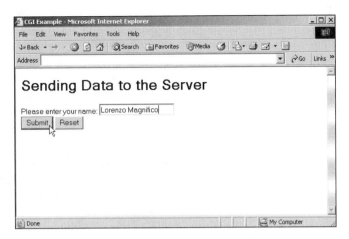

Figure 24.7 Entering data in a web page.

When the user clicks the Submit button in our web page, the data in the form, including the text in the text field, is sent to the URL I've specified in the ACTION attribute, which is the URL of our CGI script. That CGI script processes the data we've sent it and returns the web page you see in Figure 24.8.

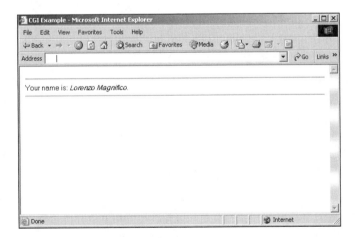

Figure 24.8 Displaying a web page from a server-side script.

To make this work, I set the form's METHOD attribute to "POST" and ACTION attribute to the URL of the script (this is a fictitious URL—if you want to use this example, replace it with the URL of the Perl script's location on your Web server) in the HTML page you see in Figure 24.7 (Listing 12-02.html):

```
<HTML>
    <HEAD>
        <TITLE>CGI Example</TITLE>
    </HEAD>

    <BODY>
        <H1>Sending Data to the Server</H1>
        <FORM METHOD="POST" ACTION="http://www.starpowder.com/12-03.cgi">
            Please enter your name:
            <INPUT TYPE="text" NAME="text" VALUE="">
            <BR>
            <INPUT TYPE="SUBMIT" NAME="Submit" VALUE="Submit">
            <INPUT TYPE="RESET">
        </FORM>
    </BODY>
</HTML>
```

Note also that I've included a Submit (<INPUT TYPE="SUBMIT">) and Reset
(<INPUT TYPE="RESET">) button. The user can click the Submit button in the
form to send the data in the form—that is, the user's name in the text
field—back to the server, and click the Reset button to reset all data in the
form's controls to its default value. (In most cases, this is used to clear the
form so that the user can start over if she enters erroneous data.) Here's
what the Perl CGI script on the server looked like (Listing 12-03.cgi):

```
#!/usr/local/bin/perl
use CGI;
$co = new CGI;

print $co->header,
$co->start_html(
    -title=>'CGI Example',
    -author=>'Steve',
    -meta=>{'keywords'=>'CGI Perl'},
),
$co->hr;
if ($co->param()) {
    print
        "Your name is: ",$co->em($co->param('text')), ".";
}
print $co->hr;
print $co->end_html;
```

Now we can take this Perl script apart to understand how it works.

CGI scripts such as this one are stored on the server and must be specially
enabled to run. The details are up to your web server; Perl runs on many
types of servers, including those that are UNIX-based and Windows-based,
and you must upload your scripts to the server. (This is commonly done
with a FTP—*File Transfer Protocol*—program, which you can find available for
free online.)

When the script is uploaded and stored on the server, you also must give it a UNIX permission setting that lets it run when accessed by browsers. A common permission setting is 755, which enables you to read, write, and execute your Perl scripts, and enables everyone else to read and execute them. For more details on installing Perl scripts on your server, check with your server's tech support.

Let's take a look at writing this Perl script. You start a script such as this one with this line, indicating where the server computer can find Perl itself—the location of Perl varies by server, but a common location is in the /usr/local/bin directory:

```
#!/usr/local/bin/perl
                .
                .
                .
```

To handle the CGI scripting, we'll use the built-in Perl CGI module, which we include in our code with the statement use CGI;. (Perl statements always end with a—non-optional—semicolon.) I'll create a new reference to a CGI object, $co, with the line $co = new CGI; (in Perl, simple variables begin with a $ to indicate they're not more complex structures like arrays) like this:

```
#!/usr/local/bin/perl
use CGI;
$co = new CGI;
                .
                .
                .
```

So how do we send data back to the browser? The CGI object $co has a built-in method for most HTML tags. To create an <HR> element, for example, you just need to call the $co->hr() method. The $co->hr() method returns the HTML text for a <HR> element (that is, simply "<HR>"); to send that back to the browser, you only have to use the Perl print statement, because all that you print from a Perl CGI script goes back to the browser automatically.

Here's how I'll start creating a new page to send to the browser using the $co object's methods. In this case, I'm sending the HTML header (a <!DOCTYPE> element) back to the browser, as well as an <HTML> element with a <HEAD> section containing a <TITLE> element, and an <HR> element (the arrow operator, ->, enables you to access the methods of an object reference in Perl):

```
#!/usr/local/bin/perl
use CGI;
$co = new CGI;
```

```
print $co->header,
$co->start_html(
    -title=>'CGI Example',
    -author=>'Steve',
    -meta=>{'keywords'=>'CGI Perl'},
),
$co->hr;
       .
       .
       .
```

That starts the creation of the web page you see in Figure 24.8. How can we read the data the user has entered into the text field we've named text? You can access the text in that text field with the param method of the $co object. This method will return true if you call it without any parameters and the user entered data into the controls in the HTML page. That means our first step is to check whether there is indeed any data waiting, using a Perl if statement (which is much like the JavaScript if statement):

```
#!/usr/local/bin/perl
use CGI;
$co = new CGI;

print $co->header,
$co->start_html(
    -title=>'CGI Example',
    -author=>'Steve',
    -meta=>{'keywords'=>'CGI Perl'},
),
$co->hr;

if ($co->param()) {
       .
       .
       .
}
       .
       .
       .
```

If there is some text in the text field named text, we can access it as $co->param('text'). In this example, I'll enclose that text with HTML <EM> tags to make the text italic—all of which means that this is how we display the text the user entered into the text field:

```
#!/usr/local/bin/perl
use CGI;
$co = new CGI;

print $co->header,
```

```
$co->start_html(
    -title=>'CGI Example',
    -author=>'Steve',
    -meta=>{'keywords'=>'CGI Perl'},
),
$co->hr;

if ($co->param()) {
    print
        "Your name is: ",$co->em($co->param('text')), ".";
}
        .
        .
        .
```

Finally, we add another <HR> element, and end the HTML document we're sending back to the browser with the end_html method:

```
#!/usr/local/bin/perl
use CGI;
$co = new CGI;

print $co->header,
$co->start_html(
    -title=>'CGI Example',
    -author=>'Steve',
    -meta=>{'keywords'=>'CGI Perl'},
),
$co->hr;
if ($co->param()) {
    print
        "Your name is: ",$co->em($co->param('text')), ".";
}
print $co->hr;
print $co->end_html;
```

That's it. That's the Perl script we need to create the results you see in Figure 24.8.

Tip

Want more information about Perl syntax? Take a look at www.perldoc.com for Perl documentation. Also take a look at www.cpan.org, the Comprehensive Perl Archive Network, for downloads (including Perl itself), documentation, and discussion of all things Perl. Another good one is www.perl.com.

As we also saw in Chapter 12, you can use JavaScript to check form data before it's sent back to the server by handling the form's onsubmit event, which occurs when the user clicks the submit button. If you return true from this event handler, the data is submitted to the server; and if you return false, the data is not submitted:

```
<HTML>
    <HEAD>
        <TITLE>CGI Example</TITLE>
        <SCRIPT LANGUAGE="JavaScript">
            <!--
            function checkData()
            {
                if(document.forms[0].text1.value == ""){
                    window.alert("Please enter your name.")
                    return false
                } else {
                    return true
                }
            }
            // -->
        </SCRIPT>
    </HEAD>

    <BODY>
        <FORM ID="form1" METHOD="POST"
            ACTION="http://www.starpowder.com/steve/12-03.cgi"
            ONSUBMIT="return checkData()">
            Please enter your name:
            <INPUT TYPE="TEXT" ID="text1" VALUE="">
            <BR>
            <INPUT TYPE="SUBMIT" NAME="Submit" VALUE="Submit">
            <INPUT TYPE="RESET">
        </FORM>
    </BODY>
</HTML>
```

To get into server-side programming in some depth, I'll take a look at a new example now, which enables you to interact with the most common HTML controls and read data from them.

Perl and HTML Controls

In this example, we'll take a look at using Perl with many HTML controls. Having some server-side experience under your belt is a good idea when you want to create full web applications, using not only JavaScript, but sending data back to the server—after all, one of JavaScript's main uses is checking user input before sending it back to the server.

In this example, we'll put together a feedback form that enables the user to submit comments about a web site, and then use a Perl script to summarize what data the user entered, displaying that data back to the user. Doing so will give us experience in reading data from HTML controls, using Perl on the server.

Tip

You could just as easily store the user's data in a file on the server. For information on file handling in Perl, take a look at www.perldoc.com. (Currently, the file-handling functions appear at www.perldoc.com/perl5.6.1/pod/perlfunc.html.)

You can see the feedback form itself in Figures 24.9 (the top half of the feedback form) and 24.10 (the bottom half). As you can see in those figures, we'll be reading data from text fields, text areas, select controls, check boxes, radio buttons, and password controls—not a bad start to CGI programming.

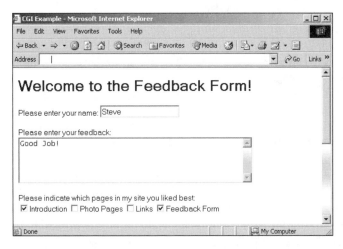

Figure 24.9   Top half of the feedback form.

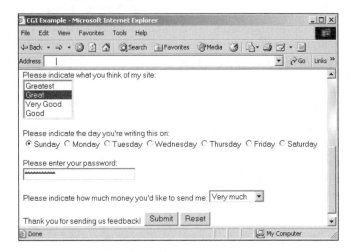

Figure 24.10   Bottom half of the feedback form.

Here's what the HTML for the feedback form looks like. Note that the URL for the ACTION attribute is fictitious; you need to use the URL of the script as placed on your server here:

(Listing 24-03.html on the web site)

```
<HTML>
    <HEAD>
        <TITLE>CGI Example</TITLE>
    </HEAD>

    <BODY>
        <H1>Welcome to the Feedback Form!</H1>
        <FORM METHOD="POST" ACTION="http://www.starpowder.com/24-04.cgi"
            ENCTYPE="application/x-www-form-urlencoded">

            Please enter your name: <INPUT TYPE="text" NAME="text" VALUE="">
            <BR>
            <BR>

            Please enter your feedback:
            <BR>
            <TEXTAREA NAME="textarea" ROWS=5 COLS=50>Good Job!</TEXTAREA>
            <BR>
            <BR>

            Please indicate which pages in my site you liked best:
            <BR>
            <INPUT TYPE="checkbox" NAME="checkboxes" VALUE="Introduction"
            ➥CHECKED>Introduction
            <INPUT TYPE="checkbox" NAME="checkboxes" VALUE="Photo Pages">Photo Pages
            <INPUT TYPE="checkbox" NAME="checkboxes" VALUE="Links">Links
            <INPUT TYPE="checkbox" NAME="checkboxes" VALUE="Feedback Form">Feedback
            ➥Form
            <BR>
            <BR>

            Please indicate what you think of my site:
            <BR>
            <SELECT NAME="list" SIZE=4>
                <OPTION  VALUE="Greatest">Greatest
                <OPTION SELECTED VALUE="Great">Great
                <OPTION  VALUE="Very Good">Very Good
                <OPTION  VALUE="Good">Good
            </SELECT>
            <BR>
            <BR>

            Please indicate the day you're writing this on:
            <BR>
            <INPUT TYPE="radio" NAME="radios" VALUE="Sunday " CHECKED>Sunday
            <INPUT TYPE="radio" NAME="radios" VALUE="Monday ">Monday
```

```
            <INPUT TYPE="radio"  NAME="radios"  VALUE="Tuesday ">Tuesday
            <INPUT TYPE="radio"  NAME="radios"  VALUE="Wednesday ">Wednesday
            <INPUT TYPE="radio"  NAME="radios"  VALUE="Thursday ">Thursday
            <INPUT TYPE="radio"  NAME="radios"  VALUE="Friday ">Friday
            <INPUT TYPE="radio"  NAME="radios"  VALUE="Saturday">Saturday
            <BR>
            <BR>

            Please enter your password:
            <BR>
            <INPUT TYPE="password" NAME="password" VALUE="open sesame" SIZE=30>
            <BR>
            <BR>

            Please indicate how much money you'd like to send me:
            <SELECT NAME="popupmenu">
                <OPTION  VALUE="Very much">Very much
                <OPTION  VALUE="A lot">A lot
                <OPTION  VALUE="Not so much">Not so much
                <OPTION  VALUE="None">None
            </SELECT>
            <BR>
            <BR>

            Thank you for sending us feedback!
            <INPUT TYPE="hidden" NAME="hiddendata" VALUE="Feedback Form 1">

            <INPUT TYPE="submit" NAME="Submit" VALUE="Submit">
            <INPUT TYPE="reset">
        </FORM>
    </BODY>
</HTML>
```

Here's the Perl script we'll develop (bear in mind that to use this script, you'll have to set the UNIX file permission of the script file to 755, and may have to change the #!/usr/local/bin/perl line to point to the Perl installation as stored on your server):

(Listing 24-04.cgi on the web site)

```
#!/usr/local/bin/perl
use CGI;
$co = new CGI;

print $co->header,
$co->start_html(
    -title=>'CGI Example',
    -author=>'Steve',
    -meta=>{'keywords'=>'CGI Perl'},
    -BGCOLOR=>'white',
    -LINK=>'red'
),
```

continues ▶

```
$co->center($co->h1('Thanks for sending us feedback.')),
$co->h3('Here is what you wrote...'),
$co->hr;

if ($co->param()) {
    print
        "Your name is: ", $co->param('text'), ".", $co->p,
        "Your feedback is: ", $co->param('textarea'), ".", $co->p,
        "Your favorite pages: ", join(", ",$co->param('checkboxes')), ".",$co->p,
        "You think my site is: ", $co->param('list'), ".", $co->p,
        "Today is ", $co->param('radios'), ".", $co->p,
        "Your password is: ", $co->param('password'), ".", $co->p,
        "How much money you want to send: ", $co->param('popupmenu'), ".", $co->p,
        "The hidden data is: \"", join(", ", $co->param('hiddendata')), "\".";
}

print $co->hr;
print $co->end_html;
```

When the user enters data into the feedback form that you see in Figures 24.9 and 24.10 and clicks the Submit button, that data is sent to our Perl script on the server. The Perl script reads the data sent to it and creates a new page summarizing that data, which it sends back to the browser. You can see that summary page in Figure 24.11.

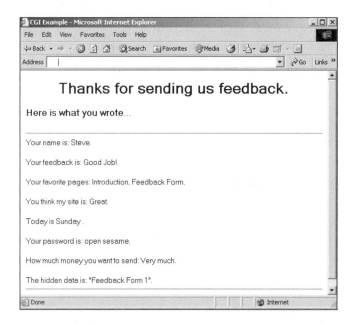

Figure 24.11 The summary of the user's feedback data.

That's what we're aiming for—a working feedback form that uses a CGI script that summarizes the data entered by the user. To make this work, we'll need to get two components set up correctly: the HTML form and its controls in the feedback form itself, and the Perl script. I'll start by taking a look at setting up the HTML form that will contain the controls we'll use.

Setting Up the Form

To send our data back to the server, the browser needs to know where to send it. You specify that with the ACTION attribute of the <FORM> element in the feedback form (substitute the URL of the Perl script on your server for the URL used here):

```
<FORM METHOD="POST" ACTION="http://www.starpowder.com/24-04.cgi"
    ENCTYPE="application/x-www-form-urlencoded">
    .
    .
    .
</FORM>
```

At the end of the form, we add Submit and Reset buttons (as discussed in Chapter 12):

```
<FORM METHOD="POST" ACTION="http://www.starpowder.com/24-04.cgi"
    ENCTYPE="application/x-www-form-urlencoded">
        .
        .
        .
    <INPUT TYPE="submit" NAME="Submit" VALUE="Submit">
    <INPUT TYPE="reset">
</FORM>
```

Now when the user clicks the Submit button, the data in the controls in this form will be sent to our CGI script for processing. The next step, then, is to add the HTML controls to this form—and to see how to use them in Perl.

Using Text Fields

I can add a text field to hold the user's name to our HTML form like this:

```
<HTML>
    <HEAD>
        <TITLE>CGI Example</TITLE>
    </HEAD>

    <BODY>
        <H1>Welcome to the Feedback Form!</H1>
        <FORM METHOD="POST" ACTION="http://www.starpowder.com/24-04.cgi"
            ENCTYPE="application/x-www-form-urlencoded">
```

continues ▶

```
            Please enter your name: <INPUT TYPE="text" NAME="text" VALUE="">
            <BR>
            <BR>
        .
        .
        .
            <INPUT TYPE="submit" NAME="Submit" VALUE="Submit">
            <INPUT TYPE="reset">
        </FORM>
      </BODY>
</HTML>
```

Now let's take a look at how to extract the data from this text field in Perl. I'll start as we've already done, by creating a new web page and using a Perl print statement to send the heading of that page back to the browser:

```perl
#!/usr/local/bin/perl
use CGI;
$co = new CGI;

print $co->header,
$co->start_html(
    -title=>'CGI Example',
    -author=>'Steve',
    -meta=>{'keywords'=>'CGI Perl'},
    -BGCOLOR=>'white',
    -LINK=>'red'
),
        .
        .
        .
```

Next, I'll add the text you see at the top of the summary page in Figure 24.11; here, the CGI h1 method creates an <H1> header, the h3 method creates an <H3> header, the center method creates a <CENTER> element, and the hr method creates an <HR> horizontal rule:

```perl
#!/usr/local/bin/perl
use CGI;
$co = new CGI;

print $co->header,
$co->start_html(
    -title=>'CGI Example',
    -author=>'Steve',
    -meta=>{'keywords'=>'CGI Perl'},
    -BGCOLOR=>'white',
    -LINK=>'red'
),
```

```
$co->center($co->h1('Thanks for sending us feedback.')),
$co->h3('Here is what you wrote...'),
$co->hr;
        .
        .
        .
```

We've already seen how to extract text from a text field; in this case, our text field is named `text`, so I can get the text from the text field and display it in the summary page this way (the CGI `p` method creates a `<P>` element):

```
#!/usr/local/bin/perl
use CGI;
$co = new CGI;

print $co->header,
$co->start_html(
    -title=>'CGI Example',
    -author=>'Steve',
    -meta=>{'keywords'=>'CGI Perl'},
    -BGCOLOR=>'white',
    -LINK=>'red'
),

$co->center($co->h1('Thanks for sending us feedback.')),
$co->h3('Here is what you wrote...'),
$co->hr;

if ($co->param()) {
    print
        "Your name is: ", $co->param('text'), ".", $co->p,
        .
        .
        .

}

print $co->hr;
print $co->end_html;
```

That's it. Next I'll take a look at handling text areas.

Using Text Areas

To enable the user to enter her feedback, I'll use a text area just named `textarea`, adding some complementary default text to this control:

```
<HTML>
    <HEAD>
        <TITLE>CGI Example</TITLE>
    </HEAD>
```

continues ▶

```
        <BODY>
            <H1>Welcome to the Feedback Form!</H1>
            <FORM METHOD="POST" ACTION="http://www.starpowder.com/24-04.cgi"
                ENCTYPE="application/x-www-form-urlencoded">
            .
            .
            .
                Please enter your feedback:
                <BR>
                <TEXTAREA NAME="textarea" ROWS="5" COLS="50">Good Job!</TEXTAREA>
                <BR>
                <BR>
            .
            .
            .
                <INPUT TYPE="submit" NAME="Submit" VALUE="Submit">
                <INPUT TYPE="reset">
            </FORM>
        </BODY>
</HTML>
```

Working with text areas is much like working with text fields in Perl—you just pass the name of the control to the param method to get the text from the control. Here's how that looks in the Perl script, where I'm displaying the text from the text area in the summary page:

```perl
#!/usr/local/bin/perl
use CGI;
$co = new CGI;

print $co->header,
$co->start_html(
    -title=>'CGI Example',
    -author=>'Steve',
    -meta=>{'keywords'=>'CGI Perl'},
    -BGCOLOR=>'white',
    -LINK=>'red'
),

$co->center($co->h1('Thanks for sending us feedback.')),
$co->h3('Here is what you wrote...'),
$co->hr;

if ($co->param()) {
    print
        .
        .
        .
        "Your feedback is: ", $co->param('textarea'), ".", $co->p,
        .
        .
        .
```

```
}

print $co->hr;

print $co->end_html;
```

Using Check Boxes

Check boxes are a little different from text fields and text areas. Here's how I add a set of check boxes to enable the user to indicate what page in the site she liked the best. Note that I'm giving all the check boxes the same name, checkboxes:

```
<HTML>
    <HEAD>
        <TITLE>CGI Example</TITLE>
    </HEAD>

    <BODY>
        <H1>Welcome to the Feedback Form!</H1>
        <FORM METHOD="POST" ACTION="http://www.starpowder.com/24-04.cgi"
            ENCTYPE="application/x-www-form-urlencoded">
            .
            .
            .
            Please indicate which pages in my site you liked best:
            <BR>
            <INPUT TYPE="checkbox" NAME="checkboxes" VALUE="Introduction"
            ➥CHECKED>Introduction
            <INPUT TYPE="checkbox" NAME="checkboxes" VALUE="Photo Pages">Photo Pages
            <INPUT TYPE="checkbox" NAME="checkboxes" VALUE="Links">Links
            <INPUT TYPE="checkbox" NAME="checkboxes" VALUE="Feedback Form">Feedback Form
            <BR>
            <BR>
            .
            .
            .
            <INPUT TYPE="submit" NAME="Submit" VALUE="Submit">
            <INPUT TYPE="reset">
        </FORM>
    </BODY>
</HTML>
```

When I pass the param method the name checkboxes in the Perl script, I'll get a *list* of the check boxes that were checked back. A *Perl list* is a construction that enables you to handle multiple items at the same time (lists and arrays can be used interchangeably in many ways in Perl), and I can concatenate all the items in a list of text items together using the join function.

Here's how I do that, putting a comma between the names of all the check boxes that were checked:

```perl
#!/usr/local/bin/perl
use CGI;
$co = new CGI;

print $co->header,
$co->start_html(
    -title=>'CGI Example',
    -author=>'Steve',
    -meta=>{'keywords'=>'CGI Perl'},
    -BGCOLOR=>'white',
    -LINK=>'red'
),

$co->center($co->h1('Thanks for sending us feedback.')),
$co->h3('Here is what you wrote...'),
$co->hr;

if ($co->param()) {
    print
        .

        .

        "Your favorite pages: ", join(", ",$co->param('checkboxes')), ".",$co->p,
        .

        .

}

print $co->hr;
print $co->end_html;
```

That's all it takes. Now the check boxes the user checked will display in the feedback form, as you see in Figure 24.11.

Using Select Controls

We also can add select controls to our feedback form. This select control enables the user to rank our site using possible values that range from "Good" to "Greatest":

```html
<HTML>
    <HEAD>
        <TITLE>CGI Example</TITLE>
    </HEAD>

    <BODY>
        <H1>Welcome to the Feedback Form!</H1>
        <FORM METHOD="POST" ACTION="http://www.starpowder.com/24-04.cgi"
```

```
            ENCTYPE="application/x-www-form-urlencoded">
    .
    .
    .
        Please indicate what you think of my site:
        <BR>
        <SELECT NAME="list" SIZE="4">
            <OPTION  VALUE="Greatest">Greatest
            <OPTION SELECTED VALUE="Great">Great
            <OPTION  VALUE="Very Good">Very Good
            <OPTION  VALUE="Good">Good
        </SELECT>
        <BR>
        <BR>
    .
    .
    .
            <INPUT TYPE="submit" NAME="Submit" VALUE="Submit">
            <INPUT TYPE="reset">
        </FORM>
    </BODY>
</HTML>
```

In multi-selection select controls, you'll get a list of selected items; because this select control allows only single selections, however, we'll get the value of the single selected item when we pass the name of this control, `select`, to the param method:

```
#!/usr/local/bin/perl
use CGI;
$co = new CGI;

print $co->header,
$co->start_html(
    -title=>'CGI Example',
    -author=>'Steve',
    -meta=>{'keywords'=>'CGI Perl'},
    -BGCOLOR=>'white',
    -LINK=>'red'
),

$co->center($co->h1('Thanks for sending us feedback.')),
$co->h3('Here is what you wrote...'),
$co->hr;

if ($co->param()) {
    print
        .
        .
        .
```

continues ▶

```
"You think my site is: ", $co->param('list'), ".", $co->p,
    .
    .
    .
}

print $co->hr;
print $co->end_html;
```

You can see the results in Figure 24.11, where the summary page is indicating that the user thought the web site was great.

Using Radio Buttons

Using radio buttons is something like using check boxes; you use the same
name for all radio buttons that you want to group together. Here's what that
looks like in a radio button group named radios, where I'm enabling the
user to indicate what day of the week it is:

```
<HTML>
    <HEAD>
        <TITLE>CGI Example</TITLE>
    </HEAD>

    <BODY>
        <H1>Welcome to the Feedback Form!</H1>
        <FORM METHOD="POST" ACTION="http://www.starpowder.com/24-04.cgi"
            ENCTYPE="application/x-www-form-urlencoded">
            .
            .
            .
            Please indicate the day you're writing this on:
            <BR>
            <INPUT TYPE="radio" NAME="radios" VALUE="Sunday " CHECKED>Sunday
            <INPUT TYPE="radio" NAME="radios" VALUE="Monday ">Monday
            <INPUT TYPE="radio" NAME="radios" VALUE="Tuesday ">Tuesday
            <INPUT TYPE="radio" NAME="radios" VALUE="Wednesday ">Wednesday
            <INPUT TYPE="radio" NAME="radios" VALUE="Thursday ">Thursday
            <INPUT TYPE="radio" NAME="radios" VALUE="Friday ">Friday
            <INPUT TYPE="radio" NAME="radios" VALUE="Saturday">Saturday
            .
            .
            .

            <INPUT TYPE="submit" NAME="Submit" VALUE="Submit">
            <INPUT TYPE="reset">
        </FORM>
    </BODY>
</HTML>
```

Because only one radio button in a group can be selected at once, we can get the value of the selected radio button in the radios group and display it in the summary page like this:

```perl
#!/usr/local/bin/perl
use CGI;
$co = new CGI;

print $co->header,
$co->start_html(
    -title=>'CGI Example',
    -author=>'Steve',
    -meta=>{'keywords'=>'CGI Perl'},
    -BGCOLOR=>'white',
    -LINK=>'red'
),

$co->center($co->h1('Thanks for sending us feedback.')),
$co->h3('Here is what you wrote...'),
$co->hr;

if ($co->param()) {
    print
        .
        .
        .
        "Today is ", $co->param('radios'), ".", $co->p,
        .
        .
        .
}

print $co->hr;
print $co->end_html;
```

You can see the results in Figure 24.11.

Using Password Controls

Password controls are much like text fields, except that they mask what you're typing. Here's how we add a password control, named password, to the feedback form:

```html
<HTML>
    <HEAD>
        <TITLE>CGI Example</TITLE>
    </HEAD>

    <BODY>
        <H1>Welcome to the Feedback Form!</H1>
        <FORM METHOD="POST" ACTION="http://www.starpowder.com/24-04.cgi"
```

continues ▶

```
                ENCTYPE="application/x-www-form-urlencoded">
          .
          .
          .

          Please enter your password:
          <BR>
          <INPUT TYPE="password" NAME="password" VALUE="open sesame" SIZE=30>
          <BR>
          <BR>
          .
          .
          .

          <INPUT TYPE="submit" NAME="Submit" VALUE="Submit">
          <INPUT TYPE="reset">
        </FORM>
    </BODY>
</HTML>
```

From Perl's point of view, handling a password control is just like handling a
text field. All we have to do is to pass the name of the control, password, to
the param method to get the text the user entered into this control:

```perl
#!/usr/local/bin/perl
use CGI;
$co = new CGI;

print $co->header,
$co->start_html(
    -title=>'CGI Example',
    -author=>'Steve',
    -meta=>{'keywords'=>'CGI Perl'},
    -BGCOLOR=>'white',
    -LINK=>'red'
),

$co->center($co->h1('Thanks for sending us feedback.')),
$co->h3('Here is what you wrote...'),
$co->hr;

if ($co->param()) {
    print
        .
        .
        .

    "Your password is: ", $co->param('password'), ".", $co->p,
        .
        .
        .

}

print $co->hr;
print $co->end_html;
```

Using Drop-Down Lists

You can make a select control appear as a drop-down list if you don't specify anything for the SIZE attribute. Here's how I do that with a drop-down list that enables the user to indicate how much money he wants to send in appreciation of our web site (compare this HTML to the select control in the topic "Using Select Controls" in this chapter, where the SIZE attribute is set to 4, which means the control will display all four items at once):

```
<HTML>
    <HEAD>
        <TITLE>CGI Example</TITLE>
    </HEAD>

    <BODY>
        <H1>Welcome to the Feedback Form!</H1>
        <FORM METHOD="POST" ACTION="http://www.starpowder.com/24-04.cgi"
            ENCTYPE="application/x-www-form-urlencoded">
            .
            .
            .

            Please indicate how much money you'd like to send me:
            <SELECT NAME="popupmenu">
                <OPTION  VALUE="Very much">Very much
                <OPTION  VALUE="A lot">A lot
                <OPTION  VALUE="Not so much">Not so much
                <OPTION  VALUE="None">None
            </SELECT>
            .
            .
            .
        </FORM>
    </BODY>
</HTML>
```

You can see this drop-down list control near the bottom of Figure 24.10. Because drop-down lists allow only single selections, we can get that selection and display it like this:

```
#!/usr/local/bin/perl
use CGI;
$co = new CGI;

print $co->header,
$co->start_html(
    -title=>'CGI Example',
    -author=>'Steve',
    -meta=>{'keywords'=>'CGI Perl'},
    -BGCOLOR=>'white',
    -LINK=>'red'
),
```

continues ▶

```
$co->center($co->h1('Thanks for sending us feedback.')),
$co->h3('Here is what you wrote...'),
$co->hr;

if ($co->param()) {
    print
         .

         .

         .
        "How much money you want to send: ", $co->param('popupmenu'), ".", $co->p,
         .

         .

         .

}

print $co->hr;
print $co->end_html;
```

That's all it takes. You can see the results in Figure 24.11.

Using Hidden Data Fields

The last of the HTML controls I'll take a look at here are hidden controls,
also called *hidden data fields*. You use hidden controls to store data that's not
immediately visible to the users (although they can see it if they view the
page's source). In this case, I'll store the name of the feedback form in a hidden control named hiddendata like this:

```
<HTML>
    <HEAD>
        <TITLE>CGI Example</TITLE>
    </HEAD>

    <BODY>
        <H1>Welcome to the Feedback Form!</H1>
        <FORM METHOD="POST" ACTION="http://www.starpowder.com/24-04.cgi"
            ENCTYPE="application/x-www-form-urlencoded">
         .

         .

         .
            <INPUT TYPE="hidden" NAME="hiddendata" VALUE="Feedback Form 1">
         .

         .

         .
            <INPUT TYPE="submit" NAME="Submit" VALUE="Submit">
            <INPUT TYPE="reset">
        </FORM>
    </BODY>
</HTML>
```

In addition, we can recover the text in the hidden control by passing its name to the param method in the Perl script like this:

```perl
#!/usr/local/bin/perl
use CGI;
$co = new CGI;

print $co->header,
$co->start_html(
    -title=>'CGI Example',
    -author=>'Steve',
    -meta=>{'keywords'=>'CGI Perl'},
    -BGCOLOR=>'white',
    -LINK=>'red'
),

$co->center($co->h1('Thanks for sending us feedback.')),
$co->h3('Here is what you wrote...'),
$co->hr;

if ($co->param()) {
    print

        .

        .

        .

        "The hidden data is: \"", join(", ", $co->param('hiddendata')), "\".";
}

print $co->hr;
print $co->end_html;
```

You can see the text we've recovered from the hidden control at the bottom of Figure 24.11.

That's it. That completes our Perl CGI example. In this example, we've seen how to display a number of HTML controls—text fields, text areas, select controls, check boxes, radio buttons, and password controls—to enable the user to enter data into those controls, and then use Perl methods to read and display that data in a summary page. That's a good start to CGI programming.

Perl is only one option for CGI programming, but it's a good one. Perl is free and is already installed on most UNIX-based servers. Both Perl and UNIX are robust server platforms. Perl documentation and examples are freely available online. As we've seen, with a little CGI code, you can handle the server side of the equation. We've been working with code in the browser throughout this book, and it's good to do a little work on the server side with a widely available tool such as Perl.

That's it for our look at the server side in this chapter—and that's it for our book. We've seen a tremendous amount of JavaScript programming here, from the very basics on up to working with the built-in browser objects, built-in JavaScript objects, HTML controls, the mouse, keyboard, images, and cross-browser issues. We've also worked with Dynamic HTML, changing web pages on-the-fly, dynamic styles, drag and drop, behaviors, data binding, regular expressions, XML and XSLT, cookies, creating your own JavaScript objects, and much more. All that's left to do is to put all this programming power to work for yourself! Best of luck with all your web projects.

Index

C

E

G

J-K

M

N

O

P

X-Z

HOW TO CONTACT US

VISIT OUR WEB SITE

WWW.NEWRIDERS.COM

On our web site, you'll find information about our other books, authors, tables of contents, and book errata. You will also find information about book registration and how to purchase our books, both domestically and internationally.

EMAIL US

Contact us at: **nrfeedback@newriders.com**

- If you have comments or questions about this book
- To report errors that you have found in this book
- If you have a book proposal to submit or are interested in writing for New Riders
- If you are an expert in a computer topic or technology and are interested in being a technical editor who reviews manuscripts for technical accuracy

Contact us at: **nreducation@newriders.com**

- If you are an instructor from an educational institution who wants to preview New Riders books for classroom use. Email should include your name, title, school, department, address, phone number, office days/hours, text in use, and enrollment, along with your request for desk/examination copies and/or additional information.

Contact us at: **nrmedia@newriders.com**

- If you are a member of the media who is interested in reviewing copies of New Riders books. Send your name, mailing address, and email address, along with the name of the publication or web site you work for.

BULK PURCHASES/CORPORATE SALES

The publisher offers discounts on this book when ordered in quantity for bulk purchases and special sales. For sales within the U.S., please contact: Corporate and Government Sales (800) 382-3419 or **corpsales@pearsontechgroup.com**. Outside of the U.S., please contact: International Sales (317) 581-3793 or **international@pearsontechgroup.com**.

WRITE TO US

New Riders Publishing
201 W. 103rd St.
Indianapolis, IN 46290-1097

CALL/FAX US

Toll-free (800) 571-5840
If outside U.S. (317) 581-3500
Ask for New Riders
FAX: (317) 581-4663

VIEW CART

search ⊙

▸ Registration already a member? Log in. ▸ Book Registration

Publishing
the Voices
that Matter

OUR AUTHORS

PRESS ROOM

| web development | design | photoshop | new media | 3-D | server technologie |

EDUCATORS

ABOUT US

CONTACT US

You already know that New Riders brings you the **Voices That Matter**.

But what does that mean? It means that New Riders brings you the

Voices that challenge your assumptions, take your talents to the next

level, or simply help you better understand the complex technical world

we're all navigating.

Visit **www.newriders.com** to find:

- ▸ **10% discount** and **free shipping** on all book purchases
- ▸ Never before published chapters
- ▸ Sample chapters and excerpts
- ▸ Author bios and interviews
- ▸ Contests and enter-to-wins
- ▸ Up-to-date industry event information
- ▸ Book reviews
- ▸ Special offers from our friends and partners
- ▸ Info on how to join our User Group program
- ▸ Ways to have your Voice heard

New
Riders

W W W . N E W R I D E R S . C O M

Colophon

This book was written and edited in Microsoft Word, and laid out in QuarkXPress. The font used for the body text is Bembo and Mono. It was printed on 50# Husky Offset Smooth paper at VonHoffmann, Inc. in Owensville, Missouri. Prepress consisted of PostScript computer-to-plate technology (filmless process). The cover was printed at Moore Langen Printing in Terre Haute, Indiana, on 12 pt., coated on one side.